★ **Cathedral of St. John the Divine** ⑫
See pages 224–5

Morningside Heights and Harlem ⑫

N

R

⑨

⑪

⑩

Upper West Side

Central Park

Upper East Side

④

⑤

Upper Midtown

Lower Midtown

⑧

RIVER

N

★ **Solomon R. Guggenheim Museum** ⑪
See pages 186–7

★ **Metropolitan Museum** ⑩
See pages 188–95

★ **United Nations** ⑧
See pages 158–61

★ **St. Patrick's Cathedral** ⑤
See pages 176–7

0 kilometers   2

0 miles   1

★ **Grand Central Terminal** ⑥
See pages 154–5

DK TRAVEL GUIDES

NEW YORK

EMPIRE STATE

DORLING KINDERSLEY *TRAVEL GUIDES*

NEW YORK

Main contributor:
ELEANOR BERMAN

DORLING KINDERSLEY
LONDON • NEW YORK • SYDNEY • MOSCOW • DELHI
www.dk.com

A DORLING KINDERSLEY BOOK

www.dk.com

PROJECT EDITOR Fay Franklin
ART EDITOR Tony Foo
EDITORS Donna Dailey, Ellen Dupont
DESIGNERS Steve Bere, Louise Parsons, Mark Stevens
EDITORIAL ASSISTANT Fiona Morgan

CONTRIBUTORS
Lester Brooks, Patricia Brooks, Susan Farewell

PHOTOGRAPHERS
Max Alexander, Dave King, Michael Moran

ILLUSTRATORS
Richard Draper, Robbie Polley, Hamish Simpson

This book was produced with the assistance of
Websters International Publishers.

Reproduced by Colourscan (Singapore)
Printed and bound by Dai Nippon Printing Co., (Hong Kong) Ltd.

First published in Great Britain in 1993
by Dorling Kindersley Limited
9 Henrietta Street, London WC2E 8PS
**Reprinted with revisions 1994, 1995 (twice),
1997, 1999, 2000**

Copyright 1993, 2000 © Dorling Kindersley Limited, London

A CIP CATALOGUE RECORD IS AVAILABLE FROM THE BRITISH LIBRARY.

ISBN 0-7513-9069-0

THROUGHOUT THIS BOOK, FLOORS ARE REFERRED TO IN ACCORDANCE
WITH AMERICAN USAGE, IE THE "FIRST FLOOR" IS AT GROUND LEVEL.

**The information in every
Dorling Kindersley Travel Guide is checked annually**.
Every effort has been made to ensure that this book is as up-to-date as
possible at the time of going to press. Some details, however, such as
telephone numbers, opening hours, prices, gallery hanging arrangements
and travel information are liable to change. The publishers cannot accept
responsibility for any consequences arising from the use of this book.
We value the views and suggestions of our readers very highly. Please write
to: Editorial Director, Dorling Kindersley Travel Guides, Dorling Kindersley,
9 Henrietta Street, London WC2E 8PS.

CONTENTS

Baseball star,
Babe Ruth
(1895–1948)

INTRODUCING
NEW YORK

South Manhattan skyline

Vesuvio Bakery, SoHo

Trump Tower, Upper Midtown

The New York City Ballet

Tug boat at the North Wind Undersea Institute Museum

Bagel from a New York deli

Solomon R. Guggenheim Museum, Upper East Side

How to Use this Guide

This EYEWITNESS TRAVEL GUIDE helps you get the most from your stay in New York with the minimum of practical difficulty. The opening section, *Introducing New York*, locates the city geographically, sets modern New York in its historical context and describes the highlights of the year. *New York at a Glance* is an overview of the city's attractions. Section two, *New York Area by Area*, guides you through the city's sightseeing areas. It describes all the main sights with maps, photographs and detailed illustrations. In addition, five planned walks take you step-by-step through special areas.

Well-researched tips on where to stay, eat, shop, and on sports and entertainment are in section three, *Travelers' Needs. Children's New York* lists highlights for young visitors, and section four, *Survival Guide*, shows you how to do everything from mailing a letter to using the subway.

NEW YORK AREA BY AREA

Manhattan has been divided into 15 sightseeing areas, each described separately. Each area opens with a portrait, summing up the area's character and history and listing all the sights to be covered. Sights are numbered and clearly located on an *Area Map*. After this comes a large-scale *Street-by-Street Map* focusing on the most interesting part of the area. Finding your way around each area is made simple by the numbering system. This refers to the order in which sights are described on the pages that follow.

Sights at a Glance lists the sights in the area by category, including: Historic Streets and Buildings, Modern Architecture, Museums and Galleries, Churches, Monuments, and Parks and Squares.

The area covered in greater detail on the *Street-by-Street Map* is shaded red.

Numbered circles pinpoint all the listed sights on the area map. Trump Tower, for example, is **❷**

1 The Area Map

For easy reference, the sights in each area are numbered and located on an Area Map. *To help the visitor, the map also shows subway stations, heliports and ferry embarkation points.*

Photographs of facades and distinctive details of buildings help you locate the sights.

Color-coding on each page makes the area easy to find in the book.

Travel tips help you reach the area quickly by public transportation.

2 The Street-by-Street Map

This gives a bird's-eye view of the heart of each sight-seeing area. The most important buildings are illustrated, to help you spot them easily as you walk around.

A locator map shows you where you are in relation to surrounding areas. The area of the *Street-by-Street Map* is shown in red.

Trump Tower ❷ is also shown on this map.

A suggested route for a walk takes you past some of the area's most interesting sights.

Red stars indicate the sights that no visitor should miss.

NEW YORK AT A GLANCE
Each map in this section
concentrates on a specific
theme: *Museums, Architecture,
Multicultural New York*, and
Celebrated New Yorkers. The
top sights are shown on the
map; other sights are
described on the two pages
following and cross-referenced
to their full entries in the
Area by Area section.

Each sightseeing area
is color-coded.

The theme is explored in greater
detail on the pages following the map.

---

3 Detailed information on each sight
*All important sights in each area are
described in depth here. They are
listed in order, following the numbering
on the opening Area Map. Practical
information is also provided.*

4 New York's major sights
*These are given two or more full pages in
the sightseeing area in which they are
found. Important buildings are dissected
to reveal their interiors; museums have
color-coded floor plans to help you find
particular exhibits.*

PRACTICAL INFORMATION
Each entry provides all the information
needed to plan a visit to the sight. The
key to the symbols is inside the back
cover.

**Map reference to Street
Finder at back of book**

Address

Sight Number

Trump Tower ❷

725 5th Ave. **Map** 12 F3.
☎ 832-2000. **M** 5th Ave–53rd St.
Garden level, shops open 10am–6pm
Mon–Sat. *Building open* 8am–10pm
daily. **Adm** free. See *Shopping* p311.
📷 ♿ *Concerts.* 🔟 🔲 🔲 🔲

Opening hours

**Services and
facilities available**

**Telephone
number**

Nearest subway station

The Visitors' Checklist
provides the practical
information you will need
to plan your visit.

The facade of each major
sight is shown to help you
spot it quickly.

Red stars indicate the
most important
exhibits or works of
art on display inside,
or the most interesting
architectural details of
the building.

A color key helps
you find your way
easily around the
collection.

Floors are referred to in
accordance with American
usage, ie the "first floor" is
at ground level.

Introducing
New York

Putting New York on the Map

NEW YORK is a city of over nine million people, covering 301 sq miles (780 sq km). The city gives its name to the state of New York, the capital of which is Albany, 156 miles (251 km) to the north. New York is also a good base from which to visit the historic towns of Boston and Philadelphia, as well as the spectacular Niagara Falls.

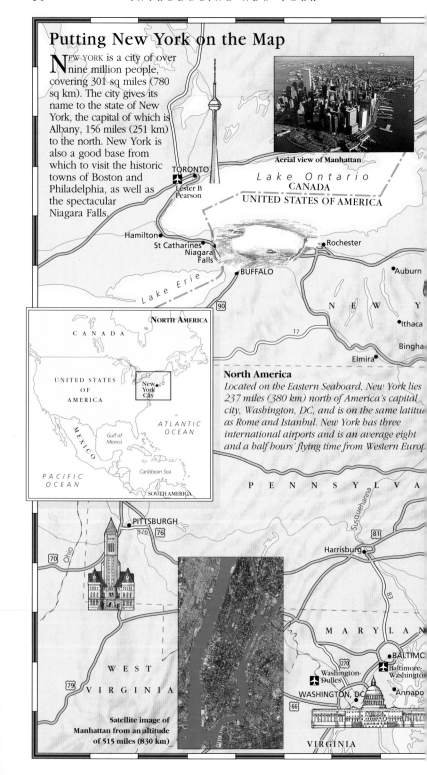

Aerial view of Manhattan

Lake Ontario

CANADA
UNITED STATES OF AMERICA

TORONTO
Lester B Pearson

Hamilton
St Catharines
Niagara Falls
● Rochester
● Auburn

BUFFALO

Lake Erie

90

N   E   W   Y

● Ithaca

17

Bingha

Elmira ●

NORTH AMERICA

CANADA

UNITED STATES
OF
AMERICA

New
York
City

ATLANTIC
OCEAN

MEXICO

Gulf of
Mexico

Caribbean Sea

PACIFIC
OCEAN

SOUTH AMERICA

North America

Located on the Eastern Seaboard, New York lies 237 miles (380 km) north of America's capital city, Washington, DC, and is on the same latitude as Rome and Istanbul. New York has three international airports and is an average eight and a half hours' flying time from Western Europe.

P   E   N   N   S   Y   L   V   A

PITTSBURGH
376   76

Ohio

70

Susquehanna

81

Harrisburg ●

83

M   A   R   Y   L   A   N

● BALTIMO

270

Baltimore-
Washington

WEST

79

VIRGINIA

Washington-
Dulles

WASHINGTON, DC

66

● Annapo

**Satellite image of
Manhattan from an altitude
of 515 miles (830 km)**

VIRGINIA

GREATER NEW YORK

Greater New York

New York City is made of five distinct boroughs: Manhattan (where the vast majority of sights are located), the Bronx, Queens, Brooklyn, and Staten Island. Details of important sights inside central New York but within the city's boundaries can be found on pages 30–53. Day trips in New York State and beyond are suggested on page 377.

see next page

Yonkers · New Rochelle · Mount Vernon · Bronx · Longisland Sound · Port Washington · Englewood · Passaic · LaGuardia · Flushing · Long Island · Valley Stream · Bloomfield · East Orange · Union City · Manhattan · East River · Newark · Jersey City · Queens · Newark · John F Kennedy (JFK) · Elizabeth · Upper New York Bay · Brooklyn · Staten Island · Lower New York Bay

ATLANTIC OCEAN

0 kilometers 10
0 miles 5

90 · Troy · Albany · MASSACHUSETTS · BOSTON
K · 88 · 90 · Worcester · Catskill Mountains · Hudson · Springfield · RHODE ISLAND · Providence
17 · Hartford · CONNECTICUT · Poughkeepsie · 91
84 · 95 · New Haven · Bridgeport · Long Island Sound
A · 87 · 80 · NEW YORK CITY · Long Island
78 · Newark · LaGuardia · John F Kennedy (JFK)

0 kilometers 100
0 miles 50

N

ntown · NEW · JERSEY · PHILADELPHIA · Camden
hia · Wilmington · 30
Dover · Atlantic City · Delaware Bay
AWARE

ATLANTIC OCEAN

Liverpool
Southampton
Gibraltar →

KEY

☐ Greater New York
✈ Airport
66 Interstate highway
═ State highway
— Major railway line
- - International boundary
- Shipping route
- - State boundary

San Juan
Panama
Recife
Rio de
Janeiro
Cape
Town

Manhattan

MOST OF THE SIGHTS described in this book lie within 15 areas of Manhattan. Each of these has its own section in the book. If you are short of time, you could restrict your sightseeing to one or two areas. Many of New York's oldest and newest buildings rub shoulders in Lower Manhattan. It is from here, too, that you can take the Staten Island ferry for breathtaking views of the famous skyline and the Statue of Liberty. The Theater District and Midtown offer Fifth Avenue's glittering shops as well as museums, entertainment and such landmark skyscrapers as the glorious Chrysler Building. Museum Mile on the Upper East Side is a cultural paradise, and, since it runs alongside Central Park, you can rest en route and watch New Yorkers at play.

PAGES 138–47
Street Finder maps
8, 11–12

PAGES 106–13
Street Finder maps
3–4

PAGES 128–37
Street Finder maps
7–8

PAGES 100–105
Street Finder map
4

Chelsea and the Garment District

Gramercy and the Flatiron District

Greenwich Village

SoHo and TriBeCa

East Village

Lower East Side

Lower Manhattan

Seaport and the Civic Center

PAGES 64–79
Street Finder maps
1–2

PAGES 80–91
Street Finder maps
1–2

PAGES 92–9
Street Finder maps
4, 5

Morningside
Heights and
Harlem

PAGES 208–17
Street Finder maps
11–12, 15–16

PAGES 218–29
Street Finder maps
19–20

Upper
West Side

Central
Park

Upper East
Side

PAGES 202–7
Street Finder maps
12, 16

eater
istrict

Upper
Midtown

Lower
Midtown

PAGES 180–201
Street Finder maps
12–13, 16–17

T   R   I   V   E   R

PAGES 148–63
Street Finder maps
9, 12, 13

PAGES 164–79
Street Finder maps
12, 13–14

PAGES 114–19
Street Finder maps
4, 5

PAGES 120–27
Street Finder maps
8, 9

0 kilometers   2

0 miles   1

THE HISTORY OF NEW YORK

FROM ITS FIRST sighting almost 500 years ago by Giovanni da Verrazano, New York's harbor was the prize that all of Europe wanted to capture. The Dutch first sent fur traders to the area in 1621, but they lost the colony they called New Amsterdam to the English in 1664. The settlement was re-christened New York and the name stayed, even after the English lost the colony in 1783, at the end of the Revolutionary War.

A shell-work cloak worn by an Indian chief

THE GROWING CITY

In the 19th century, New York grew rapidly and became a major port. Ease of shipping spawned manufacturing, commerce was king and great fortunes were made. In 1898, Manhattan was joined with the four outer boroughs to form the world's second-largest city. From 1800 to 1900, the population grew from 79,000 to 3 million people. New York City became the country's cultural and entertainment mecca as well as its business center.

THE MELTING POT

The city continued to grow as thousands of immigrants came seeking a better life. Overpopulation meant that many at first lived in slums. Today, the mix of cultures has enriched the city and become its defining quality. Its nine million inhabitants speak 80 languages.

Manhattan's skyline took shape as the city grew skyward to make space for its ever-increasing population. Throughout its history, the city has experienced alternating periods of economic decline and growth, but in both good times and bad, it remains one of the world's most vital cities.

The following pages illustrate significant periods in New York's history.

A deed signed by New Amsterdam's last Dutch governor, Peter Stuyvesant, in 1664

The southern half of Manhattan and part of Brooklyn in 1767

Early New York

MANHATTAN WAS a forested land populated by Algonquian-speaking Natives when the Dutch West India Company established a fur trading post called New Amsterdam in 1625. The first settlers built houses helter-skelter, so even today the streets of Lower Manhattan still twist. Broadway, then called by the Dutch name *Breede Wegh*, began as an Indian trail known as the Week-quaesgeek Trail. Harlem has also kept its Dutch name. The town was unruly until Peter Stuyvesant arrived to bring order. But the colony did not produce the expected revenues, and in 1664 the Dutch let it fall to the English, who renamed it New York.

Indian husk mask

GROWTH OF THE METROPOLIS
☐ *1664*   ☐ *Today*

Seal of New Netherland
The beaver pelt and wampum (Indian shell beads) on the seal were the currency of the colony of New Netherland.

FIRST VIEW OF MANHATTAN (1626)
The southern tip of Manhattan resembled a Dutch town, down to the windmill. Although shown here, the fort had not yet been built.

Dutch ships

The First New Yorkers
Algonquian-speaking Natives were the first inhabitants of Manhattan.

Iroquois Pot
Iroquois Indians were frequent visitors to early Manhattan.

Indian Village
Some Algonquians lived in longhouses on Manhattan before the Dutch arrived.

Native canoe

TIMELINE

1524 Giovanni da Verrazano sails into New York harbor

1626 Peter Minuit buys Manhattan from the Natives

1653 Wall is built for protection from attack; adjacent street is called Wall Street

1625 Dutch establish first permanent trading post

1600	1620	1640

1609 Henry Hudson sails up the Hudson River in search of the Northwest Passage

1625 First black slaves brought from Africa

1643–45 Indian skirmishes end with temporary peace treaty

1647 Peter Stuyvesant becomes colonial governor

1654 First Jewish settler arrive

Dutch Delftware
Colonists brought this popular tin-glazed earthenware pottery from Holland.

Manhattan Skyline
The Strand, now Whitehall Street, was the site of the city's first brick house.

Tiger timbers

WHERE TO SEE DUTCH NEW YORK

Dug up by workmen in 1916, these remnants of a Dutch ship, the *Tiger*, which burned in 1613, are the earliest artifacts of the period and are now in the Museum of the City of New York *(see p197)*. Rooms in this museum, as well as in the Morris-Jumel Mansion *(see p233)* and the Van Cortlandt House Museum *(see p238)*, display Dutch pottery, tiles and furniture.

Purchase of Manhattan
Peter Minuit bought the island from the Natives in 1626 for $24 worth of trinkets.

Dutch windmill

Fort Amsterdam

Peter Stuyvesant
The last Dutch governor was a tyrant who imposed strict laws – such as an edict closing all the city's taverns at 9 o'clock.

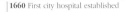

1660 First city hospital established

1664 British forces oust Dutch without a fight and change name to New York

1676 Great Dock built on East River

1698 Trinity Church dedicated

1660	1680	1700

The surrender of New Amsterdam to the British

1680s Bolting Laws give New York exclusive right to process and ship grain

1683 First New York city charter established

1689 Merchant Jacob Leisler leads revolt against taxes and takes over the city for two years

1693 Ninety-two cannons installed for protection; area becomes known as the Battery

1691 Leisler sentenced to death for treason

Colonial New York

U NDER BRITISH RULE, New York prospered and the population grew rapidly. The bolting of flour (grinding grain) was the main commercial enterprise. Shipbuilding also flourished. As the city prospered, an elite emerged that could afford a more refined way of life, and fine furniture and household silver were made for use in their homes during the Colonial period. During more than a century of governing New York, Britain proved more interested in profit than in the welfare of the colony. The Crown imposed hated taxes, and the spirit of rebellion grew, although especially in New York, loyalties were divided. On the the eve of Revolution, New York was the second-largest city in the 13 colonies, with 20,000 citizens.

Colonial gentleman

Colonial currency

GROWTH OF THE METROPOLIS

☐ *1760* ☐ *Today*

Bedroom

Colonial Street
Pigs and dogs roamed free on the streets of Colonial New York.

Dining room

Kas
This Dutch-style pine wardrobe was made in New York's Hudson River valley around 1720.

Shipping
Trade with the West Indies and Britain helped New York prosper. In some years, 200 or more vessels visited the port.

TIMELINE

1702 Lord Cornbury appointed Colonial governor; he often wore women's clothes

1711 Slave market set up at the foot of Wall Street

1720 First shipyard opens

| 1700 | 1710 | 1720 | 1730 |

1710 Iroquois chief Hendrick visits England

1732 First city theater opens

1725 *New York Gazette*, city's first newspaper, is established

Captain Kidd
The English pirate William Kidd was a respected citizen, loaning a block and tackle to help build Trinity Church (see p68).

VAN CORTLANDT HOUSE
Frederick Van Cortlandt built this Georgian-style house in 1748 on a wheat plantation in what is now the Bronx. Today a museum (see p238), it shows how a well-to-do Dutch-English family once lived.

West parlor

WHERE TO SEE COLONIAL NEW YORK
Colonial buildings are open to the public at Historic Richmond Town on Staten Island *(see p252)*. Fine examples of Colonial silver and furniture are on display at the Museum of the City of New York *(see p197)*.

Richmond Town General Store

Colonial Kitchen
Plain white cheese, called "white meat," was often served in place of meat. Waffles, introduced by the Dutch, were popular. Fresh fruit was rare, but preserved fruits were eaten.

Pewter baby bottle   **Cheese mold**   **Waffle iron**

Decorative Carvings
A face carved in stone peers over each of the front windows.

Sucket fork, for eating preserved fruits

1734 John Peter Zenger's libel trial upholds freedom of the press

1741 Slave uprising creates hysteria; 31 slaves are executed, 150 imprisoned

1754 French and Indian War begins; King's College (now Columbia University) founded

British soldier

1759 First jail built

1740   **1750**   **1760**

1733 Bowling Green becomes first city park; first ferries to Brooklyn

King's College

1762 First paid police force

1763 War ends; British gain control of North America

Revolutionary New York

George Washington, Revolutionary general

Dug up into trenches for defense, heavily shelled by British troops and scarred by recurring fires, New York suffered during the American Revolution. But despite the hardships, many continued to enjoy cricket games, horse races, balls and boxing matches. After the British took the city in 1776, it became their headquarters. The Continental army did not return to Manhattan until November 25, 1783, two years after the fighting ended.

GROWTH OF THE METROPOLIS

☐ 1776   ☐ Today

Battle Dress
The Continental (Patriot) army wore blue uniforms, while the British wore red.

British soldier

TOPPLING THE KING
New Yorkers tore down the statue of King George III in Bowling Green and melted it down to make ammunition.

Soldier's Haversack
American soldiers in the War of Independence carried their supplies in haversacks.

Battle of Harlem Heights
Washington won this battle on September 16, 1776. But he did not have enough troops to hold New York so retreated, leaving it to the British.

American soldier

Patriot

Death of a Patriot
While working behind British lines in 1776, Nathan Hale was captured and hanged by the British without trial for spying.

TIMELINE

1765 British pass Stamp Act; New Yorkers protest; Sons of Liberty formed

1767 New duties imposed with Townshend Act; after protests, the act is repealed

1770 Sons of Liberty fight British in the "Battle of Golden Hill"

1774 Rebels dump tea in New York harbor to protest taxes

1760

1770

1

1766 St. Paul's Chapel completed; Stamp Act repealed; Statue of George III erected on Bowling Green

St. Paul's Chapel

General William Howe, commander in chief of the British troops

1776 War begins; 500 ships under General Howe assemble in New York harbor

Fire Fighters
Fires had long threatened the city, but during the war a series of fires nearly destroyed it. In the wake of the patriot retreat, on September 21, 1776, a devastating fire razed Trinity Church and 1,000 houses.

Leather fire bucket

Statue of George III

General Washington Returns
Washington received a hero's welcome when he reentered New York on November 25, 1783, after the British withdrawal.

Flags of the Revolution
Washington's army flew the Continental colors, with a stripe for each of the 13 colonies and a Union Jack in the corner. The Stars and Stripes became the official flag in 1777.

First Stars and Stripes

Continental colors

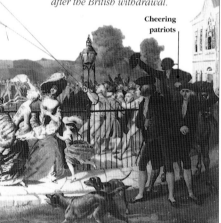

Cheering patriots

WHERE TO SEE THE REVOLUTIONARY CITY
In 1776, George Washington used the Morris-Jumel Mansion in upper Manhattan as a headquarters *(see p233)*. He also slept at the Van Cortlandt House *(see p19 and p238)*. After the war he bade farewell to his officers at Fraunces Tavern *(see p76)*.

Morris-Jumel mansion

1783 Treaty of Paris signed, US wins independence; British evacuate New York

1789 George Washington inaugurated as first president at Federal Hall

1790 US capital is moved to Philadelphia

1801 *New York Post* founded by Alexander Hamilton

1794 Bellevue Hospital opens on the East River

1790   1800

1785 New York named US capital

1792 Tontine Coffee House built – first home of the Stock Exchange

1804 Vice President Aaron Burr kills political rival Alexander Hamilton in a duel

1784 Bank of New York chartered

1791 New York Hospital, city's oldest, opens

Washington's inauguration

New York in the 19th Century

Governor De Witt Clinton

FIRMLY ESTABLISHED as the nation's largest city and preeminent seaport, New York grew increasingly wealthy. Manufacturing increased due to the ease of shipping; tycoons like John Jacob Astor made millions. The rich moved uptown; public transportation followed. With rapid growth came fires, epidemics and financial panics. Immigrants from Ireland, Germany, and other nations arrived. Some found prosperity; others crowded into slums in Lower Manhattan.

GROWTH OF THE METROPOLIS

☐ 1840   ☐ Today

Sheet Music
The Stephen Foster ballad Jeanie With the Light Brown Hair *was popular at this time.*

Croton Distributing Reservoir was built in 1842. Until then, New Yorkers had no fresh drinking water – they relied on deliveries of bottled water.

Omnibus
The horse-drawn omnibus was introduced for public transportation in 1832 and remained on New York streets until World War I.

Keeping Fit
Gymnasiums such as Dr. Rich's Institute for Physical Education were established in New York in the 1830s and 1840s.

TIMELINE

1805 First free state schools established in New York

1807 Robert Fulton launches first steamboat, on the Hudson River

1811 Randel Plan divides Manhattan into grid pattern above 14th Street

1812–14 War of 1812; British blockade New York harbor

The Constitution, *most famous ship in War of 1812*

1835 Much of old New York razed in city's worst fire

1810	1820	1830

1822 Yellow fever epidemic; people evacuate to Greenwich Village

1823 New York surpasses Boston and Philadelphia to become nation's largest city

1827 New York abolishes slavery

1837 New Yorker Samuel Morse sends first telegraph message

The Brownstone
Many brownstone row houses were built in the first half of the century. The raised stoop allowed separate entry to the parlor and ground-floor servants' quarters.

Crystal Palace was an iron and glass exhibition hall erected for the 1853 World's Fair.

THE PORT OF NEW YORK

New York's importance as a port city grew by leaps and bounds in the early 19th century. Robert Fulton launched his first steamboat, the *Clermont*, in 1807. Steamboats made travel much quicker – it now took 72 hours to reach Albany, which was both the state capital and the gateway to the West. Trade with the West by steamboat and canal boat, and with the rest of the world by clipper ship, made the fortunes of many New Yorkers.

The steamboat *Clermont*

NEW YORK IN 1855
Looking south from 42nd Street, Crystal Palace and the Croton Distributing Reservoir stood where the public library and Bryant Park are today.

Crystal Palace in Flames
On October 5, 1858, New York's Crystal Palace exhibition hall burned to the ground, just as its predecessor in London did.

Grand Canal Celebration
Ships in New York harbor lined up to celebrate the 1825 Erie Canal opening. In connecting the Great Lakes with Albany, the state capital, on the Hudson River, the canal opened a water link between the Midwest and the Port of New York. New York realized huge profits.

1849 Astor Place riots; ships set sail for California Gold Rush

Early baseball player

1845 New York Knickerbockers, first organized baseball team chartered

1842 Croton Reservoir built

1851 *New York Times* first published

1853 New York hosts first World's Fair

Clipper ship card

FOR SAN FRANCISCO

FREE TRADE

1861 Civil War begins

1857 Financial panic and depression

1858 Vaux and Olmsted design Central Park; Macy's founded

Crowds in Central Park

1863 Draft riots last four days, many die

1865 Abraham Lincoln lies in state in City Hall

1840 **1850** **1860**

The Age of Extravagance

Industrialist Andrew Carnegie

As NEW YORK'S merchant princes grew ever wealthier, the city entered into a gilded era during which many of its most opulent buildings went up. Millions were lavished on the arts with the founding of the Metropolitan Museum, Public Library and Carnegie Hall. Luxury hotels like the Plaza and the original Waldorf-Astoria were built, and elegant department stores arose to serve the wealthy. Such flamboyant figures as William "Boss" Tweed, political strongman and king of corruption, and circus man Phineas T. Barnum were also larger than life.

GROWTH OF THE METROPOLIS

☐ *1890*   ☐ *Today*

Overlooking the Park
The Dakota (1880) was the first grand luxury apartment house on the Upper West Side (see p216).

Palatial Living
Mansions lined Fifth Avenue. When it was built in 1882, W.K. Vanderbilt's Italianate palace at 660 Fifth Avenue, was one of the farthest north.

Fashion City
Lord & Taylor built a new store on Broadway's Ladies' Mile; 6th Avenue between 14th and 23rd streets was known as Fashion Row.

BATHING SUITS.

A GREAT SPECIALTY AT
LORD & TAYLOR'S, Broadway and 20th Street, N. Y.
CHEAPEST AND BEST QUALITY OF BATHING SUITS IN THE CITY.

THE ELEVATED RAILROAD
By the mid 1870s, elevated railroads or "Els" ran along 2nd, 3rd, 6th and 9th avenues. They made travel faster, but left noise, grime and pollution in their wake.

TIMELINE

1867 Brooklyn's Prospect Park completed

1868 First elevated railroad built on Greenwich Street

1870 J.D. Rockefeller founds Standard Oil

1871 The first Grand Central Depot opens on 42nd St.; "Boss" Tweed is arrested and imprisoned

1877 A.G. Bell demonstrates the telephone in New York

1865 | **1870** | **1875**

1869 First apartment house built on 18th Street; Black Friday financial crisis hits Wall Street

The interior of the Stock Exchange

1872 Bloomingdale's opens

1873 Banks fail: Stock Exchange panics

1879 St. Patrick's Cathedral completed; first city telephone exchange opened on Nassau Street

Mark Twain's Birthday
Mark Twain, whose 1873 novel The Gilded Age *portrayed the decadent lifestyle of New Yorkers, celebrated his birthday at Delmonico's.*

WHERE TO SEE THE AGE OF EXTRAVAGANCE

The Gold Room in the Henry Villard Houses *(see p174)* is a good place to experience the city's past. Formerly the Music Room, it is now a venue for afternoon tea. The Museum of the City of New York also has two period rooms *(p197)*.

The Tweed Ring
William "Boss" Tweed led Tammany Hall, which dominated city government. He stole millions in city funds.

Elevated train

Streetcar

Bowery

Smiths...

Rural Fifth Avenue
This painting by Ralph Blakelock shows a shanty-town at 86th Street. Today it is one of New York's most expensive addresses.

Nast's cartoon of "Boss" Tweed

Tammany Tiger
The Museum of the City of New York has "Boss" Tweed's cane, which sports a gold Tammany Tiger mascot on its handle.

1880 Canned fruits and meats first appear in stores; Metropolitan Museum of Art opens; streets lit by electricity

1883 Metropolitan Opera opens on Broadway; Brooklyn Bridge completed

1886 Statue of Liberty unveiled

1891 Carnegie Hall opens

1880

1885

1890

1888 Great Blizzard dumps 22 in (56 cm) of snow

1890 First moving picture shows appear in New York

Grand display of fireworks over Brooklyn Bridge, 1883

1892 Cathedral of St. John the Divine begun; Ellis Island opens

New York at the Turn of the Century

Horse-drawn carriage

By 1900, NEW YORK was a hub of American industry: 70% of the country's corporations were based there, and the port handled two-thirds of all imported goods. The rich got richer, but in the crowded slums, disease spread. Even so, immigrants kept their rich traditions alive, and political and social reform emerged. In 1900, the International Ladies' Garment Workers' Union was founded to battle for the rights of the women and children who toiled in dangerous factories for low wages. The Triangle Shirtwaist Factory fire in 1911 also sped reform.

GROWTH OF THE METROPOLIS

☐ *1914*   ☐ *Today*

Crowded Conditions
Tenements were unhealthy and overcrowded. They often lacked windows, air shafts or proper sanitary facilities.

Gateway to America
Almost five times as crowded as the rest of New York, the Lower East Side was the most densely populated place in the world.

WHERE TO SEE TURN-OF-THE-CENTURY NEW YORK

The Lower East Side Tenement Museum *(see p97)* has exhibits on tenement life.

Tailor's scissors

Hip bath

Inside a Sweatshop
Workers toiled long hours for low wages in the overcrowded sweatshops of the garment district. This view of Moe Levy's shop was taken in 1912.

Streetcars on Broadway

TIMELINE

1895 Olympia Theater is first to open in the Broadway area

1898 Five boroughs merge to form world's second-largest city

1901 Macy's opens Broadway department store

1895

1896 First bagel served in a Clinton Street bakery

1897 Waldorf-Astoria Hotel opens: the largest hotel in the world

1900 Mayor Robert Van Wyck breaks ground for city's first subway with silver shovel

1900

1903 Lyceum Theater opens – oldest Broadway house still in use

FLATIRON BUILDING

Overlooking Madison Square where Broadway, Fifth Avenue and 23rd Street meet, the 21-story tower was one of the city's first skyscrapers (1902). Triangle-shaped, it was dubbed the Flatiron Building (see p125).

Underlying steel structure

Elaborate limestone facade

Only 6 ft (185 cm) wide at apex of triangle

Supper in the Saddle

Decadent parties were all the rage. C.K.G. Billings's horseback dinner at Sherry's restaurant in 1903 was the talk of all New York.

Plaza Promenade

The section of Fifth Avenue in front of the Plaza Hotel was considered the most elegant in the city.

Ventilated hairpiece

High Fashion

In 1900 styles were stiff, with wire hoops and bustles worn beneath ornate dresses. Later, clothes became softer and more practical.

Long bustle

Wire hoops

1906 Architect Stanford White shot at Madison Square Garden, which he had built in 1890

1909 Wilbur Wright flies first plane over New York

1910 Pennsylvania Station opens

1913 Woolworth Building is world's tallest; new Grand Central Terminal opens; Harlem's Apollo Theater opens

1905

1910

1905 First crossing of the Staten Island Ferry

1907 First metered taxicabs; first Ziegfeld Follies

1911 Triangle Shirtwaist Factory fire kills 146 sweatshop workers; New York Public Library completed

Woolworth Building

New York Between the Wars

Entrance card to the Cotton Club

GROWTH OF THE METROPOLIS
☐ 1933 ☐ Today

T HE 1920S WERE a time of high living for many New Yorkers. Mayor Jimmy Walker set the pace, whether squiring chorus girls, drinking in speakeasies or watching the Yankees. But the good times ended with the 1929 stock market crash. By 1932, Walker had resigned, charged with corruption, and one-quarter of New Yorkers were unemployed. With Mayor Fiorello La Guardia's 1933 election, New York began to recover and thrive.

Exotic Costumes
Chorus girls were a major Cotton Club attraction.

THE COTTON CLUB
This Harlem nightclub was host to the best jazz in town, as first Duke Ellington and then Cab Calloway led the band. People flocked from all over the city to hear them.

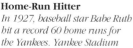

Defying Prohibition
Although alcohol was outlawed, speakeasies – semi-secret illegal drinking dens – still sold it.

Home-Run Hitter
In 1927, baseball star Babe Ruth hit a record 60 home runs for the Yankees. Yankee Stadium (see p239) became known as "the house that Ruth built."

Sawed-off shotgun concealed in violin case

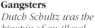

Gangsters
Dutch Schultz was the kingpin of an illegal booze racket.

TIMELINE

1918 End of World War I

1919 18th Amendment bans alcohol, launches Prohibition Era

1920 US women get the vote

Opening of the Holland Tunnel

1926 Jimmy Walker becomes mayor

1931 Empire State Building becomes world's tallest

1920

1925

1930

1924 Novelist James Baldwin is born in Harlem

1925 *The New Yorker* magazine is launched

1927 Lindbergh flies across the Atlantic; first talking movie, *The Jazz Singer*, opens; Holland Tunnel opens

1929 Stock market crash; Great Depression begins

1930 Chrysler Building completed

Big Band Leaders
Banned from many downtown clubs, black artists like Cab Calloway starred at the Cotton Club.

Broadway Melodies
The 1920s were the heyday of the Broadway musical, with a record number of plays opening.

THE GREAT DEPRESSION
The Roaring Twenties ended with the stock market crash of October 29, 1929, which set off the Depression. New York was hard hit: squatters' shacks sprang up in Central Park and thousands were out of work. But art flourished as artists went to work for the Works Projects Administration (WPA), creating outstanding murals and artworks throughout the city.

Waiting to receive benefits in 1931

Breakfast menu

Lindbergh's plane,
Spirit of St. Louis

Lindbergh's Flight
New Yorkers celebrated Lindbergh's nonstop solo flight across the Atlantic in 1927 in a variety of ways, including a breakfast in his honor.

Rockefeller Center
Millionaire John D. Rockefeller drives the final rivet to celebrate the opening of Rockefeller Center on May 1, 1939.

Mass Event
Forty-five million people visited the 1939 World's Fair in New York.

NEW YORK WORLD'S FAIR 1939

1933 Prohibition ends; Fiorello LaGuardia begins three terms as mayor

1940 Queens-Midtown Tunnel opens

1942 Times Square blacked out during World War II; Idlewild International Airport (now JFK) opens

1935 | **1940** | **1945**

1936 Parks Department headed by Robert Moses; new parks created

1939 Rockefeller Center is completed

1941 US enters World War II

1944 Black leader Adam Clayton Powell elected to Congress

Postwar New York

Since WORLD WAR II, New York has seen both the best of times and the worst. Although established as the financial capital of the world, the city itself almost went bankrupt in the 1970s. Wall Street hit its peak in the 1980s, then experienced its worst crash since 1929. In the past five years, New York has seen a dramatic drop in the crime rate and an increase in the restoration and renewal of such landmarks as Grand Central Terminal and the "new" Times Square. This constant rebuilding is emblematic of the city's position at the cultural and financial hub of the United States.

BILTMORE THEATER
201 WEST 47TH STREET, 582-5340

1967 Hippie musi Hair opens on Off Broadway, then transfers to the Biltmore Theater

1971 Pop artist Andy Warhol has a retrospective show of his work at the Whitney Museum

1953 Merce Cunningham founds dance company

1963 Pennsylvania Station razed

1966 Newspaper and transit strikes

1970 John Lindsay starts second term as mayor

1959 Guggenheim Museum opens

1945 End of World War II

1946 UN headquarters established in New York

1954 Ellis Island closes

1945	1950	1955	1960	1965	197
MAYORS:	IMPELLITERI	WAGNER	WAGNER	LINDSAY	LIN
1945	1950	1955	1960	1965	197

1964 New York World's Fair; race riots in Harlem and Bedford-Stuyvesant; Verrazano Narrows Bridge links Brooklyn and Staten Island; Beatles play at Shea Stadium

One of the most popular bands of the "swinging '60s" – The Beatles

1947 Jackie Robinson, first black baseball player in the major leagues, signs with Brooklyn Dodgers

Souvenir scarf

1968 20,000 anti-establishment hippies gather in Centra Park; student sit-ins at Columbia Universit

*Andy Warhol with actresses
Candy Darling and Ultra Violet*

Donald Trump

1975 Federal
loan saves New
York from
bankruptcy

1983 Economic boom: property prices
skyrocket; Trump Tower completed by real
estate tycoon Donald Trump, who symbolizes
the "yuppie" wealth of the 1980s

1981 New York
regains solvency

1988 Twenty-
five percent of
New Yorkers live
below the
poverty line

1990 David Dinkins,
New York's first black
mayor, takes office; Ellis
Island reopens as an
immigration museum

1977 New York
power blackout
lasts 25 hours

1987 Stock
market crash

1993 Rudolph Giuliani
takes office as mayor

1975	1980	1985	1990	1995
BEAME	KOCH	KOCH	DINKINS	GIULIANI
1975	1980	1985	1990	1995

World
e Center
oleted

1986 Shock of corruption scandals
rock Mayor Koch's administration;
Centennial
of Statue
of Liberty

1995 The
neglected
Chelsea Piers
are renovated
and open as a
mammoth
sports and
entertainment
complex
(*see p136*)

NEW YORK AT A GLANCE

THERE ARE ALMOST 300 places of interest described in the *Area by Area* section of this book. They range from the bustling New York Stock Exchange *(see pp70–71)* to Central Park's peaceful Strawberry Fields *(see p206)* and from synagogues to skyscrapers. The following 16 pages are a time-saving guide to New York's most interesting sights. Museums and architecture each have a section, and there are guides to the people and cultures that have given the city its unique character. Each sight is cross-referenced to its own full entry. Below are the top ten tourist attractions to start you off.

NEW YORK'S TOP TEN   TOURIST ATTRACTIONS

Ellis Island
See pp78–9.

Empire State Building
See pp134–5.

South Street Seaport
See p84.

Museum of Modern Art
See pp170–73.

Rockefeller Center
See p142.

Central Park
See pp202–7.

Statue of Liberty
See pp74–5.

Metropolitan Museum of Art
See pp188–95.

Brooklyn Bridge
See pp86–9.

Chinatown
See p96.

Park Avenue's relentless flow of traffic

New York's Best: Museums

NEW YORK'S MUSEUMS range from the vast scope of the Metropolitan Museum to the personal treasures of financier J. Pierpont Morgan's own collection. Several museums celebrate New York's heritage, giving visitors an insight into the people and events that made the city what it is today. This map features some highlights, with a detailed overview on pages 36 and 37.

Museum of Modern Art
The world's most comprehensive collection of modern art includes such gems as Picasso's Goat (1950).

***Intrepid* Sea-Air-Space Museum**
Situated on a large aircraft carrier on the Hudson River, this naval museum also traces the progress of flight and undersea exploration.

Pierpont Morgan Library
One of the world's finest collections of manuscripts, prints and books includes this rare French Bible from 1230.

Old Merchant's House
This perfectly preserved 1820s house belonged to a wealthy trader.

Ellis Island
This museum vividly re-creates the experiences of many millions of immigrant families.

Upper West Side

Theater District

Chelsea and the Garment District

Lower Midtown

Gramercy and the Flatiron District

Greenwich Village

SoHo and TriBeCa

East Village

Lower East Side

Lower Manhattan

Seaport and the Civic Center

Ellis Island

HUDSON RIVER

EAST RIVER

| 0 kilometers | | 2 |
| 0 miles | 1 | |

American Museum of Natural History
Dinosaurs, meteorites and much more have fascinated generations of visitors here.

Morningside Heights and Harlem

Central Park

Upper East Side

Museum of the City of New York
Costumes, works of art and household objects (such as this 1725 silver dish) create an intricate and detailed picture of New York's past.

Cooper-Hewitt Museum
A wealth of decorative arts is displayed in the handsome Upper East Side mansion of the late Andrew Carnegie.

Solomon R. Guggenheim Museum
Ellsworth Kelly's Blue, Green, Yellow, Orange, Red (1966) is part of the collection housed in Frank Lloyd Wright's only New York building.

Metropolitan Museum of Art
Of the millions of works in its collection, this 12th-dynasty Egyptian faïence hippo is the museum's own mascot.

Whitney Museum of American Art
This exceptional collection includes many views of New York. One of the best is Brooklyn Bridge: Variation on an Old Theme *(1939), by Joseph Stella.*

Frick Collection
The collection of 19th-century railroad magnate Henry Clay Frick is displayed in his former home. Masterpieces include St. Francis in the Desert *(about 1480) by Giovanni Bellini.*

Exploring New York's Museums

Richmond Town tobacco tin

YOU COULD DEVOTE an entire month to visiting New York's museums and still not do them justice. There are more than 60 museums in Manhattan alone, half that number again in the other boroughs. The wealth of art and the huge variety of offerings – from old masters to old fire engines, dinosaurs to dolls, Tibetan tapestries to African masks – is equal to that of any city in the world. Note that some museums may be closed on Monday as well as on another day. Many stay open late one or two evenings a week, and some have one evening when admission is free. Not every museum charges for admission, but donations are always welcome.

PAINTING AND SCULPTURE

NEW YORK is best known for its art museums. The **Metropolitan Museum of Art** houses an extensive collection of American art as well as world-famous masterpieces. **The Cloisters**, a branch of the "Met" in Upper Manhattan, is a treasury of medieval art and architecture. The **Frick Collection** has a superb display of Old Masters. In contrast, the **Museum of Modern Art (MoMA)** has some of the world's most famous Impressionist and modern paintings. **The Whitney Museum of American Art** and the **Solomon R. Guggenheim Museum** also specialize in modern art, the Whitney's biennial show being the foremost display of contemporary work by living artists. The cutting edge of today's art is to be seen at the **New Museum of Contemporary Art**, and the work of untrained artists can be seen

at the **Museum of American Folk Art**. The **National Academy of Design** displays a collection of 19th- and 20th-century art, donated by its members. In Harlem, the **Studio Museum** shows the work of black artists.

CRAFTS AND DESIGN

IF YOU ARE interested in textiles, porcelain and glass, embroideries and laces, wallpaper and prints, visit the **Cooper-Hewitt Museum**, the decorative arts outpost of Washington's Smithsonian Institution. The design collections at **MoMA** are as well known as the paintings, tracing the history of design from clocks to couches. The **American Craft Museum** offers the finest work of today's skilled artisans in mediums from furniture to art glass, while the **Museum of American Folk Art** presents folk forms, from quilts to canes. Silver collections are notable at the **Museum of the City of New York**. The fine displays of native art at the **Museum of the American Indian** include jewelry, rugs and pottery.

PRINTS AND PHOTOGRAPHY

THE SMALL but excellent **International Center of Photography** is the only museum in New York totally devoted to this medium. Collections can also be seen at the **Metropolitan Museum of Art** and **MoMA**, with many examples of early photography at the **Museum of the City of New York** and **Ellis Island**.

Prints and drawings by such great book illustrators as Kate Greenaway and John Tenniel are featured at the **Pierpont Morgan Library**. The **Cooper-Hewitt Museum** has examples of the use of prints in the decorative arts.

FURNITURE AND COSTUMES

THE ANNUAL exhibition of the Costume Institute at the **Metropolitan Museum of Art** is always worth a visit. Also impressive is the American Wing, with its 24 rooms of original furnishings tracing life from 1640 to the 20th century. Period rooms depicting New York in various settings, beginning with the 17th century Dutch, are on display at the **Museum of the City of New York**. There are also some house museums that give a realistic picture of furnishings and life in old New York. The **Old Merchant's House**, a preserved residence from the 1820s, was occupied by the same family for 98 years **Gracie Mansion**, the residence of the mayor, was the 1799 country house of a wealthy shipping merchant and is open periodically for public tours. The **Theodore Roosevelt Birthplace** is the brownstone where the 26th president of the United States grew up, and the **Abigail Adams Smith Museum** was part of an 18th-century estate.

Corn husk doll, American Museum of Natural History

The Peaceable Kingdom (c.1840–1845) by Edward Hicks, at the Brooklyn Museum

HISTORY

Palm pistol at the Police Academy Museum

AMERICAN HISTORY unfolds at **Federal Hall**, the first US capital: George Washington took his oath as America's first president on the balcony in April 1789. Visit the **Fraunces Tavern Museum** for a glimpse of colonial New York. **Ellis Island** and **Lower East Side Tenement Museum** re-create the hardships faced by immigrants. The new **Museum of Jewish Heritage** in Battery City is a living memorial to the Holocaust. The **NYC Fire Museum** and the **Police Academy Museum** chronicle heroism and tragedy, while the **South Street Seaport Museum** re-creates early maritime history.

TECHNOLOGY AND NATURAL HISTORY

Forest-dwelling bonga, American Museum of Natural History

SCIENCE MUSEUMS hold exhibitions from nature to space-age technology. The **American Museum of Natural History** has vast collections covering flora, fauna and cultures from around the world. Here, too, the Hayden Planetarium offers unique laser-light shows. The *Intrepid* **Sea-Air-Space Museum** is a repository of technology that chronicles military progress. It is based on the decks of an aircraft carrier.

If you missed a classic Lucille Ball sitcom or footage of the first man on the moon, the place to visit is the **Museum of Television and Radio**, which holds these and many other classics of TV and radio.

ART FROM OTHER CULTURES

ARTWORK of other nations is the focus of several special collections. Oriental art is the specialty of the **Asia Society** and the **Japan Society**. The **Jewish Museum** features major collections of Judaica and has changing exhibitions of Jewish life. **El Museo del Barrio** is dedicated to the arts of Puerto Rico, including many pre-Columbian artifacts. For an impressive review of African-American art and history, visit the **Schomburg Center for Research in Black Culture**. Finally, the **Metropolitan Museum of Art** excels in its multicultural displays of art, ranging from ancient Egypt to contemporary Africa.

Egyptian mummy, Brooklyn Museum

LIBRARIES

NEW YORK'S notable libraries, such as the **Pierpont Morgan Library**, offer some superb art collections as well as a chance to view pages from rare books. The **New York Public Library** shows a collection that includes manuscripts of many famous works.

BEYOND MANHATTAN

OTHER MUSEUMS worth a visit include **The Brooklyn Museum,** with its one and a half million paintings. The

American Museum of the Moving Image in Queens has a unique collection of motion-picture history. The **Jacques Marchais Center of Tibetan Art** is a rare find on Staten Island. Also on Staten Island is **Historic Richmond Town**, a well-restored village dating from the 1600s.

New York's Best: Architecture

E VEN WHEN FOLLOWING world trends, New York has given its own twist to the turns of architectural fashion, the style of its buildings influenced by both geography and economy. An island city, with space at a premium, must look upward to grow. This trend was reflected early on with tall, narrow town houses

and later with the city's apartment buildings and skyscrapers. Building materials such as cast-iron and brownstone were chosen for their local availability and practical appeal. The result is a city that has developed by finding flamboyant answers to practical needs. A more detailed overview of New York's architecture is on pages 40 to 41.

Apartment Buildings
The twin-towered Majestic apartment building is one of four Art Deco blocks on Central Park West.

Cast-Iron Architecture
Mass-produced cast-iron was often used for building facades. SoHo has many of the best examples, such as this building at 28–30 Greene Street.

Post-Modernism
The quirky, yet elegant, shapes of buildings like the World Financial Center, built in 1985 (see p69), mark a bold departure from the sleek steel-and-glass boxes of the 1950s and 1960s.

Brownstones
Built from local sandstone, brownstones were favored by the 19th-century middle classes. India House, built in a Florentine palazzo style on Wall Street, is typical of many brownstone commercial buildings.

Morningside Heights
and Harlem

Upper
West
Side

Central
Park

Upper East
Side

Upper
Midtown

Lower
Midtown

0 kilometers   2

0 miles   1

19th-Century Mansions
The Jewish Museum (see p184), formerly the home of Felix M. Warburg, is a fine example of the French Renaissance style that typified these mansions.

Beaux Arts
Opulent style, created for the richest of owners, is exemplified by the Beaux Arts grandeur of the Frick mansion.

Modernism
The Seagram Building's sleek bronze-and-glass walls, scant decoration and monumental scale typify postwar architecture. (See p175.)

The Skyscraper
The glory of New York architecture, these buildings expressed a perfect blend of practical engineering skill together with fabulous decoration, such as this gargoyle on the Chrysler Building.

Federal Architecture
Federal style was popular in civic architecture of the 19th century; City Hall combines it with French Renaissance influences.

Tenements
Constructed as an economic form of housing, for many these buildings were a stark introduction to new lives. Mainly built on the Lower East Side, the apartments were hopelessly over-crowded. In addition, the buildings' design, with inadequate air shafts, resulted in apartments with little or no ventilation.

Exploring New York's Architecture

A Federal-style front door

IN ITS FIRST 200 YEARS, New York, like all of America, looked to Europe for architectural inspiration. None of the buildings from the Dutch colonial period survive in Manhattan today; most were lost in the great fire of 1776 or torn down to make way for new developments in the early 1800s. Throughout the 18th and 19th centuries, the city's major architectural trends followed those of Europe. With the advent of cast-iron architecture in the 1850s, the Art Deco period and the ever-higher rise of the skyscraper, New York's architecture came into its own.

FEDERAL ARCHITECTURE

THIS AMERICAN adaptation of the Neoclassical Adam style flowered in the early decades of the new nation, featuring square buildings two or three stories tall, with low hipped roofs, balustrades and decorative elements – all carefully balanced. **City Hall** (1811, John McComb, Jr. and Joseph François Mangin) is a blend of Federal and French Renaissance influences. The restored warehouses of **Schermerhorn Row** (c1812) in the Seaport district are also in Federal style.

BROWNSTONES

PLENTIFUL AND CHEAP, the brown sandstone found in the nearby Connecticut River Valley and along the banks of the Hackensack River in New

A typical brownstone with stoop leading up to the main entrance

Jersey was the most common building material in the 1800s. It is found all over the city's residential neighborhoods, used for small homes or small

apartments – some of the best examples of brownstone can be found in **Chelsea**. Because street space was limited, these buildings were very narrow in width, but also very deep. A typical brownstone has a flight of steps, called a stoop, leading up to the living floors. Separate stairs lead down to the basement, which was originally the servants' quarters.

TENEMENTS

TENEMENTS WERE built to house the huge influx of immigrants who arrived from the 1840s up to World War I. The six-story blocks, 100 ft (30 m) long and 25 ft (8 m) wide, offered very little light and air except from tiny sidewall air shafts and windows at each end, leaving the middle rooms in darkness. The tiny apartments were called railroad flats after their similarity to railway cars. Later designs had air shafts between buildings, but these helped the spread of fire. The **Lower East Side Tenement Museum** has scale models of the old tenements.

CAST-IRON ARCHITECTURE

AN AMERICAN architectural innovation of the 19th century, cast iron was cheaper than stone or brick and allowed ornate features to be prefabricated in foundries from molds and used as building facades. Today, New York has the world's largest concentration of full and partial cast-iron facades. The best, built in the 1870s, are in the **SoHo Cast-Iron Historic District**.

The original cast-iron facade of 72–76 Greene Street, SoHo

BEAUX ARTS

THIS FRENCH school of architecture dominated public buildings and wealthy residential properties during New York's gilded age. This era (from 1880 to about 1920) produced many of the city's most prominent architects, including Richard Morris Hunt (**Carnegie Hall**, 1891; **Metropolitan Museum**, 1895), who in 1845 was the first American architect to study in Paris; Cass Gilbert (**Custom House**, 1907; **New York Life Insurance**

ARCHITECTURAL DISGUISES

Some of the most fanciful forms on the New York skyline were devised by clever architects to disguise the city's essential but utilitarian – and rather unattractive – rooftop water tanks. Look skyward to discover the ornate cupolas, spires and domes that transform the most mundane of features into veritable castles in the air. Examples that are easy to spot are atop two neighboring Fifth Avenue hotels: the Sherry Netherland at 60th Street and the Pierre at 61st Street.

Standard water tower

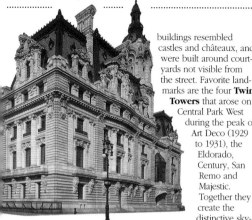

Beaux Arts mansion built for Cornelius Vanderbilt II (1843–99); it has since been demolished

Building, 1928; the **US Courthouse**, 1936; the teams of Warren & Wetmore (**Grand Central Terminal**, 1913; **Helmsley Building**, 1929; Carrère & Hastings (**New York Public Library**, 1911; **Frick mansion**, 1914); and McKim, Mead & White, the city's most famous firm of architects (**Villard Houses**, 1884; **United States General Post Office**, 1913; **Municipal Building**, 1914).

APARTMENT BUILDINGS

As the city's population grew and space became ever more precious, family homes in Manhattan became much too expensive for most New Yorkers, and even the wealthy joined the trend toward communal living. In 1884 Henry Hardenbergh's Dakota (see p216), one of the first luxury apartment buildings, started a spate of turn-of-the-century construction on the Upper West Side. Many of the

buildings resembled castles and châteaux, and were built around courtyards not visible from the street. Favorite landmarks are the four **Twin Towers** that arose on Central Park West during the peak of Art Deco (1929 to 1931), the Eldorado, Century, San Remo and Majestic. Together they create the distinctive skyline seen from the park.

SKYSCRAPERS

Although CHICAGO gave birth to the skyscraper, New York has seen some of the greatest innovations in this style. In 1902 Daniel Burnham, a Chicago architect, built the **Flatiron Building**, so tall at 300 ft (91 m) that sceptics said it would collapse. By 1913, the **Woolworth Building** had risen to 792 ft (241 m). Soon, zoning laws were passed requiring "setbacks" – upper stories were stepped back to allow light to reach street level. This suited the Art Deco style. The **Chrysler Building** (1930)

Art Deco arched pattern on the spire of the Chrysler Building

was the world's tallest until the **Empire State Building** (1931) was completed. Both are Art Deco classics, but it was Raymond Hood's **Group Health Insurance Building**, formerly the McGraw-Hill Building, that represented New York in 1932 in the *International Style* architectural survey.

The **World Trade Center** is currently the tallest building, at 1,350 ft (411 m). It represents the "glass box" Modernist style, now superseded by the Post-Modern style, such as the **Citicorp Center** (1977).

245 Fifth Avenue (Apartment Bulding)

60 Gramercy Park North (Brownstone)

Hotel Pierre (Beaux Arts)

Sherry Netherland Hotel (Beaux Arts)

Multicultural New York

WHEREVER YOU GO in New York, even in pockets of the hectic high-rise city center, you will find evidence of the richly ethnic flavor of the city. A bus ride can take you from Madras to Moscow, Hong Kong to Haiti. Immigrants are still coming to New York, though numbers are fewer than in the peak years from 1880 to 1910, when 17 million people arrived. In the 1980s, a million newcomers, largely from Caribbean countries and Asia, arrived and found their own special corner of the city. Throughout the year you will encounter crowds celebrating one of many festivals. To find out more about national celebrations and parades, see pages 50 to 53.

Hell's Kitchen
The Irish community first settled here; now they color Fifth Avenue green for St. Patrick's Day on March 17 every year.

Little Ukraine
Services are held at Taras Sevchenko Place as part of the May 17 festivities to mark the Ukrainians' conversion to Christianity.

Little Korea
Not far from Herald Square, a small enclave of Koreans has made a niche.

Chelsea and the Garment District

Greenwich Village

Gramercy and the Flatiron District

SoHo and TriBeCa

Little Italy
For ten days in September, the Italian community gathers around the Mulberry Street area, and the streets are taken over by the celebrations of the Festa di San Gennaro.

East Village

Chinatown
Every year, around the end of January, Mott Street is packed with revelers as Chinatown celebrates its New Year.

Lower Manhattan

Seaport and the Civic Center

Lower East Side

The Lower East Side
The synagogues around Rivington Street reflect the religious traditions of this old Jewish area.

0 kilometers   2

0 miles   1

Harlem
The Sunday morning gospel service at the Abyssinian Baptist Church is one of Harlem's finest.

El Barrio
The vibrant Hispanic community of Harlem's El Barrio district is centered around the street market, La Marquetta.

Yorkville
A few cafés and bierkellers remain to keep the flavor of this former uptown German district. The Steuben Day Parade is held here each September.

Upper East Side
The magnificent St. Nicholas Russian Orthodox Cathedral on East 97th Street is a reminder of the dispersed White Russian community. Mass is held in Russian each Sunday.

Little India
The restaurants of East 6th Street offer Eastern atmosphere at affordable prices.

Exploring New York's Many Cultures

Stained glass at the Cotton Club

E VEN "NATIVE" NEW YORKERS have ancestral roots in other countries. Throughout the 17th century, the Dutch and English settled here, establishing trade colonies in the New World. Soon America became a symbol of hope for the downtrodden elsewhere in Europe. Many flocked across the ocean, some penniless and with little knowledge of the language. The potato famine of the 1840s led to the first wave of Irish immigrants, followed by German and other European workers displaced by political unrest and the Industrial Revolution. Immigrants continue to enrich New York in countless ways, and today an estimated 80 languages are spoken.

Turkish immigrants arriving at former Idlewild Airport in 1963

THE JEWS

T HERE HAS BEEN a Jewish community in New York since 1654. The first synagogue, Shearith Israel, was established by refugees from a Dutch colony in Brazil and is still active today. These first settlers, Sephardic Jews of Spanish descent, included such prominent families as the Baruchs. They were followed by the German Jews, who set up successful retailing enterprises, like the Straus brothers at Macy's. Russian persecution led to the mass immigration that began in the late 1800s. By the start of World War I, there were 600,000 Jews living on the Lower East Side. Today, this area is more Hispanic than Jewish, but it holds reminders of its role as a place of refuge and new beginnings.

THE GERMANS

T HE GERMANS began to settle in New York in the 18th century. From Peter Zenger onward *(see p19)*, the city's German community has championed the freedom to express ideas and opinions. It has also produced giants of industry, such as John Jacob Astor, the city's first millionaire.

THE ITALIANS

I TALIANS FIRST came to New York in the 1830s and 1840s. Many came from northern Italy to escape the failing revolution at home. In the 1870s, poverty in southern Italy drove many more Italians across the ocean. In time, they became a potent political force in the city, exemplified by Fiorello La Guardia, one of New York's finest mayors.

THE CHINESE

T HE CHINESE were late arrivals to New York. In 1880, the population of the Mott Street district was a mere

Eastern States Buddhist Temple, in central Chinatown *(see pp96–7)*

700. By the 1940s, they were the city's fastest-growing and most upwardly mobile ethnic group, extending the old boundaries of Chinatown and establishing new neighborhoods in parts of Brooklyn and Queens. Once a closed community, Chinatown now bustles with tourists exploring the streets and markets, and sampling the restaurant food.

THE HISPANIC AMERICANS

Hispanic religious carving at El Museo del Barrio *(see p229)*

P UERTO RICANS were in New York as early as 1838, but it was not until after World War II that they arrived in large numbers in search of work. Most live in El Barrio, formerly known as Spanish Harlem. Professionals who fled Fidel Castro's Cuba have moved out of the city itself but are still very influential in Hispanic commerce and culture. Washington Heights is home to the Dominican and Colombian communities.

THE IRISH

T HE IRISH, who first arrived in New York in the 1840s, had to overcome harsh odds. Wretched with starvation, and with barely a penny to their names, they labored hard to escape the slums of Five Points and Hell's Kitchen, helping to build the modern city in the process. Many joined the police and fire-fighting forces, rising to high rank through dedication to duty. Others set up successful businesses, such as the Irish bars that act as a focus for the now-scattered New York Irish community.

THE AFRICAN AMERICANS

Arguably the best-known black inner-city community in the Western world, Harlem is noted for the Harlem Renaissance of writing *(see pp28-9)* as much as it is for great entertainment, gospel music and soul food. The move of black African Americans from the south to the north began with emancipation in the 1860s and increased markedly in the 1920s, when Harlem's black population rose from 83,000 to 204,000. Today Harlem is undergoing revitalization in many areas. The African American population has also dispersed throughout the city.

THE MELTING POT

Other new york cultures are not distinctly defined but are still easily found. Ukrainians gather in the East Village, around St. George's Ukrainian Catholic Church on East 7th Street. Little India can be spotted by the restaurants along East 6th Street. Koreans own many of the small grocery stores in Manhattan, but most tend to live in the Flushing area of Queens. The religious diversity of New York can be seen in the Islamic Center on Riverside Drive, the

A woman celebrating at the Greek Independence Day parade

Russian Orthodox Cathedral on East 97th Street *(see p197);* and the new Islamic Cultural Center on 96th Street – Manhattan's first major mosque.

THE OUTER BOROUGHS

Brooklyn is by far the most international borough. Caribbean newcomers from Jamaica and Haiti are one of the fastest-growing immigrant groups. West Indians tend to cluster along Eastern Parkway between Grand Army Plaza and Utica Avenue, the route of the lavish, exotically-costumed West Indian Day Parade in September. Recently arrived Russian Jewish immigrants have turned Brighton Beach into "Little Odessa by the Sea," and the Scandinavians and Lebanese have settled in Bay Ridge and the Finns in Sunset Park. Borough Park and Williamsburg are home to Orthodox Jews, and Midwood has an Israeli – Middle East accent. Italians live in the Bensonhurst area. Greenpoint is little Poland, and Atlantic Avenue is home to the largest Arab community in America.

The Irish were among the earliest groups to cross the Harlem River into the Bronx. Japanese executives favor the more exclusive Riverdale area. One of the most distinctive ethnic areas is Astoria, Queens, which has the largest Greek population outside the motherland. Jackson Heights is home to a large Latin American quarter, including 300,000 Colombians. Indians also favor this area and neighboring Flushing. But it is the Asians who have transformed Flushing, so much so that the local train is known as "The Orient Express."

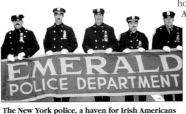

The New York police, a haven for Irish Americans

NEWCOMERS WHO MADE THEIR MARK *See also pp46–9.*

The dates mark the year these immigrants entered the US via New York.

1890	1895	1900	1905	1910	1915	1920	1925	1930	1935	1940

1893 Irving Berlin (Russia), musician

1894 Al Jolson (Lithuania), singer

1906 "Lucky Luciano" (Italy), gangster (deported 1946)

1908 Bob Hope (England), comedian

1909 Lee Strasberg (Austria), theater director

1921 Bela Lugosi (Hungary), star of *Dracula*

1932 George Balanchine (Russia), ballet choreographer

1933 Albert Einstein (Germany), scientist

1896 Samuel Goldwyn (Poland), movie mogul

1902 Joe Hill (Sweden), labor activist

1903 Frank Capra (Italy), film director

1904 Hyman Rickover (Russia), developer of nuclear submarine

1913 Rudolph Valentino (Italy), film star

1912 Claudette Colbert (France), film star

1923 Isaac Asimov (Russia), scientist and writer

1938 von Trapp family (Austria), singers

Celebrated Visitors and Residents

N̲EARLY ALL New Yorkers have immigrant roots if you go back far enough. Indeed, many of the city's most prominent residents have migrated here, coming to New York to find creative freedom and sometimes fleeing from constraints or repression in their native countries. As a result, some of the most brilliant contributions to New York's colorful history and culture have been made by first-generation immigrants and visitors.

George Balanchine (1904–8̲
The ballet choreographer migrated from Russia in 1933 and formed the New York City Ballet.

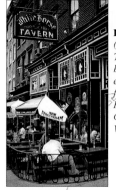

Dylan Thomas (1914–53)
The Welsh poet drank himself to a tragically early death; he frequented the White Horse Tavern in Greenwich Village.

Marcel Duchamp (1887–1968)
In 1917 the French Dadaist climbed Washington Square arch to protest against US partici- pation in World War I.

Guiseppe Garibaldi (1807–82)
A statue in Greenwich Village honors the Italian freedom fighter who spent four years in exile on Staten Island before returning to unify Italy.

Irving Berlin (1888–1989)
Born Israel Baline in Siberia, he grew up on the Lower East Side and composed the hit tune "White Christmas."

Theater District

Chelsea and the Garment District

Gramercy and the Flatiron District

Lo̲ Mi̲

Greenwich Village

East Village

SoHo & TriBeCa

Lower East Side

Seaport and the Civic Center

Lower Manhattan

Isaac Bashevis Singer
(1904–91)
The Polish Jewish novelist lived on West 86th Street for many years.

Morningside Heights and Harlem

John Audubon
(1785–1851)
America's most famous ornithologist grew up in France. His New York estate was in Washington Heights.

Marcus Garvey
(1887–1940)
During the 1920s Jamaican-born Garvey lived in Harlem, where he was an influential black leader.

Upper West Side

Central Park

John Lennon
(1940–80)
The Liverpool-born musician and his wife, Yoko Ono, made their home on the Upper West Side.

Upper East Side

Upper Midtown

Harry Houdini
(1874–1926)
The escape artist from Budapest had a vision of his death at age 52 and left his West 113th Street house weeping.

Andrew Carnegie *(1835–1919)*
The Scottish-born industrialist and philanthropist's home is now the Cooper-Hewitt Museum (see p184).

Sarah Bernhardt *(1844–1923)*
The French actress attended services at the Little Church Around the Corner (see p127) during her time in New York.

0 kilometers   2

0 miles   1

Jacob Riis *(1849–1914)*
A Danish immigrant, he slept in Bowery doorways before writing How the Other Half Lives, which helped alleviate New York's squalor.

Remarkable New Yorkers

NEW YORK HAS NOURISHED some of the best creative talents of this century. Pop art began here, and Manhattan is still the world center for modern art. The alternative writers of the 1950s and '60s – known as the Beat Generation – took inspiration from the city's jazz clubs. And since it is the financial capital, many leading world financiers have made New York their home.

WRITERS

Novelist James Baldwin

MUCH GREAT AMERICAN literature was created in New York. *Charlotte Temple, A Tale of Truth,* first published in 1791 by Susanna Rowson (c1762–1824), was a tale of seduction in the city and a best-seller for 50 years.

America's first professional author was Charles Brockden Brown (1771–1810), who came to New York in 1791. The novels of Edgar Allan Poe (1809–49), the pioneer of the modern detective story, expanded the thriller genre. Henry James (1843–1916) published *The Bostonians* (1886) and became the master of the psychological novel, and his friend Edith Wharton (1861–1937) became known for her satirical novels about American society.

American literature finally received international recognition with Washington Irving's (1783–1859) satire, *A History of New York* (1809). It earned him $2,000. Irving coined the names "Gotham" for New York and "Knickerbockers" for New Yorkers. He and James Fenimore Cooper (1789–1851), whose books gave birth to the "Western" novel, formed the Knicker-

bocker group of US writers. Greenwich Village has always attracted writers, including Herman Melville (1819–91) whose masterpiece, *Moby Dick* (1851), was very poorly received at first. Jack Kerouac (1922–69), Allen Ginsberg and William Burroughs all went to Columbia University and drank at the San Remo Café in Greenwich Village. Dylan Thomas (1914–53) lived at the Chelsea Hotel *(see p137).* Novelist Nathanael West (1902– 40) worked in the Gramercy Park Hotel, and Dashiell Hammett (1894–1961) wrote *The Maltese Falcon* while living there. James Baldwin (1924– 87), born in Harlem, wrote *Another Country* (1963) on his return to New York from Europe.

ARTISTS

THE NEW YORK School of Abstract Expressionists founded the first influential American art movement. It was launched by Hans Hofmann (1880–1966) with Franz Kline and Willem de Kooning, whose first job in America was as a housepainter. Adolph Gottlieb, Mark Rothko (1903–70) and Jackson Pollock (1912–56) went on to popularize this style. Pollock, Kline and de Kooning all had their studios on the Lower East Side.

Pop art began in New York in the 1960s with Roy Lichtenstein and

Pop artist Andy Warhol

Andy Warhol (1926– 87), who made some of his cult films at 33 Union Square. Keith Haring (1958–90) was a very prolific graffiti artist whose work as a pop artist is now receiving recognition.

Robert Mapplethorpe (1946–89) acquired notoriety for his homoerotic photos of men. Jeff Koons has now superseded him as the *bête noire* of the art establishment.

The illusionistic murals by Richard Haas enliven many walls throughout the city.

ACTORS

IN 1849 the British actor Charles Macready started a riot by saying Americans were vulgar. A mob stormed the Astor Place Opera House, where Macready was playing *Macbeth,* police opened fire, and 22 rioters were killed. In 1927 Mae West (1893–1980) spent 10 days in a workhouse on Roosevelt Island and was fined $500 for giving a lewd performance in her Broadway show *Sex.* Marc Blitzstein's radical pro-labor opera *The Cradle Will Rock* produced by Orson Welles (1915–85) and John Houseman (1902–88), was immediately banned and the show had to move to

Vaudeville actress Mae West

another theater. The actors managed to get around the ban by buying tickets and singing their roles from the audience.

The musical has been New York's special contribution to the theater. Florenz Ziegfeld's (1869–1932) *Follies* ran from 1907 to 1931. The opening of *Oklahoma!* on Broadway in 1943 began the age of musicals by Richard Rodgers (1902–79) and Oscar Hammerstein, Jr. (1895–1960).

Off Broadway, the Province-town Players at 33 MacDougal Street were the first to produce Eugene O'Neill's (1888–1953) *Beyond the Horizon* (1920). His successor as the major innovative force in US theater was Edward Albee, author of *Who's Afraid of Virginia Woolf?* (1962).

MUSICIANS AND DANCERS

LEONARD BERNSTEIN (1918–90) followed a long line of great conductors at the New York Philharmonic, including Bruno Walter (1876–1962), Arturo Toscanini (1867–1957) and Leopold Stokowski (1882–1977). Maria Callas (1923–77) was born in New York but moved to Europe.

Carnegie Hall *(see p146)* has featured Enrico Caruso (1873–1921), Bob Dylan and the Beatles. A record concert attendance was set in 1991 when Paul Simon drew a million people for his free concert in Central Park.

The legendary swinging jazz clubs of the 1930s and 1940s are now gone from 52nd Street. Plaques on "Jazz Walk" outside the CBS building honor such

Josephine Baker

famous performers as Charlie Parker (1920–55) and Josephine Baker (1906–75).

Between 1940 and 1965, New York became a world dance capital with the founding of George Balanchine's (1904–83) New York City Ballet and the American Ballet Theater. In 1958, choreographer Alvin Ailey (1931–89) started the American Dance Theater, a show-case for modern dance works by a multiracial troupe.

INDUSTRIALISTS AND ENTREPRENEURS

Tycoon Cornelius Vanderbilt

THE RAGS-TO-RICHES story is an American dream. Andrew Carnegie (1835–1919), "the steel baron with a heart of gold," started with nothing and died having given away $350 million. His beneficiaries included public libraries and universities through-out America. Many other foundations are legacies of wealthy philanthropists. Some, like Cornelius Vanderbilt (1794–1877) tried to shake off their rough begin-nings by patronizing the arts.

In business, New York's "robber barons" did what they liked with apparent impunity. Financiers Jay Gould (1836–92) and James Fisk (1834–72) beat Vanderbilt in the war for the Erie Railroad by manipu-lating stock. In September 1869 they caused Wall Street's first "Black Friday" when they tried to corner the gold market, but fled when their fraud was discovered. Gould died a happy billionaire, and Fisk was killed in a fight over a woman.

Modern entrepreneurs have included Donald Trump *(see p31)*, owner of Trump Tower, and Harry and Leona Helmsley. Despite Leona's imprisonment for tax evasion, their property empire remains intact and includes such New York sites as the Helmsley Building *(see p156)*.

ARCHITECTS

CASS GILBERT (1858–1934), who built such Neo-Gothic skyscrapers as the Woolworth Building of 1913 *(see p91)* was one of the men who literally shaped the city. His caricature can be seen in the lobby, clutching a model of his masterpiece. Stanford White (1853–1906) was as well known for his scandalous private life as for his fine Beaux Arts buildings, such as the Players Club *(p126)*. For most of his life, Frank Lloyd Wright (1867–1959) spurned city architecture. When he was persuaded to leave his mark on the city, it was in the form of the Guggenheim Museum *(pp186–7)*. German-born Ludwig Mies van der Rohe (1886–1969), who built the Seagram Building, did not believe in "inventing a new architecture every Monday morning," although some might argue that this is just what New York has always done best.

Musical producer Florenz Ziegfeld

NEW YORK THROUGH THE YEAR

SPRINGTIME IN NEW YORK sees Park Avenue filled with blooms, while Fifth Avenue goes green for St. Patrick's Day, the first of the year's many big parades. Summer in the city is hot and humid, but it is worth forsaking an air-conditioned interior to step outside, where parks and squares are the setting for free open-air music and theater. The first Monday in September marks Labor Day and the advent of comfortable temperatures and the orange-red colors of autumn. Then, as Christmas nears, the shops and streets begin to sparkle with dazzling window displays.

Dates of the events on the following pages may vary. For details consult the listings magazines *(see p353)*. The New York Convention and Visitors Bureau *(see p352)* also issues a useful quarterly free calendar of events.

SPRING

EVERY SEASON in New York brings its own tempo and temptations. In spring, the city shakes off the winter with tulips and cherry blossoms in the parks and spring fashions in the stores. Everyone window shops and gallery hops. The hugely popular St. Patrick's Day Parade draws the crowds, and thousands don their finery for the Easter Parade down Fifth Avenue.

Inventive Easter bonnets in New York's Easter Parade

MARCH

St. Patrick's Day Parade
(Mar 17), Fifth Ave, from 44th to 86th St. Green clothes, green flowers – even green beer.
Greek Independence Day Parade *(Mar 25)*, Fifth Ave, from 49th to 59th St. Greek dancing and food.
New York City Opera Spring Season *(Mar– mid-Apr)*, Lincoln Center *(p338)*.
Ringling Bros and Barnum & Bailey Circus *(late Mar– end May)*, Madison Square Garden *(p133)*.

Yellow tulips and cabs shine on Park Avenue

EASTER

Easter Flower Show *(week before Easter)*, Macy's department store *(pp132–3)*.
Easter Parade *(Easter Sun)*, Fifth Ave, from 44th to 59th St. Paraders in costumes and outrageous millinery gather around St. Patrick's Cathedral.

APRIL

Cherry Blossom Festival *(late Apr– May)*, Brooklyn Botanic Garden. Famous for Japanese cherry trees and beautifully laid out ornamental gardens.
Annual Earth Day Festival Activities *(varies)*.
Baseball *(Apr– May)*, Major league season starts for Yankees and Mets *(p344)*.
New York City Ballet Spring Season *(Apr– Jun)*, New York State Theater and Metropolitan Opera House in Lincoln Center *(p212)*.

MAY

Martin Luther King, Jr. Day Parade *(third Sun)*, Fifth Ave, from 57th to 79th St. A parade to honor the memory of the black civil rights leader who was assassinated in 1968.

Parading in national costume on Greek Independence Day

Ninth Avenue Street Festival *(mid-May)*, from W 37th to W 57th St. A feast of ethnic foods, music and dance.
Washington Square Outdoor Art Exhibit *(last weekend in May and first weekend in Jun)*. **Memorial Day** Activities *(last weekend)* A parade down Fifth Ave, festivities at South Street Seaport.

Days of Sunshine
*New York enjoys long
hours of summer sun
from June to August,
with July the month
of greatest sunshine.
The winter days are
much shorter, but
many are clear and
bright. Autumn has
more sunshine than
spring, although
both are sunny.*

SUMMER

NEW YORKERS escape the hot city streets when possible, for picnics, boat rides and the beaches. Macy's fireworks light up the Fourth of July skies, and more sparks fly when the New York Yankees and Mets baseball teams are in town. Summer also brings street fairs, outdoor concerts, and free Shakespeare and opera in Central Park.

Policeman dancing in the Puerto Rican Day Parade

JUNE

Puerto Rican Day Parade *(first Sun)*, Fifth Ave, from 44th to 86th St. Floats and marching bands.
Museum Mile Festival *(second Tue)*, Fifth Ave, from 82nd to 105th St. Free entry to museums.
Central Park Summerstage *(Jun–Aug)*, Central Park. Music and dance of every variety, almost daily, rain or shine.
Metropolitan Opera Parks Concerts. Free evening concerts in parks throughout the city *(pp338–9)*.
Goldman Memorial Band Concerts *(Jun–Aug)*, Lincoln Center *(p212)*. Traditional band concerts.

Shakespeare in the Park *(Jun–Sep)*. Broadway stars take on the bard at Delacorte Theater, Central Park *(p335)*.
Lesbian and Gay Pride Day Parade *(mid Jun)*, from Columbus Circle along Fifth Ave to Washington Sq *(p113)*.
JVC Jazz Festival *(late Jun–early Jul)*. Top jazz musicians perform in various halls in the city *(p341)*.

JULY

Macy's Firework Display *(Jul 4)*, East River. High point of the city's Independence Day celebrations.
American Crafts Festival *(late June-early July)*, Lincoln Center *(p212)*. High-quality crafts.
Mostly Mozart Festival, *(mid-Jul–end Aug)*, Avery Fisher Hall, Lincoln Center *(pp338-9)*.
NY Philharmonic Parks Concerts *(late Jul–early Aug)*. Free concerts in parks throughout the city *(p339)*.

Festivities at a summer street fair in Greenwich Village

Lincoln Center Festival *(Jul)*, Dance. opera, other performing arts from around the world. **World Trade Center** performances *(July)*.

AUGUST

Harlem Week *(mid-Aug)*. Films, art, music, dance, fashion, sports and tours.
Out-of-Doors Festival *(mid-Jul–early Sep)*, Lincoln Center. Free dance and theater performances *(p334)*.
US Open Tennis Championships *(late Aug–early Sep)*, Flushing Meadows *(p345)*.

Independence Day (July 4) fireworks display on the East River

AVERAGE MONTHLY TEMPERATURE

Temperature
The chart shows the average minimum and maximum temperatures for each month in New York. With top temperatures averaging 84° F (29° C), the city can become hot and humid. In contrast, the months of winter, although rarely below freezing, can seem bitterly cold.

AUTUMN

L ABOR DAY marks the end of the summer. The Giants and the Jets kick off the football season, the Broadway season begins and the Festa di San Gennaro in Little Italy is the high point in a succession of colorful neighborhood fairs. Macy's Thanksgiving Day Parade is the nation's symbol that the festive season has arrived.

SEPTEMBER

Richmond County Fair
(Labor Day weekend), in the grounds of Historic Richmond Town *(p252)*. New York's only authentic county fair.
West Indian Carnival
(Labor Day weekend), Brooklyn. Parade, floats, music, dancing and food.
Brazilian Festival *(early Sep)*, E 46th St, between Times Sq and Madison Ave. Brazilian music, food, and crafts.
New York is Book Country *(mid-Sep)*, Fifth Ave, from 48th to 59th Sts. Book fair.
Festa di San Gennaro *(third week)*, Little Italy *(p96)*. Ten days of festivities and processions.
New York Film Festival *(mid-Sep – early Oct)*, Lincoln Center *(p212)*. American films and international art films.
Von Steuben Day Parade *(third week)*, Upper Fifth Ave. German-American celebrations.
American Football *(season begins)*, Giants Stadium, home to the Giants and the Jets *(p344)*.

OCTOBER

Columbus Day Parade *(2nd Mon)*, Fifth Ave, from 44th to 86th Sts. Parades and music to celebrate Columbus's first sighting of America.
Pulaski Day Parade *(Sun closest to Oct 5)*, Fifth Ave, from 26th to 52nd Sts. Celebrations for Polish-American hero Casimir Pulaski.
Halloween Parade *(Oct 31)*, Greenwich Village. Brilliant event with fantastic costumes.
Big Apple Circus *(Oct–Jan)*, Damrosch Park, Lincoln Center. Special themes are presented each year *(p349)*.
Basketball *(season begins)*, Madison Square Garden. Local team is the Knicks *(p344)*.
New York City Marathon *(last Sun Oct or first Sun Nov)*. From Staten Island through all the city boroughs.

Huge Superman balloon floating above Macy's Thanksgiving Day Parade

NOVEMBER

Macy's Thanksgiving Day Parade *(fourth Thu)*, from Central Park West and W 79th St to Broadway and W 34th St. A joy for children, with floats, huge balloons and Santa.
Rockefeller Center Ice Skating Rink *(Nov– Mar)*, Open to the public. You can skate beneath the famous Christmas Tree.
Magnificent Christmas Spectacular *(Nov–Jan)*, Radio City Music Hall. Variety show, with the Rockettes.

Revelers in Greenwich Village's Halloween Parade

Exotic Caribbean carnival costume in the streets of Brooklyn

AVERAGE MONTHLY RAINFALL

Rainfall
March and August are the months of heaviest rainfall in New York. Rainfall in spring is unpredictable, so be prepared. Sudden heavy snowfalls in winter can cause chaos in the city.

◼ Rainfall

◼ Snowfall

WINTER

N EW YORK is magical at Christmas – even the stone lions at the Public Library don wreaths for the occasion, and shops become works of art. From Times Square to Chinatown, New Year celebrations punctuate the season, and Central Park becomes a winter sports arena.

Statue of Alice in Wonderland in Central Park

DECEMBER

Tree-Lighting Ceremony *(early Dec)*, Rockefeller Center *(p142)*. Lighting of the giant Christmas tree in front of the RCA Building.
Messiah Sing-In *(mid-Dec)*, Lincoln Center *(p212)*. The audience rehearses and performs under the guidance of various conductors.
Hanukkah Menorah *(mid–late Dec)*, Grand Army Plaza, Brooklyn. Lighting of the huge menorah (candelabra) every night during the eight-day Festival of Lights.
New Year's Eve. Fireworks display in Central Park *(pp204–5)*; festivities in Times Square *(p145)*; 5-mile (8-km) run in Central Park; poetry reading in St. Mark's Church.

JANUARY

National Boat Show *(mid-Jan)*, Jacob K. Javits Convention Center *(p136)*.
Chinese New Year *(late Jan/Feb)*, Chinatown *(pp96–7)*. Dragons, fireworks and food.
Winter Antiques Show *(late Jan)*, Seventh Regiment Armory *(p185)*. NYC's most prestigious antiques fair.

FEBRUARY

Black History Month. African-American events take place throughout the city.
Empire State Building Run-Up *(early Feb)*. Runners race to the 102nd floor *(pp134–5)*.
Lincoln and Washington Birthday Sales *(Feb 12–22)* Big department stores sales throughout the city.
Westminster Kennel Club Dog Show *(mid-Feb)*, Madison Square Garden *(p133)*. Major dog show.

Chinese New Year celebrations in Chinatown

PUBLIC HOLIDAYS

New Year's Day (Jan 1)
Martin Luther King Day (3rd Mon, Jan)
President's Day (mid-Feb)
Memorial Day (end May)
Independence Day (Jul 4)
Labor Day (1st Mon, Sep)
Columbus Day (2nd Mon, Oct)
Election Day (1st Tue, Nov)
Veterans Day (Nov 11)
Thanksgiving Day (4th Thu, Nov)
Christmas Day (Dec 25)

The giant Christmas tree and decorations at Rockefeller Center

The Southern Tip of Manhattan

THIS VIEW OF Lower Manhattan, seen from the Hudson River, encompasses some of the most striking modern additions to the New York skyline, including the instantly recognizable twin towers of the World Trade Center, and the newer, distinctively topped quartet of the World Financial Center. You will also catch glimpses of an earlier Manhattan: Castle Clinton set against the green space of Battery Park and, behind it, the noble Custom House building.

LOCATOR MAP

   The Southern Tip

World Financial Center
At the heart of this complex is the Winter Garden – a place to shop, dine, be entertained or just enjoy the Hudson River views (see p69).

World Trade Center
Twin 110-story steel-and-glass towers (see p72) dominate the skyline. Below is a plaza bigger than St. Mark's Square in Venice.

The Upper Room
This walkaround sculpture by Ned Smyth is one of many works of art in Battery Park City (see p72).

Detail from the *Upper Room*

An Earlier View
This 1898 photograph shows a skyline now changed beyond recognition.

Downtown Athletic Club
The Heisman Trophy for football is kept in this fine Art Deco building.

US Custom House
This magnificent 1907 Beaux Arts building now houses the Museum of the American Indian (see p73).

East Coast War Memorial
In Battery Park, a huge bronze eagle by Albino Manca honors the dead of World War II.

26 Broadway
The tower of the former Standard Oil Building resembles an oil lamp. The interior is still decorated with company symbols.

Bank of New York

17 State Street

26 Broadway

1 Liberty Plaza

Liberty View

BANK OF NEW YORK

Castle Clinton

US Custom House

American Merchant Mariners' Memorial (1991)
This sculpture by Marisol is on Pier A, the last of Manhattan's old piers. The pier also has a clock tower that chimes the hours on ships' bells.

Shrine of Mother Seton
The first US-born saint lived here (see p76).

Lower Manhattan from the East River

A{T FIRST SIGHT}, this stretch of East River shoreline, running up from the tip of Manhattan Island, is a seamless array of 20th-century office buildings. But from sea level, streets and slips are still visible, offering glimpses of old New York and the Financial District to the west. On the skyline itself, a few of the district's early skyscrapers still proudly display their ornate crowns above their more anonymous modern counterparts.

LOCATOR MAP

☐ *East River View*

India House
The handsome brownstone at One Hanover Square is one of the finest of its kind.

Vietnam Veterans Plaza
An engraved green-glass memorial dominates the former Coenties Slip, a wharf filled in to make a park in the late 19th century (see p76).

Hanover Square
A statue of one of the Dutch mayors, Abraham De Peyster, sits near the house where he was born in 1657.

One New York Plaza

55 Water Street

Barclay Bank Building

Downtown Heliport
Air-Sea Rescue and sightseeing flights operate from here.

Battery Maritime Building
This historic ferry terminal serves only Governor's Island (see p77).

Delmonico's
High society dined here a century ago.

New York Stock Exchange
Although hidden from view by more modern edifices, this is still the hub of the hectic Financial District (see pp70–71).

40 Wall Street
In the 1940s, the pyramid-topped tower of the former Bank of Manhattan was hit by a light aircraft.

70 Pine Street
Replicas of this elegant Gothic-style tower can be seen near the Pine and Cedar Street entrances.

Bank of New York
This serene 1928 interior is part of the bank set up in 1784 by Alexander Hamilton (see p21).

1 Financial Square

New York Stock Exchange

Morgan Bank
Columns from lobby to rooftop are the theme of this striking modern building.

Chase Manhattan Bank Tower

120 Wall Street

100 Old Slip
Now in the shadow of One Financial Square, the small palazzo-style First Precinct Police Department was the city's most modern police station when it was built in 1911.

Citibank Building

Carved medallion, 100 Old Slip

***Queen Elizabeth* Monument**
The ocean liner that sank in 1972 is remembered here.

South Street Seaport

As the financial district ends, the skyline, as seen from the East River or Brooklyn, changes dramatically. The corporate headquarters are replaced by the piers, low-rise streets and warehouses of the old seaport area, now restored as the South Street Seaport *(see pp82–3)*. The Civic Center lies not far inland, and a few of its monumental buildings can be seen. The Brooklyn Bridge marks the end of this stretch of skyline. Between here and midtown, apartment blocks make up the majority of riverside features.

LOCATOR MAP

☐ *South Street Area*

Stonework on the Woolworth Building

Pier 17
A focal point of the Seaport, this traditional-style leisure pier is packed with exciting shops, vendors and restaurants.

Woolworth Building
The handsomely decorated spire marks the headquarters of F.W. Woolworth's empire. It is still the finest "cathedral of commerce" ever built (see p91).

Fleet Bank Building

Seaport Plaza

Transportation Building

Bogardus Building

Maritime Crafts Center
At Pier 15, craftspeople demonstrate traditional seafaring skills such as woodcarving and model making.

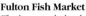

Sweets
This seafood restaurant was in this Schermerhorn Row site from 1847 to 1993.

Fulton Fish Market
The largest wholesale fish market in the US takes place at the Seaport before dawn.

Police Plaza
Five in One (1971–4), in Police Plaza, is a sculpture by Bernard Rosenthal. It represents the five boroughs of New York.

United States Courthouse
The Civic Center is marked on the skyline by the golden pyramid of architect Cass Gilbert's courthouse (see p85).

Municipal Building
Among the offices of this vast building is the Marriage Chapel, where weddings "at City Hall" actually take place. The copper statue on the skyline is Civic Fame *by Adolph Weinman (see p85).*

Surrogate's Court and Hall of Records
Archives dating back to 1664 are stored and displayed here (see p85).

Bell
Atlantic
Telephone
Company

Police
Plaza

Pace
University

Southbridge
Towers

Con Edison Mural
In 1975, artist Richard Haas re-created the Brooklyn Bridge on the side wall of a former electrical substation.

Brooklyn Bridge
Views of, and from, the bridge have made it one of New York's best-loved landmarks (see pp86–9).

Midtown Manhattan

THE SKYLINE OF midtown Manhattan is graced with some of the city's most spectacular towers and spires – from the familiar beauty of the Empire State Building's Art Deco pinnacle to the dramatic wedge shape of Citicorp's modern headquarters. As the shoreline progresses uptown, so the architecture becomes more varied; the United Nations complex dominates a long stretch, and then Beekman Place begins a strand of exclusive residential enclaves that offer the rich and famous some seclusion in this busy part of the city.

LOCATOR MAP

☐ *Midtown*

Chrysler Building
Glinting in the sun by day or lit up by night, this stainless-steel spire is, for many, the ultimate New York skyscraper (see p153).

Grand Central Terminal
Now dwarfed by its neighbors, th landmark building is full of perio details, such as this fine clock (se pp154–5).

Empire State Building
At 1250 ft (381 m), this was the tallest building in the world for many years (see p134–5).

The Highpoint

MetLife Building

Tudor City
Built in the 1920s, this complex is mock Tudor on a grand scale, with over 3,000 apartments (see p156).

United Nations
Works of art from member countries include this Barbara Hepworth sculpture, a gift from Britain (see pp158–61).

1 and 2 UN Plaza
Angular glass towers house offices and the UN Plaza Hotel (see pp156 and 280).

General Electric Building
Built of red brick in 1931, this Art Deco building has a tall spiked crown that resembles radio waves. (see p174).

Waldorf–Astoria
Twin copper-capped towers rise high above one of the city's finest hotels. The interior is also splendid (see p175).

Citicorp Center
St. Peter's Church nestles in one corner of the Citicorp Center with its raked tower (see p175).

Rockefeller Center
The outdoor skating rink and walkways of this complex of office buildings are a great place to people watch (see p142).

General
Electric
Building

The Nail, by Arnoldo Pomodoro, St. Peter's Church, Citicorp Center

866 UN Plaza

100 UN Plaza

Japan Society
Japanese culture, from avant-garde plays to ancient art, can be seen here (see p156 –7).

Beekman Tower
Now an all-suite hotel, this Art Deco tower was built in 1928 as a hotel for women who were members of US college sororities.

St. Mary's Garden
The garden at Holy Family Church is a peaceful haven.

NEW YORK
AREA BY AREA

LOWER MANHATTAN

THE OLD AND THE NEW converge at the lower tip of Manhattan, where Colonial churches and early American monuments stand in the shadow of skyscrapers. New York was born here, and this was the site of the nation's first capitol. Commerce has flourished since 1626, when Dutchman Peter Minuit made one of history's most famous property deals, purchasing the island of Man-a-hatt-ta from the Algonquian Indians for beads and goods valued at $24 *(see p17)*. The stakes have become higher, but finance remains at the heart of this part of the city: it is home to Wall Street, the Federal Reserve Bank, the World Trade Center and the Stock Exchange.

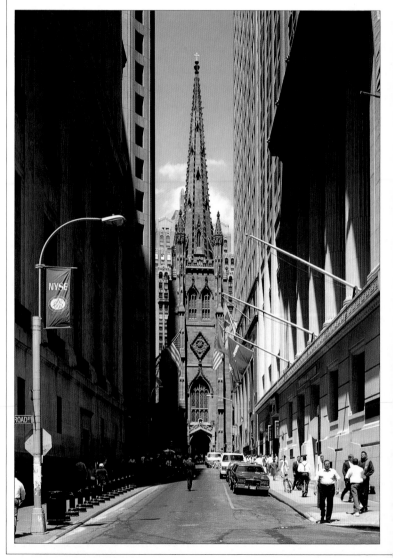

Minuit memorial on Bowling Green

Trinity Church at the foot of Wall Street

Sights at a Glance

Historic Streets and Buildings
Federal Reserve Bank **1**
Federal Hall **2**
New York Stock Exchange pp70–71 **3**
Downtown Athletic Club **8**
Cunard Building **9**
Fraunces Tavern Museum **13**
Battery Maritime Building **16**

Museums and Galleries
US Custom House **11**
Ellis Island pp78–9 **18**

Castle Clinton National Monument **20**
Museum of Jewish Heritage **21**

Monuments and Statues
Statue of Liberty pp74–5 **17**

Parks and Squares
Bowling Green **10**
Vietnam Veterans' Plaza **14**
Battery Park **19**

Boat Trips
Staten Island Ferry **15**

Churches
Trinity Church **4**
Shrine of Elizabeth Ann Seton **12**

Modern Architecture
World Financial Center **5**
World Trade Center **6**
Battery Park City **7**

Bronze statue of a bull, symbol of Wall Street, near the Custom House

Getting There
The best subway routes to the tip of Manhattan are the Lexington Ave 4 or 5 trains to Bowling Green; N or R to Whitehall St; or the 7th Ave 1 or 9 trains to South Ferry. For Wall St, take subways 2, 3, 4 or 5 to Wall St, or N or R to Rector St. The M1, M6 and M15 buses and the M22 crosstown route all serve the area.

Key

▨	Street-by-Street map
M	Subway station
⛴	Ferry boarding point
🚁	Heliport

0 meters   500

0 yards   500

Street by Street: Wall Street

No INTERSECTION has been of greater importance to the city, past or present, than the corners of Wall and Broad streets. Three important sites are located here. Federal Hall National Monument marks the place where, in 1789, George Washington was sworn in as president. Trinity Church is one of the nation's oldest Anglican parishes. The New York Stock Exchange, founded in 1817, is to this day a financial nerve center whose ups and downs cause tremors around the globe. The surrounding buildings are the very heart of New York's famous financial district.

The Marine Midland Bank rises straight up 55 stories. This dark, glass tower occupies only 40% of its site. The other 60% is a plaza in which a large red sculpture by Isamu Noguchi, *Cube*, balances on one of its points.

Trinity Building, an early 20th-century Gothic skyscraper, was designed to complement nearby Trinity Church.

The Equitable Building (1915) deprived its neighbors of light, prompting a change in the law: skyscrapers had to be set back from the street.

★ Trinity Church
Built in 1846 in a Gothic style, this is the third church on this site. Once the tallest structure in the city, the bell tower is now dwarfed by the skyscrapers that surround it. Many famous early New Yorkers are buried in the churchyard **4**

Wall Street subway (lines 4, 5)

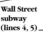

The Irving Trust Company, built in 1932, has an outer wall patterned to look like fabric. In the lobby is an Art Deco mosaic in shades of flame and gold.

26 Broadway was built as the home of the Standard Oil Trust. An oil lamp rests on top of it.

New York Stock Exchange ★
The hub of the world's financial markets is housed in a 17-story building constructed in 1903. Its visitors' center explains the history and workings of the Stock Exchange **3**

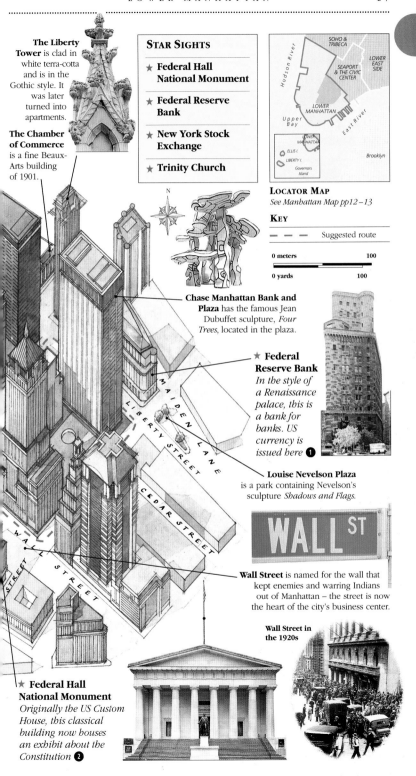

The Liberty Tower is clad in white terra-cotta and is in the Gothic style. It was later turned into apartments.

The Chamber of Commerce is a fine Beaux-Arts building of 1901.

LOCATOR MAP
See Manhattan Map pp12–13

STAR SIGHTS

★ **Federal Hall National Monument**

★ **Federal Reserve Bank**

★ **New York Stock Exchange**

★ **Trinity Church**

SOHO & TRIBECA

LOWER EAST SIDE

Hudson River

SEAPORT & THE CIVIC CENTER

LOWER MANHATTAN

Upper Bay

East River

LOWER MANHATTAN

ELLIS I.

LIBERTY I.

Governors Island

Brooklyn

KEY

— — — Suggested route

0 meters   100

0 yards   100

Chase Manhattan Bank and Plaza has the famous Jean Dubuffet sculpture, *Four Trees*, located in the plaza.

★ **Federal Reserve Bank**
In the style of a Renaissance palace, this is a bank for banks. US currency is issued here ❶

Louise Nevelson Plaza is a park containing Nevelson's sculpture *Shadows and Flags*.

WALL ST

Wall Street is named for the wall that kept enemies and warring Indians out of Manhattan – the street is now the heart of the city's business center.

Wall Street in the 1920s

★ **Federal Hall National Monument**
Originally the US Custom House, this classical building now houses an exhibit about the Constitution ❷

Federal Reserve Bank ❶

33 Liberty St. **Map** 1 C2. 720-6130. Ⓜ Wall St. **Open** 8:30am–5pm Mon–Fri. **Closed** public hols. 🚫 ♿ 📷 10:30am, 11:30am, 1:30pm and 2:30pm (call to make reservation).

Entrance to Federal Reserve Bank

THIS IS A GOVERNMENT bank *for* banks – it is one of the 12 Federal Reserve banks, and therefore issues US currency. You can identify bank notes originating from this branch by the letter B in the Federal Reserve seal on each note.

Below ground is a five-story vault that serves as the largest storehouse for gold owned by the nations of the world. Each nation's gold is stored in its own compartment within the subterranean vault, guarded by 90-ton doors. Payments between nations used to be made by physical transfers of gold, but this is no longer so.

Designed by York & Sawyer, the building was completed in 1924. It occupies a full block and is liberally adorned with fine wrought-iron grillwork. It was inspired by the palaces of the Italian Renaissance.

Federal Hall ❷

26 Wall St. **Map** 1 C3. 825-6870. Ⓜ Wall St. **Open** 9am–5pm Mon–Fri. **Closed** public holidays. 📷 ♿ 📷 📷

A BRONZE STATUE of George Washington on the steps of Federal Hall marks the site where the nation's first president took his oath of office in 1789. Thousands of New Yorkers jammed Wall and Broad streets for the occasion. They roared their approval when the Chancellor of the State of New York shouted, "Long live George Washington, President of the United States."

The present imposing structure was built between 1834 and 1842 as the United States Custom House and is one of the finest Classical designs in the city. Display rooms off the Rotunda include the Bill of Rights Room and an interactive computer exhibit about the Constitution.

New York Stock Exchange ❸

See pp70–71.

Trinity Churchyard

Trinity Church ❹

Broadway at Wall St. **Map** 1 C3. 602-0872. Ⓜ Wall St, Rector St. **Open** 7am–6pm Mon–Fri, 8am–4pm Sat, 7am–4pm Sun. 📷 11:15am Sun. 📷 except during services. 📷 2pm daily. **Concerts.** Thu 📷 📷

THIS SQUARE-TOWERED Episcopal church at the head of Wall Street is the third one on this site in one of America's oldest Anglican parishes, founded in 1697. Designed in 1846 by Richard Upjohn, it was one of the grandest churches of its day, marking the beginning of the best period of Gothic Revival architecture in America. Richard Morris Hunt's design for the sculpted brass doors was inspired by Ghiberti's *Doors of Paradise* in Florence.

Restoration has uncovered the original rosy sandstone, long buried beneath layers of city grime. The 280-ft (26-m) steeple, the tallest structure in New York until the 1860s, still commands respect despite its towering neighbors.

Many prominent early New Yorkers were members of Trinity parish. Statesman Alexander Hamilton; steamboat inventor Robert Fulton; and William Bradford, founder of New York's first newspaper in 1725, are among those buried in the venerable graveyard beside the church.

Marble-columned rotunda within Federal Hall

World Financial Center 5

West St. **Map** 1 A2. 945-0505. 1, 2, 3, 9, A, C, E to Chambers St, 1, 9, N, R to Cortlandt St. M1, M6, M9, M10, M22.

A MODEL OF URBAN design by Cesar Pelli & Associates, this development is a vital part of the revival of Lower Manhattan. Four office towers soar skyward, each topped with a different geometric shape. Some of the world's most important financial companies are headquartered here, and overpasses link the Center with its World Trade neighbor. But this is far more than an office complex.

At the heart of the Center is the dazzling Winter Garden, a vast glass-and-steel public space, flanked by 45 restaurants and shops, opening onto a lively piazza and marina on the Hudson River. The sweeping marble staircase leading down to the Winter Garden often doubles as seating for free arts and events, varying from the classic to the contemporary in music, dance and theater.

Main floor of the Winter Garden

The atrium is a sparkling vault of glass and steel, 120 ft (36 m) high.

The "hourglass" staircase is used as extra seating during concerts in the Winter Garden.

An esplanade borders the Hudson.

Cafés and shops line the atrium.

Sixteen 50-ft (15-m) palm trees from the Mojave Desert make this a 1990s version of the "palm court" of yesteryear.

Inaugurated in 1988 and still expanding, this is a place designed for people and for pleasure, and it has been hailed as the Rockefeller Center of the 21st century by even the most stringent of architectural critics.

World Financial Center viewed from the Hudson River

New York Stock Exchange ➌

I N 1790, TRADING in stocks and shares took place haphazardly on or around Wall Street, but in 1792, 24 brokers who traded under a button-wood tree at 68 Wall Street signed an agreement to deal only with one another, and the basis of the New York Stock Exchange was formed. Membership is strictly limited. In 1817, a "seat" cost $25; today it can cost up to a million dollars, and a rigorous test of suitability is required. Visitors can watch the bustle of the trading posts from a gallery overlooking the trading floor. The NYSE has weathered slumps ("bear markets") and booms ("bull markets"), and has seen advances in technology, from tickertape to microchip, turn a local market-place into a global one.

Computerized stock tickers flash a steady stream of prices as fast as the human eye is able to read them.

Ticker-tape Machine
Introduced in the 1870s, these machines printed out up-to-the-minute details of purchase prices on ribbons of paper tape.

Public entrance, Broad Street

WHAT A TRADING POST DOES

The 17 trading posts each consist of 22 groups or "sections" of traders and technology, each trading the stock of up to 10 listed companies.

Post display units show stock prices.

Free-arm CRTs display prices and trades' for the specialist.

The pages help on the busy exchange floor, bringing orders from the booths to the brokers and specialists.

The super-visor's job is to monitor the smooth and legal running of the post.

A specialist trades in just one stock at a time, quoting bids to other brokers.

Independent floor brokers handle orders for busy brokerage firms.

Commission brokers work for brokerage firms, and rush between booth and trading post, buying and selling securities (stocks and bonds) for the public.

Clerks process the orders that come into the trading post via SuperDOT computer, and log the results of trading into the Exchange's Market Data System.

The 48-Hour Day
During the 1929 Crash, stock exchange clerks worked nonstop for 48 hours. Their mood stayed cheerful despite the panic outside.

VISITORS' CHECKLIST

20 Broad St. **Map** 1 C3.
☎ 656-5168. Ⓜ 2, 3, 4, 5 to Wall St, N, R to Rector St. 🚌 M1, M6, M15. **Visitors' gallery open** 9am–4:30pm Mon–Fri (last adm: 2:45pm). **Closed** public hols. Ø
♿ 📷 🎦 **Video displays**.

Public viewing gallery

Trading post

Trading Floor
Amid the frenzy of the trading floor, 200 million shares are traded each day for more than 2,000 companies. The advanced electronics that support the Designated Order Turnaround (SuperDOT) computer are carried above the chaos in a web of gold piping.

Great Crash of 1929
On Tuesday, October 29, over 16 million shares changed hands as the stock market crashed. Investors thronged Wall Street in bewilderment but, contrary to popular myth, traders did not leap from windows in panic.

Members' entrance, Wall Street

TIMELINE

1792 Buttonwood Agreement signed on May 17	**1867** Ticker-tape machines introduced		**1903** Present Stock Exchange building opens	**1987** "Black Monday" crash, October 19. Dow Jones Index drops 508 points	
	1844 Invention of the telegraph allows trading nationwide			**1976** DOT system replaces ticker-tape	
1750	**1800**	**1850**	**1900**	**1950**	
	1817 New York Stock & Exchange Board created	**1863** Name changed to New York Stock Exchange		**1929** Wall St. Crash, October 29	
			1869 "Black Friday" gold crash, September 24		**1981** Trading posts upgraded with electronic units
	Crowds gather outside during the 1929 Crash		**1865** New Exchange Building opens at Wall and Broad Streets		

World Trade Center ⑥

Map 1 B2. Ⓜ *Chambers St, Rector St.* **Observation Deck** *Two World Trade Center.* 🄲 *323-2340.* **Open** *winter: 9:30am–9:30pm; summer: 9:30am–11:30pm daily.* **Adm charge**. 🄾 🄳 *but not to outside viewing platform.* 🄸🄸 🄿 **Commodities Exchange** *9th Floor, Four World Trade Center.* 🄲 *748-1006.* **Open** *9:30am–3pm Mon–Fri.* 🄿 🄳 🄰

THE 110-STORY twin towers of the World Trade Center dominate the skyline of lower Manhattan. The enormous weight of each building is supported by an inner wire mesh cage, instead of a steel frame, depriving workers inside of large windows. Spectacular views can be seen only from the top. Critics describe the buildings as giant, upended boxes. Built from 1966 to 1977, the complex consists of five office buildings and a hotel, connected by a vast underground concourse lined with shops and restaurants. The World Trade Center is home to 450 businesses and 50,000 workers. Large numbers of visitors come to see the unparalleled views from the observation deck or the rooftop promenade at Two World Trade Center. The express elevator takes just 58 seconds to reach the 107th floor. At One World Trade Center, make this speedy ascent to the 107th floor for drinks or dining at the Windows on the World restaurant *(see p295)*.

When you look across from one tower to the next, think of Philippe Petit who, on August 7, 1974, stepped out onto a tightrope between towers One and Two, and entertained crowds of amazed office workers for almost an hour with the ultimate high-rise balancing act.

If you've more of a head for high finance than for heights, a visitors' gallery on the ninth floor of Four World Trade Center overlooks the trading floor of the bustling Commodities Exchange.

The tightrope act in progress

Philippe Petit about to step out between the two towers in 1974

Battery Park City ⑦

Map 1 A3. Ⓜ *1,9 to Cortland St.* 🄾 🄳 🄸🄸 🄿

Battery Park City esplanade

GOVERNOR MARIO CUOMO set the tone for this project in 1983 when he urged the developers, "Give it a social purpose – give it a soul." The city's newest neighborhood is an ambitious development on 92 reclaimed acres (37 ha) along the Hudson River. The offices, buildings, restaurants, apartments, sculptures and gardens emphasize quality and are built very much on a human scale.

In due course, Battery Park City will house over 25,000 people. The most visible part is the World Financial Center, four towers centered around the Winter Garden, with its huge atrium lined with palm trees. The total cost has been estimated at $4 billion.

The esplanade along the river offers unobstructed views of the Statue of Liberty.

Downtown Athletic Club ⑧

19 West St. **Map** 1 B4. 🄲 *425-7000.* Ⓜ *4, 5 to Bowling Green. Tourists, public welcome.*

ONE OF DOWNTOWN's most striking buildings, this Art Deco creation from 1926 features a front arcade of arches with a Moorish flavor and a facade of patterned salt-glazed tiles in a range of colors from burnt orange to brown. The tiles have kept their fresh look, thanks to a natural glaze that has resisted the city soot. The rooms of the cub, open to members and their guests, have the calm, sleek atmosphere of an old-fashioned ocean liner.

Downtown Athletic Club facade

Ornate ceiling of the Cunard Building's Great Hall

Cunard Building ❾

25 Broadway. **Map** 1 C3.
📞 363-9490 Ⓜ *Bowling Green.*
Open post office hours, see **Practical Information** p361.

STEP PAST the Renaissance facade, through the brass doors and beyond the fine wrought–iron gates of what is now the US Post Office to see the elaborate, domed Great Hall of this fine building of 1921. It was here that tickets were booked on classic liners such as the *Queen Mary* and the original *Queen Elizabeth*, when the Cunard Line was the largest passenger ship company in the world.

The hall has magnificent murals and frescoes, including maps of the world by Barry Faulkner and a remarkable, ornately decorated ceiling. Paintings by Ezra Winter on the supporting vaulting show the ships of Christopher Columbus, John Cabot, Sir Francis Drake and the Viking explorer Leif Eriksson.

Bowling Green ❿

Map 1 C4. Ⓜ *Bowling Green.*

THIS TRIANGULAR plot north of Battery Park was the city's earliest park, used first as a cattle market and later as a bowling ground. A statue of King George III stood here until the signing of the Declaration of Independence,

when, as a symbol of British rule, the statue was hacked to pieces and smelted for ammunition *(see pp20–21)*. The wife of the governor of Connecticut is said to have melted down enough pieces to mold 42,000 bullets.

The fence, erected in 1771, is still standing, but minus the royal crowns that once adorned it. They met the same fate as the statue. The Green was once surrounded by elegant homes. Beyond it is the start of Broadway, which runs the length of Manhattan and, under its formal name of Route 9, all the way north to the State capital in Albany.

Top of a column at the US Custom House

Fountain at Bowling Green

US Custom House ⓫

1 Bowling Green St. **Map** 1 C4.
📞 668-6624. Ⓜ *Bowling Green.*
Open 10am–5pm daily. **Closed** Dec 25.
📷 ♿

ONE OF NEW YORK'S finest Beaux Arts designs, this 1907 granite palace by Cass Gilbert is a fitting monument to the city's role as a great seaport, incorporating the talents of the best sculptors and artists of the time. Forty-four stately Ionic columns stand guard, adorned with an ornate frieze. Four heroic sculptures by Daniel Chester French depict four continents as seated women: Asia (contemplative), America (facing optimistically forward), Europe (surrounded by symbols of past glories) and Africa (still sleeping).

Inside, murals by Reginald Marsh decorate the fine marble rotunda, showing the progress of ships into the harbor. Look to your right, opposite the entrance, to see a portrait of movie star Greta Garbo giving a press conference on board ship. In 1973 the US Customs Service moved out, leaving the building empty but for a small bankruptcy court.

The Custom House took on a new function in 1994, when the George Gustav Heye Center of the National Museum of the American Indian was finally unveiled on three floors of the building. The museum's outstanding collection of about a million artifacts along with an archive of many thousands of photographs, spans the breadth of the native cultures of North, Central and South America.

Exhibitions will include new works by contemporary Native American artists as well as changing thematic displays using exhibits drawn from the permanent collection.

Statue of Liberty ⓱

A GIFT FROM THE FRENCH to the American people, the statue was the brainchild of sculptor Frédéric-Auguste Bartholdi and has become a symbol of freedom throughout the world. In Emma Lazarus's poem, which is engraved on the base, Lady Liberty says: "Give me your tired, your poor,/ Your huddled masses yearning to breathe free." The statue loomed over Paris before its home on Bedloe's Island (now called Liberty Island) was ready. Unveiled by President Grover Cleveland on October 28, 1886, the statue was restored in time for its 100th anniversary in 1986.

★ **Golden Torch**
In 1986, a new torch replaced the corroded original. The replica's flame is coated in 24-carat gold leaf.

The crown is the highest level open to visitors.

The frame was designed by Gustave Eiffel, who later built the Eiffel Tower. The copper shell hangs on iron bars from a central iron pylon.

A central pylon anchors the 225-ton statue to its base.

354 steps lead from the entrance to the crown.

Observation deck and museum

THE STATUE
With a height of 305 ft (93 m) from ground to torch, the Statue of Liberty dominates New York harbor.

The pedestal is set within the walls of an army fort. It was the largest concrete mass ever poured.

From Her Toes to Her Torch
Three hundred molded copper sheets riveted together make up Lady Liberty.

★ **Statue of Liberty Museum**
Posters featuring the statue are among the items on display.

The original torch now stands in the main lobby.

★ **Views of Lower Manhattan**
*Lady Liberty has some of the best views of the city; see them
from the observation deck, the crown or the ferry.*

**Portrait of
Liberty**
*Bartholdi's
mother was
the model for
Liberty. The
seven rays of
her crown
represent the
seven seas
and seven
continents.*

Making the Hand
*To mold the copper shell, the hand
was made first in wood, then plaster.*

FRÉDÉRIC-AUGUSTE BARTHOLDI

The French sculptor who designed
the Statue of Liberty intended it as
a monument to the freedom he
found lacking in his own country.
He said "I will try to glorify the
Republic and Liberty over there,
in the hope that someday I will
find it again here." Bartholdi
devoted 21 years of his life to
making the statue a reality, even
traveling to America in 1871 to
talk President Ulysses S. Grant
and others into funding it and
installing it in New York's harbor.

A Model Figure
*A series of graduated
scale models enabled
Bartholdi to build the
largest metal statue
ever constructed.*

STAR FEATURES

★ **Golden Torch**

★ **Statue of Liberty
Museum**

★ **Views of Lower
Manhattan**

**Restoration
Celebration**
*On July 3, 1986,
after a $69.8
million clean-
up, the statue
was unveiled.
The $2 million
fireworks
display was the
largest ever seen
in America.*

St. Elizabeth Ann Seton Shrine **12**

7 State St. **Map** 1 C4. 269-6865.
M *Whitehall, South Ferry.* **Open**
*6:30am–5pm Mon–Fri, weekends for
services.* frequent.

**Elizabeth
Ann Seton**

Eᴌɪᴢᴀʙᴇᴛʜ ᴀɴɴ Seton
(1774–1821), the first
native-born American to be
canonized by the Catholic
Church, lived here from 1801
to 1803. Mother Seton
founded the American Sisters
of Charity, the first order of
nuns in the United States.

After the Civil War, the
Mission of Our Lady of the
Rosary turned the building
into a shelter for homeless
Irish immigrant women –
170,000 passed through on
their way to a new life in
America. The adjoining
church was built in 1883.
The Mission established and
maintains the shrine to
Mother Seton.

The house itself was built in
1793, and in 1806 a Federal
wing was added, with a
curved, columned porch. The
Georgian-style and Federal
facades have been carefully
restored according to an
1859 print. They are all that
survives of the early mansions
of Lower Manhattan.

Fraunces Tavern Museum **13**

54 Pearl St. **Map** 1 C4. 425-1778.
M *South Ferry, Bowling Green.* **Open**
*10am–4:45pm Mon–Fri, noon–4pm
Sat, Sun.* **Closed** *public hols, day after
Thanksgiving.* **Lectures, films.**

Nᴇᴡ ʏᴏʀᴋ's only full
remaining square
block of 18th-century
commercial buildings
contains an exact replica
of the Fraunces Tavern,
originally built in
1719, where George
Washington said farewell
to his officers in 1783.
The tavern had been an
early casualty of the
Revolution: the British ship
Asia shot a cannonball
through its roof in August
1775. The building was
purchased in 1904 by
the Sons of the
Revolution in the
State of New York.
Its restoration in
1907 was one of
the nation's first
efforts to preserve
its heritage.
The restaurant on
the ground floor has
wood-burning fireplaces and
great charm. Upstairs is a
museum, with changing
exhibits of paintings, prints
and decorative arts that
interpret the history and
culture of early America.

Vietnam Veterans Plaza **14**

Between Water St and South St.
Map 2 D4. **M** *Whitehall, South Ferry.*

Tʜɪs ɪs ᴀ ʀᴀᴛʜᴇʀ sterile
multilevel brick plaza with
a shopping mall below.
However, in its center is a
huge wall of translucent
green glass, engraved with
excerpts from speeches, news
stories and moving letters to
families from servicemen and
women who died in the war.

**Staten Island Ferry – one of the
city's best bargains**

Staten Island Ferry **15**

Whitehall St. **Map** 2 D5. 487-
8403. **M** *South Ferry.* **Open** *24 hrs
daily.* **No Adm charge** See
Practical Information *p353.*

Tʜᴇ ꜰɪʀsᴛ business venture
of a promising Staten
Island boy named Cornelius
Vanderbilt, who later became
the railroad magnate, the ferry
has operated since 1810,
carrying island commuters to

The 18th-century Fraunces Tavern Museum and restaurant

and from the city and offering visitors an unforgettable close-up of the harbor, the Statue of Liberty, Ellis Island and Lower Manhattan's incredible skyline. The fare is still the city's best bargain: it's free.

Battery Maritime Building ⑯

11 South St. **Map** 2 D4. South Ferry. **Not open** to the public.

FROM 1909 TO 1938, the municipal terminal for ferries to Brooklyn operated here on the site of a small wharf known as Schreijers Hoek, from which Dutch Colonial ships once set sail for the mother country. At the height of the ferry era, 17 lines made regular runs from these bustling piers, which are used now only by the Coast Guard service for Governors Island.

The building was designed in 1907. Arriving boats face 300-ft (91-m) arched openings guarded by tall, ornately scrolled columns and adorned with latticework, molding and rosettes typical of the Beaux Arts period. This is actually a false front of sheet metal and steel, painted green to resemble copper.

Ironwork railing on the Battery Maritime Building

Statue of Liberty ⑰

See pp74–5.

Ellis Island ⑱

See pp78–9.

Castle Clinton National Monument in Battery Park

Battery Park ⑲

Map 1 B4. South Ferry, Bowling Green.

NAMED FOR the cannons that once protected the harbor, the park is wedged between the water and the crush of buildings, and is one of the best places in the city for gazing out to sea. Over the years, landfill has extended the greenery far beyond its original State Street boundary.

Beaux Arts subway entrance at the corner of Battery Park

The park is rimmed with statues and monuments, such as the Netherlands Memorial Monument and memorials to New York's first Jewish immigrants and the Coast Guard. Others honored are Giovanni da Verrazano, the first explorer to see these shores, and also the poet Emma Lazarus.

Castle Clinton National Monument ⑳

Battery Park. **Map** 1 B4. 344-7220. Bowling Green, South Ferry. **Open** 8:30am–5pm daily. **Closed** Dec 25. Concerts.

CASTLE CLINTON WAS built in 1807 as a defense post for the artillery. Originally, it stood about 300 ft (91 m)

offshore, connected to Battery Park by a causeway; landfill gradually linked it to the mainland. None of its 28 guns was ever used in battle.

The fort was enclosed in 1824 and became a fashionable theater known as Castle Garden. Phineas T. Barnum introduced "Swedish nightingale" Jenny Lind here in 1850. It later preceded Ellis Island as the city's immigration center in 1855, processing 7.5 million newcomers. In 1896, the building was remodeled by McKim, Mead & White to become the New York Aquarium, a popular attraction that later moved to Coney Island in 1941 (see p247).

Now it is a monument and the main visitors' center for the National Park Service sites in Manhattan, with exhibits featuring panoramas of New York history. The complex is also the departure point for the Statue of Liberty–Ellis Island ferry (see p353).

Museum of Jewish Heritage ㉑

18 First Place. **Map** 1 B4. 968-1800. Bowling Green. **Open** 9am–5pm Sun–Wed, 9am–8pm Thu, 9am–2pm Fri. **Closed** Sat, Jewish holidays. **Adm charge** Lectures.

THE MUSEUM OF Jewish Heritage, which opened in 1997, has powerful exhibits telling the story of 20th century Jewish life and serves as a moving monument to the Holocaust. There are three main themes – pre-Nazi times, the horror of the War and finally the hope and renewal of the present day. Photographs, artifacts and films bring the story to life.

Ellis Island ⑱

ALF OF AMERICA'S population can trace its roots to Ellis Island, which served as the country's immigration depot from 1892 until 1954. Nearly 17 million people passed through its gates and dispersed across the country in the greatest wave of migration the world has ever known. Today the site is a national museum. Exhibits such as *Through America's Gate* retrace the steps through the entry inspections. *Peopling of America* is an electronic map showing the many nationalities that comprise the population. Much of this story is told with photos and the voices of actual immigrants. No other place or museum explains so well the "melting pot" that formed the unique character of New York and the nation.

Main building

The railroad office sold tickets onward to the final destination.

Rail Ticket
A special fare for emigrants led many on to California.

★ **Dormitory**
There were separate sleeping quarters for male and female detainees.

THE RESTORATION
Ellis Island lay in ruins until 1990. A $156 million renewal project replaced the copper roof domes, cleaned the mosaic tiles and restored the interior using any surviving original fixtures.

The ferry office sold tickets to New Jersey.

★ **Baggage Room**
The immigrants' meager possessions were checked here on arrival.

Great Hall ★
Immigrant families were made to wait for "processing" in the Registry Room. The old metal railings were replaced with wooden benches in 1911.

The metal and glass awning is a re-creation of the original.

Arrival Steerage passengers crowd the deck as the ship approaches Ellis Island.

Main entrance

Immigrant Family
An Italian mother and her children arrive in 1905.

STAR FEATURES

★ **Great Hall**

★ **Dormitory**

★ **Baggage Room**

Medical Examining Rooms
Immigrants with contagious diseases could be refused entry and sent back home.

SEAPORT AND THE CIVIC CENTER

Ship's figurehead, South Street Seaport

MANHATTAN'S BUSY Civic Center is the hub of the city, state and federal governments' court systems and the city's police department. In the 1880s it was the heart of the newspaper publishing business as well. The area is still a handsome enclave of imposing architecture with fine landmarks from every period in the city's history, from the 20th-century Woolworth Building to 19th-century City Hall and 18th-century St. Paul's Chapel, New York's oldest building in continuous use. Nearby is South Street Seaport. Called the "street of sails" in the 19th century because of the many ships that were moored there, the seaport underwent a decline when sailing ships became unprofitable. The area has now been restored and is home to a museum and many shops and restaurants. The Brooklyn Bridge, once the largest suspension bridge in the world, lies to the north.

SIGHTS AT A GLANCE

Historic Streets and Buildings
South Street Seaport ①
Schermerhorn Row ②
Brooklyn Bridge pp86–9 ③
Criminal Courts Building ④
New York County Courthouse ⑤
United States Courthouse ⑥
Municipal Building ⑦
Surrogate's Court, Hall of Records ⑧
Old New York County Courthouse ⑨
City Hall ⑩
Woolworth Building ⑫
AT&T Building ⑭

Churches
St. Paul's Chapel ⑬

Parks and Squares
City Hall Park and Park Row ⑪

GETTING THERE

Many subway lines serve the area: the 7th Ave/Broadway 2 and 3 trains to Park Pl; the Lexington Ave 4, 5 and 6 to Brooklyn Bridge; the 8th Ave A, C and E to Chambers St and the N and R to City Hall. By bus take the M1, M6, M9, M10, M15, M101/102 or the M22 crosstown.

KEY

▨ Street-by-Street map

Ⓜ Subway station

⛴ Riverboat boarding point

0 meters   500

0 yards   500

South Street Seaport

Street by Street: South Street Seaport

PART COMMERCIAL, part historical, the development of South Street Seaport has turned the former heart of the 19th-century port of New York, which had long been neglected, into a lively part of the city. Shops and cafés abound; tall ships are once again moored here. The South Street Seaport museum tells the story of New York's maritime past through craft demonstrations, ship tours and river cruises. Workers from Wall Street come here to eat and drink.

★ South Street Seaport
Once full of sailors and sailing ships, the seaport is now a lively complex of shops, restaurants and museums **❶**

Cannon's Walk is a 19th- and 20th-century block of buildings, with an outdoor café, shops and a very lively marketplace.

The Titanic Memorial is a lighthouse built in 1913 in memory of those who died on the *Titanic*. It now stands on Fulton Street.

To Fulton St. subway (4 blocks)

Schermerhorn Row
Built as warehouses (1811–13), the buildings now house several businesses, including the North Star Pub (see p308) and Brookstone **❷**

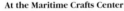

The Boat-Building Shop lets you watch as skilled craftspeople build and restore small wooden vessels.

At the Maritime Crafts Center woodcarvers and painters can be seen at work on models, ship carvings and figureheads.

Ship in a bottle

The Pilothouse was originally from a steam tugboat built in 1923 by New York Central. The Seaport's admission and information center is to be found here.

STAR SIGHTS

★ **Brooklyn Bridge**

★ **South Street Seaport**

The Consolidated Edison
electrical substation, built in
1975, has an illusionistic
mural of the Brooklyn
Bridge by Richard Haas on
one side to help it blend
in with its historic
neighbors.

LOCATOR MAP
See Manhattan Map pp12–13

KEY

– – – Suggested route

0 meters 100

0 yards 100

**Meyer's
Hotel**, built
in 1873, became
a hotel in 1881.
Now a bar, it retains a feel
of days gone by when marks-
woman Annie Oakley stayed here.

★ **Brooklyn Bridge**
*An engineering wonder when it was
built in 1883, the bridge is still
remarkable. From the pedestrian
walkway there are fine views of the
city and the bridge itself* ❸

**The Fulton Fish
Market** has been
here for over 150
years. Once sold
fresh from the boat,
the fish now come
in by road. The
market is only open
in the early morning
hours *(see p347)*.

Pier 17 offers three floors of shops,
restaurants and food stands, with
fine views from the top floor of the
Brooklyn Bridge and historic ships.

The paddlewheeler
Andrew Fletcher is
used for river cruises.
You can also sail on
the schooner *Pioneer,*
which is operated by
the South Street
Museum.

East River harbor at South Street Seaport

South Street Seaport ❶

Fulton St. **Map** 2 E2. **☎** 732-7678. **M** *Fulton St.* **Open** *10am–9pm Mon–Sat, 11am–8pm Sun.* 🅿 ♿ ✔ *Concerts.* 🍴 ⛵ **South Street Seaport Museum** ⛵ 748-8600. **Open** *10am–5pm daily (last adm: 4:30pm).* **Closed** *Tue; Jan 1, Thanksgiving, Dec 25.* **Adm charge.** 🅿 ♿ ✔ *Lectures, exhibits, films.* 🍴 ⛵

T HE HEART of New York's 19th-century seaport has been given an imaginative new lease on life. Glitzy stores and restaurants sit harmoniously beside seafaring craft, historic buildings and museum exhibits, with spectacular views of Brooklyn Bridge and the East River from the cobbled streets.

The historic ships docked alongside the piers range from the little tugboat *W.O. Decker* to the grand four-masted bark *Peking*, the second-largest sailing ship in existence. A 19th-century paddlewheeler offers atmospheric harbor cruises, and there are mini–sailing voyages on the schooner *Pioneer* .

The Fulton Fish Market has been here since 1821. Though

Fulton Fish Market at dawn

fish are no longer delivered from boats in the harbor but arrive in refrigerated trucks, many still find the busy morning action an enjoyable sight; however, you'll need to be there before dawn.

Historic seaport restaurant in Schermerhorn Row

Schermerhorn Row ❷

Fulton and South Sts. **Map** 2 D3. **M** *Fulton St.*

T HIS IS THE architectural showpiece of the seaport. Built in 1811 by shipowner and chandler Peter Schermerhorn on a piece of land reclaimed from the river, the buildings were originally warehouses and counting-houses. The opening of the Brooklyn Ferry terminus in 1814 and of Fulton Market in 1822 made the block very desirable property. The North Star Pub makes use of the nearby fish market and is justly famous for its bouillabaisse.

The Row has been restored as part of the South Street Seaport development, and it now houses a visitors' center, shops, restaurants and an ice-skating rink.

Brooklyn Bridge ❸

See pp86–9.

Criminal Courts Building ❹

100 Centre St. **Map** 4 F5. **M** *Canal St.* **Open** *9am–5pm Mon–Fri.* **Closed** *public hols.*

T HIS 1939 BUILDING is Art Moderne in style, with towers reminiscent of a Babylonian temple. The three-story-high entrance is set back in a court, behind two huge, square freestanding granite columns – an intimidating sight for the accused. The building also houses the Manhattan Detention Center for Men, which was formerly across the street in a building known as "The Tombs" because of its Egyptian-style architecture. The nickname has stuck, although the original is long gone. An aerial walkway, or "bridge of sighs," links the courts with the correctional facility across Centre Street.

The building also houses the night courts, where cases are heard from 5pm to 1am on weekdays.

Entrance to the Criminal Courts Building

New York County Courthouse ❺

60 Centre St. **Map** 2 D1. **M** *Brooklyn Br-City Hall.* **Open** *9am–5pm Mon–Fri.* **Closed** *public hols.*

B UILT TO REPLACE the Tweed Courthouse *(see p90),* this new county courthouse was completed in 1926.

The fluted Corinthian portico at the top of a wide staircase is the main feature of the hexagonal building. The austere exterior is offset by a circular-columned interior rotunda featuring Tiffany lighting fixtures and a series of rich marble and ceiling murals by Attilio Pusterla on themes of law and justice. Six wings radiate from the rotunda, each housing a single court and its facilities.

The courtroom drama *Twelve Angry Men,* starring Henry Fonda, was filmed here.

New York County Courthouse

United States Courthouse ❻

40 Centre St. **Map** 2 D1. Ⓜ
Brooklyn Br-City Hall. **Open**
9am–5pm Mon–Fri. **Closed** *public hols.*

THIS COURTHOUSE is the last work by noted architect Cass Gilbert, designer of the Woolworth Building. Begun in 1933, the year before his death, it was finished by his son. The 31-story structure is

United States Courthouse

a pyramid-topped tower set on a classical temple base. The bronzework on the doors is handsome, but the interior lacks the colorful decoration Gilbert had outlined in his sketchbooks. Aerial walkways link the building with its Police Plaza Annex.

Municipal Building ❼

1 Centre St. **Map** 1 C1. Ⓜ
Brooklyn Br-City Hall. 📷 ♿

THE MUNICIPAL Building, constructed in 1914, dominates the Civic Center and straddles Chambers Street. It was McKim, Mead & White's first skyscraper and houses government offices and a marriage chapel. The exterior, in harmony with City Hall, has no excess detail to detract from the earlier building. The most notable feature is the top, a fantasy of towers capped by Adolph Wienman's statue *Civic Fame.*

A railway passage (no longer in use) through the base, and the plaza joining the building to the IRT subway station entrance were built as concessions to modern transportation needs. The building has had a far-reaching influence on architectural style; the main building at Moscow University is said to have been modeled on its design.

Surrogate's Court, Hall of Records ❽

31 Chambers St. **Map** 1 C1. Ⓜ *City
Hall.* **Open** *9am –5pm Mon–Fri.*
Closed *public hols.* 📷 ♿ 🎞

A BEAUX ARTS triumph, the original Hall of Records was begun in 1899 and completed in 1911. The elaborate columned facade is of white Maine granite, with a high mansard roof. The figures by Henry K. Bush-Brown in the roof area represent life's stages from childhood to old age; the statues by Philip Martiny over the colonnade are of notable New Yorkers

Municipal Building

such as Peter Stuyvesant. Martiny also made the representations of New York in its infancy and New York in revolutionary times at the Chambers Street entrance.

The Paris Opéra was the inspiration for the twin marble stairways and painted ceiling of the dazzling central hall. The ceiling mosaic by William de Leftwich Dodge features the signs of the zodiac as well as symbols of record keeping.

The Hall of Records holds public records dating back to 1664. A permanent exhibition, *Windows on the Archives,* features historical papers, drawings, letters and photographs illustrating what life was like in New York from 1626 to the present.

Surrogate's Court

Brooklyn Bridge ❸

C OMPLETED IN 1883, the Brooklyn Bridge was the largest suspension bridge and the first to be constructed of steel. Engineer John A. Roebling conceived of a bridge spanning the East River while ice-bound on a ferry to Brooklyn. The bridge took 16 years to build, required 600 workers and claimed over 20 lives, including Roebling's. Most died of caisson disease (now known as the bends) after coming up from the underwater excavation chambers. When finished, the bridge linked Manhattan and Brooklyn, then two separate cities.

Souvenir medal cast for the opening of the bridge

BROOKLYN BRIDGE
From making the wire to sinking the supports, the bridge was built using new techniques.

Anchorage
The ends of the bridge's four steel cables are fastened to a series of anchor bars that are held in place by anchor plates. These are held down by giant granite vaults up to three stories high. Their vast interiors were once used for storage.

Granite vault

Cable to tower

Anchor bar

Anchor plate

Vault

Caisson
The towers rose up above caissons, each the size of four tennis courts, which provided a dry area for underwater excavation. As work went on, they sank deeper beneath the river.

Shaft

Anchor Plates
Each of the four cast-iron anchor plates holds one cable. The masonry was built up around them after they were placed in position.

Anchor plates

Central span is 1,595 ft (486 m) long

Vault

Roadway from anchorage to anchorage is 3,579 ft (1,091 m)

First Crossing

Master mechanic E.F. Farrington in 1876 was the first to cross the river on the bridge-in-progress, using a steam-driven traveler rope. His journey took 22 minutes.

VISITORS' CHECKLIST

Map 2 D2. 🅜 4, 5, 6 to Brooklyn Bridge-City Hall (Manhattan side); A, C to High St, Brooklyn Bridge (Brooklyn side). 🚌 M9, M22, M101, M102. 📷 ♿

Steel Cable Wire

Each cable contains 3,515 miles (5,657 km) of wire, galvanized with zinc for protection from the wind, rain and snow.

Brooklyn Tower (1875)

Two Gothic double arches, each 277 ft (84 m) high, one in Brooklyn, the other in Manhattan, were meant to be the portals of the cities.

JOHN A. ROEBLING

The German-born Roebling designed the bridge. In 1869, just before construction started, his foot was crushed between an incoming ferry and the ferry slip. He died three weeks later. His son, Washington Roebling, finished the bridge, but in 1872 he was taken from a caisson suffering from the bends and became partly paralyzed. His wife, under his tutelage, then took over.

Inside the Caisson

Immigrant workers broke up rocks in the riverbed.

MAKING THE CABLES

Thickness of steel wire (actual size)

End of wire

How the Cables Were Made
Each of the four main cables has 19 strands, each made of 278 steel wires. The wires were not twisted, but laid parallel.

Cable Wrapping
Wire was wound off the drum and around the cable to form a tight final wrapping.

The 19 strands of a main cable

Iron clamp

The strands were laid in order: after the bottom 12 strands were laid, the center strands were bound together.

Bolt

A massive iron clamp compressed all the strands into an even cylinder once they had been positioned.

Fireworks over the Brooklyn Bridge
Each year, the Fourth of July is celebrated with a fireworks display.

Bustling Bridge
This 1883 view from the Manhattan side shows the original two outer lanes for horse-drawn carriages, two middle lanes for cable cars and the elevated center walkway.

Panic of May 30, 1883
After a woman tripped on the bridge, panic broke out. Of the estimated 20,000 people on the bridge, 12 were crushed to death.

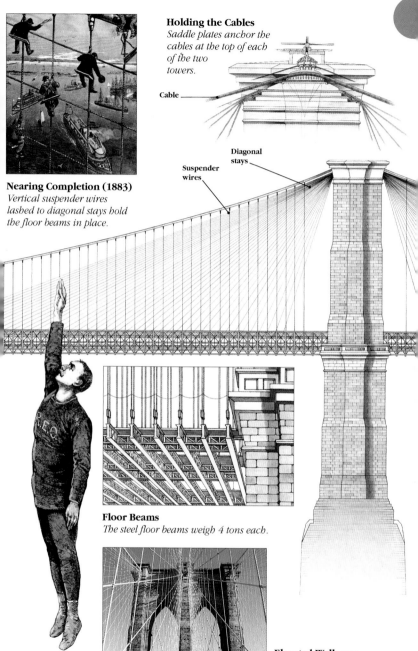

Holding the Cables
Saddle plates anchor the cables at the top of each of the two towers.

Cable

Diagonal stays

Suspender wires

Nearing Completion (1883)
Vertical suspender wires lashed to diagonal stays hold the floor beams in place.

Floor Beams
The steel floor beams weigh 4 tons each.

Odlum's Jump
Robert Odlum was the first to jump off the bridge, on a bet, in May 1885. He later died from internal bleeding.

Elevated Walkway
Poet Walt Whitman said that the view from the walkway – 18 ft (5.5 m) above the road – was "the best, most effective medicine my soul has yet partaken."

Old New York County Courthouse ❾

52 Chambers St. **Map** 1 C1.
Ⓜ *Chambers St-City Hall.* **Closed for renovation**.

THIS BUILDING is best known for the scandal it caused. It is nicknamed the "Tweed Courthouse" after the political boss who spent 20 times the budget for the building and pocketed $9 million of the total $14 million cost. "Boss" Tweed even bought a marble quarry and sold materials to the city at huge profit. Public outrage eventually led to his downfall in 1871 – ironically, he was tried in his own courthouse and died in a New York jail (*see p25*).

However, Tweed left behind a handsome Italianate building. Now used to house city offices, it has survived many threats of demolition. Work has begun on a $6.3 million renovation.

City Hall's imposing early 19th-century facade

City Hall ❿

City Hall Park. **Map** 1 C1. 📞 788-6865. Ⓜ *Brooklyn Br-City Hall.*
Open for prearranged tours only. 📷
♿ 📷 788-6865.

CITY HALL, has been the seat of the New York city government since 1812, and is one of the finest examples of early 19th-century American architecture. A stately Georgian building (with a bit of French Renaissance

P.T. Barnum's museum blazes as crowds watch from City Hall Park

influence), it was designed by John McComb, Jr., the first prominent American-born architect, and French emigré Joseph Mangin.

Marble cladding was not used for the building's rear, since it was not expected that the city would ever develop farther to the north. In 1954, a program of restoration remedied this and the interior was refurbished.

Mangin is usually given credit for the exterior, McComb for the beautiful interior with its fine domed rotunda encircled by 10 columns. The space beneath it opens onto an elegant marble stairway, leading to the splendid second-floor City Council chambers and the Governor's Room, which houses a portrait gallery of early New York leaders. This magnificent entrance has welcomed rulers and heroes for nearly 200 years. In 1865 Abraham Lincoln's body lay in state in this hall.

Stand on the steps and look to your right to see a statue of Nathan Hale, a US soldier hanged by the British as a spy in September 1776 during the Revolutionary War. His last words – "My only regret is that I have not more lives than one to offer in the service of my country" – won him a permanent place in the history books and hearts of America.

City Hall Park and Park Row ⓫

Map 1 C2. Ⓜ *Brooklyn Br-City Hall.*

THIS WAS New York's village green 250 years ago, complete with stocks and whipping post. It was the scene of pre-Revolution protests against English rule, and there is a memorial to the "Liberty Poles" (symbols of revolt) on City Hall's west lawn. The Declaration of Independence was read to George Washington and his troops here on July 9, 1776.

Later, Phineas T. Barnum's American Museum at the park's southern tip drew crowds from 1842 until it burned down in 1865. The Park Row building was the site of the Park Theater. From 1798 to 1848, the best actors of the day, such as Edmund Kean and Fanny Kemble, performed there. Park Row runs along the east side of City Hall Park. Once called "Newspaper Row," it was lined with the lofty offices of the *Sun, World, Tribune* and other papers. Printing

Statue of Benjamin Franklin in Printing House Square

House Square has a statue of Benjamin Franklin with his *Pennsylvania Gazette*.

Time has not been kind to the newspaper business. In 1893 New York had 19 daily papers; now there are four.

Woolworth Building ⑫

233 Broadway. **Map** 1 C2. **M** *City Hall.* **Open** *office hours.*

Bas-relief caricature of architect Gilbert in the Woolworth lobby

I N 1879, SALESCLERK Frank W. Woolworth opened a new kind of store, where shoppers could see and touch the goods, and everything cost five cents. The chain of stores that followed made him a fortune and changed the face of retailing forever.

The 1913 Gothic headquarters of his empire was New York's tallest building until 1930. It set the standard for the great skyscrapers.

Architect Cass Gilbert's soaring two-tiered design, adorned with gargoyles of bats and other wildlife, is topped with a pyramid roof, flying buttresses, pinnacles and four small towers. The marble interior is rich with filigree, sculptured reliefs and painted decoration, and has a high glass-tile mosaic ceiling that almost seems to glow. The lobby is one of the city's treasures. Gilbert showed his sense of humor here, in bas-relief caricatures of the founder counting out his fortune in nickels and dimes; of the real estate broker closing a deal; and of Cass Gilbert himself cradling a large model of the building. Paid for with $13.5 million in cash, the building has never had a mortgage. Woolworth's went out of business in 1997. The building is now owned by the Witkoff Group.

St. Paul's Chapel ⑬

Broadway. **Map** 1 C2. **☎** *602-0874.* **M** *Fulton St.* **Open** *9am–3pm Mon–Fri, 7am-3pm Sun.* **Closed** *most public hols.* **✝** *8am Sun.* 📷 📹 *by appt.* **Concerts**.*1pm Mon.*

I N THE LONG SHADOW of the World Trade Center stands Manhattan's only remaining church built before the

The Georgian interior of St. Paul's Chapel

Revolutionary War. It is a Georgian gem. The colorful interior, lit by Waterford chandeliers, is the setting for free concerts. The pew where newly inaugurated George Washington prayed has been preserved. In the churchyard, the Actor's Monument commemorates George Frederick Cooke, who played many great roles at the Park Theater and finally drank himself to death at the Shakespeare Tavern on Fulton Street.

AT&T Building ⑭

195 Broadway. **Map** 1 C2. **M** *Broadway-Nassau.* **Open** *office hours.*

C OLUMNS, columns everywhere mark this former headquarters designed by Welles Bosworth from 1915 to 1922. The facade is said to have more building in the world, and the interior of the building is a forest of marble pillars. The whole edifice looks like a gigantic square-topped layer cake.

A sea sprite above the door of the AT&T (American Telephone and Telegraph) Building

LOWER EAST SIDE

NOWHERE DOES the strong ethnic flavor of New York come through more clearly than in Lower Manhattan, where many immigrants first settled. Here Italians, Chinese and Jews established distinct neighborhoods, preserving their languages, customs, foods and religions in the midst of a strange land. New immigrants from many

19th-century tin, **Lower East Side Tenement Museum**

nations now occupy some of these neighborhoods of low-rise buildings, but the old flavor remains. The area brims with restaurants, some of the city's greatest bargains and a spirit found nowhere else. The composer Irving Berlin grew up here. Look-ing back on those days he said: "Everybody ought to have a Lower East Side in their life."

SIGHTS AT A GLANCE

Historic Streets and Buildings
Home Savings of America ❶
Police Headquarters Building ❷
Little Italy ❸
Chinatown ❹
Orchard Street ❽
Delancey Street ❿

Puck Building ⓬
Engine Company No. 31 ⓮

Parks and Squares
Columbus Park ❺

Museums and Galleries
Lower East Side Tenement Museum ❼

Churches and Synagogues
Eldridge Street Synagogue ❻
Bialystoker Synagogue ❾
Old St. Patrick's Cathedral ⓭

Landmark Stores
Schapiro's Winery ⓫

SEE ALSO

0 meters 500
0 yards 500

GETTING THERE
Chinatown and Little Italy can be reached by subway on the N and R or the Lexington Ave 4, 5 and 6 trains to Canal St, or by taking the M101/102 bus. The Lower East Side is served by the B and D trains to Grand St, the F train to Delancey St or the M15 bus.

KEY
▦ Street-by-Street map
Ⓜ Subway station

Dragon puppet in Chinatown at Chinese New Year

Street by Street: Little Italy and Chinatown

NEW YORK'S LARGEST and most colorful ethnic neighborhood is Chinatown, which is growing so rapidly that it is overrunning nearby Little Italy as well as the Lower East Side. Streets here teem with grocery stores, gift shops and hundreds of Chinese restaurants; even the plainest offer good food. What is left of Little Italy can be found at Mulberry and Grand streets, where old-world flavor abounds.

★ Little Italy
The scents of Italy still waft from the restaurants and bakeries of this area, once home to thousands of immigrants. ❸

★ Chinatown
Home to a thriving – and still expanding – community of Chinese immigrants, this area is famous for its restaurants and hectic street life. The area truly comes alive around the Chinese New Year in January or February ❹

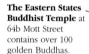

The Market on Canal Street has a wide range of bargains in new and used clothes and other goods.

Ⓜ Canal Street subway (lines N, R, 4, 5, 6)

The Eastern States Buddhist Temple at 64b Mott Street contains over 100 golden Buddhas.

The Wall of Democracy on Bayard Street is covered with newspapers and posters describing the situation in China.

Columbus Park
This park was once the site of 19th century New York's worst slum. ❺

Confucius Plaza is marked by sculptor Liu Shih's monument to the Oriental philosopher.

Chatham Square has a memorial to Chinese-American war dead.

Police Headquarters Building
The dome of this Baroque civic building towers over the City Hall area. In 1973, the police moved out; ten years later the building was turned into apartments ❷

LOCATOR MAP
See Manhattan Map pp12–13

Umberto's Clam House
serves Italian seafood. It is also known as the place where Mafia boss Joey Gallo was shot in 1972.

KEY

– – – Suggested route

0 meters   100
0 yards   100

Home Savings of America
Stanford White designed this in 1894 for the Bowery Savings Bank ❶

★**Eldridge Street Synagogue**
Although empty for decades, this lavishly decorated house of worship is being restored ❻

Bloody Angle, where Doyers Street turns sharply, was the gruesome site of many gangland ambushes during the 1920s.

STAR SIGHTS

★ **Eldridge Street Synagogue**

★ **Chinatown**

★ **Little Italy**

Home Savings of America ❶

130 Bowery. **Map** 4 F4. *Grand St, Bowery.* **Open** *banking hours.*

IMPOSING INSIDE and out, this Classical Revival building was built for the Bowery Savings Bank in 1894. Architect Stanford White designed the ornamented lime-stone facade to wrap around the rival Butchers' and Drovers' Bank, which refused to sell the corner plot. The interior is decorated with marble pillars and a ceiling scattered with gilded rosettes.

Detail from Home Savings of America

By the middle of the 20th century, the bank was a contrast to the Bowery with its vagrants and flophouses.

Police Headquarters Building ❷

240 Centre St. **Map** 4 F4. *Canal St.* **Not open** to the public.

COMPLETED IN 1909, this was a fitting home for the city's new professional police force. Corinthian columns line the main portico and the end pavilions, and the dome dom-inates the skyline. However, lack of space meant the head-quarters had to conform to an awkward, wedge-shaped site in the midst of Little Italy.

For nearly three-quarters of a century, this was where "New York's finest" came to

Stonework figures adorning the Police Headquarters Building

work. During Prohibition, Grand Street from here to the Bowery was known as "Bootleggers' Row," and alcohol was easily obtained except when a police raid was due. The liquor merchants paid handsomely for a tip-off from inside police headquarters.

The police moved to new headquarters in 1973, and in 1985 the building was converted into a luxury cooperative apartment project.

Little Italy ❸

Streets around Mulberry St. **Map** 4 F4. *Canal St.*

THE SOUTHERN Italians who came to New York in the late 19th century found themselves living in the squalor of "dumbbell" apart-ments. These were built so close together that sunlight never reached the lower windows or back-yards. With over 40,000 people living in 17 small, unsanitary blocks, diseases such as tuberculosis were rife.

Despite the privations of life on the Lower East Side, the community that grew up around Mulberry Street was lively with the colors, flavors and atmosphere of its homeland. These have lingered on, although the Italian population has

dwindled to a mere 5,000 and the boundaries of Chinatown have encroached on the traditional "Little Italy."

The most exciting time to visit is during the Feast of San Gennaro, which is held around September 19 (*see p52*). For nine days each year, Mulberry Street is renamed Via San Gennaro. On the saint's day, his shrine and relics are paraded through the streets. Throughout the feast the milling crowds enjoy music, dancing, fairground sideshows and stalls selling every conceivable kind of Italian food and drink, as well as other ethnic cuisines.

Little Italy's restaurants offer simple, rustic food served in friendly surroundings at reasonable prices.

Italian café in Little Italy

Chinatown ❹

Streets around Mott St. **Map** 4 F5. *Canal St.* **Eastern States Buddhist Temple open** 9am–8pm daily.

THE CHINATOWN of the early 20th century was primarily a male community, made up of immigrants who had first gone to California. Wages were sent home to their families in China who were prevented from joining them by US immigration laws. The men relaxed by gambling at mahjong. The community remained isolated from the rest of the city, financed and controlled by its own secret organizations, the Tongs.

Some of the Tongs were simply family associations who provided loans. Others, such as the On Leong and the Hip Sing, who were at war with one another, were criminal fraternities. Tiny, crooked Doyers Street was called "Bloody Angle"; enemies were lured there and set

A Chinese grocer tending his shop on Canal Street

upon by gang members waiting around the bend.

A truce between the Tongs in 1933 brought peace to Chinatown. By 1940 it was home to many middle-class families. Immigrants and businesses from Hong Kong also brought postwar prosperity to the community. Today over 80,000 Chinese-Americans live here.

Many people visit the neighborhood simply to feast on Chinese cuisine, but there is more to do here than eat. There are also galleries, antiques and curio shops, and Oriental festivals *(see p53).* To glimpse another side of Chinatown, step into the incense-scented dimness of

the Eastern States Buddhist Temple at 64b Mott Street, where offerings are piled up and over 100 golden Buddhas gleam in the candlelight.

Columbus Park ❺

Map 4 F5. **Ⓜ** *Canal St.*

THE TRANQUILLITY of Colum-bus Park today could not be further removed from the scene near this site in the early 1800s. The area, known as Mulberry Bend, was a red-light district, part of the infamous Five Points slum. Gangs with names like the Dead Rabbits and the Plug Uglies roamed the streets. A murder a day was common-place; even the police were afraid to pass through. Partly as a result of the writings of reformer Jacob Riis *(see p47),* the slum was finally taken down in 1892. Now the park is the only open space in all of Chinatown.

Eldridge Street Synagogue ❻

12 Eldridge St. **Map** 5 A5.
Ⓒ *219-0888.* **Ⓜ** *East Broadway.*
Open *Mon–Thu by appt only.* **▣** *Fri at sundown, Sat 10am onward* **Adm charge** ∅ **▣** *call for schedule.* **▣**

WHEN THIS HOUSE of worship was built by the Orthodox Ashkenazi from Eastern Europe in 1887, it was the most flamboyant temple in the neighborhood. But many immigrant Jews saw the Lower East Side as

just the beginning of a new life, and later moved out of this massive synagogue.

In the 1930s, the huge sanctuary, rich with stained glass, brass chandeliers, marbleized wood paneling and fine carving, was closed. Three decades later a group of citizens raised funds for preservation, and restoration is now in progress. A brief audiovisual presentation recounts the history of the synagogue and its renovation.

Even after years of neglect, the facade, with touches of Romanesque, Gothic and Moorish designs, is impressive. Inside, the Italian hand-carved ark and sculpted wooden balcony show why this build-ing was the pride of the area.

Lower East Side Tenement Museum ❼

90 Orchard St. **Map** 5 A4.
Ⓒ *431-0233.* **Ⓜ** *Delancey, Grand St.* **Open** *for* **▣** *only, 1pm, 2pm, 3pm Tue–Sun, also 11am & 4:15pm Sat, Sun.* **Closed** *Jan 1, Thanksgiving, Dec 25.* **Adm charge.** ∅ **▣**
Lectures, films, videos.

Street vendor's pushcart (1890s) from the museum

THE INTERIOR of this building was restored to re-create apartments as they appeared at different times: the late 1870s, 1916, 1918, and 1935. There were no regulations on tenement living conditions until 1879. Many rooms had no windows, and indoor plumbing was rare. The rooms give a sense of the cramped and deplorable conditions in which so many lived. The museum program includes changing exhibits about the early immigrants, slide shows and excellent walking tours of the area.

Stained glass from the Synagogue

Orchard Street ❽

Map 5 A3. **M** *Delancey, Grand St.*
See **Shopping** *p312.*

JEWISH IMMIGRANTS founded
the New York garment
industry on Orchard Street,
named after the orchards that
once stood here on James De
Lancey's colonial estate. For
many years the street was
filled with pushcarts loaded
with goods for sale, many of
which were made at home in
the teeming tenements of the
neighborhood.

The pushcarts are long
gone and not all the shop-
keepers are Jewish, but the
flavor remains and the stores
still close on Saturday, the
Jewish Sabbath. On Sunday
there is an outdoor market,
and shoppers fill the street
from Houston to Canal, looking for clothing bargains at
any of the 300 shops.

Zodiac mural from the synagogue

Bialystoker Synagogue ❾

7–11 Willett St. **Map** 5 C4.
C 475-0165. **M** *Essex St.*
❋ *frequent services.* 📷

THIS 1826 Federal-style
building was originally the
Willett Street Methodist
Church. It was bought in 1905
by Jewish immigrants from
the Bialystok province in
Poland, (now Russia) who
converted it into a synagogue.
For this reason, it faces west
instead of the traditional east.
It has a beautiful interior, with
lovely stained-glass windows,

Canal Street Market vegetable stall

a three-story carved wooden
ark and murals representing
the signs of the zodiac and
views of the Holy Land.

Delancey Street ❿

Map 5 C4. **M** *Essex St. See*
Shopping *p312.*

ONCE A MAJESTIC boulevard,
Delancey Street today is
little more than an obligatory
entrance to the Williamsburg
Bridge. The street was named
for James De Lancey, whose
farm was situated here during
colonial days. De Lancey remained loyal to George III
during the Revolution and fled
to England after the war,
before his land was seized.

Most of the stores on this
once-grand shopping street
are now run-down, but you
can still buy an authentic
English bowler hat (not to
mention an authentic
American Stetson cowboy hat,
or almost any other kind of
hat) at the Buranelli Hat
Company at 101 Delancey.

Schapiro's Winery ⓫

126 Rivington St. **Map** 5 B3.
C 674-4404. **M** *Essex St.* **Open**
*11am–5pm Mon–Thu, 10am–5pm
Sun.* **Closed,** *Jewish hols, Fri.* **Adm
charge.** 📷 ♿ 🚻 *hourly, Sun only.
Reservations necessary.*

SCHAPIRO'S was founded in
1899 so that Jewish
immigrants to New York
could have their traditional
kosher wines for the Sabbath

and holidays. It has survived
Prohibition, the Depression
and the dwindling numbers
of local Jewish residents. The
owner swears it will still be in
business when his grand-
children have grandchildren.

Today, Schapiro's produces
32 different types of wine.
Though the grapes are now
crushed in upstate New York,
fermenting and bottling are
still done on the premises.
The operation can be seen on
"quickie" tours; afterward,
you can taste the sweet, thick
wine that gave rise to
Schapiro's motto: "You can
almost cut it with a knife!"

Farther east along Rivington
Street at No. 150, Streit's
Matzoh is another long-
established neighborhood
landmark, where visitors can

Schapiro's kosher wine

watch the freshly baked unleavened bread rolling off conveyor belts behind the sales counter.

Puck Building ⑫

295–309 Lafayette St. **Map** 4 F3.
Ⓜ *Lafayette.* **Open** *to the public during business hours.* Ⓒ 274-8900.

Puck statue on building's north-east corner

THIS BLOCK-SQUARE architectural curiosity was built in 1885 by Albert and Herman Wagner. It is an adaptation of the German *Rundbogenstil*, a mid-19th-century style characterized by horizontal bands of arched windows and the skillful use of molded red brick.

The building is part of the city's publishing history. Situated on the edge of Manhattan's old printing district, from 1887 to 1916 it housed the satirical *Puck,* a magazine similar to the British *Punch.* At the turn of the century it was the largest building in the world devoted to lithography and publishing.

Today it is used as the site of some of New York's most stylish parties and artiest fashion-photography shoots. The only connection remaining to the mythical Puck is the gold-leaf statue on

the third-floor corner of Mulberry and Houston, and the smaller version over the entrance on Lafayette Street.

Walk half a block and you will see a display of *Puck* covers in Bars and Backbars at 49 East Houston.

Old St. Patrick's Cathedral ⑬

263 Mulberry St. **Map** 4 F3.
Ⓒ 226-8075.
Ⓜ *Prince St.* **Open** *daily 8am–1pm, 3:30–6pm* **Closed** *Wed.*
✝ *9:00am, Mon-Sat, 5:30pm Sat, 9:30am Sun, Spanish 11:00am Sun.*

THE FIRST St. Patrick's was begun in 1809 – one of the oldest churches in the city. When fire destroyed the original in the 1860s, it was rebuilt much as it is today. When the archdiocese moved the cathedral uptown *(see pp176–7)*, it became the local parish church, and has flourished despite a constantly changing ethnic congregation.

Below the church are vaults containing the remains of, among others, one of New York's most famous families of restaurateurs, the Delmonicos. Pierre Toussaint was also buried here. In 1990 his remains were moved from the old graveyard beside the church to a more prestigious burial place in a crypt in the uptown St. Patrick's. Born as a slave in Haiti in 1766, Toussaint was brought to New York, where he became

Old St. Patrick's Cathedral

a prosperous wig-maker as a free man. He later devoted himself to the poor, tending cholera victims and using his money to build an orphanage. The Vatican is now considering him for sainthood.

Engine Company No. 31 ⑭

87 Lafayette St. **Map** 4 F3.
Ⓒ 966-4510. Ⓜ *Canal St.*
Closed *to the public.*

IN THE 19TH CENTURY, fire stations were considered important enough to merit a building of architectural importance and the Le Brun firm was the acknowledged master of the art. This 1895 station is one of their best. The building resembles a Loire château, with its steep roof, dormers and towers, seeming almost fairy tale-like in this location.

The present day tenant is the Downtown Community Television Center, which offers courses and workshops to members but which is no longer open to the public.

Facade of Engine Company 31, in the style of a French château

SoHo and TriBeCa

ART AND architecture are the twin lures that have transformed these formerly industrial districts. SoHo (south of Houston) was threatened with demolition in the 1960s until preservationists drew attention to the rare cast-iron architecture lining the streets. The district was saved, and artists began to move into

Shopfront of a SoHo bakery

the loft spaces. Galleries, cafés and shops followed. Brunch and gallery hopping in SoHo is now a favorite weekend outing. As rents rose, many artists were priced out of SoHo and moved to TriBeCa (triangle below Canal). Now, trendy TriBeCa not only attracts galleries but also has many of the city's newest restaurants.

Sights at a Glance

Historic Streets and Buildings
Haughwout Building ❶
St. Nicholas Hotel ❷
Greene Street ❸
Singer Building ❹

Harrison Street ❾
White Street ❿

Museums and Galleries
Guggenheim Museum SoHo ❺
Museum for African Art ❼

New Museum of Contemporary Art ❻
New York City Fire Museum ❽

GETTING THERE
Take the 6th Ave D or F subway to Broadway-Lafayette; the Lexington Ave 6 to Bleecker St; or the N or R to Prince St. For Canal St, take the 7th Ave/Broadway 1 or 9; the 8th Ave A, C or E; or the Lexington Ave 4, 5, 6, N or R. Bus routes are the M1, M6, and the M21 Houston St crosstown.

| 0 meters | 500 |

| 0 yards | 500 |

KEY
☐ Street-by-Street map
Ⓜ Subway station

Cast-iron facades on Greene Street

Street by Street: SoHo Cast-Iron Historic District

THE LARGEST concentration of cast-iron architecture in the world *(see p40)* survives in the area between West Houston and Canal streets. The heart of the district is Greene Street, where 50 buildings erected between 1869 and 1895 are found on five cobblestoned blocks. The intricately designed facades were mass-produced in a foundry but are now rare works of industrial art, well suited to the character of the district.

West Broadway, as it passes through SoHo, combines striking architecture with a string of prestigious art galleries, including Charles Cowles, Hirsch & Adler, Sonnabend, Leo Castelli and Mary Boone. *(See p324.)*

Zona at 97 Greene Street stocks original and imaginative items for the home.

Creature from the Enchanted Forest

72–76 Greene Street, the "King of Greene Street," is a splendid Corinthian-columned building. It was the creation of Isaac F. Duckworth, one of the masters of cast-iron design.

Enchanted Forest casts a magic spell, just as its name suggests, selling children's toys and books in a fairy-tale forest setting. *(See p314.)*

Performing Garage is a tiny experimental theater that pioneers the work of avant-garde artists.

★ Greene Street
Of all Greene Street's fine cast-iron architecture, one of the best is 28–30, the "Queen," which was built by Duckworth in 1872, and has a tall mansard roof ❸

Canal Street-Broadway subway (2 blocks)

10–14 Greene Street dates from 1869. Note the glass circles in the risers of the iron stoop, which allowed daylight to reach the basement.

15–17 Greene Street is a late addition from 1895 in a simple Corinthian style.

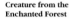

Pace Gallery is one of a group of influential galleries housed in a Tuscan-style cast-iron building by Henry Fernbach. *(See p324.)*

LOCATOR MAP
See Manhattan Map pp12–13

KEY

– – – Suggested route

Guggenheim Museum SoHo
Museum Mile's modern giant has branched out into the heart of SoHo, to rapturous acclaim ❺

★ **Singer Building**
This terra-cotta beauty was built in 1904 for the famous sewing machine company ❹

New Museum of Contemporary Art
This museum is dedicated to showing innovative work by living artists ❻

Prince Street subway station (lines N, R)

Dean & DeLuca is one of the best gourmet food stores in New York. Its range includes a global choice of coffee beans. *(See p326.)*

Richard Haas, the prolific muralist, has transformed a blank wall into a convincing cast-iron frontage.

101 Spring Street, with its simple, geometric facade and large windows, is a fine example of the style that led to the skyscraper.

St. Nicholas Hotel
During the Civil War, this former luxury hotel was used as a headquarters for the Union Army ❷

0 meters   100
0 yards   100

STAR SIGHTS

★ **Greene Street**

★ **Singer Building**

Haughwout Building
In 1857 this was a smart store, featuring the first Otis safety elevator ❶

Haughwout Building ❶

88–92 Broadway. **Map** 4 E4.
Ⓜ *Canal St.*

Haughwout Building facade

T HIS CAST-IRON building was
erected in 1857 for the
E.V. Haughwout china and
glassware company, which
once supplied the White
House. Beneath the grime,
the design is superb: rows of
windows are framed by arches
set on columns flanked by
taller columns. Mass-produced
sections repeat the pattern
over and over. The building
was the first to use a steam-
driven Otis safety elevator, an
innovation that made the
skyscraper a possibility.

St. Nicholas Hotel ❷

521–523 Broadway. **Map** 4 E4.
Ⓜ *Prince St.*

E NGLISH PARLIAMENTARIAN
W.E. Baxter, visiting New
York in 1854, reported of the
recently opened St. Nicholas
Hotel: "Every carpet is of velvet
pile; chair covers and curtains
are made of silk or satin
damask … and the embroidery
on the mosquito nettings itself

**St. Nicholas Hotel in its heyday in
the mid-19th century**

might be exhibited to royalty."
It is small wonder, then, that
it cost over $1 million to build
– and with profits of over
$50,000 for that year it must
have seemed money well
spent. Its glory was short-lived,
however. In the Civil War it
served as a Union Army headquarters. Afterward, the better
hotels followed the entertainment district uptown, and by
the mid-1870s the St. Nicholas
had closed. There is little left
on the ground floor to attest
to its former opulence, but
look up to the remains of its
once-stunning marble facade.

Greene Street ❸

Map 4 E4. Ⓜ *Canal St.*

Haas mural on Greene Street

T HIS IS THE HEART of SoHo's
Cast-Iron District. Along
five cobblestoned blocks are
50 cast-iron buildings dating
from 1869 to 1895. The block
between Broome and Spring
streets has 13 full cast-iron
facades and from 8–34 is
the longest row of cast-
iron buildings anywhere.
Those at 72–76
are known as
the "King of
Greene Street,"
but 28–30, the
"Queen," is
considered to
be the finest.
The architecture
is best appreci-
ated as a
streetscape, with row
upon row of
columned facades.
Walk into any
of the galleries housed
within to see the
spacious interior lofts.

At the corner of Greene and
Prince streets, the illusionistic
muralist Richard Haas has
created an eye-catching work,
disguising a plain brick side
wall as a cast-iron frontage.
Look for the detail of the little
gray cat, which sits primly in
an "open window."

Singer Building ❹

561–563 Broadway. **Map** 4 E3.
Ⓜ *Prince St.*

T HE "LITTLE" Singer Building
built by Ernest Flagg in
1904 is the second and
smaller Flagg structure by this
name, and many critics think
it superior to the 41-story
tower on lower Broadway
that was torn down in 1967.
The charmingly ornate
building is adorned with
wrought-iron balconies and
graceful arches painted in
striking dark green. The 12-
story facade of terra-cotta,
glass and steel was advanced
for its day, a forerunner of
the metal and glass walls to
come in the 1940s and 1950s.
The building was an office
and warehouse for the Singer
sewing machine company,
and the original Singer name
can be seen cast in iron
above the entrance to the
store on Prince Street.

**Early electric-powered
Singer sewing machine**

Guggenheim Museum SoHo **5**

575 Broadway. **Map** 4 E3. **☎** 423-3600. **M** Prince St. **Open** 10am–6pm Sun–Wed, 10am–8pm Fri, Sat. **Adm charge**.

THIS DRAMATIC gallery opened in 1992 to critical acclaim. Designed by architect Arata Isozake, it features displays that complement those at the main Guggenheim Museum (see p186).

New Museum of Contemporary Art **6**

583 Broadway. **Map** 4 E3. **☎** 219-1222. **M** Prince St. **Open** noon–6pm Wed, Sun, noon–8pm Thu, Fri, Sat. **Adm charge**. **⌀ & ✓ Lectures, readings.**

Les Enfants de Dijon by Christian Boltanski, at the New Museum

MARCIA TUCKER left her post as the Whitney Museum's Curator of Painting and Sculpture in 1977 to found this museum. Jeff Koons and the late John Cage are among those whose work has been featured in thematic shows. Tucker exhibits the kind of work she feels is missing from more traditional museums.

Museum for African Art **7**

593 Broadway. **Map** 4 E3. **☎** 966-1313 **M** Prince St. **Open** 10.30am–5.30pm Tue–Fri, noon–6pm Sat, Sun. **Adm charge**.

ONE OF ONLY two American museums devoted to African art, these galleries have been ingeniously designed by architect Maya Lin, creator of Washington's Vietnam Veteran's Memorial. The high-caliber changing shows often tour to major museums in the US and abroad. The museum also offers lectures, music and dance performances, and includes an excellent shop.

1901 La France horse-drawn steam pumper in the City Fire Museum

New York City Fire Museum **8**

278 Spring St. **Map** 4 D4. **☎** 691-1303. **M** Spring St. **Open** 10am–4pm Tue–Sun. **Adm charge**. **📷 &**

THIS SPLENDID museum is housed in a Beaux Arts–style 1904 firehouse. New York city's wonderful collection of fire-fighting equipment and memorabilia from the 18th century to 1917 includes scale models, bells and hydrants. Upstairs, a row of brilliantly gleaming fire engines is neatly lined up for an 1890 parade. Special exhibitions are sometimes held.

Harrison Street **9**

Map 4 D5. **M** Chambers St.

SURROUNDED BY modern high-rise blocks, this rare row of eight beautifully restored Federal town houses, with their pitched roofs and distinctive dormer windows, almost seems like a stage set. The houses were constructed in the late 1700s and early 1800s. Two of the buildings were designed by John McComb, Jr., New York's first major native-born architect, and were moved from Washington Street, their original site, for preservation purposes. The houses had previously been used as warehouses and were about to be razed to the ground, when, in 1969, the Landmarks Preservation Commission intervened and helped secure the necessary funding to enable them to be completely restored. They are now privately owned.

On the other side of the high-rise complex is Washington Market Park. this area was formerly the site of New York city's wholesale produce center. The market moved from this historic district and relocated to the Bronx at the beginning of the 1970s.

White Street **10**

Map 4 E5. **M** Franklin St.

WHILE NOT as fine and intricate as some of the SoHo blocks, this sampling of TriBeCa cast-iron architecture shows a considerably wide range of styles. The house at No. 2 has carefully balanced Federal features and a rare gambrel roof, in contrast with the mansard roof of No. 17 (the Alternative Museum). Numbers 8 to 10 White, designed by Silesian-born Henry Fernbach, in 1869, have impressive Tuscan columns and arches, with Neo-Renaissance shorter upper stories to give an illusion of height. In contrast, 38 White is the home of neon artist Rudi Stern's gallery, Let There Be Neon.

Rudi Stern's Let There Be Neon gallery in White Street

GREENWICH VILLAGE

NEW YORKERS call it simply "the Village," and it did indeed begin as a country village, an escape for city dwellers during the yellow fever epidemic of 1822. The crazy-quilt pattern of streets, reflecting early farm boundaries or streams, could not be made to conform to the city's grid plan, and Greenwich Village has

Jazz club flag on West 3rd Street

remained an enclave apart, a bohemian haven that has been home to many celebrated artists and writers. A popular gay district is here, but on the whole the area has become mainstream and very high-priced. Near Washington Square, it is dominated by New York University students. Nonconformists tend to live in the cheaper East Village.

SIGHTS AT A GLANCE

Historic Streets and Buildings
St. Luke's Place ❶
75½ Bedford Street ❷
Isaacs-Hendricks House ❸
Grove Court ❹
Jefferson Market Courthouse ❻
Patchin Place ❼
Salmagundi Club ❾
Washington Mews ⓬
New York University ⓭

Museums and Galleries
Forbes Magazine Building ❽

Churches
First Presbyterian Church ❿
Church of the Ascension ⓫
Judson Memorial Church ⓮

Parks and Squares
Sheridan Square ❺
Washington Square ⓯

GETTING THERE
By subway, take lines A, B, C, D, E, F or Q to West 4th St-Washington Sq, the 7th Ave 1 and 9 to Christopher St-Sheridan Sq or the R to 8th St. By bus take the M1, M5, M6 or the M8 crosstown.

0 meters 500
0 yards 500

SEE ALSO

KEY
Street-by-Street map
Ⓜ Subway station

Billboards on the corner of Christopher Street and Seventh Avenue South

Street by Street: Greenwich Village

A STROLL THROUGH HISTORIC Greenwich Village is a feast of unexpected small pleasures – charming row houses, hidden alleys and leafy courtyards. The often quirky architecture suits the bohemian air of the Village. Many famous people, particularly artists and writers, such as playwright Eugene O'Neill and actor Dustin Hoffman, have made their homes in the houses and apartments that line these old-fashioned narrow streets. By night, the Village really comes alive. Late-night coffeehouses and cafés, experimental theaters and music clubs, including some of the best jazz venues, beckon you at every turn.

The Lucille Lortel Theater is at 121 Christopher Street; it opened in 1955 with *The Threepenny Opera.*

Christopher Street, a part of New York's gay community, is lined with all kinds of shops, bookstores and bars.

Twin Peaks at 102 Bedford Street began life in 1830 as an ordinary house. It was rebuilt in 1926 by architect Clifford Daily to house artists, writers and actors. Daily believed that the quirky house would help their creativity flourish.

Grove Court
Six houses dating from 1853 to 1854 are set at the back of a leafy courtyard ❹

Chumley's at 86 Bedford Street *(see p309)*, once a speakeasy, now a restaurant, still seems secret. There is no sign outside, just a small menu.

75½ Bedford Street
Built in 1873 in an alley, this is the city's narrowest house ❷

★ **St. Luke's Place**
This beautiful row of Italianate houses was built in the 1850s ❶

To Houston Street subway (2 blocks)

The Cherry Lane Theater was founded in 1924. Originally a brewery, it was one of the first of the Off-Broadway theatres.

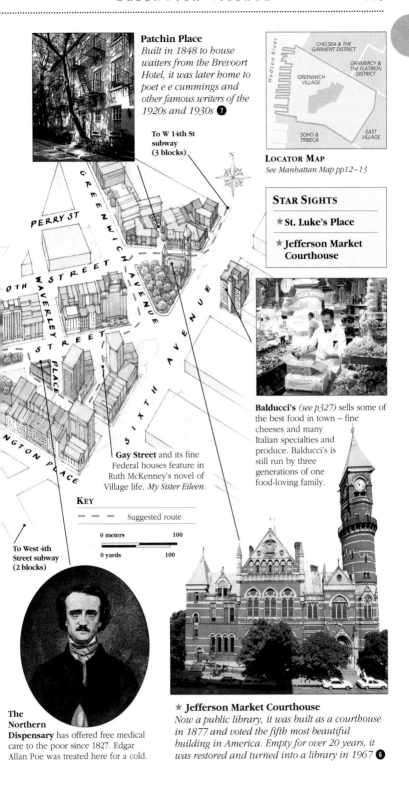

Patchin Place
Built in 1848 to house waiters from the Brevoort Hotel, it was later home to poet e e cummings and other famous writers of the 1920s and 1930s **7**

To W 14th St
subway
(3 blocks)

LOCATOR MAP
See Manhattan Map pp12–13

CHELSEA & THE
GARMENT DISTRICT

GRAMERCY &
THE FLATIRON
DISTRICT

GREENWICH
VILLAGE

Hudson River

SOHO &
TRIBECA

EAST
VILLAGE

STAR SIGHTS

★ **St. Luke's Place**

★ **Jefferson Market Courthouse**

PERRY ST

GREENWICH AVENUE

10TH STREET

WAVERLEY STREET

ST

PLACE

WASHINGTON PLACE

SIXTH AVENUE

Gay Street and its fine Federal houses feature in Ruth McKenney's novel of Village life, *My Sister Eileen*.

Balducci's *(see p327)* sells some of the best food in town – fine cheeses and many Italian specialties and produce. Balducci's is still run by three generations of one food-loving family.

KEY

– – – Suggested route

0 meters   100

0 yards   100

To West 4th
Street subway
(2 blocks)

The Northern Dispensary has offered free medical care to the poor since 1827. Edgar Allan Poe was treated here for a cold.

★ **Jefferson Market Courthouse**
Now a public library, it was built as a courthouse in 1877 and voted the fifth most beautiful building in America. Empty for over 20 years, it was restored and turned into a library in 1967 **6**

Row houses on St. Luke's Place

St. Luke's Place ❶

Map 3 C3. Ⓜ *Houston St.*

FIFTEEN ATTRACTIVE row houses, dating from the 1850s, line the north side of this street. The park opposite is named after a previous resident of St. Luke's Place, Mayor Jimmy Walker, the popular dandy who ran the city from 1926 until he was forced to resign after a financial scandal in 1932. In front of No. 6 are the lamps that always identify a mayor's home in New York. In recent years, the most recognizable house on the block has been No. 10, shown on television as the home of the Huxtable family in *The Cosby Show* (although the series sets it in Brooklyn). This is also the block where *Wait Until Dark* was filmed, starring Audrey Hepburn as a blind woman living at No. 4. Theodore Dreiser was one of several writers, including the poet Marianne Moore, who lived here. He wrote *An American Tragedy* while living at No. 16. One block north, the corner of Hudson and Morton Streets marked the edge of the Hudson River three centuries ago.

Mayor's lamp at No. 6

75½ Bedford Street ❷

Map 3 C2. Ⓜ *Houston St.* **Not open** to the public.

NEW YORK'S narrowest home, just 9½ ft (2.9 m) wide, was built in 1893 in a former passageway. The poet Edna St. Vincent Millay lived here briefly, followed by the actor John Barrymore, and later Cary Grant. The three-story building has been recently renovated and is marked by a plaque.

Just around the corner, at 38 Commerce Street, Miss Millay founded the Cherry Lane Theater in 1924 as a site for avant-garde drama. It still premieres new works. Its biggest hit was the 1960s musical *Godspell*.

Cottage on Bedford Street

Isaacs-Hendricks House ❸

77 Bedford St. **Map** 3 C2. Ⓜ *Houston St.* **Not open** to the public.

THIS IS THE OLDEST surviving home in the Village, built in 1799. The old clapboard walls are visible on the sides

Isaacs-Hendricks House

and rear; the brickwork and third floor came later. The first owner, John Isaacs, bought the land for $295 in 1794. Next came Harmon Hendricks, a copper dealer and associate of revolutionary Paul Revere. Robert Fulton, who used copper for the boilers in his steamboat, was a customer.

Grove Court ❹

Map 3 C2. Ⓜ *Christopher St/ Sheridan Sq.*

AN ENTERPRISING grocer named Samuel Cocks was responsible for this group of six town houses, fitting snugly into an area formed by the bend in the street. (The bends in this part of the Village originally marked divisions between colonial properties.) Cocks reckoned that having residents in the empty passage between Nos. 10 and 12 Grove Street would help his business at No. 18.

But residential courts, now prized as exclusive private addresses, were not considered respectable in 1854, and the lowbrow residents attracted to the area soon earned it the nickname "Mixed Ale Alley." O Henry later used this block as the setting for his 1902 work *The Last Leaf.*

The mid-19th-century town houses at Grove Court

Sheridan Square ❺

Map 3 C2. Ⓜ *Christopher St-Sheridan Sq.*

THIS IS THE HEART of the Village, where seven streets come together in such a maze that early guidebooks called it "the mousetrap." It was named after the Civil War General Philip Sheridan who became commander in chief of the US Army in 1883. His statue stands in nearby Christopher Park.

The Draft Riots of 1863 took place in the square, when mobs revolting against army service tried to lynch freed slaves. More than a century later, another famous disturbance rocked the

Sheridan Square scene

square. The Stonewall Inn on Christopher Street was a gay bar that had stayed in business (it was then illegal for gays to gather in bars) by paying off the police. However, on June 28, 1969, the patrons rebelled, and the pitched close combat that resulted found police officers barricaded inside the bar for hours while crowds taunted them from outside. It was a landmark moral victory for the budding Gay Rights movement. The inn still stands but is no longer a bar. The Village remains a focus for the city's gay community. The spirited gay Halloween Parade *(see p52)* through the Village, noted for its outrageous costumes, brings thousands out.

Pointed tower of "Old Jeff"

Jefferson Market Courthouse ❻

425 6th Ave. **Map** 4 D1. Ⓒ *243-4334.* Ⓜ *W 4th St-Washington Sq.* **Open** *10am–6pm Mon, noon–6pm Tue, Fri, 12–8pm Wed, 10am–5pm Thu, Sat.* **Closed** *Sun, public hols.* ♿

PERHAPS THE MOST treasured Village landmark, "Old Jeff" was saved from the wrecking ball and converted into a branch of the New York Public Library through a spirited campaign that began at a local Christmas party in the late 1950s.

The site became a market in 1833, named after former president Thomas Jefferson. Its fire lookout tower had a giant bell that alerted the neighborhood's volunteer fire fighters. In 1865, the founding of the municipal fire department made the bell obsolete, and the Third Judicial District, or Jefferson Market, Courthouse was built. With its Venetian Gothic–style spires and turrets, it was named one of the 10 most beautiful buildings in the country when it opened in 1877. The old

Statue of General Sheridan in Christopher Park

fire bell was installed in the tower. Here, in 1906 Harry Thaw was tried for Stanford White's murder *(see p124).*

By 1945, the market had moved, court sessions were discontinued, the four-sided clock had stopped and the building was endangered. In the 1950s, preservationists campaigned first to restore the clock and then the whole building. Architect Giorgio Cavaglieri has preserved many original details, including the stained glass and a spiral staircase that now leads to a dungeonlike reference room.

Facade and an ailanthus tree at Patchin Place

Patchin Place ❼

W 10th St. **Map** 4 D1. Ⓜ *W 4th St-Washington Sq.*

ONE OF MANY delightful unexpected pockets in the Village is this tiny block of small residences, lined with ailanthus trees planted in order to "absorb the bad air." The houses were built in the mid-19th century to house Basque waiters from the Fifth Avenue Brevoort Hotel.

Later the houses became fashionable addresses, with many writers living here. The poet e e cummings lived at No. 4 from 1923 until his death in 1962. English poet laureate John Masefield also lived on the block. So did playwright Eugene O'Neill and John Reed, whose eyewitness account of the Russian Revolution, *Ten Days That Shook The World* was filmed by Warren Beatty as *Reds.*

Toy battleship from the Forbes Magazine Collection

Forbes Building and Galleries ⓽

62 5th Ave. **Map** 4 E1. **C** 206-5548.
M 14th St-Union Sq. **Galleries open**
10am–4pm Tue, Wed, Fri, Sat (times
may vary). No strollers ⓪ **◻** Thu.

Some architectural critics
have called this 1925 limestone cube by Carrère &
Hastings pompous. It was
originally the headquarters of
the Macmillan Publishing
Company. When Macmillan
moved uptown, the late
Malcolm Forbes moved in
with his financial magazine,
Forbes. The Forbes Magazine
Galleries show Forbes's diverse
tastes, with Fabergé eggs
made for the last Russian czar;
over 500 antique toy boats;
12,000 toy soldiers; and a
signed copy of Abraham
Lincoln's Gettysburg Address,
among other presidential
memorabilia. There are also
exhibitions of paintings,
ranging from French to
American Military works.

Salmagundi Club ⓽

47 5th Ave. **Map** 4 E1.
C 255-7740. **M** 14th St-Union Sq.
Open 8.30am–midnight Mon–Fri,
8am–5pm Sat, noon–5pm Sun. ⓪

America's oldest artists club
resides in the last remain-
ing mansion on lower Fifth
Avenue. Built in 1853 for Irad
Hawley, it now houses the
American Artists' Professional
League, the American Water-
color Society and the
Greenwich Village
Society for Historic
Preservation. Wash-
ington Irving's satiric
periodical, *The Salmagundi
Papers*, gave the club its name.
Founded in 1871, the club
moved here in 1917. Periodic
art exhibits open the late 19th-
century interior to the public.

Exterior of the Salmagundi Club

First Presbyterian Church ⓵⓪

5th Ave at 12th St. **Map** 4 D1.
C 675-6150 **M** 7th Ave-Union Sq.
Open 12.15am–12.45pm Mon, Wed,
Fri, 11am–1.30pm Sun.

Designed by Joseph C.
Wells in 1846, this Gothic
church was modeled on the
Church of Saint Saviour in
Bath, England. The church is
noteworthy for its brownstone
tower. The carved wooden
plaques on the altar list every
pastor since 1716. The south
transept by McKim, Mead &
White was added in 1893.
The fence of iron and wood
was built in 1844 and then
restored in 1981.

Church of the Ascension ⓵⓵

5th Ave at 10th St. **Map** 4 E1.
C 254-8620. **M** 14th St-
Union Sq. **Open** noon–2pm,
5–7pm daily. **T** 6pm daily,
9am, 11am, 6pm Sun.
◻ (not during services).

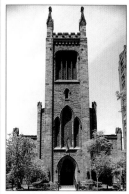

Church of the Ascension

This English Gothic Revival
church was designed in
1840–41 by Richard Upjohn,
architect of Trinity Church. The
interior was redone in 1888 by
Stanford White, with an altar
relief by Augustus Saint-
Gaudens. Above the altar
hangs *The Ascension*, a mural
by John La Farge, who also
designed some of the stained
glass. The belfry tower is lit at
night to show off the colors.
In 1844 President John
Tyler married Julia Gardiner
here; she lived in nearby
Colonnade Row *(see p118)*.

Washington Mews ⓵⓶

Washington Sq N at E 8th St.
Map 4 E2. **M** W 4th St.

Built as stables, this hidden
enclave was turned into
carriage houses around 1900.
The south side was added in
1939. Gertrude Vanderbilt
Whitney, founder of the
Whitney Museum, lived and
worked here.
On the corner of University
Place is NYU's French House,
remodeled in a French style,
where movies, lectures and
classes in French are held.

New York University ⑬

Washington Sq. **Map** 4 E2.
📞 998-1212. Ⓜ W 4th St.
Open 8:30am–8pm Mon–Fri.

Oᴿɪɢɪɴᴀʟʟʏ ᴄᴀʟʟᴇᴅ the University of the City of New York, NYU was founded in 1831 as an alternative to Episcopalian Columbia University. It is now the largest private university in America and extends for blocks around Washington Square.

Construction of the school's first building on Waverly Place sparked the Stone-cutters' Guild Riot of 1833, when contractors protested about the use of inmates from a state prison to cut stone. The National Guard had to restore order. The original building no longer exists, but a memorial with a piece of the original tower can be seen on a pedestal set into the pavement on Washington Square South. Samuel Morse's telegraph, John W. Draper's first-ever photographic

Bust of Sylvette **by Picasso, between Bleecker and West Houston streets**

portrait and Samuel Colt's six-shooter were invented here.

The Brown Building, on Washington Place near Greene Street, was the site of the Triangle Shirtwaist Company. In 1911, 146 factory workers died in a fire here, leading to new fire safety and labor laws.

A 36-ft (11-m) enlargement of Picasso's *Bust of Sylvette* is in University Village.

Judson Memorial Church ⑭

55 Washington Sq S. **Map** 4 D2.
📞 477-0351. Ⓜ W 4th St.
Open 10am–1pm, 2pm–6pm
Mon–Fri. ✝ Sun 11am.

Bᴜɪʟᴛ ɪɴ 1892, this McKim, Mead & White church is an impressive Romanesque building with stained glass by John La Farge. Designed by Stanford White, it is named after the first American missionary sent to foreign soil, Adoniram Judson, who served in Burma in 1811. A copy of his Burmese trans-lation of the Bible was put in the cornerstone when the building was dedicated.

It is the unique spirit of this church, not the architecture, that makes it stand out. Judson Memorial has played an active role in local and world concerns and has been the site of activism on issues ranging from AIDS to the arms race. It is also home to avant-garde art exhibitions and off-Off Broadway plays.

Arch on the north side of Washington Square

Washington Square ⑮

Map 4 D2. Ⓜ W 4th St.

Nᴏᴡ ᴏɴᴇ of the city's most vibrant open spaces, Washington Square was once marshland through which the quiet Minetta Brook flowed. By the late 1700s, the area had been turned into a public cemetery – when excavation began for the park, some 10,000 skeletal remains were exhumed. The square was used as a dueling ground for

a time, then as a site for public hangings until 1819. The "hanging elm" in the northwest corner remains. In 1826 the marsh was filled in and the brook diverted under-ground, where it still flows; a small sign at a fountain at the entrance to Two Fifth Avenue marks its course.

The magnificent marble arch by Stanford White, completed in 1895, replaced an earlier wooden version that had spanned lower Fifth Avenue to mark the centenary of George Washington's inaugur-ation. A stairway is hidden in the right side of the arch. In 1916, a group of artists led by Marcel Duchamp and John Sloan broke in, climbed atop the arch, and declared the "free and independent republic of Washington Square, the state of New Bohemia."

Across the street is "the Row." Now part of NYU, this block was once home to New York's most prominent families. The Delano family, writers Edith Wharton, Henry James, and John dos Passos, and artist Edward Hopper all lived here. Number 8 was once the mayor's official home.

Today students, families and free spirits mingle and enjoy the park side by side. A few drug dealers frequent the park, but it is safe by day.

Window on the corner of West 4th Street and Washington Square

EAST VILLAGE

PETER STUYVESANT had a country estate in the East Village, and in the 19th century, the Astors and Vanderbilts lived here. But around 1900, high society moved uptown and immigrants moved in. The Irish, Germans, Jews, Poles, Ukrainians and Puerto Ricans all left their mark in the area's churches, landmarks and the city's most varied

Mosaic, facade of St George's Ukrainian Catholic Church

and least expensive ethnic restaurants. In the 1950s low rents attracted the "beat generation." Later, Hippies were followed by punks. The area's experimental music clubs and theaters still feature the latest styles. Astor Place buzzes with students. To the east are Avenues A, B, C and D, an area known as "Alphabet City," which is slowly being redeveloped.

SIGHTS AT A GLANCE

Historic Streets and Buildings
Cooper Union ❶
Colonnade Row ❸
Bayard-Condict Building ❽

Museums and Galleries
Old Merchant's House ❹

Churches
St. Mark's-in-the-Bowery Church ❺
Grace Church ❻

Parks and Squares
Tompkins Square ❼

Famous Theaters
Public Theater ❷

SEE ALSO

• *Street Finder*, map 4, 5

• *Where to Stay* pp274–5

• *Restaurants* pp290–92

GETTING THERE

By subway, the Lexington Ave 6 train stop at Astor Pl is the most convenient; the area is also served by the M15 and M101/102 buses and the M8 crosstown bus.

| 0 meters | 500 |
| 0 yards | 500 |

KEY

▨ Street-by-Street map

Ⓜ Subway station

Gothic bas-relief on the facade of Grace Church

The interior of McSorley's Old Ale House

Street by Street: East Village

AT THE SPOT WHERE Tenth and Stuyvesant streets now intersect, Peter Stuyvesant's country house once stood. His grandson, also named Peter, inherited most of the property and had it divided into streets in 1787. Among the prize sites of the St. Mark's Historic District are the St. Mark's-in-the-Bowery Church, the Stuyvesant-Fish house and the 1795 home of Nicholas Stuyvesant, both on Stuyvesant Street. Many other homes in the district were built between 1871 and 1890 and still have their original stoops, lintels and other architectural details.

Astor Place subway (line 6)

Astor Place saw rioting in 1849. English actor William Macready, playing *Hamlet* at the Astor Place Opera House, criticized American actor Edwin Forrest. Forrest's fans revolted and there were 34 deaths.

Alamo is the title of the 15-ft (4.5-m) steel cube in Astor Place designed by Bernard Rosenthal. It revolves when pushed.

Colonnade Row
Now in shabby disrepair, these buildings were once expensive town houses. The houses, of which only four are left, are unified by one facade in the European style. The marble was quarried by Sing Sing prisoners ❸

Public Theater
In 1965 the late Joseph Papp convinced the city to buy the Astor Library (1849) as a home for the theater. Now restored, it sees the opening of many famous plays ❷

★ **Old Merchant's House**
This museum contains the house's original Federal, American Empire and Victorian furniture ❹

STAR SIGHTS

★ **Cooper Union**

★ **Old Merchant's House**

★ **Cooper Union**
Founded by self-made man Peter Cooper in 1859, it still provides a free education to its students ❶

The Stuyvesant-Fish House
(1803–4) was constructed out of brick. It is a classic example of a Federal-style house.

Renwick Triangle
is a group of 16 houses built in 1861 in the Italianate style.

St. Mark's-in-the-Bowery-Church
The church was built in 1799 and the steeple added in 1828 ❺

LOCATOR MAP
See Manhattan Map pp12–13

Stuyvesant Polyclinic
was founded in 1857 as the German Dispensary and it is still a health clinic. The facade is decorated with the busts of many famous physicians and scientists.

St. Mark's Place was once the main street of hippie life. It is still the hub of the East Village youth scene. Funky shops now occupy many of the basements.

Little India, the row of Indian eateries on the south side of East Sixth Street, offers a taste of India at budget prices.

Little Ukraine is home to 30,000 Ukrainians. The focus of the community is St. George's Ukrainian Catholic Church.

KEY

– – – Suggested route

0 meters 100
0 yards 100

McSorley's Old Ale House still brews its own ale and serves it in surroundings seemingly unchanged since it opened in 1854. (*See p309.*)

Great Hall at Cooper Union, where Abraham Lincoln spoke

Cooper Union **1**

30 Cooper Sq. **Map** 4 F2.
(353-4100. **M** Astor Pl.
Open by appointment only, and for
lectures and concerts in Great Hall.
Closed Jun–Aug, public hols. ✗ ♿

PETER COOPER, the wealthy
industrialist who built the
first US steam locomotive,
made the first steel rails and
was a partner in the first trans-
atlantic cable venture, had no
formal schooling. To make
education easier for others,
Cooper founded New York's
first free, nonsectarian co-
educational college. Still free,
the school inspires intense
competition for places. The
six-story building was the first
with a steel frame, made of
Cooper's own rails. The
building was renovated in
1973–74. The Great Hall was
inaugurated in 1859 by Mark
Twain, and Lincoln delivered
his "Right Makes Might"
speech there in 1860. Cooper
Union continues to sponsor a
provocative Public Forum.

Public Theater **2**

425 Lafayette St. **Map** 4 F2. **(** 260-
2400 (box office). **M** Astor Pl.
See also **Entertainment** p332.

THE LARGE redbrick and
brownstone building that
is the home of the New York
Shakespeare
Festival

began its life in 1849 as the
Astor Library, the city's first
free library, now part of the
New York Public Library. It is
a prime American example of
German Romanesque Revival
style. When the building was
threatened with demolition in
1965, Joseph Papp, founder of
the Shakespeare
Festival,
persuaded
New York City to buy
it as a home for the
company. Renovation
began in 1967,
and much of the
handsome interior
was preserved
during conversion
into six theaters.
Although much of
the work shown is
experimental, the
Public Theater was
the original home
of hit musicals *Hair*
and *A Chorus Line*.
The latter moved
uptown to become the longest-
running Broadway production.

Colonnade Row **3**

428–434 Lafayette St. **Map** 4 F2.
M Astor Pl. **Not open** to the public.

THE CORINTHIAN columns
across these four buildings
are all that remain of a once-
magnificent row of nine Greek
Revival town houses. They
were completed in 1833 by
developer Seth Geer and
were known as "Geer's Folly"
by skeptics who
thought no one
would live so far
east. They were
proved wrong
when the houses
were taken by
such eminent
citizens as John

Jacob Astor and Cornelius
Vanderbilt. Washington Irving,
author of *Rip Van Winkle* and
other classic American tales,
lived here for a time, as did
two English novelists, William
Makepeace Thackeray and
Charles Dickens. Five of the
houses were lost when the
John Wanamaker Department
Store razed them early this
century to make room for a
garage. Neglect has been cruel
to the remaining buildings.

Old Merchant's House **4**

29 E 4th St. **Map** 4 F2. **(** 777-1089.
M Astor Pl. **Open** 1–4pm Sun–Thu
and by appt. **Adm charge.** ✗ (no
flashes permitted) ▶ **Lectures** ▢

**The original 19th-century iron stove in the
kitchen of the Old Merchant's House**

THIS REMARKABLE Greek
Revival brick town house,
improbably tucked away on
an East Village block, is a
time capsule of a vanished
way of life. It still has both its
original fixtures and its
kitchen, and is filled with the
actual furniture, ornaments
and utensils of the family that
lived here for almost 100
years. Built in 1832, it was
bought in 1835 by Seabury
Tredwell, a wealthy merchant,
and stayed in the family until
Gertrude Tredwell, the last
member, died in 1933. She
had maintained her father's
home just as he would have
liked it, and a relative
opened the house as a
museum in 1936. The first-
floor parlors are very grand,
a sign of how well New
York's merchant class lived
in the 1800s.

The Public Theater on Lafayette Street

St. Mark's-in-the-Bowery Church ❺

131 E 10th St. **Map** 4 F1. 📞 *674-6377.* Ⓜ *Astor Pl.* **Open** *8:30am–4pm Mon–Fri.* ⛪ *10:30am Sun* 🚫

O NE OF New York's oldest churches, this building, dating from 1799, replaced a 1660 church on the *bouwerie* (farm) of Governor Peter Stuyvesant. He is buried here with seven generations of his descendants and many other prominent early New Yorkers. Poet W.H. Auden, who was a member of the parish, is also commemorated here.

In 1878, a grisly kidnapping took place in the churchyard, when the remains of department store magnate A.T. Stewart were removed and held for $20,000 ransom.

The church rectory at 232 East 11th Street is a little-known work, from 1900, by Ernest Flagg. He achieved renown for his Singer Building *(see p104).*

Grace Church ❻

802 Broadway. **Map** 4 F1. 📞 *254-2000.* Ⓜ *Astor Pl.* **Open** *10am–5:30pm Mon–Fri, noon–4pm Sat.* **Closed** *public hols.* ⛪ *7:30am Mon–Fri, 6pm Wed, 9am, 11am, 6pm Sun.* 🚫 ♿ *Concerts.*

J AMES RENWICK, JR., the architect of St. Patrick's Cathedral, was only 23 when he designed this church, yet many consider it his finest achievement. Its delicate early Gothic lines have a grace befitting the church's name. The interior is just as beautiful, with Pre-Raphaelite stained glass and a handsome mosaic floor.

The church's peace and serenity were briefly shattered in 1863, when Phineas T. Barnum

Tom Thumb and his bride at Grace Church

staged the wedding of midget General Tom Thumb here; the crowds turned the event into complete chaos.

The marble spire replaced a wooden steeple in 1888 amid fears that it might prove too heavy for the church – and it has since developed a distinct lean. The church is visible from afar, because it is on a bend on Broadway. Henry Brevoort forced the city to bend Broadway to divert it around his apple orchard.

Grace Church altar and window

Tompkins Square ❼

Map 5 B1. Ⓜ *2nd Ave, 1st Ave.*

T HIS ENGLISH-STYLE park has the makings of a peaceful spot, but its past has more often been dominated by strife. It was the site of America's first organized labor demonstration in 1874, the main gathering place during the neighborhood's hippie era of the 1960s and, in 1991, an arena for violent riots when the police tried to evict homeless people who had taken over the grounds. The square also contains a poignant monument to the neighborhood's greatest tragedy. A small statue of a boy

and a girl looking at a steamboat commemorates the deaths of over 1,000 local residents in the *General Slocum* steamer disaster. On June 15, 1904, the boat caught fire during a pleasure cruise on the East River. The boat was crowded with women and children from this then-German neighborhood. Many local men lost their entire families and moved away, leaving the area and its memories behind.

Bayard-Condict Building ❽

65 Bleecker St. **Map** 4 F3. Ⓜ *Bleecker St.*

T HE GRACEFUL columns, elegant filigreed terra-cotta facade and magnificent cornice on this 1898 building mark the only New York work by Louis Sullivan, the great Chicago architect who taught Frank Lloyd Wright. He died in poverty and obscurity in Chicago in 1924.

Sullivan is said to have objected vigorously to the sentimental angels supporting the Bayard-Condict Building's cornice, but he eventually gave in to the wishes of Silas Alden Condict, the owner.

Because this building is squeezed into a commercial block, it is better appreciated from a distance. Cross the street and walk a little way down Crosby Street for the best view.

The Bayard-Condict Building

GRAMERCY AND THE FLATIRON DISTRICT

FOUR SQUARES were laid out in this area by real estate developers in the 19th century to emulate the quiet, private residential areas in many European cities. Gramercy Park, still mainly residential, was one of them. The townhouses around the square

Toy in the Police Academy Museum

were designed by some of the city's best architects and occupied by some of its most prominent citizens. Today, not far away, boutiques and trendy cafés are moving to the once-dowdy stretch of lower Fifth Avenue just south of the famous Flatiron Building.

SIGHTS AT A GLANCE

Historic Streets and Buildings
New York Life Insurance Company ❷
Appellate Division of the Supreme Court of the State of New York ❸
Metropolitan Life Insurance Company ❹
Flatiron Building ❺
Ladies' Mile ❻
National Arts Club ❽
The Library at the Players ❾
Block Beautiful ⓫
Con Edison Headquarters ⓮

Museums and Galleries
Theodore Roosevelt Birthplace ❼
Police Academy Museum ⓬

Churches
The Little Church Around the Corner ⓰

Parks and Squares
Madison Square ❶
Gramercy Park ❿
Stuyvesant Square ⓭
Union Square ⓯

SEE ALSO

• **Street Finder**, maps 8, 9
• **Where to Stay** pp274–5
• **Restaurants** pp290–92

GETTING THERE

The closest subway station is at 23rd St, where the Lexington Ave No. 6 train stops. Buses to the area include the M101/102 on 3rd Ave, and the M1, M2 or M3 on 5th and Madison avenues. The crosstown bus is the M26.

0 meters   500
0 yards   500

KEY

▦ Street-by-Street map
Ⓜ Subway station

Lizard on a statue in Union Square

Con Edison Headquarters by night

Street by Street: Gramercy Park

GRAMERCY PARK AND nearby Madison Square tell a tale of two cities. Madison Square is ringed by offices and traffic and is used mainly by those who work nearby, but the fine surrounding commercial architecture and statues make it well worth visiting. It was once the home of Stanford White's famous pleasure palace, the old Madison Square Garden, a place where revelers always thronged. Gramercy Park, however, retains the air of dignified tranquility it has become known for. Here, the residences and clubs remain, set around New York's last private park, for which only those who live on the square have a key.

Statue of Diana atop the old Madison Square Garden

★ **Madison Square**
The Knickerbocker Club played baseball here in the 1840s and was the first to codify the game's rules. Today office workers enjoy the park's many statues of 19th-century figures, among them Admiral David Farragut ❶

23rd Street subway (lines N, R)

★ **Flatiron Building**
The triangle made by Fifth Avenue, Broadway and 23rd Street is the site of one of New York's most famous early skyscrapers. When it was built in 1903, it was the world's tallest building ❺

A sidewalk clock found in front of 200 Fifth Avenue marks the very end of the once-fashionable shopping area, known as Ladies' Mile.

Ladies' Mile
Broadway from Union to Madison squares was once New York's finest shopping area. A few buildings

Theodore Roosevelt Birthplace
The house is a replica of the one in which the 26th American president was born ❼

KEY

– – –   Suggested route

0 meters	100
0 yards	100

National Arts Club
This is a private club for the arts, on the south side of the park ❽

Appellate Court
This small marble palace is said to be the world's busiest courthouse ❸

MADISON AVENUE

E 26TH ST

Metropolitan Life Insurance Company
Vast vaulted entrances mark each corner ❹

23rd Street subway (line 6)

The Library at the Players
Actor Edwin Booth founded this club in 1888 ❾

LOCATOR MAP
See Manhattan Map pp12–13

CHELSEA & THE GARMENT DISTRICT

LOWER MIDTOWN

East Side

GRAMERCY & THE FLATIRON DISTRICT

GREENWICH VILLAGE

EAST VILLAGE

New York Life Insurance Company
This spectacular building by Cass Gilbert bears his trademark pyramid-shaped top ❷

STAR SIGHTS

★ **Flatiron Building**

★ **Madison Square**

Gramercy Park
Only residents can use the park itself, but all can enjoy the peace and charm of the area around it ❿

The Brotherhood Synagogue was the Friends' Meeting House from 1859 to 1975, when it became a synagogue.

The Block Beautiful
This is a tree-lined stretch of East 19th Street. No particular house is outstanding, but the street as a whole is lovely ⓫

Pete's Tavern has been here since 1903. Short story writer O. Henry, a well-known chronicler of the city, wrote "The Gift of the Magi" in the second booth.

Madison Square ❶

Map 8 F4. Ⓜ *23rd St.*

Farragut's statue, Madison Square

PLANNED AS the center of a fashionable residential district, this square became a popular entertainment center after the Civil War. It was bordered by the elegant Fifth Avenue Hotel, the Madison Square Theater and Stanford White's Madison Square Garden. The torch-bearing arm of the Statue of Liberty was exhibited here in 1884.

Quiet once again, it is a lunchtime spot for neighborhood office workers, and a place to stroll and admire the sculptures. The 1880 statue of Admiral David Farragut is by Augustus Saint-Gaudens, with a pedestal by Stanford White. Farragut was the hero of a Civil War sea battle; figures representing Courage and Loyalty arising from the waves are carved on the base. The statue of Roscoe Conkling commemorates a US senator who died of exposure during the great blizzard of 1888. The Eternal Light flagpole, by Carrère & Hastings, honors the soldiers who fell in France during World War I.

New York Life Insurance Company ❷

51 Madison Ave. **Map** 9 A3.
Ⓜ *28th St.* **Open** *office hours.*

THIS IMPOSING building was designed in 1928 by Cass Gilbert of Woolworth Building fame. The interior is a masterpiece, adorned with enormous hanging lamps, bronze doors and paneling, and a grand staircase leading, of all places, to the subway station.

Other famous buildings have stood on this site. Barnum's Hippodrome was here in 1874, then the first Madison Square Garden opened in 1879. A wide range of entertainments were put on, including the prizefights of heavyweight boxing hero John L. Sullivan in the 1880s. The next Madison Square Garden – Stanford White's legendary pleasure palace – opened on the same site in 1890. Lavish musical shows and social events were attended by New York's elite, who paid over $500 for a box at the prestigious annual horse show.

The building had street-level arcades and a tower modeled on the Giralda in Seville. A gold statue of the goddess Diana stood atop the tower. Her nudity was shocking, but far more scandalous was the decadent life and death of White himself. In 1906, while watching a revue in the roof garden, he was shot dead by millionaire Harry K. Thaw, the husband of White's former mistress, showgirl Evelyn Nesbit. The headline in the journal *Vanity Fair* summed up popular feeling: "Stanford White, Voluptuary and Pervert, Dies the Death of a Dog." The ensuing trial's revelations about decadent Broadway high society leave modern soap operas far behind.

New York Life Insurance Company's golden pyramid roof

Appellate Division of the Supreme Court of the State of New York ❸

E. 25th St. at Madison Ave. **Map** 9 A4. 🛈 *340 0400.* Ⓜ *23rd St.* **Open** *9am–5pm Mon–Fri (court in session from 2pm Tue, Wed, Thu, from 10am Fri).* **Closed** *public hols.* 🚫

APPEALS RELATING TO civil and criminal cases for New York and the Bronx are heard here, in what is widely considered to be the busiest court of its kind in the world. James Brown Lord designed the small yet noble Palladian Revival building in 1900.

Statues of *Justice* and *Study* above the Appellate Court

It is decorated with more than a dozen handsome sculptures, including Daniel Chester French's *Justice* flanked by *Power* and *Study*. During the week, the public is invited to step inside to admire the fine interior, designed by the Herter brothers, including the courtroom when it is not in session. Among the elegant details worth looking for are the fine stained-glass windows and dome, the murals and the striking cabinetwork.

Displays in the lobby often feature some of the more famous cases that have been heard in this court. Among the celebrity names that have been involved in appeals settled here are Babe Ruth, Charlie Chaplin, Fred Astaire, Harry Houdini, Theodore Dreiser and Edgar Allan Poe.

Clock tower of the Metropolitan Life Insurance Company

Metropolitan Life Insurance Company ❹

1 Madison Ave. **Map** 9 A4. 578-2211. 23rd St. **Closed** to the public, except lobby.

IN 1909, THE ADDITION of a 700-ft (210-m) tower to this 1893 building ousted the Flatiron as the tallest in the world. The huge four-sided clock has minute hands said to weigh 1000 lb (454 kg) each. The building is lit up at night, and is a familiar part of the evening skyline. It served as the company symbol "the light that never fails."

A series of historical murals by N.C. Wyeth, the famed illustrator of such classics as *Robin Hood*, *Treasure Island* and *Robinson Crusoe* (and the father of painter Andrew Wyeth), once graced the walls of the cafeteria. They are now on display in the lobby.

Flatiron Building ❺

175 5th Ave. **Map** 8 F4. 23rd St. **Open** office hours.

ORIGINALLY NAMED the Fuller Building after the construction company that owned it, this building by Chicago architect David Burnham was the tallest in the world when it was completed in 1902. One of the first buildings to use a steel frame, it heralded the era of the skyscrapers.

It soon became known as the Flatiron for its unusual triangular shape, but some called it "Burnham's folly," predicting that the winds created by the building's shape would knock it down. It has withstood the test of time, but the winds along 23rd Street did have one notable effect. In the building's early days, they drew crowds of males hoping to get a peek at women's ankles as their long skirts got blown about. Police officers had to keep people moving along, and their call, "23-skidoo" became slang for "scram."

The stretch of Fifth Avenue to the south of the building was, until recently, rather run down but is fast coming to life with chic shops such as Emporio Armani and Paul Smith, giving the area new cachet and a new name, "the Flatiron District."

Flatiron Building during its construction

Ladies' Mile ❻

Broadway (Union Sq. to Madison Sq.). **Map** 4 E1 to 8 F4. 14th St, 23rd St.

Arnold Constable store

IN THE 19TH CENTURY, the "carriage trade" came here in shiny traps from their town houses nearby, to shop at stores such as Arnold Constable (Nos. 881–887) and Lord & Taylor (No. 901). The ground-floor exteriors have changed beyond recognition; look up to see the remains of once-grand facades.

President Teddy Roosevelt

Theodore Roosevelt Birthplace ❼

28 E. 20th St. **Map** 9 A5. 260-1616 14th St.-Union Sq. **Open** 9am–5pm Wed–Sun (last adm: 4pm). **Closed** public hols. **Adm charge**. *Lectures, concerts, films, videos.*

THE RECONSTRUCTED boyhood home of the colorful 26th president displays everything from the toys with which the young Teddy played to campaign buttons and emblems of the trademark "Rough Rider" hat that Roosevelt wore in the Spanish-American War. One exhibit features his explorations and interests; the other covers his political career.

Bas-relief faces of great writers at the National Arts Club

National Arts Club **8**

15 Gramercy Pk S. **Map** 9 A5. 475-3424. **M** 14th St-Union Sq, 6 to 23rd St. **Open** for exhibitions.

DESIGNED BY Calvert Vaux in 1881–84, this large brownstone was the residence of New York governor Samuel Tilden, who condemned "Boss" Tweed *(see p25)* and established a free public library. The National Arts Club bought the home in 1906 and kept the original high ceilings and stained glass. Members have included most of the leading American artists of the late 19th and early 20th centuries. Early members were asked to donate a painting or sculpture in lieu of a subscription for life membership, and these gifts form the permanent collection. The club is open to the public several times a year for exhibitions.

The Library at the Players **9**

16 Gramercy Pk S. **Map** 9 A5. 228-7610. **M** 14th St-Union Sq, 6 to 23rd St. **Closed** exc for pre-booked group tours.

THIS TWO-STORY brownstone was the home of actor Edwin Booth, brother of John Wilkes Booth, President Lincoln's assassin. Architect Stanford White

remodeled the building as a club in 1888. Although intended primarily for actors, members have included White himself, author Mark Twain, publisher Thomas Nast and Winston Churchill, whose mother, Jennie Jerome, was born nearby. A statue of Booth playing Hamlet is across the street in Gramercy Park.

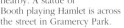

Decorative grille at The Players club

Gramercy Park **10**

Map 9 A4. **M** 23rd St.

GRAMERCY PARK is one of four squares (with Union, Stuyvesant and Madison) laid out in the 1830s and 1840s to attract society residences. It is the city's only private park, and residents in the surrounding buildings have keys to the park gate as the original owners once did. Look through the railings at the southeast corner to see Greg Wyatt's fountain, with giraffes leaping around a smiling sun.

The buildings around the square were designed by some of the city's most famous architects, including

Stanford White, whose house was located on the site of today's Gramercy Park Hotel. Particularly fine are 3 and 4, with graceful cast-iron gates and porches. The lanterns in front of 4 serve as symbols marking the house of a former mayor of the city, James Harper. Number 34 (1883) has been the home of the sculptor Daniel Chester French, the actor James Cagney and circus impresario John Ringling (who had a massive pipe organ installed in his apartment).

Block Beautiful **11**

E. 19th St. **Map** 9 A5. **M** 3rd Ave, 14th St-Union Sq, 6 to 23rd St.

House facade on the Block Beautiful on East 19th Street

THIS IS A SERENE, tree-lined block of 1920s residences, beautifully restored. None of them is exceptional on its own, but together they create a wonderfully harmonious whole. Number 132 had two famous theatrical tenants: Theda Bara, silent movie star and Hollywood's first sex symbol, and the fine Shakespearean actress Mrs. Patrick Campbell, who originated the role of Eliza Doolittle in George Bernard Shaw's *Pygmalion* in 1914. The hitching posts outside 141 and the ceramic relief of giraffes outside 147-149 are two of the many details to look for as you walk along the block.

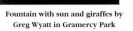

Fountain with sun and giraffes by Greg Wyatt in Gramercy Park

Police Academy Museum ⓬

235 E 20th St. **Map** 9 B4.
📞 477-9753. Ⓜ *14th St-Union Sq.*
Open *9am–3pm Mon–Fri.* **Closed** *Sat, Sun,* **public** *hols, & for meetings – call for appt.* 📷

A COLORFUL SALUTE to "New York's finest," the museum possesses one of the largest collections of police force memorabilia anywhere. On display are daily registers describing liquor raids during the Prohibition era, sensational ax murders, bank robberies and kidnappings. There is a whole arsenal of weapons – nightsticks, billy clubs and an enormous gun collection. Also on display are antique uniforms and caps, and every badge issued by the Police Department since 1845. On a more somber contemporary note, an educational exhibit details the tragic consequences of drug addiction and youth gangs.

Gangster Al Capone's gun at the Police Academy Museum

Stuyvesant Square ⓭

Map 9 B5. Ⓜ *14th St-Union Sq.*

T HIS OASIS, in the form of a pair of parks divided by Second Avenue, was part of Peter Stuyvesant's original farm in the 1600s. It was still in the Stuyvesant family when the park was designed in 1836; Peter G. Stuyvesant sold the land to the city for the nominal sum of $5 (much to the delight of those living nearby, who saw real estate values jump). A statue of Stuyvesant by Gertrude Vanderbilt Whitney stands in the park. The park separated the Stuyvesant area from the poorer Gas House district.

The towers of Con Edison (right), Metropolitan Life and the Empire State

Con Edison Headquarters ⓮

145 E 14th St. **Map** 9 A5.
Ⓜ *3rd Ave, 14th St-Union Sq.*
Closed *to the public.*

T HE CLOCK TOWER of this building, which dates from 1911, is a local landmark. It is not as tall as nearby Empire State Building, but when lit up at night, it makes an attractive showpiece. The Con Edison Energy Museum, which used to be housed next door, has now closed but the clock tower is still worth a look en route to Union square.

Union Square ⓯

Map 9 A5. Ⓜ *14th St-Union Sq.*
Farmers' Market *Mon, Wed, Fri, Sat.*

Greenmarket day at Union Square

O PENED IN 1839, this park joined Bloomingdale Road (now Broadway) with the Bowery Road (Fourth Avenue or Park), and hence its name. Later, the center of the square was lifted up for a subway to run beneath it. The park became popular with soapbox orators. During the Depression in 1930, more than 35,000 unemployed people rallied here, before marching on to City Hall to demand jobs. The square hosts a popular greenmarket where farmers from all over New York State sell their fresh produce.

The Little Church Around the Corner ⓰

1 E 29th St. **Map** 8 F3.
📞 684-6770. Ⓜ *28th St.* **Open** *9am–5pm daily.* ✝ *8, 9, 11am Sun.*
📷 ♿ ✔ *Sun after 11am service.*
Lectures, concerts, recitals.

B UILT FROM 1849 to 1856, the Episcopal Church of the Transfiguration is a tranquil retreat. It has been known by its nickname since 1870 when Joseph Jefferson tried to arrange the funeral of fellow actor George Holland. The pastor at a nearby church refused to bury a person of so lowly a profession. Instead, he suggested "the little church around the corner." The name stuck and the church has had special ties with the theater ever since. Sarah Bernhardt attended services here.

The south transept window, by John La Farge, shows Edwin Booth playing Hamlet. Jefferson's cry of "God bless the little church around the corner" is commemorated in a window in the south aisle.

CHELSEA AND THE GARMENT DISTRICT

THIS WAS OPEN farmland in 1750, but by the 1830s it was a city suburb, and in the 1870s, with the coming of the elevated railroads (*see pp24–5*), it had become quite commercial. Music halls and theaters lined 23rd Street. Fashion Row grew in the shadow of the El, with department stores serving middle-class New York. But, as fashion

Statue of garment worker, at 555 7th Avenue

moved uptown, Chelsea drifted further downhill. It became a warehouse district, until the Els were removed and New Yorkers rediscovered the charming 19th-century town houses. While Chelsea's fortunes were waning, Herald Square to the north was thriving as Macy's arrived, and New York city's retailing and garment districts grew up around it.

Inside Chelsea's Empire Diner

SIGHTS AT A GLANCE

Historic Streets and Buildings
Empire State Building
pp134–5 **2**
General Post Office **7**
General Theological
Seminary **11**

Chelsea Historic District **12**
Hugh O'Neill Dry Goods
Store **14**

Churches
Marble Collegiate Reformed
Church **1**
St. John the Baptist Church **5**

Modern Architecture
Madison Square Garden **6**
Jacob K. Javits Convention
Center **8**

Chelsea Piers Sports and
Entertainment Complex **9**

Monuments
Worth Monument **15**

Parks and Squares
Herald Square **3**

**Landmark Hotels and
Restaurants**
Empire Diner **10**
Chelsea Hotel **13**

Landmark Stores
Macy's **4**

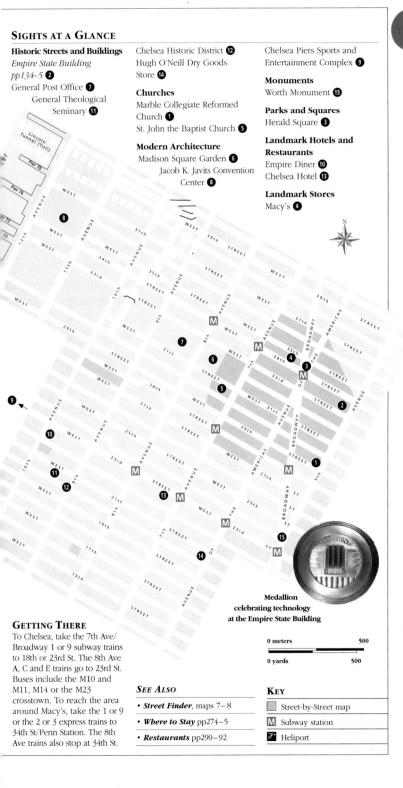

Medallion
celebrating technology
at the Empire State Building

GETTING THERE
To Chelsea, take the 7th Ave/
Broadway 1 or 9 subway trains
to 18th or 23rd St. The 8th Ave
A, C and E trains go to 23rd St.
Buses include the M10 and
M11, M14 or the M23
crosstown. To reach the area
around Macy's, take the 1 or 9
or the 2 or 3 express trains to
34th St/Penn Station. The 8th
Ave trains also stop at 34th St.

0 meters   500
0 yards   500

SEE ALSO

• *Street Finder*, maps 7–8
• *Where to Stay* pp274–5
• *Restaurants* pp290–92

KEY

Street-by-Street map

M Subway station

Heliport

Street by Street: Herald Square

HERALD SQUARE is named for the New York *Herald*, which had its office there from 1894 to 1921. Today full of shoppers, the area was once one of the raunchiest parts of New York. During the 1880s and '90s, it was known as the Tenderloin District and was filled with dance halls and bordellos. When Macy's opened in 1901, the focus moved from flesh to fashion. New York's Garment District now fills the streets near Macy's on and around Seventh Avenue, also known as Fashion Avenue. To the east on Fifth Avenue is the Empire State Building, with the city's best eagle's-eye views from the observation deck.

Fashion Avenue is another name for the stretch of Seventh Avenue around 34th Street. This area is the heart of New York's garment industry. The streets are full of men pushing racks of clothes and furs.

Manhattan Mall, Once the site of Macy's archrival, Gimbel's, holds 90 stores, 20 eateries, and a whole floor for children's wear.

34th Street-Penn Station subway (1, 2, 3, 9, A, C, E)

The Ramada Hotel Pennsylvania was a center for the 1930s big bands – Glenn Miller's song "Pennsylvania 6-5000" made its telephone number famous.

St. John the Baptist Church
A beautiful set of carved Stations of the Cross is hung on the walls of the white marble interior of this church **5**

The SJM Building is at 130 West 30th Street. Mesopotamian-style friezes adorn the outside of the building.

The Fur District is at the southern end of the Garment District. Furriers ply their trade between West 27th and 30th streets.

The Flower District, around Sixth Avenue and West 28th Street, hums with activity in the early part of the day as florists pack their vans with their highly scented, brightly colored wares.

28th Street subway (lines N, R)

★ Macy's
The biggest department store in the world has something for everyone ❹

The Greenwich Savings Bank (now the Republic National Bank) is a Greek temple to banking with huge columns on three sides.

34th Street subway (lines B, D, F, N, Q, R)

Herald Square
The New York Herald Building's clock now is situated where Broadway meets Sixth Avenue ❸

★ Empire State Building
The observation deck of this quintessential skyscraper is a great place to view the city ❷

Greeley Square is more of a traffic island than a square, but it does have a fine statue of Horace Greeley, founder of the New York *Tribune*.

Little Korea is an area of Korean businesses. In addition to shops, there are restaurants nearby on West 31st and 32nd streets.

The Life Building at 19 West 31st Street housed *Life* magazine when it was a satirical weekly. Carrère & Hastings designed the building in 1894. It is now a hotel *(see p276)*.

Marble Collegiate Church
This 1854 church was built in the Gothic Revival style. It became famous when Norman Vincent Peale was pastor here ❶

LOCATOR MAP
See Manhattan Map pp12–13

HUDSON RIVER

THEATER DISTRICT

CHELSEA & THE GARMENT DISTRICT

GREENWICH VILLAGE

GRAMERCY & THE FLATIRON DISTRICT

KEY

– – – Suggested route

| 0 meters | 100 |
| 0 yards | 100 |

STAR SIGHTS

★ **Macy's**

★ **Empire State Building**

Marble Collegiate's Tiffany stained-glass windows

Marble Collegiate Reformed Church ❶

1 W. 29th St. **Map** 8 F3. 📞 686-2770. Ⓜ 28th St. **Open** by appt only 🕐 Sep–Jun: 11:15am Sun; Jun–Sep: 10:30am Sun. 🚫 during services. ♿

THIS CHURCH is best known for its former pastor Norman Vincent Peale, who wrote *The Power of Positive Thinking*. Another positive

thinker, ex-president Richard M. Nixon, attended services here when he was a lawyer in his pre–White House days.

The church was built in 1854 using the marble blocks that give it its name. At that time, Fifth Avenue was nothing more than a dusty country road, and the cast-iron fence around the church was there to keep livestock out.

The original white and gold interior walls were replaced with a stenciled gold *fleur-de-lis* design on a soft rust background. Two stained-glass Tiffany windows, depicting Old Testament scenes, were placed in the south wall in 1893.

Empire State Building ❷

See pp134–5.

Herald Square ❸

6th Ave. **Map** 8 E2. Ⓜ 34th St-Penn Station. See **Shopping** p313.

NAMED AFTER the New York *Herald*, which occupied a fine arcaded, Italianate Stanford White building here from

1893 to 1921, the square was the hub of the rowdy Tenderloin district in the 1870s and 1880s. Theaters, such as the Manhattan Opera House, dance halls, hotels and restaurants kept the area humming with life until reformers clamped down on sleaze in the 1890s. The ornamental Bennett clock, named for James Gordon Bennett Jr., publisher of the *Herald*, is now all that is left of the Herald Building.

The Opera House was razed in 1901 to make way for Macy's and, soon after, other department stores followed, making Herald Square a mecca for shoppers. One such store was the now-defunct Gimbel Brothers Department Store, once arch rival to Macy's. (The rivalry was affectionately portrayed in the New York Christmas movie *A Miracle on 34th Street*). In 1988 the store was converted into a vertical mall with a glittery neon front. Although most of the old names have gone, Herald Square is still a key shopping district.

Macy's ❹

151 W. 34th St. **Map** 8 E2. 📞 695-4400 Ⓜ 34th St-Penn Station. **Open** 10am–8:30pm Mon, Thu, Fri; 10am–8:30pm Tue, Wed; 9am-8:30pm Sat; 11am–7pm Sun. See **Shopping** p311. **Closed** public hols.

THE "WORLD'S LARGEST STORE" covers a square block, and the merchandise inside covers just about any item you could imagine in every price range.

Macy's was founded by a former whaler named Rowland Hussey Macy, who opened a small store on West 14th Street in 1857. The store's red star logo came from Macy's tattoo, a souvenir of his sailing days.

By the time Macy died in 1877, his little store had grown to a row of 11 buildings. It was to expand further under two brothers, Isidor and Nathan Straus, who had operated Macy's china and glassware department. By 1902 Macy's had outgrown its 14th Street premises, and the firm acquired its present site. The eastern facade has a new

Macy's 34th Street facade

The nave of St. John the Baptist Church

entrance but still bears the bay windows and Corinthian pillars of the 1902 design. The 34th Street facade still has its original caryatids guarding the entrance, along with the clock, canopy and lettering. Inside, many of the original wooden escalators are still in good working order.

The sea featured again in Macy's history in 1912 – a plaque by the main entrance commemorates the death of Isidor and his wife in the sinking of the *Titanic*.

Macy's sponsors New York's renowned Thanksgiving Day parade and the Fourth of July fireworks. The store's Spring Flower Show draws thousands of visitors.

St. John the Baptist Church **5**

210 W. 31st St. **Map** 8 E3. 564-9070. 34th St-Penn Station. **Open** 6:45am–6pm daily, throughout the day.

FOUNDED IN 1840 to serve a congregation of newly arrived immigrants, today this small Roman Catholic church is almost lost in the heart of the Fur District. The exterior has a single spire. Although the brownstone facade on 30th Street is dark with city soot, many treasures lie within this dull exterior. The entrance is through the modern Friary on 31st Street.

The sanctuary by Napoleon Le Brun is a marvel of Gothic arches in glowing white marble surmounted by gilded capitals. Painted reliefs of religious scenes line the walls; sunlight streams through the stained-glass windows. Also off the Friary is the Prayer Garden, a small, green and peaceful oasis with religious statuary, a fountain and stone benches.

Madison Square Garden **6**

4 Pennsylvania Plaza. **Map** 8 D2. 465-6741. 34th St-Penn Station. **Open** Mon–Sun, times vary according to shows. **Adm charge**. See **Entertainment** p344.

THERE'S ONLY ONE good thing to be said for the razing of the extraordinarily lovely McKim, Mead & White Pennsylvania Station building in favor of this undistinguished 1968 complex: it so enraged city preservationists that they formed an alliance to ensure that such a thing would never be allowed to happen again.

Madison Square Garden itself, which sits atop underground Pennsylvania Station, is a cylinder of precast concrete, functional enough as a 20,000-seat, centrally located home for the famous New York Knickerbockers (the Knicks) basketball and New York Rangers hockey teams. It also has a packed calendar of other events: rock concerts, championship tennis and boxing, outrageously staged wrestling, the Ringling Bros. and Barnum & Bailey Circus, an antiques show, a dog show and more. There is also a 5,600-seat theater.

In spite of some recent renovation work, Madison Square Garden lacks the panache of its earlier location, which combined a truly stunning Stanford White building with equally extravagant entertainment (*see p124*).

The massive interior of Madison Square Garden

General Post Office **7**

421 8th Ave. **Map** 8 D2. 967-8585. 34th St-Penn Station. **Open** 24 hrs a day, every day, (incl public hols). See **Practical Information** p361.

DESIGNED BY McKim, Mead & White in 1913, in a style to complement their 1910 Pennsylvania Station across the street, the Post Office is a perfect example of a public building of the Beaux Arts period. The imposing, two-block-long structure has a broad staircase leading to a facade adorned with 20 Corinthian columns and a pavilion at each end. The 280-ft (85-m) inscription across it is loosely based on a description by Herodotus of the Persian Empire's postal service: "Neither snow nor rain nor heat nor gloom of night stays these couriers from the swift completion of their appointed rounds."

The Corinthian colonnade of the General Post Office

Empire State Building ❷

102nd-floor observatory

Aᴌᴛʜᴏᴜɢʜ ɪᴛ ʟᴏsᴛ its title as the world's tallest building to the World Trade Center in the 1970s, the Empire State is still New York's most famous skyscraper, a symbol of the city all over the world. Construction began only weeks before the Wall Street Crash of 1929, and by the time it opened in 1931, space was so difficult to rent that it was nicknamed "the Empty State Building." Only the immediate popularity of the observatories saved the building from bankruptcy – to date, they have attracted more than 100 million visitors.

Empire State Building

The Empire State was planned to be 86 stories high, but then a 150 ft (46 m) mooring mast for zeppelins was added. Now the mast transmits TV and radio to the city and four states.

Colored floodlighting of the top 30 floors marks special and seasonal events.

Cᴏɴsᴛʀᴜᴄᴛɪᴏɴ
The building was designed for ease and speed of construction. Everything possible was prefabricated and slotted into place at a rate of about four stories per week.

Symbols of the modern age are depicted on these bronze Art Deco medallions placed throughout the lobby.

High-speed elevators travel at up to 1,200 ft (366 m) a minute.

The framework is made from 60,000 tons of steel and was built in 23 weeks.

Aluminum panels were used instead of stone around the 6,500 windows. The steel trim masks rough edges on the facing.

Ten minutes is all it takes for fit runners to race up the 1,860 steps from the lobby to the 86th floor, in the annual Empire State Run-Up.

Ten million bricks were used to line the whole building.

Sandwich space between the floors houses the wiring, pipes and cables.

Over 200 steel and concrete piles support the 365,000-ton building.

Sᴛᴀʀ Fᴇᴀᴛᴜʀᴇs

★ **Fifth Avenue Entrance Lobby**

★ **Views from 86th- and 102nd-floor Observatories**

★ **Views from the Observatories**
The 86th floor has outdoor observation decks for bird's-eye views of Manhattan. From the 102nd floor, 1,250 ft (381 m) high, you can see more than 80 miles (125 km) on a clear day, but check the visibility rating in the lobby first.

Sky Boy
Photographer Lewis Hine documented the workers' bravery during the 1930s construction. Here, a worker climbs up a cable. The wide Hudson River appears small in the background.

Empire State 1454 ft (443 m)

Eiffel Tower 1045 ft (319 m)

Great Pyramid 350 ft (107 m)

Big Ben 220 ft (67 m)

Pecking Order
New Yorkers are justly proud of their city's symbol, which towers above the icons of other countries.

Lightning Strikes
The Empire State is a natural lightning conductor, struck up to 500 times a year. The outside deck is closed during storms, the inside viewing area open.

★ **Fifth Avenue Entrance Lobby**
A relief image of the skyscraper is superimposed on a map of New York State in the marble-lined lobby.

ENCOUNTERS IN THE SKY
The Empire State Building has been seen in many films. However, the finale from the 1933 classic *King Kong* is easily its most famous guest appearance, as the giant ape straddles the spire to do battle with army aircraft. In 1945 a real bomber flew too low over Manhattan in fog and struck the building just above the 78th floor. The luckiest escape was that of a young elevator operator whose cabin plunged 79 floors to the basement. The emergency brakes saved her life.

Jacob K. Javits Convention Center **8**

655 W. 34th St. **Map** 7 B2. **[** 216-2000. **M** 34th St-Penn Station. **Opening times** vary with shows. **Closed** on non-show days. **Adm charge.** ⊘ & ⅱ

The Convention Center – modern New York architecture at its best

STRIKINGLY MODERNISTIC in appearance, this glass building facing the Hudson, which opened in 1986, was designed by I.M. Pei to give New York the space for large-scale expositions. The 15-story building is constructed of 16,000 panes of glass, the two main halls can accommodate thousands of delegates and the lobby is high enough to hold the Statue of Liberty. In 1989 the final completion of the Galleria River Pavilion added another 40,000 sq ft (3,750 sq m) of open space and two outdoor terraces overlooking the river.

Chelsea Piers Complex **9**

11th Ave (17th & 23rd Sts) **Map** 7 B5. **[** 336-6666. **M** 14th St, 23rd St. ⊞ M23. **Open** daily. **Adm charge.**

THIS MAMMOTH complex, which opened in 1995, has converted four neglected piers into a center for a vast range of sports and leisure activities (see p31). The facilities include skating rinks, running tracks, a golf driving range, a marina, and 11 TV and film production sound stages.

Empire Diner **10**

210 10th Ave. **Map** 7 C4. **[** 243-2736. **M** 23rd St. **Open** 24hrs daily. See **Restaurants and Bars** p306.

THIS ART DECO beauty is a faithful refurbishing of a classic 1929 American diner, complete with stainless steel bar and black and chrome trim. Bette Davis reputedly declared it her favorite diner. Its cuisine and clientele are up-to-date New York style.

A 15th-century music manuscript from the Seminary's collection

General Theological Seminary **11**

20th–21st Sts. **Map** 7 C4. **[** 243-5150. **M** 23rd St. or 34th St.-Penn Station. **Open** noon–3pm Mon–Fri, 11am–3pm Sat. ⊘ &

FOUNDED IN 1817, this block-square campus accepts 150 students at a time to train for the priesthood. Clement Clarke Moore, a professor of Biblical Learning, donated the site, officially known as Chelsea Square. The earliest remaining building dates from 1836; the most modern, St. Mark's Library, was built in 1960 and holds the largest collection of Latin Bibles in the world.

The campus can be entered from Ninth Avenue only. Inside, the garden is laid out in two quadrangles like an English cathedral close: it is especially lovely in spring.

The Empire Diner before hungry club-goers arrive for breakfast

Chelsea Historic District ⑫

From 9th to 10th Aves. and from W. 20th to 21st Sts. **Map** 8 D5. Ⓜ *18th St.*

ALTHOUGH HE is more well-known as the author of "A Visit from St. Nicholas" than as an urban planner, Clement Clarke Moore owned an estate here and divided it into lots in the 1830s creating handsome rows of town houses. Restoration has since rescued many of the original buildings.

Of these, the finest are seven houses known as Cushman Row, running from 406– 418 West 20th Street, which were built from 1839–1840 for Don Alonzo Cushman. He was a merchant who also founded the Greenwich Savings Bank. He joined Moore and James N. Wells in the development of Chelsea. Rich in detail and intricate ironwork, Cushman Row is ranked with Washington Square North as supreme examples of Greek Revival architecture. Look for cast-iron wreaths around attic windows and the pineapples on the newel posts of two of the houses – old symbols of hospitality.

Farther along West 20th Street, from 446–450, there are fine examples of the Italianate style for which Chelsea is also renowned.

A house on Cushman Row

The detailed brickwork arches of windows and fanlights subtly implied the wealth of the owner, being able to afford this expensive effect.

Hugh O'Neill Dry Goods Store

Chelsea Hotel ⑬

222 W. 23rd St. **Map** 8 D4. Ⓒ 243-3700. Ⓜ *23rd St, 34 St.-Penn Station.*

FEW HOTELS ANYWHERE can match the Chelsea for artistic and literary heritage – and notoriety. Many of its former guests have been commemorated in the brass plaques on the hotel's facade.

A guest's-eye view of the Chelsea Hotel's cast-iron stairwell

They include Tennessee Williams, Mark Twain, Jack Kerouac and Brendan Behan. Dylan Thomas spent his last years here. In 1966, the hotel was the setting for the Andy Warhol movie *Chelsea Girls*, reviving its cult status, and in 1978 punk band member Sid Vicious killed his girlfriend in the hotel. For many, all this adds to the Chelsea's seedy mystique, and it still draws musicians, artists and writers who hope their names will one day be remembered.

Hugh O'Neill Dry Goods Store ⑭

655–671 6th Avenue. **Map** 8 E4. Ⓜ *23rd St.*

THOUGH THE STORE is long gone, the 1876 cast-iron columned and pilastered facade clearly shows the scale and grandeur of the emporiums that once lined Sixth Avenue from 18th to 23rd streets, the area known as Fashion Row. O'Neill, whose sign can still be seen on the facade, was a showman and super-salesman whose trademark was a shiny fleet of delivery wagons. His customers came in droves via the conveniently close Sixth Avenue El. They were not the "carriage trade" enjoyed by Ladies' Mile (*see p125*), but their numbers allowed the Row to flourish until the turn of the century, when the retailing district continued its move uptown. The grand buildings remain, and many are now under renovation. All it takes is a look upward to imagine what they were like in their heyday.

Worth Monument ⑮

5th Ave. **Map** 8 F4. Ⓜ *23rd St-Broadway.*

HIDDEN AWAY BEHIND a water meter on a triangle amid city traffic is an obelisk erected in 1857 to mark the grave of the one public figure to be buried under the streets of Manhattan. That honor belongs to General William J. Worth, a hero of the Mexican wars of the mid-1800s. A cast-iron fence of swords embedded in the ground surrounds the monument.

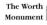

The Worth Monument

THEATER DISTRICT

IT WAS THE move of the Metropolitan Opera House to Broadway at 40th Street in 1883 that first drew lavish theaters and restaurants to this area. In the 1920s, movie palaces added the glamour of neon to Broadway, the signs getting bigger and brighter until the street became known as the "Great White Way."

Lee Lawrie design in Rockefeller Center

After World War II, the pull of the movies waned and glitter was replaced by grime. Now a redevelopment program has brought the public and the bright lights back. Pockets of calm also exist away from the bustle. Explore the Public Library or relax in Bryant Park. For the best of both worlds, though, visit Rockefeller Center.

Main Reading Room of the New York Public Library

Sights at a Glance

Historic Streets and Buildings
New York Yacht Club ❺
American Standard Building ❼
New York Public Library ❽
Times Square ❾
Group Health Insurance Building ⓫
Paramount Building ⓬
Shubert Alley ⓭
Alwyn Court Apartments ⓲

Museums
Intrepid Sea-Air-Space Museum ⓳

Modern Architecture
Rockefeller Center ❶
MONY Tower ⓮

Parks and Squares
Bryant Park ❻

Famous Theaters
Lyceum Theater ❸
New Amsterdam Theater ❿
City Center of Music and Dance ⓯
Carnegie Hall ⓰

Landmark Hotels and Restaurants
Algonquin Hotel ❹
Russian Tea Room ⓱

Landmark Stores
Diamond Row ❷

Getting There

Convenient subway routes are the 7th Ave/Broadway 1, 2, 3 and 9 trains to 50th or 42nd St, and N or R trains to 57th or 49th St. Other nearby lines include the 8th Ave A, C or E trains and 6th Ave, B, D, F or Q trains. Bus routes through the area are the M5, M6, M7, M10, M34, M42, M50, M57 and the M58 Street crosstown.

Key

	Street-by-Street map
M	Subway station
	Riverboat boarding point

See Also

• **Street Finder,** maps 8, 11–12
• **Where to Stay** pp274–75
• **Restaurants** pp290–92

0 meters   500
0 yards   500

Mermaid and dolphin fountain in the Channel Gardens

Street by Street: Rockefeller Center

THE FIRST COMPLEX in the world to integrate offices with shops, entertainment, dining and gardens, Rockefeller Center is one of the most visited sights in New York. Night and day, throughout the year, the Center is alive with people. There are workers from some of the world's major companies, shoppers browsing in the stores and tourists admiring the wealth of American art and architecture. In winter skaters glide beneath the famous Christmas tree. You can rent skates and try it. The colorful flower displays change with the seasons.

The Winter Garden has housed hit revues and musicals since 1911.

Rockefeller Center expanded to the west in the 1960s, with a series of four towers providing a bland backdrop to the older buildings.

Equitable Center has the Roy Lichtenstein *Mural with Blue Brushstroke (1984–5)* in its lobby.

50th St subway (lines 1, 9)

Cort Theater has a facade based on the Petit Trianon at Versailles, and a bust of Marie Antoinette overlooking the ticket lobby. Both *The Diary of Anne Frank* and *Sarafina!* were premiered here.

George M. Cohan's statue, in front of the TKTS booth in Duffy Square, honors the man who wrote "Give My Regards to Broadway."

GEORGE
·M·
COHAN

The Miller Building was "The Show Folks' Shoe Shop" before World War II. Four statues of American actresses by A. Stirling Cooper are all that remain to show for its former role.

Lyceum Theater
This is the oldest New York theater still in use, although it is "dark" more often than not these days. It was built in 1903 for producer Daniel Froman, who had an apartment in the building complete with a trap door looking down over the stage ❸

Detail from the facade of the Lyceum

Sun Triangle in the Lower Plaza mixes science and symbolism to show the relationship of the sun with the planets, using a reflecting pool and shining steel globes.

Radio City Music Hall
has a year-round schedule of top entertainment, but the high point is the Christmas Spectacular featuring the Rockettes chorus line. *(See p334.)*

47-50th St subway (lines B, D, F, Q)

★ **Rockefeller Center**
The towering General Electric Building is the "flagship" of the Center. It is brilliantly lit at night ❶

LOCATOR MAP
See Manhattan Map pp12–13

KEY

— — —   Suggested route

| 0 meters | 100 |
| 0 yards | 100 |

STAR SIGHTS

★ **Rockefeller Center**

★ **Diamond Row**

News, by Isamu Noguchi, is a ten-ton stainless steel panel at the main entrance to the Associated Press Building.

The ice rink at Rockefeller Plaza becomes a café area in summer.

Atlas, by Lee Lawrie, stands in the main entrance to the International Building. Cast in bronze and weighing 4,000 lb (1,800 kg) it is one of 12 works by Lawrie in the Center.

The Rainbow Room, atop the GE Building, is the place for a luxury night out, dining and dancing in a 1930s-style setting. *(See p297.)*

Channel Gardens separates the British Empire Building and La Maison Française. It is a pleasant place to sit and relax amid the floral displays and fountains.

★ **Diamond Row**
This block of West 47th Street is the hub of New York's gem trade. Almost every window gleams with jewels ❷

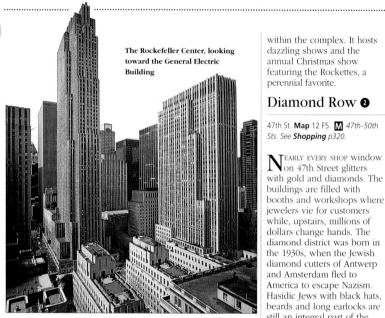

The Rockefeller Center, looking toward the General Electric Building

Rockefeller Center ❶

Map 12 F5. **M** 47th-50th Sts.
🅿 ♿ 🍴 🖥

WHEN THE New York City Landmarks Preservation Commission unanimously voted to declare Rockefeller Center a landmark in 1985, they rightly called it "the heart of New York . . . a great unifying presence in the chaotic core of midtown Manhattan."

It is the largest privately owned complex of its kind and the inspiration for dozens of cities that try to emulate its almost perfect urban mix. The Art Deco design was by a team of top architects headed by Raymond Hood. Works by 30 artists can be found in foyers, on facades, and in the gardens.

The site, once a botanic garden owned by Columbia University, was leased in 1928 by John D. Rockefeller, Jr., as an ideal central home for a new opera house. When the 1929 Depression scuttled the plans, Rockefeller, stuck with a long-term lease, decided to go ahead with his own development. The 14 buildings that were erected between 1931 and 1940 provided jobs for 225,000 people during the worst of the Depression. More development between 1957 and 1973 brought the Center to a total of 19 buildings in all.

In December 1932, Radio City Music Hall opened

Wisdom by Lee Lawrie, on the GE Building

within the complex. It hosts dazzling shows and the annual Christmas show featuring the Rockettes, a perennial favorite.

Diamond Row ❷

47th St. **Map** 12 F5. **M** 47th-50th Sts. See **Shopping** p320.

NEARLY EVERY SHOP window on 47th Street glitters with gold and diamonds. The buildings are filled with booths and workshops where jewelers vie for customers while, upstairs, millions of dollars change hands. The diamond district was born in the 1930s, when the Jewish diamond cutters of Antwerp and Amsterdam fled to America to escape Nazism. Hasidic Jews with black hats, beards and long earlocks are still an integral part of the scene. Although mainly a wholesale district, individual customers are welcome. Bring cash, compare prices, haggle, and stay away if you know nothing about the value of diamonds. In the midst of all this, look for the sign saying "Wise men fish here" – here is the Gotham Book Mart, a tiny, much-loved treasure house of literary gems *(see p322)*.

Diamond Row's main commodity

Lyceum Theater ❸

149 W 45th St. **Map** 12 E5. **C** Telecharge 239-6200. **M** 42nd St–5th Ave. See **Entertainment** p330.

THE OLDEST New York theater still active is a Baroque-style bandbox as frilly as a wedding cake. This 1903 triumph was the first theater by Herts and Tallant, later renowned for their extravagant style. The Lyceum made history with a record run of 1,600 performances of the comedy *Born Yesterday*. It was the first theater to be designated a historic landmark but, though it is safe from change, it is often dark now that the Theater District has shifted westward.

The Rose Room in the Algonquin Hotel

Algonquin Hotel ❹

59 W 44th St. **Map** 12 F5. 🅲 840-6800. Ⓜ *42nd St -5th Ave.* See **Where to Stay** *p278.*

Tʜᴇ ᴇxᴛᴇʀɪᴏʀ is a bit fussy – iron bay windows in vertical rows, red brick, too much detail – but it is the ambience, not the 1902 architecture, that makes the Algonquin special. In the 1920s, the Rose Room was home to America's best-known luncheon club, the Round Table, with literary lights such as Alexander Woollcott, Franklin P. Adams, Dorothy Parker, Robert Benchley and Harold Ross. All were associated with the *New Yorker* (Ross was the founding editor), whose 25 West 43rd Street headquarters had a back door opening into the hotel.

A recent renovation has preserved the old-fashioned, civilized feel of the Rose Room, as well as the cozy, paneled lobby where publishing types and theater-goers still like to gather for drinks, settling into comfortable armchairs and ringing a small brass bell to summon the waiters.

Statue of poet William Cullen Bryant in Bryant Park

New York Yacht Club ❺

37 W 44th St. **Map** 12 F5. Ⓜ *42nd St–5th Ave.* **Not open** to the public (access to members only).

A ᴡʜɪᴍsɪᴄᴀʟ 1899 creation, this private club has the carved sterns of 18th-century sailing ships in the three bay windows. The prows of the ships are borne up by sculpted dolphins and waves spilling over the windowsills and splashing down to the pavement.

This is the birthplace of the America's Cup yacht race, which was based in the US from 1857 to 1983. That was the year the much coveted prize was taken from the table where it had stood for more than a century, when the *Australia II* sailed to a historic victory.

The America's Cup, the coveted yachting prize

Bryant Park ❻

Map 8 F1. Ⓜ *42nd St–5th Ave.*

Iɴ 1853, ᴡɪᴛʜ the New York Public Library site still occupied by Croton Reservoir, Bryant Park (then Reservoir Park) housed a dazzling Crystal Palace, built for the World's Fair of that year *(see p23).*

In the 1960s the park was a hangout for drug dealers and other undesirables. In 1989 the city closed and renovated it, reclaiming it for workers and visitors to relax in. Food is available at lunch-time, and a Music & Dance Tickets Booth *(see p329)* offers half-price seats for same-day performances. Over seven million books lie in storage stacks beneath the park.

American Standard Building ❼

40 W 40th St. **Map** 8 F1. Ⓜ *42nd St-Grand Central.* **Not open** to the public.

Tʜɪs ᴡᴀs the first major New York work by Raymond Hood, who went on to design the News Building *(see p153)* and Rockefeller Center. The structure, from 1924, is reminiscent of the Gothic building Hood was best known for at that time, Chicago's Tribune Tower. Here, the design is sleeker, giving the building the illusion of being taller than its actual 21 stories. The black brick facade is set off by gold terra-cotta trim, evoking images of flaming coals: a comparison that would have suited its original owners well, since they made heating equipment. Stand across the street in Bryant Park to appreciate the striking golden tower top. In 1989, the building was sold to a Japanese company. After another change in ownership, the building is finally being converted into a luxury hotel.

The American Standard Building seen from Bryant Park

The New York Public Library **8**

5th Ave and 42nd St. **Map** 8 F1.
📞 869-8089. Ⓜ 42nd St–Grand
Central. **Open** Mon–Sat; hours vary.
Closed public hols. 📷 ♿ 🎫
Lectures, workshops, readings. 🛗

**The doorway leading to the Main
Reading Room**

IN 1897 THE COVETED JOB of
designing New York's main
public library was awarded to
architects Carrère & Hastings.
Their plan was influenced by
the library's first director. He
envisaged a light, quiet, airy
place for study, where millions
of books could be stored and
yet be available to readers as
promptly as possible. In the
hands of Carrère & Hastings,
his vision came true, in what
is considered the epitome of
New York's Beaux Arts period.

Built on the site of the
former Croton Reservoir (see
p22), it opened in 1911 to
immediate
acclaim,
despite
having
cost the
city $9
million.

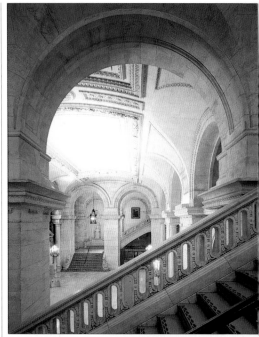

**Barrel vaults of carved
white marble over the
stairs in the Astor Hall**

The vast, paneled Main
Reading Room stretches
two full blocks and is
suffused with daylight
from the two interior
courtyards. Below it
are 88 miles (140 km)
of shelves, holding over
seven million volumes.
A staff of over 100 and
a computerized dumb-
waiter can supply any
book within 10 minutes.

The Periodicals Room
holds 10,000 current
periodicals from 128
countries. On its walls
are murals by Richard
Haas, honoring New York's
great publishing houses. The
original library combined the
collections of John
Jacob Astor and James
Lenox. Its collections
today range from
Thomas Jefferson's
handwritten copy of
the Declaration of
Independence to
T.S. Eliot's typed
copy of "The
Waste Land." More
than 1,000 queries

**One of the library's two stone lions, named
Patience and Fortitude by Mayor LaGuardia**

**The Main Reading Room, with its
original bronze reading lamps**

are answered daily, using the
vast database of the CATNYP
computer catalog.

This library is the hub of a
network of 82 branches, with
nearly seven million users.
Some branches are very well
known, such as the New York
Public Library for the Performing Arts at the Lincoln Center
(see p210) and the Schomburg
Center in Harlem (see p227).

Times Square, ablaze with neon

Times Square **❾**

Map 8 E1. **Ⓜ** *42nd St-Times Sq.*

KNOWN AS Longacre Square in the late 19th century, this was the home of horse traders, blacksmiths and stables, marking the edge of "Thieves' Lair," a haven for pickpockets. Oscar Hammerstein built the Victoria and Republic theaters in 1899; and the Republic later became Minsky's, featuring the stylishly scandal-ous Gypsy Rose Lee. Broadway blossomed, and Times Square became the heart of the Theater District.

The Depression ruined many theaters, and Broadway's "guys and dolls" were replaced by much sleazier types. The 1980s saw a huge civic plan to transform the square into a safe and vibrant place for theatergoers and tourists.

Times Square was named in 1904, after the 25-story *New York Times* tower. The *Times* moved in on New Year's Eve with a fireworks display, and the celebration has continued every year, with a countdown to midnight, when a lighted ball is lowered to mark the new year. Thousands jam the square to watch and millions more follow the events on television across the country.

In 1928, the *Times* posted election returns on the world's first moving sign, a band of 14,800 lights running around the building. The newspaper has moved on, but the ever-busy newswire remains.

New Amsterdam Theater **❿**

214 W 42nd St. Map 8 E1. **⧉** *282-2907* **Ⓜ** *42nd St-Times Sq.* **⧉** *10am-5pm Mon, 10am-12pm Tues.*

W.C. Fields (far left) and Eddie Cantor (holding top hat, right) in the 1918 *Ziegfeld Follies* at the New Amsterdam Theater

THIS WAS the most opulent theater in the United States when it opened in 1903, and the first to have an Art Nouveau interior. It was owned for a time by Florenz Ziegfeld, who produced his famous *Follies* revue here between 1914 and 1918 – with Broadway's first $5 ticket price. He remodeled the roof garden into another theater, the Aerial Gardens. This is one of the fine early theaters on 42nd Street that fell on hard times. With the rehabilitation of Times Square its fortunes rose again, and it is once more in Show Business.

The Art Deco top of the Paramount Building

Group Health Insurance Building **⓫**

330 W 42nd St. Map 8 D1. **Ⓜ** *42nd St.* **Open** office hours.

THIS 1931 design by Raymond Hood was the only New York building selected for the influential International Style survey of 1932 *(see p41)*. Its unusual design gives it a stepped profile seen from east and west, but a slab effect viewed from north or south. The exterior's horizontal bands of blue-green terra-cotta have earned it the nickname "jolly green giant." Step inside to see the classic Art Deco lobby of opaque glass and stainless steel.

One block west is Theater Row, a pleasant group of Off-Broadway theaters and cafés.

Paramount Building **⓬**

1501 Broadway. Map 8 E1. **Ⓜ** *34th St.*

THE FABULOUS ground-floor movie theater where bobby-soxers stood in line in the 1940s to hear Frank Sinatra perform is gone, but there's still a theatrical feel to the massive building designed by Rapp & Rapp in 1927. On each side are symmetrical setbacks, 14 in all, rising like building blocks to an Art Deco crown – a tower, clock and globe. In the heyday of the "Great White Way," the tower was lit, with an observation deck at the top.

Shubert Alley ®

Between W 44th and W 45th St.
Map 12 E5. Ⓜ *42nd St-Times Sq.*

THE PLAYHOUSES on the streets west of Broadway are rich in theater lore – and in notable architecture. Two classic theaters built in 1913 are the Booth (22 West 45th Street), named after actor Edwin Booth, and the Shubert (221 West 44th), after theater baron Sam S. Shubert. They form the west wall of Shubert Alley, where aspiring actors lined up, hoping for a casting in a Shubert play.

A Chorus Line ran at the Shubert until 1990, for a record 6,137 performances; Katharine Hepburn starred earlier in *The Philadelphia Story*. Across from the 44th Street end of the alley is the St. James, where Rodgers and Hammerstein made their debut with *Oklahoma!* in 1941, followed by *The King and I*. Nearby is Sardi's, the restaurant where actors waited for opening night reviews. Irving Berlin staged *The Music Box Revue* opposite the other end of the alley in 1921. His Music Box Theater has since housed many famous shows.

The tiled Moorish facade of the City Center of Music and Drama

MONY Tower ®

1740 Broadway. **Map** 12 E4.
Ⓜ *57th St.* **Not open** to the public.

BUILT IN 1950, the head office of the Mutual of New York insurance company (now MONY Financial Services) has a weather vane that tells you everything except the wind direction. The mast turns green for fair, orange for cloudy, flashing orange for rain and white for snow. Lights moving up the mast mean warmer weather; lights going down mean get out your overcoat!

City Center of Music and Dance ®

131 W 55th St. **Map** 12 E4.
Ⓒ *581-1212.* Ⓜ *57th St.* Ⓧ Ⓖ
See **Entertainment** p334.

THIS HIGHLY ornate Moorish structure with its dome of Spanish tiles was designed in 1924 as a Masonic Shriners' Temple. It was saved from the developers by Mayor La Guardia, becoming home to the New York City Opera and Ballet in 1943. When the troupes moved to Lincoln Center, City Center lived on as a major venue for dance. Renovation work has preserved the delightful excesses of the architecture.

Carnegie Hall ®

154 W 57th Street. **Map** 12 E3.
Ⓒ *903-9765.* Ⓜ *57th St, 59th St.*
Museum open *11am–4:30pm Mon, Tue, Thu, Fri & after concerts.* Ⓧ Ⓖ
Ⓒ Ⓒ See **Entertainment** p338.

FINANCED BY millionaire philanthropist Andrew Carnegie, New York's first great concert hall opened in 1891 in what was then a suburb of the city. The terra-cotta and brick Italian Renaissance–style building is said to have among the best acoustics in the world. On opening night, when Tchaikovsky was a guest conductor, all of New York's finest families were in

Auditorium of the Shubert Theater, built by Henry Herts in 1913

attendance; they waited on line for up to an hour before they could alight from their horse-drawn carriages.

For many years Carnegie Hall was home to the New York Philharmonic, under such conductors as Arturo Toscanini, Leopold Stokowski, Bruno Walter and Leonard Bernstein. Playing Carnegie Hall quickly became an international symbol of success for both classical and popular musicians.

A campaign led by violinist Isaac Stern in the late 1950s saved the building from redevelopment as offices, and in 1964 the hall was made a national landmark. Interior renovation in 1986 brought the bronze balconies and the ornamental plaster back to their original splendor. The corridors are lined with memorabilia of artists who have performed here. In 1991, a museum opened adjacent to the first-tier level, telling the story of the illustrious first 100 years of "The House that Music Built."

Millionaire Andrew Carnegie

Today, top orchestras and performers from around the world still fill Carnegie Hall with their wonderful music. A tour of the hall is also available to visitors.

Russian Tea Room ⑰

150 W 57th St. **Map** 12 E3.
Ⓒ 265-0947. Ⓜ *57th St.*
Call for details of opening times.
See Restaurants and Bars p303.

THIS RESTAURANT is a New York classic, and its location next to Carnegie Hall couldn't be better. The place is scheduled to reopen for the millennium, but owner Walter LeRoy has kept the renovated decor, the menu, and the name of a famous new chef in strictest secrecy. However, it is

The former splendorous interior of the Russian Tea Room

bound to be innovative and wonderful – and pricey, too.

Alwyn Court Apartments ⑱

180 W 58th St. **Map** 12 E3. Ⓜ *57th St.* **Not open** to the public.

YOU CAN'T miss it – not with the fanciful crowns, dragons and other French Renaissance-style terra-cotta carvings covering the exterior of this 1909 Harde and Short apartment building. The ground floor has been altered and lost its cornice in the process, but the rest of the building is intact, an intricate stone tapestry, and one of a kind in the city.

The facade follows the style of François I, whose reign saw the building of some of the finest Loire Valley châteaux, and whose symbol, a crowned salamander, can be seen above the entrance to the building at 58th Street.

Residents and their guests are fortunate to be able to enjoy the visual delights of

Salamander on Alwyn Court

the interior courtyard, which features a dazzling display of the illusionistic skills of artist Richard Haas, in which plain walls are transformed into "carved" stonework.

Flight deck of the *Intrepid*

Intrepid Sea-Air-Space Museum ⑲

Pier 86, W 46th St. **Map** 11 A5. Ⓕ 245-0072. Ⓜ *M42, M16, M27.* **Open** *Apr–Sep: 10am–5pm daily; 10am–6pm Sat-Sun; Oct–Mar:10am–5pm Wed-Sun* **Adm charge.** Ⓓ

ON THE *Intrepid*, a World War II US aircraft carrier, the hangar deck and the flight deck are open for exploration. Exhibits range from real fighter planes from the 1940s to space-age wonders like the A12, fastest spy plane in the world. The *Growler*, a guided-missile submarine, and the destroyer *Edson* are also open.

Pioneers Hall traces the development of flying and the workings of today's super-carriers; Technologies Hall looks at ocean exploration and the rockets of the future.

LOWER MIDTOWN

FROM BEAUX ARTS to Art Deco, this section of midtown boasts some fine architecture. Quiet, residential Murray Hill was named for a country estate that once occupied the site. By the turn of the century, it was home to many of New York's first families, including the financier J.P. Morgan, whose library,

Brass door, Fred F. French Building

now a museum, reveals the grandeur of the age. The commercial pace quickens at 42nd Street, near Grand Central Terminal, where tall office buildings line the streets. However, few of the newer buildings have equaled the Beaux Arts Terminal itself or such Art Deco beauties as the Chrysler Building.

SIGHTS AT A GLANCE

Historic Streets and Buildings
Grand Central Terminal pp154–5 ❷
Home Savings of America ❸
Chanin Building ❹
Chrysler Building ❺
News Building ❻
Tudor City ❼
Helmsley Building ❽
Fred F. French Building ⓬
Sniffen Court ⓯

Museums and Galleries
Pierpont Morgan Library pp162–3 ⓮
Japan Society ⓫

Modern Architecture
MetLife Building ❶
Nos. 1 and 2 United Nations Plaza ❾
United Nations pp158–61 ❿

Churches
Church of the Incarnation ⓭

GETTING THERE
By subway, take the Lexington Avenue 4, 5 or 6 trains to 42nd Street–Grand Central. Buses M15, M101/102, M1, M2, M3 and M4 run along the area's avenues, while the M34 and M42 are the crosstown buses.

Flower box in Sniffen Court

SEE ALSO

• *Street Finder*, maps 9, 12, 13

• *Where to Stay* pp274–5

• *Restaurants* pp290–92

KEY

▢ Street-by-Street map

Ⓜ Subway station

```
0 meters          500
0 yards           500
```

The stainless-steel–coated spire of the Chrysler Building

Street by Street: Lower Midtown

A WALK IN THE neighborhood allows you to see an eclectic mix of New York's architectural styles. Step back to appreciate the contours of the tallest skyscrapers, and step inside to experience the many fine interiors, from modern atriums such as those in the Philip Morris Building and Ford Foundation buildings to the ornate details of the Home Savings Bank and the soaring spaces of Grand Central Terminal.

MetLife Building
This skyscraper, built by Pan Am in 1963, towers above Park Avenue. **1**

★ **Grand Central Terminal**
The vast, vaulted interior is a splendid reminder of the heyday of train travel **2**

Grand Central-42nd St. subway (lines S, 4, 5, 6, 7)

The Philip Morris Building is the headquarters of a tobacco company. It houses a branch of the Whitney Museum, which specializes in modern American art.

Chanin Building
Built for self-made real estate mogul Irwin Chanin in 1922, this building has a fine Art Deco lobby **4**

PARK AVENUE

E 41ST ST

LEXINGTON AV

STAR SIGHTS

★ **Grand Central Terminal**

★ **Chrysler Building**

★ **Home Savings of America**

★ **Daily News Building**

The Mobil Building has a self-cleaning stainless steel facade that is embossed in geometric patterns to prevent it from warping. It was built in 1955.

Brass door, Home Savings Bank

★ **Home Savings of America**
Formerly the headquarters of the Bowery Savings Bank, this is one of the finest bank buildings in New York. Architects York & Sawyer designed it to resemble a Romanesque palace **3**

Helmsley Building

Its ornate entrance symbolized the wealth of the New York Central Railroad, the first occupants. It straddles Park Avenue near Grand Central **8**

Mailbox in the Chrysler Building

LOCATOR MAP
See Manhattan Map pp12–13

KEY

– – – Suggested route

0 meters   100
0 yards   100

★ Chrysler Building

Ornamented with automotive motifs, this Art Deco delight was built in 1930 for the Chrysler car company **5**

Worker resting during construction of the Chrysler Building

The Ford Foundation Building
is the headquarters of Ford's philanthropic arm. It has a lovely interior garden surrounded by a cube-shaped building made of pinkish gray granite, glass and steel.

Ralph J. Bunche Park

E 43RD STREET

42 ND STREET

AVENUE

SECOND AVENUE

FIRST AVENUE

Daily News ★ Building

The Art Deco home of the newspaper has a revolving globe in the lobby **6**

Tudor City
This 1928 private residential complex has 3,000 apartments. Built in the Tudor style, it features fine stonework details **7**

MetLife Building ❶

200 Park Ave. **Map** 13 A5.
M *42nd St-Grand Central.*
Open *office hours.* 🍸 🍴

Lobby of the MetLife Building

ONCE, THE SCULPTURES atop the Grand Central Terminal stood out against the sky. Then this colossus, formerly called the Pan Am Building and designed by Walter Gropius, Emery Roth and Sons and Pietro Belluschi, rose up in 1963 to block the Park Avenue view. It dwarfed the terminal and aroused universal dislike. At the time it was the largest commercial building in the world, and the dismay over its scale helped thwart a later plan to build a tower over the terminal itself.

It is ironic that the New York skies were blocked by Pan Am, a company that had opened up the skies as a means of travel for millions of people. When the company began in 1927, Charles Lindbergh, fresh from his solo trans-atlantic flight, was one of their pilots and an adviser on new routes. By 1936, Pan Am managed to introduce the first trans-Pacific passenger route, and in 1947 they introduced the first round-the-world route.

The building's famous roof-top heliport was abandoned in 1977 after a freak accident showered debris on to the surrounding streets. Now Pan Am itself has gone, too, and in 1981 the entire building was sold to the Metropolitan Life organization.

Grand Central Terminal ❷

See pp154–5.

Home Savings of America ❸

110 E 42nd St. **Map** 9 A1.
M *42nd St-Grand Central.* **Open** *banking hours.*

MANY CONSIDER this 1923 building the best work of the best bank architects of the 1920s. York & Sawyer chose the style of a Romanesque basilica for the uptown offices of the venerable Bowery Savings Bank (now Home Savings of America). An arched entry leads into the vast banking room, with a high beamed ceiling, marble mosaic floors and marble columns that support the stone arches that soar overhead.

Facade of Home Savings of America building

Between the columns are unpolished mosaic panels of marble from France and Italy. The rich detailing includes symbolic animal motifs, such as a squirrel representing thrift and a lion for power.

Chanin Building ❹

122 E 42nd St. **Map** 9 A1.
M *42nd St-Grand Central.*
Open *office hours.*

Stonework detail on the Chanin Building

ONCE THE headquarters of Irwin S. Chanin, one of New York's leading real estate developers, the 56-story tower was the first skyscraper in the Grand Central area, a harbinger of things to come. It was designed by Sloan & Robertson in 1929 and is one of the best examples of the Art Deco period. A wide bronze band, patterned with birds and fish, runs the full length of the facade; the terra-cotta base is decorated with a luxuriant tangle of stylized leaves and flowers. Inside, Radio City's sculptor René Chambellan worked on the reliefs and the bronze grills, elevator doors, mailboxes, clocks and pattern of waves in the floor. The vestibule reliefs chart the career of Chanin, who was a self-made man.

Carved detail in the banking hall of Home Savings of America

Chrysler Building ❺

405 Lexington Ave. **Map** 9 A1.
[682-3070. **M** *42nd St-Grand Central.* **Open** *office hours, lobby only.*

Entrance to the News Building

WALTER P. CHRYSLER began his career in a Union Pacific Railroad machine shop, but his passion for the motor car helped him rise swiftly to the top of the new industry, to found, in 1925, the corporation bearing his name. His wish for a headquarters in New York that symbolized his company led to a building that will always be linked with the golden age of motoring. Following Chrysler's wishes, the stainless-steel Art Deco spire resembles a car radiator grill; the building's series of stepped setbacks are emblazoned with winged radiator caps, wheels and stylized automobiles; and there are gargoyles modeled on hood ornaments from the 1929 Chrysler Plymouth.

Though it lost the title of tallest building in the world to the Empire State Building only a few months after its completion in 1930, William Van Alen's 77-story Chrysler Building and its shining crown are still among the city's best-known and most-loved landmarks.

The crowning spire was kept a secret until the last moment, when, having been built in the fire shaft, it was raised into position through the roof, ensuring that the building would be higher than the Bank of Manhattan, then just completed downtown by Van Alen's great rival, H. Craig Severance.

Van Alen was poorly rewarded for his labors. Chrysler accused him of accepting bribes from contractors and refused to pay him. Van Alen's career never recovered from the slur.

The stunning lobby, once used as a showroom for Chrysler cars, was perfectly restored in 1978. It is lavishly decorated with patterned marbles and granite from around the world and has chromed steel trim. A vast painted ceiling by Edward

Elevator door at the Chrysler Building

Trumball shows transportation scenes of the late 1920s.

Although the Chrysler Corporation never occupied the building as their headquarters, their name remains, as firm a fixture as the gargoyles.

Stainless steel gargoyle on the Chrysler Building

News Building ❻

220 E 42nd St. **Map** 9 B1.
M *42nd St-Grand Central.* **Open** *8am–6pm Mon–Fri.*

THE *DAILY NEWS* was founded in 1919, and by 1925 it was a million-seller. It was known, rather scathingly, as "the servant girl's bible," for its concentration on scandals, celebrities and murders, its readable style and its heavy use of illustration. Over the years it has stuck to what it does best, and for years the formula paid off handsomely. It revealed stories such as the romance of Edward VIII and Mrs. Simpson, and has become renowned for its punchy headlines that sum up the mood of the moment. Though in recent years it has lost money, its circulation figures are still among the highest in the United States.

Its headquarters, designed by Raymond Hood in 1930, has rows of brown and black brick alternating with windows to create a vertical striped effect. Hood's lobby is familiar to many as that of the *Daily Planet* in the 1980s *Superman* movies. It includes the world's largest interior globe, an illuminated, rotating geography lesson with details constantly updated. Bronze lines on the floor indicate the direction of world cities and the position of the planets. At night, the intricate Deco detail over the front entrance of the building is lit from within by neon.

Grand Central Terminal ❷

IN 1871 CORNELIUS VANDERBILT opened a railway station on 42nd Street. Although often revamped, it was never large enough and was finally demolished. The present station opened in 1913. This Beaux Arts gem has been a gateway to and symbol of the city ever since. Its glory is the soaring main concourse and the way it separates pedestrian and train traffic. The building has a steel frame covered with plaster and marbles. Reed & Stern were in charge of the logistical planning; Warren & Wetmore for the overall design. The restoration by architects Beyer Blinder Belle is awesome.

42nd Street colonnaded facade

Statuary on the 42nd Street Facade
Jules-Alexis Coutans sculptures of Mercury, Hercules and Minerva crown the main entrance.

Main Concourse Level

Circumferential Road

Cornelius Vanderbilt
The railroad magnate was known as the "Commodore."

Subway

Commuters use the terminal. Half a million people pass through it each day. An escalator leads up into the MetLife Building, and specialty shops and new restaurants have now opened.

Grand Central Oyster Bar
This popular spot (see p294), with its yellow Guastavino tiles, is just one of the many eateries now open in the station. As well as the individual restaurants, there is also a "food court" to suite all tastes.

STAR SIGHTS

★ **Grand Staircases**

★ **Main Concourse**

★ **Central Information**

★ **Main Concourse**
This vast pedestrian area
with its high vaulted ceiling
is dominated by three great
arched windows, 75 ft
(23 m) high on
each side.

Vaulted Ceiling
A medieval manu-
script provided the
basis for French artist
Paul Helleu's zodiac
design containing
over 2,500 stars.
Lights pinpoint the
major constellations.

The Lower Level
is linked to the other
levels by stairways,
ramps and brand
new escalators.

Grand Staircase ★
There are now two of
these double flights
of marble steps, styled
after the staircase in
Paris' Opera House,
and a vivid reminder
of the glamorous days
of early rail travel.

★ **Central Information**
This four-faced clock tops the
travel information booth on
the main concourse.

Tudor City ❼

E. 42nd St. **Map** 9 B1.
Ⓜ *42nd St.-Grand Central.*

THIS EARLY URBAN renewal effort, developed between 1925 and 1928 by the Fred F. French Company, was designed as a middle-class city within the city. Rents were modest, thanks to the "large-scale production." There are 12 buildings containing 3,000 apartments, a hotel, shops, restaurants, a post office and two small private parks, all built in the Tudor Gothic style.

Now a tranquil corner of the modern city, in the mid-19th century the area was the haunt of criminals and was known as Corcoran's Roost, after Paddy Corcoran, the leader of the notorious "Rag Gang." The East River shore was lined with glue factories, slaughterhouses, breweries and a gasworks. Some were still there when Tudor City was planned, so its buildings have few outward-facing windows from which residents might enjoy what is now a great view of the river.

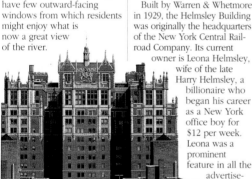

Upper stories of Tudor City

Helmsley Building ❽

230 Park Ave. **Map** 13 A5.
Ⓜ *42nd St-Grand Central.* **Open** office hours.

ONE OF THE GREAT New York views looks south down Park Avenue to the Helmsley Building straddling the busy traffic flow beneath. There is just one flaw – the monolithic MetLife Building (which was built by Pan Am as its corporate headquarters

Performance at the Japan Society

in 1963) that towers behind it, replacing the building's former backdrop, the sky.

Built by Warren & Whetmore in 1929, the Helmsley Building was originally the headquarters of the New York Central Railroad Company. Its current owner is Leona Helmsley, wife of the late Harry Helmsley, a billionaire who began his career as a New York office boy for $12 per week. Leona was a prominent feature in all the advertisements for their hotel chain – until her imprisonment in 1989 for tax evasion on a grand scale. Many observers believe that the extravagant glitter of the building's face-lift is due to Leona's over-blown taste in decor.

1 & 2 United Nations Plaza ❾

Map 13 B5. Ⓜ *42nd St.-Grand Central.*

THESE TWO GREAT columns of lovely blue-green mirrored glass are set at an angle to each other; the play of light and reflections on their gleaming sides and sloping setbacks make them seem an ever-changing, giant work of modern art. The marble and mirrored interiors are also stunning. They house streamlined modern offices and, in No. 1, the Regal United Nations Plaza Hotel *(see p280)*. Here, the guest list frequently includes many UN delegates from all over the world as well as a number of visiting heads of state. Even the stresses of international diplomacy must ease when one is floating lazily in the glassed-in swimming pool, enjoying the bird's-eye views of the city and the United Nations itself.

United Nations ❿

See pp158–61.

Japan Society ⓫

333 E 47th St. **Map** 13 B5.
☎ *832-1155.* Ⓜ *42nd St.-Grand Central.* **Gallery open** 11am–6pm Tue–Sun. Ⓝ Ⓖ Ⓕ

THE HEADQUARTERS of the Japan Society, which was founded in 1907 to foster understanding and cultural exchange between Japan and the United States, was underwritten by John D. Rockefeller III at a cost

Roman gods reclining against the Helmsley Building clock

of some $4.3 million. The striking black building with its delicate sun grilles was designed by Tokyo architects Junzo Yoshimura and George Shimamoto in 1971. It includes an auditorium, a language center, a research library, a museum gallery and serene, traditional Oriental gardens.

Changing exhibits open to the public include a variety of Japanese arts, from swords to kimonos to scrolls. The society offers programs of Japanese performing arts, lectures, language classes and many business workshops for American and Japanese executives and managers.

Fred F. French Building ⑫

521 5th Ave. **Map** 12 F5.
Ⓜ *42nd St.-Grand Central.* **Open** *office hours.*

Bᴜɪʟᴛ ɪɴ 1927 to house the best-known real estate firm of the day, this is a fabulously opulent creation. It was designed by French's chief architect, H. Douglas Ives, in collaboration with Sloan & Robertson, whose

Tiffany stained-glass window in the Church of the Incarnation

other work included the Chanin Building *(see p152).* They handsomely blended Near Eastern, ancient Egyptian and Greek styles with early Art Deco forms.

Multicolored faïence ornaments decorate the upper facade, and the water tower is hidden in a false top level of the building. Its disguise is an elaborate one, with reliefs showing a rising sun flanked by griffins and bees and symbols of virtues such as integrity and industry. Winged Assyrian beasts ride on a bronze frieze over the entrance. These exotic themes continue into the vaulted lobby, with its elaborate polychrome ceiling decoration and 25 gilt-bronze doors.

This was the first building project to employ members of the Native Canadian Caughnawaga tribe as construction workers. They did not fear heights and soon became highly sought-after scaffolders for many of the city's most famous skyscrapers.

Church of the Incarnation ⑬

205 Madison Ave. **Map** 9 A2.
📞 *689-6350.* Ⓜ *42nd St.-Grand Central.* **Open** *11:30am–2pm Mon–Wed, Fri.* 🕙 *8am–1pm Sun.* 📷 ♿ *By appointment.* ▨

Tʜɪs ᴇᴘɪsᴄᴏᴘᴀʟ church and its parish house date from 1864, when Madison Avenue was home to the elite. Its patterned sandstone and brownstone exterior is representative of the period.

The interior includes an oak communion rail by Daniel Chester French; a chancel mural, *Adoration of the Magi,* by John La Farge; and stained-glass windows by La Farge, Louis Comfort Tiffany, William Morris and Edward Burne-Jones.

Pierpont Morgan Library ⑭

See pp162–3.

Sniffen Court ⑮

150–158 E 36th St. **Map** 9 A2.
Ⓜ *33rd St.*

Hᴇʀᴇ ɪs a delightful, intimate courtyard of ten brick Romanesque revival carriage houses, built by John Sniffen in the 1850s.

They are perfectly and improbably preserved off a busy block in modern New York. The house at the south end was used as a studio by the American sculptor Malvina Hoffman, whose plaques of Greek horsemen decorate the exterior wall.

Malvina Hoffman's studio

Lobby of the Fred F. French Building

United Nations ⑩

F OUNDED IN 1945 near the end of World War II with 51 members, the United Nations now numbers some 185 nations. Its aims are to preserve world peace, promote self-determination and to aid economic and social well-being around the globe. New York was chosen as the UN headquarters, and John D. Rockefeller, Jr. donated $8.5 million for the purchase of the East River site. The chief architect was American Wallace Harrison, who worked with an international Board of Design Consultants. The 18-acre (7-ha) site is not on US territory. It is an international zone and has its own stamps and post office. Daily guided tours show visitors the various council chambers and General Assembly hall.

Flag of the United Nations

United Nations headquarters

Secretariat building

The Conference Building houses meeting rooms for the Security Council, the Trusteeship Council and the Economic and Social Council.

Trusteeship Council

★ **Security Council**
Delegates and their assistants confer around the horseshoe-shaped table while verbatim reporters and other UN staff members sit at the long table in the center.

Economic and Social Council

STAR FEATURES

★ **General Assembly**

★ **Security Council**

★ **Peace Bell**

★ **Reclining Figure**

★ **Peace Bell**
Cast from the coins of 60 nations, this gift from Japan hangs on a cypress pagoda shaped like a Shinto shrine.

Rose Garden
Twenty-five varieties of roses adorn the manicured gardens on the East River.

★ **Reclining Figure** *(1982)*
This bronze statue was a gift from the Henry Moore Foundation.

General ★
Assembly
*This is the only UN
organ in which all
member states are
represented. One
regular, three-
month session is
held each year.*

Colors of the World
*Flags of member
nations fly in front
of the UN complex.*

Non-Violence *(1988)*
*Luxembourg donated this peace
sculpture by Swedish artist Karl
Fredrik Reutersward.*

**The statue
of peace** was
a gift from
Yugoslavia.

**Visitors'
entrance**

Let Us Beat Swords Into Plowshares
*This bronze statue (1958) by Soviet
sculptor Evgeny Vuchetich symbolizes
the main goal of the United Nations.*

The Work of the United Nations

THE GOALS of the United Nations are pursued by three UN councils and a General Assembly comprising all member nations. The Secretariat carries out the administrative work of the organization. Guided tours allow visitors to see the Security Council Chamber and General Assembly Hall.

Secretary General

Translators interpret debates in Arabic, Chinese, French, Russian, Spanish or English.

Reporters

Nation delegates sit in alphabetical order by country, but who sits at the front is decided before every session by drawing lots.

Public gallery

Public entrance

GENERAL ASSEMBLY HALL

GENERAL ASSEMBLY

THE GENERAL ASSEMBLY is the governing body of the UN and has regular sessions each year from mid-September to mid-December. Special sessions are also held when the Security Council or a majority of members request one. All member states are represented with an equal vote, regardless of size. The General Assembly may discuss any international problem raised by the members or by other UN bodies. Although it cannot enact laws, recommendations strongly influence world opinion; these require a two-thirds majority vote.

Lots are drawn before each session to determine the seating in the chamber for the delegations. All 1,898 seats in the chamber are equipped with earphones that offer simultaneous translations in

several languages. The General Assembly also appoints the Secretary General (on the recommendation of the Security Council), approves the UN budgets and elects the non-permanent members of

Foucault's Pendulum **(Holland); its slowly rotating swing is proof of the earth's rotation on its axis**

the Councils. Together with the Security Council, it also appoints the judges of the International Court of Justice, based in the Netherlands.

SECURITY COUNCIL

THE MOST POWERFUL part of the UN is the Security Council. It strives to achieve

Mural symbolizing peace and freedom by Per Krohg (Norway)

international peace and security and intervenes in crises such as the fighting in Kuwait, the former Yugo-slavia and Kosovo. It is the only body whose decisions member states are obliged to obey as well as the only one in continuous session.

Five of its members – China, France, the Russian Federation, the United Kingdom and the United States – are permanent. The other nations are elected by the General Assembly to serve two-year terms.

When international conflicts arise, the Council first tries to seek agreement by mediation. If fighting breaks out, it may issue cease-fire orders and impose military or economic sanctions. It could also decide to send UN peace-keeping missions into troubled areas to separate opposing factions until issues can be resolved through diplomatic channels.

Military intervention is the Council's last resort. UN forces may be deployed, and peace-keeping forces are resident in such places as Cyprus and the Middle East.

TRUSTEESHIP COUNCIL

THE SMALLEST OF the councils, this is the only UN body whose workload is decreasing. The council was established in 1945 with the goal of fostering peaceful independence for non–self-governing territories or colonies. Since then, more than 80 colonies have gained self-rule, and the number of people living in dependent territories has been reduced from 750 million to about 3 million. The council currently consists of the five permanent members of the Security Council.

Zanetti mural (Dominican Republic) in the Conference Building depicting the struggle for peace

Trusteeship Council Chamber

ECONOMIC AND SOCIAL COUNCIL

T HE 54 MEMBERS OF this Council work to improve the standard of living and social welfare around the world, goals that consume 80% of the UN's resources. It makes recommendations to the General Assembly, to each member nation and to the UN's specialized agencies. The Council is assisted by commissions dealing with regional economic problems, human rights abuses, population, narcotics and women's rights. It also works with the International Labor Organization, the World Health Organization, UNICEF and other global welfare organizations.

SECRETARIAT

A N INTERNATIONAL STAFF of 16,000 works for the Secretariat to carry out the day-to-day work of the United Nations, providing services to all UN councils, commissions and agencies. The Secretariat is headed by the Secretary General, who

plays a key role as a spokesperson in the organization's peace-keeping efforts. The Secretary General is appointed by the General Assembly for a five-year term.

IMPORTANT EVENTS IN UN HISTORY

Soviet premier Krushchev speaking to the General Assembly in 1960

W ITH NO PERMANENT police force to deal with disputes, the UN depends on voluntary compliance and

military support from members. As a result, it has had successes and failures in its efforts to keep the peace. In 1948, the UN declared South Korea the legitimate government of Korea; two years later, it played a leading role in defending South Korea against the invading North Korean armies. In 1949, the UN helped negotiate a cease-fire between Indonesia and the Netherlands and set up a conference that led to the Dutch granting independence to Indonesia. In 1974, the People's Republic of China – long refused membership in favor of Taiwan – gained UN membership, restoring it to the international community.

The most persistent problems have been in the Middle East. When Israel was invaded by five Arab nations after it was declared a state in 1948, the UN negotiated a cease-fire; UN forces have been present in the area since 1974, but the Palestinians' status is unresolved.

The UN was instrumental in negotiating the independence of Cyprus from Britain in 1957, and in 1964 it created a UN military force in Cyprus to keep peace between the Greeks and Turks.

WORKS OF ART AT THE UN

The UN Building has acquired numerous works of art and reproductions by major artists; many have been gifts from member nations. Most of them have either a peace or international friendship theme. The legend on Norman Rockwell's *The Golden Rule* reads "Do unto others as you would have them do unto you." Marc Chagall designed a large stained-glass window as a memorial to former Secretary General Dag Hammarskjöld, who was accidentally killed while on a peace mission in 1961. A Henry Moore sculpture graces the grounds. There are many other sculptures and paintings by the artists of many nations.

***The Golden Rule* (1985), a large mosaic by Norman Rockwell**

Morgan Library 🏛

THE MORGAN LIBRARY came into being as the private collection of banker Pierpont Morgan. In 1902, architects McKim, Mead & White designed a magnificent palazzo-style building to house it. Morgan's son, J.P. Morgan, Jr., established the library as a public institution in 1924. Today it has one of the world's finest collections of rare manuscripts, prints, books and fine bindings displayed in a complex that includes the original library and J.P. Morgan, Jr.'s home.

Exterior of the original library building

★ **Garden Court**
This three-story skylit garden area links the library with the Morgan house.

Morgan House

KEY TO FLOOR PLAN

☐ Exhibition space

☐ Non-exhibition space

Forecourt Gallery

The Song of Los (1795)
Mystic poet William Blake designed and engraved this plate for one of his most innovative works.

The Nursery Alice
Lewis Carroll's characters are immortalized in John Tenniel's classic illustrations (c. 1865).

Exhibition Room

STAR EXHIBITS

★ **Livre de la Chasse**

★ **Adam and Eve by Albrecht Dürer**

★ **Garden Court**

★ **Manuscript of Mozart's Horn Concerto in E-flat Major**

Gutenberg Bible (1455)
Printed on vellum, this volume is one of only eleven surviving copies.

LIBRARY GUIDE

Mr. Morgan's Study and the original library contain some of his favorite paintings, objets d'art and rare acquisitions. Changing exhibitions provide visitors access to some of the world's significant cultural artifacts.

★ **Mozart's Horn Concerto in E-flat Major**
The six surviving leaves of this score are written in different colored inks.

VISITORS' CHECKLIST

29 E. 36th St. **Map** 9 A2.
 685-0008. 6 to 33rd St.
 M2, M3, M4 **Open**
10:30am–5pm Tues–Thu, –8pm
Fri, –6pm Sat, noon–6pm Sun.
Closed Mondays & holidays. **Adm**
charge.
Concerts, lectures, film/video
presentations.

**West Room
(Mr. Morgan's study)**

Rotunda

East Room
The walls are lined from floor to ceiling with triple tiers of bookcases. Murals show historical figures and their muses, and signs of the zodiac.

★ **Adam and Eve** (1504)
One of Albrecht Dürer's most celebrated works, this drawing reflects his quest for the perfect representation of the human figure.

Main entrance

★**Livre de la Chasse**
This copy of Gaston Phébus's illustrated book on hunting was made in about 1410.

PIERPONT MORGAN

Pierpont Morgan (1837–1913) was not only a leading financier but also one of the great collectors of his time. Rare books and original manuscripts were his passion, and inclusion in his collection was an honor. In 1909, when Morgan requested the donation of the manuscript of *Pudd'nhead Wilson*, Mark Twain responded, "One of my high ambitions is gratified."

UPPER MIDTOWN

1946 Cisitalia in the MoMA

U PMARKET NEW YORK in all its diversity is here, in this area of churches, synagogues, clubs, museums, luxury hotels, famous stores, trend-setting skyscrapers and pockets of luxury living. For almost 30 years from 1833, it was home to society names

such as Astor and Vanderbilt. In the 1950s, architectural history was made when the Lever and Seagram buildings were erected. These first great modern towers marked midtown Park Avenue's change from a residential street to a prestigious office address.

SIGHTS AT A GLANCE

Historic Streets and Buildings
Villard Houses **9**
General Electric Building **11**
Sutton Place and Beekman Place **17**
Roosevelt Island **18**
Fuller Building **20**

Modern Architecture
Trump Tower **2**
IBM Building **3**
Lever House **13**
Seagram Building **14**
Citicorp Center **15**

Museums and Galleries
Museum of Modern Art (MoMA) pp170–73 **5**
American Craft Museum **6**

Museum of Television and Radio **7**

Churches and Synagogues
St. Thomas' Church **4**
St. Patrick's Cathedral pp176–7 **8**
St. Bartholomew's Church **10**
Central Synagogue **16**

Landmark Hotels
Waldorf–Astoria **12**
Plaza Hotel **21**

Landmark Stores
Fifth Avenue **1**
Bloomingdale's **19**

SEE ALSO

- **Street Finder**, maps 12, 13–14
- **Where to Stay** pp274–5
- **Restaurants** pp290–92

KEY

Street-by-Street map

M Subway station

0 meters   500
0 yards   500

GETTING THERE
Take the Lexington Ave 4, 5 or 6 subways to 51st St, or the E or F to 5th Ave. Bus routes are the M15, M101/102 and M1, M2, M3 and M4. Crosstown buses are the M50, M57 and M58.

View down Fifth Avenue

Street by Street: Upper Midtown

THE LUXURY STORES that are synonymous with Fifth Avenue first blossomed as society moved on uptown. In 1917, Cartier's acquired the mansion of banker Morton F. Plant in exchange for a string of pearls, setting the style for other retailers to follow. But this stretch of midtown is not simply for shoppers. There are three distinctive museums and an equally diverse assembly of architectural styles to enjoy, too.

Fifth Avenue
Today's carriage rides offer a taste of past elegance ❶

American Craft Museum
This is a showcase for crafts – from ceramics to furniture ❻

The University Club was built in 1899 as an elite club for gentlemen

St. Thomas' Church
Much of the interior carving was designed by sculptor Lee Lawrie ❹

★ Museum of Modern Art
This is one of the finest collections of modern art in the world ❺

Museum of Television and Radio
Exhibitions, seasons of special screenings, live events and a vast library of historic broadcasts are offered at this media museum ❼

Fifth Avenue subway (lines E, F)

Saks Fifth Avenue has offered goods in impeccable taste to generations of New Yorkers. *(See p311.)*

★St. Patrick's Cathedral
This, the largest Catholic cathedral in the United States, is a magnificent Gothic Revival building ❽

Olympic Tower
combines offices, apartments and a skylit atrium within its sleek walls.

Villard Houses
Five handsome brownstone houses now form part of the New York Palace Hotel ❾

STAR SIGHTS

★ **Museum of Modern Art**

★ **St. Patrick's Cathedral**

Paley Park is a tiny green oasis, known as a "vest-pocket" park.

Trump Tower
Donald Trump's tower houses many expensive shops ❷

IBM Building
A restful atrium is to be found at the base of this polished black granite building ❸

Sony Building has a very distinctive "chippendale" top.

Lever House
This building is one of the most prominent "glass-box" buildings in New York ⓭

Park Avenue Plaza is a bulky glass prism containing an airy atrium.

Racquet Club, a Renaissance palazzo–style building, provides squash and tennis courts for its members.

St. Bartholomew's Church
A Byzantine dome sets this place apart from other midtown churches ❿

51st Street subway (line 6)

LOCATOR MAP
See Manhattan Map pp12–13

KEY
– – – Suggested route

0 meters   100
0 yards   100

Tiffany & Company is renowned for its discreet luxury. The store contains many precious jewels. *(See p321.)*

General Electric Building
The spiky pinnacle of this building, built in 1931, is meant to symbolize electrical waves ⓫

Waldorf-Astoria
Old-world elegance has attracted many famous guests to this hotel, including the late Duke and Duchess of Windsor ⓬

Window display at Bergdorf Goodman *(see p311)*

Fifth Avenue ❶

Map 4 F1–16 E1. Ⓜ *5th Ave-53rd St.*

In 1883, when William Henry Vanderbilt built his mansion at Fifth Avenue and 51st Street, he started a trend that resulted in palatial residences stretching as far as Central Park, built for top families such as the Astors, Belmonts and Goulds. Only a few remain to attest to the grandeur of the era.

One of these is the Cartier store at 651 Fifth Avenue, originally the home of Morton F. Plant, millionaire and commodore of the New York Yacht Club. As retailers swept north up the avenue – a trend that began in 1906 – society gradually moved to better locations uptown. In 1917, Plant moved to a new mansion at 86th Street, and legend has it that he traded his old home to Pierre Cartier for a perfectly matched string of pearls.

Fifth Avenue has been synonymous with luxury goods ever since. From Cartier at 52nd Street to Tiffany and Bergdorf Goodman at 57th, you will find a range of famous brands symbolizing wealth and social standing today, just as Vanderbilt and Astor did more than a century ago.

Trump Tower ❷

725 5th Ave. **Map** 12 F3. 〖 *832-2000.* Ⓜ *5th Ave-53rd St.* **Garden level, shops open** *10am–6pm Mon–Sat, noon–5pm Sun.* **Building open** *10am–7pm daily. See* **History** *p31.* 📷 ♿ **Concerts.** 🍴 🖥 🚻

A GLITTERING, exorbitantly expensive apartment and office tower rises above a lavish six-story atrium with layer upon layer of exclusive shops and cafés. Designed in 1983 by Der Scutt of Swanke, Hayden, Connell & Partners, the public space is lavished with pink marble, a waterfall, mirrors and glitz. It is the most opulent example of the new urban trend toward vertical shopping centers. The tower is a flamboyant monument to affluence by the developer Donald Trump, a symbol of the excesses of the 1980s.

Next door, 727 Fifth is a complete contrast: Tiffany & Co., the prestigious jewelers founded in 1837. Famed for its exquisite window displays, the store uses understated but elegant blue packaging as a status symbol in itself. Tiffany's was immortalized in New York culture by Truman Capote's *Breakfast at Tiffany's.*

Entrance to Tiffany and Co., the exclusive jewelry emporium

IBM Building ❸

590 Madison Ave. **Map** 12 F3. 〖 *745-5994.* Ⓜ *5th Ave.* **Garden Plaza open** *8am–10pm daily.* 📷 ♿

THIS 43-STORY tower was designed by Edward Larrabee Barnes. Completed in 1983, it is a sleek, five sided prism of gray-green polished granite, with a cantilevered corner at 57th Street. The Garden Plaza, a light and spacious public atrium, no longer houses a garden shop or café but it is still open for the public to wander through and admire the surroundings. Near the atrium is a work by American sculptor Michael Heizer, entitled *Levitated Mass.* Inside a low, stainless steel tank, a huge slab of granite seems to float on air while beneath it, a sheet of water flows.

In 1999, the IBM Corporation sold the building, and the future of the much-acclaimed Gallery of Science and Art is now uncertain..

Interior of the Trump Tower atrium

St. Thomas' Church

St. Thomas' Church **4**

1 W 53rd St. **Map** 12 F4.
☎ 757-7013. **M** 5th Ave-53rd St.
Open 7am–6pm daily. **✝** frequent.
♿ ⛪ 🎥 after 11am service

THIS IS THE FOURTH home for this parish and the second on this site. Today's church was built between 1909 and 1914 to replace an earlier structure destroyed in a fire in 1905. The previous building had provided the setting for most of the large, glittering Fifth Avenue high society weddings of the late 19th century. The most lavish of these was the legendary ceremony of 1895 in which heiress Consuela Vanderbilt was married to the English duke of Marlborough.

The limestone building, in French–Gothic style, has a single asymmetrical tower and an off-center nave, novel solutions to the architectural problems posed by the position, on a corner lot. The richly carved, shimmering white screens behind the altar were designed by the architect Bertram Goodhue and the sculptor Lee Lawrie. Carvings in the choir stalls, dating from the 1920s, include modern inventions such as the telephone and radio, as well as Presidents Roosevelt and Wilson, and Lee Lawrie himself.

Museum of Modern Art **5**

See pp170–73.

American Craft Museum **6**

40 W 53rd St. **Map** 12 F4.
☎ 956-3535. **M** 5th Ave-53rd St.
Open 10am–6pm Tue, Wed & Fri–Sun,
10am–8pm Thu. **Adm charge**. **♿ ⛪**
🎥 Lectures, films.

THERE IS NO BETTER place to experience the vitality of the contemporary American crafts movement than this, the showcase home of the American Crafts Council. On display are handmade quilts, ceramics, glass, textiles, wood, silver, furniture, paper and metalwork drawn from the museum's extensive collection of crafts, which date from 1900 to the present day. Founded in a brownstone on this site in 1956, the museum reopened in 1987 in the three-story atrium of an office tower. The reception desk is itself a work of art, designed and hand-carved in maple by James Schneider. The displays are not for sale.

Silver chalice by Ronald Hayes Pearson at the Craft Museum

Museum of Television and Radio **7**

25 W 52nd St. **Map** 12 F4.
☎ 621-6600. **M** 5th Ave-53rd St. **Open** noon–6pm Tue–Sun (8pm Thu). Theaters and screening rooms close 9pm Fri. **Closed** public hols. **Adm charge**. **♿ ⛪ 🎥 📷**

IN THIS one-of-a-kind repository museum, visitors can watch and listen to news and a collection of entertainment and sports documentaries from radio and television's earliest days to the present. Pop fans can see the early Beatles or a young Elvis Presley making his television debut. Sports enthusiasts can relive classic Olympic competitions. World War II footage might be chosen by students of history or by those who lived through the war. Six choices at any one time can be selected from a computer catalogue that covers a library of over 50,000 programs. The selections are then played on small private areas. There are larger screening areas and a theater for 200, where retrospectives of artists, directors and topics are shown. There are also photo exhibits, posters and memorabilia.

The museum was the brainchild of William S. Paley, who was a former head of the CBS television network. It opened in 1975 as the Museum of Broad-casting on East 53rd Street. It proved to be so popular that in 1991 it moved into this hi-tech $50 million home in a building that to many people is reminiscent of an antique radio set.

Beatles Paul, Ringo and John on the "Ed Sullivan Show" in 1964

1960s television star Lucille Ball

Museum of Modern Art ⑤

Museum facade on West 53rd Street

THE MUSEUM of Modern Art contains one of the world's best and most comprehensive collections of modern art. It was founded in 1929 by wealthy patrons and has since set the standard for other museums of its kind, including many disciplines unrecognized by other galleries. The new exhibits marking the millennium will provide a unique overview with fresh interpretations of some of this century's most compelling and powerful art.

Sculpture Garden
The Abby Aldrich Rockefeller Sculpture Garden is a beautiful and restful space.

Christina's World
(1948) Andrew Wyeth contrasts an overwhelming horizon with the minutely-studied surroundings of his handicapped neighbor.

Bird in Space *(c. 1928)*
Constantin Brancusi's elegant bronze sculpture captures the sheer essence of flight.

GALLERY GUIDE

Changing exhibitions are displayed on the first floor. Painting and sculpture are exhibited on the second and third floors. Photography is on the second floor, prints are on the third floor. Architecture and design collections are on the fourth. Films are shown on the lower level.

Main entrance

Sculpture Garden

Cisitalia '202" GT *(1946)*
This example of industrial design demonstrates the museum's eclecticism.

Fourth floor

Third floor

La Clownesse *(1896)*
This is typical of Henri de Toulouse-Lautrec's portraits of Parisian entertainers.

Second floor

Water Lilies *(c. 1920)*
Claude Monet's late triptych creates a glowing, serene environment in its own room on the second floor.

★Les Demoiselles d'Avignon
Pablo Picasso's 1907 expression-istic portrait of five prostitutes included two male customers in its early drafts. These were later left out, enabling Picasso to depict his complex feelings about women more powerfully.

First floor

★The Starry Night *(1889)*
The small size of Vincent Van Gogh's work belies its passion. This turbulent night scene remains one of the most popular paintings in the collection.

KEY TO FLOOR PLAN

☐	Architecture and Design
☐	Drawings
☐	Prints and Illustrated Books
☐	Paintings and Sculpture
☐	Photography
☐	Special exhibitions
☐	Non-exhibition space

Exploring the Collection

T HE MUSEUM OF MODERN ART houses approximately 100,000 works of art – ranging from a collection of Post-Impressionist classics to an unrivaled collection of modern American art, from fine examples of design to early masterpieces of photography and film.

1880s To 1940s
PAINTING AND SCULPTURE

The Persistence of Memory by the Surrealist Salvador Dalí (1931)

P AUL CEZANNE'S monumental *The Bather* and Vincent van Gogh's passionate and transcendent *The Starry Night* are two of the seminal works in the museum's collection of late 19th-century painting. Both Fauvism and Expressionism are well represented with works by Matisse, Derain, Kirchner and others, while Pablo Picasso's *Les Demoiselles d'Avignon* marks a transition to a new style of painting.

The museum also has an unparalleled collection of Cubist paintings, providing an overview of a movement that radically challenged our perception of the world. Among the vast display are Picasso's *Girl with a Mandolin*, Georges Braque's *Man with a Guitar* and *Soda*, and *Guitar and Flowers* by Juan Gris. Works by the Futurists, who brought color and movement to Cubism to depict the dynamic modern world, include Gino Severini's *Dynamic Hieroglyphic of the Bal Tabarin* and *Dynamism of a Soccer Player* by Umberto Boccioni, plus works by Balla, Carrà and Villon.

The geometric abstract art of the Constructivists is included in a strong display of Malevich, Lissitzky and Rodchenko: De Stijl's influence is seen in paintings by Piet Mondrian, including *Broadway Boogie Woogie*. An entire room is devoted to work by Matisse, such as *Dance I* and *The Red Studio*. Dalí, Miró and Ernst feature among the collection of bizarre, strangely beautiful Surrealist works.

POSTWAR PAINTING AND SCULPTURE

A N EXTENSIVE display of postwar art begins on the third floor, with a series of works by Bacon, Dubuffet and others. The collection of Abstract Expressionist art includes Jackson Pollock's *One [Number 31, 1950]*, Willem de Kooning's *Woman, I*, Arshile Gorky's *Agony* and *Red, Brown, and Black* by Mark Rothko. The following

Dog (1952), an oil painting by British artist Francis Bacon

galleries exhibit works such as Jasper Johns' *Flag* and Robert Rauschenberg's *First Landing Jump*, composed from urban refuse, and *Bed*, composed of bed linen. The Pop Art on show includes Roy Lichtenstein's *Girl with Ball* and *Drowning Girl*, Andy Warhol's famous *Gold Marilyn Monroe* and Claes Oldenburg's *Giant Soft Fan*.

Works after about 1965 are displayed on a rotating basis and can include pieces by Judd, Flavin, Serra and Beuys among many others.

DRAWINGS AND OTHER WORKS ON PAPER

Man with a Hat by Pablo Picasso (1912), in collage and charcoal

T HE MUSEUM of Modern Art has one of the most comprehensive collections of modern drawings anywhere in the world. This collection has a range of works in traditional mediums – pencil, ink and charcoal – and also in watercolor, gouache and collage. Some are early studies for famous paintings; Picasso's *Head of the Medical Student* is a study for *Les Demoiselles d'Avignon*. Special strengths are the works representing the School of Paris, Dada and Surrealism. The rotating exhibition in the department's second-floor galleries may include the works of Matisse, Ernst, Klee, Pollock, Dubuffet and Rauschenberg. At various times some of this collection is shown outside the drawings department to complement the museum's other exhibitions.

PRINTS AND ILLUSTRATED BOOKS

The Game of Solitaire by Jacques Villon (1903 but dated 1904)

WIDE-RANGING examples of historical and contemporary printmaking include works in such traditional techniques as lithography, etching, screenprinting and woodcuts, as well as in more experimental techniques. There are fine examples of portraiture, notably a *Self-portrait with Grimace* by Marc Chagall. The collection is strong in the works of Redon, Munch, Klee, Matisse, Picasso, Dubuffet, Villon and Johns. Prints by these and other artists are always displayed in the constantly rotating exhibition in the department's second-floor galleries.

At the entrance to the Print galleries is a reading room containing catalogs and books about prints. The first gallery has a changing survey of printed art from the 1880s up to the 1950s. The next displays art from the 1960s onward, introducing recent and contemporary work.

PHOTOGRAPHY

THE PHOTOGRAPHY collection begins with the invention of the medium around 1840. It includes pictures by fine artists, journalists, scientists and entrepreneurs, as well as amateur photographers. The first of the department's third-floor galleries is devoted to temporary exhibitions. The other galleries offer an ever-changing chronological series of the collection's highlights. Included in these are photographs by Atget, Stieglitz, Lange, Arbus, Steichen,

FILM DEPARTMENT

With a collection of some 10,000 films and four million stills, the museum offers a wide range of programs, including retrospectives of individual directors and actors, films in specific genres and experimental work, as well as a broad range of other exhibitions. Film conservation is a key part of the department's work. Today's top directors are now donating copies of their films to help fund this expensive but vital work.

Film still of Charlie Chaplin and Jackie Coogan in *The Kid* (1921)

Cartier-Bresson and Kertesz, plus a range of contemporary photographers, most notably Friedlander, Sherman and Nixon. There is an extensive variety of subject matter – covering delicate landscapes, scenes of urban desolation, abstract imagery and stylish portraiture, including some

Sunday on the Banks of the Marne, photographed by Henri Cartier-Bresson in 1939

beautiful silver-gelatin print nudes by the French Surrealist man Ray. Together, they form a complete history of photographic art and represent one of the finest collections in existence.

ARCHITECTURE AND DESIGN

THE MUSEUM of Modern Art was the first art museum to include utilitarian objects in its collection. These range from household appliances, stereo equipment, furniture, lighting, textiles and glassware to industrial ball bearings and silicon chips. Architecture is represented in the displays of scale models, drawings and photographs. Graphic design is shown in typography and posters. Architectural models and drawings are displayed in the first gallery, and selections from the design collection follow. Pinin Farina's Cisitalia car and the Bell helicopter are on permanent display in the fourth-floor galleries.

Reclining rocking chair of steam-bent beech and cane by Gebrüder Thonet (around 1900)

St. Patrick's Cathedral ⑧

See pp176–7.

Villard Houses ⑨

457 Madison Ave (New York Palace Hotel). **Map** 13 A4. ☎ *935-3960.* Ⓜ *51st St.* **Urban Center open** *11am–5pm Mon–Wed, Fri, Sat.* 📷 🚻 *See* **Restaurants and Bars** *p296.*

Henry Villard was a Bavarian immigrant who became publisher of the *New York Evening Post* and founder of the Northern Pacific Railroad. In 1881, he bought the land opposite St. Patrick's Cathedral and hired McKim, Mead & White to design town houses, one for himself, the rest for sale. The inspired result has six four-story houses built around a central court opening to the street and the church. The south wing was Villard's, but financial difficulties forced him to sell before it was finished.

Ownership passed to the Roman Catholic Archdiocese, but the houses were then threatened when the church outgrew its space in the 1970s. The problem was resolved when the Helmsley chain purchased air rights for the 51-story Helmsley (now New York) Palace Hotel. The south wing became the formal entrance to the hotel and the grand public rooms of the Villard suite, now restored to their former glory, house top French restaurant, Le Cirque. The Urban Center occupies the entire north wing and its large bookshop is the best place in New York to find architectural books on the city.

St. Bartholomew's Church

St. Bartholomew's Church ⑩

109 E 50th St. **Map** 13 A4. ☎ *751-1616.* Ⓜ *51st St.* **Open** *7:30am–6pm daily.* **Closed** *public hols exc Dec 25 & Easter.* 🚻 *frequent* 📷 ♿ **Lectures, concerts.** 🚻 *on Sundays.*

Known fondly to New Yorkers as "St. Bart's," this Byzantine structure with its ornate detail, pinkish brick, open terrace and a polychromed gold dome brought color and variety to Park Avenue in 1919.

Architect Bertram Goodhue incorporated into the design the Romanesque entrance portico created by Stanford White for the original 1903 St. Bartholomew's on Madison Avenue, and marble columns from the earlier church were used in the chapel.

St. Bartholomew's musical programs are well known, their Jazz Nativity being a special favorite. They are now concentrating on classical, choral and organ music.

General Electric Building ⑪

570 Lexington Ave. **Map** 13 A4. Ⓜ Lexington Ave. **Not open** *to the public.*

In 1931 architects Cross & Cross were commissioned to design a skyscraper that would be in keeping with its neighbor, St. Bartholomew's Church. Not an easy task, but the result won unanimous acclaim. The colors were chosen to blend and contrast, and the design of the tower complemented the church's polychrome dome.

The General Electric Building on Lexington Avenue

View the pair from the corner of Park and 50th to see how well it works. However, the General Electric is no mere backdrop but a work of art in its own right and a favorite part of the city skyline. It is an Art Deco gem from its chrome and marble lobby to its spiky "radio waves" crown.

Walk one block north on Lexington Avenue to find a place much cherished by movie fans. It is right at this spot that Marilyn Monroe, in a billowing white frock, stood so memorably in the breeze from the Lexington Avenue subway grating in the movie *The Seven-Year Itch.*

Villard Houses, now the entrance to the New York Palace Hotel

Waldorf–Astoria 🕐

301 Park Ave. **Map** 13 A5.
🅲 355-3000. Ⓜ *Lexington Ave, 53rd St.* See **Where to Stay** *p281.*

THIS ART DECO classic, which covers an entire city block, was designed by Schultze & Weaver in 1931. The earlier Waldorf–Astoria Hotel at 34th Street was demolished to make way for the Empire State Building.

Winston Churchill and New York philanthropist Grover Whalen at the Waldorf–Astoria in 1946

Still deservedly one of New York's most prestigious hotels, the Waldorf–Astoria serves, too, as a reminder of a more glamorous era in the city's history. The 625-ft (190-m) twin towers, where the Duke and Duchess of Windsor lived, have hosted numerous celebrities, including every US president since 1931. The giant lobby clock, executed for the Chicago World's Fair of 1893, is from the original hotel, and the piano in the Peacock Alley cocktail lounge belonged to Cole Porter when he was a resident of the hotel's exclusive Towers.

Lever House 🕐

390 Park Ave. **Map** 13 A4.
🅲 888-1260. Ⓜ *5th Ave-53rd St.* **Lobby and building no longer open to the public.** *Call for additional information.*

IMAGINE A PARK AVENUE lined with sturdy, residential buildings – and then imagine the sensation when they were suddenly reflected here in the first of the city's glass-walled skyscrapers, one of the most influential buildings of the modern era. The design, by

The pool at the Four Seasons in the Seagram Building

Skidmore, Owings & Merrill, is simply two rectangular slabs of stainless steel and glass, one laid horizontally, the other stacked to stand tall above it, to allow light in from every side. The crisp and bright design was always intended to symbolize many of the Lever Brothers' products – they make soaps and other cleaning products. Revolutionary though it was in 1952, Lever House is now dwarfed by the many imitators that have grown up around it, but its importance as an architectural pacesetter remains undiminished.

Lever House on Park Avenue

Seagram Building 🕐

375 Park Ave. **Map** 13 A4. 🅲 572-7000. Ⓜ *5th Ave-53rd St.* **Open** *9am–5pm Mon–Fri.* 🕐 *3pm Tue.* 🍴

SAMUEL BRONFMAN, the late head of Seagram distillers, was prepared to put up an ordinary commercial building until his architect daughter, Phyllis Lambert, intervened and persuaded him to go to the best – Mies van der Rohe.

The result, which is widely considered the best of the many Modernist buildings of the 1950s, consists of two rectangles of bronze and glass that let the light pour in.

Within is the exclusive Four Seasons Restaurant *(see p293)*, a landmark in its own right. Designer Philip Johnson has created two linked rooms, with the centerpiece of one a pool, and the other a bar that is topped by a quivering Richard Lippold sculpture.

Office workers at lunch in the spacious Citicorp atrium

Citicorp Center 🕐

153 E 53rd St. **Map** 13 A4. Ⓜ *53rd St-Lexington Ave.* **Open** *7am–11pm daily.* 🍴 🕐 **St. Peter's Lutheran Church** 🅲 *935-2200.* **Open** *9am–9pm daily* 🕐 *8:45am, 11am Sun.* **Jazz vespers** *5pm Sun.* **Concerts** *daily except Mon.* **Theater at St. Peter's Church** 🅲 *935-5800.*

AN ALUMINUM-CLAD spire built on ten-story stilts with a sliced-off roof, Citicorp Center is one of a kind and caused a sensation when it was completed in 1978. The unusual base design had to incorporate St. Peter's Lutheran Church. The church is separate both in space and design, a granite sculpture below a corner of the tower. Step inside to see the handsome modern interior and the Erol Beker Chapel by sculptor Louise Nevelson. The church is well known for its organ concerts and jazz vespers, and has a small theater. Citicorp's slanting top never functioned as a solar collector as intended, but it makes the building's outline an unmistakable landmark on the skyline.

Saint Patrick's Cathedral ⓞ

THE ROMAN CATHOLIC Church originally intended this site for use as a cemetery, but in 1850 Archbishop John Hughes decided to build a cathedral instead. Many thought that it was foolish to build so far beyond the (then) city limits, but Hughes went ahead anyway. Architect James Renwick built New York's finest Gothic Revival building, the largest Catholic cathedral in the United States. The cathedral, which seats 2,500 people, was completed in 1878, though the spires were added from 1885 to 1888.

Fifth Avenue facade

Lady Chapel ★
This chapel honors the Blessed Virgin. The stained-glass windows portray the mysteries of the rosary.

Pièta
American sculptor William O. Partridge created this statue of the Pièta in 1906; it stands at the side of the Lady Chapel.

★ Baldachin
The great baldachin rising over the high altar is made entirely of bronze. Statues of the saints and prophets adorn the four piers supporting the canopy.

STAR FEATURES

★ Baldachin

★ Great Bronze Doors

★ Lady Chapel

★ Great Organ and Rose Window

Cathedral Facade
The exterior wall is built of white marble. The spires rise 330 ft (101 m) above the pavement.

Stations of the Cross
Carved of Caen stone in Holland, these reliefs won first prize in the field of religious art at the Chicago World's Fair in 1893.

Shrine of St. Elizabeth Ann Seton
The bronze statue and screen depict the life of the first native American to be canonized a saint, who founded the Sisters of Charity (see p76).

Great Organ ★ and Rose Window
Measuring 26 ft (8 m) in diameter, the rose window shines above the great organ, which has more than 7,000 pipes.

Main entrance

Great Bronze Doors ★
The massive doors weigh 20,000 lb (9,000 kg) and are adorned with important religious figures in New York.

Central Synagogue 🔟

652 Lexington Ave. **Map** 13 A4.
C 838–5122. **M** 51st St, Lexington
Ave. **Closed for repairs until 2001**
⭐ Services held at Beir Hall at the
Community House, 123 E 55th St.

THIS IS NEW YORK'S
oldest building in
continuous use as a
synagogue. It was
designed in 1870 by
Silesian-born Henry
Fernbach, America's
first prominent Jewish
architect. He also
designed some of
SoHo's finest cast-iron
buildings. The Central
Synagogue is considered
the city's best example
of Moorish-Islamic
Revival architecture.
The congregation was
originally founded in
1846 as Ahawath
Chesed (Love of
Mercy), by 18 newly
arrived immigrants,
most of them from
Bohemia, in much
humbler surroundings
on Ludlow Street on
the Lower East Side.

The stenciled interior is a colorful mix of red, blue, ocher and gilt and was inspired by Victorian prints of a Moorish Palace in Spain called the Alhambra.

Banded "horseshoe" arches are an Hispano-Mooresque design.

The ark holds the sacred scrolls of the Jewish Holy Book, The Torah.

The twin towers represent the two columns that stood outside Solomon's Temple. The domed minarets, which rise 122 ft (37 m) are onion-shaped and made of green copper.

The facade is an understated Moorish design in local brownstone.

Sutton Place and Beekman Place 🔢

Map 13 C3, 13 C5. **M** 59th St.

SUTTON PLACE IS A posh and
pleasant neighborhood,
delightfully devoid of busy
traffic, made up of elegant
low-rise apartment houses
and town houses designed by
noted architects. The arrival of
New York society in the 1920s
transformed an area that had
once been the province of
factories and tenements.
Three Sutton Square is the
residence of the secretary-
general of the United Nations.

Look beyond Sutton Square
and 59th Street for a glimpse
of Riverview Terrace, a
private street of five ivy-
covered brownstones fronting
on the river. The tiny parks at
the end of 55th Street and
jutting out at 57th Street offer
views of the river and the
Queensboro Bridge.
    Smaller than Sutton Place,
and even more tranquil, is
Beekman Place, a virtually
private two-block enclave
of 1920s town houses and
some small-scale apartments.
Famous residents here have
included Gloria Vanderbilt,
Rex Harrison, Irving Berlin
and members of the large
Rockefeller family.
    Between Beekman and
Sutton places is River House,
a twin-towered apartment
building built in 1931. Its
squash and tennis courts, large
private yacht moorings, pool
and lavish ballroom gave it an
immediate cachet that has
stood the test of time, even

Park at Sutton Place, looking toward Queensboro Bridge and Roosevelt Island

though the moorings had to make way for FDR Drive.

At Turtle Bay Gardens, two rows of brownstone houses dating from the 1860s hide a charming Italianate garden. Among the residents enticed by this privacy have been the film stars Tyrone Power and Katharine Hepburn, and modern composer Stephen Sondheim.

Roosevelt Island 18

Map 14 D2. **M** *59th St. Tram departs from 2nd Ave-60th St.*

SINCE 1976 a Swiss cable car has offered a quick ride across the East River to Roosevelt Island, with eagle's-eye views of the city and the Queensboro Bridge.

Near the tram station are the remains of the Blackwell farmhouse, which stood from 1796 to 1804 and gave the island its name until the 1920s, when real estate development began. From the 1920s to the 1970s, the island housed a succession of hospitals, an almshouse, a jail, a workhouse and an insane asylum, and became known as Welfare Island.

In 1927, Mae West was held in the penitentiary here for eight days after a "lewd performance." She requested, and got, her silk lingerie to wear under her prison uniform. The ruins of 19th-century hospitals still remain, as does an 1872 lighthouse built by an asylum inmate.

The tram affords a thrilling ride and some fine city views; it is now part of the N and R subway lines.

Bloomingdale's store sign

Bloomingdale's 19

1000 3rd Ave. **Map** 13 A3.
C 355-5900. **M** *59th St.* **Open** *10am–8:30pm Mon–Fri, 10am–7pm Sat, 11am–7pm Sun. See* **Shopping** *p311.*

FOR A WHILE in the booming 1980s, "Bloomies" was synonymous with the good life. Founded by Joseph and Lyman Bloomingdale in 1872, this famous department store had a bargain-basement image until the 3rd Avenue El was taken down in the 1960s. Then came the store's transformation to the epitome of trendy, sophisticated shopping. But the late 1980s brought new ownership and eventual bankruptcy. While not as flashy as in the past, Bloomingdale's is open every day and remains one of the city's best-stocked stores.

Fuller Building 20

41 E 57th St. **Map** 13 A3. **C** *André Emmerich Gallery 288-1551.* **Closed to the public.** *Susan Sheehan Gallery 888-4220.* **Open** *10am–6pm Tue–Sat.* **M** *59th St.*

THIS SLIM-TOWERED black, gray and white 1929 beauty by Walker & Gillette is a prime example of geometric Art Deco design. The striking statues on either side of the clock above the entry are by Elie Nadelman. Step inside to see the intricate mosaic tile floors; one panel shows the Fuller Company's

former home in the Flatiron Building. The Fuller Building is a hive of exclusive art galleries, including the prestigious Susan Sheehan gallery.

French Renaissance–style facade of the Plaza Hotel

Plaza Hotel 21

5th Ave.& Central Park South **Map** 12 F3. **C** *759-3000.* **M** *59th St. See* **Where to Stay** *p281.*

THE CITY's grande dame of hotels was designed by Henry J. Hardenbergh, known for the Dakota *(see p216)* and the original Waldorf–Astoria. Completed in 1907 at the exorbitant cost of $12.5 million, the Plaza was proclaimed "the best hotel in the world," with 800 rooms, 500 baths, a two-story ballroom, five marble staircases, and 14- to 17-room apartments for such families as the Vanderbilts and the Goulds *(see p49).*

The 18-story cast-iron structure resembles a French Renaissance château on a larger scale. Much of the interior decoration came from Europe. The Palm Court still has mirrored walls and Italian carvings of the four seasons as supporting columns.

Former owner Donald Trump restored the hotel's original glitter (too much of it for some) with elaborate new Bavarian glass chandeliers, lush carpet and miles of gold leaf. Public areas have been refurbished without losing their original ambience.

The clock statues above the Fuller Building entrance

UPPER EAST SIDE

AT THE TURN of the century, New York society moved to the Upper East Side – and stayed. Many of the Beaux Arts mansions are now museums and embassies, but the well-to-do still occupy grand apartment buildings on Fifth and Park avenues. Chic shops and galleries line Madison. Farther east, the area includes German Yorkville in the East 80s, Hungarian Yorkville to the south and little Bohemia, with its Czech population, below 78th Street. Many Germans, Czechs and Hungarians have left the area, but their churches, restaurants, and ethnic shops still remain.

African urn, Metropolitan Museum of Art

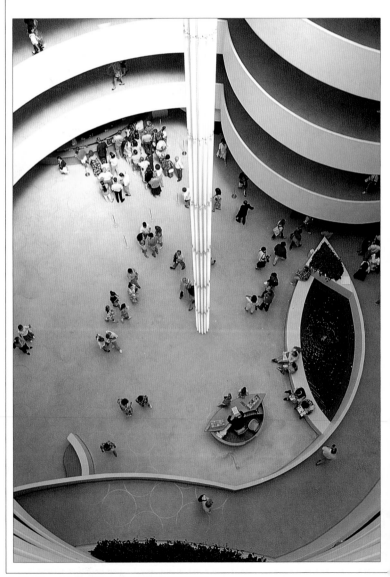

Looking down into the lobby of the Guggenheim Museum

SIGHTS AT A GLANCE

Historic Streets and Buildings
Seventh Regiment Armory **10**
Henderson Place **14**
Gracie Mansion **16**

Museums and Galleries
International Center of Photography **1**
Jewish Museum **2**
Cooper-Hewitt National Design Museum **3**
National Academy of Design **4**
Solomon R. Guggenheim Museum pp186–87 **5**
Metropolitan Museum of Art pp188–95 **6**
Whitney Museum of American Art pp198–99 **7**
Frick Collection pp200–1 **8**
Asia Society **9**
Society of Illustrators **12**
Abigail Adams Smith Museum **13**
Museum of the City of New York **19**

Churches and Synagogues
Temple Emanu-El **11**
Church of the Holy Trinity **17**
St. Nicholas Russian Orthodox Cathedral **18**

Parks and Squares
Carl Schurz Park **15**

GETTING THERE
The Lexington Ave 4 and 5 express trains stop at 59th and 86th streets. The local (No. 6) also stops at 68th, 77th and 96th streets. Buses include: M1, M2, M3 and M4 on Fifth/Madison Aves, M101/102 on Lexington/Third and M15 on First/Second. The crosstown buses are the M66, M72, M79, M86 and M96.

SEE ALSO

KEY

Street-by-Street map

M Subway station

Ferry terminal

Heliport

0 meters 500

0 yards 500

Statue of Diana, National Academy of Design

Street by Street: Museum Mile

MANY OF NEW YORK'S museums are clustered on the Upper East Side, in homes ranging from the former Frick and Carnegie mansions to the modernistic Guggenheim, designed by Frank Lloyd Wright. The displays are as varied as the architecture, running the gamut from old masters to photographs to decorative arts. Presiding over the scene is the vast Metropolitan Museum of Art, America's answer to the Louvre. Many of the museums stay open late on Tuesday evenings, and some offer free admission.

Jewish Museum
The most extensive collection of Judaica in the world is housed here. It includes coins, archaeological objects and ceremonial and religious artifacts ❷

Cooper-Hewitt Museum ★
The decorative arts, including ceramics, glass, furniture and textiles, are well represented here ❸

The Church of the Heavenly Rest was built in 1929 in the Gothic style. The madonna in the pulpit is by sculptor Malvina Hoffman.

National Academy of Design
The Academy, founded in 1825, moved here in 1940. Its fine collection includes paintings and sculptures by its members ❹

Graham House is an apartment building with a splendid Beaux Arts entrance. It was built in 1892.

★ **Solomon R. Guggenheim Museum**
Floodlit at dusk, architect Frank Lloyd Wright's building looks purple. It is in the form of a spiral. Take the elevator to the top and walk down to see one of the world's best collections of modern art ❺

STAR SIGHTS

★ **Solomon R. Guggenheim Museum**

★ **Cooper-Hewitt Museum**

**International
Center of
Photography**
*This museum
houses one of
the world's finest
photography
collections* ❶

**The facade of the
Squadron A Armory**
is all that remains of
the original building.
It is now the west
wall of the play-
ground of Hunter
High School. The
school was built
to complement
the style of
the armory.

**Public
basketball
court**

**To 96th Street
subway (2 blocks)**

**The Smithers Alcoholism
Center** occupies a mansion
that was once the home of
theatrical producer Billy Rose.

**The Synod of Bishops
of the Russian
Orthodox Church
Outside of Russia**
is housed in a
lovely 1931
mansion.

**Night
Presence
IV** (1972),
a modern
work in
rusting steel,
was created by
Louise Nevelson.
Some New
Yorkers feel it is
out of place
among its staid,
old-fashioned
neighbors on
Park Avenue.

LOCATOR MAP
See Manhattan Map pp12–13

UPPER
WEST SIDE

CENTRAL
PARK

East Side

Hell
Gate

UPPER
EAST SIDE

Roosevelt I.

UPPER
MIDTOWN

Queens

KEY

‒ ‒ ‒ Suggested route

0 meters   100

0 yards   100

At **120 and 122 East 92nd
Street** are two of the few
wooden houses left in
Manhattan. Built in 1859 and
1871, respectively, they have a
charming Italianate air.

The Marx Brothers spent their
boyhoods in a three-bedroom
apartment in a modest row house
at 179 East 93rd Street.

International Center of Photography

International Center of Photography ❶

1130 5th Ave. **Map** 16 F2.
☎ 860-1777. **M** 86th St, 96th St.
Open 10am–5pm Tue-Thu, 10am–6pm Fri–Sun. **Closed** public hols. **Adm charge**. ✗ ☑ By appt only ♿

THIS MUSEUM, often referred to as the ICP, was founded by Cornell Capa in 1974 to conserve the work of such outstanding photojournalists as his brother Robert, who was killed on assignment in 1954. The ICP's collection of 12,500 original prints includes much work by some of the world's greatest photographers, such as Ansel Adams and Henri Cartier-Bresson. There are also excellent wide-ranging exhibitions, and a program of films, lectures and classes.

One of upper Fifth Avenue's last grand residences, this brick six-story Neo-Georgian house was built in 1915 for Willard Straight, a diplomat, financier and founder of the magazines *The New Republic* and *Asia*.

Jewish Museum ❷

1109 5th Ave. **Map** 16 F2.
☎ 423-3200. **M** 86th St, 96th St.
Open 11am–5:45pm Mon, Wed, Thu, Sun, 11am–8pm Tue. **Closed** Fri, Sat, major public & Jewish hols. **Adm charge**. ✗ ♿ ☑ 🖥 ♿

THE EXQUISITE château-like residence of Felix M. Warburg, financier and leader of the Jewish community, was designed by C.P.H. Gilbert in 1908. It now houses one of the world's largest collections of Jewish fine and ceremonial art, and historical Judaica. Renovation has almost doubled the display space. The stonework in the new extension is by the stonemasons of St. John the Divine *(see pp224–5)*.

Objects have been brought here from all over the world, some at great risk of persecution to the donors. Covering 4,000 years, artifacts include Torah crowns, candelabras, kiddush cups, plates, scrolls and silver ceremonial objects.

There is a Torah ark from the Benguiat Collection, the exquisite faience entrance wall of a 16th-century Persian synagogue and the powerful *Holocaust* by sculptor George Segal. Changing exhibitions reflect Jewish life and experience around the world.

19th-century ewer and basin from Istanbul at the Jewish Museum

Cooper-Hewitt National Design Museum ❸

2 E 91st St. **Map** 16 F2. ☎ 849-8300, 849-8387. **M** 86th St. **Open** 10am–9pm Tue, 10am–5pm Wed–Sat, noon–5pm Sun. **Closed** public hols. **Adm charge**. ♿ ☑ ♿

ONE OF THE largest design collections in the world, this museum occupies the former home of industrialist Andrew Carnegie. It was amassed by the Hewitt sisters, Amy, Eleanor and Sarah. The museum opened in 1897 at Cooper Union *(see p118)*; the Smithsonian Institution acquired the collections in 1967, and the Carnegie Corporation offered the mansion.

Carnegie asked for "the most modest, plainest and most roomy house in New York," but the house set some new trends with its central

Cooper-Hewitt Museum entrance

heating, passenger elevator and air-conditioning. Visitors can enjoy the wooden staircase, rich paneling and carving and sunny solarium.

National Academy of Design ❹

1083 5th Ave. **Map** 16 F3.
☎ 369-4880. **M** 86th St. **Open** noon–5pm Wed–Sun, 10am–6pm Fri. **Adm charge** except 5–6pm Fri. ✗ ♿ ♿

MORE THAN 6,000 paintings, drawings and sculptures, including works by Thomas Eakins, Winslow Homer, Raphael Soyer and Frank Lloyd Wright, comprise the collection of the National Academy of Design, founded in 1825 by a group of artists. The group's mission was (and is) to train artists and exhibit their work. In 1940, Archer Huntington, an art patron and philanthropist, donated his house, an attractive building with patterned marble floors and decorative plaster ceilings. The grand entrance foyer has a statue of Diana by sculptor Anna Hyatt Huntington.

Statue of Diana in the National Academy of Design entrance foyer

Solomon R. Guggenheim Museum ❺

See pp186–7.

Metropolitan Museum of Art ❻

See pp188–95.

Whitney Museum of American Art ❼

See pp198–9.

Frick Collection ❽

See pp200–1.

Asia Society ❾

725 Park Ave. **Map** 13 A1.
📞 288-6400. Ⓜ 68th St.
Open 11am–6pm Tue–Sat (8pm Thu),
noon–5pm Sun. **Closed**
Mon, public hols. **Adm
charge** except 6–8pm
Thu. 🚫 ♿ 📷 🅿

Founded by
John D.
Rockefeller III
in 1956 to
increase American
understanding of
Asian culture,
the society is a
forum for 30
countries from
Japan to Iran,
Central Asia to
Australia.

Built in
1981, the
eight-story
building is
made of red

**South Asian
sculpture at the
Asia Society**

granite. It was designed by
Edward Larrabee Barnes. There
are several galleries, one
permanently devoted to
Rockefeller's own collection of
Asian sculptures, ceramics,
bronzes and wood sculptures,
amassed by him and his wife
on frequent trips to the East.

Changing exhibits show a
wide variety of Asian arts,
and the society has a full
program of films, dance,
concerts and lectures. There
is a well-stocked shop with
books on Asia.

**Entrance Hall of the Seventh
Regiment Armory**

Seventh Regiment Armory ❿

643 Park Ave. **Map** 13 A2.
📞 452-3067. Ⓜ 68th St.
Open Mon–Fri by appt only.
Closed public hols. 🚫 ♿ 📷

From the war of 1812
through two world wars,
the Seventh Regiment has
played a vital role. They were
an elite corps of "gentlemen
soldiers" from prominent
families, and their armory is
unlike any other in the US.
Within the stern fortresslike
exterior are extraordinary
rooms filled with
lavish furnishings of
the Victorian era,
objets d'art and
regimental
memorabilia.

The design by
Charles W.
Clinton, a veteran
of the regiment,
had offices facing
Park Avenue, with
a vast drill hall
stretching behind
to Lexington
Avenue. The
reception rooms
include the
Veterans' Room
and the Library
by Louis Comfort
Tiffany. The
drill hall is now
the site of the
Winter Antiques
Show *(see p53)*
and a favorite
place to hold
the city's many
charity balls.

Temple Emanu-El ⓫

1 E 65th St. **Map** 12 F2.
📞 744-1400. Ⓜ 68th St, 60th St.
Open 10am–4:30pm Sun–Fri,
12:30pm–4:45pm Sat (last adm on Fri
3:30pm) **Closed** Jewish hols.
✡ 5:30pm Sun–Thu, 5:15pm Fri,
10:30am Sat. 📷 📷 🅿

This impressive limestone
edifice of 1929 is one of
the largest synagogues in the
world, seating 2,500 in the
main sanctuary alone. It is
home to the oldest Reform
congregation in New York.
Among the many fine details
are the bronze grille doors of
the Ark, and stained glass
showing the Shield of David
and the Lion of Judah. The
dominant feature of the Fifth
Avenue exterior is the great
recessed arch enclosing a
magnificent wheel window.
The Beth-El Chapel is a
twin-domed structure with
a Byzantine influence.

The synagogue stands on
the site of the palatial home
of the legendary society
hostess Mrs. William Astor.
She left her midtown mansion
when her nephew, who was
feuding with her, built the
Waldorf Hotel next door. The
formidable Mrs. Astor moved
to the Upper East Side,
taking society with
her, while her son
built the Astoria Hotel
on the site of her
previous home.

The Ark at Temple Emanu-El

The Solomon R. Guggenheim Museum ❺

Hᴏᴍᴇ ᴛᴏ ᴏɴᴇ of the world's finest collections of modern and contemporary art, the Guggenheim building itself is perhaps the museum's greatest masterpiece. It was designed by architect Frank Lloyd Wright and has been likened to a giant white shell. As you walk along the spiral ramp that curves down and inward from the dome, and visit the new Small Rotunda and tower galleries, you will see special exhibitions featuring major works by many important 19th- and 20th-century artists. A new downtown site opened in 1992, the Guggenheim Museum SoHo (see p105).

Fifth Avenue facade

Paris Through the Window
The vibrant colors of Marc Chagall's 1913 masterpiece illumine the canvas, conjuring up images of a magical and mysterious city where nothing is quite what it appears to be.

Small Rotunda

THE SOLOMO

Sculpture terrace

Main entrance

Woman Ironing (1904)
A work from Pablo Picasso's Blue Period, this painting is his quintessential image of hard work and fatigue.

Yellow Cow (1911)
Franz Marc's work was influenced by a German back-to-nature movement.

Nude (1917)
This sleeping figure is typical of Amedeo Modigliani's stylized work.

MUSEUM GUIDE

The Great Rotunda features special exhibitions. The Small Rotunda shows some of the museum's celebrated Impressionist and Post-Impressionist holdings. The new Tower galleries feature exhibitions of work from the permanent collection as well as contemporary pieces. A fifth-floor sculpture terrace overlooks Central Park. Not all of the collection is on display at any one time.

Tower

Great
Rotunda

G E N H E I M   M U S E U M

Before the Mirror *(1876)
In trying to capture the flavor of 19th-century society, Edouard Manet often used the image of the courtesan.*

Woman Holding a Vase
Fernand Léger incorporated elements of Cubism into this work from 1927.

Black Lines *(1913) This is one of Vasily Kandinsky's earliest examples of his work in "non-objective" art.*

Woman with Yellow Hair
(1931) The gentle, voluptuous figure of Picasso's mistress often appears in his work.

FRANK LLOYD WRIGHT

During his lifetime, Wright was considered the great innovator of American architecture. Characteristic of his work are Prairie-style homes and office buildings of concrete slabs, glass bricks and tubing. Wright received the Guggenheim commission in 1942 and it was completed after his death in 1959, his only New York building.

Interior of the Guggenheim's Great Rotunda

Metropolitan Museum of Art ❻

Founded in 1870 by a group of artists and philanthropists who dreamed of an American arts institution to rival those of Europe, this collection is thought to be the most comprehensive in the Western world. Works date from prehistoric times to the present. It moved to its current site in 1880 and houses collections from all continents, including ancient Egyptian art and American sculpture and decorative art since colonial times.

The entrance of the Metropolitan Museum of Art

Robert Lehman Collection

★ **Gertrude Stein** (1905–6)
This portrait of the American writer Gertrude Stein is by Pablo Picasso. The masklike face is evidence of his debt to African and Roman art.

Pendant Mask
The kingdom of Benin (now part of Nigeria) was renowned for its art. This mask was made in the 16th century.

Seated Man with Harp
This statuette was made in the Cyclades c.3,000 BC.

Lower Floor

Gallery Guide

Most of the collections are housed on the two main floors. Works from 19 curatorial areas are in the permanent galleries, with designated galleries for temporary exhibitions. Central on the first and second floors are European painting, sculpture and decorative art. Other collections can be found radiating out from the center on both levels.

The Marriage Feast at Can[a]
This rare 16th-century pane[l] painting by Juan de Flande[s] is part of the Linsky Collecti[on].

Bust of Diderot *(1773)* *Jean Antoine Houdon's bust was made for a Russian count.*

★ **Portrait of the Princesse de Broglie** *This portrait, painted in 1853, was J.A.D. Ingres' last.*

First floor

VISITORS' CHECKLIST

1000 Fifth Ave. **Map** 16 F4.
535-7710. **M** 4, 5, 6 to 86th St. M1, M2, M3, M4. **Open** 9:30am–5:15pm Sun & Tue–Thu, 9:30am–8:45pm Fri, Sat. **Closed** Jan 1, Thanksgiving, Dec 25. **Adm charge.** Concerts, lectures, film & video presentations.

Tiffany Columns *(c.1905)* *The ornate columns are all that remain of Louis Comfort Tiffany's house on Long Island.*

STAR EXHIBITS

★ **Temple of Dendur**

★ **Portrait of the Princesse de Broglie by Ingres**

★ **Gertrude Stein by Pablo Picasso**

Main entrance

KEY TO FLOOR PLAN

☐ European painting, sculpture and decorative arts

☐ Art of Africa, Oceania and the Americas

☐ Twentieth-century art

☐ American art

☐ Egyptian art

☐ Greek and Roman art

☐ Medieval art

☐ Arms and armor

☐ Costume Institute

☐ Special exhibitions

☐ Non-exhibition space

English Armor *This was made for George Clifford around 1580.*

★ **Temple of Dendur** *(15 BC)* *The Roman emperor Augustus built this three-room temple. He is shown in its reliefs making offerings.*

Metropolitan Museum of Art: Upper Levels

Marrakech
This 1964 work is one of Frank Stella's "Moroccan" paintings. Within a square format, fluorescent strips form the painting's main focus.

Sculpture Garden
These modern sculptures, on top of the 20th-century wing, are changed annually.

Card Players *(1890)*
Paul Cézanne departed here from his traditional landscapes, still lifes and portraits to paint this scene of peasants intently playing cards.

Islamic art

Second floor

First floor

★ **Cypresses** *(1889)*
Vincent Van Gogh painted this the year before he died. The heavy brushstrokes and the swirling style mark his later work.

Eagle-headed Winged Being Pollinating the Sacred Tree *(about 900 BC)*
This relief comes from an Assyrian palace.

STAR EXHIBITS

★ **Self-portrait of 1660 by Rembrandt**

★ **George Washington Crossing the Delaware by Leutze**

★ **Cypresses by Vincent Van Gogh**

★ **Diptych by Jan van Eyck**

★ **Diptych**
(1425–30)
Flemish painter Jan van Eyck was one of the earliest masters of oil painting. These scenes of the Crucifixion and Last Judgment show him to be a forerunner of realism, too.

★ **Washington Crossing the Delaware**
In 1851 Emanuel Gottlieb Leutze painted this romanticized – and inaccurate – view of the famous crossing.

KEY TO FLOOR PLAN

- ☐ European painting, sculpture and decorative arts
- ☐ Ancient Near Eastern and Islamic art
- ☐ Twentieth-century art
- ☐ American art
- ☐ Asian art
- ☐ Greek and Roman art
- ☐ Musical instruments
- ☐ Drawings, prints and photographs
- ☐ Special exhibitions
- ▨ Non-exhibition space

Astor Court

The Death of Socrates *(1787)*
Jacques Louis David shows Socrates about to take poison rather than renounce his beliefs.

★ **Self-portrait** *(1660)*
Rembrandt painted almost 100 self-portraits. This one shows him at the age of 54.

THE ASTOR COURT

In 1979, 27 crafts-people from China, responsible for the care of Souzhou's historic gardens, came to New York to replicate a Ming-style scholar's garden in the Metropolitan Museum. They used centuries-old techniques and handmade tools that had been passed down for generations. It was the first cultural exchange between the United States and the People's Republic of China. The result is a quiet garden for meditation, a Western parallel to Souzhou's Garden of the Master of the Fishing Nets.

Exploring the Metropolitan

T HE TREASURES OF "THE MET" include a vast collection of American art and more than 3,000 European paintings, including masterpieces by Rembrandt and Vermeer. There are also many Islamic exhibits, plus the greatest collection of Egyptian art outside Cairo.

AFRICA, OCEANIA AND THE AMERICAS

A painted gold funerary mask (10th–14th century) from the necropolis of Batán Grande, Peru

N ELSON ROCKEFELLER built the Michael C. Rockefeller Wing in 1982 in memory of his son, who lost his life on an art-finding expedition in New Guinea. The wing showcases a superb collection of over 2,000 objects from Africa, the islands of the Pacific and the Americas.

Among the African works, the ivory and bronze sculptures from the royal kingdom of Benin (Nigeria) are outstanding, as is the wooden sculpture by the Dogon, Bamana and Senufo peoples of Mali. From the Pacific come carvings by the Asmat people of New Guinea and decorations and masks from the Melanesian and Polynesian islands. From Mexico and Central and South America come pre-Columbian gold, ceramics and stonework. The wing also contains fine Native American artifacts by the Inuit and other groups.

AMERICAN ART

G ILBERT STUART'S first portrait of George Washington, George Caleb Bingham's *Fur Traders Descending the Missouri*, John Singer Sargent's notorious portrait of *Madame X* and the monumental *George Washington Crossing the*

Delaware by Emanuel Leutze are among the icons of the American Wing. It holds one of the world's finest collections of American painting, including several works by Edward Hopper, and sculpture and decorative arts from colonial times to this century.

Period rooms, with original woodwork and furnishings, range from the saloon hall in which George Washington celebrated his last birthday to the elegant prairie-style living room from the Little house in Minnesota, designed by Frank Lloyd Wright in 1912.

Engelhard Court is an indoor sculpture garden with large-scale architectural elements, including the lovely stained-glass and mosaic loggia from Louis Comfort Tiffany's Long Island estate and the facade of an 1824 United States Branch Bank that stood on Wall Street.

The Lighthouse at Two Lights (1929) by Edward Hopper

ANCIENT NEAR EASTERN AND ISLAMIC ART

M ASSIVE STONE SCULPTURES of human-headed winged lions, once guardians of the 9th-century BC Assyrian

Mysterious in identity and origin, a rare 5,000-year-old copper head from the Near East

palace of Assurnasirpal II, sit at the entrance to the Ancient Near Eastern galleries. Inside is a collection spanning 7,000 years, rich in Iranian bronzes, Anatolian ivories, Sumerian sculptures, and Achaemenian and Sassanian works in silver and gold. An adjacent gallery area displays the diversity of Islamic art from the 7th to the 19th century; glass and metalwork from Egypt, Syria and Mesopotamia; royal miniatures from the courts of Persia and Mughal India; rugs of the 16th and 17th centuries; and an 18th-century room from Syria.

ARMS AND ARMOR

M OUNTED KNIGHTS in full armor charge at each other across the equestrian court here. These galleries are a favorite with children and anyone moved by medieval romance or thrilled by power.

There are suits of armor, rapiers and sabers with hilts of precious stones and gold, firearms inlaid with ivory and mother-of-pearl, plus colorful heraldic banners and shields.

The pistol of Holy Roman Emperor Charles V (16th century)

Highlights include the armor of gentleman-pirate George Clifford, a favorite of Queen Elizabeth I. The rainbow-colored armor of a 14th-century Japanese shogun and a collection of Wild West revolvers that once belonged to gunmaker Samuel Colt are also exhibited here.

ORIENTAL AND ASIAN ART

The Old Plum, a Japanese paper screen from the early Edo period (about 1650)

MANY OUTSTANDING galleries contain masterpieces of Chinese, Japanese, Korean, Indian and Southeast Asian art, dating from the second millennium BC to the 20th century. A full-scale Ming-style Chinese scholar's garden was built by craftspeople from Souzhou as part of the first cultural exchange between the United States and the People's Republic of China. The museum also has one of the finest collections of Sung and Yuan paintings in the world, Chinese Buddhist monumental sculptures, fine Chinese ceramics and jade and an important display of the arts of ancient China.

The full range of Japanese arts is represented in a breathtaking suite of ten galleries featuring chronological and thematic displays of Japanese lacquer, ceramics, painting, sculpture, textiles and screens. Indian, Southeast Asian and Korean galleries display superb sculptures and other arts from these regions.

COSTUME INSTITUTE

THERE IS ALWAYS a portion of the 45,000-piece collection of costumes, dating from the 17th century to the present, on display in these new state-of-the-art galleries. Here, the Institute maintains a definitive compendium of fashionable dress, from the elaborately embroidered dresses of the late 1600s to the shocking-pink evening dresses of Elsa Schiaparelli, complete with hats, scarves, gloves, handbags and other accessories. There are also the designs of Worth, Quant and Balenciaga, as well as gowns from the Napoleonic and Victorian eras, the costumes of the Ballets Russes and even David Bowie's sequined jockstrap.

The regional portion of the collection is rich with folk costumes from Europe, Asia, Africa and the Americas.

The Institute is so sophisticated in its understanding of conservation techniques that it has been called upon to advise NASA on the cleaning of astronauts' spacesuits.

A 17th-century European silk-and-satin doublet

DRAWINGS, PRINTS AND PHOTOGRAPHS

A NEW GALLERY regularly displays selections from the museum's incredible holdings of drawings, prints, etchings and photographs.

Michelangelo's studies of a Libyan Sibyl for the ceiling of the Sistine Chapel (1508)

The drawings collection is especially rich in Italian and French art from the 15th to the 19th century. These are exhibited on a rotating basis because of the light-sensitive nature of works on paper.

Highlights among the 4,000 drawings include works by Michelangelo, Leonardo da Vinci, Raphael, Ingres, Goya, Rubens, Rembrandt, Tiepolo and Seurat.

The encyclopedic print collection of 12,000 individual images (and almost the same number of illustrated books) includes major works by virtually every master printmaker, from an early German woodcut called *Virgin and Child* to some of Dürer's most accomplished works and Goya's *The Giant*. Influential gallery-owner Alfred Stieglitz's donation of his own extensive collection of photographs brought here such gems as Edward Steichen's *The Flatiron*. It formed the core of a photography collection that is now also particularly strong in Modernist works dating from between the world wars.

Ephemera such as posters and advertisements form another part of this collection.

EGYPTIAN ART

ONE OF THE MUSEUM'S finest and best-loved areas is the ancient Egyptian wing, which displays every one of its thousands of holdings – from the prehistoric period to the 8th century AD. Objects range from the fragmented jasper lips of a 15th-century BC queen to the massive Temple of Dendur. Other amazing archaeological finds, most of them from museum-sponsored expeditions undertaken early in the 20th century, include sculptures of the notorious Queen Hatshepsut, who seized the Theban throne in the 16th century BC; 100 carved reliefs of Amenhotpe IV's reign; and tomb figures like the blue faïence hippo that has become the museum's mascot.

Queen Tiye, wife of Amenhotpe III (1417–1379 BC)

EUROPEAN PAINTING, SCULPTURE AND DECORATIVE ARTS

THE HEART of the museum is its awe-inspiring collection of 3,000 European paintings. The Italian works include

Young Woman with a Water Jug (1660) by Jan Vermeer

Botticelli's *Last Communion of Saint Jerome* and Bronzino's *Portrait of a Young Man*. The Dutch and Flemish canvases are among the finest in the world, with Brueghel's *The Harvesters*, several works by Rubens and Van Dyck, over a dozen Rembrandts and more Vermeers than any other museum. The collection also has masterpieces by Spanish artists El Greco, Velázquez and Goya, and by French artists Poussin and Watteau.

Some of the finest Impressionist and Post impressionist canvases reside here: 30 Monets, including *Terrace at Sainte-Adresse*; 17 Cézannes; and Van Gogh's *Cypresses*.

In the Kravis wing and adjacent galleries are works from the 60,000-object collection of European sculpture and decorative arts, such as Tullio Lombardo's marble statue of Adam; a bronze statuette of a rearing horse, after a model by Leonardo; and dozens of pieces by Degas and Rodin. Period settings include the patio from a 16th-century

Spanish castle and a series of ornate 18th-century French domestic interiors known as the Wrightsman Rooms. The Petrie European Sculpture Court features French and Italian sculpture in a beautiful garden setting reminiscent of Versailles in France.

GREEK AND ROMAN ART

A ROMAN SARCOPHAGUS from Tarsus, donated in 1870, was the first work of art in the Met's collections. It can still be seen in the museum's superbly restored Greek and Roman galleries, along with breathtaking wall panels from a villa that was buried under the lava of Vesuvius in AD 79, Etruscan mirrors, Roman portrait busts, exquisite objects in glass and silver and hundreds of Greek vases. A monumental 7th-century BC statue of a youth shows the movement toward naturalism in sculpture, and the Hellenistic *Old Market Woman* demonstrates how the Greeks had mastered realism by the 2nd century BC.

An amphora by Exekias, showing a wedding (6th century BC)

LEHMAN COLLECTION

WHAT HAD BEEN one of the the finest private art collections in the world, that of investment banker Robert Lehman, came to the museum in 1971. The Lehman Wing is a dramatic glass pyramid housing an extraordinarily varied collection rich in Old Masters and 19th-century French paintings, drawings,

---

EGYPTIAN TOMB MODELS

In 1920, a Met researcher's light illuminated a room, hitherto undiscovered for 2,000 years, in the tomb of the nobleman Mekutra. Within were 23 tiny, perfect replicas of his daily life, to ensure his comfort in the next world – his house and garden, fleet of ships and herd of cattle. Mekutra himself is there, too, on his boat, inhaling a lotus's scent and enjoying the music of his singer and harpist.

A panel from the stained-glass *Death of the Virgin* window, from the 12th-century cathedral of Saint Pierre in Troyes, France

bronzes, Renaissance majolica, Venetian glass, furniture and enamels. Among the canvases are works by north–European masters; Dutch and Spanish paintings, French masterworks, Post impressionists and Fauves.

MEDIEVAL ART

THE METROPOLITAN'S medieval collection includes works dating from the 4th to the 16th century, roughly from the fall of Rome to the beginning of the Renaissance. It is split between the main museum and its uptown branch, the Cloisters *(see pp234–7)*. In the main building are a chalice once thought to be the Holy Grail, six silver Byzantine plates showing scenes from the life of David, a 1301 pulpit by Giovanni Pisano in the shape of an eagle, several monumental sculptures of the Virgin and Child, plus a huge choir screen from Spain. Other exhibits include Migration jewelry, liturgical vessels, stained glass, ivories and 14th- and 15-century tapestries.

MUSICAL INSTRUMENTS

THE WORLD'S OLDEST piano, Andrés Segovia's guitars and a sitar shaped like a peacock are some of the features of a broad and sometimes quirky collection of musical instruments that spans six continents and dates from prehistory to the present. The instruments illustrate the history of music and performance, and most of them are conserved to remain in playable condition.

Worth particular mention are instruments from the European courts of the Middle Ages and the Renaissance; rare violins; spinets and harpsichords; instruments inlaid with precious materials; a fully equipped traditional violin-maker's work-shop; as well as African drums; Asian *pi-pas;* or lutes; and Native American pipes. Visitors can use audio equipment to hear many of the instruments playing the music of their day.

Stradivari violin from Cremona, Italy (1691)

TWENTIETH-CENTURY ART

SINCE ITS FOUNDATION in 1870, the museum has been acquiring contemporary art, but it was not until 1987 that a permanent home for 20th-century art was built – the Lila Acheson Wallace Wing. Other museums in New York have larger collections of modern art, but this display space is considered among the finest. European and American works from 1900 onward are featured on three levels, starting with Europeans such as Picasso, Kandinsky and Bonnard. The collection's greatest strength lies in its collection of modern American art, with works by New York school "The Eight," including John Sloan; such Modernists as Charles Demuth and Georgia O'Keeffe; American Regionalist Grant Wood; Abstract Expressionists Willem de Kooning; and such Color Field painters as Clyfford Still.

Grant Wood's view of *The Midnight Ride of Paul Revere* (1931)

Special areas of the wing house Art Nouveau and Art Deco furniture and metalwork; a large collection of works on paper by Paul Klee; and the Sculpture Gallery, with its large-scale sculptures and canvases.

Gems of the collection include Picasso's portrait of Gertrude Stein, Matisse's *Nasturtiums and "Dance,"* Demuth's *I Saw the Figure 5 in Gold,* Jackson Pollock's *Autumn Rhythm* and Andy Warhol's last self-portrait.

Each year the Cantor Roof Garden at the top of the wing features a new installation of contemporary sculpture, especially dramatic against the backdrop of the New York skyline and Central Park.

Book cover (1916) by illustrator N.C. Wyeth

Society of Illustrators **⑫**

128 E 63rd St. **Map** 13 A2. **☎** 838-2560. **Ⓜ** Lexington Ave. **Open** 10am–5pm Wed–Fri, 10am– 8pm Tue, noon–4pm Sat. ⓐ ⓑ restricted. ⓩ ⓘ

ESTABLISHED IN 1901, this society was formed to promote the illustrator's art. Its notable roster included Charles Dana Gibson, N.C. Wyeth and Howard Pyle. It was at first concerned with education and public service, and held occasional exhibits. In 1981, the Museum of American Illustration opened in two galleries. Changing thematic exhibitions show the history of book and magazine illustration, with an annual exhibition of the year's finest American illustrations.

Abigail Adams Smith Museum **⑬**

421 E 61st St. **Map** 13 C3. **☎** 838-6878. **Ⓜ** Lexington Ave, 59th St. **Open** 11am–4pm Tue–Sun, 4pm–9pm. Jun & Jul. **Closed** Aug, public hols. **Adm charge.** ⓧ ⓩ ⓘ

BUILT IN 1799, this federal-style stone stable once belonged to Abigail Adams Smith, President John Adams's daughter. The house burned down in 1826; the stable was renovated as an inn, then as a home, and, later as a store selling colonial antiques.

It was acquired by the Colonial Dames of America in 1924 and turned into a charming re-creation of a Federal home. Costumed guides show visitors through the rooms, pointing out the treasures, including Chinese porcelain, Aubusson carpets, Sheraton chests and a Duncan Phyfe sofa. In one bedroom, a gown belonging to Abigail Adams Smith is stored in an antique wardrobe; the same room holds a baby's cradle and children's toys. An 18th-century-style garden has been planted around the house.

Henderson Place **⑭**

Map 18 D3. **Ⓜ** 86th St.

Queen Anne row houses at Henderson Place

NOW SURROUNDED by modern apartment blocks, this enclave of 24 red-brick Queen Anne row houses was built in 1882. The row houses were commissioned by John C. Henderson, a hat-maker, as a self-contained community. The elegant Lamb & Rich design has gray slate roof gables, pediments, parapets, chimneys and dormer windows forming patterns, and a turret marking the corner of each block.

Carl Schurz Park promenade

Carl Schurz Park **⑮**

Map 18 D3. **Ⓜ** 86th St.

LAID OUT IN 1891, this park along the East River has a wide promenade over the East River Drive. It offers fine vistas of the river and the turbulent waters of Hell Gate, where the river meets Long Island Sound. It is named after Carl Schurz, a native who became Secretary of the Interior (1869–75). The first part of the promenade is the John Finlay Walk, named for an editor of the *New York Times* known for his hiking prowess. One of the city's most pleasant green escapes, the park's grassy areas are filled with basking New Yorkers on sunny days.

Gracie Mansion **⑯**

East End Ave at 88th St. **Map** 18 D3. **☎** 570-4751. **Ⓜ** 86th St. **Open** 10am, 11am, 1pm, 2pm Wed for prebooked guided tours only. **Adm charge.** ⓧ ⓩ ⓘ

THIS GRACIOUS, balconied wooden 1799 country home is the official mayor's residence. Built by wealthy merchant Archibald Gracie, it is one of the best Federal houses left in New York.

The house was acquired by the city in 1887 and was the first home of the Museum of the City of New York. Mayor Fiorello La Guardia moved in in 1942 after nine years in

Front view of Gracie Mansion

office, preferring it to a 75-room palace on Riverside Drive – he said that even the modest Gracie Mansion was much too fancy for him. La Guardia, "the Little Flower" (from Fiorello), fought corruption in the city and reformed New York.

Church of the Holy Trinity ⓱

316 E 88th St. **Map** 17 B3.
☎ 289-4100. Ⓜ 86th St. **Open** 9am–5pm Mon–Fri, 7:30am–2pm Sun. 🕇 winter: 8am, 9am, 11am, 7pm Sun; 6:30pm Wed; summer: 8am, 10am. 📷

Arched doorway of the Church of the Holy Trinity

DELIGHTFULLY PLACED in a serene garden setting, this church was constructed in 1889 of glowing golden brick and terra-cotta in French Renaissance style. It boasts one of New York's best bell towers, which holds a handsome wrought-iron clock with brass hands. The arched doorway is richly decorated with carved images of the saints and prophets.

The complex was donated by Serena Rhinelander in memory of her father and grandfather. The land was part of the Rhinelander farm, which the family had owned for 100 years.

Farther down at 350 E. 88th Street is the Rhinelander Children's Center, also a gift, and the headquarters of the Children's Aid Society.

St. Nicholas Russian Orthodox Cathedral ⓲

15 E 97th St. **Map** 16 F1.
☎ 289-1915. Ⓜ 96 St. **Open** by appt. 🕇 6pm Sat, 10:00am Sun (Russian). 📷

THIS REALLY IS "Moscow on the Hudson." Built in Muscovite Baroque style in 1902, it has five onion domes crowned with crosses, and blue and yellow tiles on a red brick and white stone facade. Among the early worshipers were White Russians who had fled the first uprisings at home, mostly intellectuals and aristocrats who soon became a part of New York society. Later, there were more waves of refugees, dissidents and defectors.

The cathedral now serves a scattered community, and the congregation is small. Mass is celebrated in Russian with great pomp and dignity.

The cathedral is filled with the scent of incense. The high central sanctuary has marble columns with blue and white trim above. Ornate wooden screens trimmed with gold enclose the altar. It is unique, an unexpected find on a side street in this staid part of Manhattan.

Facade and domes of St. Nicholas Russian Cathedral

Facade of the Museum of the City of New York

Museum of the City of New York ⓳

5th Ave at 103rd St. **Map** 21 C5.
☎ 534-1672. Ⓜ 103rd St. **Open** 10am–5pm Wed–Sat, 12–5pm Sun. **Closed** public hols. **Donations** welcome. 📷 ♿ 📁 🛍

FOUNDED IN 1923 and at first housed in Gracie Mansion, this museum is dedicated to New York's development from its earliest beginnings, shown in costumes, paintings, furnishings, toys and a range of fascinating memorabilia.

Housed in this handsome Georgian Colonial building since 1932, it is noted for the period rooms from actual homes, including John D. Rockefeller's bedroom and dressing room, and for its wonderful collection of toys, dolls and dollhouses dating from 1769. Start with *The Big Apple* video, then visit the exhibition, "Broadway! 125 Years of Musical Theater." The second floor has a magnificent collection of silver objects dating from 1678 to 1984. The Alexander Hamilton Gallery contains furniture and paintings that once belonged to the first Secretary of the Treasury.

The impressive collection housed in the basement includes antique fire equipment, paintings, maps and prints all relating to city history.

Whitney Museum of American Art ❼

T HE WHITNEY MUSEUM is the foremost showcase for American art of this century. It was founded in 1930 by sculptor Gertrude Vanderbilt Whitney after the Metropolitan Museum of Art turned down her collection of works by living artists including George Bellows and Edward Hopper. In 1966 the museum moved to the present inverted pyramid building designed by Marcel Breuer. The Whitney Biennial show is the most significant survey of new trends in American art.

The cantilevered facade of the Whitney Museum

Green Coca-Cola Bottles
Andy Warhol's 1962 work is a commentary on mass production and monopoly.

The White Calico Flower
Georgia O'Keeffe's enlarged flower paintings have an abstract quality, as in this 1931 example.

Little Big Painting
The 1965 work by Roy Lichtenstein is a comic critique of Abstract Expressionist painting.

MUSEUM GUIDE
There are no permanent displays here; the only item always on exhibit is Alexander Calder's sculpture Circus, situated on the first floor. Changing exhibitions occupy the second, third and fourth floors.

Early Sunday Morning *(1930)*
Edward Hopper's paintings often convey the emptiness of American city life.

Dempsey and Firpo
In 1924, George Bellows depicted one of the most famous prizefights of the century.

Three Flags *(1958)*
Jasper Johns's use of familiar objects in an abstract form was influential in the development of Pop art.

Owh! In San Paõ *(1951)*
In this painting by Stuart Davis, abstract forms are combined with lettering to create a unique and distinctive American style.

Circus *(1926–31)*
Alexander Calder's fanciful creation is always on display.

Tango *(1919)*
This is considered Polish-born Elie Nadelman's greatest wood sculpture.

Hudson River Landscape *(1951)*
This steel sculpture is one of David Smith's most influential works.

Frick Collection ❽

THE PRICELESS ART collection of steel magnate Henry Clay Frick (1849–1919) is exhibited in a residential setting amid the furnishings of his opulent mansion, providing a rare glimpse of how the extremely wealthy lived in New York's gilded age. Frick intended the collection to be a memorial to himself and bequeathed the entire house to the nation on his death. The collection includes old master paintings, French furniture, Limoges enamels and Oriental rugs.

Fifth Avenue facade of the Frick Collection

Colonnade
Garden Court

The Harbor of Dieppe *(1826)*
J.M.W. Turner was criticized by some sceptical contemporaries for depicting this northern European port suffused with light.

The White Horse *(1819)*
John Constable based this painting on a familiar scene from his Suffolk home.

Library

West
Gallery

**Limoges
Enamel**
The collection of enamels includes The Seven Sorrows of the Virgin *(1500–50).*

Living
Hall

STAR PAINTINGS

★ **Sir Thomas More by Hans Holbein**

★ **Mall in St. James's Park by Thomas Gainsborough**

★ **Officer and the Laughing Girl by Jan Vermeer**

★ **Lady Meux by James A.M. Whistler**

★ **Sir Thomas More** *(1527)*
Holbein's portrait of Henry VIII's Lord Chancellor was painted eight years before More's execution for treason.

GALLERY GUIDE
Of special interest are the skylit West Gallery, offering oils by Vermeer, Hals and Rembrandt; the East Gallery, featuring Whistler; the Library and Dining Room, devoted to English works; and the Living Hall with works by Titian, Bellini and Holbein.

★ **Lady Meux** *(1881)*
Before marrying a brewery baron, the coquettish young Lady Meux was an actress. This was Whistler's second of three portraits of her.

East Gallery

★ **Officer and the Laughing Girl** *(1655–60)*
Jan Vermeer is unique among 17th-century Dutch painters for his bold use of light and shadow.

KEY TO FLOOR PLAN

☐ Exhibition space

☐ Non-exhibition space

Stairs to lower gallery

Main entrance

Fowling and Horticulture *(1750–52)*
François Boucher painted a series of panels for Madame de Pompadour. This one reflects her interest in exotic birds and botany.

Dining Room

Fragonard Room

The Pursuit
This is part of The Progress of Love *(1771–3 and 1790–91), by Jean-Honoré Fragonard. The series of paintings depicts the events of an idealized courtship.*

★ **Mall in St. James's Park** *(1783)*
The three central figures in Thomas Gainsborough's London landscape may be the daughters of George III.

CENTRAL PARK

THE CITY'S "BACKYARD" was created by Frederick Law Olmsted and Calvert Vaux in 1858 on an unpromising site of quarries, pig farms, swampland and shacks. Ten million cartloads of stone and earth turned it into the lush 843-acre (340-ha) park of today. There are scenic hills, lakes and lush meadows, dotted throughout with out-

Statues, Delacorte Theater *(see p206)*

crops of Manhattan bedrock and planted with more than 500,000 trees and shrubs. Over the years the park has blossomed, with playgrounds and skating rinks, plus ball fields and spaces for everything from chess and croquet to concerts and events for the thousands. Cars are banned on weekends, giving bicyclists and joggers the right-of-way.

SIGHTS AT A GLANCE

Historic Buildings
The Dairy ❶
Belvedere Castle ❸

Monuments and Statues
Strawberry Fields ❷
Bethesda Fountain and Terrace ❺
Bow Bridge ❹

Lakes and Gardens
Conservatory Water ❻
Central Park Wildlife Center ❼
Conservatory Garden ❽

SEE ALSO

- **Street Finder**, maps 12, 16

- **Restaurants** pp290–92

GETTING THERE

Subway lines B and C run the length of the park on the Upper West Side, with stops at 59th, 72nd, 81st, 86th, 96th and 103rd Sts. The 59th St/Columbus Circle stop is served by the 1 and 9 Broadway/7th Ave lines, the 8th Ave lines; the N and R Broadway local trains stop at 57th St and 5th Ave at the southern end of the park. Bus routes M1, M2, M3 and M4 run along the eastern edge of the park.

One of Central Park's mounted patrolmen

KEY

Tour map

Ⓜ Subway station

0 meters 500
0 yards 500

Bird's-eye view of the park

A Tour of Central Park

O N A SHORT VISIT, a walking tour from 59th to 79th streets takes in some of Central Park's loveliest features, from the dense wooded Ramble to the open formal spaces of Bethesda Terrace. Along the way, you will see artificial lakes and some of the 30 graceful bridges and arches, no two alike, that link some 58 miles (93 km) of footpaths, bridle paths and roads in the park. In summer the park is often several degrees cooler than the city streets around it, and thus is a favorite retreat.

★ Strawberry Fields

One of the park's most visited spots, this peaceful area was created in memory of John Lennon, who lived nearby ❷

★ Bethesda Fountain and Terrace

The richly ornamented formal terrace overlooks the Lake and the wooded shores of the Ramble ❺

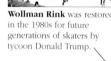

Wollman Rink was restored in the 1980s for future generations of skaters by tycoon Donald Trump.

Central Park Wildlife Center

Three climate zones are home to over 100 species of animals ❼

The Pond

Plaza Hotel *(see p179)*

Frick Collection *(see pp200–1)*

Hans Christian Andersen's statue is a favorite Central Park landmark for children. It is on the west side of Conservatory Water and is a popular site for storytelling in the summer.

★ The Dairy

This Victorian Gothic building houses the Visitor Center. Make it your first stop and pick up a calendar of park events ❶

Bow Bridge
This cast-iron bridge links the Ramble with Cherry Hill by a graceful arch, 60 ft (18 m) above the Lake 4

LOCATOR MAP
See Manhattan Map pp12–13

Alice in Wonderland is immortalized in bronze at the northern end of Conservatory Water, along with her friends the Cheshire Cat, the Mad Hatter and the Dormouse. Children love to slide down her toadstool seat.

STAR SIGHTS

★ **The Dairy**

★ **Strawberry Fields**

★ **Belvedere Castle**

★ **Bethesda Fountain**

★ **Conservatory Water**

...ota
...ding
(...216)

San Remo Apartments
(see p212)

American Museum of Natural History
(see pp214–15)

GREAT LAWN

TRANSVERSE

79TH ST

86TH ST TRANSVERSE

AVENUE

Metropolitan Museum *(see pp188–95)*

Obelisk

The Ramble is a wooded area of 37 acres (15 ha), crisscrossed by paths and streams. It is a paradise for bird-watchers – over 250 species have been spotted in the park, which is on the Atlantic migration flyway.

Reservoir

Guggenheim Museum
(see pp186–87)

★ **Belvedere Castle**
From the terraces there are unequaled views of the city and surrounding park. Within the stone walls is the Central Park Learning Center 3

★ **Conservatory Water**
From March to November, this is the scene of model boat races each Saturday. Many of the tiny craft are stored in the boathouse that adjoins the Lake 6

The Carousel, part of the park's Children's District

The Dairy ❶

Map 12 F2. 🄲 794-6564.
Ⓜ *Fifth Ave.* **Open** *Apr–Oct: 10am–5pm Tue–Sun; Nov–Mar: 110am–4pm Tue–Sun.*
Slide show. 🄸

Now used as the park information center, this charming building of natural stone was planned as part of the "Children's District" of the park, which included a playground, the Carousel, a Children's Cottage and stable. In 1873, there were cows grazing on the meadows in front of the Dairy, a ewe and her lambs feeding nearby, and chickens, guinea fowl and peacocks roaming the lawn. City children could get fresh milk and other refreshments here. Over the years, the Dairy deteriorated, being used as a shed until restoration in 1979, done according to original photographs and drawings. The Dairy is the place to begin exploring the lush and leafy park; maps and details of events can be obtained here. The less energetic can rent chess and checkers sets for use on the pretty inlaid boards of the *kinderberg*, the charming little "children's hill" nearby.

Strawberry Fields ❷

Map 12 E1. Ⓜ *72nd St.*

The restoration of this teardrop-shaped section of the park was Yoko Ono's tribute in memory of her slain husband, John Lennon. They lived in the Dakota apartments overlooking this spot *(see p216)*. Gifts for the garden came from all over the world. A mosaic set in the pathway, inscribed with the word *Imagine* (named for Lennon's famous song), was a gift from the city of Naples in Italy.

This broad expanse of the park's landscape was designed by Vaux and Olmsted. Now it is an international peace garden, with 161 species of plants (one from every country of the world), including jetbead, roses, witch hazel, birches – and strawberries.

Belvedere Castle ❸

Map 16 E4. 🄲 772-0210.
Ⓜ *81st St.* **Open** *10am–5pm Tue–Sun.* 🄸 🄳 *to main floor only.*

This stone castle atop Vista Rock, complete with tower and turrets, offers one of the best views of the park and the city from its lookout on the rooftop. Inside is the Henry Luce Nature Observatory, with a delightful exhibit telling inquisitive young visitors about the surprising variety of wildlife to be found in the park.

The view to the north from the castle allows you to look down into

Belvedere Castle with its lookout over the park

the Delacorte Theater, home to the free productions of Shakespeare in the Park every summer, featuring big-name stars *(see p335)*. The theater was the gift of George T. Delacorte. Publisher and founder of Dell paperbacks, Delacorte was a delightful philanthropist who was responsible for many of the park's pleasures.

Bow Bridge ❹

Map 16 E5. Ⓜ *72nd St.*

This is one of the park's seven original cast-iron bridges and is considered one of the finest. It was designed by Vaux as a bow tying together the two large sections of the lake. In the 19th century, when the Lake was used for ice skating, a red ball was hoisted from a bell tower on Vista Rock to signal that the ice was safe. The bridge offers expansive views of the park and the buildings bordering it on both the east and west sides.

A tranquil scene in Central Park, overlooked by exclusive apartments

An 1864 print of Bethesda Fountain and Terrace

Bethesda Fountain and Terrace ❺

Map 12 E1. **M** 72nd St.

SITUATED BETWEEN the Lake and the Mall, this is the architectural heart of the park, a formal element in the naturalistic landscape. The fountain was dedicated in 1873. The statue, *Angel of the Waters*, marked the opening of the Croton Aqueduct system in 1842, bringing the city its first supply of pure water; its name refers to a biblical account of a healing angel at the pool of Bethesda in Jerusalem. The Spanish-style detailing, such as the sculptured double staircase, tiles and friezes, is by Jacob Wrey Mould.

The terrace is one of the best spots to relax and take in some people-watching.

Conservatory Water ❻

Map 16 F5. **M** 77th St.

BETTER KNOWN as the Model Boat Pond, this stretch of water is home to model yacht races every weekend.

At the north end of the lake, a sculpture of Alice in Wonderland is a delight for children. It was commissioned by George T. Delacorte in honor of his wife. He himself is immortalized in caricature as the Mad Hatter. On the west bank, free story hours are held at a statue of Hans Christian Andersen, portrayed reading from his own story, "The Ugly Duckling," while its hero waddles at his feet. Like that of Alice, this statue is climbed on by small children, who especially like to snuggle in the author's lap.

Conservatory Water's literary links continue into adolescence: it is here that J.D. Salinger's Holden Caulfield comes to tell the ducks his troubles in *The Catcher in the Rye*.

Central Park Wildlife Center ❼

Map 12 F2. **C** 439-6500. **M** Fifth Ave. **Open** Year round 10am–5pm Mon–Fri, 10:30am–5:30pm Sat, Sun, & hols.
Adm charge. 📷 ♿ 💻 🚻

REOPENED IN 1988 after four years of reconstruction, this imaginative zoo won plaudits for its creative and humane use of small space. More than 100 species of animals are represented in three climate zones, the Tropics, the Polar Circle and the California coast. An equatorial rain forest is home to monkeys and free-flying birds, while penguins and polar bears populate an Arctic landscape that allows views both above and under water.

Near the entrance to the Tisch Children's Zoo is the much-loved Delacorte Clock, another example of the whimsical generosity of George T. Delacorte. Every half hour, bronze musical animals (such as a goat playing pan pipes) circle the clock playing nursery rhymes. Toward Willowdell Arch is another children's favorite – the memorial to Balto, lead dog of a team of huskies that made a heroic journey across Alaska to deliver serum for a diphtheria epidemic.

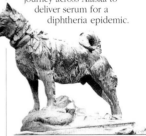

Statue of Balto, the heroic husky sled dog

Conservatory Garden ❽

Map 21 B5. **M** Central Pk N, 103rd St. **C** 860-1382.

THE VANDERBILT GATE on Fifth Avenue is the entry to three formal gardens filled with thousands of flowering trees and shrubs. The Central Garden has a large lawn with yew hedges and ends in a semicircle of hedges and shrubs crowned by a wisteria pergola. On either side are blooming gardens of Mary and Dickon, from Frances Hodgson Burnett's *The Secret Garden*. Beyond is a slope featuring thousands of native wildflowers, spreading into the park beyond. The North Garden, centered around the bronze *Fountain of the Three Dancing Maidens*, puts on a brief but brilliant display of annuals each summer.

Polar bear in the Wildlife Center

UPPER WEST SIDE

**Indian mask, Museum
of Natural History**

THIS AREA became residential only in the 1870s, when the Ninth Avenue El *(see pp24–5)* made commuting to midtown possible for the first time. When the Dakota, New York's first luxury apartment house, was built between 1880 and 1884, the city finally began to grade and level the streets. Buildings soon sprang up along Broadway and Central Park West, and today the area is bustling and diverse. The cross streets, dating mainly from the 1890s, boast many fine brownstone row houses. Many cultural institutions are here, including Lincoln Center and the American Museum of Natural History.

SIGHTS AT A GLANCE

Historic Streets and Buildings
Twin Towers of Central Park West ❶
The Dakota ❾
Pomander Walk ⓭
Riverside Drive and Park ⓮
The Dorilton ⓱

Museums and Galleries
Museum of American Folk Art ❼
New-York Historical Society ❿
American Museum of Natural History pp214–15 ⓫
Hayden Planetarium ⓬
Children's Museum of Manhattan ⓯

Famous Theaters
Lincoln Center for the Performing Arts ❷
New York State Theater ❸
Metropolitan Opera House ❹
Lincoln Center Theater ❺
Avery Fisher Hall ❻

Landmark Hotels and Restaurants
Hotel des Artistes ❽
The Ansonia ⓰

GETTING THERE
By subway, take the 6th Ave B or D, the 7th Ave/Broadway 1/9, 2 and 3, or the 8th Ave A, C and E trains. By bus, the M10 (Central Park West), M7, M11, M104 and M5 or the M66, M72, M79, M86 and M96 crosstown buses.

SEE ALSO
• *Street Finder*, maps 11, 15
• *Where to Stay* pp274–75
• *Restaurants* pp290-92

Stone figure on the facade of the Hotel des Artistes

KEY

  Street-by-Street map

 M Subway station

The facade of 14 Riverside Drive

Street by Street: Lincoln Center

Lincoln center was conceived when both the Metropolitan Opera House and the New York Philharmonic required homes, and a large tract on Manhattan's west side was in dire need of revitalization. The notion of a single complex where different performing arts could exist side by side seems natural today, but in the 1950s it was considered both daring and risky. Today Lincoln Center has proved itself by drawing audiences of five million each year. Proximity to its halls prompts both performers and arts lovers to live nearby.

★ **Lincoln Center for the Performing Arts**
Dance, music and theater come together in this fine contemporary complex. It is also a great place to sit around the reflecting fountain and people-watch ❷

Lincoln Center Theater
The Vivian Beaumont and the Mitzi E. Newhouse theaters are both housed in this building ❺

Composer Leonard Bernstein's famous musical *West Side Story,* which was based on the Romeo and Juliet theme, was set in the impoverished streets around what is now Lincoln Center. Bernstein was later instrumental in setting up the large music complex.

The Guggenheim Bandshell in Damrosch Park is the site of free concerts.

The New York State Theater
This is the home of the New York City Ballet, as well as an opera company. The theater seats 2,737 people ❸

AMSTERDAM AVENUE

COLUMBUS

W 62 ND STREET

Metropolitan Opera House
Lincoln Center's focus is the Opera House. The café at the top of the lobby offers wonderful plaza views ❹

The College Board Building is an Art Deco delight that now houses condominiums and the administrative offices of the College Board, developers of the college entrance exam.

Museum of American Folk Art
Quilting and naive painting are some of the arts displayed here 7

Early American quilt

James Dean once lived in a one-room apartment on the top floor at 19 West 68th Street.

LOCATOR MAP
see Manhattan Map pp12–13

KEY

- - - Suggested route

0 meters 100
0 yards 100

To 72nd Street subway (4 blocks)

★ **Hotel des Artistes**
Artists Isadora Duncan, Noël Coward and Norman Rockwell once lived here. It also houses a much-praised restaurant (see p296) 8

W 67TH STREET

65TH STREET

The American Broadcasting Company is housed in this castle-like building, formerly an armory.

55 Central Park West is the Art Deco apartment building that featured in the film *Ghostbusters*.

The Society for Ethical Culture was one of the city's first Art Nouveau buildings. It also houses a school.

To 59th Street subway (2 blocks)

Central Park West is home to many celebrities, who like the privacy of its exclusive apartments.

Century Apartments
The Century's twin towers are visible from the park, making it a New York landmark 1

STAR SIGHTS

★ Lincoln Center

★ Hotel des Artistes

The San Remo, a twin-towered apartment house designed by Emery Roth

Twin Towers of Central Park West ❶

Map 12 D1, 12 D2, 16 D3, 16 D5.
Ⓜ *59th St–Columbus Circle, 72nd St. Not open to public.*

AMONG THE MOST familiar landmarks on the New York skyline are the four twin-towered apartment houses on Central Park West. Built from 1929 and 1931, just before the Great Depression halted all luxury construction, they are now among the most highly sought-after residences in New York.

Admired today for their grace and architectural detail, they were designed in response to a city planning law allowing taller apartments if set backs and towers were used.

Emery Roth designed the San Remo (145 CPW), whose tenants have included Dustin Hoffman, Paul Simon and Diane Keaton. Madonna was turned down by the residents' committee and lives close by at One West 64th Street, next door to the New York Society for Ethical Culture. The towers on the Eldorado (300 CPW), also designed by Roth, are crowned by futuristic pinnacles. Celebrities here have included Groucho Marx, Marilyn Monroe and Richard Dreyfuss. The Majestic (115 CPW) and the Century (25 CPW) are both sleek classics by Art Deco designer Irwin S. Chanin.

Lincoln Center for the Performing Arts ❷

Map 11 C2. ⬛ 546-2656. Ⓜ *65th St.* ⬛ ⬛ *875-5350.* ⬛ ⬛ *See Entertainment pp338–9.*

IN MAY 1959, President Dwight D. Eisenhower traveled to New York to turn a shovelful of earth, Leonard Bernstein lifted his baton, the New York Philharmonic and the Juilliard Chorus broke into the *Hallelujah Chorus* – and New York's most important cultural center was born.

It was soon to cover 15 acres (6 ha) on the site of the slums that had been the setting for Bernstein's classic musical *West Side Story.*

The plaza fountain is by Philip Johnson, and the sculpture in the reflecting pool, *Reclining Figure*, is by Henry Moore.

Guided tours are the best way to see the complex.

New York State Theater ❸

Lincoln Center. **Map** 11 D2. ⬛ 870-5570. Ⓜ *66th St.* ⬛ ⬛ ⬛ ⬛ *See Entertainment pp334–5.*

THE HOME BASE for the highly acclaimed New York City Ballet and the New York City Opera, a troupe devoted to presenting opera at popular prices, is a Philip Johnson design. It was inaugurated in 1964.

Gargantuan white marble sculptures by Elie Nadelman dominate the vast four-story foyer. The theater seats 2,800 people. Because of its rhinestone lights and chandeliers both inside and out, some have described the theater as "a little jewel box."

Metropolitan Opera House ❹

Lincoln Center. **Map** 11 D2. ⬛ 362-6000. Ⓜ *66th St.* ⬛ ⬛ ⬛ ⬛ *See Entertainment pp338–9.*

HOME TO THE Metropolitan Opera Company and the American Ballet Theater, "the Met" is certainly the most spectacular of Lincoln Center's buildings and the focal point of the plaza. Five great arched windows offer views of the opulent foyer and two radiant murals by Marc Chagall. (You can't see them in the mornings when they are protected from the sun.)

Central plaza at Lincoln Center

Inside there are curved white marble stairs, miles of plush red carpeting and exquisite starburst crystal chandeliers

Free open-air concerts are held at the Guggenheim Bandshell

that are raised to the ceiling just before each performance. All the greats have sung here, including Maria Callas, Jessye Norman and Luciano Pavarotti. First nights are glittering, star-studded occasions.

The Guggenheim Bandshell, in Damrosch Park next to the Met, is a popular concert site featuring music from opera to jazz. The high point of the season is the Lincoln Center Out-of-Doors Festival that takes place in August.

Lincoln Center Theater ❺

Lincoln Center. **Map** 11 C2.
362-7600 (Beaumont and Newhouse), 870-1630 (Library).
66th St. See *Entertainment* pp338–9.

Two THEATERS MAKE up this innovative complex, presenting eclectic and often experimental drama.

The theaters are the 1000-seat Vivian Beaumont and the smaller, more intimate 280-seat Mitzi E. Newhouse.

Works by some of New York's best modern playwrights have been featured at the Beaumont. The theater's inaugural performance in 1962 was Arthur Miller's *After the Fall*.

The size of the Newhouse suits workshop-style plays, but it can still make the news with theatrical gems such as Robin Williams and Steve Martin in a production of

Samuel Beckett's *Waiting for Godot*. The New York Public Library for the Performing Arts (closed for renovation until late fall 2000) houses exhibits including cylinders of early Met performances and original scores and playbills.

Avery Fisher Hall ❻

Lincoln Center. **Map** 11 C2. 875-5030. 66th St. See *Entertainment* p338–9.

Home TO THE New York Philharmonic, America's oldest orchestra, as well as Lincoln Center's own Great Performers; Mostly Mozart Festival; and Jazz at Lincoln Center, Avery Fisher Hall opened in 1962 as Philharmonic Hall. While critics initially complained about the awful acoustics, several structural modifications, including one in 1992, have rendered the Hall an acoustic gem, comparing favorably with the great concert halls of the world.

For a small fee, the public can attend rehearsals on Thursday mornings.

Museum of American Folk Art ❼

Lincoln Sq. **Map** 12 D2. 977-7170. 66th St. **Open** 11:30am–7:30pm Tue–Sun.

CONCERTGOERS ATTENDING Lincoln Center events are among the many to discover and delight in this attractive, small modern gallery, which opened here in 1989 to show American folk art. The exhibits include quilts, carvings and paintings from the museum's permanent collection as well as changing displays. There are also special

programs for children and crafts demonstrations.

A huge weathervane in the shape of an American Indian and named for the legendary chief Tammany, presides over the central atrium. The museum plans a move to larger premises on West 53rd Street, but this location will remain as a branch.

Copper weathervane from the Museum of American Folk Art

Hotel des Artistes ❽

1 W 67th St. **Map** 12 D2. 362-6700. 72nd St. See *Restaurants* p296.

Built IN 1918 by George Mort Pollard, these two-story apartments were intended as working artists' studios but have attracted a variety of interesting tenants, including Alexander Woollcott, Norman Rockwell, Isadora Duncan, Rudolph Valentino and Noël Coward. The Café des Artistes is well known for its misty, romantic Howard Chandler Christy murals and its fine cuisine.

Decorative figure on the Hotel des Artistes

American Museum of Natural History ⓫

T HIS IS THE largest natural history museum in the world. Since the original building opened in 1877, the complex has grown to cover three city blocks, and today holds over 36 million artifacts. The most popular areas are the dinosaurs, meteors and the Hall of Minerals and Gems, which contains jewels valued at nearly $50 million. The new Rose Center for Earth and Space (*see p216*) adjoins the Museum.

The entrance on 77th Street

STAR EXHIBITS

★ **Barosaurus**

★ **Blue Whale**

★ **Haida Canoe**

★ **Star of India**

★ **Star of India**
This 563-carat gem is the world's largest blue star sapphire. Found in Sri Lanka, it was given to the museum by J.P. Morgan in 1901.

GALLERY GUIDE

Enter at Central Park West onto the second floor to view the barosaurus exhibit, African, Asian, Central and South American peoples and animals. First floor exhibits include ocean life, meteors, minerals and gems., and the new Hall of Biodiversity. North American Indians, birds and reptiles occupy the third floor. Dinosaurs, fossil fishes and early mammals are on the fourth floor.

★ **Blue Whale**
The blue whale is the largest of all animals, living or extinct. Its weight can exceed 150 tons. This replica is based on a female captured off the southern US coast in 1925.

★**Haida Canoe**
This 32-ft (9.7-m) seafaring war canoe of the Haida Indians was carved from the trunk of a single cedar. It stands in the 77th Street foyer.

Entrance on W. 77th St

Dinosaurs

Fourth floor

VISITORS' CHECKLIST

Central Park West at 79th St.
Map 16 D5. 769-5100.
B, C to 81st St. M7, M10,
M11, M79. **Open** 10am–5.45pm
Mon–Thu, Sun; 10am–8.45pm Fri,
Sat. Donation.

Komodo Dragons
The largest living lizards, which can grow to 10 ft (3 m), live on Komodo and other East Indian islands.

Third floor

Second floor

East African Elephants
Four of the elephants in this group were collected and mounted in the 1920s by Carl Akeley, who created the museum's Hall of African Mammals.

★ Barosaurus
The museum has the world's most complete barosaurus specimen. This exhibit, which shows a mother barosaurus rearing up to protect her baby from an attacking predator, was cast from original fossils.

Hayden Planetarium
(see p216)

First floor

Central Park West entrance

Giant Sequoia
The sequoias are among the world's oldest plants. This section has 1,342 annual rings and measures over 16 ft (4.8 m) across.

KEY TO FLOOR PLAN

☐	Dinosaurs and other fossil vertebrates
☐	Birds
☐	Fishes
☐	Mammals
☐	Meteorites, minerals and gems
☐	Human cultures
☐	Invertebrates
☐	Amphibians and reptiles
☐	Environment and ecology
☐	Memorabilia
☐	Special exhibitions
☐	Non-exhibition space

The Dakota **9**

1 W 72nd St. **Map** 12 D1. **M** *72nd St.* **Not open** *to the public.*

THE NAME AND STYLE reflect the fact that this apartment building was truly "way out West" when Henry J. Hardenberg, the architect responsible for the Plaza Hotel, designed it in 1880–84. It was New York's first luxury apartment house and was originally surrounded by squatters' shacks and wandering farm animals. Commissioned by Edward S. Clark, heir to the Singer sewing machine fortune, it is one of the city's most prestigious addresses.

The Dakota's 65 luxurious apartments have had many famous owners, including Judy Garland, Lauren Bacall, Leonard Bernstein and Boris Karloff, whose ghost is said to haunt the place. It was the setting for the film *Rosemary's Baby,* and the site of the tragic murder of former Beatle John Lennon. His widow, Yoko Ono, still lives here.

Carved Indian head over the entrance to the Dakota

New-York Historical Society **10**

170 Central Park West/77th St. **Map** 16 D5. **C** *873-3400.* **M** *81st St.* **Galleries open** *11am–5pm Tue–Sun.* **Library open** *11am–5pm Tue–Sat.* **Closed** *public hols.* **Adm charge** *for galleries.*

AUDUBON'S ORIGINAL *Birds of America* prints and over 150 Tiffany lamps are among the treasures of New York's

The Laser show at the Hayden Planetarium

oldest museum. Founded in 1804, the Society has a wide collection of paintings and decorative arts dating back to the 17th century. The portrait collection includes Gilbert Stuart's *George Washington*. There is fine furniture from the Federal period, plus an exceptional silver display.

The galleries re-opened in 1995 after a two-year closure, despite a last-minute fire and continuing financial troubles.

American Museum of Natural History **11**

See pp214–15.

Hayden Planetarium **12**

Central Park West at 81st St. **Map** 16 D4. **C** *769-5900.* **M** *81st St.* **Closed** *for major renovation and upgrading until early 2000.*

ADJOINING THE American Museum of Natural History is the new Hayden Planetarium, the centerpiece of the new Rose Center for Earth and Space. Housed within an 87-ft sphere, the Planetarium contains a technologically advanced Space Theater, the Cosmic Pathway, a 350-ft spiral ramp with a timeline chronicling 13 billion years of evolution, and a Big Bang Theater. The Hall of Planet Earth, built around dramatic rock samples and using state-of-the-art computer and video displays explaining how the Earth works, explores our planet's geologic history. Exhibits in the Hall of the Universe

present the amazing discoveries of modern astrophysics. Four zones feature hands-on interactive exhibits and extensive educational programming. The Rose Center is designed by Polshek and Partners.

Pomander Walk **13**

261–7 W 94th St. **Map** 15 C2. **M** *72nd St.*

LOOK THROUGH the gate for a delightful surprise – a double row of tiny town houses built in 1921 to look like the London mews setting of a popular play of the time.

Appropriately, it was much favored as a home by movie actors, including Rosalind Russell, Humphrey Bogart and the Gish sisters.

Facade of Pomander Walk town house

Riverside Drive and Park **14**

Map 15 B4. **M** *103rd St.*

RIVERSIDE DRIVE IS one of the city's most attractive streets – broad, with shaded, and lovely views of the Hudson River. It is lined with the opulent original town houses as well as newer apartment buildings. At 40–46, 74–77, 81–89 and 105–107 Riverside Drive are houses designed at the end of the 19th century by local architect Clarence F. True.

The curved gables, bays and arched windows seem to suit the curves of the road and the flow of the river.

The bizarrely named Cliff Dwellers' Apartments at 243 is a 1914 building with a frieze showing early Arizona cliff dwellers, complete with masks, buffalo skulls, mountain lions and rattlesnakes.

Riverside Park was designed by Frederick Law Olmsted in 1880. He also laid out Central Park *(see pp202–5)*.

Soldiers' and Sailors' monument in Riverside Park

Children's Museum of Manhattan **⑮**

212 W 83rd St. **Map** 15 C4.
☎ 721-1223. **Ⓜ** 86th St. **Open**
Sep–May: 1:30pm–5:30pm Mon, Wed, Thu; 10am–5pm Fri–Sun; Jun–Aug: 10am–5pm Wed–Sun.
Closed Jan 1, Dec 25, Thanksgiving
Adm charge. 📷 ♿ 🏛

THIS PARTICULARLY imaginative participatory museum was founded in 1973 on the premise that children learn best through play. In the "Brainatarium" the magic of the human mind is revealed in a four-minute multimedia show projected onto the domed ceiling. Using hi-tech, hands-on equipment, children can explore the five senses – not just their own, but also those of birds, insects and animals.

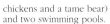

Children's Museum entrance

The Time Warner Center for Media transforms children into budding camera operators, newscasters, animators and technicians in a state-of-the-art TV studio. On weekends and holidays there are guest performers from puppeteers to storytellers in the 150-seat theater. There is also a gallery for free play.

The Ansonia **⑯**

2109 Broadway. **Map** 11 C1. **Ⓜ** 72nd St. **Not open** to the public.

THIS BEAUX ARTS gem was built in 1899 by William Earl Dodge Stokes, heir to the Phelps Dodge Company fortune, who brought French architect Paul E.M. Duboy to design a building to rival the Dakota. The hotel was converted to a condomunium in 1992. The most prominent features are the round corner tower and the two-story mansard roof adorned with single and double dormers. The building had a roof garden (complete with Dodge's menagerie: ducks,

Distinctive rounded turret of the Ansonia Hotel

chickens and a tame bear) and two swimming pools.

The hotel's thick, sound-muffling walls soon made it a favorite with the musical stars of yesteryear. Florenz Ziegfeld, Arturo Toscanini, Enrico Caruso, Leopold Stravinsky and Lily Pons were once regular guests there.

The Dorilton **⑰**

171 W 71st St. **Map** 15 C5. **Ⓜ** 72nd St. **Not open** to the public.

OPULENT DETAIL and an impressive high mansard roof adorn this apartment house. On the West 71st Street side of the building is a nine-story-high gateway. To the modern eye, the Dorilton is gloriously elaborate, but when it was first built in 1902 it provoked this reaction, reported by the *Architectural Record*: "The sight of it makes

Balcony on the Dorilton, supported by groaning figures

strong men swear and weak women shrink affrighted."

What would the critics have made of the Alexandria Condominium, at 135 West 70th Street, just a block away? Built in 1927 as the Pythian Temple, its current name stems from the lavish Egyptian-style motifs that adorned this former Masonic lodge. Many were stripped away when the building was converted to a condominium, but you can still see what the polychrome designs were like. There are lotus leaves, hieroglyphics, ornately carved columns, mythical beasts, and, in majestic splendor on the roof, two seated pharaohs.

MORNINGSIDE HEIGHTS AND HARLEM

ORNINGSIDE HEIGHTS, near the Hudson River, is home to Columbia University and two of the city's finest churches. Farther east is Hamilton Heights, situated on the border of Harlem, America's most famous black community. One way to see its highlights, which are spread over a large area, is

St. Francis of Assisi, Museo del Barrio

with one of the various tours offered, including a Sunday morning tour (*see p353*). Many tours start in Hamilton Heights, move east to the St. Nicholas Historic District, stop to enjoy the gospel choir at the Abyssinian Baptist Church, and end with a southern-style brunch at Sylvia's, Harlem's best-known restaurant.

Louis Armstrong in a stained-glass window at the new Cotton Club

SIGHTS AT A GLANCE

Historic Streets and Buildings
Columbia University **1**
St. Paul's Chapel **2**
Low Library **3**
Grant's Tomb **6**
City College of the City University of New York **7**
Hamilton Grange National Memorial **8**
Hamilton Heights Historic District **9**
St. Nicholas Historic District **10**
Mount Morris Historical District **17**

Museums and Galleries
Schomburg Center for Research into Black Culture **12**
Studio Museum in Harlem **16**
Museo del Barrio **19**

Famous Theaters
Harlem YMCA **13**
Apollo Theater **15**

Churches
Cathedral of St. John the Divine pp224–25 **4**
Riverside Church **5**
Abyssinian Baptist Church **11**

Parks and Squares
Marcus Garvey Park **18**

Landmark Restaurants
Sylvia's **14**

GETTING THERE
By subway, take the 7th Ave/Broadway local 1 and 9 trains to 116th St./Columbia University. The M4, M5, M11 and M104 buses serve the area. For Harlem, take the A, B, C or D lines to 125th St, or the M1, M2, M7 or M101/102 buses.

Carved stone column, Cathedral of St. John the Divine

SEE ALSO

- **Street Finder**, maps 19–21
- **Where to Stay** pp174–75
- **Restaurants** pp290–92

KEY

Street-by-Street map

M Subway station

0 meters 500
0 yards 500

Street by Street: Columbia University

A GREAT UNIVERSITY is as much spirit as buildings. After admiring the architecture, linger awhile on Columbia's central quadrangle in front of the Low Library, where you will see the jeans-clad future leaders of America meeting and mingling between classes. Across from the campus on both Broadway and Amsterdam Avenue are the coffee-houses and cafés where students engage in lengthy philosophical arguments, debate the topics of the day or simply unwind.

Alma Mater was sculpted by Daniel Chester French in 1903 and survived a bomb blast in the 1968 student demonstrations.

116th St./Columbia University subway (lines 1, 9)

The School of Journalism is one of Columbia's many McKim, Mead & White buildings. Founded in 1912 by publisher Joseph Pulitzer, it is the home of the Pulitzer Prize awarded for the best in letters and music.

Butler Library is Columbia's main library.

Low Library
With its imposing facade and high dome, the library dominates the main quadrangle. McKim, Mead & White designed it in 1895–97 ❸

★ **Central Quadrangle**
Columbia's first buildings were designed by McKim, Mead & White and built around a central quadrangle. This view looks across the quad toward Butler Library ❶

St. Paul's Chapel

esigned by the architects Howells &
okes in 1907, this church is known
for its fine woodwork and magni-
ficent vaulted interior. It is full of
light and has fine acoustics ❷

LOCATOR MAP
See Manhattan Map pp12–13

KEY

— — —   Suggested route

0 meters   100

0 yards   100

The Sherman Fairchild Center was built in 1977 to house the university's life sciences departments.

Student demonstrations put Columbia University in the news in 1968. The demonstrations were sparked by the university's plan to build a gymnasium in nearby Morningside Park. The protests forced the university to build elsewhere.

The Eglise de Notre Dame was built for a French-speaking congregation. Behind the altar is a replica of the grotto at Lourdes, France, the gift of a woman who believed her son was healed there.

★ **Cathedral of St. John the Divine**
If this Neo-Gothic cathedral is ever finished, it will be the largest in the

world. Although one third of the structure has not yet been built, it can hold 10,000 parishioners ❹

STAR SIGHTS

★ **Columbia University**

★ **Cathedral of St. John the Divine**

Carved stonework decorates the facade of the Cathedral.

Alma Mater statue at Low Library, Columbia University

Columbia University ❶

Main entrance at W 116th St.
Map 20 E3. 854-1754.
116th St-Columbia Univ.

THIS IS THE third location to date of one of America's oldest and finest universities. Founded in 1754 as King's College, it was first situated close to where the World Trade Center now stands.

In 1814, when a move uptown was proposed, the university approached the authorities for funding but was instead given a plot of land valued at $75,000, on which to build a new home. The university never built on the land itself, but leased it out and spent the years from 1857 to 1897 in buildings nearby. It finally sold the plot in 1985 to the leaseholders, Rockefeller Center Inc., for the sum of $400 million.

The present campus was begun in 1897 on the site of the Bloomingdale Insane Asylum. Architect Charles McKim placed the university on a terrace, serenely above street level. Its spacious lawns and plazas still create a sense of contrast in the busy city.

At last count there were over 19,000 students at this campus, 10,400 men and 8,900 women. Columbia, an Ivy League School, is noted for its law, medicine and journalism schools. Its highly distinguished faculty and alumni, past and present, include 53 Nobel laureates. Famous alumni include Isaac Asimov, J.D. Salinger, James Cagney and Joan Rivers.

St. Paul's Chapel ❷

Columbia University. **Map** 20 E3.
854-1487, 854-1540 concert info.
116th St-Columbia Univ. **Open** 10am–11pm Mon–Sat (term time), 10am–4pm (breaks). . Sun.

Interior brick vaulting of St. Paul's Chapel dome

COLUMBIA'S MOST outstanding building, built in 1904, is a mix of Italian Renaissance, Byzantine and Gothic. The interior Guastavino vaulting is of intricate patterns of aged red brick; the whole chapel is bathed in light from above.

The free organ concerts are an exceptionally fine way to appreciate the beauty and acoustics of this church. The Aeolian-Skinner pipe organ is renowned for its fine tone.

Facade of St. Paul's Chapel

Low Library ❸

Columbia University. **Map** 20 E3.
116th St-Columbia Univ.

A CLASSICAL, columned building atop three flights of stone stairs, the library was donated by Seth Low, a former mayor and college president. The statue in front of it, *Alma Mater* by Daniel Chester French, became familiar as the backdrop to the many 1968 anti–Vietnam War student demonstrations. The building is now used as offices, and its rotunda for a variety of academic and ceremonial purposes. The books have now been moved to Butler Library, across the quadrangle. The university's library collections total some six million volumes.

Cathedral of St. John the Divine ❹

See p224–5.

Riverside Church ❺

490 Riverside Dr at 122nd St.
Map 20 D2. 870-6700. 116th St-Columbia Univ. **Open** 9am–5pm daily. 10:45am Sun. with prior permission. **Carillon bell concerts** 870-6784. noon, 3pm Sun. **Theatre** 864-2929.

A 21-STORY STEEL frame with a Gothic exterior, the church design was inspired by the cathedral at Chartres. It was lavishly funded by John D. Rockefeller, Jr., in 1930. The Laura Spelman Rockefeller Memorial Carillon (in honor of Rockefeller's mother) is the largest in the world, with 74

Columbia University's main courtyard and the Low Library

bells. The 20-ton Bourdon, or hour bell, is the largest and heaviest tuned carillon bell ever cast. The organ, with its 22,000 pipes, is among the largest in the world.

At the rear of the second gallery is a figure by Jacob Epstein, *Christ in Majesty,* cast in plaster and covered in gold leaf. Another Epstein statue, *Madonna and Child,* stands in the court next to the cloister. The panels of the chancel screen honor eight men and women whose lives have exemplified the teachings of Christ. They range from Socrates and Michelangelo to Florence Nightingale and Booker T. Washington.

For quiet reflection, enter the small, secluded Christ Chapel, patterned after an 11th-century Romanesque church in France. For views, take the elevator to the 20th floor and then walk the 140 steps to the top of the 392-ft (120-m) bell tower for a fine panorama of Upper Manhattan from the windy observation deck. (This is definitely not recommended when the bells are tolling.)

Mosaic mural in Grant's Tomb showing Grant (right) and Robert E. Lee

Grant's Tomb ❻

W 122nd St and Riverside Dr.
Map 20 D2. ☎ 666-1640.
Ⓜ 116th St-Columbia Univ. **Open** 9am–5pm daily. **Closed** Jan 1, Thanksgiving, Dec 25. 📷 ✂ 🚻

Tʜɪꜱ ɢʀᴀɴᴅɪᴏꜱᴇ monument honors America's 18th president, Ulysses S. Grant, the commanding general of the Union forces in the Civil War.

The mausoleum contains the coffins of General Grant and his wife, in accordance with the president's last wish that they be buried together. After Grant's death in 1885, more than 90,000 Americans contributed $600,000 to build the sepulcher, which was inspired by Mausoleus's tomb at Halicarnassus, one of the Seven Wonders of the Ancient World. The tomb was dedicated on what

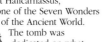

General Grant on a Civil War campaign

would have been Grant's 75th birthday, April 27, 1897. The parade of 50,000 people, along with a flotilla of 10 American and 5 European warships, took more than seven hours to pass in review.

The interior was inspired by Napoleon's tomb at Les Invalides in Paris. Each sarcophagus weighs 8.5 tons. Two exhibit rooms feature displays on Grant's personal life and his presidential and military career. Surrounding the north and east sides of the building are 17 sinuously curved mosaic benches that seem totally out of keeping with the formal architecture of the tomb. They were designed in the early 1970s by the Chilean-born Brooklyn artist Pedro Silva and built by 1,200 local volunteers under his super-vision. The colorful benches were inspired by the Spanish architect Antonio Gaudi's work in Barcelona. The mosaics depict subjects ranging from the Inuits to New York taxis to Donald Duck.

A short walk north of Grant's Tomb is another, humbler, monument. An unadorned urn on a pedestal marks the resting place of a young child who fell from the riverbank and drowned in the 18th century. His grieving father placed a marker that reads simply "Erected to the memory of an amiable child, St. Clair Pollock, died 15 July 1797 in his fifth year of his age."

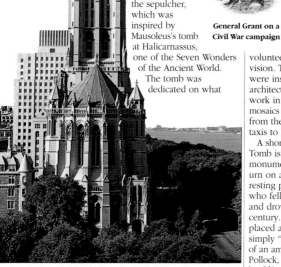

The 21-story Riverside Church, from the north

Cathedral of St. John the Divine ❹

Cram's Gothic West Front

STARTED IN 1892 and still only two-thirds finished, this will be the largest cathedral in the world. The interior is over 600 ft (180 m) long and 146 ft (45 m) wide. It was originally designed in Romanesque style by Heins and LaFarge; Ralph Adams Cram took over the project in 1911, devising a Gothic nave and west front. Medieval construction methods, such as stone supporting buttresses, continue to be used to complete the cathedral, which is also a venue for theater, music and avant-garde art.

Choir
Each of the choir's columns is 55 ft (17 m) tall and made of polished gray granite.

Nave
Rising to a height of over 100 ft (30 m), the piers of the nave are topped by graceful stone arches.

Rose Window ★
Completed in 1933, the stylized motif of the Great Rose is symbolic of the many facets of the Christian Church.

★ **West Front Entrance**
The portals of the cathedral's west front are adorned with many fine stone carvings. Some are re-creations of medieval religious sculptures. Others, such as this apocalyptic vision of New York's skyline by local stonemason Joe Kinkannon, highlight the cathedral's involve-ment in political and social issues of the day.

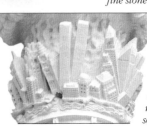

STAR FEATURES

★ **Rose Window**

★ **West Front Entrance**

★ **Bay Altars**

★ **Peace Fountain**

★ Peace Fountain
The sculpture is the creation of Greg Wyatt and represents nature in its many forms. It stands within a granite basin on the Great Lawn, south of the cathedral.

VISITORS' CHECKLIST

Amsterdam Ave at W 112th St.
Map 20 E4. 316-7540. **Box office** 662-2133. 1, 9 to Cathedral Pkwy (110th St).
M4, M5, M7, M11, M104.
Open 9am–5pm daily. **Donation welcome.**
Concerts, lectures, plays, art exhibitions.

Baptistry
The Gothic Baptistry has Italian, French and Spanish influences.

THE FINISHED DESIGN

Crossing tower

South transept

West towers

It will cost approximately $400 million to complete the cathedral. The south transept, crossing tower and west towers have yet to be finished. When the money is raised, the proposed design will take at least another 50 years to complete.

Pulpit

★ Bay Altars
The bay altar windows are devoted to human endeavor. The sports window shows feats of skill and strength.

Bishop's Chair
This is a copy from the Henry VII chapel in Westminster Abbey.

St. Ambrose Chapel
Named after a 4th-century Italian bishop, the chapel is decorated with Renaissance-style ironwork.

TIMELINE

1823 Cathedral planned for Washington Square	**1909** Pulpit designed by Henry Vaughan	**1911** Cram design replaces earlier ones	**1967** Bronze lamps from former Penn Station installed on front steps
1891 Site chosen and designated Cathedral Parkway			
1800	**1850**	**1900**	**1950**
1873 Charter granted	**1916** Ground broken for nave	**1978** Third phase of building begins, and Stonemasons' Yard opened
1888 Competition to design cathedral won by Heins & LaFarge		
1892 December 27 (St. John's Day), cornerstone laid	**1941** Work halted by World War II and does not resume until 1978	

City College of the City University of New York ❼

Main entrance at W. 138th St. and Convent Ave. **Map** 19 A2. **C** 650-7000. **M** 137th St-City College.

Set high on a hill adjoining Hamilton Heights, the original Gothic quadrangle of this college, built between 1903 and 1907, is extremely impressive. The material used for the buildings is Manhattan schist, a stone that had been excavated in building the IRT subway. Later, contemporary buildings were added to the school, which enrolls nearly 15,000 students.

Once free to all residents of New York, City College still offers an education at the city's lowest tuition rates. Three-quarters of the students are from minority groups, and a large number of them are the first in their families to attend college.

Shepard Archway at City College of the City University of New York

Hamilton Grange National Memorial ❽

287 Convent Ave. **Map** 19 A1. **C** 283-5154. **M** 137th St-City College. **Open** 9am–5pm Fri–Sun. 📷

Badly squeezed between a church and apartments is one of the city's most historic buildings, the 1802 columned wooden country home of Alexander Hamilton. He was one of the architects of the federal government system, the first secretary of the treasury and founder of the National Bank. It is his face

Statue of Alexander Hamilton at Hamilton Grange

that appears on the $10 bill. Hamilton lived here for the last two years of his life. He was killed in a duel with political rival Aaron Burr in 1804. Hamilton fired into the air.

The house was acquired by St. Luke's Episcopal Church in 1889 and moved two blocks to this "temporary" site, where it is open but awaiting further relocation and renovation.

Hamilton Heights Historic District ❾

W 141st–W 145th St. and Convent Ave. **Map** 19 A1. **M** 137th St-City College.

Originally this was a setting for the impressive country estates of the wealthy. Also known as Harlem Heights, it was developed during the 1880s following the extension of the El line (see p24) into the neighborhood. The privacy of the enclave, on a high hill above Harlem, made it a very desirable location.

The section known as Sugar Hill was highly favored by Harlem's elite – Chief Justice Thurgood Marshall, notable jazz musicians Count Basie, Duke Ellington and Cab

Calloway, and boxer Sugar Ray Robinson, five times world middleweight champion, have all lived there.

The handsome three- and four-story stone row houses were built between 1886 and 1906 mixing Flemish, Romanesque and Tudor influences. In fine condition, many are used as residences by the faculty of City College.

Row houses in Hamilton Heights

St. Nicholas Historic District ❿

202–250 W 138th & W 139th St. **Map** 19 B2. **M** 135th St (B, C).

A startling contrast to the rundown surroundings, the two blocks here, known as the King Model Houses, were built in 1891 when Harlem was considered a neighborhood for New York's gentry. They still comprise one of the city's most distinctive examples of row townhouses.

The developer, David King, chose three leading architects, who succeeded in blending their different styles to create a harmonious whole. The most famous of these was the firm of McKim, Mead & White,

Houses in St. Nicholas district

Adam Clayton Powell, Jr. (in dark suit) during a civil rights campaign

designers of the Pierpont Morgan Library *(see pp162-3)* and Villard Houses *(see p174)*, who were responsible for the northernmost row of solid brick Renaissance palaces. Their homes featured ground floor entrances rather than the typical New York brownstone stoops. Also, the elaborate parlor floors have ornate wrought-iron balconies below, as well as carved decorative medallions above their windows.

The Georgian buildings designed by Price and Luce are built of buff brick with white stone trim. James Brown Lord's section of buildings, also Georgian in architectural style, feels much closer to Victorian, with outstanding red brick facades and bases constructed of brownstone.

Successful blacks were attracted here in the 1920s and 1930s, giving it the nickname Strivers' Row. Among them were celebrated musicians W. C. Handy and Eubie Blake.

Abyssinian Baptist Church ⓫

132 W. 138th St. **Map** 19 C2.
☎ 862-7474. Ⓜ 135th St (B, C, 2, 3). ✝ 9am, 11am Sun. Groups of 10 or more need reservations.

NEW YORK'S OLDEST black church, founded in 1808, became famous through its charismatic pastor Adam Clayton Powell, Jr. (1908–72), a congressman and civil rights leader. Under his leadership it became the most powerful black church in America. A room in the church houses memorabilia from his life.

The church which is housed in a fine 1923 Gothic building, welcomes visitors to its Sunday services which feature a superb gospel choir.

Schomburg Center for Research into Black Culture ⓬

515 Malcolm X Blvd. **Map** 19 C2.
☎ 491-2200, 491-2265 for tours.
Ⓜ 135th St. (2, 3). **Open** noon–8pm Mon–Wed, 10am–6pm Thu–Sat (exhibition hours vary). **Closed** public hols. ♿ 🖤 📷

HOUSED IN a sleek contemporary complex opened in 1991, this is the largest research center of black and African culture in the United States. The immense collection was assembled by the late Arthur Schomburg, a black man of Puerto Rican descent, who was told by a teacher that there was no such thing as "black history." The Carnegie Corporation bought the collection in 1926 and gave it to the New York Public Library; Schomburg was made curator.

The library was the unofficial meeting place for writers involved in what later became known as the black literary renaissance of the 1920s, including Langston Hughes, W.E.B. Du Bois, Zora Neale Hurston and many other great writers of the day. It also hosted many literary gatherings and poetry readings.

The Schomburg Library has excellent facilities for conserving and making available the archive's treasures, which include rare books, art and recordings. The library was planned and designed to double as a cultural center and includes a theater and two art galleries which feature changing shows of art and photography.

Harlem YMCA ⓭

180 W 135th St. **Map** 19 C3.
☎ 281-4100. Ⓜ 135th St (2, 3).

Sociologist W.E.B. Du Bois

PAUL ROBESON and many others made their first stage appearances here in the early 1920s. The Krigqa Players, organized by W.E.B. Du Bois in the basement in 1928, was founded to counter the derogatory images of blacks often presented in Broadway reviews of the time. The "Y" also provided temporary lodgings for some notable new arrivals in Harlem, including writer Ralph Ellison.

Kurt Weill, Elmer Rice and Langston Hughes at the Schomburg Center

Gospel singers performing at Sylvia's during Sunday brunch

Sylvia's ⑮

328 Lenox Ave. **Map** 21 B1.
📞 996-0660. Ⓜ *125th St (2,3)*. See
Restaurants p294.

HARLEM'S BEST-KNOWN soul
food restaurant serves up
southern-fried or smothered
chicken, spicy ribs, black-eyed
peas, collard greens, candied
yams, sweet potato pie and
other Southern delicacies

Sylvia's

(see p287). Sunday brunch is
served to the accompaniment
of gospel singers.
    Take some time to explore
the market at the corner of
125th Street and Lenox
Avenue (opposite Sylvia's),
extending for a block or more
in either direction. This isn't a
food market: it sells African
clothing, jewelry and art of
varying quality.

Apollo Theater ⑯

253 W 125th St. **Map** 21 A1.
📞 531-5305. Ⓜ *125th St (A, B, C,
D)*. **Open** at showtimes. See
Entertainment p341.

THE APOLLO OPENED in 1914
as a whites-only opera
house. Its great fame came
when Frank Schiffman, a
white entrepreneur, took over
in 1934. He then opened the
theater to all races and turned

it into Harlem's best-known
showcase, with
legendary black
artists such as
Bessie Smith,
Billie Holiday,
Duke Ellington,
and Dinah
Washington
performing.
    Amateur
nights on
Wednesdays,
with winners

Apollo Theater

determined by audience
applause, were famous, and
there was a long waiting list
for performers. These amateur

nights launched the careers of
Sarah Vaughan, Pearl Bailey,
James Brown and Gladys
Knight, among others, and
they still attract hopefuls.
    The Apollo was *the* place
during the swing band era;
following World War II, a
new generation of musicians,
such as Charlie "Bird" Parker,
Dizzy Gillespie, Thelonius
Monk and Aretha Franklin,
continued the tradition.
    Rescued from decline and
refurbished in the 1980s, the
Apollo still features top black
entertainers performing the
blues, jazz, gospel and dance.

Studio Museum in Harlem ⑰

144 W 125th St. **Map** 21 B2.
📞 864-4500. Ⓜ *125th St (2, 3)*.
Open 10am–5pm Wed–Fri, 1–6pm
Sat, Sun. **Closed** Jan 1, Thanksgiving,
Dec 25. **Adm charge** except Sat. 🚫
♿ 🎁 **Lectures, children's
programs, films.** 📷

THE MUSEUM WAS founded in
1967 in a loft on upper
Fifth Avenue with the mission
of becoming the premier
center for the collection and
exhibition of the art and
artifacts of African-Americans.
    The present premises, a
five-story building on
Harlem's main commercial
street, were donated to the
museum by the New York
Bank for Savings in 1979.
The new museum opened
in 1982. There are galleries
on two levels for changing
exhibitions featuring artists
and cultural themes, and
three galleries are devoted to
the permanent collection of
works by major black artists.
    The photographic archives
comprise one of the most

Exhibition space at the Studio Museum in Harlem

complete records in existence of Harlem in its heyday. A side door opens on to a small sculpture garden.

In addition to its excellent exhibitions, the Studio Museum also maintains a national artist-in-residence program, and offers regular lectures, seminars, children's programs and film festivals. An excellent small shop sells a range of books and African crafts.

Mount Morris Historical District ⓲

W 119th–W 124th Sts. **Map** 21 B2. Ⓜ 125th St (2, 3).

YOU CAN PLAINLY see that the late 19th-century Victorian-style town houses near Marcus Garvey Park were once grand. This was a favorite neighborhood of German Jews moving up in the world from the Lower East Side. Time has not been kind, and this district shows how the area has deteriorated.

A few impressive churches, such as St. Martin's Episcopal Church, remain. There are also some interesting juxtapositions of faiths to be seen: the columned Mount Olivet Baptist Church, at 201 Lenox Avenue, was once Temple Israel, one of the most imposing synagogues in the

St. Martin's Episcopal Church on Lenox Avenue

city; and at the Ethiopian Hebrew Congregation, 1 West 123rd Street, housed in a former mansion, the choir sings in Hebrew on Saturdays.

Marcus Garvey Park ⓳

120th–124th Sts. **Map** 21 B2. Ⓜ 125th St (2,3).

The flamboyant black nationalist leader Marcus Garvey

THIS HILLY, ROCKY, two-block square of green is the site of New York's last fire watchtower, an open cast-iron structure built in 1856, with spiral stairs leading to the observation deck. The bell below the deck used to sound the alarm. Best to view it from a distance, however – this neighborhood is not recommended for carefree wandering. Previously known as Mount Morris Park, it was renamed in 1973 in honor of Marcus Garvey. He came to Harlem from Jamaica in 1916 and founded the Universal Negro Improvement Agency, which promoted self-help, racial pride and a back-to-Africa movement.

Museo del Barrio ⓴

1230 5th Ave. **Map** 21 C5. ☎ 831-7272. Ⓜ 103rd St (6). **Open** 11am–5pm Wed–Sun. **Donation expected.**

FOUNDED IN 1969, this is North America's only museum devoted to Latin American art, specializing in the culture of Puerto Rico. Exhibitions feature contemporary painting and sculpture, folk art and historical artifacts. The stars of the permanent collection are about 240 wooden Santos, carvings of the saints by folk artisans and a reconstructed *bodega* or Latino corner grocery. Exhibits change often, but some of the Santos are always on display. The pre-Columbian collection contains rare artifacts from the Caribbean. Situated at the far end of Museum Mile, this unusual museum attempts to bridge the gap between the lofty Upper East Side and the cultural heritage of El Barrio (Spanish Harlem).

Folk art at the Museo del Barrio: one of the *Three Wise Men* (left) and the *Omnipotent Hand*

FARTHER AFIELD

THOUGH OFFICIALLY part of New York City, the boroughs outside Manhattan are quite different in feel and spirit. They are residential and don't have the famous skyscrapers that are associated with New York. The difference is evident even in the way residents describe a trip to Manhattan as "going into the city." Yet the outlying areas boast many attractions, including the city's biggest zoo, botanical gardens, museums, beaches and sports arenas. For a guided walk around Brooklyn see pages 264–65.

SIGHTS AT A GLANCE

Historic Streets and Buildings
Morris-Jumel Mansion **2**
George Washington Bridge **3**
Wave Hill **5**
Yankee Stadium **10**
Grand Army Plaza **17**
Park Slope Historic District **18**
Historic Richmond Town **23**
Alice Austen House **26**

Museums and Galleries
Audubon Terrace **1**
The Cloisters pp234–37 **4**
Van Cortlandt House Museum **6**

New York Hall of Science **13**
American Museum of the Moving Image and Kaufman Astoria Studio **14**
Brooklyn Children's Museum **15**
The Brooklyn Museum pp248–51 **20**
Jacques Marchais Center of Tibetan Art **24**
Snug Harbor Cultural Center **25**

Parks and Gardens
New York Botanical Garden pp240–41 **8**
Bronx Zoo/ Wildlife Conservation Park pp242–43 **9**

Flushing Meadow-Corona Park **12**
Prospect Park **19**
Brooklyn Botanic Garden **21**

Famous Theaters
Brooklyn Academy of Music **16**

Cemeteries
Woodlawn Cemetery **7**

Beaches
City Island **11**
Coney Island **22**
Jamaica Bay Wildlife Refuge Center **27**
Jones Beach State Park **28**

KEY

Main sightseeing areas

0 kilometers 5

0 miles 3

N

SIGHTS OUTSIDE THE CENTER

Jamaica Bay

Upper Manhattan

IT WAS IN UPPER Manhattan that the 18th-century Dutch settlers established their farms. Now a suburban area with little of the bustle of downtown Manhattan, it is a good place to escape the inner city for some relaxed museum and landmark sightseeing. The Cloisters *(see pp234–37)* displays a magnificent collection of medieval art, housed within original European buildings of the period. A piece of New York history is found at the Morris-Jumel Mansion in north Harlem. From his headquarters here, George Washington mounted the defense of Manhattan in 1776.

Facade of the American Academy of Arts and Letters

Audubon Terrace ❶

Broadway at 155th St. **M** *157th St.*
American Numismatic Society **(**
234-3130. **Open** *9am – 4:30pm
Tue – Sat, 1 – 4pm Sun.* ⭕ 🚻
**American Academy of Arts and
Letters** **(** *368-5900.* **Open** *during
exhibitions.* ⭕
Hispanic Society of America
(*926-2234.* **Open** *10am – 4:30pm
Tue – Sat, 1 – 4pm Sun.* **Closed** *public
hols.* **Donation expected.** 📷 🚻

THIS 1908 complex of Classical Revival buildings by Charles Pratt Huntington is named after naturalist John James Audubon, whose estate once included this land. Audubon is buried in nearby Trinity Cemetery. His gravestone, a Celtic cross, bears the symbolic images of this adventurous artist's career: the birds he painted, his palette and brushes, and his rifles.

The complex was funded by the architect's cousin, civic benefactor Archer Milton Huntington. His dream was that it should be a center of culture and study. A central plaza contains statues by his wife, the sculptress Anna Hyatt Huntington.

Audubon Terrace contains several theme museums that are worth seeking out. The American Numismatic Society is the leading American museum devoted to coinage and medals, and has one of the world's best collections, with half a million photos and illustrations of coins. A permanent exhibition called "The World of Coins" traces the historical and political role of money, and there is a vast library.

Bronze door at the academy

The American Academy of Arts and Letters was set up to honor American writers, artists, and composers, and 75 honorary members from overseas. On the roll are writers John Steinbeck and Mark Twain, painters Andrew Wyeth and Edward Hopper, and the composer Aaron Copland. Exhibitions feature members' work. The library (for scholars, by appointment) has old manuscripts and first editions.

The Hispanic Society of America is a public museum and library based upon the personal collection of Archer M. Huntington. The Spanish Renaissance-style main gallery holds works by Goya, El Greco and Velázquez. The National Museum of the American Indian, once here, has now reopened at the Custom House *(see p73)*.

Statue of El Cid by Anna Hyatt Huntington at Audubon Terrace

Morris-Jumel Mansion ❷

Corner W 160th St and Edgecombe
Ave. 🅲 *923-8008*. Ⓜ *163rd St.*
Open *10am–4pm Wed–Sun.*
Closed *public hols.* **Adm charge.**
📷 ✍ *by appt.* ♿

Tʜɪs ɪs ᴏɴᴇ of New York's
few pre-Revolutionary
buildings. Now a museum, it
was built in 1765 for Roger
Morris. His former military
colleague George Washington
used the house as temporary
headquarters while defending
Manhattan in 1776.

The house was bought and
updated in 1810 by Stephen
Jumel, a merchant of French-
Caribbean descent, and his
wife Eliza. The pair furnished
the house with souvenirs of
their many visits to France.
Her boudoir contains her bed
and "dolphin" chair, reputedly
bought from Napoleon. Eliza's
social climbing and love
affairs scandalized New York
society. It was rumored that
she let her husband bleed to
death in 1832 so she could
inherit his fortune. She later
married Aaron Burr, aged 77,
and divorced him three years
later on the day he died.

The exterior of this wood-
sided Georgian house with its
classical portico and octagonal
wing – the earliest in the
colonies – has been restored.
The museum exhibits include
many original Jumel pieces.

The 3,500-ft (1,065-m) span of the George Washington Bridge

George Washington Bridge ❸

Ⓜ *175th St.*

Fʀᴇɴᴄʜ ᴀʀᴄʜɪᴛᴇᴄᴛ
Le Corbusier
called this "the
only seat of grace
in the disordered
city." While not as
famous a landmark
as its Brooklyn
equivalent, this
bridge by engineer
Othmar Ammann
and his architect
Cass Gilbert has its
own character and
history. Plans for a
bridge linking
Manhattan to New
Jersey had been in
the pipeline for
more than 60 years before the
Port of New York Authority
raised the $59 million needed
to fund the project. It was

The lighthouse under Washington Bridge

Ammann who suggested a
road bridge rather than the
more expensive rail link.
Work began in 1927 and the
bridge was finally opened in
1931: first across were two
young roller skaters from the
Bronx. Today the
bridge is a vital
link for commuter
traffic and is in
constant use.

Cass Gilbert had
plans to clad the
two towers with
masonry but funds
did not permit it,
leaving an elegant
skeletal structure
600 ft (183 m) in
height and 3,500
ft (1,065 m) long.
Ammann had
also allowed for a
second deck in
his original plan,
and this lower deck was
added in 1962, increasing the
bridge's capacity enormously.
Now the eastbound toll
collection shows a traffic level
of over 52 million cars per year.

Below the eastern tower is
a lighthouse that was saved
from possible demolition in
1951 by sheer force of public
pressure. The reason for this
unlikely protest has become
part of the city's mythology.
Many thousands of young
New Yorkers and children all
around the world have loved
the bedtime story *The Little
Red Lighthouse and the Great
Gray Bridge,* and wrote letters
to save the lighthouse. Author
Hildegarde Hoyt Swift wove
the tale around her two
favorite New York landmarks.

The Cloisters ❹

See pp234–37.

Morris-Jumel Mansion, built in 1765, with its original colossal portico

The Cloisters ⓸

The Cloisters seen from Fort Tryon Park

Tʜɪꜱ ᴡᴏʀʟᴅ-ꜰᴀᴍᴏᴜꜱ museum of medieval art resides in a building constructed from 1934 to 1938, incorporating medieval cloisters, chapels and halls. Sculptor George Grey Barnard founded the museum in 1914, having amassed many medieval architectural pieces and sculptures. John D. Rockefeller, Jr., funded the Metropolitan Museum of Art's 1925 purchase of the collection and donated the site at Fort Tryon Park.

Tomb Effigy of Jean d'Alluye
This tomb immortalizes the 13th-century Crusader.

Pontaut Chapter House

★ Unicorn Tapestries
The set of beautifully preserved tapestries, woven in Brussels around 1500, depicts the quest and capture of the mythical unicorn.

Boppard Stained-Glass Lancets (1440–47)
Below the lancet of Saint Catherine, angels display the arms of the coopers' guild, of which Catherine was patron.

Bonnefont Cloister

STAR EXHIBITS

- ★ **Unicorn Tapestries**

- ★ **Belles Heures de Jean, Duc de Berry**

- ★ **Annunciation Altarpiece by Robert Campin**

Trie Cloister

★ Annunciation Altarpiece (about 1425)
The Campin Room is the location of this Robert Campin of Tournai small triptych, a magnificent example of early Flemish painting.

Saint-Guilhem Cloister
Intricate floral ornamentation can be found on the capitals of this cloister.

Romanesque Hall

Upper floor

Lower floor

Main entrance

Virgin and Child Frescoes
This 12th-century fresco is from the Catalonian church of San Juan de Tredós.

KEY TO FLOOR PLAN

☐ Exhibition space
☐ Non-exhibition space

Cuxa Cloister
The reconstructed 12th-century cloister features Romanesque architectural detail and motifs.

Enthroned Virgin and Child
This elaborately carved ivory sculpture was made in England during the late 13th century.

GALLERY GUIDE
The museum is organized roughly in chronological order. It starts with the Romanesque period (1000 AD) and moves to the Gothic (1150 to 1520). Sculptures, stained glass, paintings and the gardens are on the lower floor. The Unicorn Tapestries are on the upper floor.

★ Belles Heures
This book of hours, commissioned by Jean, Duc de Berry, for his devotions, is illuminated by 94 minia-tures in tempera and gold.

Exploring The Cloisters

KNOWN PARTICULARLY for its Romanesque and Gothic architectural sculpture, The Cloisters collection also includes illuminated manuscripts, stained glass, metalwork, enamels, ivories and paintings. Among its tapestries is the renowned *Unicorn* series. The Cloisters' splendid medieval complex is unrivaled in North America.

ROMANESQUE ART

A lifesized 12th-century Spanish crucifix portraying Christ as the King of Heaven

FANCIFUL BEASTS and people, acanthus blossoms and scrollwork, top the columns around The Cloisters. Many are in the Romanesque style that flourished in the 11th and 12th centuries. The museum has numerous masterpieces of Romanesque art and architecture, showing the style's powerful rounded arches and intricate details. Highly embellished capitals and warm, pink marble typify the 12th-century Cuxa Cloister from the Pyrenees in France. A griffin, a dragon, a centaur and a basilisk are among the creatures parading over the Narbonne Arch nearby. In the Romanesque Hall, a golden-crowned Christ is depicted as triumphant over death.

In a more solemn style, the apse from the church of Saint-Martín in Fuentidueña, Spain, is a massive rounded vault constructed from 3,000 blocks of limestone. It is decorated with a 12th-century fresco of the Virgin and Child.

More than 800 years ago, Benedictine and Cistercian monks sat on the cold stone benches in the Pontaut Chapter House. By the 19th century it had become so neglected that it was used as a stable. Its ribbed vaulting is a foretaste of the Gothic style to come.

A 16th-century Flemish boxwood rosary bead from the Treasury

GOTHIC ART

WHERE ROMANESQUE art was solid, the Gothic style that followed (from 1150 to around 1520) was open, with pointed arches, glowing stained-glass windows and three-dimensional sculpture. Gothic depictions of the Virgin and Child display exquisite craftsmanship.

The Gothic Chapel's brilliantly colored windows show scenes and figures from biblical stories. Lifesized tomb sculptures include the effigy of the Crusader knight Jean d'Alluye. During the 1790s,

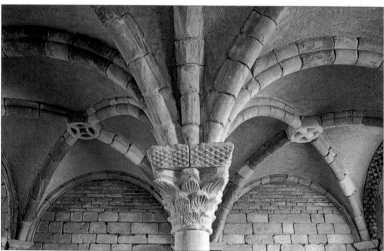

Vaulted ceiling of the Pontaut Chapter House

the statue's original home, La Clarté-Dieu Abbey in France, was vandalized, and the statue was used to bridge a stream.

In the Boppard Room, the lives of the saints are told in marvellous late Gothic stained glass from Germany.

Robert Campin's Flemish masterwork, the *Annunciation* altarpiece, is the focus of the Campin Room. It is an intimate room with furnishings that might have belonged to a wealthy 15th-century family.

MEDIEVAL GARDENS

More than 250 varieties of plants grown in the Middle Ages can be found in The Cloisters' gardens. The Bonnefont Cloister has herbal, medicinal and cooking plants. The Trie Cloister features plants shown in the *Unicorn Tapestries* and reveals the use of flowers in medieval symbolism: roses (for the Virgin Mary), pansies (the Holy Trinity) and daisies (the eye of Christ).

Bonnefont Cloister

THE TAPESTRIES

THE CLOISTERS' tapestries are full of rich imagery and symbolism, and are among the museum's most highly prized treasures. The four *Nine Heroes Tapestries* bear the coat of arms of Jean, Duc de Berry, who was a brother of the King of France and one of the greatest art patrons of the Middle Ages. These tapestries are one of only two sets that survived from the late 14th century; the other set belonged to Jean's brother, Louis, Duc d'Anjou.

Nine great heroes of the past – three pagan, three Hebrew, three Christian – are shown with members of the medieval court, from cardinals, knights and damsels to musicians.

In an adjacent room is the magnificent *Hunt of the Unicorn*, a series of seven tapestries woven in Brussels around 1500. It depicts the symbolic hunt of the mythical unicorn and capture by a maiden.

Although they were misused in the 19th century to protect fruit trees from frost damage,

the tapestries are remarkably well preserved. They are also astonishing in detail, with

Julius Caesar, entertained by court musicians, in a *Nine Heroes* tapestry

literally hundreds of minutely observed plants and animals. Their story can be read as a tale of courtly love, but the series is also an allegory for the Crucifixion and the Resurrection of Christ.

THE TREASURY

IN MEDIEVAL TIMES, precious objects were stored in sanctuaries for safekeeping. At the Cloisters, they are to be found in the Treasury.

The collection includes several Gothic illuminated "books of hours." These were used for the private devotions of the nobility, such as the Limbourg brothers' *Belles Heures*, made for Jean, Duc de Berry, in 1410, and the tiny, palm-sized version by Gothic master Jean Pucelle for the Queen of France, around 1325.

Other religious artifacts range from a 13th-century English ivory Virgin to the 14th-century silver gilt and enamel reliquary shrine thought to have belonged to Queen Elizabeth of Hungary, along with censers, chalices, candlesticks and crucifixes.

Curiosities here include the "Monkey Cup," an enameled beaker probably made for the 15th-century Burgundian court, showing mischievous monkeys robbing a sleeping peddler; an intricately carved rosary bead the size of a walnut; a 13th-century boat-shaped, jeweled saltcellar; and one of the oldest full sets of playing cards in existence.

Hunting images and symbols depicted on a 15th-century deck of playing cards

The west parlor of the Van Cortlandt House Museum

The Bronx

ONCE A prosperous suburb with a famous Grand Concourse lined with apartment buildings for the wealthy, the Bronx has now become an unfortunate symbol of urban decay. Still, diverse ethnic communities, unique resources and charming areas, such as Riverdale at the northern end, remain. Two major, outstanding attractions are the Bronx Zoo and the New York Botanical Garden. New Yorkers still flock to see baseball at Yankee Stadium, now more than 50 years old. (see p239).

Wave Hill **5**

W 249th St. and Independence Ave, Riverdale. **[** (718) 549-3200. **M** 231st St. then bus Bx7, 10, 24. **Open** 9am–5:30pm Tue–Sun (9am–4:30pm mid-Oct to mid-May). **Adm charge** Sat, Sun; free Nov–Mar.

WHEN CITY concrete begins to overwhelm, come to this 28-acre (11-ha) oasis of calm and beauty, with its fine views over to the New Jersey Palisades across the Hudson River. The former estate of financier and conservationist George W. Perkins, Wave Hill has had a long series of distinguished tenants, including Theodore Roosevelt, Mark Twain and

Arturo Toscanini. Perkins also owned neighboring estates, underneath which he built a subterranean recreation center complete with bowling alley, and a tunnel leading into the main building.

The house and the grounds are open to the public. The house is frequently used for concerts. They often take place in the grand Armor Hall, designed in 1928 for Bashford Dean, who was then the curator of the collection of arms and armor at the Metropolitan Museum of Art.

The gardens were originally designed by Viennese landscape gardener, Albert Millard. There are also greenhouses, lawns, an herb garden and woodlands. Exhibitions range from sculpture to horticulture.

The adjoining Riverdale Park has attractive woodland and paths along the river.

The interior of the grand Armor Hall at Wave Hill

Van Cortlandt House Museum **6**

Van Cortlandt Park. **[** (718) 543-3344. **M** 242nd St, Van Cortlandt Park. **Open** 10am–3pm Tue–Fri, 11am–4pm Sat, Sun (last adm: 30 mins before closing). **Closed** most public hols. **Adm charge**. **◙ ☑ ♿** See **The History of New York** pp18–19.

The facade of Van Cortlandt House

A RESTORED 1748 Georgian Colonial country manor built of rough stone, this was originally the family home of Frederick Van Cortlandt, a New Yorker who inherited great wealth and was related to many of the influential and rich families of his day.

The dining room was used as one of General George Washington's headquarters; the ground behind the house was once the scene of skirmishing during the Revolutionary War.

The interior has American period furnishings as well as a superb collection of delftware and a complete 17th-century Dutch bedroom.

On the exterior, look for the carved faces in the keystones over the windows.

Woodlawn Cemetery ❼

Jerome and Bainbridge Aves.
🄲 *(718) 920-0500.* Ⓜ *Woodlawn.*
Open *9am–4:30pm daily.* **Office
closed** *public hols, Sun.* 🚫 ♿ 📷

F OR A GLIMPSE into another
kind of social history, visit
Woodlawn Cemetery, the
burial place of many a wealthy
and distinguished New Yorker.

Memorials
and tomb-
stones are set
in beautiful
grounds. F.W.
Woolworth
and many
members of
his family are
interred in a
mausoleum

**Entrance to the
Woolworth
mausoleum**

only a little
less ornate
than the
building that
carries the family name. The
pink marble vault of meat
magnate Herman Armour is
oddly reminiscent of a ham.

Other New York notables
buried here include Mayor
Fiorello La Guardia, Roland
Macy, the founder of the
great department store,
author Herman Melville and
jazz legend Duke Ellington.

New York Botanical Garden ❽

See pp240–41.

Bronx Zoo/ Wildlife Conservation Park ❾

See pp242–43.

Yankee Stadium ❿

E 161st St at River Ave, Highbridge.
🄲 *(718) 293-6000.* Ⓜ *161st St.*
See **Entertainment** *pp344–45.*

T HIS IS THE HOME of the New
York Yankees baseball
team. Among Yankee heroes
are two of the greatest players of all time: Babe Ruth and
Joe DiMaggio (who was also
famous for marrying, in 1954,

the legendary
actress Marilyn
Monroe).

The stadium
was completed
in 1923 by
Jacob Ruppert,
the owner of
the Yankees. It
became known
as "the house
that Ruth built"
after the
famous left-
hander Babe

Joe DiMaggio in action at Yankee Stadium in 1941

Ruth. The Stadium had a face-
lift in the mid-1970s, and now
seats up to 54,000 people
who come for sports,
concerts and other events.
Take the children along, too.

City Island ⓫

610 City Island Ave. Ⓜ *6 to Pelham
Parkway, then Bx29 to City Island.*
**North Wind Undersea Institute
Museum** 🄲 *(718) 885-0701.* **Open**
12pm–4pm Mon–Fri (5pm Sat & Sun)

S ITUATED JUST off the
northeast shore
of the Bronx, City
Island is a small
nautical outpost
with a very New
England feel – it
seems a world
apart from
New York City,
and offers a
refreshing
change of
pace. Its scenic
marinas are
filled with sail-
boats, and its
seafood restaurants
would satisfy any

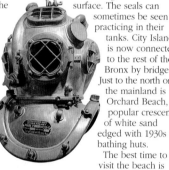

**Diving helmet at the
North Wind Undersea
Institute Museum**

sailor's appetite. Several
America's Cup winners have
been built in its boatyards.

The main entrance of the
North Wind Undersea Institute
Museum is constructed from
the gaping 9-ft (2.75-m) jaw of
a whale. It houses displays on
the history of whaling and the
only seals in the world that
work for the police force. They
are trained to retrieve sunken
weapons and drugs and to
undo the seat belts in sub-
merged cars or planes and
then to bring humans to the
surface. The seals can
sometimes be seen
practicing in their
tanks. City Island
is now connected
to the rest of the
Bronx by bridge.
Just to the north on
the mainland is
Orchard Beach, a
popular crescent
of white sand
edged with 1930s
bathing huts.

The best time to
visit the beach is
during the week,
when it is less
crowded.

An old tugboat at the North Wind Undersea Institute Museum

New York Botanical Garden ●

Hibiscus

THE NEW YORK Botanical garden
is 250 acres of dazzling beauty
and hands-on enjoyment. From the
nation's most glorious Victorian
glasshouse to the 12-acre Everett
Children's Adventure Garden it is
alive with things to discover. One
of the oldest and largest botanical gardens in
the world, the Garden has 28 specialty gardens
and plant collections, and 40 acres of uncut
forest. The spectacular Enid A. Haupt conservatory has been restored as *A World of Plants*,
with misty tropical
rain forests and
dramatic deserts.

Entrance to Enid A. Haupt Conservatory

**Old World
Desert**

**Display
gallery**

Rock Garden
*Giant boulders, ledges,
streams and a waterfall
create an alpine habitat
for plants from the world's
rocky and mountainous
regions* ④

Botanical Garden Forest
*One of New York City's last surviving
natural forest areas includes red oak,
white ash, tulip trees and maples* ⑤

**Americas'
Deserts**

Children's Adventure Garden
*Kids can discover the wonders of
ecology and the plant world* ⑧

Entrance

③
②
①

⑥

④ ⑤

⑧

⑦

Entrance

LOCATOR MAP

Rose Garden
*Over 2,700 roses
have been planted in
the Peggy Rockefeller
Rose Garden, laid
out in 1988 accord-
ing to the original
1915 design* ⑦

Palms of the Americas

One hundred of these majestic palms soar into a 90-ft glass dome. A tranquil reflecting pool is surrounded by tropical plants.

The Enid A. Haupt Conservatory consists of 11 interconnecting glass galleries housing *A World of Plants*, including rain forests, deserts, aquatic plants, and seasonal displays ①

Demonstration Gardens
Colorful displays are designed to inspire visitors with ideas for their own gardens ③

Tropical pool

Tropical flora

Jane Watson Irwin Perennial Garden
Flowering perennials are arranged in dramatic patterns according to height, shade, color and blooming time ②

Tropical Lowland Rainforest

Aquatic plants

Main entrance

Tropical New World Upland Rainforest

Garden Café
Abigail Kirsch's new Garden Café is a delightful spot to enjoy a full lunch or light refreshments and snacks. You can eat indoors, or enjoy the food outside on terraces that overlook the Demonstration Gardens ⑥

Bronx Zoo/Wildlife Conservation Park ❾

OPENED IN 1899, the Bronx Zoo/Wildlife Conservation Park is the largest urban zoo in the US, home to some 6,500 animals of over 600 species, living in realistic representations of their natural habitats. The Park is a leader in the perpetuation of endangered species, such as the Indian rhinoceros and the snow leopard. Its 265 acres of woods, streams and parklands include a children's zoo (seasonal) and a shuttle train that transports visitors around the sprawling park. Visitors are also free to walk around. For the best overview of the different areas of the park take the Skyfari cable car, open seasonally.

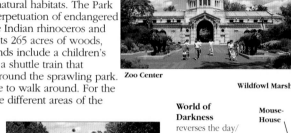

Zoo Center

Wildfowl Marsh

World of Darkness reverses the day/night cycle so visitors can see nocturnal animals like bats and sugar gliders in action.

Mouse-House

Skyfari cable car

Carter Giraffe Building

★ **African Plains**
Zebras, lions, cheetahs and gazelles roam the African Plains. Predators and prey are separated by a moat.

Africa
Oryxes find shelter under an African hut.

Asia entrance

Camel Rides
Children enjoy such seasonal experiences as camel rides and other attractions.

Bengali Express monorail

★ **JungleWorld**
A climate-controlled tropical rain forest harbors mammals, birds and reptiles from South Asia. The animals are kept apart from visitors by ravines, streams and cliffs.

Monkeys in JungleWorld

Baboon Reserve
*Visitors walk along a dry
riverbed to see wildlife in an
Ethiopian mountain habitat.*

Children's Zoo
*Kids can crawl
through a prairie dog
tunnel, climb on a
spiderweb, try on a
turtle shell, and pet
and feed the animals.*

The Zoo Center
houses elephants,
rhinos and tapirs.

**Southern Boulevard
entrance**

**World of
Reptiles**

Aquatic Bird House

Aitken Aviary

Rainey Gate entrance

**Monkey
House**

★ **World of
Birds**
*Exotic birds soar
free in the lush
surroundings of a rain
forest. Simulated
tropical thunder-
storms occur
every day, and
an artificial
waterfall rushes
down a 50-ft (15-m)
fiberglass cliff.*

**Greater
hornbill**

**Bronxdale
entrance**

**Himalayan
Highlands**
*Endangered species,
such as snow leopards
and red pandas, are
kept here.*

★ **Wild Asia**
*The Bengali Express monorail journeys
through forests and meadows of an Asian
habitat, where elephants, rhinoceroses
and Siberian tigers roam free.*

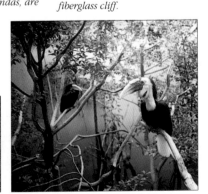

Queens

A BIG, SPRAWLING borough, Queens has a wide variety of attractions and residential and commercial areas, including a business district known as Long Island City. Development of the borough accelerated after 1909, when the construction of Queensboro Bridge made commuting easier. The city's main airports are here, and there are various ethnic enclaves too, including the Greek neighborhood of Astoria, and some Asian communities in Flushing, a district popular with varied ethnic groups.

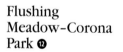

A 1900 Mutoscope at the Museum of the Moving Image

Flushing Meadow–Corona Park ⑫

Ⓜ *Willets Point-Shea Stadium. See* **Entertainment** *pp344–45.*

THE SITE of New York's two World's Fairs now offers expansive waterside picnic grounds and a multitude of attractions. These include the 50,000-seat Shea Stadium, the home of the New York Mets baseball team and a popular site for rock concerts. Flushing Meadow is also home to the US Tennis Center, where the prestigious United States Open is played. The courts are open for would-be Agassis, Grafs and Everts for the remainder of the year. In the 1920s this area was known as the Corona Dump, a nightmarish place of salt marshes and great piles of smoldering trash. In *The Great Gatsby*, author F. Scott Fitzgerald dubbed it the "valley of ashes." It reeked of rotting garbage and glowed red at night. New York's Parks' Commissioner Robert Moses was the driving force behind its transformation. A whole mountain of rubbish was removed and the river was totally re-channeled. The marsh was drained and sewage works were built, helping to restore the area. This site was to serve as the site for the 1939 World's Fair, at which a world on the brink of war saluted the elusive notion of world peace.

The Unisphere, symbol of the 1964 fair, still dominates the remains of the fairground. This giant hollow ball of green steel, built by the US Steel Corporation, is 12 stories high and weighs a massive 350 tons.

The 1964 World's Fair Unisphere at Flushing Meadow-Corona Park

New York Hall of Science ⑬

46th Ave and 111th St Flushing Meadows, Corona Park. Ⓒ (718) 699-0005. Ⓜ *111th St.* **Open** *9:30am–2pm Mon–Wed, 9:30am–5pm Thu–Sun.* **Closed** *public hols.* **Adm charge** . ▣ ⓑ ▯

THE SCIENCE PAVILION built for the 1964 World's Fair was designed with stained glass set in concrete panels. It is now a hands-on museum for science and technology, with exhibits on color, light and physics. Children love to watch the giant video screens that can magnify a drop of water, and the interactive video and laser optical exhibits

The concrete curtain wall of the New York Hall of Science

American Museum of the Moving Image and Kaufman Astoria Studio ⑭

35th Ave at 36th St, Astoria. **Museum** Ⓒ (718) 784-4520. **Studio** Ⓒ (718) 392-5600. Ⓜ *36th St.* **Museum open** *noon–5pm Tue–Fri, 11am–6pm Sat, Sun.* **Adm charge**. **Studio not open** *to public.* ▣ ⓑ ▯

IN NEW YORK's filmmaking heyday, Rudolph Valentino, W.C. Fields, the Marx Brothers and Gloria Swanson all made films here in the city's largest studio, opened by Paramount Pictures in 1920. When the movies went west, the army took over, making training films here from 1941 to 1971.

The complex stood empty until the 1970s when Astoria Motion Picture and Television Foundation was founded to preserve it. *The Wiz,* Sidney

Poster at the Museum of the Moving Image

Lumet's $24 million musical starring Michael Jackson and Diana Ross, was made here, helping to pay for restoration. Today, the studios house the largest moviemaking facilities on the East Coast and are again in full use. *The Cotton Club* and Woody Allen's *Radio Days* were filmed here.

In 1981 one of the studio buildings was transformed into the American Museum of the Moving Image, with interactive displays on production and theaters for the screening of movies and television.

There is a lot of kitsch and memorabilia on display, from Annie Hall's outfits to the Star Trek costumes. The main gallery on the second floor draws from the permanent collection, containing over 60,000 movie artifacts. These include exhibits such as a mirror in which you can see your own head reflected above the body of Sylvester Stallone in *Rocky*, Marilyn Monroe in *The Seven Year Itch* or Eddie Murphy in *Beverly Hills Cop*.

"Behind the Screen" looks at every aspect of filmmaking, including editing, sound and costumes. Visitors can walk through the original set for Paul Newman's 1988 version of *The Glass Menagerie*. The main floor theater presents film and video programs, from early silent movies to the most avant-garde.

Head for 31st Street for Astoria's big Greek enclave. Here and along Ditmars Boulevard and Broadway are legions of *zacharoplasteia* (pastry shops), *tavernas* (restaurants), nightclubs, 11 Greek Orthodox churches and a Greek cinema. Greek religious processions are very moving, if you're lucky enough to see one.

Brooklyn

The bandstand at Prospect Park *(see p246)*

IF BROOKLYN were a separate city, it would be the USA's fourth largest. It has a character all of its own. Many entertainment greats – Mel Brooks, Phil Silvers, Woody Allen and Neil Simon among them – celebrate their birthplace with great affection and humor. Brooklyn is the ultimate melting pot, with West Indians, Hasidic Jews, Russians, Italians and Arabs, to mention only a few groups, living side by side. Among the diverse neighborhoods are the historic residential districts of Park Slope and Brooklyn Heights.

Brooklyn Children's Museum ⑮

145 Brooklyn Ave. 🄲 *(718) 735-4432.* 🄼 *Kingston.* **Open** *2–5pm Wed–Fri, 10am–5pm Sat, Sun. Jul, Aug; 10am–5pm Mon, noon–6:30pm Wed–Sun.* **Closed** *Jan 1, Thanksgiving, Dec 25.* **Donation expected.** ♿ 🚻

THE BROOKLYN Children's Museum was the first to be designed especially for children and was founded in 1899. Since then, it has been a model, inspiration and consultant to the development of more than 250 museums for children across the country and all over the world. Housed in a high-tech, specially designed underground building dating from 1976, it is one of the most imaginative children's museums anywhere.

The layout of the building is a maze of complex inter-connected passageways running off the main "people tube" – a huge drainage pipe that connects the four levels. This is not a passive place where children are meant to stand around and stare – the emphasis is on involvement and hands-on exhibits. Everywhere you look there are curiosities to be discovered, experienced, made or played with. There is even a walk-on piano like the one in the film *Big* – children of every age find it quite irresistible.

Special exhibitions and events are designed to help children learn about the planet, resolve their fears or problems, understand other cultures and discover the past. The squeals of laughter and delight that are always heard are a sign of this well-designed and clever museum's success in teaching children and the young at heart.

A mask from the Children's Museum

The facade of the Brooklyn Academy of Music

Brooklyn Academy of Music ⑯

30 Lafayette Ave. 🅒 (718) 636-4100. 🅜 Atlantic Ave. **Adm charge**. 🚫 ♿ 🅞 See **Entertainment** pp338–9.

HOME TO THE Brooklyn Philharmonic, the Academy (known as BAM) is Brooklyn's leading cultural venue and the oldest, founded in 1858. It offers outstanding performances, often tending toward the innovative and avant-garde.

The classic 1908 building was designed by Herts & Tallant, and inaugurated with a production of Gounod's opera *Faust* featuring the legendary Neapolitan tenor Enrico Caruso. The list of the greats who have performed here is endless and includes actress Sarah Bernhardt, ballerina Anna Pavlova, musicians Pablo Casals and Sergei Rachmaninoff, poets Edna St. Vincent Millay and Carl Sandburg, and statesman Winston Churchill. Many international touring groups have made appearances here, including Britain's Royal Shakespeare Company.

The BAM Next Wave Festival has presented a number of well-known contemporary artists, including musicians Philip Glass and David Byrne, performance artist Laurie Anderson, and choreographers Pina Bausch and Mark Morris. The Brooklyn Academy of Music also runs the Majestic Theater nearby, once a movie theater and now used for dance, drama and music events.

Grand Army Plaza ⑰

Plaza St at Flatbush Ave. 🅒 (718) 965-8951. 🅜 Grand Army Plaza. **Arch open** for occasional exhibitions.

The Soldiers' and Sailors' Arch at Grand Army Plaza

FREDERICK LAW OLMSTED and Calvert Vaux laid out this grand oval in 1870 as a gateway to Prospect Park. The Soldiers' and Sailors' Arch and its sculptures were added in 1892 as a tribute to the Union Army. The bust of John F. Kennedy here is the only official New York monument to him.

In June, the plaza is the center of the Welcome Back to Brooklyn Festival for the famous – and not-so-famous – people born in Brooklyn.

Park Slope Historic District ⑱

Streets from Prospect Park W below Flatbush Ave. to 8th/7th/5th avenues. 🅜 Grand Army Plaza.

Relief work on the Montauk Club

THIS WONDERFUL enclave of beautiful Victorian town houses was developed on the edge of Prospect Park in the 1880s. It served the upper-middle-class professionals who were able to commute into Manhattan after the Brooklyn Bridge was opened in 1883. The shady streets are lined with two- to five-story houses in every architectural style popular in the late 19th century, some with the towers, turrets and curlicues so representative of the era. Particularly fine examples are in Romanesque Revival style, with rounded entry arches.

The Montauk Club at 25 Eighth Avenue combines the style of Venice's Ca' d'Oro palazzo with the friezes and gargoyles of the Montauk Indians, after whom this popular 19th-century gathering place was named.

Prospect Park ⑲

🅒 (718) 965-8951. 🅕 (718) 965-8999. 🅜 Grand Army Plaza. 🅣 (718) 788-8500.

DESIGNERS OLMSTED and Vaux considered this park, opened in 1867, better than their earlier Central Park. The Long Meadow, a sweep of broad lawns and grand vistas, is the longest unbroken swath of green space in New York.

Olmsted's belief was that "a feeling of relief is experienced by entering them [the parks] on escaping from the cramped, confining and controlling circumstances of the streets of the town." That

The facade of the Brooklyn Public Library on Grand Army Plaza

vision is still as true today as it was a century ago.

Among the many notable features are Stanford White's colonnaded Croquet Shelter, and the pools and weeping willows of the Vale of Cashmere. The Music Grove bandstand shows Japanese influences and hosts both jazz and classical music concerts throughout the summer.

A favorite feature of the park is the Camperdown Elm, an ancient and twisted tree planted in 1872. The Friends of Prospect Park raise money to keep it and all the park trees healthy. This old elm has inspired many poems and paintings. Prospect Park has a wide variety of landscapes, from classical gardens dotted with statues to rocky glens with running brooks. A guided tour with a ranger is the best way to see the park.

Carousel horse in Prospect Park

The Brooklyn Museum 20

See pp248–51.

Brooklyn Botanic Garden 21

900 Washington Ave. 🄲 (718) 623-7200. Ⓜ *Prospect Pk, Eastern Pkwy.* **Grounds open** *Apr–Sep: 8am–6pm Tue–Fri (10am Sat & Sun); Oct–Mar: 8am–4:30pm (10am Sat & Sun).* **Closed** *Jan 1, Thanksgiving, Dec 25.* **Adm charge** *for Japanese Garden, free Tue & Sat.* 🄾 🄱 🄲 🄷 🄿

THOUGH IT is not vast in size, you will find that this 50-acre (20-ha) garden holds many delights. The area was designed by the Olmsted Brothers in 1910 and features a traditional Elizabethan-style "knot" herb garden and one of North America's largest collections of roses.

The central showpiece is a Japanese hill-and-pond garden, complete with both a teahouse and Shinto shrine. In late April and early May the park promenade is aglow with delicate Japanese cherry blossoms, which have prompted an annual festival featuring typical Japanese culture, food and music.

April is also the time for tourists to appreciate Magnolia Plaza, where some 80 trees display their beautiful, creamy blossoms against a backdrop of daffodils on Boulder Hill.

The Fragrance Garden is planted in raised beds, where the heavily scented, textured and flavored plants are all labeled in Braille, giving blind visitors an opportunity to identify them as well.

The new conservatory now houses one of America's largest bonsai collections and some rare rain forest trees, which are providing scientists with medicinal extracts to produce life-saving drugs.

A beluga whale at the New York Aquarium

Coney Island 22

Boardwalk and W 8th St, Coney Island. Ⓜ *Stillwell Ave, Coney Island.* **New York Aquarium** 🄲 *(718) 265-3400.* **Open** *10am–6pm daily.*

IN THE MID-19TH century, Brooklyn poet Walt Whitman composed many of his works on Coney Island, accompanied by the roar of the surf. At that time it was untamed Atlantic coastline, the tip of the nose on the great "whale" to which the poet compared Long Island.

By the 1920s, Coney Island was starting to bill itself as the "World's Largest Playground." It had grown from three huge fairgrounds built between 1887 and 1904 (Luna Park, Dreamland and Steeplechase Park), providing a popular combination of hair-raising rides and nearby beaches. The subway arrived in 1920, and the addition of the boardwalk in 1921 ensured Coney Island's popularity throughout the Depression. Here was an escape from the city that cost little more than a few nickels.

A main attraction is the New York Aquarium, moved here from Battery Park in 1955 and worth a day's visit. Today, Coney Island remains an exciting experience for all ages: the boardwalk yields ocean views, the wooden Cyclone roller coaster evokes screams and tourists can still enjoy Nathan's Famous hot dogs.

Brooklyn Botanic Garden lily pond

The Brooklyn Museum of Art ⑱

W HEN IT OPENED in 1897, the Brooklyn Museum building, designed to be the largest cultural edifice in the world, was the greatest achievement of New York architects McKim, Mead & White. Though only one-fifth completed, the museum is today one of the most impressive cultural institutions in the United States, with a permanent encyclopedic collection of some 1.5 million objects, which are housed in a grand structure of 560,000 sq ft (41,805 sq m).

North facade, designed by Stanford White

Chinese Jar
Cobalt blue fishes and water plants adorn this 14th-century Yuan dynasty blue-and-white ceramic jar.

KEY TO FLOOR PLAN

☐ African, Oceanic and New World art

☐ Asian art

☐ Prints, drawings and photographs

☐ Classical and Egyptian art

☐ Decorative arts

☐ Painting and sculpture

☐ Williamsburg murals

☐ Special exhibitions

☐ Non-exhibition space

★ **Paracas Textile**
Over 2,000 years old, a woven mantle from Peru still glows with color.

Mother and Child
Figurines like this are carved by the Luluwa tribe of Zaire as amulets for pregnant or nursing women.

Third floor

Second floor

Sculpture Garden

West wing

First floor

Portico and main entrance

★ **Storm in the Rocky Mountains** *(1866)*
A trip to the American West inspired this painting by Albert Bierstadt.

★ **The Ducal Palace at Venice** *(1908)*
The magical light of Venice was brilliantly captured by Impressionist Claude Monet.

★ **Parlor, Nicholas Schenk House**
This room re-creates middle-class life in 1820's Brooklyn.

Alexander the Great
The military leader was portrayed in alabaster in the 1st century BC.

Ibis Coffin *(332–330 BC)*
The sacred bird of ancient Egypt merited a splendid coffin of gold leaf and silver.

GALLERY GUIDE
The collection is on five floors, with African, Oceanic and New World art on the first; prints, drawings and Asian art on the second; Egyptian, Classical and ancient Middle Eastern art on the third; decorative art on the fourth; and American, European and contemporary art on the fifth. There is special exhibition space on the first and fourth floors.

STAR EXHIBITS

★ **Paracas Textile**

★ **The Ducal Palace at Venice by Claude Monet**

★ **Storm in the Rocky Mountains – Mount Rosalie by Albert Bierstadt**

★ **Parlor, Nicholas Schenk House**

Fifth floor

Fourth floor

Exploring the Collection

THE BROOKLYN MUSEUM houses one of the finest art collections in the United States. Its strengths include an outstanding collection of Native American art from the Southwest; 28 American period rooms; exquisite examples of ancient Egyptian and Islamic art; and many important American and European paintings.

AFRICAN, OCEANIC AND NEW WORLD ART

THE BROOKLYN Museum set a precedent in the United States in 1923 by exhibiting African objects as works of art rather than as artifacts. Since then, the African art collection has grown steadily in both importance and size.

Exhibits include a rare intricately carved ivory gong from the Benin kingdom of 16th-century Nigeria, one of only five in existence.

The museum also has a notable collection of Native American work, including totem poles, textiles and pottery. A 19th-century deerskin shirt, once worn by a chief of the Blackfoot tribe, depicts his brave and daring exploits in battle.

Ancient American artistic traditions are represented by Peruvian textiles, Central American gold and Mexican sculpture. A beautifully preserved tunic from Peru, dating from AD 600, is so tightly woven that its vibrant symbolic designs appear to have been painted onto the cloth rather than woven in the traditional manner.

The Oceanic collection includes sculpture from the Solomon Islands, Papua New Guinea and New Zealand.

ASIAN ART

CHANGING EXHIBITIONS from the museum's permanent collection of Chinese, Japanese, Korean, Indian, Southeast Asian and Islamic art are always on display. Japanese and Chinese paintings, Indian miniatures and Islamic calligraphy complement the Asian sculpture, textiles and ceramics. The collections of Japanese folk art, Chinese cloisonné (enamel work) and Oriental carpets are of particular note. Good examples of Buddhist art range from a variety of Chinese, Indian and Southeast Asian Buddhas to a mandala-patterned temple banner from 14th-century Tibet, painted in rich, luminous watercolors.

Seated Buddha torso in limestone, from India (late 3rd century AD)

DECORATIVE ARTS

THE FOCUS of the decorative arts department is a very stylish assembly of 28 superb American period rooms.

The earliest is from a 17th-century Brooklyn Dutch house. It served as a parlor, dining room and sleeping area, with the enclosed "bed boxes" built against the wall opposite the fireplace. The Moorish Smoking Room, from John D. Rockefeller's brownstone house, is an opulent example of elegant New York living during the 1880s. In complete contrast, the most recent room is a 1928–30 Art Deco study from a Park Avenue apartment, including a walk-in bar that was hidden behind paneling during the Prohibition era (see pp28–29).

Normandie **chrome pitcher, by Peter Müller-Munk (1935)**

Blackfoot tribe deerskin shirt, decorated with porcupine quills and glass beads (19th century)

Also on exhibit is a wide selection from the museum's vast collection of furniture, ceramics, glass, pewter, silver and metalware, including a 1930s pitcher whose shape was inspired by the stacks of the ocean liner *Normandie*.

EGYPTIAN, CLASSICAL AND ANCIENT MIDDLE EASTERN ART

RECOGNIZED AS among the world's finest, the Egyptian collection holds many masterpieces. It begins with an early female figure dating from 3500 BC, and encompasses sculptures, statues, tomb paintings and reliefs as well as funerary paraphernalia. Of the latter, the most unusual is the coffin of an ibis, probably recovered from the vast animal cemetery of Tuna el-Gebel in Middle Egypt. The ibis was a sacred bird representing the god Thoth, and this coffin is made of solid silver and wood overlaid with gold leaf, with rock crystal for the bird's eyes. These galleries have been renovated into a state-of-the-art, high-tech installation.

Among the artifacts from the Greek and Roman civilizations are statuary, pottery, bronzes, jewelry and mosaics.

Among the Ancient Near and Middle Eastern exhibits are an extensive collection of pottery and 12 alabaster reliefs from the Assyrian palace of King Ashur-nasir-pal II. These date from around 883-859 BC and depict the king fighting, overseeing his crops and purifying the "sacred tree," a major icon in Assyrian religion.

PAINTING AND SCULPTURE

THIS SECTION contains works from the 14th century to the present, including a well-known and outstanding 19th-century French art collection with works by Degas, Rodin, Monet, Cézanne, Matisse and Pissarro. It also boasts one of the largest holdings of Spanish

Pierre de Wiessant **(about 1886) by Auguste Rodin, from his** *Burghers of Calais* **group**

Colonial paintings and one of the best collections of North American paintings to be found in the United States.

The museum's 20th-century American collection includes, appropriately, *Brooklyn Bridge* by Georgia O'Keeffe.

The Sculpture Garden has a collection of architectural ornamentation taken from demolished New York buildings, including statues that were rescued from the original Penn Station.

PRINTS, DRAWINGS AND PHOTOGRAPHS

THE PRINTS section displays examples by many masters, ranging from a rare woodcut print by Dürer entitled *The Great Triumphal Chariot* and works by Piranesi to an excellent Impressionist and Post-Impressionist collection. This includes works by Toulouse-Lautrec and Mary Cassatt, the only American woman associated with the Impressionist movement. There are lithographs by James McNeill Whistler, Winslow Homer engravings, and a superb selection of

Rotherhide, **an etching by James McNeill Whistler (1860)**

drawings by Fragonard, Paul Klee, Van Gogh, Picasso and Gorky, among others, many of them in black and white.

The photography collection consists mainly of works by major 20th-century American photographers, including a 1924 portrait of Mary Pickford by Edward Steichen and work by Margaret Bourke-White and Berenice Abbott. Contemporary examples include photographs by Robert Mapplethorpe.

Sandstone reliefs from Thebes in Egypt (around 760–656 BC), depicting the great god Amun-Re and his consort Mut

Staten Island

APART FROM the famous ferry ride, Staten Island and its attractions are not well known to New Yorkers in general. Residents feel so ignored, they've talked about seceding from the city. Visitors who venture beyond the ferry terminal, however, will be pleasantly surprised to find hills, lakes and greenery, with expanses of open space, amazing harbor views and well-preserved early New York buildings. One of the biggest surprises here is a cache of Tibetan art hidden away in a replica of a Buddhist temple.

Historic Richmond Town ㉓

441 Clarke Ave. 📞 (718) 351-1611. 🚌 S74 from ferry. **Open** Jan–Mar: 1–5pm Wed–Fri; Apr–Jun & Sep–Dec: 1–5pm Wed–Sun; Jul–Aug: 10am–5pm Wed–Fri, 1–5pm Sat & Sun. **Adm charge**. 📷 ♿ 🎬 🎁

Cologne at the General Store

THERE ARE NOW 29 buildings, 14 of which are open to the public, in New York's only restored village and outdoor museum. The village was first named Coccles-town, after the local shellfish, but was soon corrupted to "Cuckoldstown," much to the annoyance of the residents. By the end of the Revolutionary War the new name of Richmondtown had been adopted. It was the county seat until Staten Island was made part of the city in 1898, and has been preserved as an example of an early New York settlement.

The Voorlezer House, built in the Dutch era before 1696, is the oldest elementary school to be found in the country. The Stephens General Store, which opened in 1837, doubled as the local post office. It has been well restored, right down to the contents of the shelves. The complex, set on 103 acres (42 ha), includes wagon sheds, a courthouse built in 1837, houses, several shops and a tavern. There are also seasonal workshops where traditional rural crafts are demonstrated to visitors. St. Andrew's Church (1708) and its old graveyard are just across the Mill Pond stream, and the Historical Society Museum is in the County Clerk's and Surrogate's Office. The toy room is a delight.

The Voorlezer House at Richmond Town

Jacques Marchais Center of Tibetan Art ㉔

338 Lighthouse Ave. 📞 (718) 987-3500. 🚌 S74 from ferry. **Open** Apr–Nov: 1–5pm Wed–Sun; (4:45pm: last adm) Dec–Mar: 1–5pm Wed–Fri. **Closed** public hols. **Adm charge**. 📷 🎬 🎁

A HILLTOP provides a very tranquil setting for one of the largest collections of privately owned Tibetan art outside Tibet. The main building is a replica of a mountain temple with an authentic altar

in three tiers, crowded with gold, silver and bronze figures.

Another building is used as a library. The garden has some stone sculptures, including life-size Buddhas. The museum was built in 1947 by Mrs. Harry Klauber, a dealer in Asian art trading under the name of Jacques Marchais. The Dalai Lama paid his first visit here in 1991.

A gazebo at the Snug Harbor Cultural Center

Snug Harbor Cultural Center ㉕

1000 Richmond Terrace. 📞 (718) 448-2500. 🚌 S40 from ferry to Snug Harbor Gate. **Grounds open** dawn–dusk daily. **Gallery and Children's Museum open** noon–5pm Tue–Sun. **Closed** Jan 1, Thanksgiving, Dec 25. ♿ limited. 🎬 🎁

FOUNDED IN 1801 as a haven for aged sailors, Snug Harbor is now an arts center complex of 28 historical buildings in various stages of restoration. There are five stately Greek Revival gems, dating from 1831 to 1880. The oldest, the Main Hall, is the Newhouse Center for Contemporary Art, but the ships at sea in the stained-glass windows are a reminder of its origins.

Sacred sculpture at the Jacques Marchais Center of Tibetan Art

Other buildings house the award-winning Staten Island Children's Museum and the Veterans Memorial Hall, a restored chapel now used for indoor performances.

An annual sculpture festival and summer shows are held on the lawns. The grounds include the Staten Island Botanical Garden, with its noted orchid collection and a beautiful rose garden.

Snug Harbor is the legacy of a Scottish sailor, Robert Richard Randall, who became rich during the Revolutionary War, some say by piracy, and bequeathed his wealth to care for less fortunate seamen. His estate's trustees bought the property so that the sailors could enjoy its harbor views.

Clear Comfort, Alice Austen's lifetime residence

Alice Austen House 26

2 Hylan Blvd. (718) 816-4506.
S 51 from ferry to Hylan Blvd.
Open noon–5pm Thu–Sun. **Closed**
Jan, Feb, public hols. **Donation**
limited.

CLEAR COMFORT is a delightfully named small cottage built around 1710, in a setting with splendid harbor views. This was the home of the

photographer Alice Austen. Born in 1866, she lived in this house for most of her life. She documented life on the island, in Manhattan, and also on trips to other parts of the country and on her travels to Europe. She lost all her money in the stock market crash of 1929 and her poverty forced her into a public poorhouse at the age of 84. One year later, her photographic talent was finally recognized by *Life* magazine, which published an article about her, earning her enough money to enter a nursing home. She left 3,500 negatives dating from 1880 to 1930. Today the Friends of Alice Austen House mounts exhibitions of her best work.

Even Farther Afield

The village of Broad Channel at Jamaica Bay

Jamaica Bay Wildlife Refuge Center 27

Cross Bay Blvd at Broad Channel.
(718) 318-4340. Broad
Channel. **Open** 8:30am–5pm daily.

THE MARSHES and uplands of the Refuge cover an area almost the size of Manhattan. Over 300 species of birds live here either seasonally or all year round. Situated on the main Atlantic migratory path, the Refuge is at its best in spring and autumn, when the skies are filled with skeins of geese and ducks. The park rangers conduct hikes and nature walks for weekend visitors – be sure to wear

suitable shoes and clothes, and take along a zoom lens camera or binoculars to get the best from your visit. The only village at Jamaica Bay is named Broad Channel, a small collection of houses on pilings along the Cross Bay Boulevard. The Refuge and a 10-mile (16-km) stretch of beach and boardwalk at nearby Rockaway, are accessible by subway straight from the heart of Manhattan.

Jones Beach State Park 28

(516) 785-1600.
Long Island Railroad from Penn Station to Jones Beach. **Operates**
late May–Labor Day. (718) 217-
5477. **Jones Beach Theater**
(516) 221-1000.
Beaches open late May –Labor Day .

JONES BEACH was the creation of New York's Parks' Commissioner Robert Moses (*see p244*), who transformed this narrow spit of land into Long Island's most accessible

and popular beach in 1929. There are sand dunes, surf on the Atlantic side and sheltered water in the bay. There is also miniature golf, swimming pools, restaurants and the Jones Beach Theater, which hosts a variety of open-air concerts in the summer.

Robert Moses State Park is on the next island to the east, Fire Island, which is over 30 miles (48 km) long, yet less than 900 yds (800 m) across. Areas of the island are totally unspoiled and unpopulated, with long stretches of white sands, making it a great place for walking and bicycling in peaceful surroundings.

Fire Island's communities are small and very varied – some are favored by singles looking for the company of the opposite sex, others are sedate and family-orientated, others are favorites with New York's large gay community.

Sunbathers basking at Jones Beach

FIVE GUIDED WALKS

WALKING IN NEW YORK is an excellent way to discover the human scale of the city. The following ten pages explore the unique character and charm of New York through five thematic walks. These range from an exploration of Greenwich Village and SoHo's literary and artistic connections *(see pp260–1)* to a trip across the Brooklyn Bridge for spectacular views and a glimpse of 19th-century New York *(see pp264–5)*.

In addition, each of the 15 areas of Manhattan described in the *Area by Area* section of this book has a short

Sculpture outside US Custom House, Lower Manhattan

walk on its *Street-by-Street* map, taking you past many of the interesting sights in that area. Various organizations and enthusiasts run walking tours of the city. These range from serious appraisals of architectural history to a guide to the ghosts of Broadway. Details of tour organizers are listed on page 353, or you can consult the listings in *New York* magazine. As in any major city, take extra care of your personal belongings while walking *(see p356–7)*. Plan your route ahead; walk only during daylight hours; and, whenever possible, go in a group.

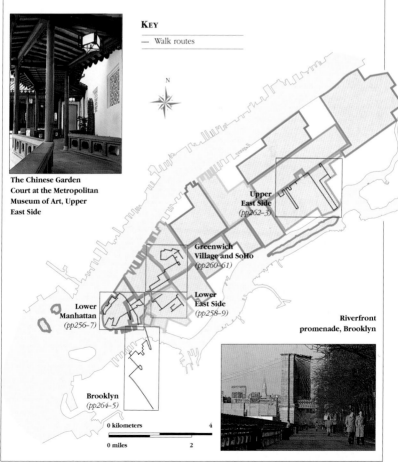

KEY

----- Walk routes

N

The Chinese Garden Court at the Metropolitan Museum of Art, Upper East Side

Upper East Side *(pp262–3)*

Greenwich Village and SoHo *(pp260–61)*

Lower East Side *(pp258–9)*

Lower Manhattan *(pp256–7)*

Riverfront promenade, Brooklyn

Brooklyn *(pp264–5)*

0 kilometers   4

0 miles   2

Relaxing in Grove Street, Greenwich Village

A Two-Hour Walk in Lower Manhattan

Tʜɪs ᴡᴀʟᴋ takes in the tip of Manhattan from its colonial sites to the World Financial Center, passing through the streets of the financial district. There are detours to the historic South Street Seaport as well as to New York's newest neighborhood, Battery Park City. For more details on Lower Manhattan sights, see pages 64–79; for South Street Seaport sights, see pages 80–91.

Battery Park and Federal New York

Start at Battery Park ①, the tip of the island, named for the line of cannons that once protected the harbor. Visit Castle Clinton, an 1807 fort, to see dioramas of a changing New York. The shoreline is much farther out than it used to be; much of the edge of Manhattan is built on landfill, including most of this park.

Walk a little farther inland past the many statues and monuments and the handsome Beaux Arts US Custom House ②. The building is the new home of the Museum of the American Indian. Ironically, it was near to this spot, in 1626, that Peter Minuit acquired Manhattan Island from the local Indians, in exchange for $24 worth of beads and other trinkets.

Cross the street to Bowling Green, the city's first park, dating from 1633; turn right on Whitehall, then left to Pearl Street (which, as the old shoreline, was once scattered with pearly shells). You will soon come to the Fraunces Tavern ③, a restoration of the 1719 building where George

Minuit memorial, Bowling Green

Washington bade farewell to his troops after the Revolutionary War. It is now a restaurant with a small museum upstairs. Also in this block are the last few small-scale Federal-style buildings to be found in the financial district.

The Canyon of Wall Street

Walk up Broad Street, an avenue once split by a canal leading to the river. This was eventually filled in, resulting in one of the wider streets downtown. At Wall Street, look left between the high-rises to Trinity Church, a square-towered structure built in 1846. Try to imagine a New York in which this 280-ft (85-m) steeple was the tallest point in New York (until 1860). Among the many prominent early New Yorkers buried in the graveyard is Alexander Hamilton, whose ghost is said to haunt the nearby grave of Matthew Davis, Aaron Burr's second in the duel that took Hamilton's life.

At the junction of Broad and Wall Street stands the New York Stock Exchange ④. On weekdays, visitors can look down at the trading floor from a balcony. Nearby at 26 Wall Street is Federal Hall ⑤ where, in 1789, crowds of cheering New Yorkers saw George Washington take his oath of office as president.

From Nassau Street to City Hall

Turn uptown at Nassau Street, a continuation of Broad Street, to see some of modern New York at Chase Plaza ⑥, the first open plaza in the financial district. At the north end of the plaza on Liberty Street is the massive, ornate Federal Reserve Bank ⑦, built in 1924 and famed for its five stories of

The tower of City Hall ⑨

bullion vaults. At the far end of the block is the Legion Memorial Square, which was renamed Louise Nevelson

The Immigrants' Memorial at Castle Clinton

Key

— Walk route

- - Detour route

⚡ Good viewing point

Ⓜ Subway station

The *Peking*, a four-masted bark, in South Street Seaport ⑫

Georgian City Hall ⑨, the
seat of New York city
government since 1812.

Turn back to 233
Broadway, the Woolworth
Building ⑩, a 1913
skyscraper that has never
been surpassed in design.
Inside is a marvelous
interior and mosaic
ceiling.

Two blocks farther
south is St. Paul's
Chapel ⑪, where
Washington prayed
after being sworn
into office. As the
city's oldest public
building in constant
use, this Georgian
gem was built
in what was
then a
wheat field.
The Hudson
once flowed
along the edge of
the churchyard.

George Washington,
Federal Hall ⑤

South Street Seaport

Past the church, a left turn at
Fulton Street and a short walk
brings you on to South Street
Seaport ⑫ for a waterfront
lunch and a tour of one of
the tall ships. The red brick
Georgian-Federal buildings
on Schermerhorn Row have
been beautifully restored and
now look brand-new, but this
is an authentic block of early
1800s warehouses and
countinghouses. The North
Star Pub, on
South Street, is
a good place
for a beer. For
a water view,
stop off at the
informal cafés
on Pier 17.

From South Street to Battery Park City

Return along Fulton Street
past Broadway and then cut
through the courtyard behind
the twin towers of the World
Trade Center ⑬ and detour
for the views from the
107th-floor observation
deck. Across the street
is the new World
Financial Center ⑭, a
vital part of the
revival of lower New
York. (Use the over-
pass from the north
tower of the World
Trade Center or
cross at Vesey
Street.) The Winter
Garden is a vast glass
and steel atrium
filled with tall palms,
opening onto a
landscaped
promenade and a
marina on the
Hudson River. Just
before you reach Battery Park
City ⑮ at the end of the
promenade, visit the Museum
of Jewish Heritage *(see p 77).*

Winter Garden at the World
Financial Center ⑭

Plaza
after the
artist, who has
seven sculptures on
display here. Note the
small 1815 building at
90 Maiden Lane
opposite the south
side of the plaza, a
surprising survivor
in the high-rise
financial dist-
rict. The fine
cast-iron front
was added in
1872. Continue
north to Park
Row ⑧ and
the graceful

St. Paul's Chapel ⑪

A 90-Minute Walk in the Lower East Side

THIS WALK PASSES through some of the old immigrant neighborhoods that have given New York its unique texture, and gives you the chance to experience a taste of the character, cultures, and cuisine of some of New York's most vibrant communities. Sunday is the best day for local outdoor activity. For more details on sights in the Lower East Side see pages 92–9.

The Lower East Side

Begin at the Lower East Side Tenement Museum ① at 97 Orchard Street between Delancey and Broome. This original tenement building is being restored to show how immigrants lived at the turn of the century. It features a gallery of exhibits on the immigrant experience, giving insights for the remainder of your walk.

Orchard Street itself ② was the center of the Jewish Lower East Side. The pushcarts that once lined the block are gone, but the shops selling fashionable merchandise at discount prices still remain. The stores close on Saturday, the Jewish

An 1885 iron from the Lower East Side Tenement Museum ①

Sabbath, and so Sunday is the traditional shopping day.

Much of the Jewish population has moved, but reminders are many. Turn left at Grand Street and right at Essex to 35 Essex, the Essex Street Pickle Company ③, the shop in the film *Crossing Delancey*. Barrels of pickles are outside and people line up to buy. Just a few steps down Hester Street brings you to Kadouri Import (dried fruits, nuts and lots of spices) and Gertel's, an old Jewish bakery. Go back up Essex, cross Delancey and at Rivington, turn right for tours and tastings at Schapiro's Winery ④ at 126 Rivington. At 150 is Streit's Matzoh, the largest manufacturer of unleavened bread in New York.

A cultural mixture

Go back along Rivington Street. Have a look at the Spanish *bodegas* and the Chinese grocers supplying the new restaurants in this once-Jewish area. This is a rather gritty street and requires caution, but it shows a true picture of the new immigrant life. Walk across the street. At the corner of Forsyth, a synagogue has been converted to a Spanish church ⑤. Once back on Rivington Street, turn right on to Eldridge

which is a typical tenement street. At the junction of Grand and Eldridge streets you will find the hub of the textile area, good for discount towels and linens. Just beyond Canal Street is the Eldridge Street Synagogue ⑥, which was the first Eastern European synagogue in New York. It is now undergoing a program of restoration.

KEY

— Walk route

-- Detour route

⁙ Good viewing point

Ⓜ Subway station

Clothes vendors at Orchard Street market ②

The Essex Street Pickle Company ③

Pretzel seller on Orchard Street ②

Kam Man Food Products at 200 Canal Street

Chinatown

Return to Canal Street and turn left. At the entry to the Manhattan Bridge, you'll see the World Trade Center towering in the distance, framed in stark contrast by the nearby tenements. Cross the Bowery; you'll see many jewelry shops, the remnants of the original Diamond District ⑦. As you continue, they give way to stalls selling an exotic array of vegetables, and butcher shops with rows of roast ducks in the windows. At 200 Canal Street is Kam Man Food Products. One of the largest Chinese markets in the area, it is a fascinating place to explore.

Turn left from Canal to Mott Street and you'll know you are right in the heart of Chinatown by all the Chinese neon signs. Even the banks and phone booths are shaped like pagodas. There are hundreds of restaurants here, from holes-in-the-wall to haute cuisine, all offering a chance to taste unusual fare. For spiritual sustenance. visit the Eastern States Buddhist Temple ⑧.

At Bayard Street, turn left to see all the Chinese political posters and messages on the Wall of Democracy, then turn back and to the right, to Mulberry Street. The curve next to Columbus Park was Mulberry Bend ⑨, once notorious for gang murders and mayhem.

An Italian deli in Little Italy ⑩

Little Italy

Turn and walk the other way on Mulberry Street and you are suddenly in Little Italy ⑩. Small in area though it is, and encroached on by Chinatown, this is still a wonderful neighborhood full of old-world restaurants and stores selling homemade pasta, sausages, breads and pastries. The Italian population has dwindled over the years, as the younger generation has moved out. But a staunch community still remains, as does the area's Italian atmosphere.

The big event of the year is the Feast of San Gennaro, named for the patron saint of Naples. For eleven nights every September, Mulberry Street is jammed with thousands of locals and visitors enjoying the parades and the Italian food, with rows of stalls selling sizzling sausages.

Little Italy's foothold is Mott to Mulberry on Hester and then from Hester to Grand on Mulberry. If you turn right on to Grand Street you'll soon find yourself passing rows of Chinese grocers again.

A 90-Minute Walk in Greenwich Village and SoHo

A STROLL THROUGH the patchwork quilt of streets in Greenwich Village takes you to where New York's best-known writers and artists have lived, worked and played, and ends with a tour of SoHo's galleries and museums, where today's artists show their work. For more details on sights in Greenwich Village, see pages 106–13, and for SoHo sights, see pages 100–5.

Facade in Washington Mews ⑬

Author Mark Twain, who lived on 10th Street

West 10th Street

The junction of 8th Street and 6th Avenue ① has many book, music and clothing stores nearby. Walk up Sixth to West Ninth Street to see (on the left) Jefferson Market Courthouse ② and (on the right) Balducci's gourmet market.

Turn right at West 10th Street ③ to the Alexander Onassis Center for Hellenic Studies. A passageway at the front once led up to the Tile Club, a gathering place for the artists of the Tenth Street Studio,

where Augustus Saint-Gaudens, John LaFarge and Winslow Homer lived. Mark Twain lived at 24 West 10th Street, and Edward Albee at 50 West 10th.

Back across Sixth Avenue is Milligan Place ④, a cluster of 19th-century houses, and Patchin Place ⑤, where the poets e e cummings and John Masefield both lived.

Farther on is the Ninth Circle bar ⑥ which, when it first opened in 1898, was known as "Regnaneschi's." It was the subject of John Sloan's painting *Regnaneschi's Saturday Night.* Playwright Edward Albee first saw the question "Who's afraid of Virginia Woolf?" scrawled on a mirror here.

The doorway of Chumley's ⑩

Greenwich Village

Turn left at Waverly Place past the Three Lives Bookstore, a typical Village literary gathering spot, to Christopher Street and to the triangular Northern Dispensary ⑦.

Follow Grove Street along Christopher Park to Sheridan Square, the busy hub of the

Village. The Circle Repertory Theater ⑧, which premiered plays by Pulitzer Prizewinner Lanford Wilson, is now closed.

Cross Seventh Avenue and bear left on to Grove Street. At the corner of Bedford Street, you can't miss "Twin Peaks" ⑨, a home for artists in the 1920s. Turn right to see Bedford: the unmarked door is Chumley's ⑩, a saloon not much changed since 1928 when it was a speakeasy *(see p28).* Writers Dylan Thomas, Simone de Beauvoir, Ernest Hemingway, William Faulkner, J.D. Salinger, Jack Kerouac and many others drank here. Covers of their books line the walls. 75 Bedford is the narrowest house in the Village, once the home of feminist poet Edna St. Vincent Millay.

Walk up Carmine to Sixth Avenue and turn right at Waverly Place. At 116 Waverly ⑪, Anne Charlotte Lynch, an English teacher, held weekly gatherings in her town house for such eminent friends as Herman Melville and Edgar Allan Poe, who gave his first reading of *The Raven* here.

A detour left of half a block will bring you to MacDougal Alley ⑫, a lane of carriage houses in which Gertrude Vanderbilt Whitney had her studio. She opened the first Whitney Museum here in 1932, just behind the studio.

TIPS FOR WALKERS

Starting point: 8th St/6th Ave.
Length: 2 miles (3.2 km).
Getting there: Take subway train A, B, C, D, E or F to West Fourth Street-Washington Square station (Eighth Street exit). Fifth Avenue buses M2 and M3 stop at Eighth Street. From here, walk one block west to Sixth. The M5 bus loops around Washington Square back to Sixth Avenue and Eighth Street.
Stopping-off points: The Pink Tea Cup, 42 Grove Street, is good for lunch. The SoHo Kitchen & Bar, 103 Greene Street, is a typical soaring SoHo space, also known for its superb selection of wines.

Washington Square

Once back on MacDougal, turn left to Washington Square North, to see the finest Greek Revival houses in the United States. Writer Henry James set his *Washington Square* in No. 18, his grandmother's home.

Then pause at Fifth Avenue to look back at Washington Square Park for a perfect view

Washington Square Park and Arch

0 meters 500

0 yards 500

KEY

— Walk route

❧ Good viewing point

Ⓜ Subway station

of the twin towers of the World Trade Center framed by the Washington Square Arch.

Go across to Two Fifth Avenue; opposite is Washington Mews ⑬, an elegant carriage house complex. John Dos Passos, Edward Hopper and Rockwell Kent lived in the studio at No. 14a at various times.

Go back up Washington Square North, past some elegant houses. Writer Edith Wharton lived at Seven Washington Square North. Walk beneath the arch and across Washington Square Park. On the left as you leave the park, is the fine Judson Memorial Church and Tower ⑭ by Stanford White and the NYU Loeb Student Center. The Center was once a boarding house, known as the "house of genius," and is where Theodore Dreiser wrote *An American Tragedy.*

SoHo

Walk south on Thompson, a typical Village street lined with clubs, cafés and shops. Turn left at Houston, SoHo's northern limit, and right on West Broadway, lined with some of the city's most famous galleries along with chic and arty boutiques.

Turn left at Spring Street for yet more tempting shops, then right at Greene Street ⑮, the heart of the Cast-Iron Historic District. Many of these fine buildings now house clusters of galleries. Turn left at the end of Greene Street to Canal Street, the end of SoHo, to see how quickly New York can change. This noisy street is full of hawkers and discount electronics stores. You can explore bargains for the next two blocks and then turn left up Broadway, soon finding yourself on the cutting edge of art, at the New Museum of Contemporary Art at 583 Broadway and the Guggenheim Museum SoHo ⑯ found at 575 Broadway *(see p105).*

Cast-iron facade, Greene Street ⑮

A Two-Hour Walk in the Upper East Side

A PROMENADE ALONG upper Fifth Avenue and its environs will take you past the best remaining examples of New York's turn-of-the-century gilded age. A detour through the old German district of Yorkville leads to a riverside stroll to Gracie Mansion, official residence of the city's mayor, dating from 1799. For details on Upper East Side sights, see pages 180–201.

0 meters 500
0 yards 500

From the Frick to the Met
Begin at the Frick mansion ①, built for coal magnate Henry Clay Frick in 1913–14. Allow some extra time to see Frick's art collection (pp200–1). Many such mansions were built as New York's first families outdid each other with miniature Versailles, Loire-style châteaux and even Venetian palazzos. Most of the ones still standing have now become either institutions or museums. The apartment building opposite the Frick is typical of those where today's affluent New Yorkers live.

East on 70th are two of the city's top art galleries, the Knoedler Gallery and Hirschl & Adler ②. Walk up Madison to the corner of 72nd Street, to the big Polo-Ralph Lauren store ③, the 1898 French Renaissance home of Gertrude Rhinelander Waldo. Wander inside to see the elegant restored interior.

Walk back toward Fifth on the north side of 72nd, past two 1890s limestone beauties, now the Lycée Français de New York ④. Continue along Fifth Avenue to 73rd Street. Turn east to 11, Joseph Pulitzer's former home ⑤.

A few blocks on, between Lexington and Third, is a fine row of town houses ⑥. Back on Fifth, walk to 75th Street, to see No. 1,

Church of the Holy Trinity ⑰

KEY
— Walk route
❊ Good viewing point
Ⓜ Subway station

the former residence of Edward S. Harkness, son of a founder of Standard Oil. It is now the Common-Fund ⑦. At 1 East 78th, the tobacco millionaire James B. Duke's 18th-century French-style château has now become the New York University Institute of Fine Arts ⑧. At 79th Street and Fifth, the former home of financier Payne Whitney, is the French Embassy ⑨ and 2 East 79th is the Ukrainian Institute of America ⑩. On the southeast corner of 82nd is Duke-Semans House ⑪, one of the few grand Fifth Avenue residences still privately owned. Save another day for The Metropolitan Museum of Art ⑫ at 82nd.

Ukrainian Institute of America ⑩

Carl Schurz Park Promenade

TIPS FOR WALKERS

Starting point: Frick Collection.
Length: 3 miles (4.8 km).
Getting there: Take subway train 6 to 68th Street and Lexington, then walk west (left) three blocks to Fifth Avenue. Or take the M1, M2, M3 or M4 bus up Madison Avenue to 70th Street and walk one block west.
Stopping-off points: The cafés at the Whitney and Guggenheim museums are pleasant. Or sample the German fare at Ideal, a restaurant at 322 E. 86th Street, or try the Heidelberg Café on Second Avenue off 86th Street. Madison Avenue between 92nd and 93rd has many places to eat, including Sarabeth's Kitchen, with its excellent weekend brunch.

Yorkville

Turn east on 86th Street for the vestiges of German Yorkville – Bremen House ⑬, Kleine Konditorei and Ideal, a restaurant that

serves large portions. Cross Second Avenue, then turn right to the Heidelberg Café and German deli, Schaller & Weber ⑭.

East River and Gracie Mansion

Henderson Place ⑮ at East End Avenue is a cluster of 24 red-brick Queen Anne town houses. Carl Schurz Park opposite was named after the city's most prominent German immigrant, editor of *Harper's Weekly* and the *New York Post*. The park promenade atop the east River Drive leads to a view of Hell Gate, where the Harlem River, Long Island Sound and New York harbor meet. From the walkway you can see the back of Gracie Mansion ⑯, the mayor's official residence. The path west along the fence leads to a better view. Walk west on 88th Street past the Church of the Holy Trinity ⑰ and at Lexington Avenue go to 92nd Street and west past two of the few wooden houses left in Manhattan ⑱.

The Cooper-Hewitt Museum ⑳

Carnegie Hill

Back on Fifth Avenue, turn downtown past the Felix Warburg Mansion of 1908, now the Jewish Museum ⑲, and continue to 91st Street and the huge Andrew Carnegie home, now the Cooper-Hewitt Museum ⑳. Built in 1902 in the style of an English country manor, it gave the area the unofficial name of Carnegie Hill. The James Burden House ㉑ at 7 East 91st Street, built for Vanderbilt heiress Adele Sloan in 1905, has a spiral staircase under a stained glass skylight that was known in society as "the stairway to heaven." At 1 East 91st, the financier Otto Kahn's Italian Renaissance-style residence was a showplace with a drive-through porch and interior courtyard. It is now the Convent of the Sacred Heart School.

Wooden houses on 92nd Street ⑱

A Three-Hour Walk in Brooklyn

A TRIP ACROSS New York's most famous crossing leads to Brooklyn Heights, the city's first suburb. This neighborhood has a 19th-century feel, mixed with a hint of Middle Eastern cultures. The riverfront promenade has unrivaled views of Manhattan. For more details on sights in Brooklyn, see pages 245–51.

Brooklyn Bridge–Worth Street
550yards/500m

Fire Station on Old Fulton Street

Fulton Ferry Landing

About 3,580 ft (1 km) long, the Brooklyn Bridge span yields thrilling views of the lower New York skyline and prize photo opportunities. Take a taxi, or, if feeling energetic, walk across to Brooklyn.

On the far side, follow the Tillary Street sign to the right, turn right at the bottom of the stairs, then take the first path through the park and walk down Cadman Plaza West ① under the Brooklyn-Queens Expressway; here Cadman becomes Old Fulton Street. You can see the bridge on the right as you head to the river at Water Street and the Fulton Ferry landing ②. During the Revolutionary War, George Washington's troops fled to Manhattan from here. In 1814, this was the depot for the ferry connecting Brooklyn and Manhattan Island. This transformed Brooklyn Heights from a predominantly farming area to a residential district. The area is full of character and is still a very popular place to live. To the right is the River Café ③. This restaurant's fine cuisine and spectacular views of the Manhattan skyline make it one of New York's most exceptional dining spots.

Eagle Warehouse ④

Brooklyn Heights

From the landing, turn right up steep Everitt Street up Columbia Heights, past the former Eagle Warehouse ④ of 1893 to Middagh Street and along the streets of Brooklyn Heights. 24 Middagh ⑤ is one of the oldest, built in 1824.

Next turn right on Willow and left on Cranberry; here the town houses range from wooden clapboards to brick Federal-style to brownstones. Except for cars and a few modern buildings, you could be in the 19th century.

Many famous people have lived here. Truman Capote wrote *Breakfast at Tiffany's* and *In Cold Blood* in the basement of 70 Willow, and Arthur Miller once owned 155 Willow. Walt Whitman lived on Cranberry Street when he was editor of the *Brooklyn Eagle*. He set the type for his *Leaves of Grass* at a print shop near the corner of Cranberry and Fulton. The town houses now on the site are called Whitman Close.

Turn right along Hicks. The Hicks family, local farmers, inspired the name "hick" for a yokel. Turn left on Orange Street to the Plymouth Church ⑥, home of Henry Ward Beecher, an antislavery preacher. His sister, Harriet Beecher Stowe,

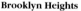

Entrance to the River Café

Truman Capote with feathered friend

wrote *Uncle Tom's Cabin*. At Clark Street are marquees of once-luxurious hotels, such as the Towers. Follow Clark Street to 142 Columbia Heights, where Norman Mailer lives ⑦. Invalid Washington Roebling lived at 110 – using a telescope, he directed the construction of Brooklyn Bridge from his room.

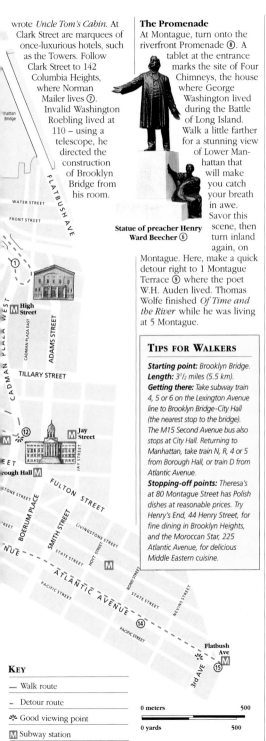

Statue of preacher Henry Ward Beecher ⑥

The Promenade
At Montague, turn onto the riverfront Promenade ⑧. A tablet at the entrance marks the site of Four Chimneys, the house where George Washington lived during the Battle of Long Island. Walk a little farther for a stunning view of Lower Manhattan that will make you catch your breath in awe. Savor this scene, then turn inland again, on Montague. Here, make a quick detour right to 1 Montague Terrace ⑨ where the poet W.H. Auden lived. Thomas Wolfe finished *Of Time and the River* while he was living at 5 Montague.

TIPS FOR WALKERS

Starting point: *Brooklyn Bridge.*
Length: *3¹/₂ miles (5.5 km).*
Getting there: *Take subway train 4, 5 or 6 on the Lexington Avenue line to Brooklyn Bridge-City Hall (the nearest stop to the bridge). The M15 Second Avenue bus also stops at City Hall. Returning to Manhattan, take train N, R, 4 or 5 from Borough Hall, or train D from Atlantic Avenue.*
Stopping-off points: *Theresa's at 80 Montague Street has Polish dishes at reasonable prices. Try Henry's End, 44 Henry Street, for fine dining in Brooklyn Heights, and the Moroccan Star, 225 Atlantic Avenue, for delicious Middle Eastern cuisine.*

The old Montague Street trolley, which led to the river and the ferry

Montague and Clinton Streets
Once back on Montague Street, walk to the heart of Brooklyn Heights, with all its cafés and boutiques. The baseball team, the Brooklyn Dodgers, got their name from dodging the trolley cars that once ran down the street. Walk to the intersection of Montague and Clinton to see the stained glass of the 1834 Church of St. Ann and the Holy Trinity ⑩. Walk a block left on Clinton to Pierrepont Street for the Brooklyn Historical Society ⑪. A block farther, at Court Street, is the 1849 Borough Hall ⑫, and the subway taking you back to Manhattan.

Brooklyn's Dodgers, who got their name from dodging trolley cars

Atlantic Avenue
Another option is to stay on Clinton and walk five short blocks to Atlantic Avenue. A left turn here leads to a whole string of Middle Eastern emporia ⑬, such as Sahadi Imports at 187 Atlantic Avenue, with a huge selection of foods. Rashid at 191 sells Arabic publications and records; and the Damascus Bakery at 195 makes the most delicious filo pastries. Two blocks on are numerous antique shops ⑭. At Flatbush Avenue, look left to the Brooklyn Academy of Music ⑮ and the grand front of the Williamsburg Savings Bank. Watch for signs to the subway back to Manhattan.

KEY

— Walk route

-- Detour route

✲ Good viewing point

Ⓜ Subway station

0 meters _____ 500
0 yards _____ 500

RENAISSANCE

SAMSUNG
SAMSUNG
SAMSUNG

SUNTORY
WHISKY

Enjoy
Coke

AT THE DOUGLAS
FAIRBANKS THEATRE

TRAVELERS' NEEDS

WHERE TO STAY

WITH OVER 65,000 hotel rooms available, New York offers something for everyone. The top hotels are not quite as expensive as those in Paris or London, but the best news for visitors is the increase in budget hotels. While many of these are basic rather than charming, they offer good value. Other budget options are furnished apartments and studios and bed and breakfast in private homes, as well as youth hostels and YMCAs. From an inspection of over 200 hotels, we have selected 72 as the best of their kind. *Choosing a Hotel (pp274–45)* helps you make a choice based on your needs, but for more detailed descriptions, turn to the listings on pages 276–83. The map on page 272 highlights ten hotels, chosen as the best in their category.

Cole Porter's piano, in the Waldorf–Astoria bar *(see p281)*

Bathroom at the Paramount Hotel *(see p277)*

WHERE TO LOOK

THE EAST SIDE, roughly between 59th and 77th streets, is the traditional location for luxury hotels, but the renovation of certain landmark midtown properties, such as the St. Regis, and new hotels in famous chains from the Far East, such as the Peninsula Group, have increased competition in this price range.

Business travelers tend to favor midtown, especially the moderately priced hotels lining Lexington Avenue near Grand Central Terminal.

Those seeking relative quiet with access to midtown should look in the Murray Hill area, while theater lovers should note the revival of the Times Square area. Hotels within walking distance of theaters offer an advantage, since performances tend to end at the same time and cabs are hard to come by.

There are a number of good, inexpensive hotels around Herald Square, which is convenient for shopping. The Upper West Side hotels are also less expensive. This popular residential area is convenient for Lincoln Center and offers easy access to public transportation.

The **New York Convention and Visitors Bureau** publishes a free, annually updated leaflet called "The New York Hotel Guide," listing current rates, toll-free numbers and fax numbers. Staff will offer advice about hotels but do not make reservations.

HOTEL PRICES

SOME HOTELS offer seasonal promotional rates and other off-peak reductions. For example, business travelers vacate hotels at the end of the working week, and you can take advantage of bargain weekend deals, even in luxury hotels, as prices drop *(see Special Breaks p270)*. There is a growing number of all-suite hotels available in every price category. Suites offer extra space plus cooking facilities and a refrigerator. Most suites can accommodate up to four people, which makes them popular with families.

Café Botanica at the Essex House Hotel *(see p278)*

HIDDEN EXTRAS

WHEN CALCULATING the cost of hotels in New York, it is not enough simply to take into consideration the quoted room price. Hotel rooms have long been subject to extra taxes, but the former sliding scale, which favored rates under $100, has now given way to a blanket 13.25% hotel tax, plus $2 per night per room fee.

Several hotels now include continental breakfast in the room price. This is a big

Lobby phones, to reach a guest staying in the hotel.

Suite at the Millenium *(see p276)*

saving, since standard hotel continental breakfast prices, before tax and tip, start at about $5 and soar to around $15 in some of the luxury hotels. To save money, head for the nearest deli or coffee shop and leave the hotel to business people having power breakfasts.

Hotel telephone charges are usually high; it may well be cheaper to use the pay phone in the lobby, particularly when calling overseas.

Tips are expected in the United States. Staff who take your luggage to the room are usually tipped a minimum of $1 per bag – more in a luxury hotel. The concierge need not be tipped for normal services such as arranging transportation or making dinner reservations, but should be rewarded for exceptional services.

When you order from room service, check the menu to see whether a service charge will also be included in the bill; if not, a 15% tip is customary. Solo travelers will find that single room rates are usually at least 80% of the double rate and are sometimes the same as for two people.

FACILITIES

ALTHOUGH you'd expect hotel rooms in New York City to be noisy, most windows are double- or even triple-glazed to keep out the noise. Air-conditioning is almost a standard feature, so there is no need to open the windows in hot weather. Even so, some rooms are obviously quieter than others, if they are at the back of the hotel or overlooking a courtyard – check when reserving.

Television, radio and at least one telephone are usually provided in every room, even in modest lodgings, and most hotel bedrooms have private bathrooms. In budget and mid-priced hotels a shower, rather than a tub is the norm. Many mid-range hotels now offer fax outlets and machines in each room, a health club or exercise room and a full concierge service. Luxury facilities include mini-bars in the room, dual phones, private phone message systems and electronic checkout.

The hotels listed here are all within a few minutes' walk of a large number of shops and restaurants. Very few hotels have their own parking, but valets may park your car in areas reserved for guests' use in nearby public garages. A reduced (but still expensive) daily parking fee is normally offered. If there is no concierge at the hotel, front desk staff will be able to help with tourist information and to answer any queries.

The Art Deco lobby of the Edison Hotel *(see p277)*

How to Reserve

It is advisable to make hotel reservations at least one month in advance. While it's unlikely that the hotel will be fully booked, you may well find that the best rooms and suites have been taken, especially if a major convention is taking place. The busiest periods are at Easter, the New York Marathon week in late October or early November, Thanksgiving and Christmas.

Reserve directly with the hotel by telephone, letter or fax. Written confirmation of your telephone booking will be required, probably with a deposit as a guarantee of your arrival; any cancellation fees may be deducted from this. You can pay by credit card, international bank draft or money order, or US traveler's check. Advise the staff if you are going to arrive at the hotel after 6pm or you will lose your reservation, unless you have prepaid with a credit card.

You can also book a hotel through your travel agent or airline. Most hotels have a toll-free telephone number for use in the United States, but these numbers do not work from Europe and the UK. If the hotel is part of an international chain, an affiliated hotel in your country should be able to reserve a room for you.

Special Rates

Hotels are busiest during the week, when business travelers are in the city, so most of them offer budget packages to encourage more weekend business. It's often possible to move from a standard to a luxury room for the weekend at the same rate.

A lower corporate rate is usually available to employees

Lobby of the St. Regis Hotel (*see p282*)

of large companies. But quite often, reservation clerks will grant corporate discounts on request without asking for a company affiliation.

Some reservation agencies offer discount rates. A good travel agent should be able to get the best current rates, but compare prices by contacting directly a discount reservation service such as Express (*see p269*). They offer discounts between 20% and 50% on bookings, depending on the time of year. You reserve by credit card and receive a voucher, which you should present to the hotel.

Package tours can also provide savings on the usual price. These rates may not oblige you to stay with a tour group, only to use their air and hotel arrangements. These packages may also include airport transfers, an additional saving. Airlines frequently have their own special deals, particularly during slow travel seasons. Again, a knowledgeable travel agent should be able to tell you the current best deals, but newspapers often advertise special, limited offers that can be booked directly. At off-peak times you may net even bigger savings than with the package plans.

Directory

Disabled Travelers

Mayor's Office for People with Disabilities
52 Chambers St, Room 206, NY, NY 10007.
☎ 788-2830.

Bed and Breakfast

Abode Bed and Breakfast Inc
PO Box 20022, NY, NY 10021. ☎ 472-2000.

At Home in NY
PO Box 407, NY, NY 10185.
☎ 956-3125/0407.
FAX 247-3294.

Bed & Breakfast (& Books)
35 W 92nd St, Apt 2C, NY, NY 10025.
☎ 865-8740.

Bed & Breakfast in Manhattan
PO Box 533, NY NY 10150.
☎ 472-2528.
FAX 988-9818.

Bed & Breakfast Network of New York
130 Barrow St, Suite 508, NY, NY 10014.
☎ 645-8134 / (800) 900-8134.

City Lights Bed & Breakfast Ltd
PO Box 20355, Cherokee Stn, NY, NY 10021.
☎ 737-7049.

New World Bed and Breakfast Ltd
150 5th Ave, Suite 711, NY, NY 10011.
☎ 675-5600.

Urban Ventures, Inc.
PO Box 426, Planetarium Station, NY, NY 10024.
☎ 594-5650.

Youth Hostels and Dormitories

Hosteling International, NY
891 Amsterdam Ave at W 103rd St, NY, NY 10025. **Map** 20 E5.
☎ 932-2300.

92nd St Y
1395 Lexington Ave, NY, NY 10128. **Map** 17 A2.
☎ 415-5650.

YMCA-Vanderbilt
224 E 47th St, NY, NY 10017. **Map** 13 A5.
☎ 756-9600.

YMCA-West Side
5 W 63rd St, NY, NY 10023. **Map** 12 D2.
☎ 875-4273.

Student Lodgings

NYU Summer Housing
8 Washington Place, NY, NY 10003. ☎ 998-4621.

Airport Hotels

See p364-5 for details of the hotels to be found at the two major New York airports, **JFK** *and* **Newark**.

DISABLED TRAVELERS

By LAW, NEW hotels must provide facilities for disabled visitors, and many older buildings have been renovated to comply, too. Guide dogs are allowed in most hotels, but it is advisable to check when reserving.

This guide's disabled access information is based upon each hotel's own assessment of its suitability. Let the hotel know of any specific needs when booking. The **Mayor's Office for People With Disabilities** also offers information about hotels.

TRAVELING WITH CHILDREN

AMERICAN HOTELS generally have a very welcoming attitude toward children. Cots or cribs and lists of baby-sitters are normally widely available, and most hotel restaurants are happy to cater to young guests.

Traveling with children can be cheaper than anticipated. Many hotels do not charge for children if they stay in their parents' room, or make only a small charge for an extra bed. There is usually a limit of one or two children per room in these cases, and most hotels stipulate that the children must be under a certain age, often 12. Parents of older children are expected to pay the full price, although the age limit is occasionally extended to 18. Ask about family rates when reserving.

BED-AND-BREAKFAST

THERE IS AN increasing number of bed-and-breakfast accommodations to be had in private apartments. This varies from a room in an apartment with an owner-host in residence to an entire apartment to yourself, with its own kitchen and bathroom, yours while the owner is away.

Staying in a private apartment enables you to feel at home in a New York neighborhood and to visit local restaurants, usually far more reasonably priced than

Entrance to the Peninsula Hotel
(see p281)

those in tourist areas. Bed-and-breakfast lodgings can be found through many free booking services. Some booking agencies have a two-night minimum. Rates for unhosted apartments vary from about $70 to $200, and for a double room range from $60 to $90 a night, depending on whether you have a private bathroom. There is a wide range of apartments, from spacious and luxurious to cramped and dowdy. Your costs will rise if the address is remote, requiring frequent cabs. Ask about location and amenities when you reserve.

YOUTH AND BUDGET ACCOMMODATIONS

A YOUTH HOSTEL and many YMCA dormitories offer lodgings for those on a tight budget. For the longer-term visitor, the **92nd Street Y**, a nonsectarian hostel and lively cultural center situated in the Upper East Side, has good-value rooms from about $30 to $50 a night.

There are no campsites in Manhattan, and, sadly, youth hostels are not as prevalent in New York as they are in large European cities.

Sky-high swimming pool at the UN Plaza Hotel *(see p280)*

New York's Best: Hotels

NEW YORK hotels range from the ultimate in luxury to the surprisingly cheap and cheerful. All are within easy reach of shops, restaurants and transportation. Some are of historical or literary interest; some are streamlined and hi-tech; others are old-fashioned and cozy. From this wide variety, certain hotels stand out, whether for character, comfort or good value. The hotels shown here have been selected from the listings on pages 276–83 as the best in their particular style or price range.

Plaza
This land-mark hotel has been part of New York life for over 100 years. Re-furbishing has restored its early glamor. (See p281.)

Wyndham
Book well in advance for a winning com-bination of homey charm and low prices.
(See p280.)

Theater District

Paramount
Chic designer Philippe Starck set the style of this ultra-smart, yet sensibly-priced, hotel.
(See p278.)

Chelsea and the Garment District

Lower Midtown

Greenwich Village

Gramercy and the Flatiron District

SoHo and TriBeCa

Seaport and the Civic Center

Lower East Side

Lower Manhattan

Algonquin
Sip a cocktail in the spot where literary wit Dorothy Parker and her circle gathered in the 1920s.
(See p278 and p143.)

Box Tree
Two brownstones have been converted into an intimate yet sumptuous inn, complete with superb restaurant. (See p281.)

Carlyle
Old-world elegance, stunning views of Central Park and the mellow jazz notes of Bobby Short in the Café Carlyle combine to make this luxury hotel superb. (See p282.)

Lowell
Luxurious suites offer all the comforts of a country house on the Upper East Side. There are also two restaurants on the premises. (See p282.)

Four Seasons
Modern fittings and hi-tech gadgetry combine with superlative service at an I. M. Pei-designed hotel. (See p281.)

0 kilometres　　　2
0 miles　　　1

Pickwick Arms
Midtown's best bargain offers no-frills value for money in the heart of Manhattan. An unexpected bonus are the fine views of the encircling skyline from the simple, pleasant roof terrace. (See p280.)

Regal United Nations Plaza
The soaring views from the bedrooms are outdone only by those from the glassed-in, 27th-floor pool. (See p280.)

Choosing a Hotel

THE 72 HOTELS listed in the following pages have all been individually inspected and assessed to help you make an informed decision. All the hotels are in Manhattan itself, within easy walking distance of museums, shops, and restaurants. They are listed alphabetically in their price category.

		NUMBER OF ROOMS	LARGE ROOMS	BUSINESS FACILITIES	CHILDREN'S FACILITIES	RECOMMENDED RESTAURANT	CONCIERGE	QUIET LOCATION	24-HOUR ROOM SERVICE
LOWER MANHATTAN (See p276)									
Millenium Hilton	$$$$	561		■	●		●		●
NY Marriott Financial Center	$$$$	504		■	●		●		
SoHo Grand Hotel	$$$$$	367		■					●
GREENWICH VILLAGE (See p276)									
Washington Square Hotel	$$	170					■	■	
GRAMERCY AND THE FLATIRON DISTRICT (See p276)									
Carlton	$$$	171		■	●			■	
The Inn at Irving Place	$$$$	12	●					■	
Roger Williams	$$$$	186	●					■	
CHELSEA AND THE GARMENT DISTRICT (See p276)									
Best Western Manhattan	$	183							
Herald Square Hotel	$	120							
Hotel Metro	$$	180		■					
Stanford	$$	130			●				
THEATER DISTRICT (See pp277–9)									
Best Western Ambassador	$	70		■					
Days Hotel Midtown	$$	366		■					
Edison	$$	900							
Hampshire Hotel and Suites	$$	200		■					
Howard Johnson Plaza	$$	300		■	●				
Ramada Milford Plaza	$$	1300		■					
Wellington	$$	617		■					
Doubletree Guest Suites	$$$	460		■	●		●		
Iroquois	$$$	106		■					
The Mansfield	$$$	124					●		
Paramount	$$$	610		■	●	■	●		●
Salisbury	$$$	196	●						
Algonquin	$$$$	165		■					
Crowne Plaza	$$$$	770	●	■	●		●		●
Essex House	$$$$	597		■	●	■	●		●
Michelangelo	$$$$	178	●	■	●		●		
Millennium Broadway	$$$$	627		■	●				
Royalton	$$$$	169		■	●	■	●		●
St. Moritz	$$$$	695							
Le Parker Meridien	$$$$$	700		■			●		●
Rihga Royal	$$$$$	500	●	■	●		●		●
LOWER MIDTOWN (See pp279–80)									
Quality Hotel	$$	189		■					
Helmsley Middletowne	$$	190						■	

Price categories for a double room per night, including tax and service:
$ under $150
$$ $150–$220
$$$ $220–$300
$$$$ $300–$400
$$$$$ over $400

CONCIERGE
Concierge available to advise, make reservations, etc

BUSINESS FACILITIES
Message service; fax for guests; desk and telephone in each room; meeting room within the hotel.

CHILDREN'S FACILITIES
Family rooms; cots or cribs; babysitting service; children's portions; high chairs in dining area.

QUIET LOCATION
Quiet, residential neighborhood or quiet street in a busy area.

	Price	Number of Rooms	Large Rooms	Business Facilities	Children's Facilities	Recommended Restaurant	Concierge	Quiet Location	24-Hour Room Service
Jolly Madison Towers	$$$	225	●	■					
Roger Smith	$$$	130	●	■	●				
Doral Court	$$$$	199	●	■		■	●	■	
Doral Park Avenue	$$$$	188		■		■	●	■	
Doral Tuscany	$$$$	121		■		■	●	■	
Morgans	$$$$	113		■	●		●	■	●
Regal United Nations Plaza	$$$$	427		■	●	■	●		●
Sheraton Russell	$$$$	146	●	■		■	●	■	●
UPPER MIDTOWN (See pp280–82)									
Pickwick Arms	$	370					●	■	
Wyndham	$$	200	●					■	
W. New York	$$$	720		■			●		
Fitzpatrick Manhattan Hotel	$$	92		■			●		●
Hotel Benjamin	$$$$	209	●	■	●		●		
The Elysée	$$$$	99		■	●				
Plaza	$$$$	804	●	■	●	■	●		●
Waldorf–Astoria	$$$$	1380	●	■	●	■	●		●
Box Tree	$$$$$	13		■		■		■	●
Four Seasons	$$$$$	370	●	■		■	●		●
New York Palace	$$$$$	800	●	■	●	■	●		●
Peninsula	$$$$$	242	●	■	●	■	●		●
Pierre	$$$$$	202	●	■	●	■	●		●
St. Regis	$$$$$	314	●	■	●	■	●		●
Westin Central Park South	$$$$$	207	●	■	●	■	●		●
UPPER EAST SIDE (See pp282–3)									
Franklin	$$$	53		■	●			■	●
Hotel Wales	$$$	87		■			●	■	
Surrey Hotel	$$$$	130	●	■		■	●	■	●
Mark	$$$$$	180	●	■	●	■	●		●
Carlyle	$$$$$	190	●	■	●	■	●		●
Lowell	$$$$$	67	●		●	■	●	■	●
Plaza Athénée	$$$$$	152		■		■	●	■	●
Regency	$$$$$	384	●	■	●	■	●		●
Stanhope	$$$$$	183	●	■	●	■	●	■	●
UPPER WEST SIDE (See p283)									
Beacon	$$	100					●	■	
Empire	$$	381		■	●	■	●		
Excelsior	$$	196	●					■	
Milburn	$$	111	●	■	●		◐	■	●
On The Ave	$$	251	●						
Mayflower	$$$	377	●	■				■	

LOWER MANHATTAN

Millenium Hilton

55 Church St, NY, NY 10007.
Map 1 B2. 693-2001
FAX 571-2316. **Rooms:** 561.

AE, DC, MC, V, JCB. $$$$

At 58 stories high, the sleek
Millenium is designed to appeal to
the well-heeled who have business near Wall Street. Rooms are
not particularly large, but make
excellent use of space with furnishings that give the illusion of
being built-in. Bathrooms are in
dramatic black marble, lighting
fixtures are the very latest design,
and there are conveniences such
as two-line telephones with
speaker and conference capa-
bilities, voice mail, and a video
system that can be used to order
room service or settle the bill.
Most rooms face the World Trade
Center; lower floors overlook the
courtyard while higher locations
offer a view of the river. Some of
the most pleasant views are from
the side, where the fitness center
and large pool face the leafy
churchyard of St. Paul's Chapel.

New York Marriott Financial Center

85 West St, NY, NY 10006. **Map** 1 B3.
385-4900. FAX 227-8136. **Rooms:**
504.

AE, DC, MC, V, JCB. $$$$

The standard rooms and amenities
of this hotel are redeemed by some
welcome features, such as an
indoor pool and health club and
the outstanding views of the
Hudson River from higher floors.
Rates drop substantially on weekends, making this a good base for
exploring Lower Manhattan.

SoHo Grand Hotel

310 West Broadway, NY, NY 10013.
Map 4 E4. 965-3000. FAX 965-
3200. **Rooms:** 367.

AE, DC, MC, V, JCB.
$$$$$

The first hotel in arty SoHo
opened in 1996, a stylish, well-
located haven in an area ideal for
browsing. The two-level lobby,
designed to evoke the architectural spirit of the neighborhood,
boasts massive brick and cast stone
columns, exposed steel ceiling
beams, and a staircase of translucent glass and iron suspended by
cables. Guest rooms in neutral
tones offer king-size beds and

two-line phones with voice mail.
Vintage photographs of New York
adorn the walls. The hotel
includes a fitness room and a
bistro that serves American fare.

GREENWICH VILLAGE

Washington Square Hotel

103 Waverly Pl, NY, NY 10011.
Map 4 E2. 777-9515.
FAX 979-8373. **Rooms:** 170.

AE, MC, V, JCB. $$

This small hotel, just off the square
in the heart of Greenwich Village,
has tiny rooms but much to recom-
mend it nevertheless. Marble,
lattice-work, and plants give an
old-world look to the lobby, while
the narrow hallways are accented
with Mexican tiles. The rooms are
decorated with cheerful fabrics,
bathrooms are new, and there is a
restaurant and a small fitness
center. Above all, it is the only
hotel in the center of the Village.

GRAMERCY AND THE FLATIRON DISTRICT

Carlton

22 E 29th St, NY, NY 10016. **Map** 8 F3.
532-4100. FAX 889-8683.
Rooms: 171.

AE, DC, MC, V, JCB $$

Extensive renovation of this Beaux
Arts building is transforming it from
a budget option to a moderate first
class hotel, although there is no
fixed completion date for the work.
The hotel is conveniently situated
for the shops of 34th Street.

The Inn at Irving Place

56 Irving Place, NY, NY 10003. **Map** 9
A5. 533-4600. FAX 533-4611.
Rooms: 12.

AE, MC, V, JCB. $$$$

This discreet 19th-century town
house is straight out of a Jane
Austen novel. The sitting room
with high ceilings and ornate
plasterwork and the 12 guest
rooms are filled with antiques
denoting understated elegance.
Bedrooms have brass, iron, or
carved headboards, Victorian
armoires, wooden-armed settees,
chaise longues, and period lamps,
and each has a fireplace (non-
working). The 20th-century
intrudes only with additions such
as dual line telephones, cable
television and videos. Guests can

enjoy breakfast in a charming
dining room/bar, where an elegant
five-course tea is also served in
the afternoon. The neighborhood,
near Gramercy Park, is another
evocation of Old New York.

Roger Williams

131 Madison Ave, NY, NY 10016.
Map 9 A3. 448-7000. FAX 576-
4343. **Rooms:** 186.

AE, DC, MC, V. $$$$

Complete renovation by Gotham
Hospitality Group has turned the
Roger Williams into a spiffy hotel
that fits the Gotham model. Rooms
include CD players and VCRs,
music in the lobby, and a
complimentary breakfast.

CHELSEA AND THE GARMENT DISTRICT

Best Western Manhattan

17 W 32nd St, NY, NY 10001.
Map 8 E3. 736-1600. FAX 563-
4007. **Rooms:** 183.

AE, DC, MC,
V, JCB. $

This new budget entry on the "Little
Korea" block is a winner, recently
renovated with fresh black-and-
white décor, stylish contemporary
furnishings, and new bathroom
fixtures. The theme is New York,
with attractive Manhattan photos
in the halls and fun touches like
a Statue of Liberty lamp in each
room. Comfortable suites accommodate four and are an excellent
choice for families.

Herald Square Hotel

19 W 31st St, NY, NY 10001.
Map 8 F3. 279-4017. FAX 643-
9208. **Rooms:** 120. 108.

AE, MC, V, JCB. $
See p131.

This tiny budget hideaway has
been renovated with taste. The
gilded cherub over the front door
remains from the time when the
Beaux Arts building, designed by
Carrere and Hastings, was the first
home of *Life Magazine*, a satirical
magazine in its earliest incarnation.
Vintage *Life* covers now adorn the
hallways. The rooms are quite
small but pleasantly decorated and
bathrooms are modern. The
location near Macy's is very convenient for Herald Square shopping
and the Javits Convention Center.
The neighborhood, unfortunately,
lacks a wide range of restaurants,
but "Little Korea" is only a
block away, with a variety of
inexpensive eateries.

Hotel Metro

45 W 35th St, NY, NY 10001.
Map 7 C2. **(** 947-2500. **FAX** 279-1310. **Rooms:** 180. 🛏 🎬 📺 ⌨
🌆 🗄 🍴 🛗 ᱚ 🌐 🗄 ℹ
🎫 AE, DC, MC, V. ⑤⑤

A bright, recent arrival, the Metro
sets a breezy, sophisticated tone
with a spacious contemporary
Deco-Revival lobby and walls
adorned with oversized Greta Garbo
and Marlene Dietrich photos, old
movie posters, and vintage New
York scenes. Rooms are a good
size with a tailored black-and-tan
color scheme, striped wallpaper,
and amenities such as refrigerators
and hair dryers. There is a small
exercise room on the top floor,
and the roof terrace, with its views
of the Empire State Building,
becomes an outdoor bar during
the summer months. Guests can
also enjoy a spacious double sitting room off the lobby where a
complimentary breakfast is served
and coffee is available throughout
the day. Understandably popular
with younger visitors in the
fashion industry, the Hotel Metro
is a well-priced choice for all.

Stanford

43 W 32nd St, NY, NY 10001.
Map 8 F3. **(** 563-1480. **FAX** 629-0043. **Rooms:** 130. 🛏 🗄 ᱚ 📺
🍴 🛗 ᱚ ℹ 🎫 AE, DC,
MC, V., JCB ⑤

Particularly popular with Asian
visitors, this clean, modern hotel
on the "Little Korea" block is a
great bargain. In addition to the
standard hotel facilities of a telephone, TV and radio, each comfortable room has a small
refrigerator. The Stanford offers an
American coffee shop as well as
the Gam Mee Ok restaurant, which
features good Korean cuisine.
The location is convenient for
Herald Square as well as Madison
Square Garden and the Javits
Convention Center (see p136).

THEATER DISTRICT

Best Western Ambassador

132 W 45th St, NY, NY 10036.
Map 12 E5. **(** 921-7600.
FAX 719-0171. **Rooms:** 70. 🛏 ᱚ ᱚ
📺 🗄 ᱚ 🌐 ℹ 🍴 🎫 AE, DC, MC,
V, JCB. ⑤

This modest, reasonably priced
choice in a convenient location for
theater-goers has recently been remodeled with attractive new
furnishings and bathrooms. A free
continental breakfast is available in
the hotel lobby.

Days Hotel Midtown

790 8th Ave, NY, NY 10019. **Map** 12
D5. **(** (1800) 572-6232. **FAX** 974-0291. **Rooms:** 366. 🛏 ᱚ 📺
ᱚ 🗄 🍴 🌐 🍴 🛗 ℹ
🎫 AE, DC, MC, V. ⑤⑤

Location is the main attraction at
this otherwise predictable Loews
chain hotel in the Theater District.
The entire hotel was recently
renovated, including the lobby,
which has some sleek banquettes
and an attractive Art Deco
chandelier. The rates are
moderate, especially for families,
as children under 12 can stay in
their parents' room free. Definitely
worth consideration.

Edison

228 W 47th St, NY, NY 10036.
Map 12 E5. **(** 840-5000.
FAX 596-6850. **Rooms:** 900. 🛏 ᱚ
ᱚ 📺 ᱚ 🗄 ᱚ 🍴 🛗 ℹ
🎫 AE, DC, MC, V, JCB. ⑤⑤

After its recent restoration, this
vintage building has become one
of the best value hotels to be
found in the Theater District. The
Art Deco lobby, brass doorways,
and period light fixtures of the
original 1931 hotel have all been
beautifully restored. Rooms have
also been refurbished, and now
boast updated bathrooms and some
new furnishings. The hotel has a
café, restaurant, and bar.

Hampshire Hotel and Suites

157 W 47th St, NY, NY 10036.
Map 12 D5. **(** 768-7573.
FAX 768-3403. **Rooms:** 200. 🛏 ᱚ
ᱚ 📺 ᱚ 🗄 ᱚ 🌐 🍴 🛗 ℹ
🎫 AE, DC, MC, V, JCB. ⑤⑤

A multilingual staff welcomes
guests from all parts of the world
at this modest hotel. It is convenient for theater-goers, has small,
recently renovated bedrooms with
new bathroom fixtures, and offers
complimentary continental breakfasts. No frills, but decent value.

Howard Johnson Plaza

851 8th Ave, NY, NY 10019.
Map 12 D4. **(** 581-4100.
FAX 974-7502. **Rooms:** 300. 🛏 ᱚ
ᱚ 📺 ᱚ 🗄 ᱚ 🌐 🍴 🛗
🎫 AE, DC, MC, V, JCB. ⑤⑤

Although it has the name of a chain
of motels, this lodging is also under
upmarket Loews management, and
it may exceed your expectations.
Comfortable, decent-sized rooms
have recently been refurbished.
Many rooms have spacious areas
for seating and lots of work space,
and there is an on-site restaurant.
A garage is available for parking.

Children under 18 can stay free
with their parents. For the price,
it's a reasonable choice.

Ramada Milford Plaza

270 W 45th St, NY, NY 10036.
Map 11 C5. **(** 869-3600.
FAX 642-4694. **Rooms:** 1300.
🛏 ᱚ 🌐 📺 ᱚ 🗄 🌐
🌐 🍴 🛗 ℹ 🎫 AE, DC, MC, V,
JCB. ⑤⑤

Big and bustling, this 28-story,
1300-roomed hotel is a favorite
with tour groups who appreciate
its location in the heart of the
Theater District. Don't expect frills,
but there are conveniences such as
exercise equipment and a
restaurant and bar on site, as well
as videos available on request.

Wellington

7th Ave at 55th St, NY, NY 10019.
Map 12 E4. **(** 247-3900.
FAX 581-1719. **Rooms:** 617.
🛏 ᱚ 🌐 📺 🗄 🌐 🌐 🍴 🛗
🍴 🛗 ℹ 🎫 AE, DC, MC, V, JCB.
⑤⑤

A favorite with tour groups,
this big budget hotel offers a
convenient midtown location and
amenities that include a coffee
shop, lounge, and restaurant on
the premises. Smallish rooms
offer updated baths; suites and a
number of rooms also provide
kitchenettes. Family rooms with
two bathrooms are also available.

Doubletree Guest Suites

1568 Broadway, NY, NY 10036.
Map 12 E5. **(** 719-1600.
FAX 921-5212. **Rooms:** 460.
🛏 ᱚ 🌐 📺 ᱚ 🗄 ᱚ 🌆 🌐
🌐 🌐 🍴 ℹ 🎫 AE, DC, MC, V.
⑤⑤⑤

Broadway buffs, business travelers,
and families will find spacious
quarters here and a quiet haven
from the busy scene outside. Part
of a 43-story office building atop
the Palace Theater, the setting is
suitably dramatic for the Theater
District, with a sky-lit third-floor
lobby, klieg lighting, and sleek
playful Deco décor. The well-
equipped two-room suites offer
three phone lines with call waiting
and voice mail, two remote-control
TV sets, a bar, refrigerator,
microwave, coffee maker, and
ironing board. Guests also have
free use of a fitness center and
children's playroom, access to a
café, and room service from
6am–4am. Everyone gets the
Doubletree trademark chocolate
chip cookies at night.

For key to symbols see p271

Iroquois

49 W 44th St, NY, NY 10036.
Map 12 F5. **☎** 840-3080.
FAX 398-1754. *Rooms: 106.* ▥ **1**
▥ **TV** ▤ ▦ **Ⅵ** ▥ **Ⅱ ⅰ**
☑ *AE, DC, MC, V, JCB.* **⑤⑤⑤**

Famous for being the home of the legendary actor James Dean from 1951–3, this hotel has recently undergone major renovation, both inside and out. It has grown from a budget hotel to one of understated elegance and luxury, including a new, first-class restaurant. It is well located for shopping and theaters.

The Mansfield

12 W 44th St, NY, NY 10036. **Map** 11
B5. **☎** 944-6050. **FAX** 764-4477.
Rooms: 124. ▥ **TV** ▦ ▥
▥ **P ⅰ** **☑** *AE, MC, V.* **⑤⑤⑤**

Adding to the hotel riches on this block is this treasure built in 1904 as a lodging for wealthy bachelors. It has recently been restored by the Gotham Hospitality Group, whose architecturally interesting and moderately priced hotels are an increasing and welcome presence in the city. The original cast iron detailing and stonework, coffered ceilings, graceful mahogany, and steel staircases have been restored. Rooms are chic modern, with sleigh beds made of iron and wire mesh, and sleek stainless steel washbasins in the bathroom. On the main floor are a sitting room with a period skylight and a lovely book-lined library where a harpist plays and concerts are held. Rates include parking, breakfast, complimentary cappuccino all day and an after-theater dessert buffet, as well as a library of tapes, CDs, and videos for the TV, video, and CD player in every room.

Paramount

235 W 46th St, NY, NY 10036.
Map 12 E5. **☎** 764-5500. **FAX** 354-
5237. *Rooms: 610.* ▥ **1** ▦ **24**
TV ▦ ▤ **Ⅵ** ▥ **Ⅺ** ▥ **Y Ⅱ ⅰ**
☑ *AE, DC, MC, V, JCB.* **⑤⑤⑤**

Philippe Starck's spectacular floating stairway and lighting, inspired by the art of Joan Miró, are the first things you see in the Paramount Hotel. Ian Schrager designed it for the young and hip and to prove that inexpensive hotels need not be boring. Playful design manage to distract from the tiny rooms. Amenities include a children's play room and a branch of Dean & DeLuca *(see p326)*, with take-out food. There's a business center, and a video library to supply the video recorders in every room. The bar, known as Whiskey, is one of the hottest spots in town.

Salisbury

123 W 57th St, NY, NY 10019.
Map 12 E3. **☎** 246-1300. **FAX** 977-
7752. *Rooms: 196.* ▥ **1** ▦ **TV**
▥ ▤ **Ⅵ ⅰ** ▥ **☑** *AE, DC, MC, V,*
JCB. **⑤⑤⑤**

Comfortably old-fashioned, the Salisbury is a really good deal in a wonderful location. It is right across from Carnegie Hall and an easy walk to the best Fifth Avenue shops. Rooms are fairly undistinguished, but a decent size, and many of them have well-equipped kitchenettes, a bonus for families. The ambience is friendly and warm, and the neighborhood is convenient and safe.

Algonquin

59 W 44th St, NY, NY 10036. **Map** 12
F5. **☎** 840-6800. **FAX** 944-1419.
Rooms: 165. ▥ ▦ **TV** ▦ ▥ **Ⅵ**
▥ **Ⅺ** ▥ **Y Ⅱ ⅰ** **☑** *AE, DC,*
MC, V, JCB. **⑤⑤⑤⑤** *See p143.*

The Round Table of the 1920s may have gone, but the Algonquin still maintains its famous literary tradition. It is a favorite haunt of publishers, writers, and theatrical types – even the friendly bartender is rumored to have written a couple of novels. Renovation has considerably freshened the décor and modernized most bathroom fixtures, but the old-fashioned feel of the rooms, which make up in coziness what they lack in size, has been very carefully preserved.

Crowne Plaza

1605 Broadway, NY, NY 10019.
Map 12 E4. **☎** 977-4000.
FAX 315-6164. *Rooms: 770.* ▥ **1**
▦ **24** **TV** **Y** ▤ ▥ **Ⅵ** ▤ ▦
▥ **Ⅺ** ▥ **Ⅵ** ▥ **P Y Ⅱ ⅰ**
☑ *AE, DC, MC, V, JCB.* **⑤⑤⑤**

For those who want a really big hotel right on Broadway, there is much to recommend the Crowne Plaza, aptly described by one reviewer as "brassy and classy." Public spaces are flashy and fun and, while their furnishings are predictable, the rooms are large, and higher floors have some really great views of New York or the Hudson River. Guests can choose from three restaurants and have the use of a well-equipped business center, a health club, and the added luxury of New York's largest indoor hotel swimming pool.

Essex House

160 Central Park S, NY, NY 10019.
Map 12 E3. **☎** 247-0300.
FAX 315-1839. *Rooms: 597.* ▥ ▦
▦ **24** **TV** **Y** ▤ ▥ **Ⅵ** ▥ **Ⅺ** ▥
▥ ▥ **P Y Ⅱ ⅰ** **☑** *AE, DC,*
MC, V. **⑤⑤⑤⑤**

A multimillion dollar renovation by the Nikko hotel chain of Japan has transformed the Essex House into dramatic Art Deco. There are stunning black marble columns standing tall in the lobby, coffered ceilings, etched brass elevator doors and newly enlarged windows, through which views of Central Park can be enjoyed. Rooms are not overly large, but guests who have views of the park may never actually notice. All of the rooms are decorated in tasteful, traditional English-style décor, and guests are treated to bathrobes, shoe shines, turn-down service, and 24-hour room service. The hotel also offers a health spa and a business center.

Michelangelo

152 W 51st St, NY, NY 10019.
Map 12 E4. **☎** 765-1900.
FAX 581-7618. *Rooms: 178.* ▥ ▦
24 **TV** ▤ ▥ **Ⅵ** ▥ **Ⅺ** ▥ **P**
Y Ⅱ ⅰ **☑** *AE, DC, MC, V, JCB.*
⑤⑤⑤

A classy hotel situated just off Broadway, this New York outpost of Italy's Starhotels has spacious rooms averaging 475 sq ft (46 sq m) and an unusual choice of room furnishings: Empire, Country French, or Art Deco. Marble bathrooms come with oversize tubs and TVs. Guests enjoy a complimentary continental breakfast, videos and a video library, and a 24-hour fitness facility. Business travelers can choose SmartDesk rooms, conveniently equipped with computers, printer/fax/ copiers, and fax modems.

Millennium Broadway

145 W 44th St, NY, NY 10036.
Map 12 E5. **☎** 768-4400.
FAX 768-0847. *Rooms: 627.* ▥ **1**
▦ **TV** ▤ ▥ **Ⅵ** ▤ ▥ **Ⅺ** ▥
▥ **P Y Ⅱ ⅰ** **☑** *AE, DC, MC,*
V, JCB. **⑤⑤⑤⑤**

Sleek and streamlined, this high-tech mecca boasts a striking modernistic lobby and staff dressed all in robotlike gray. Rooms are fairly small for the price, but are compensated for by a large cache of gadgetry, which includes voice mail in four languages and an in-room system that allows guests to access airline schedules and restaurant menus, order tickets, and make theater reservations, review accounts, and then check out of the hotel electronically. Hotel amenities include a fitness center and a business center. The Millennium Broadway is especially recommended for business travellers, who can make use of the extensive meeting room and conference facilities.

Royalton

44 W 44th St, NY, NY 10036.
Map 12 F5. **C** 869-4400.
FAX 869-8965. **Rooms:** 169. ⚓ 1
⚏ 24 TV ⚑ ⚑ ≡ ⚑ ⚑ ⚑
⚑ P ⚑ ¶¶ ℹ 🅰 AE, DC, MC,
V. $$$$

Ian Schrager, who began revolutionizing New York hotels with Morgans on Madison Avenue, really pulled out all the stops with the amazing Royalton. Philippe Starck's design includes a space-age lobby, curving hallways, and rooms rigged out like first-class cabins in a sleek ocean liner, with big beds built in like bunks. Who likes this sort of thing? Well, the celebrity guest list includes directors David Lynch and Oliver Stone, actors Dudley Moore, Sean Penn, and John Malkovich, the Manhattan Transfer singing group, and other musical stars including Hammer and heavy-metal band Guns 'n' Roses. The 44 restaurant attracts trendy editorial types for lunch, and the small round bar, aptly called 44 Round, is equally popular.

St. Moritz

50 Central Park S, NY, NY 10019.
Map 12 E3. **C** 752-7760.
FAX 688-6619. **Rooms:** 695. ⚓ 1
⚏ TV ⚑ ⚑ ≡ ⚑ P ⚑ ¶¶ ℹ
🅰 AE, DC, MC, V, JCB. $$$

Standing in a superb location opposite Central Park, and with one of the best sidewalk cafés in the city, the refurbished St. Moritz is a solid choice in the moderate-price category – especially for rooms facing the park. While not posh, the décor is comfortable, and most bathrooms have been updated. Rumplemayer's, the famous ice-cream parlor, is just off the lobby. Don't count the calories, just enjoy the experience.

Le Parker Meridien

119 W 56th St, NY, NY 10019.
Map 12 E3. **C** 245-5000.
FAX 708-7477. **Rooms:** 700. ⚓ 1
⚏ 24 TV ⚑ ⚑ ≡ ⚑ ⚑ ⚑
⚑ ⚑ P ⚑ ¶¶ ℹ 🅰 AE,
DC, MC, V, JCB. $$$$$

The two main attractions at Le Parker Meridien are the soaring public spaces and the exceptionally good fitness facilities. There is a rooftop pool, jogging track, squash courts, and racquetball court, plus a well-equipped health club. The entrance, a two-story, block-long arcade, is very impressive, and the colorful Montparnasse bar is a great place for a relaxing drink. Recently refurbished rooms are in a chic Neo-Classical motif and come with fax, hairdryer, and CD player.

Rihga Royal

151 W 54th St, NY, NY 10019.
Map 12 E4. **C** 307-5000.
FAX 765-6530. **Rooms:** 500. ⚓ 24
TV ⚑ ⚑ ≡ ⚑ ⚑ ⚑ ⚑
P ⚑ ¶¶ ℹ 🅰 AE, DC, MC, V,
JCB. $$$$$

In the line-up of the many luxury hotels near Broadway, the all-suite Rihga Royal really does stand out: at 54 stories high, it is one of New York's tallest hotels. Rooms on the upper floors offer spectacular panoramic views. Each elegant suite has a living room with bay windows and one or two bedrooms, separated with mirrored French doors. Décor is classic and comfortable, and amenities in the rooms include dressing areas, minibars with icemakers, three telephones, two TVs, including cable TV and movie channels, a video, and an electronic room safe. Guests can also make the most of a business and fitness center, free newspapers, shoe shines, and the added convenience of a shuttle bus from the hotel to Wall Street.

LOWER MIDTOWN

Quality Hotel

3 E 40th St, NY, NY 10016. **Map** 8 F1.
C 447-1500. **FAX** 213-0972.
Rooms: 189. ⚓ 1 ⚏ TV ⚑ ⚑
⚑ ⚑ ⚑ ⚑ ¶¶ ℹ 🅰 AE, DC,
MC, V, JCB. $$

A Canadian company, which is best known for its motels, has provided this clean, contemporary, no-frills midtown hotel with very reasonable rates. The décor is motel-like, but the rooms are fitted out with functional work tables, comfortable sitting areas, remote-control TV, clock radios, and guests receive complimentary morning newspapers and coffee. Many rooms have sofa beds for children, who can stay free in their parents' room. The location is convenient for theaters and good shopping.

Helmsley Middletowne

148 E 48th St, NY, NY 10017.
Map 13 A5. **C** 755-3000.
FAX 832-0261. **Rooms:** 190. ⚓ 1
⚏ TV ⚑ ≡ ⚑ ⚑ P 🅰 AE,
DC, MC, V, JCB. $$

Of the city's several Helmsley hotels, the Middletowne Hotel is the least glitzy and the best bargain. It is a good bet for those who like the ambience of a smaller hotel but who also want a safe, convenient East Side location. The lobby is tiny, the rooms are small, but the bedrooms have a

pleasant atmosphere, as they have been redecorated in bright colors and fresh fabrics. All rooms have refrigerators, and many come with kitchenettes.

Jolly Madison Towers

22 E 38th St, NY, NY 10016.
C 802-0600.
FAX 447-0747. **Rooms:** 225. ⚓ 1
⚏ TV ⚑ ⚑ ⚑ ⚑ Y ¶¶ ℹ
🅰 AE, DC, MC, V. $$$

A comfortable midrange hotel, the Madison Towers is nothing fancy – but then neither are the rates. The rooms are reasonably large and are being redecorated by the Jolly chain from Italy. The hotel offers a good health spa equipped with whirlpool and sauna. The pleasant Whaler Bar has a fireplace and murals with a nautical theme.

Roger Smith

501 Lexington Ave, NY, NY 10017.
Map 13 A1. **C** 755-1400.
FAX 758-4061. **Rooms:** 130. ⚓ 1
⚏ TV ≡ ⚑ ⚑ ⚑ ⚑ ⚑ P
Y ¶¶ ℹ 🅰 AE, DC, MC, V.
$$$

This used to be just yet another commonplace commercial hotel, but some artistic new owners have done wonders. The lobby has been transformed with paintings and sculpture, and all the rooms have been refurbished; no two are alike, and some have four-poster beds. Continental breakfast is offered on the balcony level, and Lily's Restaurant serves good continental food.

Doral Court

130 E 39th St, NY, NY 10016.
Map 9 A1. **C** 685-1100.
FAX 889-0287. **Rooms:** 199. ⚓ 1
⚏ TV Y ⚑ ≡ ⚑ ⚑ ⚑ ⚑ P
¶¶ ℹ 🅰 AE, DC, MC, V.
$$$$

This is the least assuming of three popular Doral properties in the civilized Murray Hill area, and the Doral Court is an appealing hotel. Among its many features are a small, warm, wood-paneled lobby and cheerful, light and airy rooms with entry foyers, walk-in closets, dressing areas and fluffy bathrobes. The best extra is guest privileges at the nearby Doral Fitness Center. Ask for one of the four rooms on the 15th floor for terraces with skyline views.

Doral Park Avenue

70 Park Ave, NY, NY 10016. **Map** 9 A1.
C 687-7050. **FAX** 973-2440.
Rooms: 188. ⚓ 1 ⚏ TV Y ≡
⚑ ⚑ ⚑ ⚑ Y ¶¶ ℹ 🅰 AE,
DC, MC, V. $$$$

A Murray Hill oasis attracting sophisticated travelers who prefer smaller hotels, the Doral Park Avenue has distinctive Neo-Classical décor. Tranquil bedrooms in muted colors have such luxurious amenities as marble bathrooms, well-stocked minibars, and TV movies. Guests also have use of the Doral Fitness Center. In warm weather, the Odyssey Lounge moves outside with a pleasant sidewalk café.

Doral Tuscany

120 E 39th St, NY, NY 10016.
Map 9 A1. 686-1600. **FAX** 779-7822. *Rooms:* 121. *AE, DC, MC, V.* $$$$

The most expensive of the Murray Hill Doral trio, the Tuscany attracts a loyal clientele who appreciate the fresh flowers, walk-in closets, TV and telephone in the bathroom, and refrigerators stocked with soft drinks. Guests can use the Doral Fitness Center across the street, or request exercise bicycles in their rooms. The aptly named Time and Again restaurant has a good reputation.

Morgans

237 Madison Ave, NY, NY 10016.
Map 9 A3. 686-0300. **FAX** 779-8352. *Rooms:* 113. *AE, DC, MC, V.* $$$$

There are no hotel clichés at this first hot property of Ian Schrager, not even a sign out front. French designer Andrée Putnam's black-and-white minimalist world is clean and uncluttered, from the optical-illusion cube carpeting in the lobby to the bold tiles and stainless steel sinks in the bathrooms. Furniture in the smallish rooms is functional – built-in sofas, window seats that lift to accommodate suitcases and clutter. All rooms come with a CD player and private phone line; fax and computers are available on request. There is complimentary continental breakfast, afternoon tea service, and dining at the Asia de Cuba restaurant.

Regal United Nations Plaza Hotel

1 United Nations Plaza, NY, NY 10017.
Map 13 C5. 758-1234. **FAX** 702-5051. *Rooms:* 427. *AE, DC, MC, V, JCB.* $$$$ See p156.

There is no more dramatic setting in New York than Kevin Roche's soaring skyscraper towering above the city, which is usually filled with an international clientele

from the nearby United Nations. The sleek, marble lobby has chrome accents and massive floral bouquets are displayed here. Pastel-hued and very comfortable modern bedrooms begin on the 28th floor and provide truly spectacular views. The 27th floor has a fitness center and a glass-enclosed swimming pool, and on the 38th floor is the only indoor hotel tennis court in Manhattan. The artwork throughout the hotel is unique, taken from the hotel's collection of antique tapestries and textiles gathered from every UN country. The hotel also offers butler service, and provides a free shuttle bus to business locations and to the Theater District.

Sheraton Russell

45 Park Ave, NY, NY 10016. **Map** 9 A2. 685-7676. **FAX** 889-3193. *Rooms:* 146. *AE, DC, MC, JCB.* $$$$

The Sheraton Russell (formerly the Sheraton Park Avenue) is decorated in English style, with wood-paneled walls, Chippendale furnishings, and an entire library of leather-bound books. Bedrooms are comfortable, with long floral curtains, mantelpieces, and prints of old New York on the walls. It has a fine restaurant and a bar, and a concierge is always on duty. It is understated and quietly situated.

UPPER MIDTOWN

Pickwick Arms

230 E 51st St, NY, NY 10022.
Map 13 B4. 355-0300.
FAX 755-5029. *Rooms:* 370. 235. *AE, DC, MC, V, JCB.* $

With a good and safe Eastside address, this is the best Midtown choice in the budget range. The comfortable lobby is adorned with columns, sofas, and a sparkling chandelier. Plain but pleasant bedrooms offer TV, a small safe, and room service. The single rooms with a shared bathroom are very cheap. The studios offer extra space and a sofa bed for additional family members. On the premises are a French bistro and Mediterranean restaurant. It's a good hotel to relax in and enjoy the city views from the attractive rooftop garden.

Wyndham

42 W 58th St, NY, NY 10019.
Map 12 F3. 753-3500. **FAX** 754-5638. *Rooms:* 200. *AE, DC, MC, V.* $$

It is important to book well in advance to get a room in the hotel that many consider to be New York's best buy. The very homey warm atmosphere is enhanced by the fact the owners themselves reside here. Exceptionally large rooms are individually furnished and decorated and, although a little threadbare in places, they all have a personal charm and warmth. This is a favorite place for actors, especially those seeking long-term lodgings during a Broadway run. The restaurant is currently undergoing renovation and is due to reopen in the late fall of 2000.

W. New York

541 Lexington Ave, NY, NY 10022.
Map 13 A5. 755-1200.
FAX 319-8344. *Rooms:* 720. *AE, DC, MC, V, JCB.* $$$

One of several decent commercial hotels near Grand Central, the W. New York provides a very good bargain. It has well-decorated, moderately priced lodgings and offers extras such as a complimentary health club with a sauna and squash courts, a 24-hour café and a convenient and money-saving laundry room. The hotel is also popular with tour groups, which accounts for the occasional lines at the check-in counter.

Fitzpatrick Manhattan Hotel

687 Lexington Ave, NY, NY 10022.
Map 13 A3. 355-0100.
FAX 355-1371. *Rooms:* 92. *AE, DC, MC, V, JCB.* $$$

Emerald-green carpet, Waterford chandeliers, and lots of Irish prints are unmistakable clues that this is a new American outpost for a Dublin-based hotelier. Further hints include a portrait of the Irish president and suites named after past presidents of the Irish Republic. This is a renovation of a former apartment hotel with just 92 rooms, more than half of them suites, which are much better value than the rather small single rooms. Amenities offered to the guests include cable TV, voice mail, computer, and fax outlets. Guests also get membership privileges at the Excelsior Club, an excellent nearby fitness center. Fitzers, the in-house restaurant and bar, offers dishea featuring a good choice of produce that reflects the hotel's character, including delicious Dublin Bay prawns and oak-smoked salmon.

Hotel Benjamin

125 E 50th St, NY, NY 10022. **Map** 13
A4. █ 715-2500, 888-4 BENJAMIN.
█ 715-2525. **Rooms**: 209. █ █
█ █ █ █ █ █ █ █ █ █
█ AE, DC, MC, V. $$$$$

The Benjamin, in a carefully
restored 1927 building, is an
Executive Suite Hotel offering elegant rooms and suites in intimate,
boutique-style settings. Its business
center has every amenity for the
traveling executive. The excellent
American Place restaurant is here.

The Elysee

60 E 54th St, NY, NY 10022.
█ 753-1066. █ 980-9278.
Rooms: 99. █ █ █ █ █ █
█ █ █ █ █ █ █
█ AE, DC, MC, V, JCB. $$$$$

In a world of look-alike hotels,
the 99-room Elysee stands out.
Named rather than numbered
rooms have a homelike quality,
each individually furnished with
comfortable reading areas and
antique pieces such as fruitwood
commodes or carved desks that
look as though they might have
been in the family for years. Some
rooms have kitchenettes and
terraces, and all have sleek, marble
baths. Rates include continental
breakfast as well as afternoon tea
served in a pretty second-floor
sitting room, where the menu
changes to complimentary wine
and cheese after 5pm. The murals
in the Monkey Bar are famous,
including Hirschfeld caricatures of
Tallulah Bankhead, Joe DiMaggio,
the Gish Sisters, Tennessee
Williams, and other former residents of the hotel. The Piano Suite
boasts a Steinway once
belonged to Vladimir Horowitz.

Plaza

5th Ave at 59th St, NY, NY 10019.
Map 12 F3. █ 759-3000. █ 759-
3167. **Rooms**: 804. █ █ █ █
█ █ █ █ █ █ █ █ █
█ █ █ █ AE, DC, MC, V, JCB.
$$$$$ See p179.

There are ritzier hotels and more
elaborate rooms in New York, but
for location, lobby, and history,
nothing compares with the Plaza.
It is a National Landmark, a local
fixture, and has been a favorite for
almost 100 years. The Plaza
presides over Grand Army Plaza
at the entrance to Central Park,
and rooms facing the park have
fabulous green vistas. The rates are
higher on weekends, but you get a
restaurant credit for some fine
meals at the several restaurants in
the hotel. Other amenities include a
boutique, gift shops, a barber, and
hair salon.

Waldorf–Astoria

301 Park Ave, NY, NY 10022.
Map 13 A5. █ 355-3000.
█ 872-7272. **Rooms**: 1380.
█ █ █ █ █ █ █ █ █
█ █ █ █ █ █ █ █ █
█ AE, DC, MC, V, JCB. $$$$$
See p175.

There are really two Waldorfs: the
big business-orientated hotel and
the ultra-exclusive Towers, with its
own private entrance and chic
concierge and some of the most
elaborate and beautifully furnished
quarters in the city. The Towers is
the frequent choice of presidents
and visiting top dignitaries. The
main lobby is quite magnificent. It
has been restored to its 1931 Art
Deco glory, with bas-relief friezes
and grillwork setting off the
beautifully painted murals, deep
mahogany paneling, and elegant
marble columns. The marvelous
giant clock, dating from 1893, once
stood in the legendary original
hotel on 34th Street. Famous
Peacock Alley is still a very
popular place to go for drinks.

Box Tree

250 E 49th St, NY, NY 10017.
Map 13 B5. █ 758-8320.
█ 308-3899. **Rooms**: 13.
█ █ █ █ █ █ █
█ █ █ █ AE, DC, MC, V.
$$$$$

Only the red carpet on the front
steps gives a clue that these two
town houses in a row of look-
alike brownstones are actually
New York's most unusual lodging.
The Box Tree is an opulent 13-
room inn with its own restaurant.
It reflects the extravagant tastes of
Bulgarian-born owner, Augustin
Paege, who, having bought the
brownstone next door, hopes to
increase the number of rooms
available. The rooms are small but
sumptuous, with formal curtains,
chandeliers, fur throws, and working marble fireplaces. Each room
has an individual theme, from
Chinese to English Gothic or 1930s
Paris. Rates are high, but they do
include a substantial restaurant
credit per night. Children under
the age of five are not welcome.

Four Seasons

57 E 57th St, NY, NY 10022.
█ 758-5700. █ 758-5711.
Rooms: 370. █ █ █ █ █ █ █
█ █ █ █ █ █ █ █ █ █ █
█ █ █ █ AE, DC, MC, V, JCB.
$$$$$

IM Pei's 52-story triumph is an
updated, slim, soaring limestone
evocation of New York's Art Deco
prime. Breaking the predictable
mold of traditional Old World

décor found in the city's luxury
hotels, the soaring pillared 33-ft
high (10-m) grand foyer is as austere and awesome as a monument.
Rooms are the city's largest with
exquisite custom-made modernistic furnishings and bedside
buttons for everything – to open
the curtains, pull down the blinds,
turn off the lights. Many have
foyers and dressing rooms, and all
have enormous marble bathrooms
with giant tubs and separate glass
stall showers. Lacking no amenity
and with peerless service, the Four
Seasons was accorded five-star
status just after it opened in 1993.
For those who wish for luxury in
an urbane modern mode and can
afford the lofty tab, this is New
York's prime lodging.

New York Palace

455 Madison Ave, NY, NY 10022.
█ 888-7000. █ 303 6000. **Rooms**:
800. █ █ █ █ █ █ █ █ █
█ █ █ █ █ █ █ █ █ █ █
█ █ AE, DC, MC, V, JCB.
$$$$$

The New York Palace incorporates
an unusual blend of the opulent
1882 landmark Villard Houses with
a contemporary 55-story tower.
Oversize guest rooms have been
handsomely refurbished in traditional European style, with a safe,
minibar, and fax machine installed
in every room. Rooms on the
upper floors have dazzling views.
Other amenities include a spa and
fitness center, and a well-equipped
business center. There is a lobby
cafe and olive bar, in addition to
one of Manhattan's finest and most
celebrated restaurants, Le Cirque
2000 (see p296), located in the
south wing of the historic Villard
Houses. Treat yourself to a
culinary experience, just this once!

Peninsula

700 5th Ave, NY, NY 10019. **Map** 12
F4. █ 247-2200. █ 903-3949.
Rooms: 242. █ █ █ █ █ █ █
█ █ █ █ █ █ █ █ █ █ █
█ █ █ AE, DC, MC, V, JCB.
$$$$$

Since the Peninsula group from
Hong Kong took over at the hotel,
things have been looking up at the
1905 Beaux Arts landmark, the
former Gotham Hotel. Guests go
up a sweeping double stairway
to the elegant lobby with its
antiques and floral arrangements.
The Art Nouveau bedrooms are
gracious and some of the baths
have 6 ft (2 m) whirlpool tubs. A
highlight of the hotel is the
rooftop-level fitness center, health
spa, and pool. The Pen-Top bar
opens onto a terrace in summer
and is always pleasant for a drink
and a grand view of the city.

Pierre

2 E 61st St, NY, NY 10021. **Map 12 F3.** 838-8000. **FAX** 940-8109.
Rooms: 202. *AE, DC, MC, V, JCB.*
$$$$$$

Limousines stand outside the door, awaiting the presidents who are among the clientele of this luxurious and pampering hotel. The Pierre is a member of Canada's highly esteemed Four Seasons group. Half the rooms are leased on a permanent basis. Both lobby and bedrooms are full of antiques and old-world elegance, and are lovelier than ever after recent refurbishing. Amenities and service are excellent, and the Café Pierre is one of New York's top places for business breakfasts.

St. Regis

2 E 55th St, NY, NY 10022.
Map 12 F4. 753-4500.
FAX 787-3447. **Rooms:** 314. *AE, DC, MC, V, JCB.* $$$$$$

John Jacob Astor's Beaux Arts beauty, the toast of New York society back in 1904, has emerged from a $100 million, three-year restoration looking almost as good as new. Decorated in muted blues and greens, the high-ceilinged rooms contain silk wall coverings and Louis XV reproduction furniture. The St. Regis Roof is the scene of glittering social events, and Maxfield Parrish's mural of King Cole once more reigns behind the King Cole Bar. The price for all this luxury is one of the highest room rates in the entire city.

Westin Central Park South

112 Central Park South, NY, NY 10019. **Map 12 E3.** 757-1900.
FAX 757-9620. **Rooms:** 228. *AE, DC, MC, V, JCB.* $$$$$$

Once called the Ritz-Carlton, lavish renovation has completely changed the décor of this building and made this one of New York's most elegant boutique hotels. The look is old-world European, with crystal chandeliers, Oriental rugs, and many gilt-trimmed French furnishings. Guest rooms have been enlarged and the splendid Central Park views need no improvement. The Fantino restaurant offers a northern Italian menu, and the bar remains a favorite gathering place. Guests can also enjoy the full breakfast buffet.

UPPER EAST SIDE

Franklin

164 E 87th St, NY, NY 10028.
369-1000. **FAX** 369-8000.
Rooms: 53. *AE, DC, MC ,V.* $$$

The Gotham hoteliers have transformed the 53-room Franklin Hotel into a reasonably priced entry compensating for small space with high style. Tall bouquets and an original Picasso print greet guests in the tiny lobby. Sandblasted steel, polished black granite, rich cherrywood, and soft black leather are used throughout. Custom furnishings and built-ins are designed to fool the eye. Each room comes with a video and TV, and a library offers free videos of classic films. Rates include complimentary continental breakfast as well as on-site parking. The neighborhood is rich in museums, shops, and restaurants.

Hotel Wales

1295 Madison Ave, NY, NY 10128.
Map 17 A3. 876-6000.
FAX 860-7000. **Rooms:** 87. *AE, DC, MC, V.* $$$

A small turn-of-the-century, almost European hotel, this Gotham Hospitality Group property is one of a kind in New York. While far from luxurious, it has genteel charm, thanks to caring renovation that has restored the fireplaces, marble stairs, and oak wood paneling of the original 1901 hotel. The marble sinks and brass fixtures in the bathrooms are also originals. Complimentary breakfast and tea are served in a Victorian parlor on the second floor, decorated with charming antique illustrations from children's books. The room also hosts musical recitals and Sunday chamber music concerts. The location is perfect for museum-hopping, and the neighborhood has a wide choice of restaurants.

Surrey Hotel

20 E 76th St, NY, NY 10021. **Map 16 F5.** 288-3700. **FAX** 628-1549.
Rooms: 130. *AE, DC, MC, V.* $$$$

Set amid the exclusive boutiques and galleries of Madison Avenue, the Surrey exudes the charm and grace of 18th century England. The one- and two-bedroom suites are spacious, and the lobby is an elegant oasis of calm with its crystal sconces and leather sofas. Indeed, the entire hotel seems wonderfully civilized. A fully equipped fitness center is open 24 hours a day, and Daniel Boulud's Café Boulud gets rave reviews for it's exquisite French cuisine.

Mark

25 E 77th St, NY, NY 10021. **Map 16 F5.** 744-4300. **FAX** 744-2749.
Rooms: 180. *AE, DC, MC, V, JCB.* $$$$$

Discreet, contemporary elegance is the hallmark of this Upper East Side sanctuary, with Biedermeier furniture, marble floors, and 18th-century Piranesi prints on the walls. There is a 24-hour concierge service. The bedrooms have formal curtains matching the bedspreads, fresh plants, antique prints, and bathrooms in marble or black-and-white Italian ceramic tile. Fine linen and down pillows are used in all rooms and most have pantries with minibars. The Edwardian, wood-paneled Mark's Restaurant gets high marks from reviewers, and its drawing room ambience makes it a favorite spot for afternoon tea.

Carlyle

35 E 76th St, NY, NY 10021.
Map 16 F5. 744-1600.
FAX 717-4682. **Rooms:** 190. *AE, DC, MC, V.* $$$$$

A hushed lobby, filled with antiques and tapestries, welcomes guests to what many consider to be New York's best hotel. An Upper East Side luxury outpost, the Carlyle has a reputation for exceptional personal service. The rooms are large and in understated good taste, decorated in traditional style and floral prints. Each has a kitchenette as well as a video, stereo, CD player, dedicated fax line and a multiple-line, hands-free phone. Several of the rooms have private terraces and dining rooms. A fitness center and sauna are available to all guests. Despite its subdued luxury, the Carlyle is lively by night, a popular spot for drinks amid the amusing murals in Bemelmans' Bar, and songs by cabaret star Bobby Short in the Café Carlyle.

Lowell

28 E 63rd St, NY, NY 10021. **Map 13 A2.** 838-1400. **FAX** 319-4230.
Rooms: 67. *AE, DC, MC, V, JCB.* $$$$$

This intimate, luxurious all-suite hotel was built in 1926 and retains its old-world charm. Service is excellent, and the 61 suites offer wood-burning fireplaces, libraries, real plants, fresh flowers, marble baths, and full kitchens. Eclectic decor mixes French, Art Deco, and Oriental pieces, always in the best of taste. The Pembroke Room on the second floor seats just 35 people and is a delightful place for tea or weekend brunch in a serene setting of lace curtains and discreet European character. The Post House restaurant is also highly regarded.

Plaza Athénée

37 E 64th St, NY, NY 10021.
Map 12 F2. 734-9100.
FAX 772 0958. **Rooms**: 152.
AE, DC, MC, V, JCB.

This is New York's version of an elite enclave. It is very exclusive, with opulently appointed, albeit small, rooms and a host of amenities, including fresh flowers, shoe trees, safes, kitchenettes, bathrobes, and room humidifiers. Décor is Louis XVI and every room has a replica of the gilt clock found in the famous Paris hotel of the same name. The hotel's restaurant, Le Régence, receives good reviews for its food, served beneath a cloud-painted ceiling (*see p297*). The reader survey in *Institutional Investor Magazine* has often named the hotel number one in Manhattan.

Regency

540 Park Ave, NY, NY 10021. **Map** 13 A2. 759-4100. FAX 826-5674.
Rooms: 384. AE, DC, MC, V, JCB.

Hollywood moguls are likely to be among those alighting from the limousines in front of the Regency, many of them bound for magnificent suites. The name reflects the Regency décor that the rooms share, and the lobby is filled with mirrors and gilt. The Regency's 540 Restaurant is where New York's "power breakfast" was born; you can see the bigwigs almost every morning, wheeling and dealing over muffins and croissants. The hotel gives first-class service to all guests and has every amenity.

Stanhope

995 5th Ave, NY, NY 10028. **Map** 17 A4. 288-5800. FAX 517-0088.
Rooms: 183. AE, DC, MC, V.

Small and opulent, the Stanhope stands in a superb spot right across the street from the Metropolitan Museum of Art. It has a Parisian-style terrace café, which is one of

the city's most popular. The public rooms are heavily adorned with French antiques. Each of the bedrooms is furnished with Louis XVI reproduction furniture and, besides the usual conveniences, comes equipped with CD and cassette players. Even if you can't afford to stay here, it is worth coming for tea in Le Salon, a room with the feel of an indoor garden.

UPPER WEST SIDE

Beacon

2130 Broadway, NY, NY 10023.
Map 15 C5. 787-1100.
FAX 724-0839. **Rooms**: 100.
AE, DC, MC, V, JCB.

The most stylish of the budget hotels sprouting on the Upper West Side, the Beacon is named after the famous theater next door. The recently refurbished lobby is chic, with a floor of black and white tiles and an Oriental-style rug. Bedroom furnishings are unimaginative but adequately comfortable, and rooms are equipped with full kitchenettes.

Empire

44 W 63rd St, NY, NY 10023. **Map** 12 D2. 265-7400 FAX 315-0349.
Rooms: 381. AE, DC, MC, V.

The old Empire has a totally new lease on life, thanks to fairly recent stylish renovations. The high-ceilinged lobby now has the look of a Tudor castle, with some unusual wrought-iron candelabra and a beautiful carved mantelpiece. Rooms are pleasantly decorated with floral patterns. The hotel is almost close enough to Lincoln Center to hear the arias. Music lovers will be pleased to note that each room comes equipped not only with TV and video but with a stereo, tape deck, and CD player. The Empire Café is convenient for pre-concert dining.

Excelsior

45 W 81st St, NY, NY 10024. **Map** 15 D4. 362-9200. FAX 721-2994.
Rooms: 196. AE, MC, V.

An understated, reliable option on the Upper West Side, the Excelsior has a gracious, welcoming lobby and large, comfortable, old-fashioned rooms that lack fancy furnishings. Most of the accommodations are in suite form, but even individual rooms come equipped with money-saving kitchens. Good

restaurants abound in the neighborhood. For the best views, ask for a front room overlooking the Museum of Natural History.

Milburn

242 W 76th St, NY, NY 10023.
Map 16 D5. 362-1006.
FAX 721-5476. **Rooms**: 111.
AE, DC, MC, V.

Newly refurbished and pleasantly decorated with art posters, this modest West Side hotel offers some reasonably sized studios (the best buys) and a few two-room suites, all with fully equipped kitchens, including a microwave and a refrigerator. Bathrooms are new, and there is an in-house laundry for guests' use. The location is convenient for the Lincoln Center and for the many interesting shops and restaurants to be found on increasingly trendy Broadway and the rest of the Upper West Side.

On The Ave

2178 Broadway, NY, NY 10024.
Map 15 C5. 362-1100.
FAX 787-9521. **Rooms**: 251. AE, DC, MC, V.

The new On The Ave is a good find for budget-watchers. This recently renovated lodging is decorated in sparse Art Deco style, with bright, abstract modern art downstairs and some whimsical touches in the rooms. The location can't be beat for all the Upper West Side sites, and restaurants. Guests can use the fitness equipment at the nearby Equinox. The new ground-floor restaurant is getting good reviews.

Mayflower

15 Central Park West, NY, NY 10023.
Map 12 D2. 265-0060.
FAX 265-2026. **Rooms**: 377.
AE, DC, MC, V, JCB.

Situated opposite Central Park and an easy walk from Lincoln Center, the Mayflower has a genteel air – perhaps shabbily genteel is a better description; the rooms are well overdue for renovation. It remains pleasantly comfortable and unpretentious though, and bedrooms have the added convenience of small kitchenettes and refrigerators. The hotel is very popular with those who appreciate the location and the frequent opportunities to rub elbows with Lincoln Center performers at the Conservatory Café. Park views from rooms at the front on the higher floors are glorious and are well worth the extra expense.

For key to symbols see p271

RESTAURANTS AND BARS

NEW YORKERS love to eat well, and there are over 25,000 restaurants in the five boroughs catering to their wishes. City dwellers avidly read restaurant reviews in magazines such as *New York* to ensure that they are seen in the latest fashionable eatery. "In" places and cuisine change with great regularity, while some favorite places simply remain

The classic Manhattan cocktail

popular. The restaurants in our listings have been selected as the best that New York can offer. *Choosing a Restaurant* on pages 290–92 will help narrow down your choice, and the map on page 288 shows the highlights of the list. For lighter refreshment and casual meals, see *Light Meals and Snacks* on pages 304–305.

RESTAURANT MENUS

MEALS IN MOST of the better restaurants consist of three courses: the appetizer (or starter), an entrée (the main course) and a dessert. Virtually all New York restaurants, except fast-food places, serve you rolls or bread and butter just after you're seated, at no extra charge – it's all part of the expected service. In some fine restaurants you may be offered a complimentary appetizer, such as a small

Street-corner hot dog stand

dollop of mousse or a tiny triangle of quiche. Appetizers at the better restaurants are often the chef's most creative dishes – many diners request two appetizers and no entrée. Italian menus offer a pasta dish as a second course before the main course, but in many places pasta is considered a main course. Coffee or tea and a dessert ordinarily conclude the meal in restaurants above the coffee-shop level. Your coffee cup may be refilled until you refuse any more.

The cheeseboard is a rarity in New York restaurants, although a few of the better French restaurants offer one.

PRICES

YOU WILL ALWAYS find a restaurant in New York to suit your budget. At inexpensive coffee shops, diners and fast food chains, $5 will buy you a filling meal. There are also hundreds of acceptable, even first-rate, restaurants where you can eat well at a moderate cost – around $20 per person for a filling and decent meal, not including drinks – in attractive surroundings. For dinner at a trendy New American venue with a star chef, the bill could be upward of $40 to $60 per person, excluding drinks. Many top restaurants do, however, offer fixed-price (or, as they are known in New York, prix-fixe) meals. These are normally much cheaper than items on the à la carte menu. Lunch is also less expensive than dinner in such places, and because of the profusion of business diners, lunch is also the busiest period of the day.

TAXES AND TIPPING

NEW YORK CITY sales tax of 8.25% will be added to your bill. Service is not usually included. Tipping can run from 10% at a coffee shop to 25% at the fanciest places, with 15% an average fair tip. Many New Yorkers just double the sales tax for a tip.

The bill is known as the "check" in New York, as all

A typical New York deli *(see p304)*

over the US. Commonly accepted credit cards are VISA, MasterCard and American Express. Traveler's checks are also taken in many restaurants. Luncheonettes and coffee shops accept cash only. In fast-food chains, you order at the counter and pay cash in advance.

DINING ON A BUDGET

DESPITE THE TALES of $200 business lunches, there are ways to stretch a meal budget in New York.

Order fewer courses than you would normally. American portions are huge, and an appetizer is often big enough for a light main course. You could share one with your companion or choose two appetizers and no entrée.

"Specials of the day" may be more expensive than items on the printed menu, so be sure to check prices.

Ask your waiter if there is a prix-fixe menu. Many expensive restaurants offer this at lunch and dinner – in the early evening it may often be called the pre-theater menu. Or try a prix-fixe lunch buffet. These are popular in

Interior of Zen Palate *(see p301)*

Indian restaurants and other places and are very reasonably priced meals.

Go to bars featuring "happy hours." They often offer a variety of hors d'oeuvres, like Spanish *tapas*, which can make a meal in themselves. If you want to simply see inside the restaurants every visitor has heard about, just go to have a drink and soak up the atmosphere. Avoid breakfast in your hotel. Even its coffee shop is likely to be more expensive than an outside coffee shop or deli. Many restaurants post their menus or will let you see them before you are seated, good for checking prices in advance.

HOURS

BREAKFAST HOURS are usually from 7 to 10:30 or 11am. Sunday brunch is a popular meal, served at most better restaurants between about 11am and 3pm. Lunch runs from 11:30am or noon to 2:30pm at most places, but the busiest time of the day

Poolside at the Four Seasons *(see p293)*

is 1pm. Dinner is usually served from 5:30 to 6pm onward. The most popular time is around 7:30 to 8pm.

Some restaurants stop serving at 10pm during the week, or 11pm on Friday and Saturday. Certain informal restaurants, especially Chinese, are open from 11:30am to 10pm. Coffee shops are open long hours, from 7am to midnight or even 24 hours.

DRESS CODES

FEW RESTAURANTS demand that male diners dress formally, though a jacket is required at classy restaurants, and jacket and tie at the very best. At most places, for both men and women, "casual but

Waiting in style at a bar in Grand Central Terminal *(see p309)*

chic" suffices. Women tend to dress up when dining at the expensive restaurants. If unsure, check the dress code when making a reservation.

RESERVATIONS

IT IS PRUDENT to make reservations at any restaurant above the luncheonette/fast food level, especially on weekends. A few of the trendiest restaurants won't even accept reservations except for groups of six or more. It is essential to make reservations for lunch at a midtown restaurant. But you may still be seated at the bar, even if you have booked a table.

SMOKING

SMOKING IS now illegal in restaurants with 35 or more seats. Many places provide separate rooms for smokers, but phone ahead for details.

CHILDREN

WHEN EATING out with children, ask if there's a child's menu with half-portions. The prices are reduced, sometimes by half. Children are accepted in most New York restaurants, but if yours are unpredictable stick to casual spots, Chinatown Chinese or family-run Italian restaurants, burger bars, delis, cafés, fast food chains and luncheonettes. A few of the better restaurants have facilities for babies or toddlers; others may not be so well equipped. Dining out in the more formal New York restaurants is certainly not a family affair.

WHEELCHAIR ACCESS

WHILE MANY restaurants may be able to accommodate a wheelchair, it is always best to mention your requirements when making your reservation. Many smaller places cannot cater to disabled customers because of lack of space.

USING THE LISTINGS
Key to symbols in the listings on pp293–303.

🌀 telephone number
🍴 fixed-price menu available
V vegetarian or vegetarian specialties
🪑 high chairs and/or children's portions
🌿 outdoor eating
♿ wheelchair access to all or part of restaurant
👔 jacket and tie required
🎵 live music
🍷 excellent wine list
★ highly recommended
💳 credit cards accepted
AE American Express
DC Diners Club
MC MasterCard/Access
V VISA
JCB Japanese Credit Bureau

Price categories for a three-course meal for one, including a half-bottle of house wine and all unavoidable extra charges (sales tax and service):

$ Under $25
$$ $25–$35
$$$ $35–$50
$$$$ $50–$70
$$$$$ Over $70

What to Eat in New York

Hot dog

THE VARIETY OF FOOD found in New York is as varied as its cultural and ethnic makeup, and you can find virtually any food you want. For a hearty simple meal, such as marinated vegetables, pasta or salami and cheese, visit one of the Italian restaurants found in every neighborhood. For a more sophisticated meal try a Japanese restaurant for sushi and sashimi – as good in New York as anywhere in Japan. Or try such traditional Jewish foods as pastrami, blintzes and bagels, found in most delis and coffee shops. Spicy curries can be found in the many Indian restaurants around Manhattan. If you are really hungry, visit a steakhouse for juicy steaks, fresh seafood and some especially wicked desserts.

Bagel
This chewy Jewish bread roll is most popularly served with lox (smoked salmon) and cream cheese.

Pancakes
Thick, sweet pancakes are usually served with maple syrup as breakfast. Fresh or dried fruit may be mixed into the batter before cooking.

Bacon is often sweet-cured and fried very crisp.

"Home fries" are chunky sautéed potatoes.

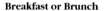

Whole-wheat toast

Eggs "over easy" are lightly fried on both sides.

French Toast
A breakfast dish of sliced bread dipped in egg then fried and often served with syrup.

Breakfast or Brunch
Breakfast (or brunch if eaten midmorning) can consist of anything from home fries, eggs, bacon and toast to sweet pancakes or croissants, often with unlimited coffee.

Egg Cream
This drink is made with milk, chocolate syrup and carbonated soda water.

Corned Beef on Rye
Cured beef is served on rye bread with mild mustard and a pickled dill gherkin.

Burger and Fries "To Go"
A hamburger and french fries may come with salad and onion rings.

Giant Pretzel
This savory bread twist is sold on many street corners.

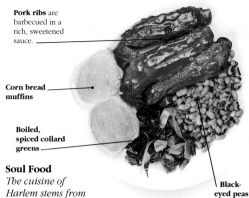

Pork ribs are barbecued in a rich, sweetened sauce.

Corn bread muffins

Boiled, spiced collard greens

Black-eyed peas

Clam Chowder
The Manhattan version of this shellfish soup is made with tomatoes and garnished with crackers.

Soul Food
The cuisine of Harlem stems from America's Deep South. Simple foods are cooked with spices for a unique flavor.

Pizza
The street food of Italian festivals is available all over the city – this uptown version is topped with artichoke hearts.

Sushi
Japanese cuisine, like this ultrafresh raw fish and rice, is a New York favorite.

Dim Sum
Tiny steamed dumplings, stuffed with fish, meat or vegetables, are a speciality of Chinese cuisine.

Waldorf Salad
Created in the 1930s at the Waldorf Hotel, it's made out of apples, nuts and lettuce.

Cappuccino and Cookies
Frothy coffee sprinkled with chocolate is served with cookies in New York cafés.

Apple Pie à la Mode
This traditional American dessert is only "à la mode" when served with ice cream.

New York Cheesecake
This thick, baked Jewish dessert may be served plain or glazed with fruit.

Banana Split
Some New York ice cream concoctions will feed a family. No one will mind if you order extra spoons and share.

New York's Best: Restaurants, Cafés and Bars

RESTAURANTS CAN BE FOUND all over New York, catering to all tastes and budgets and open at all times of the day or night. New York's eating habits reflect the city's ethnic heritage, past and present, as new immigrant groups make New York their home. Witness the enduring popularity of Italian, Chinese and Japanese restaurants and the traditional Jewish deli. In the more than 40 pages of restaurant listings in the New York telephone directory, you can find virtually every imaginable cuisine, from Californian, New American, Cajun and southern barbecue to Thai, Vietnamese, Indian, Afghan, Burmese and Philippine. The restaurants here are just a few favorites, selected from the listings on pages 293 to 303 as the best in their particular field.

Carnegie Delicatessen
Try the giant "pastrami on rye" at this typical deli. (See p306.)

Zen Palate
The excellent vegetarian cuisine offered here is a clever blend of Oriental styles. (See p301.)

Union Square Café
This is the place to sample New American cuisine at its best. Seafood and desserts are both excellent. (See p295.)

Florent
This bistro is open around the clock for authentic food and atmosphere. (See p306.)

Caffè Vivaldi
Of many charming coffeehouses in New York, this is a favorite for its delicious sticky pastries. (See p306.)

Golden Unicorn
Chinatown's best Chinese food is served here. Their range of dim sum is not to be missed. (See p299.)

McSorley's Old Ale House
For atmosphere alone, try this bar. Sample the potent house beer with care. (See p308.)

Greenwich Village

Gramercy the Fla Distr

SoHo and TriBeCa

Lower Manhattan

Seaport and the Civic Center

HUDSON RIVER

N

Upper West Side

Central Park

Café des Artistes
This New York classic is famed for both its saucy 1930s murals and its chocolate dessert tray.
(See p296.)

Upper East Side

*ater
trict*

*Upper
Midtown*

Lower Midtown

Mezzaluna
It's just a short walk from Museum Mile to some of the best pizzas in town.
(See p306.)

Serendipity 3
Eccentric Victoriana amuses the adults, but kids vote this café a hit for its ice-cream sundaes.
(See p306.)

The Four Seasons
Outstanding European and American food is served in two stunning rooms, one paneled in rosewood, the other centered around a pool. (See p293.)

Oyster Bar, Grand Central Terminal
The best seafood restaurant in Manhattan is this vaulted, golden room in the historic train station. The all-American wine list is excellent, too. (See p294.)

Hatsuhana
The freshest and most varied sushi available makes this Japanese restaurant stand out from the rest. Take a seat at the sushi bar and watch the skilled chefs at work. (See p300.)

0 kilometers 2

0 miles 1

Choosing a Restaurant

THE RESTAURANTS in this section have been selected for their good value or exceptional food. The chart highlights some factors that may influence your choice. For details see pages 293–303. Details of *Light Meals and Snacks* are on pages 304–6 and for some of New York's best *Bars* see pages 307–9.

	Page Number	Fixed-Price Menu	Late Opening	Children's Facilities	Tables Outside	Quiet Restaurant	Vegetarian Dishes	Seafood Specialties
LOWER MANHATTAN								
Layla *(Middle Eastern)* $$$	302	●	■	●	■		■	
Hudson River Club *(American)* $$$$	294	●		●				
Windows on the World *(American)* ★ $$$$$	295	●				●		
SEAPORT AND THE CIVIC CENTER								
Bo Ky *(Chinese)* $	299	●		●				
LOWER EAST SIDE								
Canton *(Chinese)* $$	299							
Oriental Garden *(Chinese)* $$	300		■	●				●
Golden Unicorn *(Chinese)* $$$	299	●	■	●				
Sammy's Famous Roumanian *(Jewish/Romanian)* $$$	303							
SOHO AND TRIBECA								
Penang *(Malaysian)* $	301		■				■	
Mekong *(Vietnamese)* $$	301	●			■		■	
Saalam Bombay *(Indian)* $$	302	●			■		■	
Savoy *(Mediterranean)* $$	294			●		●	■	●
Honmura An *(Japanese)* $$$	300	●				●	■	●
Provence *(French)* $$$	297		■	●	■			
Alison on Dominick Street *(French)* $$$$	295					●		●
Montrachet *(French)* ★ $$$$	297	●		●				
TriBeCa Grill *(American)* $$$	295	●					■	
Zoë *(American)* $$$	295			●			■	●
Chanterelle *(French)* $$$$$	296	●				●		
GREENWICH VILLAGE								
Moustache *(Middle Eastern)* $	302	●	■				■	
Cendrillon *(Malaysian/Philipino)* $$	301	●						
Cent' Anni *(Italian)* $$$	298						■	
Riodizio *(Brazilian)* $$$	303		■				■	
Il Mulino *(Italian)* $$$$	298		■	●			■	
La Métairie *(French)* $$$$	297		■				■	
Nobu *(Japanese)* ★ $$$$	300	●		●		●	■	●
Gotham Bar & Grill *(American)* $$$$$	293	●		●				
EAST VILLAGE								
Iso *(Japanese)* $$$	300	●	■					●
GRAMERCY AND THE FLATIRON DISTRICT								
An American Place *(American)* $$$	293			●			■	
Les Halles *(French)* $$$	295		■		■		■	
Mesa Grill *(American)* $$$	294					●		●
Periyali *(Greek)* $$$	303				■			
Verbena *(American)* $$$	295			●	■	●	■	●
Gramercy Tavern *(American)* ★ $$$$	294	●					■	
Lola *(Caribbean)* $$$	303		■	●				●
Union Square Cafe *(American)* ★ $$$$	295			●			■	●
The Water Club *(American)* $$$$$	295	●	■		■			●

Price categories include a three-course meal for one, half a bottle of house wine, and all unavoidable extra charges such as sales tax and service.
$ under $25
$$ $25–$35
$$$ $35–$50
$$$$ $50–$70
$$$$$ over $70.

★ Means highly recommended.

FIXED-PRICE MENU
A fixed price for a set meal that is less expensive than normal menu prices.
LATE OPENING
Last orders at or after 11:30pm excluding Sunday.
CHILDREN'S FACILITIES
High chairs and/or child portions.
QUIET RESTAURANT
No piped music; peaceful atmosphere.
VEGETARIAN DISHES
Vegetarian restaurant, or restaurant with good vegetarian selection.

Restaurant	Price	Page Number	Fixed-Price Menu	Late Opening	Children's Facilities	Tables Outside	Quiet Restaurant	Vegetarian Dishes	Seafood Specialties
CHELSEA AND THE GARMENT DISTRICT									
Da Umberto *(Italian)*	$$$$	298							●
Le Madri *(Italian)* ★	$$$$	298		●		●		●	
THEATER DISTRICT									
Afghan Kebab House *(Afghan)*	$	302	●						
Red Garlic *(Thai)*	$	301	●		●			●	
Jewel of India *(Indian)*	$$	302	●						
Tang Pavilion *(Chinese)*	$$	300	●						
Zen Palate *(Southeast Asian)*	$$	301	●	●				●	
B Smith's *(American)*	$$$	293						●	
Cabana Carioca *(Brazilian)*	$$$	303			●				
Orso *(Italian)*	$$$	298		●				●	
Tapika *(American)*	$$$	294	●					●	
Barbetta *(Italian)* ★	$$$$	297	●	●		●	●		
Osteria del Circo *(Italian)* ★	$$$$	298			●			●	
Remi *(Italian)*	$$$$	299			●	●			
Trattoria Dell'Arte *(Italian)*	$$$$	299		●				●	●
Le Bernardin *(French)*	$$$$$	295	●						●
Les Célébrités *(French)* ★	$$$$$	296	●		●		●		
Palio *(Italian)*	$$$$$	298	●					●	
The Rainbow Room *(American)* ★	$$$$$	294	●	●	●			●	●
Russian Tea Room *(Russian)*	$$$$$	303	●	●				●	●
San Domenico *(Italian)* ★	$$$$$	299		●			●		●
LOWER MIDTOWN									
Ambassador Grill *(American)*	$$$	293	●		●		●	●	
Grand Central Oyster Bar *(American)* ★	$$$	294			●				●
Les Halles *(French)*	$$$	296		●		●		●	
Tropica *(Caribbean)*	$$$$	303			●			●	●
Sparks Steakhouse *(American)*	$$$$$	294							●
UPPER MIDTOWN									
Zarela *(Mexican)*	$$	303						●	
Arizona 206 *(American)*	$$$	293		●	●			●	
Chin Chin *(Chinese)*	$$$	299	●	●	●	●		●	
Le Colonial *(Vietnamese)*	$$$	301	●					●	
Dawat *(Indian)*	$$$	302	●					●	
Il Nido *(Italian)*	$$$	298			●			●	
Shun Lee Palace *(Chinese)*	$$$	300	●						●
Aquavit *(Scandinavian)*	$$$$	302	●					●	●
Bice *(Italian)*	$$$$	297				●			
La Caravelle *(French)*	$$$$	296	●				●		
Darbar *(Indian)*	$$$$	302			●		●	●	
Felidia *(Italian)*	$$$$	298						●	
Hatsuhana *(Japanese)*	$$$$	300	●						●
Inagiku *(Japanese)*	$$$$	300							●
Lespinasse *(French)* ★	$$$$	297					●	●	
Lutèce *(French)*	$$$$	297	●						
Sushisay *(Japanese)*	$$$$	300							●
Vong *(Thai)* ★	$$$$	301	●			●	●	●	

Price categories include a three-course meal for one, half a bottle of house wine, and all unavoidable extra charges such as sales tax and service.
$ under $25
$$ $25–$35
$$$ $35–$50
$$$$ $50–$70
$$$$$ over $70.

★ Means highly recommended.

FIXED-PRICE MENU A fixed price for a set meal that is less expensive than normal menu prices.
LATE OPENING Last orders at or after 11:30pm excluding Sunday.
CHILDREN'S FACILITIES High chairs and/or child portions.
QUIET RESTAURANT No piped music; peaceful atmosphere.
VEGETARIAN DISHES Vegetarian restaurant, or restaurant with good vegetarian selection.

Restaurant	Price	Page Number	Fixed-Price Menu	Late Opening	Children's Facilities	Tables Outside	Quiet Restaurant	Vegetarian Dishes	Seafood Specialties
La Côte Basque (French)	$$$$$	296	●				●		
The Four Seasons (American) ★	$$$$$	293	●				●		●
La Grenouille (French)	$$$$$	296	●		●			■	
Le Périgord (French)	$$$$$	297	●				●		●
The '21' Club (American)	$$$$$	295	●				●	■	
UPPER EAST SIDE									
Owen Thai (Thai)	$$	301							●
Pamir (Afghan)	$$	302						■	
Arcadia (American) ★	$$$$	293	●		●	■			
Coco Pazzo (Italian)	$$$$	298						■	
Daniel (French) ★	$$$$	296	●		●	■			
Jo Jo (French)	$$$$	296		■			●		
Aureole (American) ★	$$$$$	293	●			■	●	●	
Le Cirque 2000 (French) ★	$$$$$	296	●						●
Le Régence (French)	$$$$$	297	●						●
Parioli Romanissimo (Italian)	$$$$$	298						■	
Sign of the Dove (American)	$$$$$	294	●			■	●		
UPPER WEST SIDE									
Lemongrass Grill (Thai)	$	301	●	■					
Barney Greengrass (Jewish)	$$	302	●		●			■	
Monsoon (Thai/Vietnamese)	$$	301	●	■				■	
Ollie's Noodle Shop & Grill (Chinese)	$$	299		■	●				●
Rain (Southeast Asian)	$$	301			●			■	
Santa Fe (American)	$$	294		■				■	
Carmine's (Italian)	$$$	297			●				
Shun Lee West (Chinese)	$$$	300		■				■	
Picholine (French/Mediterranean)	$$$	303	●	■	●				
Café des Artistes (French) ★	$$$$	296	●	■					●
MORNINGSIDE HEIGHTS AND HARLEM									
Sylvia's (American)	$	294			●				
The Terrace (French)	$$$$	297	●			■			●
BROOKLYN									
Moroccan Star (Moroccan)	$	302	●		●				
Gage & Tollner (American)	$$$	293	●		●				●
Peter Luger (American)	$$$$	294	●		●				
The River Café (American) ★	$$$$$	294	●			■			
QUEENS									
The Water's Edge (American)	$$$$$	295			●	■			●

AMERICAN

Three types of American cuisine are likely to be found in New York restaurants: Standard American, New American, and Regional American.

Standard American cuisine generally consists of grilled meats, deep-fried seafood, french fries, and fresh tossed salads. Served in huge portions at reasonable prices, this food will be found in restaurants in almost every neighborhood.

New American cuisine is a spin-off from French nouvelle cuisine. Portions are generally small – and foods are chosen for interesting textures and color combinations. Adapting the old, regional recipes and using fresh local ingredients with the infusion of Oriental items – such as ginger, soy, garlic, curry, and fresh cilantro – has become a touchstone of this cooking style. New American restaurants are easily among the very best and most expensive in New York.

Also to be found in the city is Regional American food. Cuisines in this category range from New England's seafood to the South's barbecued ribs and soul food, which is traditionally eaten by African-Americans. Cajun cuisine may include blackened fish, crayfish, or gumbo (soup, stew with poultry, rice, seafood, tomatoes, and sausage). Californian cuisine uses mainly natural, fresh ingredients, often combining Asian food with nouvelle techniques. Restaurants serving regional food tend be in the middle of the price range.

Ambassador Grill

United Nations Plaza Hotel, 1 United Nations Plaza. **Map** 13 C5. **C** 702-5014. **Open** 7–11am Mon–Sat, 7–10:30am Sun, noon–2:30pm Mon–Sat, 11am–1:45pm Sun, 5–10:30 daily. 🍴 👤 V ♿ 🎵 🈂 🌣 AE, DC, MC, V. $$$

American cuisine, with a French flourish, is served to a mixed clientele of UN business people and mature East Siders. Prices are reasonable, considering the quality of the food and the locality. By far the best buy is the all-you-can-eat Sunday lobster-and-champagne brunch buffet (two seatings).

An American Place

125 E. 50th St. **Map** 13 A4. **C** 715-2702. **Open** 11:45am–2:30pm Mon–Fri, 5:45–9:30pm Mon–Sat. V 👤 ♿ 🎵 🈂 AE, DC, MC, V. $$$

Chef-proprietor Larry Forgione has made a name for himself and his New American cooking style. Relocated uptown in the new Benjamin Hotel, this restaurant has excellent American cuisine. The menu changes frequently, and the daily specials never disappoint your palate.

Arcadia

21 E 62nd St. **Map** 12 F2. **C** 223-2900. **Open** noon–2:30pm Mon–Sat, 6–10pm Mon–Thu (10:30pm Fri, Sat). **Closed** some hols. 🍴 👤 ♿ 🌣 🈂 🌣 AE, DC, MC, V. $$$$

For the practicing gourmet, a visit to this smart, uptown brownstone is essential. The chef/co-owner Anne Rosenzweig is one of the top young New American chefs. Virtually everything on the menu is appealing, and dining here can be a memorable experience. Unfortunately, its popularity means it gets a bit crowded, and the noise levels can then become intrusive.

Arizona 206

206 E 60th St. **Map** 13 B3. **C** 838-0440. **Open** noon–3pm Mon–Sat, 5:30–11:30pm Fri, Sat, 5:30–10:30pm Sun. V 🈂 AE, DC, MC, V. $$

For a different experience, step into this adobe-like interior, with its whitewashed walls, cozy wood fires, wood tables and knotty pine floors. An imaginative blend of the southwest with New American flair produces dishes such as barbecued *foie gras* and roasted quail with polenta. Dinner is the best time to eat here, though it's noisy and crowded. The attached Arizona 206 Café is cheaper, with a different menu, but also wonderful food.

Aureole

34 E 61st St. **Map** 12 F3. **C** 319-1660. **Open** noon–2:30pm Mon–Fri, 5:30–11pm Mon–Sat. 🍴 ♿ 🌣 V 🈂 🈂 🌣 🈂 AE, DC, MC, V. $$$$

In an old, well-restored brownstone, long, narrow rooms are brightened by floral arrangements and bas relief decorations. The garden is the place to be in warm weather. The American-cum-French menu changes often and offers a rare dining experience. Recent gems include oak-smoked salmon with vegetable citrus salad, and Maine cod wrapped in eggplant (aubergine) with shrimp. A prix-fixe menu offers excellent value for rarefied food.

B Smith's

771 8th Ave. **Map** 12 D5. **C** 247-2222. **Open** noon–11pm Mon–Thu, noon–12:30pm Fri, Sat, noon–10:30pm Sun. ♿ 🎵 🈂 AE, DC, V, MC. $$$

Run by Barbara Smith, a former model, this high-ceilinged restaurant is a magnet for New York's showbiz types and after-theater crowd. Surprisingly, the stylish Southern and Mediterranean food is both good and reasonably priced. Upstairs, in a vast glass-enclosed space, is B Smith's Rooftop Café, where there is live music every night of the week.

The Four Seasons

99 E 52nd St. **Map** 1 3A. **C** 754-9494. **Open** noon–2:30pm, 5–9:30pm Mon–Fri, noon–2pm, 5–11pm Sat. **Closed** some hols. 🍴 ♿ 🈂 🈂 occasionally. 🈂 🌣 🈂 AE, DC, MC, V, JCB. $$$$$

This restaurant, established in 1961, continues to attract power-lunch regulars to its magnificent, high-ceilinged Grill Room. More romantic, and a good place for a pre-theater prix-fixe dinner, is the spacious Pool Room, with its marble pool. Wherever you sit, you'll enjoy a consistently delicious meal of New American and continental dishes. The game dishes, including fillet of buffalo, baby lamb, and all meat dishes are superb, and don't miss the dessert cart. This will be an expensive treat that will not disappoint.

Gage & Tollner

372 Fulton St, Brooklyn. **C** (718) 875-5181. **Open** 11:30am–3:30pm Mon–Fri, 5–10pm Mon–Thu (11pm Fri), 3:30–11pm Sat. 🍴 👤 ♿ 🈂 AE, DC, MC, V. $$$

It's worth the subway ride to Gage & Tollner for this seafood, served in a restaurant that could pass as a set for the movie *Gaslight*. Oysters and broiled clam-bellies are here, as are South Carolina specialties like Charleston she-crab soup (crab meat and crab eggs mixed with cream, onion and sherry). At lunch the clientele is mostly local politicos; at night it's more eclectic and interesting, but take a taxi.

Gotham Bar & Grill

12 E 12th St. **Map** 4 E1. **C** 620-4020. **Open** noon–2:30pm Mon–Fri, 5:30–10pm Sun–Thu, 5:30–11pm Fri, Sat, 5:30–9:30pm Sun. 🈂 🍴 V 👤 🈂 🈂 AE, DC, MC, V. $$$$$

Housed in a former warehouse, amid a Neo-Classical setting of columns, high ceilings, and a pink marble bar, you will find what is probably the best food in this part of town. Alfred Portale is a young and gifted French-trained chef whose seafood dishes are wonderful, but who also has a flair with game such as grilled saddle of rabbit. It is pricey, but makes for a great New American food experience.

Gramercy Tavern

42 E 20th St. **Map** 8 F5.
🕐 477-0777. **Open** noon–11pm
Sun–Thu, noon–midnight Fri, Sat.
🍴 👍 ⚡ 🅅 🆃 ★ 🅴 AE, DC,
MC, V. ⑤⑤⑤⑤

This newcomer, the creation of
Danny Meyer of the Union Square
Café, has inventive New American
fare in a setting that could pass for
a French country inn. You might
try such dishes as roasted scallops
with truffle *coulis* or marinated
salmon with minted *couscous* and
crème fraîche. Desserts are uni-
formly wonderful. Food in the
Tavern Room is also good and
much less expensive.

Grand Central Oyster Bar

Grand Central Station, Lower Level.
Map 9 A1. 🕐 490-6650. **Open**
11:30am to last sitting at 9:30pm
Mon–Fri, 5:30 –9:30pm Sat. **Closed**
some hols. 🅃 👍 ★ 🅴 AE,
DC, MC, V, JCB. ⑤⑤⑤

Some of the best seafood in New
York is served in this cavernous,
simple space below the city's
grand railroad station. At lunch you
can't hear yourself think, let alone
talk, as sound bounces off the
vaulted tile arches and ceilings.
But the fish and shellfish are always
fresh and simply prepared – and
surprisingly well-priced. There's
also a lengthy California wine list.

Hudson River Club

250 Vesey St. **Map** 1 A2. 🕐 786-
1500. **Open** 11:30am–2:30pm Mon–
Fri, 5–9:30pm Mon–Sat, noon–7pm
Sun. **Closed** some hols. 🍴 🅃
🆃 👍 🅴 AE, DC, MC, V. ⑤⑤⑤⑤

Situated on the second floor in
one of the World Financial Center
towers, this elegant clublike
restaurant offers views of the
harbor and the Statue of Liberty.
The original menu highlights the
foods and wines of the Hudson
River Valley for a stylish clientele.

Mesa Grill

102 5th Ave. **Map** 8 F5. 🕐 807-
7400. **Open** noon–2:15pm Mon–Fri,
11:30am–3pm Sat, Sun, 5:30–10pm
Mon–Thu, 5:30–10:30pm Fri, Sat. 👍
🅴 AE, DC, MC, V. ⑤⑤⑤

Spicy, inventive renderings of
southwestern US dishes, mainly
from Arizona and New Mexico,
are served in a former clothing
showroom, now turned into a
spacious and colorful evocation
of the West. It attracts the trend-
setting crowd with its unusual
combinations of grilled foods
at very reasonable prices.

Peter Luger Steakhouse

178 Broadway, Brooklyn. 🕐 (718)
387-7400. **Open** 11:45am–10pm
Mon–Thu, 11:45am–11pm Fri, Sat,
1–10pm Sun. 🍴 🅃 👍 ⑤⑤⑤⑤

Carnivores call this the best steakhouse in all five boroughs and
worth the taxi ride to indulge in
an enormous, well-charred porter-
house steak or double lamb chops.
The main dining room resembles a
German beerhall, with oak wain-
scoting and exposed wood beams
and the same kind of intimacy. The
waiters deal with their customers
with a brusque good humor – rare
for New York steakhouses.

The Rainbow Room

65th floor, GE Building, 30 Rockefeller
Plaza. **Map** 12 F5. 🕐 632-5000.
Open 5:30pm–1am Tue–Sat, 6–9pm
Sun. 🍴 👍 🅅 🅃 🆃 🎵 ★
🅴 AE, MC. ⑤⑤⑤⑤⑤

This is definitely a place for
special occasions, with splendid
American, French, and continental
food, dancing to a live band, and
a celestial view of New York.
The luxurious Art Deco setting
anticipates a comparable check.

The River Café

1 Water St, Brooklyn. **Map** 12 F5.
🕐 (718) 522-5200. **Open** noon–
11pm daily. 🍴 👍 🅅 🎵 🆃 🅃
★ 🅴 AE, DC, MC, V. ⑤⑤⑤⑤⑤

This delightful restaurant has spectacular skyline views of Manhattan,
and also features creative New
American cooking with excellent
seafood, prix fixe and six-course
menus. Nighttime is the lovers'
favorite here, but views are great
at lunch and brunch, and it's easier
to reserve a window table then.

Santa Fe

72 W 69th St. **Map** 11 C1. 🕐 724-
0822. **Open** noon–11pm Mon, noon–
midnight Tue–Fri, 11:30am–midnight
Sat, 11:30am–11pm Sun. 👍 ⚡ 🅅
🅴 AE, DC, MC, V. ⑤⑤

A good bet for Lincoln Center-
goers, this decorative southwestern restaurant with its own
fireplace has been dishing up good,
spicy New Mexican fare for years.

Savoy

70 Prince St. **Map** 4 D3. 🕐 219-
8570. **Open** noon–3pm Mon–Sat,
6–10:30pm Mon–Thu, 6–11pm
Fri, Sat, 6–10pm Sun. ⚡ 🅅 🅃
🅴 AE, DC, MC, V. ⑤⑤⑤

With its welcoming fireplace,
Savoy is a hit with SoHo's successful artistic types who can afford
the prices. The menu sometimes
tends to be too creative, pairing
too many competing flavors. But it
is always intriguing, emphasizing
fresh, locally grown ingredients,
such as *penne* with rabbit,
chanterelles, corn, and walnuts.

Sign of the Dove

Park Ave South at E 25th St. **Map** 13
B2. 🕐 861-8080. **Open**
noon–2:30pm Tue–Sun, 5:30–11pm
Mon–Fri, 5:30–11:30pm Sat,
6–10pm Sun. 🍴 🎵 🔲 🅴 AE,
DC, MC, V. ⑤⑤⑤⑤⑤

Now in an elegant new setting,
this restaurant has lost none of its
appeal. Couples gravitate to this
romantic hideaway of small rooms
with well-spaced tables, mirrors,
and quiet waiters. It is one of the
city's prime restaurants for its
elegant New American/French
food, such as fillet with *foie gras*.

Sparks Steakhouse

210 E 46th St. **Map** 13 B5.
🕐 687-4855. **Open** noon–3pm
Mon–Fri, 5–11pm Mon–Thu,
5–11:30pm Fri, Sat. 👍 🅃 🅴 AE,
DC, MC, V. ⑤⑤⑤⑤⑤

This machismo place, which may
remind you of *The Godfather*, is a
business lunch favorite. As such,
the decibel level rises quickly.
Steaks are the main menu item,
though there are good lobsters too.
The wine list is exceptional.
Service is typically brusque.

Sylvia's

328 Lenox Ave. **Map** 21 B1.
🕐 996-0660. **Open** 8am–10:30pm
Mon–Sat, 12:30pm–7pm Sun.
Closed Christmas. 🅃 👍 🎵
🅴 AE, DC, MC, V. ⑤ See p228.

For a unique American cuisine
experience, head for this soul food
heaven in Harlem (going by taxi is
recommended). Barbecued ribs,
fried chicken, black-eyed peas,
collard greens, and ham are a
few things to try in this homey
outpost of South Carolina home
cooking, where the waiters may
call you "dear." The Sunday
gospel brunch is also terrific.

Tapika

950 8th Ave. **Map** 13 D5. 🕐 397-
3737. **Open** noon–12:30pm daily,
5:30–10:30pm Mon–Thu, 5:30–
11:15pm Fri, Sat, 5–10pm Sun.
Closed July & Aug. 🍴 👍 🅅 🅃
🅴 AE, DC, MC, V. ⑤⑤⑤

Tapika has more going for it than
just its Carnegie Hall location. The
colorful décor was designed by
David Rockwell (who also did

Nobu), and the southwestern cuisine is brightly innovative. You might try coriander-crusted tuna or tequila-cured salmon. Brunch is great too.

TriBeCa Grill

375 Greenwich St. **Map** 4 D5. 941-3900. **Open** 11:30am–3pm Mon–Fri, 5:30–10:45pm Mon–Thu, 5:30–11:15pm Fri, Sat, 11:30am–3pm, 5:30–9:15pm Sun. ᵀᵉ 🎵 V 🚻 🏧 🍴 🍽 *AE, DC, MC, V.* ⑤⑤⑤⑤

You may see co-owner Robert De Niro here, as well as many other stars, especially at the large round bar that is the centerpiece of this brick-walled bistro. The inventive American food is surprisingly good, despite the frenetic nature of the place. Save room for one of the many delicious desserts.

The "21" Club

21 W 52nd St. **Map** 12 F4. 582-7200. **Open** noon–2:30pm, 5:30–10:30pm Mon–Fri; 5:30–11:15pm Sat. **Closed** Sat in May–Aug. ᵀᵉ V 🚻 🏧 🎵 🍴 🍽 *AE, DC, MC, V.* ⑤⑤⑤⑤⑤

This former speakeasy, in three attached brownstones with a black iron fence and jockey statues outside, has developed a younger showbiz-and-political clientele for the overpriced American food and somewhat formal town house ambience. New owners, the Orient-Express Hotels, Inc., suggest more changes in the near future.

Union Square Café

21 E 16th. **Map** 8 F5. 243-4020. **Open** noon–2:30pm, 6–10:15pm Mon–Thu, 6–11:15pm Fri, Sat, 5:30–9:45pm Sun. V 🚻 🏧 ★ 🍽 *AE, DC, MC, V.* ⑤⑤⑤⑤

This is one of New York's premier restaurants, famous for its imaginative American/Italian/French dishes. Attractive but not ostentatious, the café is moderately priced, despite all the hype, and the staff is unusually friendly. Everything on the seasonal menu is delicious, from a first course of rosemary gnocchi with gorgonzola, walnuts, pancetta, and leeks to a main course of commeal-and-sage-fried rabbit with creamy polenta. Desserts are also superb.

Verbena

54 Irving Place. **Map** 9 A5. 260-5454. **Open** noon–2:30pm, 5–10pm Mon, Tue, 5–11pm Wed–Sat, 5–9pm Sun. ⚓ 🎵 V 🚻 🏧 🍴 *AE, DC, MC, V.* ⑤⑤⑤

This new restaurant with a charming herb garden at the back has a youthful chef-owner, Diane Forley,

who uses the best natural ingredients in a creative New American menu. Memorable moments include butternut squash ravioli, oxtail terrine, and seared tuna with minted cucumber. Brunch in the garden is very nice.

The Water Club

East River & 30th St. **Map** 9 C3. 683-3333. **Open** noon–11:30pm daily. ᵀᵉ 🚻 🎵 🍴 🍽 *AE, DC, MC, V.* ⑤⑤⑤⑤⑤

Located on a glass-enclosed, skylit pier that connects two large barges, the Water Club offers sweeping East River views and some intriguing seafood dishes, such as spiced seared yellowfin tuna and sautéed red snapper with lobster dumplings.

The Water's Edge

44th Drive & East River, Long Island City. (718) 482-0033. **Open** noon–3pm Mon–Fri, 6–11pm Mon–Sat. 🚹 🚻 🎵 🍴 🍽 *AE, DC, MC, V, JCB.* ⑤⑤⑤⑤⑤

From this large dining room's windows, you'll have a wide-angle view of the Chrysler Building and other Manhattan landmarks across the river. New American food prepared with a certain amount of flair and live music add to the often magical experience here. There's a free ferry service from 34th Street to the restaurant dock.

Windows on the World

1 World Trade Center, 107th Fl, West St. **Map** 1 B2. 938-1111. **Open** 5–9pm Sun–Wed, 5–10pm Thu–Sat, 11–2pm Sat, Sun brunch at the bar. ᵀᵉ 🚹 🚻 🍴 🍽 ★ *AE, DC, MC, V.* ⑤⑤⑤⑤⑤

Located 107 stories above the harbor in the World Trade Center, with stunning views, this is an ideal place for seeing events in the harbor, such as the Fourth of July celebrations. Recent elaborate renovations have made the place even more attractive. The food is expensive, but a prix-fixe menu helps considerably. It is a membership club at breakfast and lunch, with an extra charge for non-members.

Zoë

90 Prince St. **Map** 4 E3. 966-6722. **Open** noon–3pm Tue–Sat, 11:30am–3pm Sun, 6–10:30pm Mon–Fri, 5:30–11:30pm Sat, 5:30–10pm Sun. V 🚹 🚻 🍴 🍽 *AE, DC, MC, V.* ⑤⑤⑤⑤

This 19th-century landmark building, has loftlike high ceilings, high columns, and an open kitchen. The SoHo artists and young professional clientele appreciate the New American cuisine, extensive microbrewery beer, and American wine lists. Grilled meats and fish are specialties, such as grilled loin of lamb with potato-horseradish gratin and herb-roasted salmon.

FRENCH

Fine dining in New York usually means French. The fashionable, long-established French restaurants tend to be expensive, serving haute cuisine in a setting profuse with fresh floral arrangements. Most are located on the Upper East Side. In many of them the chef-proprietor is French with long restaurant experience. Some places in the Theater District are less fancily decorated and less pricey, though still traditional in menu. Many newer places feature nouvelle cuisine and can also be very costly. Prix-fixe lunch, dinner, and pre-theater menus lower the prices.

Bistros have become newly popular as a means of serving simple French fare at lower prices in informal settings with less fussiness. All three types, haute, nouvelle, and bistro, are at their very best in New York.

Alison on Dominick Street

38 Dominick St. **Map** 4 D4. 727-1188. **Open** 5:30–10:30pm Mon–Thu, 5:30–10:45pm Fri, Sat, 5:30–9:30pm Sun. 🍽 *AE, DC, MC, V.* ⑤⑤⑤⑤

You'll find a creative rendering of French/Mediterranean/New American cuisines in this rather out-of-the-way, romantic place. The setting is sleek and stylish. The bar at the front is a scene in itself, and the dining room is dark, cozy, and conducive to intimate dining.

Le Bernardin

155 W 51st St. **Map** 10 E4. 489-1515. **Open** noon–2:30pm Mon–Fri, 5:30–11:30pm daily. **Closed** some hols. ᵀᵉ 🚻 🍴 🍽 *AE, DC, MC, V, JCB.* ⑤⑤⑤⑤⑤

To New York food-lovers, seafood and Le Bernardin are synonymous. This is a large and beautiful, if somewhat austere, room with teak ceiling, pale blue walls, and tapestry-covered chairs. The fish is served undercooked to let the freshness speak for itself and is minimally sauced. While very expensive, for a seafood fancier it is worth every penny. You might consider the prix-fixe lunch.

For key to symbols *see p285*

Café des Artistes

1 W 67th St. **Map** 12 D2. **〔** 877-3500. **Open** noon–3pm, 5:30pm–midnight Mon–Sat, 10am–3pm, 5–11pm Sun. **Closed** Christmas Day. 〔◎〕 **T** after 5pm. ★ ☑ AE, DC, MC, V. $$$$

This boisterous, jolly café is on everyone's list of favorites. The 1934 murals of frolicking nymphs, by Howard Chandler Christy, set the light-hearted tone, and the excellent French food extends it. Desserts are a specialty here, especially the Hungarian *tortes* (small cakes), and lavish chocolate creations that only the very strong-willed can resist. The theater and media personalities who drop by add to the *joie de vivre*.

La Caravelle

33 W 55th St. **Map** 12 F4.
〔 586-4252. **Open** 12:30–2:30pm Mon–Fri, 5:30–10:30pm Mon–Sat. 〔◎〕 **T** ☑ ☑ AE, DC, JCB, MC, V. $$$$

For over 30 years this bastion of haute cuisine has been serving classic French food in a comfortable, softly lit room to an upscale, regular clientele. With a new chef, there have been some new flourishes in the kitchen, but the fresh *foie gras*, Dover sole, and other seafood dishes are old favorites that are consistently good. Lunch, dinner, and pre-theater prix fixe menus are also available.

Les Célébrités

Essex House Hotel, 155 W 58th St. **Map** 12 E3. **〔** 484-5113. **Open** 6–9:30m Tue–Sat. 〔◎〕 ⚹ ☑ **T** ☑ ★ ☑ AE, DC, MC, V. $$$$$

Within a short space of time, this luxurious dining room, off the lobby of the Essex House Hotel, has become one of New York's top French restaurants. The setting is sumptuous in a theatrical way, with huge gilded columns, thick carpeting, paintings by showbiz people – and a mere 14 tables. The food is remarkably good with many elegant touches, such as veal tenderloin filled with *foie gras*, truffles, and wild mushrooms, or rabbit loin and leg stuffed with eggplant (aubergine) caviar and black olives.

Chanterelle

2 Harrison St. **Map** 4 D5. **〔** 966-6960. **Open** noon–2:30pm Tue–Sat, 5:30–11:30pm Mon–Sat. **Closed** some hols. 〔◎〕 ☑ **T** ☑ AE, DC, MC, V. $$$$$

This TriBeCa establishment seats 60 people in a handsome setting,

with high ceilings, wood walls, columns, and stunning flower arrangements. The creative French menu changes daily, but you might encounter such dishes as striped bass with sage and red butter or salmon sauté with fresh rhubarb. Desserts are wonderful, and there is a cheese tray, a rarity in New York. At lunch there is an à la carte and prix-fixe menu; at dinner only prix-fixe and tasting menus.

Le Cirque 2000

455 Madison Ave. **Map** 13 A2.
〔 794-9292. **Open** 11:45am–2:45pm, 5:45–11pm Mon–Sat, 11:30am–2:30pm, 5:30–10:30pm Sun. 〔◎〕 ☑ **T** ☑ ★ ☑ AE, DC, MC, V. $$$$$

Sirio Maccioni has set up his big top in the baronial splendor of the Villard Houses (*see p174*), and the reputation of this long-time New York favorite is intact. The team in charge of the $1-million-plus kitchen will be working its magic once again, with dishes like porcini risotto, sole with wild baby asparagus, and white-and-dark chocolate harlequin mousse.

La Côte Basque

60 W 55th St. **Map** 12 F4. **〔** 688-6525. **Open** noon–2pm Mon–Sat, 5:30–10:30pm Mon–Thu, 5:30–11pm Fri, Sat, 5–10pm Sun. **Closed** some hols. 〔◎〕 ☑ **T** ☑ ☑ AE, DC, JCB, MC, V. $$$$$

In a new location just a block from the old, this outpost of traditional French cuisine continues to serve its classic *cassoulets*, with more modern dishes such as roast duckling in a honey/Grand Marnier/black cherry sauce. The setting is as comfortable as ever. Even the mural of the Basque Coast and the old wooden beams have been transported to the new site. The upscale, knowledgeable clientele appreciate one of the city's most extensive wine lists.

Daniel

60 E 65th St. **Map** 13 A2. **〔** 288-0033. **Open** noon–2:30pm, 5:45–10:30pm Mon–Sat. 〔◎〕 ⚡ ☑ ☑ **T** ☑ ★ ☑ AE, DC, MC, V. $$$$

Chef-owner Daniel Boulud, formerly of Le Cirque, has created a floral bower with fabulous displays of seasonal flowers as a backdrop for some of the very best modern French cooking in town. It would be hard to surpass the honey and cumin-glazed leg of venison with *foie gras* or a seasonal dish like shad roe sautéed with sun-dried tomatoes, toasted almonds, and

black olives. The entire menu, at lunch or dinner, is a catalogue of unusual and inspiring creations, beautifully executed. The lunch and dinner prix-fixe menus, while not cheap, offer excellent value in this otherwise ultra-expensive restaurant. The wine list, as you would expect, is exemplary.

La Grenouille

3 E 52nd St. **Map** 12 F4. **〔** 752-1495. **Open** noon–2:30pm, 5:30–11:15pm Tue–Sat. **Closed** August. 〔◎〕 ☑ ☑ **T** ☑ ☑ AE, DC, MC, V. $$$$$

La Grenouille has everything one expects of a superior French restaurant: dazzling floral displays, unobtrusive service, expertly prepared food, and an extensive wine list. Lunch is the time to be here, both for the well-priced prix fixe menu and to people-watch the fashion industry clientele.

Les Halles

411 Park Ave South. **Map** 9 A3.
〔 679-4111. **Open** noon–midnight daily. ☑ ☑ AE, DC, MC, V. $$$

This classic French brasserie is named after the original *Les Halles* quarter in Paris. Situated on the premises of a butcher shop, the specialty is, unsurprisingly, meat dishes, using only the best cuts. Favorites include *steak frites, filet mignon au poivre,* or *charcuterie* served with *choucroute* (the French version of *sauerkraut*). The atmosphere is festive, and very French, with a smoking section and tight seating for that intimate tête-à-tête.

Jo Jo

160 E 64th St. **Map** 13 A2. **〔** 223-5656. **Open** noon–2:30pm, 6–11:30pm Mon–Fri, 5:30–11pm Sat. ☑ ☑ AE, DC, MC, V. $$$$

Jo Jo is the creation of chef Jean-Georges Vongerichten, who also owns Vong. The setting is a Paris-style town house. The quieter upstairs is best for a tête-à-tête meal, but the downstairs dining room with mirrored walls is more glamorous and livelier. The prices aren't too hefty for some very good, inventive bistro food. There's also a prix fixe lunch menu.

Lespinasse

St. Regis Hotel, 2 E 55th St.. **Map** 12 F4. **〔** 339-6719. **Open** 7–10am noon–2pm, 5:30–10pm Tue–Sat. ☑ ⚡ ☑ ☑ **T** ★ ☑ AE, DC, MC, V. $$$$$

One of New York's most expensive restaurants, Lespinasse is also one of the very best. The dining room is sedate to the point of dullness, relieved by a few dignified floral displays. But it's the food here that matters, elegant French with an Asian accent. Words can't convey the finesse of dishes such as quail salad with endive in an almond-honey vinaigrette, herbed risotto with mushroom *fricasée*, and seared loin and *confit* of rabbit in rosemary-mustard sauce. Desserts are also spectacular. There is an interesting, if pricey, four-course vegetarian tasting menu.

Lutèce

249 E 50th St. **Map** 13 B4.
[752-2225. **Open** noon–2pm Tue–Fri, 6–10pm Mon–Thu, 5:30–10:30pm Fri, Sat. **Closed** Mon July & Aug, some hols. 🍴 🕹 🍴 ❤ 🍴 AE, DC, JCB, MC. $$$$$

For decades, this was New York's authoritative French restaurant. But with the advent of many other excellent restaurants, Lutèce has lost some of its luster. Its country look, however, is still appealing, and it remains an attractive place to dine – try the grilled squab with asparagus and morels or guinea hen baked in cabbage leaves. There's a prix fixe menu making an occasional splurge more possible.

La Métairie

189 W 10th St. **Map** 3 C2. [989-0343. **Open** 5:30pm–midnight Mon–Fri, noon–midnight Sat, Sun. 🕹 📺 ❤ 🍴 AE, DC, MC, V $$$$$

This tiny, crowded bistro, with room for a mere 20 customers, not only has plenty of charm, but good robust, country French food, and a setting that is marvelous for a romantic dinner for two.

Montrachet

239 W Broadway. **Map** 4 E5. [219-2777. **Open** noon–2pm Fri, 6–10pm Mon–Thu, 6–11pm Fri, Sat. 🍴 🏃 🕹 ❤ ★ ❤ AE, DC, MC, V. $$$$$

In this popular TriBeCa restaurant, the three large, high-ceilinged loft-like dining rooms are spacious but unpretentious. The menu offers a panoply of inventive contemporary French dishes – and desserts must be sampled. The extensive wine list is well-priced as is the food, especially the lunch specials.

Le Périgord

405 E 52nd St. **Map** 13 C4. [755-6244. **Open** noon–3pm Mon–Fri, 5:30–10pm daily. **Closed** Sun July & Aug, some hols. 🍴 🕹 ❤ 🍴 AE, DC, MC, V. $$$$$

This established restaurant is a favorite of UN people who appreciate impeccably prepared dishes, with service to match, in a setting of quiet elegance. Fresh flowers, soft lighting, and a low noise level all add up to a superlative dining experience.

Provence

38 MacDougal St. **Map** 4 D3. [475-7500. **Open** noon–3pm, 6–11pm daily. **Closed** Dec 25, Jan 1. 🏃 📺 ❤ 🍴 AE. $$$

This is a well-priced Greenwich Village bistro whose country French décor, dried flowers, and garden for warm-weather dining all suggest Provence. A menu of café fare includes braised monkfish, Provençal fish soup, pan-roasted lamb with ratatouille, and other southern French favorites.

Le Régence

Hotel Plaza Athénée, 37 E 64th St. **Map** 13 A2. [606-4647. **Open** 7–10am, noon–2:30pm, 6–9:30pm daily. 🍴 🕹 🍴 ❤ AE, DC, MC, V. $$$$$

Crystal chandeliers and a cloud-painted ceiling add to the classical splendor of this dining experience. Dishes are prepared with great inventiveness, making this a most memorable French restaurant. It is expensive, but there's a prix fixe dinner menu.

The Terrace

400 W 119th St. **Map** 20 F3. [666-9490. **Open** noon–2:30pm Tue–Fri, 6–10pm Tue–Sat. 🍴 🎵 📺 ❤ AE, DC, MC, V. $$$$$

Although somewhat overpriced, everything is redeemed by the breathtaking view of the city. Service can be erratic, but the setting invites lovers with its candlelit tables and compelling French menu. Take a taxi there and back, as the neighborhood is dubious.

ITALIAN

Italian restaurants vie with Chinese for being the most popular with New Yorkers and the most prolific. Little Italy and Greenwich Village have long been strongholds of southern Italian cooking, but northern Italian cuisine has become increasingly popular in the 1990s, and restaurants featuring it have blossomed all over the city. The southern cuisine consists of hearty, more peasant-style food, while northern cuisine is more sophisticated. Another difference is price: southern Italian restaurants range from cheap to moderate;

northern ones are more expensive. In southern Italian restaurants you may find formica-topped tables and a cheerful, noisy, informal atmosphere. The food usually features soups, many shrimp and veal entrées, vegetable dishes such as eggplant (aubergine) parmigiana (eggplant, cheese and tomato sauce), plenty of rich tomato-based sauces, and deep-fried mozzarella.

Northern Italian restaurants have a tendency to be more formal, elegant, and pricey. They feature a variety of pastas in rich cream and cheese sauces, polenta, gnocchi, risotto, game birds, venison, truffles, many kinds of wild mushrooms, diverse herbs and breads such as *foccacia* and *bruschetta*.

Barbetta

321 W 46th St. **Map** 12 D5. [246-9171. **Open** noon, 5pm–midnight Mon–Sat. 🍴 🕹 🍴 🎵 📺 ❤ ★ ❤ AE, DC, MC, V, JCB. $$$$$

In warm weather the beautiful garden of this 19th-century town house is so tranquil it's hard to believe that Broadway is just a stone's throw away (literally). The excellent Piedmontese Italian food is pricey, but a prix fixe pretheater menu offers good value. There is an extensive wine list.

Bice

7 E 54th St. **Map** 12 F4. [688-1999. **Open** noon–midnight Mon–Sat, noon–11pm Sun. 📺 🕹 ❤ AE, DC, MC, V. $$$$

A magnet for the rich, famous, and expense account types, this Art Deco offspring of Milan's Bice is packed steadily. It is no wonder: the northern Italian food is light with freshly made pastas, such as lobster ravioli or pasta with quail and arugula. The check is as heady as the ambience and the staff's snobbish attitudes.

Carmine's

2450 Broadway. **Map** 15 C2. [362-2200. **Open** 11:30am–3pm Mon-Fri, 5–11pm Mon–Thu, 5pm–midnight Fri, 11:30am–midnight Sat, 2–10pm Sun. **Closed** Dec 25. 🏃 🕹 ❤ AE, DC, MC, V. $$$

Carmine's is the sort of southern Italian restaurant you would expect to find in Little Italy, but with Upper West Side casualness. This Sicilian restaurant is best enjoyed with families who like plates piled high with food for relatively little money – and those who don't mind an uneven culinary performance and the possibility of waiting in long lines. Another branch is located at 200 W 44th St. (221-3800).

Cent' Anni

50 Carmine St. **Map** 4 D3. **[** 989-
9494. **Open** noon–4pm Mon–Sat,
5:30–10:45pm daily. **Closed** Dec 25,
Jan 1. **V** **&** **!** **✉** AE, DC, MC, V.
$$$

This West Village favorite earns
good reviews for its robust,
Florentine-style food and unusual
Tuscan wines at pretty reasonable
prices. Service can be erratic, and
crowds ensure high noise levels.
For a classic Village experience,
however, it's fine. You might try
the grigliata mista (mixed grill plate
of rabbit, lamb, sausage, and quail).

Coco Pazzo

23 E 74th St. **Map** 16 F5. **[** 794-
0205. **Open** noon–3pm, 6–11:30pm
daily. **Closed** one wk Aug. **V** **&**
✉ AE, DC, MC, V. **$$$$**

This trendy, softly lit, contempo-
rary-looking trattoria is a favorite
with beautiful people and is part
of the Le Madri stable of stylish,
upscale Italian restaurants. The
tables are close together, the noise
level can be distracting, and the
service can be slow, but these
points should not deter the
dedicated food-lover from the
remarkable risotto with seafood
and the assortment of delicious,
mostly northern specialties.

Da Umberto

107 W 17th St. **Map** 8 E5.
[989-0303. **Open** noon–3pm
Mon–Fri, 5:30–11pm Mon–Thu,
5:30–11:30pm Fri, Sat. **Closed** Dec
25, Jan 1. **✉** AE. **$$$$**

In a tawny, softly lit front dining
room and an airier skylit one in
the back, which is probably the
brighter lunch choice, hearty
Tuscan fare, strong on game and
roasts, is served. You can watch
through glass windows as large
portions of baked pheasant with
herbs and pork studded with garlic
are dished up in the kitchen. It's a
pretty good value for the money.

Felidia

243 E 58th St. **Map** 13 B3.
[758-1479. **Open** noon–2:30pm
Mon–Fri, 5–10:30pm Mon–Thu,
5–11:30pm Fri–Sat. **V** **!** **✉**
AE, DC, MC, V. **$$$$$**

Dinner in this much-acclaimed
restaurant in an East Side
brownstone is comfortably rustic,
with rows of brightly polished
copper pots, partial brick walls,
and open wine racks. The Italian
regional food derives mostly from
Trieste, with dishes such as gnocchi
al ragu d'agrello (potato dumplings
with lamb ragu and artichokes)

and krafi all' Istriana (fresh pasta
"pillows" stuffed with three cheeses,
raisins, rum, and citrus rind).

Le Madri

168 W 18th St. **Map** 8 E5. **[** 727-
8022. **Open** noon–3pm, 5:30–11pm
daily. **Closed** one wk Sep. **V** **!** **!**
★ **✉** AE, MC, V. **$$$**

Named after the female cooks,
"the mothers," who turn out some
of the most exquisite northern
Italian food in the city, Le Madri
continues to shine as one of New
York's most fashionable restaurants.
The dining room is low-key but
enlivened by lavish floral arrangements and food displays. Risotto,
osso buco (veal shank stew),
gourmet pizzas, and various pastas
are among the specialties. There
are good vegetarian dishes as well.

Il Mulino

86 W 3rd St. **Map** 4 D3. **[** 673-3783.
Open noon–2:30pm Mon–Fri, 5–
11pm Mon–Sat. **Closed** July, some
hols. **V** **!** **!** **✉** AE, MC, V.
$$$$

Almost too dark at dinner, Il
Mulino's exposed brick walls, bent-
wood chairs, and cramped quarters
seem more agreeable at lunch when
there are fewer customers. Aficionados love the lagniappe (small
appetizer) of delicious fried zucchi-
ni (courgette), served the minute
you sit down. Less agreeable is the
long wait at the bar before you are
seated, even with a reservation.
Though expensive, this is the best
Italian in Greenwich Village.

Il Nido

251 E 53rd St. **Map** 13 B4.
[753-8450. **Open** noon–3pm,
5:30–11pm Mon–Sat. **Closed** Jul 4,
Thanksgiving, Dec 25. **V** **!** **!** **✉**
AE, DC, MC, V. **$$$**

One of the first northern Italian
restaurants in New York, Il Nido
has been overshadowed recently
by newer stars. But its charming
Tuscan farmhouse interior prepares
you for many delicious dishes, like
the risotto Nido and grilled scampi
with anchovy caper sauce. A place
for upscale and business clientele,
dining here is a fairly dressy affair.

Orso

322 W 46th St. **Map** 12 D5.
[489-7212. **Open** noon–11:45
Sun–Tue, Thu, Fri, 11:30am–11:45
Wed, Sat. **Closed** Dec 25. **V**
✉ MC, V. **$$$**

There are many Theater District
Italian restaurants, but only one
Orso, a favorite of journalists,

theater people and their agents.
Its Broadway convenience, cheerful décor, with open kitchen and
bright skylight, large pizzas, and
other Italian standbys, contribute
to its bustling popularity. There is
a respectable Italian wine list. The
limited menu has enough choices
at medium prices, especially
pastas, to keep you satisfied.

Osteria del Circo

120 W 55th St. **Map** 11 B4. **[** 265-
3636. **Open** 11:30am–2:30pm
Mon–Sat, 5:30–10:30pm Sun–Tue,
5:30–11pm Wed, Thu, 5:30–11:30pm
Fri, Sat. **&** **✂** **V** **!** ★ **✉** AE,
MC, V. **$$$$**

It is no wonder that Circo is so
dazzling. It has the imprimatur
of Sirio Maccioni, owner of the
fabulous Le Cirque 2000, whose
sons run this newcomer with
similar panache. The circus motif
with bright banners overhead can
be seen throughout the stylish restaurant; even the tables are set as
though inside a big, open circus
tent. One can watch the chefs at
work in the open kitchen. The
food is refined northern Italian.
Flash-seared beef carpaccio in an
aromatic herb crust, gnocchi with
shrimp and black truffle ragu, and
calamaretti ripieni (squid filled
with shrimp and vegetables) are
among many notable dishes. This
is not a place to worry about the
price; just sit back, enjoy the high-
powered celebrity scene, and
savor the wonderful food.

Palio

151 W 51st St. **Map** 12 E4. **[** 245-
4850. **Open** noon–3pm Mon–Fri,
5:30–11pm Mon–Sat. **Closed** some
hols. **¶** **☰** **V** **&** **!** **!** **✉** AE,
DC, MC, V. **$$$$$**

Palio is a favorite of upscale
Broadwayites and office workers
in the Equitable Assurance Tower,
in which the restaurant is located.
The restaurant has a popular
street-level bar with a vivid, 124-ft
(38-m) long, wrap-around mural of
Siena's famous Palio (horse race
festival) by Sandro Chia. Upstairs,
the dining room is pretty, though
northern Italian food can be uneven
– superb one evening, routine the
next. Dishes to savor include filet
steak in a hazelnut crust, loin of
venison in a juniper berry sauce,
and the risottos. A pleasant quick
lunch at the bar and a pretheater
menu are also available.

Parioli Romanissimo

24 E 81st St. **Map** 16 F4.
[288-2391. **Open** 5:30–11pm
Mon–Sat. **&** **✂** **V** **!** **✉** AE, DC,
MC, V. **$$$$$**

This handsome, low-key restaurant housed in an Upper East Side town house has the aura of a private club, complete with fireplace. In this setting the classic Italian cuisine and service are virtually flawless, as indeed they should be at the rarefied prices charged. This is possibly the priciest Italian restaurant in town.

Remi

145 W 53rd St. **Map** 12 E4. 581-4242. **Open** noon–2pm Mon– Fri, 5:30–11:30pm Mon–Sat, 5:30–10pm Sun. **Closed** Thanksgiving, Dec 25. AE, DC, MC, V.

For deal-makers at lunch and the pre- and post-theater crowd at dinner, this lively, noisy restaurant is the place to be seen. Adam Tihany designed the spectacular décor (he also did Osteria del Circo). There is a mural of Venice, reddish Brazilian maple floors with stripes of birch, comfortable chairs and banquettes, and a glass wall facing a flower-bedecked atrium, where diners may eat in mild weather. The service is very attentive and the fine Venetian food is prepared with gusto. The pasta dishes, such as the homemade ravioli Marco Polo, filled with fresh tuna and ginger in a light tomato sauce, are especially creative. Desserts are stunning, as is the lengthy Italian wine list, which includes more than four dozen types of grappa.

San Domenico

240 Central Park South. **Map** 12 E3. 265-5959. **Open** noon–2:30pm Mon–Fri, 5:30–11pm Mon–Thu, 5:30–midnight Fri, Sat, 5:30–10pm Sun. ★ AE, DC, MC, V.

Soft lighting, Florentine terracotta floors, well-spaced chairs, supple leather chairs, and impeccable service make this a luxurious and romantic setting for some of the best and most imaginative northern Italian food in town. Risotto with white truffles, snails in brown sauce, and grilled eel in vine leaves with balsamic vinegar are a few of the many superlative dishes on the menu. A well-priced pretheater menu is available early evening.

Trattoria dell'Arte

900 7th Ave. **Map** 12 E3. 245-9800. **Open** 11:45–2:30pm , 5–11:30pm Mon–Sat, 11am–10:30pm Sun. **Closed** Christmas Day. AE, DC, MC, V.

The two main advantages here, according to the Carnegie Hall-going clientele, are the bright,

clever Milton Glazer interior designs and what is possibly the biggest antipasto bar in the city. Share an amazingly well-priced platter of delicious antipasto items, enjoy the exuberant décor of "body parts" sculpture, people-watch the celebrities who gather here, and then head across the street for the music. The rest of the menu, even the pizza, is somewhat uninspired.

CHINESE

Chinese restaurants are as numerous as Italian ones in New York. They range from take-out outlets and cheap eateries – found in almost every neighborhood and extensively throughout Chinatown – to more formal, expensive restaurants, located mostly in Midtown or on the Upper East Side. For those visitors dining on a tight budget, a Chinese meal is probably the best option.

Many Chinese restaurants in New York are of the chop suey-chow mein variety, Americanized for decades. The better Chinese restaurants are as good as any to be found outside Hong Kong and Taiwan. A large local Chinese population has created a much more demanding clientele. On the whole, by far the most authentic places can be found in Chinatown, while the uptown restaurants tend to be more chic, serving, in some instances, Westernized nouvelle Chinese fare.

Szechuan and Hunan cooking swept New York in the 1970s, creating a demand for the hot, sour and peppery cuisines of those regions of China. Of late, New Yorkers have become more interested in the delicate subtlety of Cantonese cooking. Most Chinese restaurants have large menus, enabling you to sample both spicy and mild dishes. Desserts at Chinese restaurants tend to be limited, usually to ice cream, canned lychees or pineapple.

Dim sum, which are small steamed or fried dumplings and other nibbles, are mainly served in Chinatown on weekend mornings and early afternoons, and are treated as a Chinese brunch. Diners choose their dishes from trolleys wheeled from table to table, generally drinking hot tea as an accompaniment.

Bo Ky

80 Bayard St. **Map** 4 F5. 406-2292. **Open** 8am–9:30pm daily. **Closed** two days Chinese New Year.

This noisy and bustling, no-frills Chinatown restaurant has shared tables and waiters who speak

limited English. But the many seafood noodle dishes and soups are filling, delicious, and a real bargain. The Vietnamese items on the menu are often the best.

Canton

45 Division St. **Map** 5 A5. 226-4441. **Open** noon–10pm Wed–Thu, noon–10:30pm Fri, Sat, noon–9:30pm Sun. **Closed** 5 weeks July–mid-August.

The Canton offers better standards than those usually found in Chinatown restaurants, in décor, service, and food. Prices are also higher, but its ardent fans think it's worth it, especially for the Cantonese seafood dishes. No credit cards are accepted, nor is there a license for alcohol, but you may bring your own wine or beer.

Chin Chin

216 E 49th St. **Map** 13 B5. 888-4555. **Open** noon–11:45pm Mon–Fri, 5–11:45pm Sat, 5–11 Sun. AE, DC, MC, V.

An upscale Chinese restaurant with Western décor, Chin Chin has a wide and interesting range of dishes from all over China (many prepared with a Western accent). Try some of the offbeat items, such as vegetable duck pie with crepes or Chinese ratatouille casserole. As Chinese restaurants go, this is on the pricey side.

Golden Unicorn

18 E Broadway. **Map** 5 A5. 941-0911. **Open** 9am–11pm daily. AE, MC, V.

This large, mirrored, two-story Hong Kong-style palace has some of the most delicious *dim sum* in town, as well as savory Cantonese dishes. Noise, crowds and staff outfitted with walkie-talkies may be unsettling, but the large numbers of Chinese families attest to the restaurant's authenticity. Try the special shark-fin dumpling in fragrant broth.

Ollie's Noodle Shop & Grille

2315 Broadway. **Map** 15 C4. 362-3111. **Open** 11:30am–midnight daily. AE, MC, V.

In this plain luncheonette-style noodle restaurant there are many different soups available. These come with wontons, vegetables, meats and/or seafood, and are hearty, satisfying and particularly budget-friendly.

For key to symbols see p285

Oriental Garden

14 Elizabeth St. **Map** 4 F5.
🄲 *619-0085.* **Open** *8:30am–1am
daily.* 🏃 🅴 AE. $$

Expect to share formica-topped
tables with strangers in this jam-
packed, noisy restaurant. Don't let
the dreary décor or occasional
surly waiter put you off, for the
seafood is among Chinatown's
best. *Dim sum* and other
Cantonese dishes are also good.

Shun Lee Palace

155 E 55th St. **Map** 13 A4.
🄲 *371-8844.* **Open** *noon–11:30pm
daily.* **Closed** *Thanksgiving.* 🅱 🆃
🅴 AE, DC, MC, V. $$$

In the forefront of East Side
Chinese chic for more than 20
years, this popular place has a
devoted clientele for its spacious
elegance and slightly upscale
Cantonese and Szechuan menu
(there's even a spa-cuisine menu
for the diet-conscious). The wine
list is long for a Chinese restaurant,
and prices are very fair for the
neighborhood. The casserole
dishes are house specialties.

Shun Lee West

43 W 65th St. **Map** 11 D2.
🄲 *595-8895.* **Open** *noon–midnight
daily.* **Closed** *Thanksgiving.* 🆅 🅱
🅴 AE, DC, MC, V. $$$

Handy for the Lincoln Center, this
West Side cousin of Shun Lee
Palace has just as devoted a
coterie, though both food and
service can be slightly erratic,
especially at peak times. When
"on," its Szechuan dishes have
real sizzle and snap. Regional
winners include softshell crab in
black bean sauce and dry,
shredded Szechuan beef.

Tang Pavilion

65 W 55th St. **Map** 11 B4.
🄲 *956-6888.* **Open** *11:30am–
10:30pm daily.* 🎶 🆅 🆅
🅴 AE, DC, MC, V. $$

Finding such a low-key and
pleasantly upscale Chinese
restaurant near Carnegie Hall is
good news. That the food is so
tasty and prices so fair makes the
Tang Pavilion even more of an
asset. You might try the Shanghai
specialties, a rarity in New York.

JAPANESE

After Chinese, Japanese restaurants are the most common Asian
restaurants in New York, and they
serve perhaps the best Japanese
food this side of Tokyo. Most are
located in the Midtown area and

serve traditional dishes, such as
sukiyaki (vegetables and meat
simmered in broth), *tempura* (vegetables or seafood deep-fried in
gossamer-light batter) and *teriyaki*
(meat or chicken marinated several times in soy sauce, sweet rice
wine, and sugar, dried, then grilled).

Many Japanese restaurants have
sushi bars in the front or back,
where you can sit and eat, choosing from a tempting array of fresh,
uncooked seafood in a display
case in front of you. Sushi (cooked,
vinegared rice wrapped around
raw fish or barely-cooked shrimp)
and sashimi (raw fish accompanied by rice and a dip of soy,
ginger, and *wasabi*, Japanese horse-
radish) are very popular and are
most often eaten with chopsticks.

Hatsuhana

17 E 48th St. **Map** 12 F5.
🄲 *355-3345.* **Open** *11:45am–
2:45pm, 5:30–10pm Mon–Fri,
5–10pm Sat.* 🎶 🅴 AE, DC,
MC, V. $$$$

Just why this Japanese sushi and
sashimi restaurant is so revered
and constantly so crowded may
not seem apparent at first glance.
But connoisseurs have long since
considered it to have the very
best, freshest, and most varied
sushi in town. The best seats in
the house are at the sushi bar,
where you can watch the skilled
chefs carry out their work.

Honmura An

170 Mercer St. **Map** 4 E3.
🄲 *334-5253.* **Open** *noon–2:30pm
Wed–Sat, 6–10pm Tue–Thu, 6–
10:30pm Fri, Sat, 6–9:30pm Sun.*
Closed *1st week Jan, July 4th
weekend, Labor Day weekend.*
🎶 🆅 🅴 AE, DC, MC, V. $$$

The elegant and stylish Honmura
An raises noodle-making to an art
form, and its SoHo setting adds to
its artistic appeal. The homemade
udon and soba noodle dishes are
particularly delicious.

Inagiku

Waldorf-Astoria Hotel, 301 Park Ave.
Map 13 A5. 🄲 *355-0440.* **Open**
*noon–2pm Mon–Fri, 5:30–
10pm daily.* **Closed** *some hols.*
🅱 🅴 AE, DC, JCB, MC, V.
$$$$

With its tasteful, formal Japanese
décor, kimono-clad waitresses,
and tatami-mat dining rooms,
Inagiku is a unique dining expe-
rience. Specialties are *tempura*,
teriyaki, and the traditional *Kaiseki*,
a full course dinner consisting of a
dozen or so dishes served in a
designated order. The large selec-
tion of ingredients is seasonal.

Iso

175 2nd Ave. **Map** 4 F1.
🄲 *777-0361.* **Open** *5:30pm–
midnight Mon–Sat.* **Closed** *some
hols, one week summer.* 🎶
🅴 AE, MC, V. $$$

Iso combines walls hung with
modern art, the freshest sushi
imaginable, and a casual East
Village ambience. Add moderate
prices and it's no wonder this has
become a neighborhood favorite.

Nobu

105 Hudson St. **Map** 3 B1. 🄲 *219-
0500.* **Open** *11:45–2:30pm, 5:45–
11pm daily.* 🎶 🅱 🆅 🏃 ★ 🅴
AE, DC, MC, V. $$$$

Nobu has become a "hot ticket"
for its superb sushi and sashimi
and the iconoclastic whimsy of
its chef's creations (in which non-
Japanese ingredients are added to
classic dishes). A clever décor fits
the arty TriBeCa locale perfectly.
Prices are rather high, but offbeat
delights such as rock shrimp
tempura with spicy red pepper oil
and Kumamoto oysters with Maui
onion salsa give a new fillip to the
Japanese menu. Try Next Door
Nobu (344-4445) for a less pricey
menu and no waiting.

Sushisay

38 E 51st St. **Map** 13 A4. 🄲 *755-
1780.* **Open** *noon–2:15pm,
5:30–10pm Mon–Fri, 5pm–9pm Sat.*
🅴 AE, DC, MC, V. $$$$

This understated and tranquil
Japanese dining room is just
below street level. Sushi and
sashimi are the best choices here,
especially at the always-crowded
sushi bar, where you can select
favorites from the display. Service is
cheerful and quick at the sushi
bar, but can be slow elsewhere.
Go for the sushi; dishes on the
regular menu are more humdrum.

SOUTHEAST ASIAN

The Thai mania never took too
strong a hold in New York. Many
of the hole-in-the-wall Thai restaurants known for spicy food and
modest prices have given way to
more sophisticated restaurants that
combine Thai and European
cuisines, using Thai ingredients,
such as lemongrass, *galanga*
(similar to ginger root), kaffir lime
leaves, garlic, tamarind, cilantro
and hot chili oil, and western
cooking techniques.

There has been a recent upsurge
in New York of other Southeast
Asian restaurants, especially
Vietnamese, which often have
an overlay of the French in

presentation and décor. The "Europeanizing" of these cuisines has led to a toning down of the spiciness, though there is still enough sizzle for most Western palates.

Cendrillon

45 Mercer St. **Map** 4 E2.
📞 343-9012. **Open** 11am–11pm, Tue–Sun. 🍴 👶 🎵 ♿ *AE, DC, MC, V.* ⑤⑤

The setting is a spacious, restful one in bustling SoHo, the food is Malaysian and Filipino, artistically presented, and the prices are modest. Sweet potato noodle with spicy grilled squid is one of many pleasing dishes.

Le Colonial

149 E 57th St. **Map** 13 B3.
📞 752-0808. **Open** noon–2pm Mon–Fri, 5:30–11pm Mon–Fri, 5:30–midnight Sat, 5–10pm Sun. 🍴 ♿ 👶 ♿ *AE, DC, MC, V.* ⑤⑤⑤

A celebrity favorite, Le Colonial uses pre-war Vietnam as a theme, but its Vietnamese food and well-dressed clientele are strictly 1990s. The food can be very spicy, but it's always fresh, low in calories, and quite delicious. Try the tasty, crisp-seared whole red snapper or the Vietnamese ravioli and shrimp in coconut curry sauce.

Lemongrass Grill

2534 Broadway. **Map** 15 C4.
📞 666-0888. **Open** 11:30am–11pm Mon–Fri, 11:30am–midnight Sat, 1–11:30pm Sun. 🍴 👶 ♿ 🗽 *AE, MC, V.* ⑤

Countering other restaurants' moves upmarket, this inexpensive Thai restaurant offers fiery delights that include delicious soups and noodle dishes, served in a tropical setting. There are other branches in Greenwich Village and Brooklyn.

Mekong

44 Prince St. **Map** 4 D3. 📞 343-8169. **Open** 11am–11pm daily. 🍴 👶 ♿ 🗽 🎵 ♿ *AE, MC, V.* ⑤⑤

Softly lit but not fancy, this cheerful little Vietnamese restaurant does a good job of serving authentic dishes at prices reasonable for its SoHo location.

Monsoon

435 Amsterdam Ave. **Map** 15 C4.
📞 580-8686. **Open** 11:30am–11:30pm Mon–Thu. 🍴 ♿ 🗽 *AE, MC, V.* ⑤⑤

With a successful blend of Thai and Vietnamese dishes, Monsoon is popular for its surprisingly low prices and satisfying amalgam of both cuisines.

Owen Thai

1485 1st Ave. **Map** 17 C5.
📞 249-5700. **Open** 5–11pm Mon–Fri, 5–11:30pm Sat, Sun. ♿ *AE, MC, V.* ⑤⑤

You will find reasonably authentic, well-spiced Thai food in Owen Thai's romantic setting of spacious tables and comfortable chairs, which is enhanced by helpful staff. Prices range from inexpensive to high, depending on what you choose from the varied menu.

Penang

109 Spring St. **Map** 3 C4.
📞 274-8883. **Open** 11:30am–midnight Mon–Thu, 11:30–1am Fri, Sat, 1–11pm Sun. 👶 🗽 ♿ *AE, MC, V.* ⑤

This has become a popular SoHo hangout for its unusual, slightly exotic Malaysian food and vibrant tropical setting. The pompano fish in black bean sauce is one of many delicious dishes to choose from. There is a slightly cheaper branch in Queens (718-321-2078).

Rain

100 W 82nd St. **Map** 15 B4.
📞 501-0776. **Open** noon–3pm Mon–Fri, 6–11pm Mon–Thu, 6pm–midnight Fri, 5pm–midnight Sat, 5–10pm Sun. ♿ 🗽 ♿ 👶 🗽 *AE, MC, V.* ⑤⑤

Trendy, noisy, and crowded, this new restaurant brings touches of Thailand, Vietnam, and Malaysia to its menu. A haunt of celebrities, the restaurant boasts good food, like crispy whole fish, and a huge beer list. Service can be a little slow at times.

Red Garlic

916 8th Ave. **Map** 12 D5.
📞 489-5237. **Open** 11am–3pm, 5–11:30pm Mon–Fri, 4–11:30pm Sat, 4–11pm Sun. 🍴 👶 ♿ 👶 ♿ *AE, DC, MC, V.* ⑤⑤

Décor is just a notch above the diner level in this tiny, crowded restaurant – the former Siam Inn – but the authentic food compensates, and the price is right – low. Hot, fresh, spicy Thai dishes are served in generous portions by friendly staff. *Plalad prig* (deep-fried seabass in a chili-garlic sauce) is one of many very good dishes. The prix fixe dinner is a good option and represents excellent value.

Vong

200 E 54th St. **Map** 13 A4.
📞 486-9592. **Open** noon–2:30pm, 6–11pm Mon–Fri, 5:30–11:30pm Sat, 5:30–10pm Sun. 🍴 ♿ 🗽 ♿ ★ *AE, DC, MC, V.* ⑤⑤⑤⑤

Probably the hippest of the French-accented Thai restaurants, the copper-toned Vong looks as beautiful as its elegantly presented food tastes. Memorable dishes include sweetbreads roasted on a licorice satay and sautéed *fois gras* with ginger and mango. Desserts are as mouth-watering as the rest of the menu. Prices are moderate for the quality of the food.

Zen Palate

663 9th Ave. **Map** 12 D3. 📞 582-1669. **Open** 11:30am–11pm daily. 🍴 👶 ♿ 👶 ♿ *AE, DC, MC, V.*

Zen Palate is a stylish vegetarian restaurant located in the Theater District. Many dishes with a Thai, Chinese and Japanese flair are served. There is another branch located at 34 E Union Square (614-9291). A take-out service is available at both branches.

INDIAN AND AFGHAN

Indian restaurants in New York have become more adventurous, but they still have a way to go to match the standard of Indian restaurants in London, for example. Even so, they offer some of the best dining values in the city, with many featuring a bargain lunchtime buffet. Some of the cheapest restaurants can be found on E 6th Street between 1st and 2nd Avenues. Most Indian menus feature curries and other lamb, chicken, shrimp, and vegetable dishes. Due to New York's scarcity of pure vegetarian restaurants, Indian ones make a fine substitute. Some restaurants have tandoori ovens and specialize in chicken dishes and breads baked in the oven's dry heat. While most Indian restaurants have liquor licences, the best drink with Indian food is beer. For non-drinkers, a yogurt-based drink called lassi is a refreshing option, while mango lassi makes a good alternative to traditional Indian desserts, which can sometimes seem overly sweet.

There are just a few Afghan restaurants in New York, also reasonably priced and informal. Afghan food is similar to Indian, with some interesting variations, though less spicy and diverse.

For key to symbols *see p285*

Afghan Kebab House

764 9th Ave. **Map** 12 D4.
█ 307-1612. **Open** 11am–11pm
Mon–Sat. 🍴 & ⑤

This is one of three Afghan restaurants offering remarkable value and zesty Afghan fare, especially their kebabs. The menu differs slightly at each site, but tiny space and minimal décor prevail at each one. None has a liquor license but you may bring your own bottle. The other restaurants are Afghan Kebab House II at 1345 2nd Ave (517-2776) and Afghan Kebab House III at 155 W 46th St (768-3835).

Darbar

44 W 56th St. **Map** 12 F3. █ 265-
1850. **Open** noon–3pm daily, 5:30–
11pm Mon–Thu, 5:30–11:30pm Fri,
Sat, 5:30–10:30pm Sun. V &
🃏 AE, DC, MC, V. ⑤⑤⑤⑤

At Darbar, consistently reliable, well-seasoned northern Indian food is served in surroundings congenial to privacy. The restaurant is multilevel and handsome. Try the many fine vegetarian dishes.

Dawat

210 E 58th St. **Map** 13 B3.
█ 355-7555. **Open** 11:30am–3pm
Mon–Sat, 5:30–11pm Sun–Thu,
5:30–11:30pm Fri, Sat. 🍴 V &
🃏 AE, DC, MC, V. ⑤⑤⑤

The imprimatur of famous Indian food writer Madhur Jaffrey, who acts as a consultant, is all over this Indian menu, which features haute (and hot) food in a cool pastel décor. Unusual and exquisitely seasoned dishes are the hallmark here. The surprise is the moderate cost for such originality. *Bhindi masala*, okra flavored with browned onions and dried mango, is one of many delights.

Jewel of India

15 W 44th St. **Map** 12 F5.
█ 869-5544. **Open** noon–3pm,
5:30–11pm daily. 🍴 V &
🃏 AE, DC, MC, V. ⑤⑤

The just-off 5th Avenue location is perfect for theater-goers and shoppers. Once inside, you've stepped into a north Indian oasis, where the service, décor and food are Indian at its finest. Tandoori and à la carte dishes are well priced, but the real buys here are the prix fixe dinner, lunch buffet, and business lunch. There are also delicious free nibbles during happy hour.

Pamir

1437 2nd Ave. **Map** 17 B5. █ 734-
3791. **Open** 5–11pm Tue–Sun. V
& 🃏 MC, V. ⑤⑤

This modest, well-priced Afghan restaurant has built a following for its reliable lamb dishes, kebabs, yogurt sauces and hearty accoutrements. Service is eager and helpful and the setting is cozy. Sometimes there are long waits for a table on weekends, but most feel the food is worth the wait.

Saalam Bombay

317 Greenwich St. **Map** 1 B1.
█ 226-9400. **Open** noon–3pm,
5:30–11pm Sun–Fri. 🍴 V
🃏 AE, DC, MC, V. ⑤⑤

This newcomer brings grace and elegance to its TriBeCa location with a menu best described as Indian haute cuisine. A good time to sample the many unusual dishes is at the bargain-priced lunch buffet on weekdays.

EUROPEAN AND MIDDLE EASTERN

If you look hard enough, you might find any national cuisine in New York, but not necessarily in large numbers. The following are a few of the best in a range of European and Middle Eastern cuisines. Mediterranean cooking is enjoying a big vogue in New York, partially because of its healthy nature – fresh seafood, grilled meats, tomatoes, olives, peppers, garlic, olive oil, and herbs. In most Greek restaurants, for example, you'll find salads with feta cheese, stuffed eggplant (aubergine), vine leaves and peppers, roast lamb, seafood dishes, *spanakopita* (spinach pie baked in filo pastry), and honeyed sweets like *baklava*.

Moroccan chefs create dishes such as roast chicken or lamb with prunes or figs and almonds, and *couscous* (steamed semolina with a meat and vegetable stew).

There are very few northern European restaurants in New York. Scandinavian restaurants specialize in seafood and tend to be formal and pricey. Russian and Jewish/Romanian restaurants are informal on the whole, though not inexpensive. (For Jewish kosher specialties, *see Delis, p304*.)

Aquavit

13 W 54th St. **Map** 12 F4.
█ 307-7311. **Open** noon–3pm,
5:30–10:30pm daily. 🍴 V
🃏 AE, DC, MC, V. ⑤⑤⑤⑤

This is one of New York's most arresting and elegant restaurants, occupying space in the late Nelson Rockefeller's town house. The main dining room (The Atrium) is an eight-story, glass-topped atrium with birch trees, a waterfall,

and kites hung overhead – extremely pleasant at lunchtime. Aquavit's speciality is Scandinavian cuisine with an emphasis on the Swedish. The salmon is superb; all fish dishes are impeccably prepared. Pan-roasted Arctic venison is also memorable. Though the à la carte menu is very pricey, Aquavit offers a prix-fixe menu at lunch and dinner, a pretheater menu, and a five-course tasting menu at dinner. Lighter, cheaper fare is available upstairs at Café Aquavit, overlooking the Atrium.

Barney Greengrass

541 Amsterdam Ave. **Map** 15 C3.
█ 724-4707. **Open** 8:30am– 4pm
Tue–Fri, 8:30am–5pm Sat–Sun. 🍴
 V & ⑤⑤

This landmark Jewish restaurant is to lox (smoked salmon) what Tiffany's is to jewelry. Known for its fabulous smoked fish, Barney Greengrass also serves great borscht and a typical Jewish brunch of bagels, lox, and cream cheese. The lines can be long at peak times.

Layla

211 Broadway. **Map** 1 C2.
█ 431-0700. **Open** noon–2:15pm
Fri only, 5:30–11:30pm daily. 🍴 &
 V 🎵& AE, DC, MC, V.
⑤⑤⑤

From the owner of Nobu and TriBeCa Grill now comes Layla, a dream version of Middle Eastern cuisine. Not specifically Turkish, Moroccan, or Egyptian, the food at this glitzy new TriBeCa "in" place evokes the spirit of the Middle East in such creations as *falafel* and cumin-scented swordfish kebabs on *couscous*. Be sure to sample the *meze*, a delicious assortment of appetizers. There's even belly dancing, and the *meze* bar stays open until midnight.

Moroccan Star

205 Atlantic Ave, Brooklyn.
█ (718) 643-0800. **Open** noon–
10pm daily. 🍴 & AE, MC, V.
⑤

The Moroccan Star twinkles on a street known for its modestly priced Middle Eastern restaurants. There are wonderful Moroccan dishes on the menu, like chicken *tajine* (stew), *b'stilla* (chicken pie), and lamb dishes. These are served in friendly, family style with family-run simplicity. Prices are low.

Moustache

90 Bedford St. **Map** 3 C2.
█ 229-2220. **Open** noon–midnight
daily. 🍴 & V ⑤
One of two branches.

This tiny West Village spot is a find for zesty Middle Eastern dishes like *falafel*, *ouzi*, and *babaganough*, all dished up at modest prices. Even the pita bread is baked fresh.

Periyali

35 W 20th St. **Map** 8 F5.
【 463-7890. **Open** noon–2:30pm Mon–Fri, 5:30–10:30pm Mon–Sat.
🖬 🍽 *AE, DC, MC, V.* $$$

The white stucco walls of Periyali, the tiled floors, and dark-beamed upscale taverna décor may transport you in spirit to a Greek island, though the billowy tent ceiling is more designer fantasy. The nouvelle Greek food, somewhat gentrified and more expensive than most tavernas, can be terrific. Try the *spanakopita* and seafood dishes such as charcoal-grilled octopus and whole sea bass anointed with lemon, herbs, and olive oil.

Picholine

35 W 64th St. **Map** 11 C2.
【 724-8585. **Open** 11:45am–2pm Tue–Sat, 5:30–11:45pm Mon–Sat, 5–10pm Sun. 🍽 🛇 🕊 🔆
🍽 *AE, DC, MC, V.* $$$

Near Lincoln Center, this new French-Mediterranean restaurant has much going for it: a quietly appealing décor that reflects the color of the olives on each table (for which the restaurant is named), its tasty Mediterranean food, and an award-winning wine list and cheese cart that are remarkable for their breadth. The Moroccan spiced loin of lamb is one of many intriguing dishes that are making a name for the chef Terry Brennan.

The Russian Tea Room

150 W 57th St. **Map** 12 E3.
【 265-0947. **Open** 11:30am– midnight Mon–Fri, 11am–mid- night Sat, Sun. 🍽 🛇 🎵
🕯 at dinner. 🍽 *AE, DC, MC, V.*
$$$$$

No one knows for sure what the food at this glamorous, famous restaurant will be when it reopens in 2000 after a major renovation. With a new (and secret) celebrity chef at the helm it is guaranteed to be innovative and wonderful – and probably pricey too.

Sammy's Famous Roumanian

157 Chrystie St. **Map** 5 A4.
【 673-0330. **Open** 3:30–10:30pm Sun–Thu, 3:30pm–midnight Fri, Sat.
🍽 *AE, MC, V.* $$$$$

Sammy's isn't Kosher, but Jewish-Romanian. This noisy, no-décor-to-speak-of place is where you'll catch the essence of the New York Jewish experience. You don't have to be Jewish to enjoy the "let it all hang out" atmosphere of live music, loud talk, and much laughing. It is famous for its stuffed cabbage, chopped chicken liver, stuffed *derma* (boiled and baked sausages), and the huge portions. On each table are ingredients to make a terrific egg cream: milk and seltzer water, with chocolate syrup to add. Skip the boring desserts.

SOUTH AMERICAN AND CARIBBEAN

Despite the influx of people from Latin America and the Caribbean to New York, there are only a few mainstream restaurants that feature their cuisines. Caribbean restaurants use ingredients such as coconut, banana, garlic, rice, and beans. They also have lots of peppery dishes such as conch stews and black bean soup.

Brazilian restaurants offer good value, an upbeat, casual ambience, and a number of authentic, homey dishes. Look for the national dish, *feijoada*, a stew of black beans and various meats and vegetables.

Mexican restaurants in New York generally offer standard Tex-Mex food. *Enchiladas* (chicken or beef-stuffed corn tortilla, covered in melted cheese), *tamales* (filled cornmeal parcels, wrapped and steamed in corn husks), *fajitas* (strips of grilled beef), refried beans, and *quesadillas* (crisp pastry filled with melted cheese) are among the dishes to expect.

Cabana Carioca

123 W 45th St. **Map** 12 E5.
【 581-8088. **Open** noon–11pm Sun–Thu, noon–midnight Fri, Sat.
🕯 🎵 🍽 *AE, DC, MC, V.* $$$

Of a number of Brazilian restaurants on 45th Street that have sprung up over the last few years, this moderately priced one on three levels is without doubt one of the best. Arrive feeling hungry, as portions are huge in this funky place with nonstop music, decorative folk art frescoes on the walls, and a high decibel level bouncing off them. *Feijoada* is served on Wednesday and Saturday, but you will always find hearty steak dishes, chicken, cod, and seafood. After a few gulps of *caipirinha*, the favorite Brazilian drink made of *pinga* (a sugar cane liquor) and fresh lemon, you may find the noise less bothersome and may even join in.

Lola

30 W 22nd St. **Map** 8 F4.
【 675-6700. **Open** noon–3pm Tue–Fri, 6pm–midnight daily, 9am– 2:30pm, 6pm–midnight Sun. 🕯 🕊
🎵 🍽 *AE, DC, MC, V.* $$$$

Lola's is a handsomely converted, high-ceilinged loft serving hot 'n' sassy Caribbean dishes as well as some American and Italian food, such as venison, pasta, and seafood. The best of the many wonderful dishes is the fiery 100-spices Caribbean fried chicken. Lola has departed, but remaining are live rhythm-and-blues nights and a Gospel choir Sunday brunch that rocks the rafters.

Riodizio

417 Lafayette St. **Map** 4 F2.
【 529-1313. **Open** 5:30am–10pm Sun–Thu, 5:30–11:30pm Fri, Sat. 🕊
🛇 🕯 🍽 *AE, DC, MC, V.* $$$

This Brazilian-style rotisserie has a prime location near the Public Theater in the heart of Greenwich Village. Handsome and spacious, it is a great value for the ultrahungry.

Tropica

MetLife Bldg, 200 Park Ave.
Map 13 A5. **【** 867-6767. **Open** 11:30am–3pm, 5:30–10pm Mon–Fri.
Closed some hols. 🍽 🛇 🕯 🕊
🍽 *AE, DC, MC, V.* $$$$

This attractive restaurant evokes the tropics with its palms, airy upper levels, latticework, and wicker chairs. The Caribbean food is more imaginative than its bustling business lunch crowd might demand. Seafood is good here; try the roasted cod with *saké* (Japanese rice wine) and black bean sauce. It is pricey, as the location dictates, but definitely worth the money for the adventurous.

Zarela

953 2nd Ave. **Map** 13 B4.
【 644-6740. **Open** noon–3pm Mon–Fri, 5pm–11pm Mon–Thu, 5pm–11:30pm Fri, Sat, 5pm–10pm Sun. 🎵 🍽 *AE, DC, MC, V.* $$

Light years from the standard Tex-Mex fare, Zarela's is upscale in every way – menu, crowd (which is youthful), and especially the price. You'll find authentic *tamales* and *enchiladas* as starters only. Fresh seafood is featured strongly here, prepared with subtle sophistication in the style of Mexico's coastal region. Try the delicious tuna marinated in Oaxacan *mole* sauce and seared rare, or whole grilled trout rubbed with *chipotle* paste with a tasty lime/onion/coriander sauce.

For key to symbols see p285

Light Meals and Snacks

Y OU CAN GET A SNACK almost anywhere and anytime in Manhattan. New Yorkers seem to eat endlessly – on street corners, in bars, luncheonettes, delis, before and after work, and long into the night. Casual eating in New York might include soft pretzels or char-roasted chestnuts from a corner stand; a huge sandwich from a deli; a Greek *gyro* sandwich (roasted lamb in pita bread) from street vendors; a pretheater snack at a café or coffee bar; or a post-party binge at an all-night diner or bistro. While street fare is generally cheap, the quality and culinary skills vary greatly.

DELIS

D ELICATESSENS are a New York institution, a great source for a hefty lunchtime sandwich. Try the wonderful corned beef and pastrami sandwiches at the famous **Carnegie Delicatessen**, considered by many to be New York's best deli.

Some delis, such as **Katz's Deli**, cater to those who enjoy traditional kosher food. Most deli business is, however, takeout and as such delis are bustling places serving huge sandwiches at relatively cheap prices. Counter staff are typically surly and impatient, and rudeness has almost become a trademark of the **Stage Deli**, which is now more of a tourist stop than the showbiz favorite it used to be.

For New York ethnic Jewish flavor, try the **Second Avenue Delicatessen**, well-known for its homemade soups, pickles, corned beef sandwiches, chopped liver, and other kosher goodies. **Zabar's** is a takeout heaven for yuppies who put up with the crowds for superb smoked fish, pickles, and salads.

Aficionados say the best pastrami sandwiches and other favorites are to be found at the **Pastrami King** in Queens.

CAFÉS, BISTROS AND BRASSERIES

C AFÉS, BISTROS, and the larger brasseries have become "in" places in New York in recent years. Try **Balthazar** on Spring St. for "brilliantly faux" everything except the menu, which is stellar. The **Café Centro**, above Grand

Central, is particularly busy and noisy during lunchtime, and is a favorite with business types. The Provençal/ Mediterranean fare includes fish soups and some succulent desserts. **The Brasserie**, a longtime landmark, has reliable French food and is open 24 hours a day. **Bistro du Nord** on Madison Ave serves a variety of good French/American fare with an inventive flair. Downtown, **Odeon** is a TriBeCa favorite for its brasserie menu and late hours. **Raoul's** in SoHo is a French bistro with a relaxed ambience that keeps artists and other habitués coming back for reliable, informal food. **Elephant and Castle**, a minimally decorated café, is a Greenwich Village standby for soup-salad-omelette lunches and other light snacks. Its real forte is breakfast and brunch, served in ample portions at modest prices. The bar scene is lively too. Tiny **Chez Jacqueline** is also a favored Village spot. Its French bistro fare and proximity to several off-Broadway theaters make it popular with the young, hip, and international crowd for a moderately priced dinner or late supper.

In the Theater District, try the Cuban **Victor's Café 52**. Large, lively, and Latin, it is known for authentic Cuban food served in giant portions at medium prices. **Chez Josephine** is an exuberant bistro-cabaret with live jazz piano playing. The scene is the main attraction here, and the French food is excellent. **La Boite en Bois**, small but delightfully French, serves delicious French bistro

food and is conveniently close to Lincoln Center. In the same vicinity is **Vince and Eddie's**, a tiny gem known for reliable, often superb American food.

Sarabeth's, on the Upper West Side, defies categorizing, but might best be dubbed a café. The best time to visit is for breakfast or weekend brunch, when families wolf down waffles, French toast, pancakes, and omelettes. There are two other branches, one of which is located in the Whitney Museum of Art.

The Gramercy Park area's **Les Halles** is about as all-out French bistro as New York gets. At its late-night peak, the decibel level is high, but regulars think the *frites* and beef dishes are worth the noise and crowds.

PIZZERIAS

P IZZA IS AVAILABLE all over New York, from street stands and fast-food places that sell it by the slice for a few dollars, to a traditional Neapolitan pizzeria.

Some pizzerias offer something more. **Arturo's Pizzeria** uses a coal oven for crisp, thin-crusted bases with the added inducement of live jazz. **Mezzogiorno** has a Tuscan menu and wonderful pizzas with unusual toppings. The crowded **Mezzaluna** also specializes in brick-oven, thin-crusted pizza, as does **John's Pizzeria**, whose many fans (including Woody Allen) consider it to be Manhattan's best.

Brooklyn boasts a top pizzeria in Coney Island's **Totonno Pizzeria**, which is well worth the trip for real pizza aficionados.Generally, pizza parlors are good places to go for a cheap, simple meal, especially with children. Most places won't take reservations, so the popular ones may have long lines.

HAMBURGER PLACES

Y OUR NOSE may lead you to some of the cheaper burger and hot dog stands on the street. However, there are many places in New York where you can buy a better quality burger, even though prices for a top grade all-beef burger can go up to $10.

Hamburger Harry's offers reasonably priced, large, juicy, and mesquite-grilled burgers, with a choice of over a dozen toppings and a huge fresh salad. **Hard Rock Café** is a well-known chain which serves hearty portions in a lively atmosphere.

Bright and basic, the five outlets of **Jackson Hole** offer fat, juicy, meaty burgers in 28 varieties popular with kids. Adults might prefer less glare and smarter décor, but they will like the low prices. It's also a good place to try the quintessential New York drink, the egg cream *(see p286)*.

The **Beer Bar** at Café Centro is where professional types like to hang out. Besides an unusual beer menu, the burgers are delicious.

New York's best burgers may well be found at the **Corner Bistro** in Greenwich Village. Not only are the burgers tasty and reasonably priced, but the beer selection is good, too, and the 4am closing makes this a great late-night stop.

DINERS AND LUNCHEONETTES

DINERS and luncheonettes, also called sandwich or coffee shops, can be found all over town. Food is usually indifferent but served in huge, cheap platefuls. Despite the name luncheonette, such places are usually open from breakfast until late evening, and you can stop in at almost any hour for coffee and something basic and filling to eat.

A recent trend with diners has seen 1990s replicas of the old 1930s cheap-eats places. One such retro-diner is the chic Empire Diner *(see p136)*. The **Broadway Diner** in Midtown is a faithful re-creation of a 1940s diner. It offers a good American breakfast, including thick-cut fries and homemade corned beef hash with poached eggs.

Jerry's attracts a SoHo art and celebrity crowd who love

the inventive sandwiches, salads, desserts and huge breakfasts. Also attracting a hip art crowd is **Florent**, a West Village diner with reliable French food served around the clock. The **Kiev** is very plain, but famous for its Jewish-Eastern European specialties, like borscht. The **Coffee Shop** in Union Square serves Brazilian-American fare and is open all night.

On the Upper East Side, Eli Zabar's **E.A.T.** sells top quality, but pricey Jewish favorites – like mushroom-barley soup and *challah* bread, as well as some sinful desserts.

Devotees swear by **Viand**, a spic-and-span East Side luncheonette, with cheap, ample American breakfasts, good burgers, egg creams, and the best turkey sandwiches in town. **Veselka** is not the usual New York sandwich shop – what makes it special is the Polish/Ukrainian food, all at rock-bottom prices.

TEAROOMS

ABOUT THE ONLY PLACE you can be absolutely sure of getting a cup of real, brewed tea is at a formal, prix fixe afternoon tea in a lounge at one of New York's great hotels, from 3pm to 5pm.

Afternoon tea in the **Plaza Hotel**'s Palm Court has cream cakes and hot buttered scones galore. For an extra stylish tea, on Chippendale furniture, visit the **Carlyle** hotel. The **Hotel Pierre** offers one of the better buys in hotel prix fixe teas. Tea at the **Waldorf–Astoria** comes with Devonshire cream, while the elegant tea at the **Stanhope** hotel is abundant enough to carry you through to a late dinner.

A variation on tea themes can be found in a new chain of teahouses called **Saint's Alp**. These delightful spots serving frothy, flavored, colorful tea drinks poured over crushed ice can be found at 51 Mott Street near Chinatown and in the new Times Square area. Teatime, Japanese style, can be enjoyed at **The Tea Box** located in the Takashimaya department store.

COFFEE AND CAKES

YOU CAN GET a decent cup of coffee for as little as 75 cents, with endless free refills, at most diners, luncheonettes, and coffee shops. There is a new trend for coffee bars that serve a variety of gourmet and specialty coffees, such as cappuccino, espresso and caffè latte. Some ice cream parlors and patisseries also serve good coffee, along with decadently luscious pastries.

Some of the most charming coffee houses are in Little Italy, such as **Caffè Biondo**, which serves cappuccino and sinful sweets, and **Caffè Vivaldi** with relatively cheap coffees, teas, and desserts served on marble tables. **Caffè Ferrara**, going strong since 1892, has moderately-priced Italian pastries, good coffee, and outdoor seating. **Caffè Dante** is a favorite with students who like to sit outside in warm weather.

The European-style outdoor **Fledermaus Café**, in the South Street Seaport, serves fine coffee and is a good place to watch the passing scene.

The **Candy Bar and Grill**, in Chelsea, offers a selection of excellent Viennese pastries and coffees *mit schlag* (with whipped cream) in a cozy turn-of-the-century setting. The modern Austrian dishes make this a worthwhile dinner stop as well. At **Caffè Bianco**, uptown, desserts are fabulous, the coffee is good, and prices are low. The much pricier **Café Guy Pascal** has delicious French pastries as does **Payard Patisserie**. **Sant' Ambroeus** is a luxurious outpost of the Milanese *pasticceria*, with decadent desserts and an espresso bar. **Rumpelmayer's** is New York's quintessential old-fashioned ice cream parlor and is the best place to have an egg cream *(see p286)* or an ice cream fantasia. A close runner-up is **Serendipity 3**, famous for its Victoriana, elaborate ice cream creations, coffee, and mid-afternoon snacks. **Barnes & Noble Café** is a happy refuge for coffee and a pastry while browsing at one of New York's largest bookstores.

DIRECTORY

LOWER EAST SIDE

Caffè Biondo
141 Mulberry St.
Map 4 F5.

Caffè Ferrara
195 Grand St.
Map 4 F4.

Fledermaus Café
199 Water St.
Map 2 E2.

Katz's Deli
205 E Houston St.
Map 5 A3.

Saint's Alp
51 Mott St
Map 4 F 4.

SoHo AND TriBeCa

Jerry's
101 Prince St.
Map 4 D3.

Mezzogiorno
195 Spring St.
Map 4 D4.

Odeon
145 W Broadway.
Map 1 B1.

Raoul's
180 Prince St.
Map 4 D3.

GREENWICH VILLAGE

Arturo's Pizzeria
106 W Houston St.
Map 4 E3.

Balthazar
80 Spring St.
Map 3 E4.

Caffè Dante
79 MacDougal St.
Map 4 D3.

Caffè Vivaldi
32 Jones St. **Map** 3 C2.

Chez Jacqueline
73 MacDougal St.
Map 4 D2.

Corner Bistro
331 W 4th St.
Map 3 C1.

Elephant and Castle
68 Greenwich Ave.
Map 3 C1.

Florent
69 Gansevoort St
Map 3 B1.

EAST VILLAGE

Kiev
117 2nd Ave.
Map 4 2F.

Second Avenue Delicatessen
156 2nd Ave.
Map 4 F1.

Veselka
144 2nd Ave.
Map 4 F1.

GRAMERCY AND THE FLATIRON

The Coffee Shop
29 Union Sq.
Map 9 A5.

Les Halles
411 Park Ave.
Map 9 A3.

CHELSEA AND THE GARMENT DISTRICT

Candy Bar and Grill
131 8th Ave.
Map 8 D2.

THEATER DISTRICT

Broadway Diner
1726 Broadway.
Map 12 E4.

Carnegie Delicatessen
854 7th Ave.
Map 12 E4.

Chez Josephine
414 W 42nd St.
Map 7 B1.

Hamburger Harry's
145 W 45th St.
Map 12 E4.

Hard Rock Café
221 W 57th St.
Map 12 E3.

Rumpelmayer's
St. Moritz Hotel,
50 Central Park S.
Map 12 F3.

Stage Deli
834 7th Ave.
Map 12 E4.

Victor's Café 52
236 W 52nd St.
Map 11 B4.

EAST SIDE MIDTOWN

Beer Bar at Café Centro
MetLife Building,
200 Park Ave. **Map** 9 A2.

UPPER MIDTOWN

Barnes & Noble Café
Citicorp Building,
160 E. 54th St. **Map** 13 A4.

The Brasserie
100 E 53rd St. **Map** 13 A4.

Plaza Hotel
Palm Court, 768 5th Ave.
Map 12 F3.

The Tea Box
Takashimaya, 693 5th Ave.
Map 12 F2.

Waldorf–Astoria
301 Park Ave.
Map 13 A5.

UPPER EAST SIDE

Bistro du Nord
1312 Madison Ave.
Map 17 A2.

Caffè Bianco
1486 2nd Ave.
Map 17 B5.

Carlyle
35 E 76th St.
Map 17 A5.

Café Guy Pascal
1231 Madison Ave.
Map 17 A3.

E.A.T.
2 E 61st St.
Map 12 F3.

Hotel Pierre
2 E 61st St.
Map 12 F3.

Jackson Hole
232 E 64th St.
Map 13 B2.

John's Pizzeria
408 E 64th St.
Map 13 C2.
One of several branches.

Mezzaluna
1295 3rd Ave.
Map 17 B5.

Payard Patisserie
1032 Lexington Ave.
Map 13 A1.

Sant' Ambroeus
1000 Madison Ave.
Map 17 A5.

Serendipity 3
225 E 60th St.
Map 13 B5.

Stanhope
995 5th Ave.
Map 17 A4.

Viand
1011 Madison Ave.
Map 17 A5.

UPPER WEST SIDE

La Boite en Bois
75 W 68th St.
Map 11 C1.

Sarabeth's
423 Amsterdam Ave.
Map 15 C4.

Whitney Museum
945 Madison Ave
Map 17 A5.

Vince and Eddie's
70 W 68th St.
Map 11 C1.

Zabar's
2245 Broadway.
Map 15 C2.

BROOKLYN

Totonno Pizzeria
1524 Neptune Ave.
Map 7 C5.

QUEENS

Pastrami King
124 Queens Blvd,
Kew Gardens.

New York Bars

NEW YORK BARS play a huge role in the life and culture of the city. Many New Yorkers spend the evening in a succession of bars, because each usually offers something more than just alcohol. There may be additional inducements, like excellent food, live music, dancing, or a particularly large selection of beers. Brew pubs, which serve meals and brew beer on the premises, are a recent phenomenon. Bars suiting every taste and budget are to be found all over the city.

RULES AND CONVENTIONS

BARS GENERALLY stay open from around 11am to midnight. Some stay open to 2 or 4am, when they must close by law. Many bars have a "happy hour" between 5pm and 7pm, when they offer twofers (two drinks for the price of one) and a variety of free snacks. Bartenders also have the right to refuse to serve anyone they consider having had too much to drink.

The legal minimum drinking age is 21; if the bartender suspects you are younger, you'll be "carded," or asked to show some identification to prove your age. Children are not usually taken into bars.

It is common to "run a tab" and pay your bill just before you leave. Tipping the bartender is expected – 10% of the bill or about 50 cents for a single drink. Shots are not premeasured, so if you want a bigger drink, it can help to "belly up" to the bar and tip the bartender accordingly for his or her generosity. If you sit at a table, you'll be served there and be charged more.

A round of drinks can be expensive. A good way to save money is by buying a quart (95 cl) or a half gallon (190 cl) pitcher of beer.

Avoid the "free drinks for ladies" bars, which are often just pick-up joints. Some of New York's pubs did not admit women until forced by law to do so, a few years ago. Even today, many women feel uncomfortable drinking alone in certain places. Safer bets for single women are hotel bars or singles bars, although it may still be difficult to avoid harassment.

WHAT TO DRINK

YOU CAN GET almost any alcoholic drink you fancy in New York bars; the most popular drink is ice-cold beer. Mainstream bars serve standard beers from big producers like Budweiser, Coors, and Miller, and high-profile imports such as Bass ale, Becks and Heineken, and even draft Guinness. Some bars, especially the old pubs and certain chic new bars, have a much wider variety of beers, imported and small domestics. These include locally made products by some of New York's microbreweries, and the popular Brooklyn Lager. There is a vogue now, especially among the young, for microbrewery products. A microbrewery is a small producer of flavorful beers often based on traditional European (German/Belgian/English) styles.

Other popular drinks include cocktails; rum and coke; dry martinis; Scotch or bourbon, either "straight up" (without ice) or on the rocks (with ice); vodka-and-tonic and gin-and-tonic. Wine is also widely available at bars, although the "wine bar" concept has been replaced by the "olive bar."

FOOD

ALL BARS SERVE some sort of food throughout the day. It is usually convenience food like burgers, fries, salads, sandwiches and small snacks like delicious spicy chicken wings. Happy hour is an excellent time to fill up on free snacks and hot hors d'oeuvres in New York bars. Most bar kitchens stop serving food just before midnight.

FASHIONABLE BARS

YOU MAY have to line up to watch the bored and beautiful at **BB's** (formerly the Bowery Bar) – one of the hippest bars on the current scene. The bar's pretentiousness belies its humble beginnings as a gas station.

Much more fun is the funky late night scene at **Bar Six**, a West Village hangout for the cool and quirky, with microbrewery beers and food that has a Moroccan accent. Also downtown is **SoHo Kitchen and Bar**, a handsome loftlike space with tiered dining areas, a long brick bar, good pizzas, a lengthy wine lists with some 400 wines, and a good range of beers. The **Odeon** is another good place to catch the lively SoHo–TriBeCa scene.

On the Upper East Side, the bar at **Mortimer's** is a place to observe what passes these days for high society without paying exorbitant prices for the restaurant's ordinary food.

There is a new vogue for cigar bars that encourage smokers. **The Cigar Room at Trumpets** has a 36 premium cigar menu and a large single malt Scotch list. Its attached *intime* dining room is also cigar-friendly. At **Bar and Books** you can inhale, sip, and nibble snacks before a fireplace in a club-like library setting, with live jazz on weekends. In the same venue is the Beekman Bar and Book.

BARS WITH VIEWS

FINANCIAL TYPES gravitate towards the **Edward Moran Bar and Grill** in the World Financial Center for a beer and the views from the terrace of the harbor and Statue of Liberty. **The Greatest Bar on Earth** also offers a view of the statue, and the city in general. In warm weather **BP Café**, a friendly outdoor café, is the latest Midtown scene. The **Tavern on the Green** has magical views of Central Park. Inside, the glitz may overwhelm you, but the garden is a pure delight.

HISTORIC AND LITERARY BARS

IF YOU SAMPLE only one New York bar, it should probably be **McSorley's Old Alehouse**, an Irish saloon, often dubbed "McSurly's" because of the staff. It's been on the same site since 1854, making it one of New York's oldest bars. It offers a good choice of beers and a tasty lunch. Try the chili.

The Ear Inn dates from 1812 when the first tavern opened on this SoHo site. Now the haunt of poets and writers, its dark, cramped interior and long wooden bar ooze authenticity.

Greenwich Village has some of the city's oldest bars, such as **Chumley's**, which retains its character as a Prohibition-era speakeasy. It's particularly snug in winter, when an open fire burns in the hearth.

Dylan Thomas's old favorite, the **White Horse Tavern**, is an unpretentious 1880s landmark still going strong and crowded with literary and collegiate types. There's an outdoor café used in warm weather.

Peculier Pub is a beer-lover's paradise, with over 360 varieties of beer from all over the world. You must, however, be willing to tolerate the sometimes snappish and uninformed staff.

A good, though rather touristy, place for a drink in the financial district is the atmospheric **Fraunces Tavern**, first built in 1719 (see p76). Another oldie, dating to 1864, is **Pete's Tavern**, a prime hangout in the Gramercy Park area that is busy until 2am. It is known for its Victorian feel, its house brew called Pete's Ale, and the many beers on tap. In the same area, the **Old Town Bar** has been a typically Irish pub since 1892 and is now favored largely by advertising types.

No longer the celebrity scene it once was, **Sardi's** is still a hangout for *New York Times* reporters and is worth a stop to inspect the "who's who" celebrity caricatures lining the walls and for the generous drinks served in the second floor bar.

After work, crowds head to **P. J. Clarke's**, a long time favorite New York saloon dating back to the 1890s, with Irish bartenders and an incredibly bustling *après*-office scene. **Elaine's**, also on the East Side, remains a haunt of New York and visiting literary types. Sit close to Elaine's table where the meeting-and-greeting action takes place. The food is nothing much.

Near Carnegie Hall is the unobtrusive **P. J. Carney's**, which has been a watering hole for musicians and artists since 1927. It serves Irish ales and a good shepherd's pie.

YOUNG HANGOUTS

BREW PUBS, where the house beer is brewed on the premises, are currently the rage with the 20s-to-30s crowd, as are bars with sizable beer lists that feature a variety of microbrewery and imported beers. **The Chelsea Brewing Company** is a large, fun-filled brewpub situated in the Chelsea Piers sports complex, overlooking the Hudson River. In the nearby Gramercy neighborhood you will find the **Heartland Brewery**, which is the busiest, and, some think, best of the new brew pubs, with five beers, including the outstanding India Pale Ale, and many seasonals, such as cranberry and pumpkin ales.

The **Westside Brewing Company** uptown is a favorite youth and neighborhood hangout, popular for its house ales and fruit beers. Also popular is the **Yorkville Brewery & Tavern**, which has a sports bar feel in what used to be a German neighborhood. The beer list is extensive, and there is typical pub fare served at the bar.

Brews in the Garment District has a huge beer list, good grub, and an upstairs club with live music, making it a pub-crawlers' favorite.

For homesick Brits, the **Manchester** is a name to reckon with. In a cozy publike setting, you'll find Watneys or Newcastle Brown Ale on tap, just two of 18 draft beers and 40 bottled ones not widely available in New York.

In the East Village is bustling **d.b.a.**. Depending on whom you ask, the initials might stand for "don't bother to ask" or "draft beer available". There are 14 draft beers on tap, along with scores of microbrews and 50 single malt whiskeys to choose from.

A popular beer stop uptown for the college-age crowd is the loud and noisy **Brother Jimmy's BBQ**, where you can snack on old-fashioned southern barbequed ribs.

In the South Street Seaport, the **North Star Pub** is housed in a building dating back to 1821. It has much to recommend it to those in search of a good selection of English and Irish beers on tap and some 70 single malt whiskies.

Park Slope Brewery Company, in two Brooklyn locations, is another brew pub favored by the young for its 12 home brews and seasonal beers, as well as its decent pub grub and lively ambience.

SINGLES BARS

THE CHANCE TO MEET new people is offered in singles bars, which are still extremely popular. These are located all over the city, with a large concentration in midtown on the East Side. Prices in such places can be inflated, with beer costing $3 and up.

The Art Deco styled **Beer Bar**, with its interesting beer list and beer-tasting menus, is currently new and "with it." There is a frenetic singles scene at **Live Bait**, which is good for model-gazing and for its passable southern food.

GAY AND LESBIAN BARS

GAY BARS CAN be be found in Greenwich Village, with many also in SoHo, the East Village, Chelsea, and Murray Hill. Lesbian bars are mostly in Greenwich Village and the East Village. For current listings, check the *Native* newspaper and the *Village Voice* or call the Gay and Lesbian Switchboard (see p343).

HOTEL BARS

CENTRALLY LOCATED in midtown, the Algonquin Hotel (see p143) was a famous literary haunt in the 1920s and early 1930s. Its Lobby

Bar and Blue Bar are both good places for a quiet pre-dinner or pretheater drink.

The round bar in the handsome lobby lounge of the trendy **Royalton Hotel** is a perfect spot for a drink while watching the theatrical crowds drifting in and out. This is a favorite meeting place for Conde-Nast staffers. Also in the Theater District, the **Whiskey Bar** in the Paramount Hotel has floor-to-ceiling windows and is usually frequented by fashion and theater types.

In Lower Midtown is the **Sun Garden**, a glassed-in, tiered space, particularly pleasant on bright afternoons when the sun streams through the glass.

The **Bull and Bear** in the Waldorf–Astoria, dating back to the Prohibition era, exudes comfort and a sense of history. There are many exotic drinks and Bull and Bear ale on tap.

Uptown, the **Oak Room** at the Plaza Hotel is a posh place to impress people, drink, and converse in earnest tones – but at a high price. The **King**

Cole Room at the St. Regis Hotel is named after the mural behind the bar, by Maxfield Parrish, which adds color to a stylish room.

For nostalgic British visitors and anglophile New Yorkers, **Journeys** in the Essex House Hotel has an English club ambience, with hunting prints and mahogany paneling.

Drinks are a bargain at **Randolf's** in the Warwick Hotel, especially during happy hour, when free, delicious snacks are served.

DIRECTORY

LOWER MANHATTAN

BB's
40 E 4th St. **Map** 4 F2.

Edward Moran Bar and Grill
World Financial Center. 250 Vesey St. **Map** 1 B2.

Fraunces Tavern
54 Pearl St. **Map** 1 C4.

The Greatest Bar on Earth
1 World Trade Center, Church St. **Map** 1 B2.

North Star Pub
93 South St, South St Seaport. **Map** 2 D3.

SOHO AND TRIBECA

The Ear Inn
326 Spring St. **Map** 3 C4.

Odeon
145 W Broadway. **Map** 4 E4.

SoHo Kitchen and Bar
103 Greene St. **Map** 4 E3.

GREENWICH VILLAGE

Bar Six
502 6th Ave. **Map** 4 D1.

Chumley's
86 Bedford St. **Map** 3 C2.

Peculier Pub
145 Bleecker St. **Map** 4 D3.

White Horse Tavern
567 Hudson St. **Map** 3 C1.

EAST VILLAGE

d.b.a.
41 1st Ave. **Map** 5 A1.

McSorley's Old Alehouse
15 E 7th St. **Map** 4 F2.

GRAMERCY

Heartland Brewery
35 Union Square W. **Map** 9 A5.

Live Bait
14 E 23rd St. **Map** 8 F4.

Old Town Bar
45 E 18th St. **Map** 8 F5.

Pete's Tavern
129 E 18th St. **Map** 9 A5.

CHELSEA AND THE GARMENT DISTRICT

Brews
156 E 34th St. **Map** 9 A2.

Chelsea Brewing Company
Pier 59 11th Ave. **Map** 7 B5.

THEATER DISTRICT

P. J. Carney's
906 7th Ave. **Map** 12 E3.

Randolf's
Warwick Hotel, 65 W 54th St. **Map** 12 F4.

Royalton Hotel
44 W 44th St. Fifth Ave. **Map** 12 F5

Sardi's
234 W 44th St. **Map** 12 F5.

Whiskey Bar
Paramount Hotel, 235 W 46th St. **Map** 12 E5.

LOWER MIDTOWN

Beer Bar
Metlife Bldg, 200 Park Ave. **Map** 9 A2.

BP Café
Bryant Park, 25 W 40th St. **Map** 7 B1.
Open summertime only.

The Cigar Room at Trumpets
Grand Hyatt Hotel, Grand Central Station, E 42nd St. **Map** 13 A5.

Sun Garden
Grand Hyatt Hotel, Grand Central, 42nd St. **Map** 9 A1.

UPPER MIDTOWN

Bar and Books
889 1st Ave. **Map** 13 C2.

Bull and Bear
Ground fl, Waldorf–Astoria Hotel, Lexington Ave at E 49th St. **Map** 13 A5.

King Cole Room
St Regis Hotel, 2 E 55th St. **Map** 12 F5.

Manchester
920 2nd Ave. **Map** 13 B5.

Oak Room
Plaza Hotel, 768 5th Ave. **Map** 12 F3.

P. J. Clarke's
915 3rd Ave. **Map** 13 B4.

UPPER EAST SIDE

Brother Jimmy's BBQ
1461 1st Ave. **Map** 17 C3.

Elaine's
1703 2nd Ave. **Map** 17 B4.

Mortimer's
1057 Lexington Ave. **Map** 17 A5.

Yorkville Brewery and Tavern
1359 1st Ave. **Map** 13 C1.

UPPER WEST SIDE

Journeys
Essex House Hotel, 160 Central Park S. **Map** 12 E3.

Tavern on the Green
Central Park, W 67th St. **Map** 12 D2.

Westside Brewing Company
340 Amsterdam Ave. **Map** 15 C2.

BROOKLYN

Park Slope Brewing Company
356 6th Ave. **Map** 4 D1.
One of several branches.

SHOPPING

A VISITOR to New York will inevitably include shopping in his or her action plan. The city is the consumer capital of the world: a shopper's paradise that is a constant source of entertainment, with dazzling window displays and a staggering variety of goods for sale. Everything is available here, from high fashion to rare children's books, state-of-the-art electronics and a mouthwatering array of exotic food. Whether you are looking for a personal Hovercraft, read-in-the-dark eyeglass attachments, a designer bed for your pet gerbil or a Wurlitzer jukebox, this is the city of your dreams. Whether you have $50,000 or $5, New York is the place to spend it.

Tiffany's clock

BEST BUYS

N EW YORK is a bargain hunter's dream, with huge discounts on anything from household goods to designer clothes. Some of the best shops are on Orchard Street and Grand Street on the Lower East Side, where designer goods are sold at

The 1920s-style Henri Bendel store (see p311)

20–50% below the retail price. You can find just about every imaginable item of clothing here, in addition to tableware, shoes, home furnishings and electronics. Shops in this area are closed on Saturday – the Jewish Sabbath – but are usually open all day Sunday.

Another great area for fashion bargain hunters is the trendy Garment District, roughly between Sixth and Eighth avenues from 30th to 40th Street. The hub of it – Seventh Avenue – was renamed as Fashion Avenue in the early 1970s. Here, many different designers and manufacturers have showrooms, some of which are open to the public. They also have sales of many of their samples, announced on notices posted around the

area. Often the best time to go and visit these stores is just before one of the major gift-giving holidays.

SALES

O NE WORD you are likely to see all over the city, no matter what time of year you visit, is "Sale." So before you pay full price for anything, check the sale goods first. The best sales are during New York's sale seasons, which run from mid-June until the end of July and from December 26 until February. For information, look for ads in the local papers. A word of warning: along midtown Fifth Avenue there are signs announcing "Lost Our Lease" sales. But many of the shops have had these signs up for years and are best avoided.

HOW TO PAY

M OST SHOPS accept major credit cards, although there will often be a minimum purchase price. If you want to use your traveler's checks, identification is needed. Personal checks drawn in another currency will be refused. Some stores only take cash, especially during sales.

The Bulgari entrance at Hotel Pierre (see p282)

OPENING HOURS

M OST SHOPS in New York are normally open from 10am to 6pm, Monday to Saturday. Many department stores, though, are open all day Sunday and until 9pm at least two nights a week. The best time to avoid crowds is weekday mornings. The most crowded times are lunch hours (noon to 2:30pm), Saturday mornings, sales and holidays.

TAXES

T HE NEW YORK city sales tax, 8.25%, is added to the price when you pay. But you may still be asked to pay duty on goods at customs if you exceed the allowance. However, if the goods are sent direct, you won't have to pay sales tax.

Designer dress at a New York sale

SHOPPING TOURS

IF YOU CAN'T face the thought of braving the stores by yourself, why not go on one of the many shopping tours available in New York? Apart from visiting the main department stores, options include a visit to private designer showrooms, auction houses and fashion shows. Some operators will customize tours to suit your requirements.

Convention Tours Unlimited
(545-1160.

Doorway to Design
(221-1111.

Guide Service of New York
(408-3332.

The Intrepid New Yorker
(534-5071.

Window displays at Bloomingdale's (see p179)

DEPARTMENT STORES

MOST OF New York's large department stores are in midtown Manhattan. Be sure to allow plenty of time to explore the ones you are interested in, because all these stores tend to be enormous, with an amazing range of goods. If at all possible, avoid going at weekends and around vacation times – the crowds can be overwhelming. Prices are often high, but you can get bargains during sales.

Stores such as Saks Fifth Avenue, Bloomingdale's and Macy's provide a diverse and extraordinary range of shopping services, including doing the shopping for you. But then you would miss out on what may be the shopping experience of a lifetime.

Barney's New York is a favorite among young professional New Yorkers. It specializes in excellent, but expensive, designer clothes. A branch for men only is located in the glittering World Financial Center.

Bergdorf Goodman is luxurious, very elegant and understated. It carries high-quality contemporary fashions at high prices, specializing in European designers. The men's store is right across the street.

Almost every visitor to New York includes **Bloomingdale's** (see p179) on their sightseeing list. Bloomingdale's is the Hollywood film star of the department stores, with many eye-catching displays and seductive goods. Its ambience is that of a luxurious wonderland, filled with young and old New Yorkers seeking out the newest in fashion. The linen and fine china departments have an undisputed reputation for quality. Check out the gourmet food section– it has a shop devoted entirely to caviar. Extensive shopping services and amenities include a noted restaurant, Le Train Bleu, with its view of the Queensboro Bridge

Everything found in **Henri Bendel's**, from the Art Deco jewels to beautiful handmade shoes, is displayed as though each were a priceless work of art. The store, which is laid out in a series of 1920s-style boutiques, is exclusive and sophisticated, and has a good selection of creative and innovative women's fashions.

Lord & Taylor is renowned for its classic and much more conservative fashions for men and women. The store places an emphasis on US designers.

A magnificent display offering household goods

You need comfy shoes and lots of spare time to wander.

Macy's, the self-proclaimed largest store in the world (see p132–3), sprawls over an entire city block. It has ten floors and sells everything imaginable from can openers to massive antiques.

Saks Fifth Avenue is synonymous with style and elegance. It has long been considered one of the city's high-quality department stores, with service to match. It sells stunning designer clothes for men, women and children.

ADDRESSES

Barney's New York
660 Madison Ave.
Map 13 A3.
(826-8900.
Upper Level, 2 World Financial Center.
Map 1 A2.
(945-1600.

Bergdorf Goodman
754 5th Ave. **Map** 12 F3.
(753-7300.

Bloomingdale's
1000 3rd Ave. **Map** 13 B3.
(705-2000.

Henri Bendel
712 5th Ave. **Map** 12 F4.
(247-1100.

Lord & Taylor
424 5th Ave. **Map** 8 F1.
(391-3344.

Macy's
151 W 34th St. **Map** 8 E2.
(695-4400.

Saks Fifth Avenue
611 5th Ave. **Map** 12 F4.
(753-4000.

New York's Best: Shopping

Designer shoes from Madison Avenue

I N A CITY where you can literally shop 24 hours a day, the best plan is to shop the way New Yorkers do, by neighborhood. Each has its own character and specialties. Here are highlights of the best shopping districts – where they are and what you will find in each. If time is very tight, head for one of the huge department stores *(see p311),* or if window shopping is your preference, stroll along Fifth Avenue, home to Manhattan's most glittering stores *(see opposite).* For great bargains in a truly ethnic area, try the Lower East Side.

Greenwich and East Villages
Explore around Eighth Street and St. Mark's Place for shoes and avant-garde fashions, books, ethnic goods and flea markets. Move to lower Broadway for antiques (often "retro" 20th century). (See pp108–9 and pp116–17.)

SoHo
The area bordered by Sixth Avenue, Lafayette, Houston and Canal streets is bustling with contemporary art galleries, antiques, crafts, exclusive or unusual gifts and fashions. Weekend brunchtime gallery-hopping is very popular. (See pp102–3.)

Lower East Side
Sunday is the day when New Yorkers and visitors flock to Canal, Delancey, Orchard and Essex streets for great bargains in fashions, shoes, jewelry, electronics and household goods. (See pp94–95.)

South Street Seaport
This is a browser's paradise of crafts, gifts, toys, souvenirs, antiquarian and new books, and antiques with a seafaring connection. (See pp82–83.)

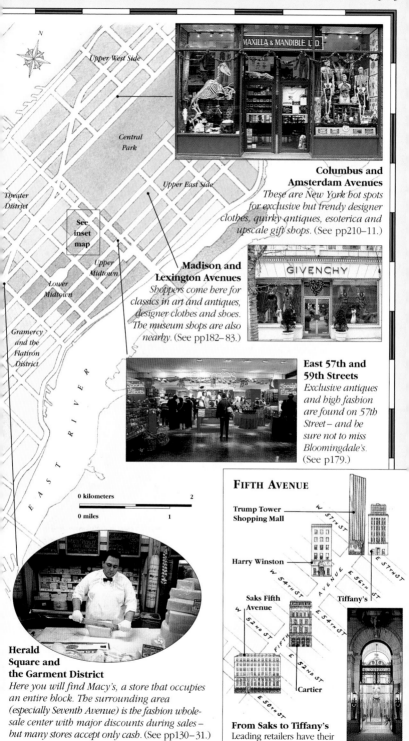

Columbus and Amsterdam Avenues
These are New York hot spots for exclusive but trendy designer clothes, quirky antiques, esoterica and upscale gift shops. (See pp210–11.)

Madison and Lexington Avenues
Shoppers come here for classics in art and antiques, designer clothes and shoes. The museum shops are also nearby. (See pp182–83.)

East 57th and 59th Streets
Exclusive antiques and high fashion are found on 57th Street – and be sure not to miss Bloomingdale's. (See p179.)

Herald Square and the Garment District
Here you will find Macy's, a store that occupies an entire block. The surrounding area (especially Seventh Avenue) is the fashion wholesale center with major discounts during sales – but many stores accept only cash. (See pp130–31.)

FIFTH AVENUE

Trump Tower Shopping Mall

Harry Winston

Saks Fifth Avenue

Tiffany's

Cartier

From Saks to Tiffany's
Leading retailers have their flagship store on world-famous Fifth Avenue.

Harry Winston
(see p320)

0 kilometers 2
0 miles 1

New York Originals

NEW YORK IS A CITY where just about any kind of shop, no matter how esoteric, will always attract customers. Dozens of tiny shops scattered around the city specialize in unusual merchandise, from butterflies and bones to traditional Tibetan treasures and Shamrock sprigs from Ireland. Coming across these in some tucked-away corner is what makes shopping in New York such an entertaining experience.

SPECIALTY SHOPS

FOR BEAUTIFUL BRASS, onyx and pewter chess sets, and the opportunity to play a decent game, make a move to the **Chess Shop**. For every type of pen **Arthur Brown & Bros.** stocks an enormous range, including such names as Mont Blanc and Schaeffer. **Big City Kites and Darts** has kites in different kinds of weird and wonderful shapes from fiery dragons to cuddly teddy bears, plus enough accessories to satisfy even the most dedicated kite flyer. For those with a bit more energy, **Blades** sells and rents out skates and also the trendiest skateboards plus all the safety equipment to go with them.

If you're looking for different or unusual buttons, a visit to **Tender Buttons**, which stocks millions, is a must. Whether you want enamel, wood or Navajo silver buttons – or perhaps want your own buttons made into cuff links or earrings – here you'll find just what you want – and more.

Leo Kaplan Ltd. is the place to go if you are a keen collector of paperweights and **Rita Ford's Music Boxes**, a 19th-century style shop, stocks a tuneful and extensive range of music boxes.

The **New York Firefighter's Friend** sells an intriguing range of items related purely to fire-fighting, including toy fire engines, firemen's jackets, badges, scaled-down uniforms for children, stuffed toy dalmatians and a wide selection of T-shirts including a popular one with NYFD (New York Fire Department) on one side and "Keep back 200 feet" on the other.

For the true romantic who wants to impress, everything sold by **Only Hearts** is heart-shaped, including pillows, soap and jewelry. If you are artistic, or if you wish to buy a present for someone who is, visit the **Pearl Paint Co.**, which stocks everything you could need. The **Magickal Childe** is an occult emporium full of potions, tarot cards and fragrant incense (note: there's no phone here and hours are erratic). Step straight into the space age at **Star Magic** to buy celestial maps, holograms, prisms and scientific toys.

Cologne made especially for George Washington and the official soap of the White House during the Eisenhower era are just some of the many fascinating items for sale at **Caswell-Massey Ltd.**, the oldest pharmacy in the city.

Guitar gurus will want to visit **Rudy's**, Manny's or Sam Ash's guitar shop. Not only is there a chance you'll bump into Eric Clapton or Lou Reed – both have their guitars made in this area – but you'll find the widest and best choice of instruments in the city.

Bibliophiles will find a range of gifts in both the **New York Public Library Shop** (see p144) (such as bookends of the lions guarding the main entrance) and the **Pierpont Morgan Library shop** (see pp162–3), including book-marks and writing paper.

University logos and college colors dominate the many knickknacks and accessories are at **The Yale Club** gift shop and **The Princeton Club**. **Hebrew Religious Articles** carries one of the largest selections of Jewish religious items in the city.

The Cathedral Shop at the Cathedral of St. John the Divine is a large store selling books, artworks, herbs, jewelry and religious items made locally.

MEMORABILIA

AT LINCOLN CENTER, the **Metropolitan Opera Shop** has records, cards, librettos, small binoculars and many other opera-related items. The **Performing Arts Shop** downstairs is a real treasure trove of theater, opera, ballet and music memorabilia. For ballet fans, everything from Nureyev T-shirts to dance records can be found at the **Ballet Shop**. For thousands of rare and classic film stills and posters visit **Jerry Ohlinger's Movie Material Store**.

If you're looking for an old Wurlitzer jukebox or a Coke machine, go to **Back Pages Antiques**. The **Carnegie Hall Shop** carries musically themed cards, T-shirts, games, posters, tote bags and much more. For something truly original and very American, be sure to visit **Lost City Arts** and **Urban Archaeology** in SoHo. Between these two shops, you'll unearth all sorts of relics from America's past, from Barbie Doll lunch boxes to furniture from traditional ice-cream parlors.

TOYS, GAMES AND GADGETS

FOR CHILDREN'S GIFTS, don't miss the legendary **F.A.O. Schwarz**. This is a massive store crammed from floor to ceiling with luxury toy cars, enormous stuffed animals and every kind of electronic toy imaginable. There are shoulder-to-shoulder crowds at Christmas, when you might have to line up to get in.

The **Children's General Store** is one of the city's newest – and cleverest – children's toy stores.

The **Enchanted Forest** (see p102) is a magical experience for children. Its handmade toys are artfully displayed among the trees of the delightful interior, built by a theatrical set designer.

Penny Whistle Toys sells a huge selection of quality toys, games and all kinds of different dolls.

For games for both children and adults, the **Game Show** has puzzles and games galore, from real classics like Monopoly to the latest yuppie favorite. **Red Caboose** is for fans of model railways. **Toys 'R' Us** doesn't have Schwarz's style but it does stock over a million toys for all ages at reasonable prices.

If you're looking for a more bizarre, unusual kind of present, then go to **Little Rickie** on First Avenue. You will find a large collection of weird and wonderful toys and trinkets from all over the world, to amaze and amuse people of all ages.

MUSEUM SHOPS

SOME OF NEW YORK'S best souvenirs can be found in the city's many museum shops. In addition to the usual range of books, posters and cards, there are reproductions of the exhibits on display, including jewelry and sculpture. The **American Craft Museum** (see p169) has an excellent selection of American crafts as well as original works for sale. In addition to realistic model dinosaurs, rubber animals, minerals, and rocks,

the **American Museum of Natural History** (see pp214–15) has a variety of recycled products and earth-awareness gifts, which include posters, bags and T-shirts with environmental messages, and a large selection Native American handicrafts. There is also a kids' shop with reasonably priced items such as shell sets, magnets and toys.

The **Asia Society Book-store and Gift Shop** (see p185) has a striking selection of Oriental prints, posters, art books, toys and jewelry. Items related to interior design are offered at the **Cooper-Hewitt** (see p184). One of New York's largest collections of Jewish ceremonial objects, including menorahs and Kiddush cups, books and jewelry, is found in the small shop at the **Jewish Museum** (see p184).

For reproduction prints of famous paintings, and other exquisite gifts a visit to the **Metropolitan Museum of Art** (see pp188–95) gift shop is a must. There is also an enormous book department The traditional **Museum of American Folk Art** (see p213) prides itself on its

American country crafts, including wooden toys, quilts and weathervanes, which are mostly original. Works by craftspeople who currently have pieces on display in the museum are also sold.

The **Museum of the City of New York** (see p197), specializes in pictures of old New York. The **Museum of Modern Art/MOMA Design Store** (see pp170–73) has a highly praised selection of innovative home furnishings, toys and kitchenware inspired by international designers such as Frank Lloyd Wright and Le Corbusier.

For a selection of nautical items, including charts, maps, model ships and scrimshaw, go to the **South Street Seaport Museum Shops** (see pp82–85). The **Whitney Museum's Store Next Door** (see pp198–9) stocks only American-made items, including jewelry, wooden toys and books and posters complementing current exhibitions. The **Museum of Jewish Heritage** (see p77) has an interesting gift shop with an unusual array of gifts, souvenirs and educational material about Jewish life. Open to ticketed visitors only.

THE BEST OF THE IMPORTS

NEW YORK is a massive melting pot of different nationalities, cultures and ethnic groups, all of which have made their mark on New York's diverse culture in one way or another. Many ethnic shops specialize in food or goods of a particular group. Some of the most interesting and unusual shops include **Alaska on Madison**, which has a huge collection of Eskimo art, and the **Chinese Porcelain Company,** for exquisite Chinese decorative arts and furniture. **Back From Guatemala** has jewelry and decorative arts from Central and South America, and **Himalayan Crafts and Tours** stocks everything

from paintings to Tibetan rugs. A wonderful collection of emerald green goods and items with a Celtic theme can be found in **Shamrock Imports**, which also sells hand-knitted Irish sweaters. **Things Japanese** has beautifully made crafts and unusual books. **Surma** is a Ukrainian general store that sells hand painted eggs and linens. **Common Ground** sells Native American baskets, weavings and jewelry, and **Tibet West** sells textiles and colorful jewelry.

ADDRESSES

Alaska on Madison
937 Madison Ave. **Map** 17 A1.
(879-1782.

Back From Guatemala
306 E 6th St. **Map** 5 A2.
(260-7010.

Chinese Porcelain Company
475 Park Ave. **Map** 13 A3.
(838-7744.

Common Ground
19 Greenwich Ave. **Map** 1 B1.
(989-4178.

Himalayan Crafts and Tours
2007 Broadway. **Map** 11 C1.
(787-8500.

Shamrock Imports
Manhattan Mall, 901 Sixth Ave.
Map 8 E1.
(564-7474.

Surma
11 E 7th St. **Map** 4 F2.
(477-0729.

Things Japanese
127 E 60th St.
Map 13 A3.
(371-4661.

Tibet West
19 Christopher St. **Map** 3 C2.
(255-3416.

DIRECTORY

SPECIALTY SHOPS

Arthur Brown & Bros.
2 W 46th St.
Map 12 F5.
C 575-5555.

Big City Kites and Darts
1210 Lexington Ave.
Map 17 A4.
C 472-2623.

Blades
120 W 72nd St.
Map 11 C1.
C 787-3911.
One of several branches.

Caswell-Massey Ltd.
518 Lexington Ave.
Map 13 A5.
C 755-2254.

The Cathedral Shop
Cathedral of St. John the Divine, 1047 Amsterdam Ave. **Map** 20 E4.
C 222-7200.

Hebrew Religious Articles
45 Essex St.
Map 5 B4.
C 674-1770.

Leo Kaplan Ltd.
967 Madison Ave.
Map 17 A5.
C 249-6766.

Magickal Childe
35 W 19th St.
Map 8 F5.

New York Firefighter's Friend
263 Lafayette St.
Map 4 F3.
C 226-3142.

New York Public Library Shop
5th Ave at 42nd St.
Map 8 F1.
C 930-0678.

Only Hearts
386 Columbus Ave.
Map 15 D5.
C 724-5608.

Pearl Paint Co
308 Canal St.
Map 4 E5
C 431-7932

Pierpont Morgan Library Shop
Madison Ave at 36th St.
Map 9 A2.
C 685-0610.

The Princeton Club
15 W 43rd St. **Map** 8 F1.
C 596-1200.

Rita Ford's Music Boxes
19 E 65th St. **Map** 12 F2.
C 535-6717.

Rudy's
169 W 48th St. **Map** 12 E5.
C 391-1699.

Star Magic
745 Broadway. **Map** 4 E2.
C 228-7770.

Tender Buttons
143 E 62nd St.
Map 13 A2.
C 758-7004.

The Chess Shop
230 Thompson St.
Map 4 D3.
C 475-9580.

The Yale Club
50 Vanderbilt Ave.
Map 13 A5.
C 661-2070.

MEMORABILIA

Back Pages Antiques
125 Greene St.
Map 4 E4.
C 460-5998.

Ballet Company
1887 Broadway.
Map 12 D2.
C 246-6893.

The Carnegie Hall Shop
881 7th Ave.
Map 12 E3.
C 903-9610.

Jerry Ohlinger's Movie Material Store
242 W 14th St.
Map 3 C1.
C 989-0869.

Lost City Arts
275 Lafayette St.
Map 4 F3.
C 941-8025.

Metropolitan Opera Shop
Metropolitan Opera House, Lincoln Center, 136 W 65th St.
Map 11 C2.
C 580-4090.

Performing Arts Shop
Metropolitan Opera House, Lincoln Center, 136 W 65th St.
Map 11 C2.
C 580-4356.

Urban Archaeology
285 Lafayette St.
Map 4 F3.
C 431-6969.

TOYS, GAMES AND GADGETS

The Children's General Store
2473 Broadway.
Map 15 C4.
C 580-2723.

The Enchanted Forest
85 Mercer St.
Map 4 E4.
C 925-6677.

F.A.O. Schwarz
767 5th Ave.
Map 12 F3.
C 644-9400.

Game Show
474 6th Ave.
Map 12 E5.
C 633-6328.

Little Rickie
49½ 1st Ave.
Map 5 A2.
C 505-6467.

Penny Whistle Toys
448 Columbus Ave.
Map 16 D4.
C 873-9090.
One of several branches.

Red Caboose
23 W 45th St.
Map 12 F5.
C 575-0155.

Toys 'R' Us
Herald Center, 1293 Broadway.
Map 8 E2.
C 594-8697.

MUSEUM SHOPS

American Craft Museum
40 W 53rd St. **Map** 12 F4.
C 956-6047.

American Museum of Natural History
W 79th St at Central Park West. **Map** 16 D5.
C 769-5150.

Asia Society Bookstore and Gift Shop
725 Park Ave. **Map** 13 A1.
C 288-6400.

Cooper-Hewitt
2 E 91st St. **Map** 16 F2.
C 860-6878.

Jewish Museum
1109 5th Ave. **Map** 16 F2.
C 423-3200.

Metropolitan Museum of Art
5th Ave at 82nd St.
Map 16 F4.
C 535-7710.

Museum of American Folk Art
2 Lincoln Sq. **Map** 12 D2.
C 496-2966.

Museum of the City of New York
5th Ave at 103rd St.
Map 21 C5.
C 534-1672.

Museum of Jewish Heritage
18 First Place, Battery Park City.
Map 1 B4.
C 968-1800.

Museum of Modern Art/MOMA Design Store
44 W 53rd St.
Map 12 F4.
C 767-1050.

South St. Seaport Museum Shops
207 Front St. **Map** 2 D2.
C 748-8600.

The Whitney Museum's Store Next Door
943 Madison Ave.
Map 13 A1.
C 606-0200.

Fashion

WHETHER YOU'RE LOOKING for a secondhand pair of 501s or the kind of ballgown Ivana Trump would be proud to wear, you're sure to find it in New York. The city is the fashion capital of America and an important center of clothing manufacture and design. New York's clothing stores, like its restaurants, reflect the city's dramatically different styles and cultures. To save time it's probably best to visit one area at a time and wander from store to store. Alternatively, visit one of the major department stores for an excellent selection of fashion for everyone.

AMERICAN DESIGNERS

MANY AMERICAN designers sell their creations in boutiques within the large department stores, or have exclusive shops of their own. One of the most famous is Geoffrey Beene, known for sophisticated looks that are casual and comfortable.

Bill Blass is the king of American fashion whose clothes feature loads of different colors, wild patterns, innovative shapes and a lot of wit. Liz Claiborne's designs are always elegantly simple, casual and reasonably priced, including everything you could possibly need from tennis whites to casual professional wear for women.

The late Perry Ellis's style lives on with clothes designed by Marc Jacobs, known for his sportswear. James Galanos is an exclusive designer for the rich and famous, making one-of-a-kind *couture* clothes, and Betsey Johnson is popular with women able to wear figure-hugging fashions in fabulous fabrics.

In recent years, Donna Karan has become a name that appears everywhere. Her simple, stylish and great-looking designs work for everything from work-out clothes to black tie wear. Calvin Klein now has his name on place settings and sunglasses in addition to underwear, jeans and a whole range of clothes. He is renowned for comfortable, sensuous and well-fitting – as well as very hip – looks. Ralph Lauren is well known for his aristocratic and expensive clothes, a "look" favored by the exclusive and posh Ivy League, horsey set. For those with a taste for more experimental designs, Joan Vass specializes in moderately priced but exciting, colorful and innovative knitwear.

DISCOUNT DESIGNER CLOTHES

IF YOU'RE on the lookout for discount designer clothes, **Designer Resale**, **Encore** and **Michael's** sell a wide range. Oscar de la Renta, Ungaro and Armani are just some of the leading labels available. Clothes are either new or worn but near-perfect.

MEN'S CLOTHES

IN THE CENTER of midtown, you'll find two of the city's most highly regarded menswear stores: **Brooks Brothers** and **Paul Stuart**. Brooks Brothers is something of a New York institution, famous for its traditional, conservative clothing such as smart button-down shirts and Chinos. There's an ultra-conservative woman's line too. Paul Stuart prides itself on its very British look and offers a stylish array of superbly tailored fashions.

Go to the high-quality department store **Bergdorf Goodman Men** to find beautifully made Turnbull & Asser shirts and marvelous suits by Gianfranco Ferré or Hugo Boss.

Barney's New York has one of the most comprehensive men's departments in America, with a truly massive range of clothes and accessories. A smaller Barney's, at the World Financial Center, specializes in even smarter business clothes and suits for professionals. The **Polo/Ralph Lauren** department store is packed from floor to ceiling with the so-called king of American Sportswear's simple and timeless fashions as well as his many stylish accessories.

Matsuda sells very expensive, avant-garde Japanese chic for men and women. **Bijan Designer for Men** is so exclusive that clothes can be seen only by appointment.

The Custom Shop Shirtmakers specializes in custom-made suits and shirts in beautiful materials. Go to **Burberry Limited** if you are looking for classic British trenchcoats.

J. Press sells classic, conservative yet elegant clothes. Uptown designer menswear boutiques include the renowned **Beau Brummel** with a selection of very stylish European clothes and for superb designer bargains, check out **Moe Ginsburg** for one of New York's largest selections of men's Italian clothing. Women, be advised: many of these men's stores also carry striking women's fashions.

CHILDREN'S CLOTHES

IN ADDITION to an excellent selection within the large department stores, there are several shops around the city that sell children's clothing exclusively. A good example is **Bonpoint**, which has a world of French-style charm.

Gapkids and BabyGap shops, often in the **Gap** shops, have comfortable, long-lasting cotton overalls, sweat pants, denim jackets, sweatshirts and leggings. The wonderfully named **Peanut Butter & Jane** sells trendy but particularly comfortable togs. **Space Kiddets** has everything from bibs and booties to cowboy and cowgirl clothes.

WOMEN'S CLOTHES

WOMEN'S FASHION is subject to design trends, and New York stores keep pace with them all. Most of the city's most fashionable shops are found in the midtown area around Madison and Fifth avenues. These include some of the major department stores (*see p311*), which stock a range of American designers, including Donna Karan, Ralph Lauren and Bill Blass.

Leading international names such as **Chanel**, **Fendi**, and **Valentino** also have shops here, as does one of the outstanding American designers, **Geoffrey Beene**. There is also a handful of popular ready-to-wear stores, including **Ann Taylor**, which is much favored by young, busy professionals looking for stylish, comfortable clothing.

Right at the heart of this area stands the pink-marbled Trump Tower, which houses a selection of exclusive shops.

Madison Avenue is packed with designers for the smart set, who have everything you could ever need, including **Givenchy** who sells show-stopping formal gowns at phenomenal prices, Valentino who has classic Italian clothes and **Emanuel Ungaro** who is relatively unintimidating and has something to suit most tastes and physiques from beautifully tailored jackets to more matronly full-figured and boldly patterned print dresses. **Missoni** is famous for richly textured sweaters in sumptuous wools and colorful patterns. **Yves St Laurent Rive Gauche** has evening gowns, one-of-a-kind jackets, silks and extravagant blouses and beautifully cut pants suits.

Sophisticated Italian looks are also available from Italian style kings **Giorgio Armani** and **Gianni Versace**. **Romeo Gigli's** Milanese clothing is so exclusive that his shop has no name on the door. **Gucci**, one of the oldest Italian shops in America, is only for the wealthy and status-conscious.

The Upper West Side has many shops competing for attention with contemporary fashions, including **Betsey Johnson's** shop, with her whimsical, relatively inexpensive designs. **Calvin Klein** now has a store on the East Side, specializing in ultra-hip, casual fashions. **French Connection** is known for its affordable separates, both casual and for the office. **Variazioni** is *the* place to get a little black dress.

The villages – the East Village in particular – are the best places to go for second-hand clothing and 1950s rock 'n' roll gear, with ever-changing interesting shops run by new and young designers and art school graduates. For a range of affordable, well-cut clothes from classic to casual, try **APC**.

Cheap Jack's carries a huge selection of second-hand Levi's as well as hundreds of denim and leather jackets. **Dorothy's Closet** has classic dresses from the 1920s to the 1960s. **Big Drop** has a great selection of perfectly fitting little black dresses.

Screaming Mimi's is where you could unearth that pair of velvet bell-bottoms or go-go boots you've always dreamed of having. A more main-stream shop is **The Gap**, a chain store selling lots of moderately-priced, casual and comfortable clothes for men, women and children.

Recently SoHo has come to rival Madison Avenue for designer boutiques specializing in expensive but interesting clothes – the fashions here are far more avant-garde. You'll find **Yohji Yamamoto**, among other exclusive stores. **Comme des Garçons** sells minimalist Japanese chic.

More accessible is one of SoHo's most famous stores, the **Canal Jean Co.**, which has all the latest SoHo looks at affordable prices.

What Comes Around Goes Around is the place to go for vintage jeans. Go to **Wearable Energy** for wall-to-wall spandex.

SIZE CHART

For Australian sizes follow the British and American conversions.

Children's clothing

American	2-3	4-5	6-6x	7-8	10	12	14	16 (size)
British	2-3	4-5	6-7	8-9	10-11	12	14	14+ (years)
Continental	2-3	4-5	6-7	8-9	10-11	12	14	14+ (years)

Children's shoes

American	$7\frac{1}{2}$	$8\frac{1}{2}$	$9\frac{1}{2}$	$10\frac{1}{2}$	$11\frac{1}{2}$	$12\frac{1}{2}$	$13\frac{1}{2}$	$1\frac{1}{2}$	$2\frac{1}{2}$
British	7	8	9	10	11	12	13	1	2
Continental	24	$25\frac{1}{2}$	27	28	29	30	32	33	34

Women's dresses, coats and skirts

American	4	6	8	10	12	14	16	18
British	6	8	10	12	14	16	18	20
Continental	38	40	42	44	46	48	50	52

Women's blouses and sweaters

American	6	8	10	12	14	16	18
British	30	32	34	36	38	40	42
Continental	40	42	44	46	48	50	52

Women's shoes

American	5	6	7	8	9	10	11
British	3	4	5	6	7	8	9
Continental	36	37	38	39	40	41	44

Men's suits

American	34	36	38	40	42	44	46	48
British	34	36	38	40	42	44	46	48
Continental	44	46	48	50	52	54	56	58

Men's shirts

American	14	15	$15\frac{1}{2}$	16	$16\frac{1}{2}$	17	$17\frac{1}{2}$	18
British	14	15	$15\frac{1}{2}$	16	$16\frac{1}{2}$	17	$17\frac{1}{2}$	18
Continental	36	38	39	41	42	43	44	45

Men's shoes

American	7	$7\frac{1}{2}$	8	$8\frac{1}{2}$	$9\frac{1}{2}$	$10\frac{1}{2}$	11	$11\frac{1}{2}$
British	6	7	$7\frac{1}{2}$	8	9	10	11	12
Continental	39	40	41	42	43	44	45	46

DIRECTORY

DISCOUNT DESIGNER CLOTHES

Designer Resale
324 E 81st St.
Map 17 B4.
(734-3639.

Encore
1132 Madison Ave.
Map 17 A4.
(879-2850.

Michael's
1041 Madison Ave.
Map 17 A5.
(737-7273.

MEN'S CLOTHES

Barney's New York
660 Madison Ave.
Map 13 A3.
(593-7800.

Beau Brummel
421 West Broadway.
Map 4 E3.
(219-2666.
One of several branches.

Bergdorf Goodman Men
754 5th Ave.
Map 12 F3.
(753-7300.

Bijan Designer for Men
699 5th Ave.
Map 12 F4.
(758-7500.

Brooks Brothers
346 Madison Ave.
Map 9 A1.
(682-8800.

Burberry Limited
9 E 57th St.
Map 12 F3.
(371-5010.

The Custom Shop Shirtmakers
618 5th Ave. **Map** 12 F4.
(245-2499.
One of several branches.

J. Press
7 E 44th St. **Map** 12 F5.
(687-7642.

Matsuda
156 5th Ave.
Map 8 F4.
(645-5151.

Moe Ginsburg
162 5th Ave.
Map 8 F4.
(242-3482.

Paul Stuart
Madison Ave at 45th St.
Map 13 A5.
(682-0320.

Polo/Ralph Lauren
Madison Ave at 72nd St.
Map 13 A1.
(606-2100.

CHILDREN'S CLOTHES

Bonpoint
1269 Madison Ave.
Map 17 A3.
(722-7720.

Gapkids
60 W 34th St. **Map** 8 F2.
(643-8995.
One of several branches.

Peanut Butter & Jane
617 Hudson St.
Map 3 B1.
(620-7952.

Space Kiddets
46 E 21st St. **Map** 8 F4.
(420-9878.

WOMEN'S CLOTHES

Ann Taylor
645 Madison Ave.
Map 13 A3.
(832-2010.
One of several branches.

APC
131 Mercer St.
Map 4 E3.
(966-9685.

Betsey Johnson
248 Columbus Ave.
Map 16 D4.
(362-3364.
One of several branches.

Big Drop
174 Spring St.
Map 3 C4.
(966-4299.

Calvin Klein
654 Madison Ave.
Map 13 A3.
(292-9000.

Canal Jean Co
504 Broadway.
Map 4 E4.
(226-0737.

Chanel
15 E 57th St.
Map 12 F3.
(355-5050.

Cheap Jack's
841 Broadway.
Map 4 E1.
(777-9564.

Comme des Garçons
116 Wooster Street.
Map 4 E3.
(219-0660.

Dorothy's Closet
335 Bleecker St.
Map 3 C2.
(206-6414.

Emanuel Ungaro
792 Madison Ave.
Map 13 A2.
(249-4090.

Fendi
720 5th Ave.
Map 12 F3.
(767-0100.

French Connection
304 Columbus Ave.
Map 12 D1.
(496-1470.
One of several branches.

The Gap
250 W 57th St.
Map 12 D3.
(315-2250.
One of many branches.

Geoffrey Beene
783 5th Ave.
Map 12 F3.
(935-0470.

Gianni Versace
816 Madison Ave.
Map 13 A2.
(744-5572.

Giorgio Armani
760 Madison Ave.
Map 13 A2.
(988-9191.

Givenchy
954 Madison Ave.
Map 13 A1.
(772-1040.

Gucci
685 5th Ave.
Map 12 F4.
(826-2600.

Missoni
836 Madison Ave.
Map 13 A1.
(517-9339.

Romeo Gigli
21 E 69th St.
Map 10 F1.
(744-9121.

Screaming Mimi's
382 Lafayette St.
Map 4 F2.
(677-6464.

Valentino
745 Madison Ave.
Map 13 A2.
(772-6969.

Variazioni
309 Columbus Ave.
Map 16 D2.
(874-7474.

Wearable Energy
73 W Houston St.
Map 4 D3.
(475-0026.

What Comes Around Goes Around
351 West Broadway.
Map 4 E4.
(343-9303.

Yohji Yamamoto
103 Grand St.
Map 4 E4.
(966-9066.

Yves St Laurent Rive Gauche
855 Madison Ave.
Map 13 A1.
(472-5299.

Accessories

IN ADDITION TO the following shops, all of the major Manhattan department stores have extensive accessory departments stocking a range of hats, gloves, bags, jewelry, watches, scarves, shoes and umbrellas.

JEWELRY

MIDTOWN FIFTH AVENUE is where to find the most dazzling jewelers. By day, windows glisten with gems from around the world; by night they are empty – the jewels safely locked away. The most sensational shops are all within a couple of blocks of one another and include the museum-like **Harry Winston**, which showcases its coveted jewels from around the world. **Buccellati** is well respected for its innovative Italian creations and excellent workmanship. **Bulgari** has an impressive collection that ranges in price from a mere couple of hundred to over a million dollars.

Housed in a Renaissance-style palazzo, **Cartier** is a jewel in itself and sells its beautiful baubles at unthinkable prices. **Tiffany & Co.** has ten floors of glittering crystal, diamonds and other jewels just waiting to be packed up for you and taken away in the store's signature sky blue boxes.

Diamond Row, a one-block area on 47th Street (between Fifth and Sixth avenues), is lined with shops displaying hundreds of thousands of dollars worth of diamonds, gold, pearls and other exotic jewels from around the world. Try not to miss the **Jewelry Exchange**, a complex where 60 different crafts-people sell their ware direct to the public. Boisterous bargaining is very much alive here, so be prepared to play the game.

HATS

NEW YORK'S OLDEST hat shop is **Worth & Worth**, which also has the largest collection of hats in the city. You can get everything you could possibly want here, ranging from original Australian bush hats to silk toppers and the most romantic, magical frothy concoctions. Or try **Lola Millinery** for some unique, whimsical hats. **Suzanne Millinery** is the hat-maker to the stars, as she has proved very popular with celebrities such as Whoopi Goldberg and Ivana Trump.

UMBRELLAS

THE MINUTE IT STARTS to rain in New York, hundreds of street vendors selling umbrellas seem to sprout like mushrooms. Their umbrellas, which sell at just a few dollars, are without doubt the cheapest in the city, but unlikely to last much longer than the downpour itself. For good-quality umbrellas, you'll find a fine selection of Briggs of London at **Worth & Worth**. There is a wide range of styles at **Uncle Sam**, from small Mickey Mouse styles that start at about $10 to enormous tentlike umbrellas, and both trendy patterns and more traditional tartans and stripes at **Barney's New York**. World-famous **Gucci** has umbrellas to match its ties. There are expensive and telescopic ones found at **Hanae Mori**, and doorman-sized ones in solid black or in the university's traditional colors of black and orange at **The Princeton Club**. **The Yale Club** has blue ones emblazoned with a white "Y".

HANDBAGS AND BRIEFCASES

TWICE A YEAR, during the January and August sales, a serpentine line of buyers wraps around the corner of 48th Street and Madison Avenue waiting to get into **Crouch & Fitzgerald**. An old New York institution, selling handbags, briefcases and luggage. All the well-known brands are sold here, including Judith Leiber, Ghurka, Dooney & Bourke and Louis Vuitton, as well as the firm's own line. Elsewhere in the city are such exclusive shops as **Bottega Veneta** and **Prada**, where handbags are displayed like precious art, with prices to match. Younger and trendier places include **Furla**, well-respected for its Italian designs, and the stylish **Il Bisonte**. Current must-have designer Rafé Totengco's soft suede pastel pouches are found at **TG-170** and **Big Drop**. **The Coach Store** is known for its simple, classic leather handbags.

For discount designer handbags go to the legendary **Fine & Klein**, and for bargain briefcases from slim envelopes to thick lawyer's bags, a visit to the **Altman Luggage Company** is a must.

SHOES AND BOOTS

MANHATTAN SHOE stores are well renowned for their extensive selections of shoes and boots, and if you shop around you are sure to find what you want at a fairly reasonable price.

Most of the large department stores in New York also have shoe departments where you can find designer-label shoes in addition to other brands. **Bloomingdale's** *(see p179)* has a huge women's footwear department, and **Brooks Brothers** has one of the best selections of traditional men's shoes in the city.

For both men's and women's shoes, the most exclusive shops are around the midtown area. **Martinez Valero** has beautiful shoes made from suede and leather, in various elegant styles. **Ferragamo** sells classic styles crafted in Florence. Go to **Botticelli** for whimsical shoe fashions. For stylish shoes at decent prices, head for **Sigerson Morrison** in Little Italy.

For cowboy boots, head for **Billy Martin's**. There's an enormous selection of handmade boots, from basic, no-frills "ropers," which real American cowboys wear, to crocodile leather boots that sell for thousands of dollars. Billy Martin's also stocks all sorts of western garb and accessories, so you can clothe yourself in western gear from head to toe. For beautiful custom-made boots, try **Buffalo Chips Bootery**.

For the latest and best in children's shoes, **East Side Kids** stocks the trendiest fashions for kids. **Little Eric**

has unusual, eye-catching footwear and **Shoofly** has imported shoes in all styles. **Harry's** carries a wonderful selection of sensible shoes.

For discounted shoes, the greatest concentration of shops is around West 34th Street and West 8th Street between Fifth and Sixth avenues, and Orchard Street on the Lower East Side.

LINGERIE

EXPENSIVE imports from Europe, which are sexy yet elegant, can be found at **La Petite Coquette**.

More affordable is **Victoria's Secret**, which offers two floors of beautifully made lingerie in satin, silk and many other fine fabrics.

Books and Music

As the publishing capital of America, it's not surprising that New York has the country's best selection of bookstores. These range from vast general interest stores to hundreds of esoteric bookstores specializing in everything from sci-fi to suspense, selling new books and old. Music lovers will also find sounds for all tastes at reasonable prices, plus thousands of rare recordings.

GENERAL INTEREST BOOKSTORES

One of the most well-known of New York's bookstores – for best prices as well as selection of titles – is **Barnes & Noble** on Fifth Avenue, reputedly the world's largest bookstore and packed high with over three million books on every imaginable subject. There are other branches, such as the sales annex across the street, with thousands of amazing bargains.

Several blocks away is the main branch of New York's famous **Strand Book Store**. The Strand, as those in the know refer to it, has an astonishing two million copies of new and secondhand books at some of the best prices in town. There is also a large rare book room for first editions. **Tower Books** is as comprehensive as its music counterpart, as it stocks an enormous collection of literature, in particular a specialty art section as well as strange, more obscure books. **Coliseum Books** has a vast selection of paperbacks. The two branches of **Borders Books & Music** offer a choice of cds and books of all genres.

In midtown, **Rizzoli** has an enormous selection of photography, foreign language, music and art books plus children's books and videos. **Gotham Book Mart**, a New York institution, is a tiny shop with hundreds of out-of-print books and limited editions.

Shakespeare & Co. offers a sensational selection of titles and is open late every night.

SPECIALTY BOOKSTORES

For the best selection of art books in the city, visit **Hacker Art Books**. **Urban Center Books** has titles on urban planning and other conservation issues. The city's largest selection of out-of-print books, especially for art and literature, can be found at **Academy Book Store**. Rare books, books out-of-print and old books about New York are the *raison d'être* of **JN Bartfield Books**. The **Biography Bookshop** is the only midtown store specializing in diaries, letters, biographies and autobiographies. Theater buffs should try **Applause Theater & Cinema Books**.

For hundreds of titles on science, business, technology and computers visit **McGraw-Hill Bookstore**.

Books on murder and suspense are the focus of two shops: **Murder Ink** and **Mysterious Bookshop**.

Try **Forbidden Planet** for old and new science fiction books and comics. The **Village Comics** has thousands of old and new comics to suit all tastes. **Bank Street Book Store** has one of the best selections of current children's books. Visit **Books of Wonder** for a variety of hardcover and rare children's books.

Travelers' Choice specializes in travel guides, maps, videos and travel accessories. **The Complete Traveler** also stocks a wide selection of brand-new and antique travel books and guides for your trip, on everywhere from Alabama to Zimbabwe. The staff is very knowledgeable and more than helpful. **The Civilized Traveler** carries travel accessories, from portable high-tech gadgets to an array of leather bags. There are also travel videos for rent, an ongoing schedule of lectures and seminars on worldwide travel issues, some by well-known travelers, and special interest trip services.

For an excellent range of maps visit the large **Rand McNally Map & Travel Store** and the **Hagstrom Map & Travel Store**. Cookbooks are on the menu at **Kitchen Arts & Letters**, with many out-of-print books and first editions.

Radicals should head for **Revolution Books** or **St. Mark's Bookstore**, which also has an excellent selection of literary and art titles.

The **Oscar Wilde Memorial Bookshop** has a wide selection of gay and lesbian texts.

RECORDS, TAPES AND COMPACT DISCS

The best Manhattan record-store chain is **Tower Records**, whose three stores have everything from bebop to rap. **HMV** and **Virgin** follow a close second. **J&R Music World** is a complete home entertainment store with one of the best CD selections in the city. **Record Explosion** carries many budget CDs.

For out-of-print records, go to **Gryphon Records**, a treasure trove for collectors. The **Academy Book Store** has an excellent choice of classical, jazz and opera recordings. **Footlight Records** is for lovers of Broadway musicals and film soundtracks, and **House of Oldies** has a massive stock of deleted and rare records to suit all tastes. **Bleecker Bob's Golden Oldies** Record Shop has everything from imports, rock and punk to rare jazz. Try **Midnight Records** for imports, reissues, American garage rock and psychedelia.

SHEET MUSIC

Just behind Carnegie Hall is one of the best stores for classical sheet music, **Joseph Patelson Music House Ltd**. The **Frank Music Company** has a huge collection of classical music scores. **Charles Colin Publications** specializes in jazz. For chart music and pop tunes try **Colony Record and Music Center** in the Brill Building.

DIRECTORY

GENERAL INTEREST BOOKSTORES

Barnes & Noble
105 5th Ave. **Map** 8 F5.
(807-0099.
One of several branches.

Borders Books & Music
5 World Trade Center.
Map 1 B2.
(839-0049.
One of two branches.

Coliseum Books
1771 Broadway.
Map 12 D3.
(757-8381.

Gotham Book Mart
41 W 47th St. **Map** 12 F5.
(719-4448.

Rizzoli
31 W 57th St.
Map 12 F3.
(759-2424.
One of several branches.

Shakespeare & Co
716 Broadway.
Map 4 E2.
(529-1330.

939 Lexington Ave.
Map 13 A1.
(570-0201.

Strand Book Store
828 Broadway.
Map 4 E1.
(473-1452.

Tower Books
383 Lafayette St.
Map 4 F2.
(228-5100.

SPECIALITY BOOKSTORES

Academy Book Store
10 W 18th St.
Map 8 F5.
(242-4848.

Applause Theater & Cinema Books
211 W 71st St.
Map 11 C1.
(496-7511.

Bank Street Book Store
610 W 112th St.
Map 21 A4.
(678-1654.

Biography Bookshop
400 Bleecker St.
Map 3 C2.
(807-8655.

Books of Wonder
16 W 18th St.
Map 8 E5.
(989-3270.

The Civilized Traveler
2003 Broadway.
Map 11 C1.
(875-0306.

The Complete Traveler
199 Madison Ave.
Map 9 A2.
(685-9007

Forbidden Planet
840 Broadway.
Map 4 E1.
(473-1576.

Hacker Art Books
45 W 57th St.
Map 12 F3.
(688-7600.

Hagstrom Map & Travel Store
57 W 43rd St.
Map 8 F1.
(398-1222.

JN Bartfield Books
30 W 57th St.
Map 12 F3.
(245-8890.

Kitchen Arts & Letters
1435 Lexington Ave.
Map 17 A2.
(876-5550.

McGraw-Hill Bookstore
1221 6th Ave.
Map 12 E4.
(512-4100.

Murder Ink
2486 Broadway.
Map 15 C2.
(362-8905.

Mysterious Bookshop
129 W 56th St.
Map 12 E3.
(765-0900.

Oscar Wilde Memorial Bookshop
15 Christopher St.
Map 3 C2.
(255-8097.

Rand McNally Map & Travel Store
150 E 52nd St.
Map 13 A4.
(758-7488.

Revolution Books
9 W 19th St.
Map 7 C5.
(691-3345.

St. Mark's Bookshop
31 3rd Ave.
Map 5 A2.
(260-7853.

Travelers' Choice
2 Wooster St.
Map 4 E4.
(941-1535.

Urban Center Books
457 Madison Ave.
Map 13 A4.
(935-3592.

Village Comics
214 Sullivan St.
Map 4 D2.
(777-2770.

RECORDS, TAPES, COMPACT DISCS

Academy Book Store
See Specialty Bookshops.

Bleecker Bob's Golden Oldies
118 W 3rd St.
Map 4 D2.
(475-9677.

Footlight Records
113 E 12th St.
Map 4 F1.
(533-1572.

Gryphon Records
233 W 72nd St.
Map 11 D1.
(874-1588.

HMV
2081 Broadway.
Map 15 C5.
(721-5900.
One of several branches.

House of Oldies
35 Carmine St.
Map 4 D3.
(243-0500.

J&R Music World
15, 23, 27 & 33 Park Row.
Map 1 C2.
(732-8600.

Midnight Records
263 W 23rd St.
Map 8 D4.
(675-2768.

Record Explosion
507 5th Ave. **Map** 8 F1.
(661-6642.
One of several branches.

Tower Records
692 Broadway.
Map 4 E2.
(505-1500.
One of three branches.

Virgin Megastore
45th & Broadway.
Map 12 E5.
(921-1020.

SHEET MUSIC

Charles Colin Publications
315 W 53rd St.
Map 12 D4.
(581-1480.

Colony Record and Music Center
1619 Broadway.
Map 12 E4.
(265-2050.

Frank Music Company
250 W 54th St.
Map 12 D4.
(582-1999.

Joseph Patelson Music House Ltd
160 W 56th St.
Map 12 E4.
(757-5587.

Art and Antiques

ANY ART-LOVING VISITOR to New York could easily spend several days gallery-hopping around the several hundred galleries found throughout New York. Antique lovers can find an exciting variety of goods, including Americana and many bargains, at the many flea markets; or they can browse through European and American fine antiques in one of the more exclusive antiques centers. To find out what's happening, pick up the free monthly *Art Now Gallery Guide*, available at most galleries, or check the local papers.

ART GALLERIES

ONE OF THE MOST well known galleries in New York is **Leo Castelli**, an important showcase for Pop Art during the early 1960s and now spotlighting new artists. **Mary Boone Gallery** features Neo-Expressionist artists such as Julian Schnabel. The **Pace Gallery** exhibits current stars, especially well-known painter-photographers, and the trendy gallery **Gorney, Bravin & Lee** deals in contemporary art and sculpture. The **John Weber Gallery** features new talent but is famous for its many Minimalists and Conceptualists. **Postmasters** is a treasure trove of conceptual pieces.

Among the exclusive 57th Street galleries is the venerable **Sidney Janis Gallery**, which displays 20th-century masters; **Marian Goodman Gallery** features the European avant-garde. **Holly Solomon Gallery** in SoHo has European and American contemporary painting, drawing and sculpture

Along the Upper East Side is **Knoedler & Company**, which exhibits contemporary paintings by modern masters. **Gagosian Gallery** has great works by Lichtenstein and Johns, and the **Hirschl & Adler Galleries** feature a good selection of European and American fine art.

AMERICAN FOLK ART

IF YOU'RE in the market for American folk art, go to **Susan Parrish Antiques** and to **Kelter-Malcé** for a selection of hooked rugs and other Americana. Similar goods are at **Brian Windsor**.

Laura Fisher sells everything from decoys to hooked rugs.

ANTIQUES CENTERS AND SECONDHAND ANTIQUES

IN ADDITION TO hundreds of small shops selling everything from tiger teeth to multimillion-dollar paintings, Manhattan is home to **The Manhattan Art & Antiques Center**, which has dozens of dealers under one roof. **Chelsea Antiques** is home to more than 100 galleries and even has a small cafe. **Irving Barber Shop Antiques** is filled with fabulous secondhand finds at astoundingly good prices.

AMERICAN FURNITURE

FOR FURNITURE from the 17th-, 18th- and 19th-centuries, try **Bernard Levy & S. Dean**, **Eagles Antiques**, **Leigh Keno American Furniture** or the highly regarded **Israel Sack**. **Judith James Milne** sells early American country furniture and a splendid collection of quilts. Go to **Woodard & Greenstein American Antiques & Quilts** for a truly wonderful selection of Shaker pieces.

Collectors of Art Deco or Art Nouveau furniture should pay a visit to **Alan Moss**, which is full of furniture and decorative items. **Macklowe Gallery & Modernism** has a massive collection of fine Art Nouveau furniture. **Minna Rosenblatt** and **Lillian Nassau** have Tiffany lamps and many Art Nouveau and Art Deco pieces.

New York has a handful of retro shops, though numbers are growing all the time. Two of the best are **Depression Modern** and **Mood Indigo**, which have treasures from the 1930s and 1940s.

INTERNATIONAL ANTIQUES

IF YOU'RE LOOKING for English antiques, try **Florian Papp** and **Kentshire Galleries**. For European pieces, you'll have plenty of choices; try **Betty Jane Bart Antiques**, **Kurt Gluckselig Antiques**, **The Little Antique Shop**, **Linda Horn Antiques**, **La Belle Epoque**, and **Pierre Deux**. Oriental dealers include **Doris Leslie Blau**, **E. & J. Frankel** and **Flying Cranes Antiques**.

FLEA MARKETS

NEW YORK HAS a number of year-round weekend markets. The best time to go is at the crack of dawn. Most flea markets officially open at 9 or 10am, but the haggling starts as early as 6am. If you arrive early, you may be lucky enough to unearth some valuable piece of definitively cultural Americana like a Barbie lunch box or a Soupy Sales record, for example.

Visit the **Annex Antiques Fair and Flea Market** for everything from secondhand clothing to antique furniture. The weekend **Canal Street Flea Market** has bric-a-brac; the **Columbus Avenue Flea Market** has new and second-hand clothing and furniture. For further information on all street fairs and flea markets, check Friday's *New York Times*.

AUCTION HOUSES

MANHATTAN'S TWO most celebrated auction houses are **Christie's** and **Sotheby's**, selling collectibles ranging from coins, jewels, and vintage wines to fine and decorative arts.

Items for sale are usually previewed several days before the auctions. For further information on previews and auctions, check the Friday and Sunday editions of the *New York Times*.

DIRECTORY

ART GALLERIES

Gagosian Gallery
980 Madison Ave.
Map 17 A5.
744-2313.

Hirschl & Adler Galleries
21 E 70th St. **Map** 12 F1.
535-8810.
One of several branches.

Holly Solomon Gallery
172 Mercer St. **Map** 4 E3.
941-5777.

Gorney, Bravin & Lee
534 W 26 St. **Map** 7 C4.
352-8372.

John Weber Gallery
529 W 20th St. **Map** 7 C5.
691-5711.

Knoedler & Company
19 E 70th St. **Map** 13 A1.
794-0550.

Leo Castelli
59 E 79th St.
Map 17 A4.
249-4470.

Marian Goodman Gallery
24 W 57th St. **Map** 12 F3.
977-7160.

Mary Boone Gallery
745 5th Ave.
Map 12 F3.
752-2929.

Pace Gallery
32 E 57th St. **Map** 12 F3.
421-3292.

Postmasters
80 Greene St. **Map** 4 E2.
941-5711.

Sidney Janis Gallery
110 W 57th St.
Map 12 E3.
586-0110.

AMERICAN FOLK ART

Brian Windsor
272 Lafayette St.
Map 4 F4.
274-0411.

Kelter-Malcé
74 Jane St.
Map 3 C1.
989-6760.

Laura Fisher
Manhattan Art & Antiques Center, 1050 2nd Ave.
Map 13 B4.
838-2596.

Susan Parrish Antiques
390 Bleecker St.
Map 3 C2.
645-5020.

ANTIQUE CENTERS AND SECOND-HAND ANTIQUES

Chelsea Antiques
110 W 25th St.
Map 8 E4.
929-0909.

Irving Barber Shop Antiques
210 E 21st St.
Map 9 A4.
no phone.

The Manhattan Arts & Antiques Center
1050 2nd Ave.
Map 13 A3.
355-4400.

AMERICAN FURNITURE

Alan Moss
436 Lafayette St.
Map 4 F2.
473-1310.

Bernard Levy & S. Dean
24 E 84th St.
Map 16 F4.
628-7088.

Depression Modern
150 Sullivan St.
Map 4 D3.
982-5699.

Eagles Antiques
1097 Madison Ave.
Map 17 A5.
772-3266.

Israel Sack
730 5th Ave.
Map 12 F3.
399-6562.

Judith James Milne
506 E 74th St.
Map 17 C5.
472-0107.

Leigh Keno American Furniture
980 Madison Ave.
Map 17 A5.
734-2381.

Lillian Nassau
220 E 57th St. **Map** 13 B3.
759-6062.

Macklowe Gallery & Modernism
667 Madison Ave.
Map 13 A3.
644-6400.

Minna Rosenblatt
961 Madison Ave.
Map 17 A5.
288-0250.

Mood Indigo
181 Prince St.
Map 4 E3.
254-1176.

Woodard & Greenstein American Antiques
506 E 74th St.
Map 17 A5.
988-2906.

INTERNATIONAL ANTIQUES

La Belle Epoque
280 Columbus Ave.
Map 12 D1.
362-1770.

Betty Jane Bart Antiques
1225 Madison Ave.
Map 17 A3.
410-2702.

Doris Leslie Blau
724 5th Ave.
Map 12 F3.
586-5511.
By appointment only.

E & J Frankel
1040 Madison Ave.
Map 17 A5.
879-5733.

Florian Papp
962 Madison Ave.
Map 17 A5.
288-6770.

Flying Cranes Antiques
1050 2nd Ave.
Map 13 B4.
223-4600.

Kentshire Galleries
37 E 12th St. **Map** 4 E1.
673-6644.

Kurt Gluckselig Antiques
1050 2nd Ave.
Map 13 B4.
758-1805.

Linda Horn Antiques
1015 Madison Ave.
Map 17 A5.
772-1122.

The Little Antique Shop
44 E 11th St.
Map 4 E1.
673-5173.

Pierre Deux
367 Bleecker St.
Map 3 C2.
243-7740.
One of several branches.

FLEA MARKETS

Annex Antiques Fair and Flea Market
24th to 27th Sts at 6th Ave.
Map 8 E4.
243-5343.
Open Sat and Sun.

Canal Street Flea Market
335 Canal St.
Map 4 E5.
Open every weekend
Mar–Dec.

Columbus Avenue Flea Market
Columbus Ave, between 76th and 77th St.
Map 16 D5.
721-0900.
Open Sun.

AUCTION HOUSES

Christie's
20 Rockefeller Plaza.
Map 12 F5.
636-2000.

Sotheby's
1334 York Ave.
Map 13 C1.
606-7000.

Food and Household Goods

NEW YORK'S STRIKING cultural and ethnic diversity is celebrated in its food – the city's food shops provide a truly international feast. There is also a dazzling array of household goods, electronics and photographic equipment available almost everywhere you turn.

GOURMET GROCERIES

SCATTERED AROUND town are several famous food emporiums that are tourist attractions in themselves. Remember, too, to visit the department stores, which often rival the specialty food stores.

Balducci's in Greenwich Village is a real Italian delight, with its own brands of cold meats, pastas, salami and fish. Food has been elevated to an art form at **Dean & DeLuca**, a chic delicatessen – don't miss the huge selection of take-out food. **Russ & Daughters** is one of the oldest gourmet shops, known as an "appetizing" store, full of ethnic food and famous for cream cheese, chocolates and bagels. **The Gourmet Garage** sells all kinds of delicious fresh food, in particular organic produce. **Zabar's** is perhaps the finest food store in the world, with huge crowds jostling for the excellent smoked salmon, bagels, caviar, cheese and coffee.

William Poll has a good selection of picnic hampers as well as a great variety of prepared dishes. For pâté de foie gras, Scottish smoked salmon, caviar and handmade chocolates, go to **Caviarteria**.

SPECIALTY FOOD AND WINE SHOPS

FABULOUS BREAD and cake shops abound but one of the best is **Poseidon Greek Bakery**, renowned for its filo pastry. **H & H Bagels** bakes 60,000 of the best bagels in Manhattan every day. **Vesuvio** has Italian bread and some unusual pepper biscuits. Try **Fung Wong** for delicious Chinese pastries or purchase a traditional Sicilian loaf from **A. Zito & Son's Bakery**.

Great confectionery shops include **Li-Lac** for handmade chocolates and **Mondel**

Chocolates for chocolate animals. **Economy Candy** has a huge selection of dried fruit but for a real treat go to **Teuscher**, which has fresh champagne truffles flown in direct from Switzerland.

Myers of Keswick imports English food. For something more exotic, **Kam Man Food Products** is an Oriental grocery selling Chinese, Thai, and other oriental products. The **Italian Food Center** has great olive oils, dried pastas and sausages, and try **Raffeto's Corporation** for every kind of pasta. Go to **Jefferson Market** for meat and fish, and **Citarella's** for its fine seafood. **Angelica's Herbs and Spices** has a selection of 2,000 varieties of herbs and spices.

For fine burgundies, **Acker, Merrall & Condit** is a good choice. Go to **Garnet Liquors** for fine wines and champagnes at bargain prices. **SoHo Wines and Spirits** has an extensive selection of single-malt Scotch whisky. **Sherry-Lehmann** is New York's leading wine merchant.

New York also has many fine coffee stores. Among the best are **Oren's**, **The Sensuous Bean** and **Porto Rico Importing Company**, each with a mouth-watering selection. For fruit and vegetables at reasonable prices, visit a farmers' market, but get there early. Among the most popular are **City Hall**, **Upper West Side**, **St. Mark's in-the-Bowery**, and **Union Square**. For information about the city's markets, phone: 788-7900.

HOUSEHOLD GOODS

MOST OF THE department stores offer a wide range of household goods. For a specialized shop, try **Broadway Panhandler**, a cook's heaven with outstanding baking and pastry-making

equipment. **Bridge Kitchenware** is a household name among most restaurateurs. **Williams-Sonoma** has many cooking utensils and cookbooks. **Zabar's** has a great selection of cooking utensils.

Baccarat, **Daum**, **Lalique** and **Villeroy & Boch** are where you'll find the finest crystal, china and silverware. Other fashionable shops include **Orrefors Crystal**, **Kosta Boda** and **Tiffany & Co**. Go to **Avventura** for crystal and china and, for the best of inexpensive, utilitarian American china, visit **Fishs Eddy**. Also visit **Ceramica**, which stocks lovely handmade Italian pottery, and **La Terrine** and **Steuben Glass** for hand-painted ceramics.

Inexpensive linens can be found in most department stores, but for silk sheets and luxurious linens, visit **Porthault** and **Pratesi**. **ABC Carpet & Home** has an enviable reputation for home furnishings as does **Bed, Bath & Beyond** for its bed linens, kitchen and bath accessories. For the lowest prices, shop-hop on Grand Street on the Lower East Side.

ELECTRONICS AND PHOTOGRAPHIC EQUIPMENT

PERHAPS THE MOST competitive retailers in New York are the ones that sell electronics, and it pays to shop around. If you're buying electrical goods to take to Europe, make sure they have compatible voltages and formats (many in the US are made to different standards).

B & H Photo sells equipment from cameras to fax machines. Another popular shop for electrical equipment is **Compusa**. **J&R Music World** sells very competitively priced equipment and has possibly the best CD selection in the city. **The Wiz** is a large electronics chain that offers a wide range of equipment and games. Check the papers for **Willoughby's**; they have good sales on photographic equipment and supplies.

DIRECTORY

GOURMET GROCERIES

Balducci's
424 Ave of the Americas.
Map 4 D1.
🕻 673-2600.

Caviarteria
29 E 60th St. **Map** 12 F3.
🕻 759-7410.

Dean & DeLuca
560 Broadway. **Map** 4 E3.
🕻 226-6800.

Gourmet Garage
453 Broome St. **Map** 4 E4.
🕻 941-5850.
One of several branches.

Russ & Daughters
179 E Houston St.
Map 5 A3.
🕻 475-4880.

William Poll
1051 Lexington Ave.
Map 17 A5.
🕻 288-0501.

Zabar's
2245 Broadway.
Map 15 C4.
🕻 787-2000.

SPECIALTY FOOD AND WINE SHOPS

A Zito & Son's Bakery
259 Bleecker St. **Map** 3 C2.
🕻 929-6139.

Acker, Merrall & Condit
160 W 72nd St.
Map 11 C1.
🕻 787-1700.

Angelica's Herbs and Spices
147 1st Ave.
Map 5 A1.
🕻 677-1549.

Citarella's
2135 Broadway.
Map 15 C5.
🕻 874-0383.

City Hall Green Market
Centre St and Chambers St.
Map 1 C1.

Economy Candy
108 Rivington St.
Map 5 A3.
🕻 254-1531.

Fung Wong
30 Mott St. **Map** 4 F3.
🕻 267-4037.

Garnet Liquors
929 Lexington Ave.
Map 13 A1.
🕻 772-3211.

H & H Bagels
2239 Broadway.
Map 15 C4. 🕻 595-8000.
One of two branches.

Italian Food Center
186 Grand St. **Map** 15 C4.
🕻 925-2954.

Jefferson Market
450 Ave of the Americas.
Map 12 E5. 🕻 533-3377.

Kam Man Food Products
200 Canal St. **Map** 4 F5.
🕻 571-0330.

Li-Lac
120 Christopher St.
Map 3 C2. 🕻 242-7374.

Mondel Chocolates
2913 Broadway.
Map 20 E3. 🕻 864-2111.

Myers of Keswick
634 Hudson St.
Map 3 C2.
🕻 691-4194.

Oren's
1144 Lexington Ave.
Map 17 A4. 🕻 472-6830.

Porto Rico Importing Company
201 Bleecker St. **Map** 3 C2.
🕻 477-5421.

Poseidon Greek Bakery
629 9th Ave. **Map** 12 D5.
🕻 757-6173.

Raffeto's Corporation
144 West Houston St.
Map 4 D3. 🕻 777-1261.

St Mark's in-the-Bowery Greenmarket
E 10th St at 2nd Ave.
Map 4 F1.

The Sensuous Bean
66 W 70th St. **Map** 12 D1.
🕻 724-7725.

Sherry-Lehmann
679 Madison Ave.
Map 13 A3.
🕻 838-7500.

SoHo Wines and Spirits
461 W Broadway.
Map 4 E4.
🕻 777-4332.

Teuscher
25 E 61st St. **Map** 12 F3.
🕻 751-8482.

Union Square Greenmarket
E 17th St and Broadway.
Map 8 F5.

Upper West Side Greenmarket
Columbus Ave at 77th St.
Map 16 D5.

Vesuvio
160 Prince St. **Map** 4 E3.
🕻 925-8248.

HOUSEHOLD GOODS

ABC Carpet & Home
888 Broadway.
Map 8 F5.
🕻 473-3000.

Bed, Bath & Beyond
610 Ave of the Americas
Map 8 F5.
🕻 255-3550.

Avventura
463 Amsterdam Ave.
Map 15 C4.
🕻 769-2510.

Baccarat
625 Madison Ave.
Map 13 A3.
🕻 826-4100.

Bridge Kitchenware
214 E 52nd St.
Map 13 B4.
🕻 688-4220.

Bro'adway Panhandler
477 Broome St.
Map 4 E4.
🕻 966-3434.

Ceramica
59 Thompson St.
Map 4 D4.
🕻 941-1307.

Daum
694 Madison Ave.
Map 13 A3.
🕻 355-2060.

Fishs Eddy
2176 Broadway.
Map 15 C5.
🕻 873-8819.

Kosta Boda
58 E 57th St.
Map 12 F3.
🕻 753-3442.

Lalique
680 Madison Ave.
Map 13 A3.
🕻 355-6550.

Orrefors Crystal
58 E 57th St.
Map 13 A3.
🕻 753-3442.

Porthault
18 E 69th St. **Map** 12 F1.
🕻 688-1660.

Pratesi
829 Madison Ave.
Map 13 A2.
🕻 288-2315.

Steuben Glass
715 5th Ave. **Map** 12 F3.
🕻 752-1441.

La Terrine
1024 Lexington Ave.
Map 13 A1.
🕻 988-3366.

Tiffany & Co
See p321.

Villeroy & Boch
974 Madison Ave.
Map 17 A5.
🕻 535-2500.

Williams-Sonoma
20 E 60th St. **Map** 12 F3.
🕻 980-5155.
One of several branches.

Zabar's
See Gourmet Groceries.

ELECTRONICS AND PHOTOGRAPHIC EQUIPMENT

B & H Photo
420 9th Ave. **Map** 8 D2.
🕻 444-6630.

J&R Music World
See p322.

The Wiz
212 E 57th St. **Map** 13 A3.
🕻 754-1600.
One of several branches.

Compusa
420 5th Ave. **Map** 8 F1.
🕻 764-6224.
One of several branches.

Willoughby's
136 W 32nd St.
Map 8 E3.
🕻 564-1600.

ENTERTAINMENT IN NEW YORK

N EW YORK CITY IS a non-stop entertainment extravaganza, every day, all year round. Whatever your taste, you can be sure the city will satisfy it on both a grand and an intimate scale. The challenge is to take advantage of as many of the entertainments as possible. If it's theater, you can enjoy a mainstream success on Broadway or take a chance on an experimental production

Performance by the New York City Ballet

in a loft. If it's music, there's the magnificence of opera at the Met or a jazz group blowing in a club in the Village. You can catch a spectacle of avant-garde dance in a café or try your own avant-garde dancing in one of the city's warehouse-sized clubs. Movie theaters abound. But perhaps best of all is wandering and watching the vast show that is New York.

PRACTICAL INFORMATION

F IND OUT what you can choose from in the arts and leisure listings of the *New York Times* and the *Village Voice* newspapers and *Time Out New York* (referred

TKTS discount ticket booth

to as TONY) and *The New Yorker* magazines. These briefly describe the entertainment and tell you which credit cards are accepted. At your hotel ask for *Where*, a free weekly magazine containing maps and information on the many different attractions.

Hotel staff may be able to answer some of your questions and should also carry a wide selection of brochures and leaflets. They may also be willing to reserve tickets for you. Some hotel TVs have a New York visitor information channel.

The **Times Square Visitors Information Bureau** is an official distribution center for entertainment literature and schedules of events, selling theatre tickets and sightseeing tours. They also have free and discount tickets such as

"twofers" – which used to mean two for the price of one but now just refers to a hefty discount. **NYC On Stage** is a telephone hotline for theater, dance and music; **Broadway Line** gives brief descriptions of current shows, schedules and the different prices; while **Moviefone** gives recorded information on all the films, and **ClubFone** (777-2582) has information on nightlife.

BOOKING TICKETS

P OPULAR SHOWS may well be sold out for weeks ahead, so purchase your seats well in advance. Theater box offices are open daily, except on Sundays, from 10am until one hour after the performance begins. Call in person or telephone the box office or a ticket agency and order your seats by credit card. The

biggest agencies are **Telecharge**, **Ticketmaster** and **Ticket Central**. A small handling fee of a few dollars will always be charged.

An independent ticket agent may also be able to find seats – one to try is **Prestige Entertainment**; others are listed in the New York Yellow Pages. Fees will vary according to demand.

Broadway Ticket Center in the Times Square Visitors Center sells full-price tickets.

DISCOUNT TICKETS

D ISCOUNT tickets for plays and musicals are sold on the day of performance by nonprofit **TKTS** booths. Discounts range from 25% to 50%, but the price will include a small handling fee and must be paid for in cash or by traveler's check.

The TKTS booth on Broadway sells matinée tickets from 10am to 2pm every Wednesday and Saturday; evening tickets are sold from 3pm to 8pm, and Sunday tickets from 11am until 7pm. The booth at the 2 World Trade Center mezzanine sells tickets from 11am to 5:30pm Monday to Friday and 11am to 3:30pm on Saturday. Saturday matinée tickets can be bought here on Fridays.

You can purchase day-of-performance tickets from **Ticketmaster** at discounts of 10 to 75% (with a small commission charge) by telephone.

Bobby Short singing at the Café Carlyle (*p343*)

The Booth Theater on Broadway *(see p333)*

Ticketmaster also sells tickets via its own website. If you have internet access, the address is www.ticketmaster.com. The **Hit Show Club** sells vouchers that can be exchanged at theater box offices for discounted tickets.

Some shows offer standing-room tickets on the day at a bargain price. It's often the only way to catch a sold-out show on short notice.

"SCALPERS" AND TOUTS

I F YOU BUY from a "scalper" (a ticket tout), tickets for the wrong day or wrong price, counterfeit tickets and outrageous prices are among the risks. The police often monitor sports and theater venues for scalpers and their customers.

FREE TICKETS

F REE TICKETS to TV shows, concerts and special events are offered at the **Times Square Visitors Information Bureau,** which is open from 8:30am to 6pm Monday to Friday and 9am to 5pm on weekends. "Cheap Thrills" in the *Village Voice* lists such events as poetry readings, recitals and experimental films. During the popular New York Shakespeare Festival, free tickets are given out on a first-come, first-served basis and are restricted to one ticket per person. The line forms at

noon on the day of the performance at the **Delacorte Theater**, in Central Park. Take a picnic basket and blankets.

Free tickets for TV video-taping sessions are available by writing to the networks or from their on-street agents at **Rockefeller Center.**

Royale Theater at night *(see p333)*

HANDICAPPED ACCESS

B ROADWAY THEATERS reserve a few spaces and cut-price tickets for the disabled. Call **Ticketmaster** or **Telecharge** well in advance for information about shows and also to reserve tickets. For Off-Broadway theaters, call their box offices. Some theaters offer useful equipment for the hearing-impaired. **Tap** can arrange sign language for Broadway theaters, and **Hands On** for Off-Broadway.

USEFUL ADDRESSES

Broadway Line
📞 563-2929.

Delacorte Theater
Entrance via 81st St
at Central Park W.
Map 16 E4.
📞 861-7277.
Summer time only.

Hands On
📞 672-4898 (Voice/TDD).

Hit Show Club
8th floor, 630 5th Ave.
Map 12 D5.
📞 581-4211.

Moviefone
(see p337)
📞 777-FILM.

Prestige Entertainment
📞 697-7788.

Network Tickets
ABC.
67th St and Columbus Ave.
📞 456-3537.

CBS.
524 W 57th St.
📞 975-2476

NYC On Stage
1501 Broadway.
Map 12 D2
📞 768-1818.

Tap (Theatre Access Project)
📞 221-1103 (Voice),
719-4537 (TDD).

Telecharge
📞 239-6200.

Ticket Central
📞 279-4200.

Ticketmaster
📞 307-4100.

Times Square Visitors Center
1560 Broadway.
Map 12 E5.
www.newyork.citysearch.com

TKTS
Broadway at W 47th St.
Map 12 E5.

2 World Trade Center.
Map 1 B2.

New York's Best: Entertainment

Greenwich Village jazz club

Nᴇᴡ ʏᴏʀᴋ is one of the great entertainment capitals of the world. Top names in every branch of the arts are drawn here to perform and often to live and work. Major sporting events are also constant, and as for nightlife, New York lives up to its reputation as "the city that never sleeps." From the huge choice offered, there are some venues and events that stand out as classics of their kind; this selection has been chosen from the listings on pages 332 to 347 as among those not to be missed. Even if you experience only one of them, you will have been part of something as essentially New York as the Empire State Building.

Limelight
Nightclubs come and go, but this converted church has become a firm favorite with New York's night owls.
(See p342.)

Chelsea and Garment Dist

Greenwich Village

Madison Square Garden
Top sporting action is found at "the Garden," including home games for basketball's New York Knicks and ice hockey's Rangers, plus the Golden Gloves boxing tournament. (See p344.)

SoHo and TriBeCa

Eas Vill

Seaport and the Civic Center

Lower East Side

Lower Manhattan

H U D S O N   R I V E R

Film Forum
At New York's most stylish arts movie theater you can see the latest foreign and American independent releases or catch up with a classic in a wide range of retrospectives. (See p336.)

Village Vanguard
The jazz clubs of Greenwich Village have played host to all the great names in jazz. Fans can catch the stars of today and tomorrow at the world-famous Village Vanguard and the Blue Note. (See p340.)

N

Upper
West Side

Central
Park

Upper
East
Side

Upper
Midtown

ercy
the
iron
rict

EAST RIVER

Philharmonic Rehearsals
*The Thursday-morning
rehearsals at Avery Fisher
Hall are often open to
the public at a fraction of
the normal ticket price.*
(See p338.)

Metropolitan Opera House
*Reserve well ahead and prepare
to pay high prices to see the giants
of the opera world.* (See p338.)

**Shakespeare in
Central Park**
*If you are a
summer visitor,
set aside a day
to get one of
the rare free
tickets for the
Delacorte
Theater's open-air Shakespeare
featuring top Hollywood and
Broadway names.* (See p332.)

The Nutcracker
*The Christmas event for children of
every age is performed each year at
Lincoln Center by the New York City
Ballet.* (See p334.)

0 kilometers   2

0 miles   1

The Fantasticks
*The tiny Sullivan
Street Playhouse
has been home to
America's longest-
running play since
May 1960. New
Yorkers who saw it
when they were
young are now
taking their own
children to the
show.* (See p332.)

Carnegie Hall
*Conveniently situated in the
Theater District, Carnegie Hall is
famous the world over as a showcase for the best in the musical arts.
A backstage tour gives a fascinating insight into "the house that
music built."* (See p338.)

Theater and Dance

NEW YORK IS FAMOUS for its extravagant musicals and its ferocious critics. It is one of the world's greatest theater and dance centers, featuring every kind of production imaginable. Whether your preference is for the glitz and glamour of a Broadway blockbuster or something truly experimental, you'll find it here.

BROADWAY

BROADWAY HAS long been synonymous with New York's Theater District, but the majority of Broadway theaters are actually scattered between 41st and 53rd streets and from Sixth to Ninth avenues, with a few around the much-improved Times Square. Most were built between 1910 and 1930, during the heyday of vaudeville and the likes of the famous Ziegfeld Follies. The **Lyceum** (see p142) is the oldest theater still in operation (1903), and the **Ford Center for the Performing Arts** and the **New Amsterdam Theater** are the newest (1997). Broadway theaters experienced a slump during the 1980s but are now enjoying a revival because of cutting costs, using big names to draw in the crowds and benefiting from urban renewal of the Broadway district.

This is where you will find the "power productions" – the big, highly publicized dramas, musicals and revivals starring many Hollywood luminaries in (it is hoped) sure-fire money earners. Recent hits include such international imports as *Les Misérables;* New York originals like *Ragtime,* the most popular children's favorite *The Lion King,* and great revivals like *Cabaret* .

OFF-BROADWAY AND OFF-OFF-BROADWAY

THERE ARE about 20 Off-Broadway stages and 300 Off-Off-Broadway stages whose works will sometimes transfer to Broadway. Off-Broadway theaters have from 100 to 499 seats, and Off-Off-Broadway showplaces have fewer than 100. Both range from the well-appointed to the improvised, sited in lofts, churches and even garages.

Off-Broadway became very popular during the 1950s as a reaction to the commercialism of Broadway. It was also an ideal place for more cautious producers to try out works considered too avant-garde or unsuitable for Broadway at a much lower operating costs. During the last two decades, Off-Off-Broadway theaters have become the venue for the more experimental pieces by these same producers.

Off-Broadway theaters are found all over Manhattan – from Greenwich Village's **Sullivan Street Playhouse** (where the longest-running show in New York, *The Fantasticks,* plays) to Central Park's open-air **Delacorte Theater**. Some are even in the traditional Broadway district, such as the **Manhattan Theater Club**. Farther afield are the **Brooklyn Academy of Music (BAM)** (see p246), the **Manhattan Theater Club** and the **92nd Street Y**. In these venues you will always find lively, unusual and experimental showcases for new talent as well as lots of uninhibited productions.

The Off-Broadway theatres mounted the first productions in New York of the works of playwrights Sean O'Casey, Tennessee Williams, Eugene O'Neill, Samuel Beckett, Jean Genet, Eugene Ionesco and David Mamet. They host new and very often irreverent treatments of the classics, and every imaginable theatrical presentation is floated.

Sometimes a more intimate, smaller Off-Broadway stage suits a production much better than a larger more established theater would, as proved by such long-running successes as *The Fantasticks* and the *Three-penny Opera.* Of course, there are flops occasionally – but that's show business.

PERFORMANCE THEATER

THIS EXTREMELY avant-garde art form can be found in several Off- and Off-Off-Broadway locations. Accurate descriptions and categorizations are almost impossible, but expect the bizarre and outlandish. The most likely venues to find this are **La MaMa**, **P.S. 122**, **HERE**, **92nd Street Y**, **Symphony Space** and the Joseph Papp **Public Theater** (see p118). The latter is perhaps the most influential theater in New York. It was founded in the 1950s by the late director Joseph Papp, who introduced neighborhood tours to bring theater to people who had never seen it before.

The Public Theater created hits like *Hair* and *A Chorus Line;* it is most famous for its free summer performances of Shakespeare at the Delacorte Theater in Central Park (see p206). It usually has several productions running, and at 6pm on the day of performance, "Quiktix" tickets (limited to two per person) are sold in the Public Theater lobby.

THEATER SCHOOLS

NEW YORK is the best place in the country to see actors learning their trade. Foremost among the acting schools is **The Actors' Studio**. The late Lee Strasberg, the advocate of method acting – in which the actor aims for complete identification with the character being played – was its guru. His students included Dustin Hoffman, Al Pacino and Marilyn Monroe. "In progress" productions feature trainees and are usually open to the public. Sandy Meisner trained many actors, including the late Lee Remick, at the **Neighborhood Playhouse School of the Theater**. Its plays are also open to the public. The **New Dramatists** began in 1949 to develop new playwrights, helping the careers of the likes of William Inge. Play readings are open to the public and free.

BROADWAY THEATERS

① Ambassador
215 W 49th St.
239-6200.

② Barrymore
243 W 47th St.
239-6200.

③ Belasco
111 W 44th St.
239-6200.

④ Booth
222 W 45th St.
239-6200.

⑤ Broadhurst
235 W 44th St.
239-6200.

⑥ Broadway
1681 Broadway.
239-6200.

⑦ Brooks Atkinson
256 W 47th St.
307-4100.

⑧ Cort
138 W 48th St.
239-6200.

⑨ Eugene O'Neill
230 W 49th St.
239-6200.

⑩ Gershwin
222 W 51st St.
307-4100.

⑪ John Golden
252 W 45th St.
239-6200.

⑫ Helen Hayes
240 W 44th St.
307-4100.

⑬ Imperial
249 W 45th St.
239-6200.

⑭ Longacre
220 W 48th St.
239-6200.

⑮ Lunt–Fontanne
205 W 46th St.
307-4100.

⑯ Lyceum
149 W 45th St.
239-6200.

⑰ Majestic
245 W 44th St.
239-6200.

⑱ Marquis
1535 Broadway.
307-4100.

⑲ Martin Beck
302 W 45th St.
239-6200.

⑳ Minskoff
Broadway at 45th St.
307-4100.

㉑ Music Box
239 W 45th St.
239-6200.

㉒ Nederlander
208 W 41st St.
307-4100.

㉓ Neil Simon
250 W 52nd St.
307-4100.

㉔ Palace
1564 Broadway.
307-4100.

㉕ Plymouth
236 W 45th St.
239-6200.

㉖ Richard Rodgers
226 W 46th St.
307-4100.

㉗ Roundabout
1530 Broadway.
869-8400.

㉘ Royale
242 W 45th St.
239-6200.

㉙ St. James
246 W 44th St.
239-6200.

㉚ Shubert
225 W 44th St.
239-6200.

㉛ Virginia
245 W 52nd St.
239-6200.

㉜ Walter Kerr
219 W 48th St.
239-6200.

㉝ Winter Garden
1634 Broadway.
239-6200.

For other theaters *see p335.*

BALLET

AT THE HEART of the dance world is Lincoln Center (see p212), where the New York City Ballet performs pieces in the **New York State Theater**. This company was created by the legendary brilliant choreographer George Balanchine (see p46) and is probably still the best in the world. The current director, Peter Martins, was one of Balanchine's best dancers and continues the strict policy of ensemble dancing rather than "star turns." The season runs from November to February and late April to early June. The ballet school at the **Juilliard Dance Theater** also presents a spring workshop every year, and this is a good chance to see budding stars.

The American Ballet Theatre appears at the **Metropolitan Opera House**, which also hosts many visiting foreign companies, such as the Kirov, Bolshoi and Royal ballets. Its repertoire includes 19th-century classics, such as Swan Lake, and works by modern choreographers like Twyla Tharp and Paul Taylor.

CONTEMPORARY DANCE

NEW YORK is the center of many of the most important movements in modern dance. The **Dance Theater of Harlem** is world famous for its modern, traditional and ethnic productions. Other havens of experimental dance include the **92nd Street Y** and the **Merce Cunningham Studio** in Greenwich Village. The unusual **Dance Theater Workshop** has a packed program as well as an art gallery. **The Kitchen**, **La MaMa**, **Symphony Space** and **P.S. 122** are all multimedia venues with the latest in contemporary dance, performance art and avant-garde music. Choreographer Mark Morris's company performs at the **Manhattan Center**. **City Center** (see p146), a favorite venue for dance fans, used to house the New York City Ballet and the American Ballet Theater before Lincoln Center was built. As well as

featuring the Joffrey Ballet, City Center has held performances by all the great contemporary artists, including Alvin Ailey's blend of modern, jazz and blues and the companies of modern dance masters Merce Cunningham and Paul Taylor. Avoid the mezzanine as the view is restricted.

The city's single most active venue for dance is probably the **Joyce Theater**, where such well-established companies as the Feld Ballet, along with bold newcomers and visiting troupes, perform.

Each spring the Festival of Black Dance at the **Brooklyn Academy of Music (BAM)** (see p246) features everything from ethnic dance to hip-hop. During autumn the "Next Wave" festival of music and dance is held, celebrating international and American avant-garde dance and music. During winter the American Ballet Festival is held here.

During June, **New York University** (see p113) holds a Summer Residency Festival with lecture-demonstrations, rehearsals and performances, and **Dancing in the Streets** organizes summertime dance performances all over the city.

Throughout the month of August, **Lincoln Center Out of Doors** has a program of free dance events on the plaza, with such experimental groups as the American Tap Dance Orchestra.

The **World Financial Center** (see p69) has a free series at the Winter Garden, with such dance companies as the National Dance Institute.

At different times of the year, **Radio City Music Hall** holds several accomplished and spectacular shows, with different companies from all over the world. At Christmas and Easter, it features the Rockettes dance troupe.

Choreographers and dance companies frequently present works-in-progress and recitals to the public. Among the most interesting venue for these is **Alvin Ailey's Repertory Ensemble**. The **Hunter College Dance Company** performs new works by its student choreographers, and the **Isadora Duncan Inter-**national **Center for Dance** re-creates her original dances. For contemporary choreographers the best place to go is **Juilliard Dance Theater**.

PRICES

THEATER is extremely expensive to produce, and ticket prices tend to reflect this. Even Off- and Off-Off-Broadway tickets are not cheap anymore. At one time, all tickets to previews of new plays sold at a much-reduced price, but not so today. Preview tickets are easier to get hold of, though, and it's fun to see a show before the reviews are in so you're able to make up your own mind.

For Broadway theater you can expect to pay $60 or more; for musicals, up to $85; Off-Broadway, $25 to $40. For dance, $20 to $50 is the usual range, with up to $115 for the American Ballet Theatre. The **Music and Dance Booth** (see p329) in Bryant Park sells half-price day-of-performance tickets, worth the wait.

TIMES OF PERFORMANCE

THE GENERAL RULES for theater hours are: closed on Mondays (except for most musicals), with matinees on Wednesdays, Saturdays and sometimes Sundays. Matinees usually begin at 2pm, with evening performances at 8pm. Be sure to check the correct dates and times of the performance beforehand.

BACKSTAGE TOURS AND LECTURES

FOR THOSE INTERESTED in the mechanics of the theater and anecdotes on the stars, **Backstage on Broadway** conducts backstage tours. The **92nd Street Y** organizes talks giving an insider's view of the theater, with famous directors, actors and choreographers taking part. Writers are often invited along to read or discuss their current works. **Radio City Music Hall** also holds tours.

DIRECTORY

OFF-BROADWAY

92nd Street Y
Lexington Ave.
Map 17 A2.
☎ 415-5420.

Actors' Playhouse
100 Seventh Ave S.
Map 3 C1.
☎ 463-0060.

American Place
111 W 46th St.
Map 12 E5.
☎ 840-3074.

Brooklyn Academy of Music
30 Lafayette St., Brooklyn.
☎ (718) 636-4100.

HERE Art Center
145 6th Ave.
Map 4 D4.
☎ 647-0202.

Circle in the Square – Downtown
159 Bleecker St.
Map 4 D3.
☎ 254-6330.

Delacorte Theater
Central Park. (81st St.)
Map 16 E4.
☎ 861-7277.
Summer time only.

John Houseman
450 W 42nd St.
Map 7 C1.
☎ 967-9077.

Lambs Theater
130 W 44th St.
Map 12 E5.
☎ 997-1780.

Manhattan Theater Club
311 W 43rd St.
Map 8 D1.
☎ 399-3030.

New York Theater Workshop
79 E 4th St.
Map 4 F2.
☎ 460-5475.

Public Theater
425 Lafayette St.
Map 4 F2.
☎ 539-8500.

Sullivan Street Playhouse
181 Sullivan St.
Map 4 D3.
☎ 674-3838.

Symphony Space
2537 Broadway.
Map 15 C2.
☎ 864-5400.

Vivian Beaumont
Lincoln Center.
Map 11 C2.
☎ 362-7600.

OFF-OFF-BROADWAY

Bouwerie Lane Theater
330 Bowery. **Map** 4 F2.
☎ 677-0060.

The Kitchen
512 W 19th St. **Map** 7 C5.
☎ 255-5793.

Living Theater
☎ 865-3957.
Touring group. Call for info.

Performing Garage
33 Wooster St.
Map 4 E4.
☎ 966-3651.

Theater at St. Peter's Church
Citicorp Center, 619 Lexington Ave.
Map 13 A4.
☎ 935-5824.

PERFORMANCE THEATER

92nd Street Y
See Off-Broadway.

HERE
See Off-Broadway.

La MaMa
74a E 4th St. **Map** 4 F2.
☎ 475-7710.

P.S. 122
150 First Ave. **Map** 5 A1.
☎ 477-5288.

Public Theater
See Off-Broadway.

Symphony Space
See Off-Broadway.

THEATER SCHOOLS

The Actors' Studio
432 W 44th St.
Map 11 C5.
☎ 757-0870.

Neighborhood Playhouse School of the Theater
340 E 54th St.
Map 13 B4.
☎ 688-3770.

New Dramatists
424 W 44th. **Map** 11 C5.
☎ 757-6960.

DANCE

92nd Street Y
See Off-Broadway.

Alvin Ailey American Dance Center
211 W 61st St. **Map** 11 3C.
☎ 767-0590.

Brooklyn Academy of Music
See Off-Broadway.

City Center
131 W 55th St.
Map 12 E4.
☎ 581-7907.

Dance Theater of Harlem
466 W 152nd St.
☎ 690-2800.

Dance Theater Workshop
219 W 19th St. **Map** 8 E5.
☎ 924-0077.

Dancing in the Streets
131 Varick St. **Map** 4 D4.
☎ 989-6830.

Hunter College Dance Company
695 Park Ave.
Map 13 A1.
☎ 772-4490.

Isadora Duncan International Center for Dance
91 Claremont Ave.
Map 20 D2.
☎ 662-4591.

Joyce Theater
175 Eighth Ave at 19th St.
Map 8 D5.
☎ 242-0800.

Juilliard Dance Theater
60 Lincoln Center Plaza, W 65th St.
Map 11 C2.
☎ 769-7406.

The Kitchen
See Off-Off Broadway.

La MaMa
See Performance Theatre.

Lincoln Center Out of Doors
Lincoln Center, Broadway at 64th St. **Map** 11 C2.
☎ 362-6000.

Manhattan Center
311 W 34th St.
Map 8 D2.
☎ 307-4100.

Merce Cunningham Studio
55 Bethune St.
Map 3 B2.
☎ 255-8240.

Metropolitan Opera House
Lincoln Center, Broadway at 65th St.
Map 11 C2.
☎ 362-6000.

Music and Dance Booth
See page 329.

New York State Theater
Lincoln Center, Broadway at 65th St. **Map** 11 C2.
☎ 870-5570.

New York University
Tisch Hall, 111 Second Ave.
Map 4 F1.
☎ 998-1984.

P.S. 122
See Performance Theater.

Radio City Music Hall
50th St at Ave of the Americas. **Map** 12 F4.
☎ 247-4777.

Symphony Space
See Off-Broadway.

World Financial Center
West St between Vesey and Liberty St. **Map** 1 B2.
☎ 945-0505.

BACKSTAGE TOURS

92nd Street Y
See Off-Broadway.

Backstage on Broadway
☎ 575-8065.

Radio City Music Hall
☎ 632-4041.

Movies

NEW YORK is a film buff's paradise. Apart from new US releases, which show months in advance of other countries, many classic and foreign films are screened here.

The city has always been the testing ground for new developments in films, and it continues to be a hotbed of new and innovative talent. Many of the movies' most famous directors – Spike Lee, Martin Scorsese and Woody Allen – were born and raised in New York, and the city's influence can be seen in many of their films. They, and others, can often be seen filming on the streets of the city; many of New York's landmarks have become famous after appearing in films. Most of the TV networks based in New York offer free tickets to the taping of their shows. Watching a show, such as *The David Letterman Show,* is popular with visitors.

FIRST-RUN MOVIES

NEW YORK REVIEWS and box office returns are so vital to a film's success that most major American films have their premieres in Manhattan's theaters. First-run films are shown mainly at the City Cinema chains, Loews, United Artists and Cineplex Odeon, which are scattered around the city. Some theaters have recorded information giving the names and duration of the different films showing, with starting times and ticket prices.

Programs start at 10am or 11am and are repeated every two to three hours until midnight. You should expect to line up for most evening and weekend performances of the more popular films. Making reservations using a credit card is possible at some theaters for an additional charge of about $1 per ticket. Matinées (usually before 4pm) are easier to get into. Senior citizens pay a reduced price for tickets: the required age may be over 60, 62 or 65 depending on the policy of the theater.

NEW YORK FILM FESTIVAL

A HIGH POINT of the year for film buffs is the New York Film Festival, now in its third decade. Organized by the **Film Society of Lincoln Center**, the festival starts in late September and continues for two weeks at the many Lincoln Center theaters. Outstanding new films from the United States and abroad are entered in a competition that has no prizes except for the huge prestige of winning an award. Many of the films shown during the festival are later released and can usually be seen only in art houses.

FOREIGN FILMS AND ART HOUSES

FOR THE LATEST foreign and independent films, go to the **Angelika Film Center**, which has six screens and an upscale coffee bar. Other good places are the 4-screen **Rose Cinemas** at the Brooklyn Academy of Music, the stylish **Film Forum**, and **Lincoln Plaza Cinema**. The Plaza has a busy program of foreign and art films. For

FILM RATINGS

Films in the United States are graded as follows:
G General audiences; all ages admitted.
PG Parental guidance suggested; some material unsuitable for children.
PG-13 Parents strongly cautioned; some material inappropriate for children under age 13.
R Restricted. Children under 17 need to be accompanied by a parent or an adult guardian.
NC-17 No children under 17 admitted.

ON LOCATION

Many New York locations have played starring roles in films. Here are a few:

The Brill Building (1141 Broadway) contained Burt Lancaster's penthouse in *Sweet Smell of Success.*
The Brooklyn Bridge was a great backdrop in Spike Lee's *Mo' Better Blues.*
Brooklyn Heights and the **Metropolitan Opera** appeared in *Moonstruck.*
Central Park has shown up in countless films, including *Love Story* and *Marathon Man.*
55 Central Park West will be remembered as Sigourney Weaver's home in *Ghostbusters.*
Chinatown played a major role in *Year of the Dragon.*
The Dakota was where Mia Farrow lived in the classic *Rosemary's Baby.*
The Empire State Building is still standing after *King Kong*'s last heroic battle.
Grand Central Station is famous for Robert Walker's meeting with Judy Garland in *Under the Clock* and the magical ballroom sequence in *The Fisher King.*
Harlem's tenements were the seedy settings for the jazz musicians and dancers in *The Cotton Club.*
Katz's Deli was the setting for the café scene between Billy Crystal and Meg Ryan in *When Harry Met Sally…*
Little Italy appeared in *The Godfather I* and *II.*
Madison Square Garden was the setting for the dramatic climax of *The Manchurian Candidate.*
The Russian Tea Room was where Dustin Hoffman had lunch with his agent in *Tootsie.*
Tiffany & Co. was Audrey Hepburn's favorite shop in *Breakfast at Tiffany's.*
The United Nations Building featured in the thriller *North by Northwest.*
Washington Square Park was where Robert Redford and Jane Fonda walked *Barefoot in the Park.*

Asian, Indian and Chinese films, you should visit the **Asia Society**. The **French Institute** screens many French films with English subtitles and plays host to the Asian American International Film Festival. The **Quad Cinema** shows a wide selection of foreign films, often quite rare. **Cinema Village** runs special film events, such as the Festival of Animation.

The **Walter Reade Theater** houses the Film Society of the Lincoln Center, offering retrospectives of international movies as well as celebrations of contemporary works, such as the popular annual Spanish Cinema Now festival.

CLASSIC FILMS AND MUSEUMS

RETROSPECTIVES OF films by particular directors or featuring specific actors are shown at the **Public Theater** and the **Whitney Museum of American Art** *(see pp198–9)*. The extensive **Museum of Modern Art** *(see pp170-3)* is one of the best places to see a wide range of classic and silent movies. The museum also screens films on art and cultural subjects. The

American Museum of the Moving Image *(see p244)* screens old films and also has many exhibits of memorabilia from the film industry. The **Museum of Television & Radio** *(see p169)* has regular screenings of classic films; you can also see or hear specific television or radio programs. Students interested in classic, new and experimental movies will appreciate the really huge wealth of material at the **Anthology Film Archives**.

"Naturemax," which is at the **American Museum of Natural History**, shows environmental films using the most up-to-date technology – like IMAX, 70-mm film that has incredible clarity of image – projected onto huge screens.

On Saturday mornings, take your young filmgoers to the **Film Society of Lincoln Center,** where special children's shows are held.

TELEVISION SHOWS

A NUMBER of TV programs originate in New York. By writing several months in advance, you may be able to see one or more of them as they are being taped for broadcast. The highly popular David Letterman show is one

of the most popular. To request free tickets from **ABC** and **CBS**, write to each company individually. Another good source of free tickets is the Times Square Visitors Information Bureau *(see p352)*. On weekday mornings on Fifth Avenue around **Rockefeller Plaza**, free tickets for a number of TV programs are sometimes distributed by the program's production staff. There's absolutely no way that you can plan for this. It's simply a matter of good luck and being in the right place at the right time.

For those who want to get a glimpse behind the scenes of TV, NBC organizes tours around the studios, usually from 9am to 4pm on Monday to Saturday.

CHOOSING WHAT TO SEE

I F YOU FEEL bewildered by the huge range of films offered in New York, check the detailed listings in the art sections of *New York* magazine, the *New York Times*, the *Village Voice* and *The New Yorker*. "Moviefone," a free telephone service, gives recorded information of all films.

FILM HOUSES

ABC
See p329.

American Museum of the Moving Image
35th Ave and 36th St
Astoria, Queens.
(718) 784-0077.

American Museum of Natural History
Central Park W at 79th St.
Map 16 D5.
769-5650.

Angelika Film Center
18 W Houston St.
Map 4 E3. *995-2000.*

Anthology Film Archives
32 2nd Ave at 2nd St.
Map 5 C2.
505-5181.

Asia Society
725 Park Ave.
Map 13 A1.
517-2742.

Rose Cinemas
Brooklyn Academy of Music.
(718) 623-2770

CBS
See p329.

Cinema Village
22 E 12th St.
Map 4 F1.
924-3363.

Film Forum
209 W Houston St.
Map 3 C3.
727-8110.

French Institute
55 E 59th St.
Map 12 F3.
355-6160.

Lincoln Plaza Cinema
1886 Broadway.
Map 12 D2.
757-2280.

Moviefone
777-FILM.

Museum of Modern Art
11 W 53rd St.
Map 12 F4.
708-9480.

Museum of Television & Radio
25 W 52nd St.
Map 12 F4.
621-6600.

New York Film Festival
875-5600.

Public Theater
425 Lafayette St.
Map 4 F4.
539-8500.

Quad Cinema
34 W 13th St.
Map 4 D1.
225-8800.

Rockefeller Plaza
47th–50th St, 5th Ave.
Map 12 F5.

Walter Reade Theater/Film Society of the Lincoln Center
70 Lincoln Center Plaza.
Map 12 D2.
875-5600.

Whitney Museum of American Art
945 Madison Ave.
Map 13 A1.
570-3600.

Classical and Contemporary Music

NEW YORKERS HAVE A voracious appetite for music. Live concerts by the world's most celebrated musical performers may be enjoyed at famous halls throughout the year, and younger, newer artists and exotic imports always find receptive audiences.

TICKETS

FIND OUT WHAT you can choose from in New York by checking out the listings in the *New York Times* and the *Village Voice* and in *Time Out New York* and *The New Yorker* magazines.

CLASSICAL MUSIC

THE ORCHESTRA in residence at **Avery Fisher Hall** in Lincoln Center *(see p213)* is the New York Philharmonic. It is also the annual site for the popular "Mostly Mozart" series and Young People's Concerts. **Alice Tully Hall**, in Lincoln Center, is an acoustic gem and home to the Chamber Music Society.

One of the world's premier concert halls is the revamped **Carnegie Hall** *(see p146)*. Upstairs in the Weill Recital Hall there are quality performances for reasonable prices.

The **Brooklyn Academy of Music (BAM)** *(see p246)* is the home of the Brooklyn Philharmonic. The **New Jersey Performance Arts Center** in Newark is the newest star in the music venue scene. Classical music, dance, opera, jazz and world music all find an audience here.

The **Merkin Concert Hall** is host to some top chamber ensembles and soloists. For really excellent acoustics, go to the **Town Hall**. The **92nd Street Y's** Kaufmann Concert Hall also offers a lively menu of music and dance. Popular museum venues include the

Museum of Modern Art's sculpture garden for chamber and contemporary music. There's also the **Frick Collection** and **Symphony Space**, both of which offer a varied program ranging from gospel to Gershwin, classical to ethnic. The beautiful Grace Rainey Rogers Auditorium in the **Metropolitan Museum of Art** is for chamber music and soloists, while the **Florence Gould Hall**, at the Alliance Française, presents a varied program of chamber music and orchestral pieces.

The **Juilliard School of Music** and the **Mannes College of Music** are both considered excellent. Their students and faculties give free recitals, and there are shows by leading orchestras, chamber music groups and opera companies. The **Manhattan School of Music** offers an excellent program of over 400 events per year, from classical to jazz.

At 9:45am on the Thursdays of the New York Philharmonic concerts, the evening show is rehearsed at **Avery Fisher Hall** in Lincoln Center. Audiences are often admitted to listen, and rehearsal tickets are available at low prices. The **Kosciuszko Foundation** is a good venue for chamber music. The annual Chopin Competition is held here.

OPERA

DOMINATING the city's operatic scene is **Lincoln Center** *(see p212)*, home to the New York City Opera, and the **Metropolitan Opera House**, which has its own operatic company. The Met is the jewel in the crown, offering top international performers, but it is often criticized for being unadventurous. More accessible and dynamic is the New York City Opera. Its performances

range from *Madame Butterfly* to *South Pacific*, with subtitles above the stage to help the audience understand the plot. Lower-priced quality performances are staged by the up-and-coming singers at the **Village Light Opera Group**, the **Amato Opera Theater**, the **Kaye Playhouse** at Hunter College, and the students at the **Juilliard Opera Center** in Lincoln Center.

CONTEMPORARY MUSIC

NEW YORK is one of the most important places in the world for contemporary music. Exotic, ethnic and experimental music is played in many first-rate venues. The **Brooklyn Academy of Music (BAM)** is the standard bearer of the avant-garde. Each autumn the Academy holds a festival of music and dance called "Next Wave," which has helped launch many musical careers.

An annual festival of serious modern music called "Bang on a Can" is performed at the **Ethical Culture Society Hall** and features works by Steve Reich, Pierre Boulez and John Cage. Experimentalists, such as Davie Weinstein with his "audio-visual acid test" music – a mix of CD players, amplified instruments, keyboards and sound effects – perform at the **Dance Theater Workshop**.

Other venues include the **Asia Society** *(see p185)*, with its jewel of a theater for many visiting Asian performers, and **St. Peter's Church**.

BACKSTAGE TOURS

BEHIND-THE-SCENES tours are offered by **Lincoln Center** and **Carnegie Hall**.

RELIGIOUS MUSIC

FEW EXPERIENCES are more moving than an Easter concert in the vast **Cathedral of St. John the Divine** *(see pp224–5)*. Seasonal music is also offered at many of the city's museums and in almost every other available space – from Grand Central Terminal's

---

CLASSICAL RADIO

New York has three FM radio stations that broadcast classical music: WQXR at 96.3, the National Public Radio station WNYC at 93.9 and WKCR 89.9.

main concourse (see pp154–5) to bank and hotel lobbies. For jazz vespers in a stunning modern building, visit **St. Peter's Church** (see p175). Most of these concerts are free for everyone, but you are encouraged to contribute.

ALFRESCO

FREE OUTDOOR concerts during the summer can be found in **Bryant Park**, **Washington Square** and **Lincoln Center's Damrosch Park**. The annual concerts on Central Park's Great Lawn and in Brooklyn's Prospect Park are performed by the New York Philharmonic and the Metropolitan Opera. In good weather, keep a look out for all the strolling musicians who perform at South Street Seaport, right on the steps of the **Metropolitan Museum of Art** (see pp188–95) and also around Washington Square.

MUSIC FOR FREE

THROUGHOUT the year free musical performances are given at the **Citicorp Atrium** (see p175), **The Cloisters** (see pp234–7) and the **Whitney Museum's** Philip Morris Building (see p150). Sunday-afternoon recitals are held at **The Dairy** in Central Park (see p206). You will also find music in the Winter Garden and Plaza of the **World Financial Center** (see p69) and **Federal Hall** (see p68). At **Lincoln Center**, be sure not to miss the exciting free performances held in the **Juilliard School of Music**.

Other very popular venues include the **Greenwich House Music School** (where student recitals are free) and the **Theodore Roosevelt Birthplace** (see p125).

Free concerts and talks in churches include **St. Paul's Chapel** and **Trinity Church Wall Street**. (see p68).

MUSIC VENUES

92nd Street Y
1395 Lexington Ave.
Map 17 A2.
(996-1100.

Amato Opera Theater
319 Bowery at 2nd St.
Map 4 F2.
(228-8200.

Asia Society
70th St at Park Ave.
Map 13 A1.
(517-2742.

Backstage Tours
(903-9790.

Brooklyn Academy of Music
30 Lafayette Ave, Brooklyn.
((718) 636-4100.

Bryant Park
Map 8 F1.
(983-4143.

Carnegie Hall
881 7th Ave. **Map** 12 E3.
(247-7800.

Cathedral of St John the Divine
Amsterdam Ave and 112th St.
Map 20 E4.
(316-7400.

Citicorp Atrium
Lexington Ave at 53rd St.
Map 13 A4.
(559-9095.

The Cloisters
Fort Tryon Park.
(923-3700.

The Dairy
Central Park.
Map 12 F2.
(794-6564.

Dance Theater Workshop
See Dance p335.

Ethical Culture Society Hall
2 W 64th St. **Map** 12 D2.
(874-5210.

Federal Hall
Broad St at Wall St.
Map 1 C3.
(866-2086.

Florence Gould Hall (at the Alliance Française)
55 E 59th St. **Map** 13 A3.
(355-6160.

Frick Collection
1 E 70th St. **Map** 12 F1.
(288-0700.

Greenwich House Music School
46 Barrow St. **Map** 3 C2.
(242-4770.

Kaye Playhouse
695 Park Ave.
Map 13 A1
(772-4448.

Kosciuszko Foundation
15 E 65th St. **Map** 12 F2
(734-2130.

Lincoln Center
155 W 65th St.
Map 11 C2.
(546-2656.

Alice Tully Hall
(875-5050.

Avery Fisher Hall
(875-5030.

Damrosch Park
(875-5596.

Juilliard Opera Center
(769-7406.

Juilliard School of Music
(799-5000.

Metropolitan Opera House
(362-6000.

Manhattan School of Music
120 Claremont Ave.
Map 20 E2.
(749-2802.

Mannes College of Music
150 W 85th St.
Map 15 D3.
(580-0210.

Merkin Hall
129 W 67th St. **Map** 11 D2.
(501-3330.

Metropolitan Museum of Art
5th Ave at 82nd St.
Map 16 F4.
(570-3949.

Museum of Modern Art
Sculpture garden
11 W 53rd St. **Map** 12 F4.
(708-9480.

New Jersey Performance Arts Center
1 Center St, Newark, NJ
(888-466-5722.

NYC On Stage
1501 Broadway.
Map 12 D2.
(768-1818.

St Paul's Chapel
Broadway at Fulton St.
Map 1 C2.
(602-0876.

St Peter's Church
54th St at Lexington Ave.
Map 13 A4.
(935-2200.

Symphony Space
2537 Broadway.
Map 15 C2.
(864-5400.

Theodore Roosevelt Birthplace
28 E 20th St. **Map** 8 F5.
(260-1616.

Town Hall
123 W 43rd St. **Map** 8 E1.
(840-2824.

Trinity Church
Broadway at Wall St.
Map 1 C3.
(602-0800.

Village Light Opera Group
227 W 27th St. **Map** 8 E3.
(243-6281.

Washington Square
Map 4 D2.

Whitney Museum
Park Ave at 42nd St.
Map 9 A1 (878-2550.

World Financial Center
West St at Vesey St
(945-0505.

Rock, Jazz and World Music

THERE'S EVERY IMAGINABLE form of music in New York, from international stadium rock to the sounds of the 1960s, from Dixieland jazz or country blues, soul and world music to talented street musicians. The city's music scene changes at a dizzying pace, with many new arrivals (and departures) almost daily, so there's no way to predict what you may find when you arrive. Musical standards also vary.

PRICES AND PLACES

AT CLUBS, EXPECT a cover charge and possibly a one- or two-drink minimum (at $5 or more) requirement. The prices for concerts range from $8 to $75 for the major venues, with about $12 to $25 the norm. Many of the smaller concert venues are arranged for seating in certain areas and dancing in others – often with different prices for each.

The top international bands are usually to be found in the huge arenas at **Shea Stadium** in Flushing Meadows or at the **Meadowlands** and **Madison Square Garden** *(see p133)*. Here the likes of Elton John, Bruce Springsteen and the Stones perform. Tickets for these events sell out very fast, so buy as many as you need as soon as you hear of a concert, unless you don't mind paying a lot for them through an agent or a scalper. During the summer, big outdoor concerts are held at Jones Beach *(see p253)* and **Central Park SummerStage**.

Medium-sized venues for mainstream bands include the Art Deco palace of **Radio City Music Hall** and the **Beacon Theater**, by far the most popular live-music venue in the Upper West Side area.

Many leading rock venues are basically bars with music. They will often book different bands every night, so check the listings in the *New York Times*, *Village Voice* or *Time Out New York* or phone the place to find out what's happening and at what time during that particular week.

ROCK MUSIC

ROCK COMES IN many forms: gothic, industrial, techno, psychedelic, post-punk funk,

indie and alternative music are among the latest crazes. If you prefer to see more of a band than a giant video screen, the following venues have a much more intimate, friendly atmosphere. **CBGB**, New York's sleazy, dungeon-like cradle of new wave, launched such bands as Talking Heads and Blondie in the 1970s and is still a showcase for new indie bands.

The **Knitting Factory** has live jazz and new music. The **Limelight** is a good bet for the latest sounds and the newest groups. **The Mercury Lounge** is another of the most happening music spots, featuring hot new bands being groomed for MTV. **Tramps** is in a loft where relatively unknown rock groups play, as do the occasional famous country and blues musicians.

Mega-star Bruce Springsteen played his first recorded concert in the 1970s at the **Bottom Line**, and it still remains a record industry showcase for new and up-and-coming bands.

Bands appearing at the **Acme Underground** are mostly up-and-coming acts, given a chance to find fame in the rock music world. Located in the old meat-packing district, **The Cooler** is a hip new home for ravers. Alternative rock, avant-garde jazz and innovative DJs make this a great place to dance. The subterranean space is huge and wild.

The **Hammerstein Ballroom** at the Manhattan Center in midtown hosts techno, progressive and alternative bands. **Roulette** has avant-garde sounds performed by such appropriately named groups as Woof, Quack and Miaow.

JAZZ

THE ORIGINAL Cotton Club and Connie's Inn, which were once crucibles of jazz, are long gone, as are the former speakeasies of West 52nd Street. But living legends such as Maynard Ferguson still play, while others carry on the old traditions of Dave Brubeck, Les Paul, Duke Ellington, Count Basie and other big bands.

In Greenwich Village, jazz temples from the 1930s survive and continue to foster great music. Foremost among them is the **Village Vanguard**, where some of the most highly revered jazz memories linger and newer ones are being fashioned by such groups as the McCoy Tyner and Branford Marsalis trios. **Blue Note** hosts big bands at high prices but has an excellent atmosphere.

The **Knitting Factory** and the well-known **Bottom Line** tend to feature much more contemporary and avant-garde jazz, while **Zinno** offers an appealing blend of northern Italian food and guest appearances by some top-flight musicians.

Birdland features ex-Mingus alumni and musicians such as Bud Shank. Expect the great sounds of Dixieland jazz or small unknown groups in **Cajun**, a friendly New Orleans–style restaurant.

Café Carlyle, an East Side spot famed for mellow jazz pianist and singer Bobby Short, now also features clarinetist-filmmaker Woody Allen playing with Eddy Davis and his New Orleans Jazz Band

One of the hottest tickets in town is the Sunday jazz brunch at **Sweet Basil**, which often features the trumpeter Doc Cheatham and his band. A sophisticated newcomer, club and restaurant **Iridium** features progressive jazz. **Fez Under Time Café** presents the Mingus Big Band workshop every Thursday. If you're in New York in June, be sure not to miss the annual **JVC Jazz Festival**, where such famous jazz and blues icons as Oscar Peterson, Nina Simone and B.B. King play at various clubs all around Manhattan. For information, phone ahead.

Jazz at Lincoln Center events are scheduled throughout the year, including concerts by the renowned Lincoln Center Jazz Orchestra under the direction of Wynton Marsalis. The music ranges from Duke Ellington's New York sounds to Johnny Dodds' traditional New Orleans-style jazz.

FOLK AND COUNTRY MUSIC

FOLK, ROCK MUSIC and R&B (rhythm and blues) can be found at the famed but much-faded **Bitter End**, which once

showcased James Taylor and Joni Mitchell but now specializes in new talent as does **Kenny's Castaways**.

The **Fast Folk Café** is an atmospheric place with a "New Voices Showcase" every month. Also good for folk music, and worth checking out, is the **Sidewalk Café**.

BLUES, SOUL AND WORLD MUSIC

FOR BLUES, soul and world music, options include the **Apollo Theater** in Harlem (see p228). For nearly 60 years the near-legendary Wednesday Amateur Nights have been responsible for "discovering" and launching stars such as James Brown and Dionne Warwick.

The **Cotton Club** is no longer located in its original spot, but it offers good blues, jazz and a Sunday real Gospel brunch on Harlem's main street. **Chicago B.L.U.E.S.** is now considered to be best blues club in the city and you'll hear more than Chicago sounds there. Don't miss "Mambo Mondays" with Nestor Torres at **SOB's** (Sounds of Brazil), a world music club specializing in the many Afro-Latin rhythms. **Terra Blues** is a bar which doubles up as an interesting music venue. The blues artists that appear can range from authentic Chicago acoustic players to more modern blues acts. Finally, there's **Wetlands**, for classic soul and 60's sounds.

DIRECTORY

MUSIC VENUES

Beacon Theater
2124 Broadway.
Map 15 C5.
496-7070.

Central Park SummerStage
Rumsey Playfield.
Map 12 F1.
360-2777.

Madison Square Garden
7th Ave 33rd St.
Map 8 E2.
465-MSG1.

Meadowlands
50 Route 120
East Rutherford, N.J.
(201) 935-3900.

Radio City Music Hall
See Dance p335.

Shea Stadium
126th St at Roosevelt Ave.
Flushing, Queens.
(718) 507-8499.

ROCK MUSIC

Acme Underground
9 Great Jones St.
Map 4 F2. 677-6963.

Bottom Line
15 W 4th St. Map 4 D2.
228-6300.

CBGB
315 Bowery. Map 4 F2.
982-4052.

The Cooler
416 W 14th St. Map 3 B1.
229-0785.

Knitting Factory
74 Leonard St. Map 4 E5.
219-3055.

Limelight
660 6th Ave. Map 8 F4.
807-7780.

Mercury Lounge
217 E Houston St.
Map 5 A3. 260-4700.

Hammerstein Ballroom
311 W 34th St. Map 8 D2.
564-4882.

Roulette
228 W Broadway. Map 4 E5.
219-8242.

Tramps
51 W 21st St. Map 8 F4.
727-7788.

JAZZ

Birdland
315 W 44th St. Map 12 D5.
581-3080.

Blue Note
131 W 3rd St. Map 4 D2.
475-8592.

Café Carlyle
35 E 76th St. Map 17 A5.
570-7189.

Cajun
129 8th Ave. Map 8 D5.
691-6174.

Fez Under Time Café
380 Lafayette St. Map 4 F2.
533-7000.

Iridium
48 W 63rd St. Map 12 D2.
582 2121.

Jazz at Lincoln Center
875-5299.

JVC Jazz Festival
501-1390.

Knitting Factory
See Rock Music.

Sweet Basil
88 7th Ave S. Map 8 E5.
242-1785.

Village Vanguard
178 7th Ave South.
Map 3 C1.
255-4037.

Zinno
126 W 13th St. Map 3 C1.
924-5182.

FOLK AND COUNTRY

Bitter End
147 Bleecker St. Map 4 E3.
673-7030.

Fast Folk Café
41 North Moore St.
Map 4 D5. 274-1636.

Kenny's Castaways
157 Bleecker St. Map 4 E3.
473-9870.

Sidewalk Café
94 Ave A.
Map 5 B2.
473-7373.

BLUES, SOUL AND WORLD MUSIC

Apollo Theater
253 W 125 St.
Map 19 A1.
531-5305.

Chicago B.L.U.E.S.
73 8th Ave.
Map 3 C1.
924-9755.

Cotton Club
656 W 125th St.
Map 22 F2.
663-7980.

SOB's
204 Varick St.
Map 4 D3.
243-4940.

Terra Blues
149 Bleecker St.
Map 4 E3.
777-7776.

Wetlands
161 Hudson St.
Map 4 D5.
966-4225.

Clubs, Dance Halls and Piano Bars

NEW YORK'S NIGHTLIFE and club scene is legendary, and deservedly so. Whatever your preference – be it for a noisy disco, stand-up comedy or the soothing melodies of a Harry Connick, Jr., sound-alike in a piano bar – you'll be really amazed at the choice. There was a rash of big discos in the 1980s, but relatively few of these have survived the recent trend toward the comfort and style of supper clubs.

WHEN AND WHERE

THE BEST and hippest time for clubbing is during the week – it's also a lot cheaper. Take a fair amount of money and some ID to prove you're old enough to drink (which is over 21) – but beware, all the drinks are very expensive.

The trendiest clubs roll on until 4am or later. Fashions and club nights change all the time, so go to Tower Records on Broadway for all the latest leaflets, check club details in the listings magazines *(see p328)* and read the *Village Voice*. The most interesting places nowadays are often popularized by word of mouth. Your best bet is to go somewhere like the **Limelight** and hope someone will tell you where to go on to – often invitations to other clubs are given out there as well.

DANCING

NEW YORKERS thrive on music and dancing. The dance floors available all around the city range from the always-crowded **The Greatest Bar on Earth** – for jazz, dancing, a 107th-floor view and snacks – to a few huge basketball-court-sized places, such as **Roseland**. This has ballroom dancing every Thursday and Sunday and is New York's classic Broadway ballroom, revealing a tantalizing glimpse of older Broadway culture. It also has a good megasize, 700-seater, restaurant with a fully stocked bar.

For mainstream danceable music, the **Rainbow Room** is reliable. If you want to sample something really different, try **Barbetta**, where Boris and Yvgeny play a combination of gypsy music and Viennese waltzes. The **Copacabana**, which when it originally opened starred the likes of Dean Martin and Frank Sinatra, is now a disco alternating with live bands. It also stages wild parties on the last Thursday of every month, with go-go boys, drag queens and disco divas.

The **Limelight**, which is a mixed venue with ground-floor dancing and spectator seats up in the balconies, was renovated in 1998, and the new, improved club is well worth a visit. It always advertises upcoming events. To reserve tickets ahead, call Ticketmaster *(see p329)*.

Some of the most popular clubs for disco dancing, which also feature the latest music groups, are Ritz, Acme Underground, Marquee, CBGB, Tramps, and the Knitting Factory *(see p340)*. Few of these have strict membership policies. Be sure to get there early and be prepared to line up for entry.

NIGHTCLUBS

NIGHTCLUBS are the places to see a show. New York shows are less flashy than in the 1940s and 1950s but still have a variety of acts. Expect to pay a cover charge; many of the clubs also require that you have at least two drinks.

Catch a Rising Star adjoins a Spanish restaurant and often has vocalists singing hits from Broadway musicals. **Maxim's** usually has one room open that features revues, plus another with singers. For some spectacular views, an elegant room, revues plus singers, go to the **Rainbow & Stars**. **Swing Street Café** is a theater supper club. The chic **Supper Club** surrounds you with gold lamé draperies and features big band music downstairs. Cabaret singers perform upstairs in their intimate Blue Room. **Tatou** is very expensive to eat in, and acts range from jazz to disco. Central Park has a revered indoors/outdoors club, **Tavern on the Green**, which offers jazz in its Chestnut Room.

GAY AND LESBIAN VENUES

THE PAST TWO decades have seen the arrival of clubs and restaurants specifically geared to gay and lesbian clientele. Although the entertainment is varied, transvestite revues predominate. Though all the clubs are open to heterosexuals and often to the opposite sex, too, some can make "interlopers" feel extremely uncomfortable. The current popular gay cabarets include the **Duplex**, which has a mix of stand-up comics, comedy sketches and singers. The very fashionable nightclubs and bars for men include the trendy uptown **Town House**, a piano bar with restaurant, and **Julius**, known as Greenwich Village's top neighborhood bar. **Don't Tell Mama** is a long-established gay bar, that presents good musical revues and spoofs.

Henrietta Hudson and **Crazy Nanny's** cater solely to women, as does **Grolier**. **Marie's Crisis** piano bar is a mixed venue and **Splash** is open daily with a happy hour between 5pm and 9pm.

The *Village Voice* has good listings of what's happening in the gay communities, and the *Gay Yellow Pages* covers the gay scene. If you need more information, phone the **Gay and Lesbian Switchboard**.

COMEDY SHOWCASES

MANY OF New York's best current comedy clubs or showcases have evolved from earlier "improvisational" comedy. Leading the pack are the **Boston Comedy Club**, the **Original Improv** and

Caroline's. Also good for a visit are the **Comic Strip**, **Stand-Up New York**, **NY Comedy Club**, **55 Grove St.**, **Dangerfield's**, and **Comedy Cellar**. Each club presents a nightly batch of comics.

PIANO BARS AND HOTEL "ROOMS"

C ABARETS HAVE become a New York institution. Such cozy, just-for-listening places are often called "rooms" and are located in hotels. Most operate from Tuesday to Saturday (usually with a cover charge or drink minimum) and most take credit cards.

The **Algonquin's** Oak Room has song stylists such as Michael Feinstein. For a classic piano lounge with a panoramic Manhattan view, visit the **Beekman Tower**. The "long-distance hummer" award goes to Bobby Short, who has played his piano for over 25 years at the Café Carlyle in the **Carlyle Hotel**. Woody Allen often plays there with Eddy Davis's New Orleans Jazz Band. In the same hotel is Bemelman's Bar, with whimsical murals and attracting a relaxed crowd who enjoy first-class crooners.

Hear tinkling keys and fine songs in the lounge of the **Drake Swissôtel**. Performers such as Barbara Cook play the **Hilton Hotel's** Mirage Lounge, and Café Pierre's singer-pianist Kathleen Landis holds court at the **Pierre Hotel**. Piano music can also be heard at the Ambassador Lounge in the **Regal UN Plaza Hotel**.

DIRECTORY

DANCING

Barbetta
321 W 46th St.
Map 12 D5.
📞 246-9171.

Copacabana
617 W 57th St.
Map 11 B3.
📞 582-2672.

The Greatest Bar on Earth
1 World Trade Center.
Map 1 B2.
📞 524-7000.

Knitting Factory
See p341.

Limelight
See p341.

Rainbow Room
30 Rockefeller Plaza.
Map 12 F4.
📞 632-5100.

Roseland
239 W 52nd St.
Map 12 E4.
📞 247-0200.

NIGHTCLUBS

Catch a Rising Star
253 W 28th St.
Map 8 E3.
📞 244-3005.

Maxim's
680 Madison Ave.
Map 13 A3.
📞 751-5111.

Rainbow & Stars
30 Rockefeller Plaza.
Map 12 F4.
📞 632-5000.

Supper Club
240 W 47th St.
Map 12 D5.
📞 921-1940.

Swing Street Café
253 E 52nd St.
Map 13 B4.
📞 754-4862.

Tatou
151 E 50th St. Map 13 A4.
📞 753-1144.

Tavern on the Green
Central Park west side at 67th St.
Map 12 D2.
📞 873-3200.

GAY AND LESBIAN VENUES

Crazy Nanny's
21 7th Ave South.
Map 3 C1.
📞 366-6312.

Don't Tell Mama
343 W 46th St.
Map 12 D5.
📞 757-0788.

Duplex
61 Christopher St.
Map 3 C2.
📞 255-5438.

Gay and Lesbian Switchboard
📞 989-0999.

Henrietta Hudson
438 Hudson St.
Map 3 C3.
📞 243-9079.

Julius
159 W 10th St.
Map 4 D1.
📞 929-9672.

Marie's Crisis Café
59 Grove St.
Map 3 C2.
📞 243-9323.

Town House
236 E 58th St.
Map 13 B4.
📞 754-4649.

COMEDY SHOWCASES

55 Grove St
Map 3 C2.
📞 366-5438.

Boston Comedy Club
82 W 3rd St. Map 4 D2.
📞 477-1000.

Caroline's
1626 Broadway.
Map 12 E5.
📞 757-4100.

Comedy Cellar
117 MacDougal St.
Map 4 D2.
📞 254-3480.

Comic Strip
1568 2nd Ave.
Map 17 B4.
📞 861-9386.

Dangerfield's
1118 1st Ave.
Map 13 C3.
📞 593-1650.

The Improv
346 W 46th St.
Map 12 D5.
📞 475-6147.

NY Comedy Club
241 E 34th St. Map 9 B4.
📞 696-5233.

Stand-Up New York
236 W 78th St.
Map 15 C5.
📞 595-0850.

PIANO BARS AND HOTEL "ROOMS"

Algonquin Hotel
Oak Room, 59 W 44th St.
Map 12 F5.
📞 840-6800.

Beekman Tower
3 Mitchell Pl.
Map 13 C5.
📞 355-7300.

Carlyle Hotel
35 E 76th St.
Map 17 A5.
📞 744-1600.

Drake Swissôtel
67 E 56th St.
Map 13 A3.
📞 421-0900.

Hilton Hotel
Mirage Lounge. 53 Ave of the Americas. Map 12 E4.
📞 586-7000.

Pierre Hotel
Café Pierre, 2 E 61st St.
Map 12 F3.
📞 940-8185.

Regal UN Plaza Hotel
1 UN Plaza at 44th St.
Map 13 C5.
📞 758-1234.

Sports and Fitness

NEW YORKERS ARE SPORTS CRAZY, and there are activities to suit every taste. If you're a doer not a viewer, you can choose from health clubs and horseback riding to pumping iron and swimming, playing tennis or jogging. Spectator sports are provided by two professional baseball teams, two hockey teams, a basketball team and two football teams, while for tennis fans there are the US Open and Virginia Slims tournaments.

TICKETS

THE EASIEST WAY to get hold of your tickets is through Ticketron or Ticketmaster (see p329). For the big games, you may need a ticket agent.

FOOTBALL

THE CITY'S two professional football teams are the New York Giants and the New York Jets. They both play their home games across the river at **Giants Stadium** in New Jersey. Tickets for the Giants are almost impossible to obtain, but they may be available for the Jets.

BASEBALL

TO CAPTURE the essence of this American institution, first time spectators should go to **Yankee Stadium**, home of the New York Yankees. **Shea Stadium**, the Mets' base, is also convenient. The season runs from April to September.

BASKETBALL

THE NEW YORK KNICKS play their home games from October to April at **Madison Square Garden**; you may also catch the ever-popular Harlem Globetrotters there.

BICYCLING

THE BEST PLACE to cycle is in Central Park during the weekend, when it is closed to cars. Bikes may be rented from **West Side Bicycle Store**.

BOXING

PROFESSIONAL boxing matches are more often seen on Paramount's wide TV screen than in the flesh at **Madison Square Garden**.

FITNESS CENTERS, GYMS AND HEALTH CLUBS

MOST MAJOR HOTELS have fitness centers. Check out the **Chelsea Piers Sports & Entertainment Complex**; there's something for everyone at this enormous facility. Many of the commercial gyms and health clubs are open only to those with an annual membership, but it is possible to use the facilities at a **Y** if you are a member.

GOLF

PRACTICE YOUR swing at the **Randalls Island Golf Center, Chelsea Golf Club** or play mini-golf at the **Wollman Memorial Rink**. The city owns several courses in the boroughs, such as **Pelham Bay Park** in the Bronx and **Silver Lake** on Staten Island. To make a reservation, phone 225-GOLF.

HORSE RIDING AND RACING

THE ONLY riding stable in Manhattan is **Claremont Riding Academy**. You can ride in its indoor arena or go trotting in Central Park.

Harness racing, in which horses pull sulkies (small carts), takes place year-round at **Yonkers Raceway**. Flat races are held daily, except Tuesday, October to May at the **Aqueduct Race Track**, and May to October at the **Belmont Park Race Track**.

ICE HOCKEY

THE ICE FLIES, as do the players' fists, when the New York Rangers meet their competition at **Madison Square Garden**. The season runs from October to April.

ICE-SKATING

THERE ARE TWO good places to go ice skating out of doors. One is the **Rockefeller Plaza Rink**, which looks beautiful at Christmas. The other is **Wollman Rink**, which has ice-skating in winter, roller skating and mini-golf. For indoor sites, try the **Sky Rink** at Chelsea Piers or **Ice Studio**.

INDOOR SPORTS AND RACQUET GAMES

A LARGE SPORTS complex called **Hackers, Hitters & Hoops** has batting cages, mini-golf, Ping-Pong, racquetball and other activities. There's also the **Printing House Fitness & Racquet Center** and **Chelsea Piers**.

JOGGING

SOME PARKS are safe for joggers, others are not, so be guided by your concierge. None is safe after dark, at dusk or before dawn. The most popular route is around the reservoir in Central Park. The **International Running Center** has weekly running clinics and races.

MARATHON

TO BE ONE of the 25,000 who enter the New York Marathon, you have to sign up six months in advance. The race is held on the first Sunday in November. Phone 860-4455 for information.

SPORTS BARS

TOP BARS include **The Sporting Club**, which has a huge electronic scoreboard with right-up-to-the-second information, plus nine life-sized TV screens. At **Mickey Mantle's** you can watch the action on ten elephantine video screens.

SWIMMING

MANY MANHATTAN hotels have pools with free access during your stay. You can also swim and surf at the Surfside 3 Maritime Center at Chelsea Piers overlooking the Hudson River.

Try the spectacular Jones Beach State Park (see p253) along Long Island's shoreline.

TENNIS

THE TOP TENNIS tournament in New York is the US Open, played each August at the **National Tennis Center**. Also good is the women's Virginia Slims Championships in November at **Madison Square Garden** (see p133).

If you want to play tennis rather than watch it, look in the telephone directory under "Tennis Courts: Public and Private." For private courts, you can expect to pay up to about $50 an hour. For public courts, you will need a $50 permit, available from the **NY City Parks & Recreation Department**. You will also need an identity card before you are allowed to play. Courts must be reserved at least a week in advance. **Crosstown Tennis** and the **Manhattan Plaza Tennis Center** are two possibilities.

TRACK AND FIELD

THE MILLROSE GAMES are normally held in early February, and the Amateur Athletic Union (AAU) championships, where most of the top athletes usually appear, are held in late February at **Madison Square Garden**.

OTHER ACTIVITIES

IN CENTRAL PARK, options include renting rowboats from **Loeb Boathouse** or playing chess – pick up the pieces from The Dairy (see p206). Bowling is available at the **AMF Chelsea Piers Bowl**. Pool can be played in bars and pool halls such as **Chelsea Billiards**.

Farther afield, try a deep-sea fishing trip from **Sheepshead Bay** in Brooklyn.

SPORTS ADDRESSES

Aqueduct Race Track
Ozone Park, Queens.
(718) 641-4700.

Belmont Park Race Track
Hempstead Turnpike,
Long Island.
(718) 641-4700.

Chelsea Billiards
54 W 21st St.
Map 8 E4.
989-0096.

Claremont Riding Academy
175 W 89th St.
Map 15 C3.
724-5100.

Crosstown Tennis
14 W 31st St.
Map 8 F3.
947-5780.

Giants Stadium
Meadowlands
East Rutherford, N.J.
(201) 935-8222.
New York Giants.
(201) 935-8500.
New York Jets.

Hackers, Hitters & Hoops
123 W 18th St.
Map 8 E5.
929-7482.

Ice Studio
1034 Lexington Ave.
Map 17 A5.
535-0304.

International Running Center
9 E 89th St.
Map 17 A3.
860-4455.

Chelsea Piers Sports & Entertainment Complex
Piers 59- 62 at 11th Ave.
Map 7 B4-5.
336-6800.

Loeb Boathouse
Central Park. Map 16 F5.
517-4723.

Madison Square Garden
7th Ave at 33rd St.
Map 8 E2.
465-MSG1.

Manhattan Plaza Racquet Club
450 W 43rd St. Map 7 C1.
594-0554.

Mickey Mantle's
42 Central Park South.
Map 12 E3.
688-7777.

National Tennis Center
Flushing Meadow Park,
Queens.
(718) 760-6200.

NY City Parks & Recreation Department
Arsenal Building
64th St and 5th Ave.
Map 12 F2. 408-0100.

Pelham Bay Park
Bronx.
(718) 885-3368.

Plaza Rink
Rockefeller Center.
1 Rockefeller Plaza, 5th Ave.
Map 12 F5.
332-7654.

Printing House Fitness & Racquet Center
421 Hudson St. Map 3 C3.
243-3777.

Randalls Island Golf Center
Randalls Island.
Map 22 F2.
427-5689.

Shea Stadium
126th St at Roosevelt Ave,
Flushing, Queens.
(718) 507-TIXX or
(718) 507-8499.

Sheepshead Bay
(For information on fishing trips call Mike's Tackle & Bait Shop.)
(718) 646-9261.

Silver Lake
915 Victory Blvd
Staten Island.
(718) 447-5686 or
(718) 225-4653.

The Sporting Club
99 Hudson St.
Map 4 D5.
219-0900.

West Side Bicycle Store
231 W 96th St .
Map 15 C2.
663-7531.

Wollman Memorial Rink
Central Park,
5th Ave at 59th St.
Map 12 F2.
396-1010.

Yankee Stadium
River Ave at 161st St
The Bronx.
(718) 293-6000.

YMCA 47th St
224 E 47th St.
Map 13 B5.
756-9600

Y at 92nd St
1395 Lexington Ave.
Map 17 A2.
427-6000.

YMCA West Side
5 W 63rd St.
Map 12 D2.
787-4400.

Yonkers Raceway
Yonkers
Westchester County.
(914) 968-4200.

Late-Night New York

NEW YORK IS INDEED a city that never sleeps. If you wake up in the middle of the night – with a craving for fresh bread, a need to be entertained or an urge to watch the sun rise over the Manhattan skyline – there are always plenty of options to choose from.

BARS AND CLUBS

THE BEST and friendliest bars are often the Irish ones. Sing-alongs happen at **Mitch's Place** on Thursdays, and daily (except Mondays) at **Tommy Makem's**. Have a late-night dry martini at the **Temple Bar**. The best piano bars are in the hotels: try the Café Carlyle in the **Carlyle Hotel** or the Oak Room in the **Algonquin Hotel**.

For hot American jazz until 4am, go to **Sweet Basil** or the **Blue Note**. Traditional jazz and swing entertain the diners and dancers at the **Rainbow Room** and the **Red Blazer Too**. **Cornelia Street Café** is a snug and lively nook for prose, poetry and theater readings. Poetry, theater and Latin music can be found at the **Nuyorican Poets Café**.

MIDNIGHT MOVIES

SPECIAL MIDNIGHT showings and a youthful crowd can be found at the Angelika Film Center and the Film Forum (see pp336–7). New multiplexes often show movies at midnight on weekends

SHOPS

SHAKESPEARE & Company Booksellers on Broadway and the St. Mark's Bookshop are open until late. The Upper West Side branch of HMV is open until midnight, the East Side branch until 10pm. Both Tower Records branches shut at midnight, as does Gryphon Records. Bleecker Bob's Golden Oldies Record Shop stays open until 3am on weekends (see Shopping pp322-3). Late-night video stores include the enormous **Palmer Video Store** and **Mrs. Hudson's Video Store**, both of which are located on Hudson.

Late-night video stores include the enormous **Palmer Video Store** on Hudson and **Video Access**.

Among the many Village clothing stores that stay open late on weekends are the **Antique Boutique** (open until midnight) and **Trash and Vaudeville** (open till 8pm on Fridays and Saturdays). For aspirin and other health essentials, **Rite Aid Pharmacy** is open 24 hours a day and **Plaza Pharmacy** until 11pm every night.

TAKE-OUT FOOD AND GROCERIES

A FEW TAKE-OUT food stores are open 24 hours a day, including the **Delmonico Gourmet Food Market** and the **West Side Supermarket**. Many Korean greengrocers also stay open all night. The **Food Emporium** is a supermarket chain open until midnight (around the clock at the York Avenue branch). On Saturdays, **Zabar's** stays open until midnight. Liquor stores are usually open until 10pm and many deliver.

For the best in bagels, go to **H & H Bagels East**, **Bagels On The Square** and **Jumbo Bagels and Bialys.** There are many pizzerias and Chinese restaurants that stay open late, and most deliver. Many ice cream parlors are also open late.

DINING

CLUBBERS AND the trendy set often frequent **La Jumelle**, **Florent** and **Les Halles** for good French dishes. Twentysomethings will seek out the **Coffee Shop** for late-night beer and Brazilian food. You'll find delicious and legendary sandwiches at the **Carnegie Deli**. **Caffè Reggio** in Greenwich Village has been a favorite for late-night coffee and desserts since 1927. It is also possible to find good food in dinner clubs. **Le Bar Bat** is popular for its bat cave décor and Vietnamese cuisine. **Tatou's** offers jazz and real old-fashioned Creole food, and at the 1930s **Rainbow Room**, the continental dishes add to the magic of this special place.

SPORTS

THERE IS round-the-clock play at **Chelsea Billiards** or until 5am at the **Billiard Club** on weekends. Have late-night beers and burgers with the New York University crowd at **Bowlmore Lanes** bowling alley.

SERVICES

MIDNIGHT EXPRESS CLEANERS, of Long Island City, picks up garments in Manhattan until midnight and has them ready the next day. It also delivers until midnight. **Tudor City Flowers** will take your order for flowers 24 hours a day. On Thursdays hairdresser **George Michael of Madison Avenue/Madora Inc** is open until 10pm and will also make house calls.

TOURS AND VIEWS

ONE OF NEW YORK'S most enjoyable walks is along the Hudson River at the World Financial Center's **Battery Park City**, open (and safe) at all hours. Piers 16 and 17 at South Street Seaport attract strollers and revelers all night long and the **Harbor Lights** restaurant on Pier 17 is open until 4am for a middle of the night pick-me-up. Or enjoy the city lights by taking a **Circle Line** two-hour tour of the nighttime harbor.

Try the Riverview Terrace at Sutton Place: the benches offer a peaceful and quiet place to watch the sun rise over the East River, Roosevelt Island and Queens. Two of the most sensational views with the Manhattan backdrop are (looking west) from the **River Café** and (looking east) from **Arthur's Landing** restaurant.

Take a trip on the **Staten Island Ferry** (see p76) to see the Statue of Liberty and the Manhattan skyline in the dawn light, or a take a taxi across Brooklyn Bridge (see pp86–9) to watch the sun rise over New York harbor. Go to the **Beekman Tower Hotel's** Top of the Tower for some panoramas of the city's East

Side up to 1am. The ultimate view is from the **Empire State Building**: its Observation Deck (see pp134–5) stays open until midnight. Have breakfast 107 floors up, at the World Trade Center's **Windows on the World** restaurant, overlooking the city, river and harbor.

Château Stables has rides in horse-drawn carriages and

Island Helicopter runs spectacular flights over the city at night. If you want something a little bit different, try one of **Marvelous Manhattan Tours'** escorted evening barhopping walks, or see the night lights with **Happy Apple Tours**. And if you still can't sleep, visit the bustling downtown **Fulton Fish Market** at 6am.

DIRECTORY

BARS AND CLUBS

Algonquin Hotel
See Piano Bars p343.

Blue Note
See Jazz p341.

Carlyle Hotel
See Piano Bars p343.

Cornelia Street Café
29 Cornelia St. **Map** 4 D2.
📞 989-9318.

Mitch's Place
134 Reade St. **Map** 1 B1.
📞 226-8928.

Nuyorican Poets Café
236 E 3rd St. **Map** 5 A2.
📞 505-8183.

Rainbow Room
See Dancing p343.

Red Blazer Too
32 W 37th St. **Map** 8 F2.
📞 262-3112.

Sweet Basil
See Jazz p341.

Temple Bar
332 Lafayette St.
Map 4 F4.
📞 925-4242.

Tommy Makem's
130 E 57th St. **Map** 12 E3.
📞 759-9040.

SHOPS

Antique Boutique
712 Broadway. **Map** 4 E2.
📞 460-8830.

Rite Aid Pharmacy
See Survival Guide p357.

Mrs. Hudson's Video Library
573 Hudson St.
Map 3 C2.
📞 989-1050.

Palmer Video Store
470 Hudson St. **Map** 3 C3.
📞 463-9377.

Plaza Pharmacy
251 E 86th St. **Map** 17 B3.
📞 427-6940.

Trash and Vaudeville
4 St. Mark's Pl. **Map** 5 A2.
📞 982-3590.

TAKE-OUT FOOD AND GROCERIES

Bagels On The Square
7 Carmine St. **Map** 4 D3.
📞 691-3041.

Delmonico Gourmet Food Market
55 E 59th St. **Map** 12 F3.
📞 751-5559.

Food Emporium
1498 York Ave.
Map 17 C4.
📞 879-9555.

H & H Bagels East
1551 2nd Ave. **Map** 17 B4.
📞 734-7441.

Jumbo Bagels and Bialys
1070 2nd Ave. **Map** 13 B3.
📞 355-6185.

West Side Supermarket
2171 Broadway. **Map** 15 C5.
📞 595-2536.

Zabar's
2245 Broadway. **Map** 15 3C.
📞 787-2000.

DINING

Caffè Reggio
119 MacDougal St.
Map 4 D2.
📞 475-9557.

Carnegie Deli
Restaurants and Bars p306.

Coffee Shop
Restaurants and Bars p306.

Florent
Restaurants and Bars p306.

La Jumelle
55 Grand St. **Map** 4 E4.
📞 941-9651.

Le Bar Bat
311 West 57th St.
Map 12 D3.
📞 307-7228.

Les Halles
Restaurants and Bars p296.

Rainbow Room
Restaurants and Bars p297.

Tatou
151 East 50th St.
Map 13 A4.
📞 753-1144.

SPORTS

Billiard Club
220 W 19th St.
Map 8 E5.
📞 206-POOL.

Bowlmore Lanes
110 University Pl.
Map 4 E1.
📞 255-8188.

Chelsea Billiards
See Sport p345.

SERVICES

George Michael of MadisonAvenue/ Madora Inc
420 Madison Ave.
Map 13 A5.
📞 752-1177.

Midnight Express Cleaners
3838 13th St.**Map** 14 F1
📞 921-0111.

Tudor City Flowers
5 Tudor City Place.
Map 9 B1.
📞 986-1490.

TOURS AND VIEWS

Arthur's Landing
Port Imperial Marina,
Pershing Circle,
Weehawken, NJ.
📞 (201) 867-0777.

Battery Park City
West St. **Map** 1 A3.

Beekman Tower Hotel
1st Ave 49th St.
Map 13 C5.
📞 355-7300.

Château Stables
608 W 48th St.
Map 15 B3.
📞 246-0520.

Circle Line
W 42nd St. **Map** 15 B3
📞 563-3200 .

Marvelous Manhattan Tours
📞 (800) 926-8795.

Empire State Building
See pp134–5.

Fulton Fish Market Tours
📞 748-8590.

Happy Apple Tours
📞 (800) 421-4518.

Harbour Lights
89 Fulton St.
Map 2 D2.
📞 227-2800.

Island Helicopter
📞 683-4575.

River Café
See Restaurants and Bars p294.

Staten Island Ferry
See Getting Around New York p76.

Windows on the World
See Restaurants and Bars p295.

CHILDREN'S NEW YORK

YOUNG VISITORS soon catch the contagious excitement in the air in New York. Attractions for all ages abound, and plenty are designed especially for children. More than a dozen theater companies, two zoos and three imaginative museums are for just the young, backed up with special events at many museums and parks. The chance to visit a TV studio is a treat, and New York's own Big Apple Circus is a perennial delight. With more to do than can ever be squeezed into a single visit, you'll never hear the cry "I'm bored!" Best of all, there's no need to spend a fortune to have fun.

A young visitor making New York his very own playground

PRACTICAL ADVICE

NEW YORK is family-friendly. Many of its hotels allow children in parents' rooms free, and will supply cots or cribs if needed. Most museums charge half price or less for children, while others are free. Children under 44 in (112 cm) also ride free on subways and buses when accompanied by an adult. Travel between 9am and 4pm to avoid rush hours.

Supplies such as diapers and medicines are readily available, and the Rite Aid Pharmacy (see p357) is open 24 hours a day. Finding changing tables in public toilets is less easy, but no one objects if a counter is used. Best bets are the facilities in libraries, hotels and department stores. Most hotels will arrange baby-sitters; another reliable source is the **Baby Sitters' Guild**.

To find out more about the range of current activities for children, get a copy of the free quarterly calendar of events, available from the New York Convention and Visitors Bureau (see p352). Weekly listings can be found in *New York* magazine.

NEW YORK ADVENTURES

THE CITY can seem like a giant amusement park for youngsters. Elevators whisk you sky-high for bird's-eye views from atop the world's highest buildings. You can set sail on the classic **Circle Line** tour around Manhattan; the sailboat **Petrel**; a tall ship from South Street Seaport (see p84) or a paddlewheeler from the marina at E. 23rd St; or the free round-trip on the Staten Island Ferry (see p76). The Roosevelt Island Tram (see p179) is a Swiss cable car offering an airborne ride over the East River. Central Park (see pp202–7) is a source of rides of every kind – from the old-fashioned charm of the carousel to real horseback and ponycart rides. Children

Skating with Santa at Rockefeller Center

who prefer a faster pace can join the in-line skaters who cruise around the traffic-free park every weekend.

Cooling off in a playground in Central Park

MUSEUMS

WHILE MANY of New York's museums appeal to all ages, some are designed just for the young. High on the list is the imaginative Children's Museum of Manhattan (see p217), a multimedia world in which children can produce their own videos and newscasts. Farther afield are the **Staten Island Children's Museum**, where a huge climb-through anthill is one of the favorite items, and the Brooklyn Children's Museum (see p245). The *Intrepid* Sea-Air-Space Museum (see p147) is a real air-craft carrier, with exhibits including the fastest spy plane in the world. Finally, be sure to see the dino-saur displays at the American Museum of Natural History (see pp214–15).

OUTDOOR FUN

IN SUMMER, all of New York comes out to play. Central Park is a child's wonderland, from skating rinks to boating lakes, bicycle paths to miniature golf. The park has free entertainment galore – such as guided walks by park rangers on Saturdays, toy sailboat races and summer storytelling. The Central Park Wildlife Center and the smaller Tisch Children's Zoo are all-time favorites.

Children of all ages will be fascinated by the Bronx Zoo/Wildlife Conservation Park which is home to over 700 species (see pp242–3). **Orchard** and **Rockaway** beaches and Coney Island (see p247) are just a subway ride away. Winter brings the chance to skate at Rockefeller Center (see p142) or in Central Park on a rink fringed with views of skyscrapers.

INDOOR FUN

NEW YORK children's theater is of a quality and variety matching that for adults. Some favorite companies are the **Paper Bag Players** and **Theaterworks USA**, whose shows sell out fast; get schedules and reserve seats early.

The New York City Ballet's annual Christmas production of *The Nutcracker* at Lincoln Center (see p212) opens at about the same time that the **Big Apple Circus** sets up its tent nearby. Ringling Brothers and Barnum & Bailey Circus is in action at Madison Square Garden (see p133) for several weeks each spring.

Opportunities for youngsters to work off energy in winter are many, from indoor skating rinks to bowling alleys.

SHOPPING

THERE WILL be no complaints about shopping trips if they include **F.A.O. Schwarz**,

Centerpiece clock at toy store F.A.O. Schwarz

one of the world's biggest and best toy stores with a vast range of wonderful items. Another favorite among children is **Enchanted Forest**, and youngsters are welcomed for storytelling sessions at children's bookstores, such as **Books of Wonder**.

EATING OUT

HAMBURGER-and-pasta joint **Ottomanelli's Café** is very popular with children, and even adults find it hard to finish their huge burgers. The lively **Hard Rock Café** is another hit, and most children enjoy the foods sold around Chinatown and Little Italy. For a quick hot snack, pizza-by-the-slice is worth a try, or stave off hunger pangs with pretzels and hot dogs from street vendors. Sure to sweeten young dispositions are the legendary ice-cream parlors, **Rumplemayer's** (see p305) and **Peppermint Park**. If all else fails, there are scores of fast food places, including McDonalds, with more than 40 branches dotted throughout Manhattan.

Storytelling session at South Street Seaport

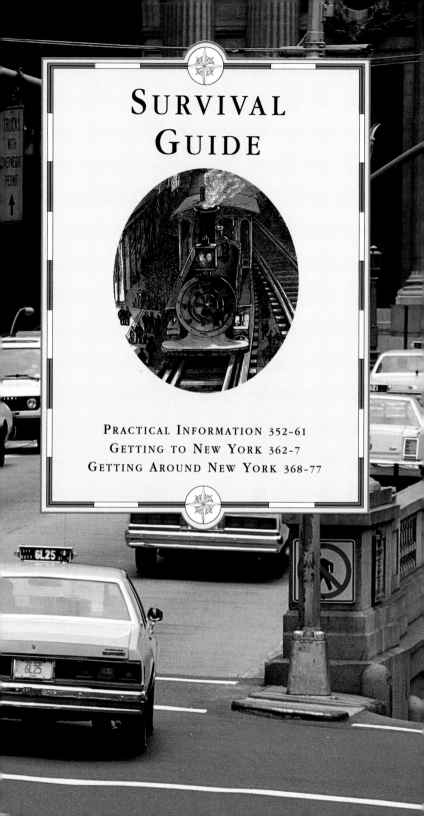

SURVIVAL
GUIDE

PRACTICAL INFORMATION

VISITORS TO New York are treated very much the same as anyone else. While you may not be given special treatment, as long as you follow a few guidelines on personal security *(see pp356–7)* you'll be able to explore the city as freely as any native New Yorker. Buses and subway trains *(pp372–5)*

Visitors resting on the steps of the Metropolitan Museum of Art

are reliable and cheap; there are lots of cash machines *(pp358–9)*, and money can be easily exchanged at banks, hotels and foreign money brokers. The wide range of prices offered by all the many hotels *(pp274–5)*, restaurants *(pp290–92)* and entertainment venues *(pp328–47)* means your New York trip can be both fun and affordable.

SIGHTSEEING TIPS

NEW YORK'S rush hours extend from 8 to 10am, 11:30am to 1:30pm and 4:30 to 6:30pm, Monday to Friday. During these times, every form of public transportation will be crowded, and the streets will be much harder to navigate on foot.

It's worth trying to visit a cluster of sights in the same area – see the *Street-by-Street* plans of each area – instead of exhausting yourself rushing from one distant attraction to another. Buses are a comfortable and reliable way to get around, and you'll see the city as you travel.

It's best to avoid passing through certain areas of the city, especially at particular times *(pp356–7)*. Public toilets in bus stations and subways should always be avoided. They attract drug users and the homeless, even when there's an attendant. Both Penn Station and Grand Central have clean and safe restrooms.

If you need help with street directions or, for whatever reason, feel a need to get off the street, try and find a hotel doorman. There is one on duty at the entrance to most hotels 24 hours a day.

OPENING HOURS

BUSINESS HOURS are generally from 9am to 5pm with no lunchtime closing. Only banks close earlier, at 3pm, although

some do have longer hours (8am–6pm) and are open on Saturday mornings. Many museums close on Mondays and major holidays. Some open on Tuesday or Thursday evenings during certain seasons (phone for details).

MUSEUMS

IN NEW YORK, *museums* is used as a blanket term to include institutions that offer diverse holdings. The city's museums are described on pages 34 to 37. Museums in the city either charge admission, starting at around $2, or ask for a "donation." There are usually discounts for senior citizens, students and children. The leading museums schedule free guided tours and lectures. Museum Mile *(see pp182–3)*, on or near Fifth Avenue, groups a number of major museums close together. Of these, the Frick Collection and the Cooper-Hewitt are small enough to see in one or two hours, but the larger Guggenheim and Whitney museums may take far longer than this.

Hotel doorman

ETIQUETTE

IT IS ILLEGAL to smoke in *any* public place or building in New York. Some restaurants now provide separate rooms for smokers, but it is best to phone ahead for details.

Business travelers need not bring a gift for their hosts. Such tokens are not expected

and may even be considered improper. If you do bring something, it should be something inexpensive and preferably representative of where you live.

Tipping is an integral part of New York life: for taxi drivers leave 10 to 15%; waiters 15 to 20%, cocktail waiters 15%, hotel room service 10% (when not added to the bill); coat check $1; hotel maids $1 or $2 per day after the first day; hotel bellhops about $1 per bag; hair stylists 15 to 20% and barbers 10 to 20%.

TOURIST INFORMATION

ADVICE ON ANY aspect of life in New York is available from the **New York Convention and Visitors Bureau**. Its literature racks and information desk attendants provide information. The 24-hour touch-tone phone service offers help outside office hours.

Useful information
New York Convention and Visitors Bureau, 810 7th Ave. **Map** 12 E4.
[484-1222, or www.nycvisit.com.
Open 9am–6pm Mon–Fri,
10am–6pm Sat, Sun.

Information racks at the New York Convention and Visitors Bureau

ENTERTAINMENT LISTINGS

A NUMBER of inexpensive or even free publications listing current exhibitions and leisure activities are available at newsstands, hotels or galleries throughout New York.

Among the more popular ones are *New York* magazine, *The New Yorker's* "Goings On About Town" roster and *Time Out New York*, which list offerings at the city's many museums, clubs, theaters, galleries, restaurants, cinemas, colleges and libraries, plus impending auctions. The *Village Voice* focuses on events in SoHo, TriBeCa and Greenwich Village, plus other major cultural activity in the city. The *New York Times* Friday and Sunday editions list current visual and performing arts events in their respective "Weekend" and "Arts and Leisure" sections. *Art News* is a monthly magazine that lists major art events and auctions and reviews exhibits.

There are also various free magazines. The weekly *Where* is distributed through hotel concierges and lists major museums, their opening hours, locations and any exhibitions. *Art Now/New York Gallery Guide* is released in art galleries each month. It lists current exhibitions and has useful maps showing where they are located.

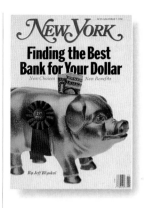

New York **magazine has weekly comprehensive entertainment listings for all of New York**

GUIDED TOURS

However you want to see New York – with the help of a pre-recorded walk or by an exciting trip in a helicopter, boat or horse-drawn carriage – organized sight-seeing trips, planned by someone else, can save a lot of time, effort and often money.

Boat Tours

Circle Line
Sightseeing Yachts
Pier 83, W 42nd St.
Map 7 A1.   -
☎ 563-3200.
A three-hour trip circum-navigating Manhattan.

Circle Line Statue of Liberty Ferry
South Ferry, Battery Park.
Map 1 C4.
☎ 269-5755.

Spirit of New York
W 23rd and 8th Ave.
Map 8 D4.
☎ 741-4266. *Cruises include lunch or dinner.*

Dept. of Transportation
Staten Island Ferry
South Ferry.
Map 2 D4.
☎ (718) 727-2508.
Manhattan–Staten Island.

World Yacht, Inc
Pier 81 W 41st St.
Map 2 D5.
☎ 630-8100.
Cruises include lunch, dinner and entertainment.

Helicopter tour

Carriage Tours

59th St at Fifth Ave and along Central Park S.
*Horse-drawn carriages gather outside the Plaza Hotel (***Map** 12 F3*), days and evenings. The usual itinerary takes in Central Park.*

Bus Tours

Allied Tours
165 W 46th St.
Map 12 E5.
☎ 869-5100.

Gray Line of New York
42nd St and 8th Ave.
Map 8 D1.
☎ 397-2600.

Short Line Tours/American Sightseeing NY
166 W 46th St.
Map 12 F5.
☎ 800-631-8405.

Helicopter Tours

Helicopter Flight Services
Sightseeing, Mon-Fri at Pier 6 and East River,
Map 2 D4.
Sat-Sun, Heliport at W 30th St and Twelfth Ave.
Map 7 B3.
☎ 355-0801.

Walking Tours

Backstage on Broadway
228 W 47th St.
Map 12 E5.
☎ 564-1343.
Behind-the-scenes tours of Broadway shows.

Big Onion Walking Tours
PO Box 250201,
Columbia University.
Map 20 E3.
☎ 439-1090.
Historical and ethnic.

CityWalks
410 W 20th St. **Map** 7 C5.
☎ 989-2456.
Historic neighborhoods – Private Tours.

Harlem Spirituals, Inc.
690 8th Ave.
Map 8 D1.
☎ 757-0425.
Harlem's history and culture.

Museum of the City of New York
103rd St and Fifth Ave.
Map 21 C5.
☎ 534-1672.
Architecture and history.

NBC Studio Tour
30 Rockefeller Plaza.
Map 12 F5.
☎ 664-7174.

92nd Street Y
1395 Lexington Ave.
Map 17 B5.
☎ 427-6000.
Culture and history.

Talk-a-Walk
30 Waterside Plaza.
Map 9 C4.
☎ 686-0356.
Recorded itineraries.

Carriage ride in Central Park

DISABLED TRAVELERS

DISABLED PEOPLE will find New York more accessible than most cities. All of the city's buses have ramps that can be lowered to help people in wheelchairs board. The buses also "kneel" to help those with restricted mobility.

Hotels, large stores and office buildings are also often well equipped for wheelchair access, and some museums offer tours for the deaf, blind and disabled. Several city theaters have systems to aid hearing-impaired patrons as do a growing number of telephones. *Access Guide to New York City*, free from the **Junior League of the City of New York**, lists buildings accessible to the disabled.

Useful information Junior League of the City of New York, 130 E 80th St. **Map** 17 A4. **(** 288-6220.
The Mayor's Office for People with Disabilities. **(** 788-2830.

A New York city bus "kneeling" to help the elderly board

CUSTOMS AND IMMIGRATION

AT PRESENT ALL British and Canadian passport holders, whether they are on vacation, business travelers or students, do not need visas if they are staying in the US for 90 days or less. Australians and New Zealanders require passports, visas and onward passage tickets. Some nationals also must show proof they have $500 or more. Check with a travel agent if in any doubt.

Customs allowances per person when you enter the US are 200 cigarettes, 50 cigars or 4.4 pounds (2 kilograms) of tobacco; no more than 2 pints (1 liter) of alcohol; gifts which are worth no more than $100; no meat or meat products (even in cans), seeds, growing plants or fresh fruit.

Upon arrival at one of New York's airports, you should follow signs stating "other than American passports" to immigration counters where your passport will then be inspected and stamped. Once you have reclaimed your baggage from the appropriate area (again, follow the signs), you will be approached by a Customs officer. He or she will examine the Customs declaration you should have received and filled in on your flight and direct you either toward the exit or to a Customs inspector who will then search your luggage.

According to American Customs officials, only 5% of all travelers will have to have their luggage searched. There are no red or green Customs channels – you're cleared and free to go once the Customs officer has seen your fully completed declaration.

STUDENT TRAVELERS

MANY MUSEUMS and theaters allow students a discount on admission. To receive this, however, you will need to carry proof of your student status at all times.

An International Student ID Card can be purchased quite cheaply, provided you have the right credentials, from the **Council Travel**, which has three branches in New York. At the same time, ask for a copy of the *ISIC Student Handbook*. This invaluable booklet identifies places and services throughout the US that offer a range of discounts to card holders. Included are accommodations, various museums, theaters, tours and attractions, nightclubs, restaurants and even Carey transportation (buses from Manhattan to New York's airports, *see p363*).

Normally, it is extremely difficult to obtain permission to work in the US; students are an exception. Any branch of the Student Travel Association in the UK, Australia or New Zealand will be able to help you with details of working holidays in New York. In London, contact the **Council on International Educational Exchange**.

STUDENT INFORMATION

Bunac
895 Amsterdam Ave. **Map** 20 E5.
(316-5312.
Summer time only.

Council on International Educational Exchange
205 E 42nd St. **Map** 9 B1.
(822-2600.

52 Poland St, London W1V 4JQ
(0171-478 2000.

Council Travel
254 Greene St. **Map** 4 E2.
(254-2525.
Also at the two NY addresses above.

CONVERSION CHART

Bear in mind that 1 US pint (0.5 liter) is a smaller measure than 1 UK pint (0.6 liter).

Imperial system:
1 inch = 2.5 centimeters
1 foot = 30 centimeters
1 mile = 1.6 kilometers
1 ounce = 28 grams
1 pound = 454 grams
1 US pint = 0.5 liter
1 US gallon = 3.8 liters

Metric system:
1 millimeter = 0.04 inch
1 centimeter = 0.4 inch
1 meter = 3 feet 3 inches
1 kilometer = 0.6 mile
1 gram = 0.04 ounce

International Student ID Card

New York daily newspapers

A newspaper vending machine

NEWSPAPERS, TELEVISION AND RADIO

YOU CAN BUY foreign newspapers, usually the previous day's issue, at **Hotalings**. Vendors are also at airports, hotels and newsstands near international business areas like the World Trade Center and Wall Street.

Comprehensive schedules of TV programs can be found in the weekly *TV Guide* magazine and the television section of Sunday's *New York Times*.

The choice of TV stations available in New York is vast. CBS operates on channel 2, NBC on channel 4, ABC on channel 7 and WNYW (Fox) on channel 5. PBS offers cultural and educational fare, including some vintage BBC programs, on channel 13. Cable TV offers everything from the Arts and Entertainment Network (channel 16) to public access programs.

AM radio stations include WCBS News (880Hz) and WFAN Sports (660Hz). Among many FM stations are WNEW rock (102.7M), WBGO jazz (88.3M) and WQXR classical (96.3M).

Useful information Hotalings,142 W 42nd St. **Map** 8 E1. (840-1868.

ELECTRICAL APPLIANCES

ALL AMERICAN electric current flows at a standardized 110 to 120 volts AC (alternating

current). You will need to bring an adapter plug and a voltage con-vertor that fits standard US electrical outlets. US plugs have two flat prongs.

Most modern New York hotels provide wall-mounted electric hair dryers in bathrooms. In addition, some hotels have wall plugs capable of powering both 110- and 220-volt electric shavers, but little else – not even radios. It can, in fact, be dangerous to connect anything more powerful. If you bring along sophisticated electrical appliances with you, be certain to take a battery pack as well. You will also need an adapter to recharge your spare batteries. Few New York hotel rooms provide irons or coffee- or tea-makers. However, room service should be able to provide you with an iron upon request.

Standard plug

EMBASSIES AND CONSULATES

Australian Consulate General
150 E 42nd St. **Map** 9 A1.
(351-6500.

British Consulate General
845 Third Ave. **Map** 13 B4.
(745-0202.

Canadian Consulate General
1251 Sixth Ave and 50th St.
Map 12 E4. (596-1783.

Consulate General of Ireland
345 Park Ave. **Map** 13 A4.
(319-2555.

New Zealand Embassy
37 Observatory Circle, NW,
Washington, DC 20008.
((202) 328-4800.

RELIGIOUS SERVICES

THERE ARE SOME 4,000 places of worship in New York, catering to almost any faith. Most hotels have lists of local organizations and service times. Among the leading churches and temples are:

Baptist
Riverside Church
122nd St at Riverside Dr.
Map 20 D2.
(870-6700.

Catholic
St. Patrick's Cathedral
Fifth Ave at 50th St.
Map 12 F4.
(753-2261.

Episcopal
St. Bartholomew's
109 E 50th St. **Map** 13 A4.
(751-1616.

Jewish
Reform
Temple Emanu-El
Fifth Ave at 65th St.
Map 12 F2.
(744-1400.

Orthodox
Fifth Avenue Synagogue
5 E 62nd St. **Map** 12 F2.
(838-2122.

Lutheran
St. Peter's
619 Lexington Ave. **Map** 17 A4.
(935-2200.

Methodist
Christ Church United Methodist
520 Park Ave. **Map** 13 A3.
(838-3036.

Riverside Church

Personal Security and Health

Police badge

IN 1998, NEW YORK was rated the safest among large US cities with a population of more than one million. This ranks New York 166th among cities with population of over one hundred thousand. The city's police force concentrates on foot and bicycle patrols in tourist areas, and security has been beefed up in midtown, in the transportation system and at airports. While there are places where any traveler would be foolish to tread after dark – and sometimes in daylight – if you keep your wits about you and stick to the following guidelines, you should enjoy a trouble-free visit.

Curtis Sliwa, founder of the Guardian Angels

LAW ENFORCEMENT

THE NEW YORK police department has around-the-clock foot, horse, bike and car patrols. These are concentrated in specific areas at critical times – for instance, the theater district during show times. There are police who ride the subways and buses, and the recent dramatic drop in crime statistics reflects this..

You may also see youths wearing red berets. As their T-shirts proclaim, they are Guardian Angels. Always unarmed, these safety patrols "police" the subways and midtown streets. Although tolerated by the police and often a welcome sight, they have no official powers.

GUIDELINES ON SAFETY

BE ALERT and walk as if you know where you're going. Avoid making eye contact and confrontations with down-and-outs.

If someone asks you for money, be careful; do not be drawn into conversation.

Never use deserted streets. At night, if you can't afford a taxi, try to travel with a group and avoid such areas as the Lower East Side, Chinatown, midtown west of Broadway (except the Lincoln Center plaza) and, uptown, generally north of 82nd Street. Even the side streets around Times Square and the Broadway theaters can be unsafe. The Financial District (except for the World Financial Center) is deserted after business hours, and some TriBeCa and SoHo streets can be risky after dark if you are alone.

Parks are often used for drug dealing. They are safest when there is a crowd for a rally, concert or other event. If you want to go for a jog, ask your hotel concierge for a map of safe routes and follow his or her

advice. Keep your wallet in an inconspicuous place and have enough change handy for phone calls and bus fares. It's best not to have to dig into your purse or wallet while standing in line. Never stop to count your money on the street. Defeat purse snatchers by carrying your bag with the clasp facing toward you and the shoulder strap diagonally across your body.

Leave valuable jewelry at home or stored at your hotel. If you wear it casually, it may mark you as a target for robbery or harassment.

Do not allow anyone except hotel and airport personnel to carry your luggage or parcels.

Stow your valuables and camera in a locked suitcase or dresser or closet safe when you do leave your hotel room.

Mounted police officers

LOST AND FOUND

THE CHANCES are poor of recovering anything lost in New York City. There is no citywide lost and found.

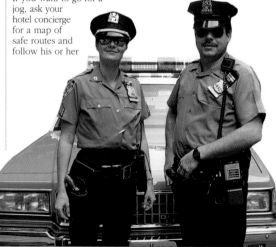

Two armed New York City police officers

Cap and badge worn by city police

The lost-and-found rooms at Grand Central and Penn Station are well-run, well-stocked and very helpful.

USEFUL INFORMATION

Lost and Found Offices
Bus and subway services
(712-4500.

Taxis
(692-8294.

Missing Credit Cards
American Express
((800) 528-4800 (free).

Diners Club
((800) 234-6377 (free).

JCB
((800) 366-4522 (free).

MasterCard
((800) 627-8372 (free).

VISA
((800) 336-8472 (free).

TRAVEL INSURANCE

TRAVEL INSURANCE is highly recommended, mainly because of the high cost of medical care. There are many types of coverage, with prices dependent on the length of your trip and the number of people covered on the policy.

Among the most important features are: accidental death, dismemberment, emergency medical and dental care, trip cancellation, and baggage and travel document loss. There are many policies that include all these items. Your travel agent or insurance company should recommend a suitable policy.

MEDICAL TREATMENT

BE PREPARED to undergo an expensive experience: some of the city's practitioners and facilities are among the best around, and medical fees in the US are unregulated. Be sure to protect yourself well with insurance. A few physicians and dentists may accept credit cards, but they are much more likely to want payment in cash or traveler's checks. Hospitals accept most credit cards *(see p358)*.

A 24-hour pharmacy, one of several in the city

EMERGENCIES

IN THE EVENT of your being involved in a medical emergency, proceed at once to a **Hospital Emergency Room**. Should you need an ambulance, telephone 911 and one will be sent. If your medical insurance is properly in order, you won't have to worry about costs.

Unless you are impoverished, it is better to avoid the city-owned hospitals listed in the telephone book Blue Pages. Instead, choose one of the many private hospitals listed in the Yellow Pages. Dial 411 and ask the operator to give you the number of the nearest public or private hospital. Other options include asking your hotel to call a doctor or dentist to visit you in your room, or finding one yourself through the **NY Hotel Urgent Medical Services** (737-1212), **Dial-A-Doctor** or **NYU Dental Care**. For more general advice and information call **Travelers' Aid**, a national organization geared to helping travelers.

CRISIS INFORMATION

All Emergencies
(911 (or 0). This alerts police, fire and medical services.

Dial-A-Doctor
(971-9692.

Crime Victims Hot Line
(577-7777.

NYU Dental Care
(998-9487, 998-9988, 998-9828 (weekends).

Hospital Emergency Rooms
St. Vincent's.
11th St and Seventh Ave.
Map 3 C1.
(604-7998.

St. Luke's Roosevelt.
58th St and Ninth Ave.
Map 12 D3.
(523-6800.

National Organization of Women (NOW)
(260-4422.

Pharmacy (24-hour)
Rite Aid
200 W 70th St.
Map 11 C1.
(787-2903.

Poison Control Center
(764-7667.

Robberies, Muggings or Assaults
(911 for instant police help.

Sex Crimes Report Line
(267-7273.

Travelers' Aid
(944-0013.

New York ambulance

Banking and Currency

Nᴇᴡ ʏᴏʀᴋ ɪꜱ ᴛʜᴇ ɴᴀᴛɪᴏɴ'ꜱ banking center. It has a wealth of local, regional and major national banks, plus some retail branches of the leading foreign banks. Fleet Bank and Barclays are well represented in New York; the banks of Australia, Canada, Ireland, Scotland, Tokyo, and Turkey all have offices or branches.

Banking

Nᴇᴡ ʏᴏʀᴋ banks are generally open weekdays from 9am to 3pm. There are, however, a number of banks that open earlier or close late evening to suit commuters' needs. Tellers are behind a counter. At most banks, all the tellers will cash traveler's checks and exchange your foreign currency.

Automated teller machine (ATM)

Automated Teller Machines

Aᴄᴏɴᴠᴇɴɪᴇɴᴛ development in banking has been the introduction of the automated teller machine (ATM). These are found in nearly all bank lobbies and enable you to obtain American currency 24 hours a day by electronically tapping into your own bank account. ATMs usually issue American banknotes in $20 denominations.

Before you leave for New York, check with your bank about which New York City banks and ATM systems will accept your bank card and what fees and commissions will be charged on each transaction. Most ATM machines are in either the Cirrus or Plus network. They accept various US bank cards, MasterCard and VISA cards and certain others. Among the many advantages of ATMs is the swift, secure exchange of your money at the wholesale rate used between the banks when they make their million-dollar deals.

On a more cautionary note, be aware of your surroundings when using an unlocked ATM. It is best to use them only in daylight hours or when the streets are crowded.

Credit Cards

Mᴀꜱᴛᴇʀᴄᴀʀᴅ, American Express, VISA, JCB and Diners Card are widely accepted throughout the United States, regardless of which company or bank issues them. These cards can also be used to obtain cash advances from various ATM machines. They may also be upgraded to confer higher spending limits. In the US you can use a credit card to pay for nearly everything imaginable, from groceries to restaurant and hotel bills, and telephone orders for movie and theater tickets. Major expenses such as tours, travel packages and expensive rentals are all best paid for by credit card. Try to avoid carrying huge sums of money around with you.

Cashing Checks

Dᴏʟʟᴀʀ ᴛʀᴀᴠᴇʟᴇʀ'ꜱ checks issued by American Express and Thomas Cook are widely accepted without a fee by most of New York's department stores, shops, hotels and restaurants. Traveler's checks in other currencies, including sterling, are not universally accepted. They can usually be

Foreign currency exchange counter at Chequepoint USA

exchanged by your hotel cashier, but may require a visit to a bank. Exchange rates are printed daily in the *New York Times* and *Wall Street Journal*, and may be posted in the windows of banks that invite currency-exchange business. American Express checks are always exchanged without a fee at American Express offices. Major hotels have cashiers equipped to exchange your traveler's checks.

Foreign exchange brokers are few. Among the most solidly established are **Thomas Cook Currency Services Inc.** and **MTB**. The ones listed on the opposite page have late hours. Others are listed in the city's telephone Yellow Pages under *Foreign Money Brokers*. Expect to pay a fee, which will vary widely from one place to the next, plus a commission.

There are scores of hole-in-the-wall check-cashing shops in Manhattan. They are listed in the Yellow Pages classified section. They may not be willing to cash your traveler's checks though, and they are very unlikely to accept or cash foreign checks.

Exchange Addresses

Thomas Cook Currency Services
1590 Broadway
Map 12 E5. ☏ 265-6049.
One of several branches.

MTB Banking Corporation
90 Broad St.
Map 1 C3. ☏ 858-3300.

Coins

American coins (actual size shown) come in 25-, 10-, 5- and 1-cent pieces. 50-cent and $1 coins are also minted but are rarely used. Each value of coin has a more popular name: 25-cent pieces are called quarters, 10-cent pieces are called dimes, 5-cent pieces are called nickels and 1-cent pieces are known as pennies.

**25-cent coin
(a quarter)**

**10-cent coin
(a dime)**

**5-cent coin
(a nickel)**

**1-cent coin
(a penny)**

**Emblem on US
currency**

Bank Notes

Units of currency in the United States are dollars and cents. There are 100 cents to a dollar. Notes (bills) come in $1, $5, $10, $20, $50 and $100s. All bills are the same color, so check the amount carefully. The new $20, $50, and $100 bills are now in circulation; they have very large numbers.

FINANCIAL SERVICES

American Express
822 Lexington Ave. **Map** 13 A2.
🅒 758-6510. **Open** 9am–6pm
Mon–Fri, 10am–4pm Sat.
Helpline 🅒 (800) 221-7282

Avis Currency Exchange
1451 Broadway.
Map 8 E1. 🅒 944-7600.
Open 10am–8pm Mon–Fri,
noon–8pm Sat & Sun.

Cirrus
🅒 (800) 424-7787

Chequepoint USA
22 Central Park South.
Map 12 F3. 🅒 750-2400.
Open 8am–8pm Sun–Fri.

Plus
🅒 (800) 843-7587

Thomas Cook
1590 Broadway. **Map** 12 E5.
🅒 265-6049.
Open 9am–7pm Mon–Sat,
9am–5pm Sun. Also at 317
Madison Ave 🅒 883-0400.
🅒 (800) CURRENCY. **Refund
Assistance** 🅒 (800) 223-7373
Open 9am–5pm Mon–Sun.

1-dollar bill ($1)

5-dollar bill ($5)

20-dollar bill ($20)

50-dollar bill ($50)

100-dollar bill ($100)

Using New York's Phones

Sign for public payphones

Pᴜʙʟɪᴄ ᴘᴀʏᴘʜᴏɴᴇꜱ can be found at many street corners, in hotel and office lobbies, restaurants, bars, theaters and department stores. Few use credit cards, but you can now buy prepaid phone cards. Most phones are coin-operated and take 5-, 10- and 25-cent coins. Hotels are free to set their own rates, and so calls made from your room can be more expensive than using a public payphone. Avoid this by making calls from a public phone in the lobby.

PUBLIC TELEPHONES

Tʜᴇ ꜱᴛᴀɴᴅᴀʀᴅ payphone has a hand receiver and 12-button key pad and is pillar- or wall-mounted. In some locations the payphone may belong to an independent company. These phones often look similar to those of Bell Atlantic but usually work differently. The independents are usually more expensive and definitely less reliable.

Regulations require each public payphone to post information about charges, toll-free numbers and how to make calls using other carriers. Look for the Bell Atlantic Telephone Company name or logo on the box to be sure the phone will reach all numbers at the standard rates. To complain about service, call the **Public Service Commission**. Useful **information** Public Service Commission ☎ *(800) 342-3355 (tollfree number).*

Independently operated payphone

PAYPHONE CHARGES

Wɪᴛʜɪɴ the New York boroughs, the standard charge, around 25 cents, buys three minutes' talking time. If your call lasts longer, the operator will request additional payment.

Many newsstands now sell prepaid phone cards for long-distance calls; they can be bought in $5, $10, and $25 amounts. The cards offer substantial savings compared to standard rates. However, the calls are connected over the Internet and so the sound quality is not as good as calls using a standard carrier

USING A COIN-OPERATED PHONE

1 Lift the receiver.

3 Dial or press the number.

Coins
Make sure you have the correct coins available before you dial.

2 Insert the necessary coin or coins. The coin drops as soon as you insert it.

4 If you do not want to complete your call or it does not get through, retrieve the coin(s) by pressing the coin return.

5 If the call is answered and you talk longer than the allotted three minutes, the operator will interrupt and ask you to deposit more coins. Payphones do not give change.

5 cents

10 cents

25 cents

A Bell Atlantic Telephone Company phone stand

International long-distance rates for calls dialed direct vary from country to country. For calls to the UK, the discount rate starts at 1pm, then drops to an economy rate from 6pm until 7am the next day.

USEFUL NUMBERS

Directory Inquiries
📞 *411; 10-10-9000.*

Main Post Office
📞 *967-8585.*

Operator Assistance
📞 *0.*

Speaking Clock
📞 *976-1616.*

International Directory Inquiries
📞 *00.*

REACHING THE RIGHT NUMBER

• Five area codes are used in New York: 212 , 917, 646 for Manhattan; the other boroughs use 718 and 347. 800, 888, and 877 prefixes mean the call will be free.
• To call a number outside your own area, first dial 1. For example, to dial Queens from Manhattan dial 1 (718) (number).
• To call long distance from a payphone: dial 0 followed by the area code and then the number. The operator will answer and tell you how much money you need to deposit.
• To make an international direct call: dial 011 followed by the country code (New Zealand; 64, Australia: 61; UK: 44), then the city or area code (minus the first 0) and the local number.
• To make an international call via the operator: dial 01 followed by the country code, the city code (minus the first 0) and then the local number.
• International Directory Inquiries are on 00. If you have problems, call international operator assistance on 01.
• **In an emergency, dial 911.**

Sending A Letter

US state mail logo

APART FROM post offices, letters can be mailed at your hotel concierge desk (which usually also sells stamps); in letter slots in office building lobbies; in air, rail and bus terminals; and in the occasional street mailbox. These are always painted blue, or red, white and blue. Mail in most mailboxes is not picked up on weekends. Post offices are shown on the *Street Finder* maps *(see pp378–9)*.

POSTAL SERVICES

THE CITY'S main **General Post Office** is open 24 hours a day. Stamps can be bought here or from branch offices (a handy one is in the Empire State Building) or from coin-operated machines in pharmacies, department stores and bus and train stations. All letters go first class.

The federal post office offers three special delivery services: **Express Mail** service for next-day delivery, **Priority Mail** service for two-day delivery, and **International Express Mail** for overseas. Priority Mail will also pick up letters on weekdays for an extra charge. Private express mail can be

Colorful US stamps

arranged through hotel concierges or with one of the delivery services listed in the telephone book such as **DHL, Federal Express,** or **UPS**.

Useful information General Post Office, 421 Eighth Ave. **Map** 8 D2. 📞 *967-8585.* Priority and Express Mail 📞 *(800) 222-1811.* FedEx 📞 *(800) 463-3339.* DHL 📞 *(800) 225-5345.* UPS. 📞 *(800) 742-5877*

HELD MAIL

MAIL will be held for you for 30 days at the General Post Office's General Delivery window. Mail can be sent to other post offices by giving the zip code or name. Address mail with: Name, General Delivery, US Post Office, New York, NY10001.

Express Mail   Priority Mail

Mailboxes
Mailboxes can be few and far between on New York streets, and it may be easier to find a post office (see Street Finder pp378–9). *Instructions on how to use each mailbox are written on the box. If you use Express or Priority services, weigh your letters at a post office to figure out the postage needed.*

Standard mailbox

GETTING TO NEW YORK

M ANY INTERNATIONAL airlines have direct flights to New York. It is also very well served by charter and domestic services. Price wars between airlines have reduced fares, and domestic flights now prove a viable alternative to bus and train tickets; group tour package prices are often

Aerial view of Manhattan

unbeatable. The *QE2* is one of several cruise ships that dock in the city. Long-distance trains serving New York are clean and comfortable. Interstate and long distance buses are comfortable, with air-conditioning and on-board toilets. For information on arriving in New York see the map on pages 366–7.

AIR TRAVEL

N EW YORK CAN be reached by air direct from most major cities. The flight from London takes about eight hours. However, there are no direct flights from Australia or New Zealand. Instead, the airlines fly to the West coast, which takes around 14 hours, land, refuel and then continue on to New York.

Among the main carriers to New York are **Air Canada**, **Delta**, **Canadian Air**, **Continental**, **British Airways**, **American Airlines**, **Virgin Atlantic** and **United Airlines**. All international flights arrive at Newark or JFK airports *(see pp364–5)*.

APEX (Advance Purchase Excursion) tickets for the scheduled airlines are usually the cheapest return fares apart from package tours. But they must be bought in advance and are valid for a stay of 7 to 30 days. Some airlines offer cheaper fares if you limit your stay to specified periods. Senior citizens may also receive discounts.

AIRLINE NUMBERS

Major Carriers

Air Canada
[(800) 488-1800 (tollfree).

American Airlines
[(800) 433-7300 (tollfree).

British Airways
[(800) 247-9297 (tollfree).

Canadian Air
[(800) 426-7000 (tollfree).

Continental
[(800) 231-0856 (tollfree).

Delta
[(800) 241-4141 (tollfree).

United Airlines
[(800) 241-6522 (tollfree).

Virgin Atlantic
[(800) 862-8621 (tollfree).

SEA TRAVEL

N EW YORK IS a regular port of call for the *QE2* which docks there, via Southampton, 25 times a year. It also makes

Long-distance Greyhound bus

voyages to Australia and New Zealand. Sea travel offers an expensive, but relaxing, way of traveling to New York. Ships dock at the Hudson River piers in mid-town Manhattan.

LONG-DISTANCE BUSES

A LL LONG-DISTANCE buses such as **Greyhound Lines** arrive in the city at the **Port Authority Bus Terminal**. Buses from here also connect with the three airports. With over 6,000 buses arriving and leaving daily and carrying some 172,000 passengers, the atmosphere is chaotic. Many hotels are also accessible directly from the terminal.
Useful information Greyhound Bus Lines [(800) 231-2222. (24 hrs). Port Authority Bus Terminal. W 40th St and Eighth Ave. **Map** 8 D1. [564-8484 (24 hrs).

TRAIN TRAVEL

A MTRAK TRAINS from Canada, upstate, southern, northeastern and western states all stop at Penn Station *(see p376)*. Metro North lines from upstate and Connecticut arrive at Grand Central Terminal.

Ocean liner approaching Manhattan

New York Airports

Transatlantic jet

THE THREE MAIN airports (Newark, JFK and La Guardia) are all well connected to central Manhattan. Look for uniformed "skycaps" – scarlet-capped porters wearing distinctive badges, who will help you with your luggage. Never trust anyone else to help carry your bags – you may never see them again. Taxi dispatchers will help you into a licensed taxi at the taxi area.

GETTING INTO MANHATTAN

THE GROUND Transportation center at each airport will give you information on the ways you can continue your trip. The most useful services, operating from LaGuardia and JFK, are the **New York Airport Service** and **Gray Line Air Shuttle**. The former stops at Grand Central; the latter will drop you anywhere in Manhattan between 23rd and 63rd streets. New Jersey Transit buses and **Olympia Airport Express** also go to Manhattan.

Shared vehicle rides are offered at JFK and LaGuardia by **Classic Airport Share Ride** and **Westchester Express**. The "A" subway connects with a shuttle bus and takes passengers to and from JFK. The M60 bus goes to and from LaGuardia. Many car rental firms have

Signs for connections to Manhattan at La Guardia

courtesy telephones at the baggage-claim areas. Telephone numbers for your advance reservations are listed on page 370.

BUS COMPANIES

New York Airport Service
☎ (718) 706-9658.

Classic Airport Share Ride ☎ (516) 567-5100.

Gray Line Air Shuttle ☎ 315-3006.

Olympia Airport Express ☎ 964-6233.

Westchester Express ☎ (800) 532-3730.

Taxi dispatcher

LA GUARDIA (LGA)

PRINCIPALLY SERVING business travelers, La Guardia lies 8 miles (13 km) east of Manhattan on the north side of Long Island in Queens.

Upon arrival, you can rent luggage trolleys cheaply from the baggage-claim area next to the luggage carousels. Skycaps are on hand to assist you. Baggage can also be left in the Tele-Trip business center on the departure level. Foreign exchange desks are located around the Central Terminal.

Uniformed taxi dispatchers at the airport are on duty at peak hours; or ask one of the Port Authority Police for help. Only use yellow taxis licensed by the city. The cost of tolls, plus a small surcharge after 8pm and all day Sunday, will be added to the fare shown on the meter (about $25–$40 to central Manhattan). **Useful information** Airport Information Service ☎ (718) 533-3400.

Check-in desk at La Guardia

PLAN OF LA GUARDIA AIRPORT

A frequent free bus service runs between each of the terminals and parking areas. Buses and taxis into the city and its suburbs depart from the first floor of the Central Terminal building.

Central Terminal building

Marine Air Terminal

Delta Shuttle Terminal

USAirways Terminal

USAirways Shuttle

Delta Terminal

Grand Central Parkway to New York

KEY

🅿 Parking

🚌 Bus service between terminals

JFK Airport

N EW YORK'S main inter-national airport, JFK, lies 15 miles (24 km) southeast of Manhattan, in the borough of Queens. American Airlines, British Airways, Delta, TWA, and United have their own arrivals buildings, complete with customs and immigration facilities. Other international airlines use Terminals 1, 2 or 4. Note that the terminals have all been recently renumbered.

Luggage trolleys are free

Airport information signs at JFK

Main Hall at the International Arrivals Building, JFK

for arriving passengers in the meeting area. Foreign ex-change offices are located in all terminals.

The Ground Transportation desk is on the ground level near the baggage-claim. Transportation into Manhattan can be arranged here 24 hours a day. The quickest way to reach Manhattan is by heli-copter; the price for a 15-minute flight is double or more the cost of a taxi fare. Courtesy phones are provided by the car rental companies.

Most have shuttle service to their rental offices. Taxis wait outside the terminals. A trip into Manhattan normally takes up to an hour; there is a flat fee of $30 plus tolls.

The New York Airport Service bus service is reliable, inexpensive, safe, and operates 24 hours a day. For early morning flights there are hotels very near the airport. City hotels can be booked at the Meegan Services reservation desk.

Useful Addresses

Airport Information Service
🛈 *(718) 244-4444.*

Hilton JFK Airport
138–10 135th Ave, Queens.
☎ *(718) 322-8700.*

Holiday Inn JFK
144–02 135th Ave, Queens.
☎ *(718) 659-0200.*

American Airlines (8)

British Airways
United Airlines (7)

TWA (6) (Domestic flights)

Terminal 9

Van Wyck Expressway to New York

P Parking

Terminal 1

Terminal 2

TWA (5) (International flights)

Garage

Terminal (4)

Delta Airlines (3)

Key

P Parking

🚌 Bus stops for all buses

Plan of JFK Airport

Free Airline Connection buses operate between terminals – allow half an hour for distant connections. They usually leave every 5–15 minutes, 24 hours a day. For a faster, but more expensive, transfer, take a taxi. All buses and cabs leave from clearly marked stands just outside the air terminal arrival areas.

NEWARK AIRPORT

Bus terminal at Newark Airport

KEY

🅿 Parking

🚌 Bus stop

▬ Inter-terminal monorail

Terminal B
(International Arrivals)

Terminal C

Terminal A

Marriott Hotel

Roads to Manhattan

PLAN OF NEWARK AIRPORT

Free Airline Connection buses offer a 24-hour service between terminals every 5–15 minutes. Allow about 30 minutes for the farthest terminals. Taxis are also available. A monorail links all three terminals with the parking lots. All buses and taxis leave from outside the air terminal arrival areas.

NEWARK, NEW YORK'S second largest international airport, is located about 16 miles (26 km) southwest of Manhattan, in New Jersey.

All international flights arrive at Terminal "B." Baggage trolleys are free for arriving international passengers. There is no baggage room. Foreign exchange desks are available in each terminal.

The Ground Transportation services desk, open 24 hours a day, is next to the baggage-claim area. Courtesy phones are provided by limousine and car rental firms. Many of these have a free shuttle service to their rental offices.

If you want a taxi, line up at one of the many taxi stands located outside most arrival areas. Uniformed taxi dispatchers will also help you hail a cab. Never accept a ride into town from anyone who approaches you in the terminal: they may not have

insurance and could charge an outrageous fare. The trip into Manhattan takes about 40–60 minutes and will cost you up to $40-$45.

Buses can take anywhere from 40 minutes to over an hour to reach Manhattan, but cost about $10. Electronic boards around the terminal list departure times of all these services.

For early morning flights, there are hotels located in and around the airport grounds. City hotels can be booked on arrival through the courtesy phones that are linked directly to various Manhattan

hotels. At Newark, these are located in all three terminals.

USEFUL ADDRESSES

Port Authority at Newark Airport
📞 (973) 961-6000.
Parking 📞 (888) 397-4636.

Holiday Inn International
1000 Spring St, Elizabeth, N.J.
📞 (800) 465-4329.

Marriott Hotel
Newark Airport grounds.
📞 (800) 228-9290.

Monitors for ground transportation information, Newark Airport

Arriving in New York

THIS MAP SHOWS the links between New York's three airports and the center of Manhattan. It also illustrates rail connections linking New York to the rest of the United States and Canada. Travel information, including travel times for subway, bus, rail and helicopter services, is listed in each information box. The passenger ship terminal, once New York's key point of arrival for the flood of post-war immigrants, is located a short distance from the center of Manhattan. Port Authority Bus Terminal, on the west side, provides services across the city.

Ships at the passenger terminal

KEY

✈	Airport *see pp363–5*
⚓	Seaport *see p362*
🚆	Rail link *see p362*
🚌	Bus station/link *see p362*
Ⓜ	Subway link *see pp374–5*
⛴	Water shuttle
🚁	Helicopter link *see p364*
—	New York Airport Service and Gray Line Air Shuttle *see p363*
—	Water shuttle
—	Helicopter *see p364*
—	Long Island Rail Road *see pp376–7*
—	New Jersey Transit buses *see p363*
—	Olympia Airport Express *see p363*
—	Shuttle bus *see p364*
—	Subway line, A train *see p374*

 PASSENGER SHIP TERMINAL
Piers 88–92 for QE2 and other cruise ship arrivals and departures.

Passenger Ship Terminal

🚌 **PORT AUTHORITY BUS TERMINAL**
All long-distance buses arrive and depart here; links to all city airports.

Port Authority Bus Terminal

🚆 **PENN STATION**
*Long-distance trains from **Canada** and other US states arrive and depart here; daily commuter train services to **Long Island** and **New Jersey**.*
🚆 *Amtrak, Long Island Rail Road and New Jersey Transit services.*
Ⓜ *A, C, E, 1, 2, 3, 9.*

Penn Station

Chelsea and the Garment District

Greenwich Village

Gray Line Air Shuttle buses take passenger to any point between 23rd and 63rd street

SoHo and TriBeCa

East Village

Seaport and the Civic Center

Lower East Side

World Trade Center
🚆 *Metro-North.*
Ⓜ *A, C, E, 2, 3.*

Lower Manhattan

Pier 11

 NEWARK
Bus service to central Manhattan every 20–30 mins.
🚌 ***Olympia Airport Express** every 20–30 mins to the **World Trade Center**, **Penn Station** and **Grand Central Terminal**.*
🚌 ***New Jersey Transit** buses every 15–20 mins to the **Port Authority Bus Terminal**.*

Delta Water Shuttle from La Guardia

Amtrak railroad train

Morningside
Heights
and Harlem

Upper West
Side

Central Park

Grand Central Terminal

Upper
East Side

🚇 GRAND CENTRAL
Daily commuter train service to
upstate **New York** and **Connecticut**.
🚆 Metro-North.
Ⓜ 4, 5, 6, 7.

Upper
Midtown

**Grand Central
Terminal**

Lower
Midtown

**East 34th
St. Pier**

**NYC
Heliport**

✈ LA GUARDIA
Buses to Grand Central Terminal
every 20 mins. Train services every 5–
10 mins. Water shuttle to city center.
🚌 **New York Airport Service**
every 20–30 mins to **Grand
Central**, **Port Authority** and
midtown hotels.
🚌 Gray Line Air Shuttle service
to your choice of destination (see
box at center of map).
🚌 Shuttle bus to **Jamaica**,
Queens, station of the **Long
Island Rail Road** every half hour
(1 hr); then trains every 5–10 mins
to **Penn Station** (25 mins).
🚢 Delta Water Shuttle to **Wall St**
and **E 34th St**, Mon–Fri (30 mins).

Jamaica
🚆 Long Island Rail
Road

Helicopter service from JFK

Howard Beach
Ⓜ A

✈ JFK
Bus service to Grand Central and
Port Authority every 20 mins. Trains
every 5–10 mins to Penn Station.
Subway to city center.
🚌 **New York Airport Service**
every 20 mins to **Grand Central,
Port Authority Bus Terminal** and
midtown hotels (45 mins–1 hr).
🚌 Gray Line Air Shuttle service
to your choice of destination (see
box at center of map).
Ⓜ Shuttle buses from all terminals
to Howard Beach stop of the A train
subway to city center (1hr 30 mins).
🚁 **New York Helicopter** makes
frequent departures from TWA
International Terminal Gate 37 to
34th Street Heliport.

0 kilometers		2
0 miles		1

GETTING AROUND NEW YORK

WITH OVER SIX thousand miles of streets, walking around New York could prove difficult. But the city is a network of districts and many of the major sites can be visited area by area. Taxis are best for door-to-door transit but can be held up in traffic jams, especially during rush hours. The city's bus service is reliable and cheap but often slow. Subways are quick, reliable and cheap, and make stops throughout central Manhattan. There are no weekly or day passes valid for all public transportation, but buses and trains have their own forms of travel passes.

Stretch limousine, the preferred vehicle for New York's glitterati

NEGOTIATING THE AVENUES AND STREETS

MANHATTAN'S avenues run approximately north to south; its streets (except in the older areas) run east to west. Fifth Avenue is used as an arbitrary center line for the measurement of East and West addresses; Five West 40th Street is, for example, a few doors west of Fifth Avenue on 40th Street, and Five East 40th is a few doors to the east.

Most streets in midtown are one-way. In general, traffic is eastbound on even-numbered streets and westbound on odd-numbered streets. Avenues also tend to be one-way, alternating northbound or southbound.

First, Third (above 23rd Street), Madison, Eighth, Avenue of the Americas (6th Ave) and Tenth avenues, are all northbound, while Second, Lexington, Fifth, Seventh, and Ninth avenues and Broadway below 59th Street are southbound. There is two-way traffic on York, Park, Eleventh and Twelfth avenues and Broadway above 60th Street.

Although most city blocks north of Houston Street are rectangular, they are not very uniform: east–west blocks are three or even four times longer than north–south blocks.

When asking directions from a New Yorker, you may get confused over certain streets. For instance, Avenue of the Americas is also Sixth Avenue, and Seventh Avenue is often called Fashion Avenue. Many intersections and plazas have titles commemorating famous people and events.

Rush-hour gridlock in Manhattan

FINDING AN ADDRESS

A useful formula has been devised to help pinpoint any **Avenue Address**. By dropping the last digit of the address, dividing the remainder by 2, then adding or subtracting the **Key Number** given here, you will discover the nearest cross street. For example: To find No. 826 Lexington Avenue, first you have to drop the 6; divide 82 by 2, which is 41; then add **22** (the key number). Therefore, the nearest cross street is 63rd Street.

A road sign for Madison Avenue positioned at an intersection with a street

Avenue Address	Key Number	Avenue Address	Key Number
1st Ave	+3	9th Ave	+13
2nd Ave	+3	10th Ave	+14
3rd Ave	+10	Amsterdam Ave	+60
4th Ave	+8	Audubon Ave	+165
5th Ave, up to 200	+13	Broadway above	
5th Ave, up to 400	+16	23rd St	-30
5th Ave, up to 600	+18	Central Park W, divide	
5th Ave, up to 775	+20	full number by 10	+60
5th Ave 775–1286,		Columbus Ave	+60
do not divide by 2	-18	Convent Ave	+127
5th Ave, up to 1500	+45	Lenox Ave	+110
5th Ave, up to 2000	+24	Lexington Ave	+22
(6th) Ave of the		Madison Ave	+26
Americas	-12	Park Ave	+35
7th Ave below		Park Ave South	+08
110th St	+12	Riverside Drive, divide	
7th Ave above		full number by 10	+72
110th St	+20	St Nicholas Ave	+110
8th Ave	+10	West End Ave	+60

However, the maps in this guide use the place names that most New Yorkers know and regularly use.

PLANNING YOUR JOURNEY

T HE STREETS and sidewalks are busiest during the rush hours – 8 to 10am, 11:30am to 1:30pm and 4:30 to 6:30pm, Monday to Friday. Throughout these periods it is better to face the crowds on foot than attempt any journey by bus, taxi or subway. At other times of day and during certain holiday periods (see p53), the traffic is often much lighter and you should reach your destination quickly.

There are, of course, a few exceptions. Fifth Avenue should always be avoided on parade days (St. Patrick's Day and Thanksgiving Day are the worst). Celebrity visits or one of the regular demonstrations at City Hall (see p90) can cause major disruption to the traffic. The area around Seventh Avenue, south of 42nd Street, is likely to be busy during the day with the truck and handcart traffic of New York's garment industry.

WALKING

M OST INTERSECTIONS between avenues and streets have lampposts with name-markers and electric traffic signals. The traffic lights show red (stop) and green (go) for vehicles and "Walk–Don't Walk" for pedestrians. You

Pedestrian crossing

Do not cross the street

You may cross the street

Staten Island Ferry leaving Battery Park

Circle Line tour boat

FERRIES
There are two ferries of interest to visitors (see also p353): the Circle Line runs a ferry to the Statue of Liberty and Ellis Island several times each day from Battery Park at the southern tip of Manhattan. The 24-hour Staten Island ferry from Battery Park travels the channel, offering splendid views of Manhattan, the Statue of Liberty, Ellis Island, the bridges and Governors Island. The round trip is the best bargain in New York; it's free.

will quickly come to realize, however, that most New York pedestrians rely on their eyes and judgment rather than on the numerous "Walk" signs.

Remember that vehicles keep to the right. There are no cautionary "Look Left" signs to alert you to the direction of oncoming traffic. There are, however, numerous one-way streets, so it's best to look both ways before you cross. Beware, too, of cars, trucks and taxis turning the corner behind you as you start to cross the street.

There are pedestrian crossings at some intersections. These are officially designated pedestrian crossing points (at Rockefeller Center for instance) and are closely monitored by the police. The city has a few underground walkways for pedestrians in Central Park.

CYCLING

F OR VISITORS who want to cycle around New York it is safer on the park pathways (Central Park and along the East and Hudson rivers) and to use them only in daylight hours. You can rent bikes at West Side Bicycle Store.
Useful information West Side Bicycle Store, W 96th St & Broadway. **Map** 15 C2 [663-7531.

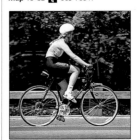
Cyclist in Central Park

Driving in New York

HEAVY TRAFFIC AND EXPENSIVE rental cars make driving in New York a frustrating experience. You must wear a seat belt. The speed limit is 30 mph (48 km/h) – which is difficult to exceed because of Manhattan's pot-holes and traffic. Most streets are one-way, and there are traffic lights at every corner. Driving is on the right.

Traffic on Sixth Avenue

RENTING A CAR

TO RENT A CAR you must be able to prove that you are at least 25 years old. You will need a valid driver's license (for foreign visitors an International Driver's License is useful) and a credit card or you will have to pay a large deposit.

Unless you are adequately covered by your own insurance policy, you should also take out damage and liability protection, as vandalism and theft are common. Refill with gas before you return the car or you'll pay double the normal price for fuel. It is cheaper to rent a car in the city than at the airports.

TRAFFIC SIGNS

Black-and-white markings on many street crossings mean that pedestrians have right of way. At intersections, they indicate that traffic should keep out when the light is red. Unlike the rest of New York State, you can never turn right on a red light unless there is a sign indicating otherwise.

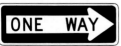

Traffic flows in a single direction

PARKING

PARKING IN Manhattan is difficult and costly. Parking areas and parking garages post their rates at the entrance. Some hotels include parking charges in their room rates.

In some areas there are meters at the curb for short-term (20–60 minutes) parking. Don't be tempted to park at out-of-order meters – you may receive a parking ticket. Yellow street and curb markings mean no parking.

"Alternate-side" parking applies on most of the city's side streets. Cars may usually be left all day and night but must be moved to the other side of the street before 8am the next day. For specific information call the **Transportation Department.**

PENALTIES

IF YOU RECEIVE a parking ticket, you have seven days to pay the required fine or to appeal against it. If you have any queries about your ticket call the **Parking Violations Bureau** between 8:30am and 7pm on any weekday.

New York's tow-away brigades are extremely active, and one-third of cars towed suffer damage. If you cannot

Entry prohibited

50 mph (80 km/h) speed limit

Give way to all vehicles

Stop at intersection

find your car at its parking place, first of all call the traffic department's tow-away office. The pound is open 24 hours a day, Monday to Saturday. You can redeem your car for a hefty fine of $150, plus $10 per day storage fee. Traveler's checks, certified checks, money orders and cash are all accepted. There is an ATM machine *(see p358)* on the premises. If you have rented the car, the contract must be produced, and only the authorized driver (with license) may redeem the car. If it is not there, report its loss to the police.

Useful information Police emergencies only (*911*; Parking Violations Bureau (*477-4430*; Traffic Dept, Tow Pound, Pier 76, W 38th St and Twelfth Ave., and at the uptown 207th St. pound. **Map** 7 1B. (*788-7800*; Transportation Dept (*225-5368*.

Police Department traffic officer

CAR RENTAL AGENCIES

IF YOU NEED TO rent a car while in New York, agencies are listed in the telephone directory under *Automobile Renting*. The major rental companies include:

Avis
(*(800) 331-1212*.

Budget
(*(800) 527-0700*.

Dollar
(*(800) 800-4000*.

Hertz
(*(800) 654-3131*.

National
(*(800) 227-7368*.

New York's Taxis

New York taxi cab

ALL LICENSED TAXI cabs are yellow. If their roof numbers are lit up, they are available and can be flagged down. Occupied cabs have their top lights switched off. Taxis that are not on duty have their "Off-Duty" sign lit. Only licensed cabs are authorized to pick up people who hail them from the street; accepting a ride from anyone else can be dangerous and expensive.

TAKING A CAB

EVERY YELLOW CAB has a meter, and many can issue printed receipts. A taxi can carry up to four passengers with a single fare covering everyone on board.

Taxi stands are scarce; hotels, Penn Station and Grand Central Terminal are by far the best places to seek cabs.

Licensed taxis undergo periodic inspections and are insured against accidents and losses. Non-licensed or "gypsy" cabs are unlikely to have these safeguards, but they can be an alternative.

Once the cab driver accepts a passenger the meter starts ticking at $2. The fare increases 30 cents after each additional 292 yards (320 meters). Surcharges will then be added for waiting time and trips between 8pm and 6am. A few drivers now accept credit cards but most will want to be paid in cash. Tip the driver about 15%.

Cab driving is a traditional occupation of newly arrived immigrants and, as such, communication can be a problem. Although owners of licensed cabs must pass exams in English comprehension and the layout of the city, they will not necessarily understand either. Make sure your driver understands exactly

A printed receipt available from most taxi cabs

where you want to go before you start your ride.

By law, a driver must take you anywhere in the city unless the off-duty sign is lit and the roof light is off. The driver should not ask you your destination until after you've sat down, and must follow your requests not to smoke, to open or close a window, and to pick up or drop off passengers as you direct. If he or she doesn't comply you can then report them to the **Taxi & Limousine Commission**.

Each yellow cab displays the driver's photograph and registered number next to the meter. Drivers can be sullen, or try to overcharge or not cooperate with some of your requests. Make a note of the driver's number or the license or receipt number (if you have requested one), and report it to a policeman.

Heavy one-way traffic on one of the city's avenues

TAXI NUMBERS

Taxi & Limousine Commission
(302-8294 or 676-1000 for *general information.*

Lost and Found
(302-8294.

If you would prefer to use a taxi that has been radio-dispatched, rather than hailing one on the street, call:

Allstate Car & Limousine
((800) 453-4099 (toll free).

Chris Limousines
((718) 356-3232.

Sabra Travel, Inc.
(777-7171
or (800) 722-7122 (toll free).

A meter will display your fare as it mounts up. Additional costs are then shown separately.

The roof-light illuminates the cab's number as well as the driver's "Off-Duty" sign.

Charge rates are listed clearly on the outside of the front passenger door.

Traveling by Bus

THE CITY'S MORE THAN 4,000 blue-and-white buses cover more than 200 routes in the five boroughs. Many run 24 hours a day, every day. The buses are modern, clean and air-conditioned. Traveling by bus is a good way to take in many of New York's sights. Buses are also considered very safe and tend not to get too crowded. Smoking is forbidden on all public buses, and animals (except guide dogs) are not allowed.

The fare box is just inside the entrance doors, next to the driver.

FARE

YOU CAN PAY THE FARE with a MetroCard *(see p374)*, a token or exact change (coins only). Bus drivers cannot make change, and fare boxes do not accept bills or pennies. You can buy the MetroCard or tokens at any subway station booth.

Subway or bus token

If you pay with a MetroCard, a free bus-to-subway, subway-to-bus, or bus-to-bus transfer is electronically placed on the card. If you pay with a token or exact change, you get a free bus-to-bus transfer, valid for an hour. Be sure to ask the driver when you pay. There are discount fares for senior citizens and the disabled. All buses can "kneel," which helps elderly people board *(see p354)* and are also accessible to wheelchairs via a platform at the rear.

Bus transfer

RIDING THE BUS

BUSES WILL STOP only at the designated bus stops. They follow north–south routes on the major avenues, stopping every two or three blocks. Crosstown buses, running east–west, stop at every block *(see p368)*. Many routes run a 24-hour daily service, which becomes a lot less frequent during the evening and at night; other bus services operate only during the peak hours of 7am to 10pm.

Bus stops are marked by red, white and blue signs and yellow paint along the curb. Most also have bus shelters. A route map and schedule is posted at each stop. When you have identified your bus, enter at the front door and put your MetroCard or token in the fare box. Request a transfer if you will be changing to another bus. The

Bus stops often have three-sided, glass-walled shelters.

This bus map shows the route and main stopping-off points for route M15.

majority of New York's bus drivers are very friendly and will call out your stop if you ask them to.

To request a stop when traveling on the bus, press the vertical call strip between the windows. A "Stop Requested" sign near the driver will light up.

Leave through the double door located toward the rear of the bus. The driver will activate the door release as soon as the bus has stopped, but you then have to push the door to open it. If you do not keep a firm grip on the door handle it is liable to swing back and hit you, so take care.

Route numbers appear on the front and side of the bus.

Enter the bus through the doors at the front.

RECOGNIZING YOUR BUS

Each bus stop serves more than one route, so look for the route number posted on the lighted strip above the windshield on the front of the bus. Ask the driver if he or she will be stopping at your destination or close to it.

Exit the bus through the double doors toward the rear.

LONG-DISTANCE & COMMUTER BUSES

BUSES TO THE rest of the US and Canada leave from the **Port Authority Bus Terminal**. Another terminal, at the Manhattan end of the George Washington Bridge, is for local buses to northern New Jersey and New York's Rockland County.

Bus tickets at Port Authority are on sale in the main concourse. The long-distance bus companies, Greyhound, Peter Pan, and Adirondack and the commuter Short Line and NJ Transit have their own ticket counters. There are no reservations taken on any of these bus lines.

There are bathrooms open from 6am to 10pm, but caution is advised. The homeless congregate in Port Authority.

A Greyhound bus arriving in New York en route to Port Authority

BUS INFORMATION

Route Maps
Available from MTA, 370 Jay St, Brooklyn, NY 11201 or NYC Visitors Center, 810 7th Ave (212-484-1222).

MTA Travel Information
(718) 330-1234 (24 hrs).

Port Authority Bus Terminal
West 40th St and Eighth Ave.
Map 8 D1.
564-8484.

George Washington Bridge Terminal
178th St. and Broadway.
564-1114.

Lost Property
(212) 712-4500.

SIGHTSEEING BY BUS

For a pleasant and cheap alternative to a tour bus, hop on a city bus and see New York with the New Yorkers. Bus routes M1 and M6 down Fifth and Seventh Avenues to the Battery, returning north via the Wall Street area, Madison Avenue, and Sixth Avenue. Route M5 gives fine views of the Hudson River as buses travel north on Riverside Drive to the George Washington Bridge at 178th Street. Route M104 travels from the United Nations at First Avenue across 42nd Street, through Times Square, then follows Broadway north by Lincoln Center to Columbia University at 125th Street.

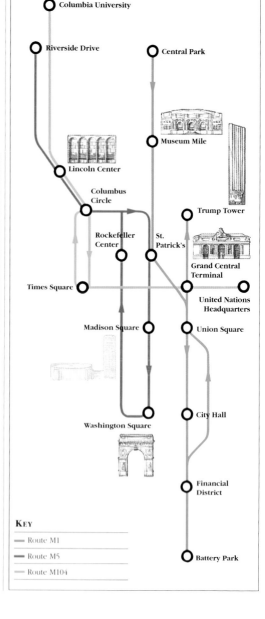

- Columbia University
- Riverside Drive
- Central Park
- Museum Mile
- Lincoln Center
- Columbus Circle
- Trump Tower
- Rockefeller Center
- St. Patrick's
- Grand Central Terminal
- Times Square
- United Nations Headquarters
- Madison Square
- Union Square
- City Hall
- Washington Square
- Financial District
- Battery Park

KEY
— Route M1
— Route M5
— Route M104

Using the Subway

New York subway logo

THE SUBWAY is the quickest and most reliable way to travel in the city. The vast system extends over 233 route miles (375 km) and has 468 stations. Most routes operate 24 hours a day throughout the year. Night services are less frequent, and fewer trains run on weekends. In the last few years the subway system has been completely upgraded, and the trains are now air-conditioned, well lit, safer and much more comfortable.

NEW YORK SUBWAY

MANY SUBWAY entrances are marked by illuminated spheres: green where the station booth is manned around the clock, red means restricted entry. Others are marked by a sign bearing the name of the station and the numbers or letters of the routes passing through it.

The subway system runs 24 hours a day, but some routes do have restricted operating times. The basic service is between 6am and midnight.

Bear in mind that there are two types of trains. Local trains stop at all stations, and express trains are faster and stop at fewer stations. Both types of stops are distinguished on every subway map.

In general, the safest, but most crowded, times to travel are between the rush hours of 8am to 6pm. Use common sense, stand in the "Off-Hour Waiting Area" on the platforms, and always be sure of where you are going when you use the subway. It is safe to travel to outer boroughs, although it is not a good idea for anyone to travel alone after midnight. Use the central cars and avoid eye contact with unsavory characters. In an emergency, contact the guard at the station.

Subway information New York City Transit Authority 【 *(718) 330-1234.* Metrocard Customer Service 【 *(212) 638-7622.*

SUBWAY FARE

THE FARE is the same no matter how far you travel on the subway. Since 1997, use of the new MetroCard has greatly increased, and the MTA is phasing out tokens as a means of fare. Many different types of MetroCards exist, providing flexibility for passengers. The price of the MetroCard ranges from $5 to $80 depending on the number of trips you plan to take. Ask at the booth for information.

MetroCard

READING THE SUBWAY MAP

Each route is identified on the subway map *(see inside back cover)* by color, by the names of the stations at each end of the line, and by a letter or number. For instance, the green (6) route links Woodlawn and Utica Avenues, and is served by number 4 trains. Local and express stops and interchange points are identified. The letters and numbers below the station names indicate which routes serve that particular station. A letter or number in heavy type indicates that trains on that route stop there between 6am and midnight; letters in lighter type mean that the route is served by a part-time service only; a boxed letter or number shows the last stop on the line. The maps posted in all the subway stations have a comprehensive guide that explains the trains and timetable of each route.

This station's green sphere shows that it is staffed continuously

Line letter

Local stop

Express stop

Express and local stop

Free local transfers

Free express transfers

42 Street– Times Square

N·R S

1·2·3 7 9

Express and local stops

Light type
Part-time service

Free transfers from line to line

Boxed type
Last stop on this line (full or part-time)

Bold type Full-time service

MAKING A TRIP BY SUBWAY

1 There is a map of the subway system on the back inside cover of this book. Large-scale maps are also positioned in prominent areas in every station, usually very near the token booth.

the map

Subway map

Booth with agent

2 Buy a MetroCard or token from a booth or a vending machine.

Vending machine

3 Use the card or token to pass through the turnstile onto the platform.

4 Follow the directions for the train you want. For safety, stay in sight of the booth as you wait for your train; at night, stay in one of the yellow off-hours waiting areas.

Entry turnstile

→ **Uptown Local** ① ⑨

Off-hours waiting area

5 Each train displays its route number or letter in the appropriate color and the names of the terminal stations.

Route indicator

6 Once aboard, you will find a system map next to the door on each side of the car. Use it to follow your progress. Stops are announced on the public address system, and you will also see the station names at each platform. The doors are operated by the driver. For safety, be sure to enter a well-populated car.

7 After leaving the train, look for signs giving directions to the exit. If you need to change trains, just follow the signs to the connecting platforms.

→ **Exit** 33 St 7 Av Penn Station Madison Square Garden Amtrack LIRR NJ Transit

Traveling by Train

NEW YORK HAS TWO main train stations. Grand Central Terminal is served by commuter trains from New York's suburbs and Connecticut, while Pennsylvania (Penn) Station is the terminal for long-distance services from the rest of the US and also Canada. Most commuter trains have no buffet cars on board, so it's best to buy any food and drink you want before boarding the train. Seat reservations are available only on the long-distance intercity services.

An Amtrak train

GRAND CENTRAL TERMINAL

GRAND CENTRAL Terminal (*see pp154–5*) on Park Avenue between 41st and 42nd streets is the main terminal for **Metro-North Rail-road** trains (Hudson, New Haven and Harlem lines), which run north and east of New York and serve southwest Connec-ticut and West-chester, Dutchess, and Putnam counties. From Grand Central you might travel by train to such destinations as the Bronx Zoo (*see pp242–3*), the New York

Botanical Garden and President Franklin D. Roosevelt's Hyde Park estate.

The 4, 5 and 6 trains on the green (Lexington) line and number 7 on the purple (Flushing) line serve Grand Central subway station, below the main terminal. A shuttle service links Grand Central to Times Square. Many bus lines stop at Grand Central.

PENN STATION

PENN STATION, between Seventh and Eighth avenues and from 31st to 33rd streets, is a modern terminal that was rebuilt in 1963 under-neath the Madison Square Garden com-plex (*see p133*). Commuter trains, New Jersey Transit trains and **Amtrak** trains from Canada and other parts of the US terminate at this station. There are no luggage trolleys, but redcap porters will help.

You will find taxis at street level. Buses run downtown on Seventh Avenue and uptown on Eighth Avenue. The blue (8th Avenue) subway lines, A, C, and E run on the Eighth Avenue side of the station; the red (Broadway) lines, 1, 2, 3 and 4 run on the Seventh Avenue side of the station. The ticket counters and waiting rooms are one level below; the trains leave from an even lower level.

From Penn Station, you could head for New Jersey and Long Island or farther on Amtrak trains to such destina-

Grand Central Terminal

tions as Canada, Philadelphia or Washington. Also in Penn Station are ticket offices and departure points of the **Long Island Rail Road (LIRR)**, mainly a commuter line, but with trains to such Long Island resorts, as the Hamptons and Montauk Point.

PATH TRAINS

PATH TRAINS operate round the clock between New Jersey stations (Harrison, Hoboken, Jersey City and Newark) and Penn Station in Manhattan. They also stop at Christopher Street, the World Trade Center, 9th, 14th, 23rd and 33rd streets and Avenue of the Americas (6th Avenue).

LIRR train at Penn Station

AMTRAK

AMTRAK IS THE US national railroad passenger service linking New York with other US cities and Canada. Some Amtrak trains have cars with reclining seats; others have dining facilities and lounge cars. Sleeper cars are available on all long-distance routes. The new express trains operate on certain Amtrak routes, such as the **Acela** between Boston and Wash-ington via New York.

Tickets can be bought at Penn Station, as well as from Amtrak Travel Centers. Buy your ticket before getting on the train as there is a penalty for buying tickets on board. Senior citizens receive a 15% discount; the conductor will ask for proof of age. There are no student discounts. Seat reservations made by phone with a credit card need to be made at least 10 days in advance of travel if you want the tickets mailed to you.

Amtrak also offers a Great American Vacations package and various promotional fares during the year. Ask for information when you book.

Information board at Penn Station

TICKETS AND TRAVEL

TICKETING AREAS at all train stations are well lit and generally crowded at all times of the day. Ticket offices will accept most credit cards, as well as cash. There are a variety of ticket types, most based on a one-way fare; a return fare is twice the single fare. If you are planning a number of trips, Metro-North and LIRR offer weekly passes that will save you money.

Train times, destination and gate numbers are continually updated on numerous large information boards. Watch for signs indicating the major interim stops and transfer points, listed next to the gate for departing trains. Wait for the opening of the gate posted for your train. Metro-North and LIRR cars are all one class, and have no reserved seating. Amtrak trains offer both services. The conductor will ask to see your ticket after the train has left the station.

Penn Station and Grand Central Terminal have good facilities, including bathrooms, banks, shops, bars and restaurants.

TRAIN INFORMATION

Amtrak Travel Centers
12 West 51st St. **Map** *12 F4.*
1 East 59th St. **Map** *12 F3.*
1 World Trade Center. **Map** *1 B2.*
C *(800) USA-RAIL or*
(800) 872-7245.

Long Island Rail Road (LIRR)
C *(718) 217-LIRR (Information).*
C *(718) 558 8384 (Lost property).*

Acela
C *(800) 523-8720.*

Metro-North
C *532-4900 (Information).*
C *340-2555 (Lost property).*

PATH Trains
C *(800) 234-7284*

DAY TRIPS BY TRAIN

There are some beautiful places outside New York city, which, if your time allows, are well worth a visit. Below is a list of some recommended sights within 125 miles (200 km) of New York city center. For further details, call the New York Convention and Visitors Bureau *(see p352).*

A scenic view of Tarrytown

Stony Brook
Peaceful north shore village. Entrance to the Three Villages historic district.
🚆 *58 miles (93 km) east. Long Island Rail Road from Penn Station. 2 hrs.*

The Hamptons
Chic bars and boutiques in a weathered, historic setting. The Beverly Hills of Long Island.
🚆 *100 miles (161 km) east. Long Island Rail Road from Penn Station. 2 hrs, 50 min.*

Montauk Point
State park on the eastern-most tip of Long Island; windswept ocean views.
🚆 *120 miles (193 km). LIRR from Penn Station. 3 hrs.*

Westbury House, Old Westbury
John Phipps's 1906 re-creation of a Charles II mansion with exquisite English formal gardens.
🚆 *24 miles (39 km) east. Long Island Rail Road from Penn Station. 40 min.*

Tarrytown
Washington Irving's home "Sunnyside" and Jay Gould's mansion.
🚆 *25 miles (40 km) north. Metro-North from Grand Central, then taxi. 40–50 min.*

Hyde Park
Springwood estate of Franklin D. Roosevelt and the Vanderbilt mansion.
🚆 *74 miles (119 km) north. Metro-North from Grand Central to Poughkeepsie, then bus. 2 hrs.*

New Haven, Connecticut
Home of Yale University.
🚆 *74 miles (119 km). Metro-North from Grand Central Terminal. 1 hr, 46 min.*

Hartford, Connecticut
Mark Twain's riverboat-style house, Atheneum Museum and Old State House.
🚆 *112 miles (180 km) north. Amtrak from Penn Station. 2 hrs, 45 min.*

Winterthur, Delaware
Henry du Pont's collection of Early American art, museum and gardens.
🚆 *116 miles (187 km) south. Amtrak from Penn Station to Wilmington, then bus to Winterthur. 2 hrs.*

Yale University in New Haven, Connecticut

STREET FINDER

THE MAP REFERENCES given with all sights, hotels, restaurants, bars, shops and entertainment venues described in this book refer to the maps in this section (*see* How Map References Work *opposite*). These maps cover the whole of Manhattan. A complete index of street names and all the places of interest marked on the maps can be found on the following pages.

The key map *(below)* shows the areas covered by the *Street Finder*, within the various districts. The maps include all of Manhattan's sight-seeing areas (which are color-coded), with all the districts important for hotels, restaurants, bars, shops, theaters and entertainment.

Browsing at South Street Seaport

0 kilometers   2

0 miles   1

Inset on Map 1

KEY TO STREET FINDER

Major sight

Other sight

Station building

M Subway station

⬛ Heliport

⛴ Ferry terminal

🚌 Bus terminal

🚊 Tram terminal

P Parking

ℹ Tourist information office

✚ Hospital with emergency unit

🚓 Police station

✝ Church

✡ Synagogue

⊠ Post office

═ Railway line

One way street

Pedestrian street

SCALE OF MAP PAGES

0 meters   200
                        1:12,500
0 yards   200

Inset on Map 19

HOW THE MAP REFERENCES WORK

The first figure tells you which Street Finder map to turn to.

Theodore Roosevelt Birthplace ❼

28 E 20th St. **Map 9** A5. 📞 260-1616. M 14th St-Union Sq. **Open** 9am–5pm Wed–Sun (last adm: 4:30pm). **Closed** public hols. **Adm charge.** 📷 🎦 Lectures, concerts, films & video. 🚻

A letter and number give the grid reference. Letters go across the map's top and bottom, numbers on its sides.

The map continues on map 5 of the *Street Finder.*

Street Finder Index

Each place name is followed by its borough (unless in Manhattan) and then by its Street Finder reference

Each place name is followed by its borough (unless in Manhattan) and then by its Street Finder reference

Each place name is followed by its borough (unless in Manhattan) and then by its Street Finder reference

Each place name is followed by its borough (unless in Manhattan) and then by its Street Finder reference

NORTH 9TH STREET
NORTH 8TH STREET
NORTH 7TH STREET
NORTH 6TH AVENUE STREET
NORTHAVENUE AVENUE STREET
NORTH 5TH STREET

1

EAST

NORTH 4TH STREET
KENT WYTHE
Athletic
Field
NORTH 3RD STREET
STREET
BERRY
#215
METROPOLITAN AVENUE
RIVER
NORTH 1ST STREET

2

(EAST RIVER DRIVE)
RIVER
GRAND STREET
SOUTH 1ST STREET

MANGIN STREET
SOUTH 2ND STREET
BARUCH PLACE
PARK
SOUTH 3RD STREET
FRANKLIN
SOUTH 4TH STREET
SOUTH 5TH STREET

3

Williamsburg Bridge
SOUTH 6TH STREET
BERRY STREET
STREET
#375
DUNHAM
PLACE
SOUTH
D. ROOSEVELT
BROADWAY
EAST
SOUTH 8TH STREET
LEWIS STREET
STREET
SOUTH 9TH ST
SAMUEL A
AVENUE
SPIEGEL SQUARE
□ Fireboat Station
RIVER
SOUTH 11TH ST

4

CHERRY STREET
DRIVE
PARK
Wallabout
CORLEARS
STREET
HOOK PARK
Channel
DIVISION AVENUE
VIADUCT
Corlears
Hook

PIER 44
US Naval Reserve
Center

5

Wallabout Bay

Hudson River

CONRAIL
PIERS
(ABANDONED)

PIER 99
PIER 98
PIER 97
PIER 96
PIER 95
PIER 94
PIER 92

N. Y. C. Passenger Ship Terminal
(Port Authority)

PIER 90
PIER 88
PIER 86

Intrepid Sea-Air-Space Museum

PIER 84

HENRY HUDSON PARKWAY
MILLER HIGHWAY

FREEDOM PLACE

WEST END AVENUE

WEST 72ND STREET
WEST 71ST STREET
WEST 70TH STREET

WEST SIDE

WEST 66TH STREET
WEST 65TH STREET
WEST 64TH STREET

WEST 61ST STREET
WEST 60TH STREET
WEST 59TH STREET
WEST 58TH STREET

WEST 57TH STREET

WEST 56TH STREET
WEST 55TH STREET
WEST 54TH STREET

DE WITT
CLINTON
PARK

WEST 53RD STREET
WEST 52ND STREET
WEST 51ST STREET
WEST 50TH STREET

TWELFTH AVENUE

ELEVENTH AVENUE

WEST 49TH STREET
WEST 48TH STREET
WEST 47TH STREET
WEST 46TH STREET
WEST 45TH STREET
WEST 44TH STREET

TENTH AVENUE

VERDI
SQUARE
M 72nd Street
SHERMAN SQUARE
The Dorilton

AMSTERDAM
BROADWAY

The Juilliard School
Alice Tully Hall
Lincoln Center
Metropolitan Opera House
DAMROSCH PARK
Guggenheim Bandshell
Fordham University
Roosevelt Hospital Center

TWELFTH AVE

WEST 130TH STREET

ST CLAIR PLACE

WEST 125TH STREET

CONVENT HILL

CONVENT AVENUE

ST NICHOLAS TERRACE

ST NICHOLAS AVENUE

#4020

#1401

WEST 129TH STREET

WEST 126TH STREET

WEST 128TH STREET

125th Street
M

(MARTIN LUTHER KING, JR BOULEVARD)

OLD BROADWAY

WEST 127TH STREET

WEST 126TH STREET

TIEMANN PLACE

CLAREMONT AVENUE

BROADWAY

AMSTERDAM

ROOSEVELT SQUARE

WEST 125TH STREET
M 125th Street

LA SALLE STREET

HANCOCK PLACE

#388   #323

HANCOCK SQUARE

HENRY HUDSON PARKWAY 9A

RIVERSIDE DRIVE EAST

RIVERSIDE DRIVE WEST

Grant's Tomb

WEST 123RD STREET

WEST 123RD STREET

Jewish Theological Seminary

WEST 122ND STREET

WEST 122ND STREET

MANHATTAN STREET

Riverside Church

AVENUE

WEST 121ST STREET

REINHOLD NIEBUHR PLACE

WEST 121ST STREET

Teachers' College, Columbia University

WEST 120TH STREET

WEST 120TH STREET

RIVERSIDE PARK

RIVERSIDE DRIVE

W 119TH ST

#1181

Pedestrian Bridge

WEST 119TH STREET

MORNINGSIDE PARK

MORNINGSIDE AVENUE

WEST 118TH STREET

St Paul's Chapel

WEST 117TH STREET

Lou Library

Columbia

A H Sulzberger Plaza

3

M 116th Street-Columbia University

W 115TH ST

University

Butler Library

WEST 114TH STREET

MORNINGSIDE DRIVE

WEST 116TH STREET

WEST 115TH STREET

St Luke's Hospital Center

BROADWAY

WEST 113TH STREET

WEST 112TH STREET

Cathedral of St John the Divine

WEST 111TH STREET

M 110th Street-Cathedral Parkway

#380

#2824

CATHEDRAL   PARKWAY

#595   #370   #311

WEST 109TH STREET

AMSTERDAM

MANHATTAN AVENUE

COLUMBUS AVENUE

RIVERSIDE DRIVE

WEST 108TH STREET

WEST 107TH STREET

STRAUS PARK

BROADWAY

WEST 106TH STREET (DUKE ELLINGTON BOULEVARD)

WEST END AVENUE

WEST 105TH STREET

AVENUE

AVENUE

WEST 104TH STREET

AVENUE

WEST 103RD STREET   M 103rd Street

#695   #2625   #856

General Index

Acknowledgments

DORLING KINDERSLEY would like to thank the many people whose help and assistance contributed to the preparation of this book.

MAIN CONTRIBUTOR
Eleanor Berman has lived in New York for almost 40 years. Her travel articles are widely published and she is the author of *Away for the Weekend: New York*, a favorite since 1982. Her other books include *Away for the Weekend* guides for the Mid-Atlantic, New England and Northern California, *Travelling on Your Own* and *Reflections of Washington, DC.*

MUSEUM CONTRIBUTORS
Michelle Menendez, Lucy O'Brien, Heidi Rosenau, Elyse Topalian, Sally Williams.

DORLING KINDERSLEY wishes to thank the following editors and researchers at Websters International Publishers: Sandy Carr, Matthew Barrell, Sara Harper, Miriam Lloyd, Ava-Lee Tanner, Celia Woolfrey.

ADDITIONAL PHOTOGRAPHY
Edward Hueber, Eliot Kaufman, Karen Kent, Norman McGrath, Howard Millard, Paul Solomon, Chuck Spang, Chris Stevens.

ADDITIONAL ILLUSTRATIONS
Steve Gyapay, Kevin Jones, Dinwiddie MacLaren, Janos Marffy, Chris D. Orr, Nick Shewring, John Woodcock.

CARTOGRAPHY
MAPS Andrew Heritage, James Mills-Hicks, Chez Picthall, John Plumer (Dorling Kindersley Cartography)
Advanced Illustration (Cheshire), Contour Publishing (Derby), Europmap Ltd (Berkshire). Street Finder maps: ERA-Maptec Ltd (Dublin) adapted with permission from original survey and mapping by Shobunsha (Japan).

CARTOGRAPHIC RESEARCH
Roger Bullen, Tony Chambers, Ruth Duxbury, Ailsa Heritage, Jayne Parsons, Laura Porter, Donna Rispoli, Joan Russell, Jill Tinsley, Andrew Thompson.

DESIGN AND EDITORIAL
MANAGING EDITOR Douglas Amrine
MANAGING ART EDITORS Stephen Knowlden, Geoff Manders
SENIOR EDITOR Georgina Matthews
SERIES DESIGN CONSULTANT Peter Luff
EDITORIAL DIRECTOR David Lamb
ART DIRECTOR Anne-Marie Bulat
PRODUCTION CONTROLLER Hilary Stephens
PICTURE RESEARCH Susan Mennell, Sarah Moule
DTP DESIGNER Andy Wilkinson
Keith Addison, Ron Boudreau, Linda Cabasin, Michelle Clark, Carey Combe, Diana Craig, Maggie Crowley, Guy Dimond, Tom Fraser, Alex Gray, Marcus Hardy, Sasha Heseltine, Pippa Hurst, Kim Inglis, Jane Middleton, Helen Partington, Leigh Priest, Nicki Rawson, Marisa Renzullo, Ellen Root, Liz Rowe, Anaïs Scott, Anna Streiffert, Clare Sullivan, Andrew Szudek.

SPECIAL ASSISTANCE
Beyer Blinder Belle, John Beatty at the Cotton Club, Peter Casey at the New York Public Library, Nicky Clifford, Linda Corcoran at the Bronx Zoo, Audrey Manley at the Morgan Library, Jane Fischer, Deborah Gaines at the New York Convention and Visitors Bureau, Dawn Geigerich at the Queens Museum of Art, Peggy Harrington at St. John the Divine, Pamela Herrick at the Van Cortlandt House, Marguerite Lavin at the Museum of the City of New York, Robert Makla at the Friends of Central Park, Gary Miller at the New York Stock Exchange, Laura Mogil at the American Museum of Natural History, Fred Olsson at the Shubert Organization, Dominique Palermo at the Police Academy Museum, Royal Canadian Pancake House, Lydia Ruth and Laura I. Fries at the Empire State Building, David Schwartz at the American Museum of the Moving Image, Joy Sienkiewicz at the South Street Seaport Museum, Barbara Orlando at the Metropolitan Transit Authority, the staff at the Lower East Side Tenement Museum, Msgr. Anthony Dalla Valla at St. Patrick's Cathedral.

RESEARCH ASSISTANCE
Christa Griffin, B. Kaczorowski, Steve McClure, Sabra Moore, Jeff Mulligan, Marc Svensson, Malissa Taylor, Vicky Weiner, Steven Weinstein.

PHOTOGRAPHIC REFERENCE
Duncan Petersen Publishers Ltd.

PHOTOGRAPHY PERMISSIONS
DORLING KINDERSLEY would like to thank the following for their kind permission to photograph at their establishments:
American Craft Museum, American Museum of Natural History, Aunt Len's Doll and Toy Museum, Balducci's, Home Savings of America, Brooklyn Children's Museum, The Cloisters, Columbia University, Eldridge Street Project, Federal Hall, Rockefeller Group, Trump Tower.

PICTURE CREDITS
t = top; tc = top center; tr = top right; cla = center left above; ca = center above; cra = center right above; cl = center left; c = center; cr = center right; clb = center left below; cb = center below; crb = center right below; bl = bottom left; bc = bottom center; br = bottom right.

Works of art have been reproduced with the permission of the following copyright holders:
© ADAGP, Paris and DACS, London 1993: 67cl (*Four Trees*, April 1971–July 1972, by Jean Dubuffet), 105cl, 170bl, 186tl, 187crb, 199crb; *Alice In Wonderland*, 1959 © Jose de Creeft/ DACS, London/VAGA, New York 1993: 53cl, 205cl; © DACS 1993: 34tr, 113tc, 160tr (donated by the Norwegian Government, 1952), 171cb, 172cr, 186bl, 187cra, 187bl, 188cla; © Estate of STUART DAVIS/DACS, London/VAGA, New York 1993: 199cr; © DEMART PRO ARTE BV/DACS 1993: 172cl; *The American Merchant Mariners Memorial*, 1991, © MARISOL ESCOBAR/DACS, London/VAGA, New York 1993: 55bc; © JASPER JOHNS/DACS, London/VAGA, New York 1993: 199ca; © ROY LICHTENSTEIN/DACS 1993: 140tr

(commissioned by The Equitable Life Assurance Society of the United States), 173tl, 198clb; © Estate of DAVID SMITH/DACS, London/VAGA, New York 1993: 199bl.
© 1993 THE GEORGIA O'KEEFFE FOUNDATION/ARS, New York: 198c; © 1993 FRANK STELLA/ARS, New York: 190tr.
By permission of ELLSWORTH KELLY: 35cr.
By permission of E JAN NADELMAN: 199br.
Printed by permission of the NORMAN ROCKWELL FAMILY TRUST © 1961 the Norman Rockwell Family Trust: 161br.
© 1993 THE ANDY WARHOL FOUNDATION FOR THE VISUAL ARTS, INC: 198cla.
© THE WHITNEY MUSEUM OF AMERICAN ART, NY: 35br (*The Brooklyn Bridge: Variation On An Old Theme*, 1939, by Joseph Stella), 198bl.

The Publishers are grateful to the following museums, companies and picture libraries for permission to reproduce their photographs:

ALGONQUIN HOTEL, N.Y.: 272bl; AQUARIUS, UK: 169c; AMERICAN MUSEUM-HAYDEN PLANETARIUM, NY: 216tl; AMERICAN MUSEUM OF THE MOVING IMAGE: Carson Collection © Bruce Polin 245t; AMERICAN MUSEUM OF NATURAL HISTORY: 37bl, 214ca; ASHMOLEAN MUSEUM, Oxford: 15tc; THE ASIA SOCIETY, NY: 185cl; AVERY ARCHITECTURAL AND FINE ART LIBRARY, Columbia University in the City of New York: 135cl; AVERY FISHER HALL: © N McGrath 1976 331tr.

© THE GEORGE BALANCHINE TRUST: *Apollo*, choreography by George Balanchine, photo by P Kolnik 5tc; *Stravinsky Violin Concerto*, choreography by George Balanchine, photo by P Kolnik 328tc; George Balanchine's *The Nutcracker*, SM, photo by P Kolnik 331cb; THE BETTMANN ARCHIVE, NY: 16bcl, 17cra, 17cr, 17bl, 18cl, 20cbr, 20bl, 20–21, 23br, 25cra, 26cla, 26cra, 26crb, 30cla, 31tl, 41tl, 43cbl, 47cr, 47bc, 49c, 54-55b, 71tl, 74cla, 79crb, 79br, 109bl, 175cla, 183br, 207t, 210cl, 223cr, 229t, 239tr, 265tl; BETTMANN NEWSPHOTOS/REUTERS: 31tr; BETTMANN/ UPI: 27cra, 27bc, 28bcr, 29br, 30cra, 30bl, 30br, 44cl, 47cra, 48cl, 49bl, 72c, 72ca, 78cl, 151c, 161c, 264br, 265cr; BLOOMINGDALE'S: 27cbr; BFI: courtesy of Paramount Pictures 46b; © Roy Export Company Establishment 173tr; THE BRITISH LIBRARY, London: 14; BROOKLYN HISTORICAL SOCIETY: (detail) 89tl; THE BROOKLYN MUSEUM: 34clb (*Climbing Into The Promised Land*, 1908, photo by Lewis Wick Hine), 36bl, 37c, 248cra, 248bl, 249t, 249cra, 249c, 249bl, 250t, 250br, 251cr, 251bl; The Cantor Collection 251cl; photo by J Kerr 248c, 250bl; photo by P Warchol 249cr; BROWN BROTHERS: 67br, 71bl, 82cra, 90t, 104br.

CAMERA PRESS: 28cbr, 28bl, 31cb, 125cr; R Open 48tr; T Spencer 30cb; THE CARLYLE HOTEL, NY: 273tr, 328bc; CARNEGIE HALL: © H. Grossman 331br; J ALLAN CASH: 31bl, 362cr; CATHEDRAL OF ST. JOHN THE DIVINE: Greg Wyatt 1985, 225tl; CBS ENTERTAINMENT/DESILU TOO: "Vacation from Marriage" 169br; CHELSEA PIERS: Fred George 31bl; COLORIFIC!: A Clifton 373cl; Colorific/ Black Star: 79cra; T Cowell 221cr; R Fraser 74t; H Matsumoto 368cr, 371tr; D Moore 29bl; T Spiegel 13cr, 348tr; CORBIS UK: Gail Mooney 205b; CULVER

PICTURES, INC: (inset) 9, 17crb, 18cbl, 19bl, 21tl, 21br, 24tl, 24cl, 27cb, 27bl, 46tr, 47cb, 48br, 49tr, 74bl, 75cra, 75cb, 76tl, 78crb, 83c, 83crb, 119bl, 122tc, 125bl, 135cr, 145c, 147cl, 227t, 227bc, 227cr, 257bl, 259crb.

DAILY EAGLE: (detail) 89cl; DAILY NEWS: 354tl, 354tr.

ESSEX HOUSE, NY: 268cr; COLLECTION THE EQUITABLE LIFE ASSURANCE SOCIETY: Photo by G Gorgoni 140tr; ESTO: P Aaron 330bl; MARY EVANS PICTURE LIBRARY: 22br, 46clb, 47br, 87br, 104bl.

CHRIS FAIRCLOUGH COLOUR LIBRARY: 369bcl; THE FORBES MAGAZINE COLLECTION, NY: 112tl; FOUR SEASONS HOTEL: Peter Vitale 273cr; FRAUNCES TAVERN MUSEUM, NY: From the exhibit "Come All You Gallant Heroes" The World of the Revolutionary Soldier December 4, 1991 to August 14, 1992: 20cla; Copyright THE FRICK COLLECTION, NY: 35bl (*St Francis In The Desert* by Giovanni Bellini), 200ca, 200cl, 200clb, 200b, 201tl, 201ca, 201cr, 201bc, 201br.

GARRARD THE CROWN JEWELLERS: 143c; THE SOLOMON R GUGGENHEIM MUSEUM, NY: *Blue, Green, Yellow, Orange, Red*, 1966, by Ellsworth Kelly, photo by D Aronowitz 35cr; photo by D Heald 186tl, 186bl, 186bc, 186br, 187t, 187cra, 187crb, 187bl.

ROBERT HARDING PICTURE LIBRARY: 362tc, 362bl; HARPERS NEW MONTHLY MAGAZINE: 87tl; HARPERS WEEKLY: 351c; MILTON HEBALD: *Prospero and Miranda* 203t, *Romeo and Juliet* 331cr; THE HOTEL MILLENIUM, NY: 269tl.

THE IMAGE BANK: front endpaper bl, 89br; M Hilaire 75t; P McConville 377c; M Melford 10t, 377br; P Miller 367tr; A Satterwhite 75br.

THE JEWISH MUSEUM, NY: 182tr, 184c.

Copyright © 1993 K-III MAGAZINE CORPORATION: All rights reserved. Reprinted with the permission of *New York* Magazine 352tr; THE KOBAL COLLECTION: 211tc.

FRANK LESLIE'S ILLUSTRATED NEWSPAPER: 86br, 87tr, 267c; LIBRARY OF CONGRESS: 18bc, 21cla, 25bl, 25br; LIFE MAGAZINE © Time Warner Inc/Katz/A Feininger: 8–9; GEORG JOHN LOBER: *Hans Christian Anderson*, 1956, 204br; THE LOWELL HOTEL, NY: 273cl; MARY ANN LYNCH: 310bc, 356cl.

MADISON SQUARE GARDEN: 132r, 330cr; MAGNUM PHOTOS: © H Cartier-Bresson 173c; Erwitt 33cr; G Peres 12br, 92; JACQUES MARCHAIS CENTER OF TIBETAN ART: 252bc; METRO-NORTH COMMUTER RAILROAD: F English 154tr, 154cla; THE METRO-POLITAN MUSEUM OF ART, NY: 33bl (*Young Woman With A Waterjug* by Johannes Vermeer), 35crb (*Figure of a Hippopotamus*, faience, Egypt, 12th Dynasty), 180tc, 188cla, 188clb, 188bc, 188br, 189tl, 189tr, 189cr, 189bl, (photo Al Mozell) 189br, 190tr, 190c, 190bl, 190br, 191tl, 191tr, 191c, 191bl, 192tl, 192tr, 192c, 192b, (detail) 193tl, 193tr, 193b, 194t, 194cl, 194cr, 194b, 195tl, 195cr, 195bl, 234tr, 234cl, 234cr, 234b, 235ca, 235cr, 235bl, 235br, 236tl, 236tr, 237tr, 237c, 237b; METROPOLITAN TRANSIT AUTHORITY: 372bca, 374t, 375cla/ca; MORRIS-JUMEL MANSION, INC NY: 17tl; A

Rosario 21crb; THE MUSEUM OF THE CITY OF NEW YORK: 15b, 16cra, 16–17, 17tr, 18ca, 19crb (photo J Parnell), 20tl, 20cb, 22tl (attributed to Samuel Lovett Waldo), 22cla, 22clb, 23cr, 23crb, 23bc, 24cb, 25tl, 25crb, 25cb, 26bl, 27tr, 28tl, 28cr, 29tc, 29c, 30tr, 35tr (silver porringer), 87cr (Talfour); THE MUSEUM OF MODERN ART, NY: 33ca (*The Starry Night* by Vincent Van Gogh, 1889), 34t (*The Goat* by Pablo Picasso, 1950), 6bl (Cisitalia "202" GT car), 165tc, 170c, 170bl, 171tc, 171cra, 171crb, 171cb, 171bl, 172cl, 172cr, 172bc, 173tl, 173b.

NATIONAL BASEBALL LIBRARY, Cooperstown, NY: 4tr, 23bl, 28cl; NATIONAL MUSEUM OF THE AMERICAN INDIAN/SMITHSONIAN INSTITUTION: 16c; NATIONAL PARK SERVICE: Ellis Island Immigration Museum 78ca, 78br; Statue of Liberty National Monument 75bl; THE NEW MUSEUM OF CONTEMPORARY ART, NY: 105cl; NEW YORK BOTANICAL GARDEN: Jason Green 240cr; Tori Butt 240b, 241t/cl/b; NEW YORK CITY TRANSIT AUTHORITY: 374bc; Phil Bartley 375tc, 375ca, 375cl; Collection of THE NEW YORK HISTORICAL SOCIETY: 47tr; THE NEW YORKER MAGAZINE INC: Cover drawing by Rea Irvin, © 1925, 1953, All rights reserved, 28bcl; THE NEW YORK PALACE, NY: 25tr; NEW YORK POST: 354tl; NEW YORK PUBLIC LIBRARY: Special Collection Office, Schomburg Center for Research in Black Culture 28ca, 29cla; Stokes Collection 21tr; NEW YORK STATE DEPARTMENT OF MOTOR VEHICLES: 370b; THE NEW YORK TIMES: 354tl; NPA: © CNES 1993 10b; THE PENINSULA, NY: 271bc; PERFORMING ARTS LIBRARY: Clive Barda: 210bl; Collection of THE PIERPONT MORGAN LIBRARY, NY: 34cr (*Blanche of Castille and King Louis IX of France, author dictating to a scribe,* moralized Bible, c1230); 162bc, Devon Jarvis 162clb; *Song of Los* David A. Loggie (gift of Mrs Landon K Thorne) 162cl, *Biblia Latina* David A. Loggie 162b; 163tl, 163c, 163bl, 163br; POPPERFOTO: 29cra, 29cr, 71crb, 260cla; PLAZA HOTEL, NY: 272tr.

COLLECTION OF THE QUEENS MUSEUM OF ART: purchased with funds from the George and Mollie Wolfe World's Fair Fund 29cbr; Official souvenir, purchase 30cbr.

RENSSELAER POLYTECHNIC INSTITUTE: 86–87, 87bl; REX FEATURES LTD: 376tl; Sipa-Press 52tr, 52br; Courtesy of the ROCKEFELLER CENTER © The Rockefeller Group, Inc: 29cbl.

LUIS SANGUINO: *The Immigrants,* 1973, 256b; THE ST. REGIS, NY: 270c; SCIENTIFIC AMERICAN: 18 May 1878 edition 86tr; 9 November 1878 edition 88bl; THE SOCIETY OF ILLUSTRATORS: 196tl; SPECTRUM COLOUR LIBRARY: 376bl; FRANK SPOONER PICTURES: Gamma 158cl; Gamma/B Gysenbergh 367tl; Liaison/Gamma/ Anderson front end-paper clb, 158tl, 159cla; Liaison/Levy/Halebian: 42tr, 45c; Sygma/ A Tannenbaum 47ca.

TURNER ENTERTAINMENT COMPANY: 135br, 183br.

UNITED AIRLINES: Goldstag 363tl; UNITED NATIONS, NY: 159cra, 160tr, 160bc, 161tc, 161cla, 161br; UNITED NATIONS PHOTO: 158tr; © US POSTAL SERVICE: 361t, © THE US POSTAL SERVICE 1981: 361ca, © US POSTAL SERVICE 1991: 361c. Used with permission; UN PLAZA HYATT HOTEL, NY: 273bl.

© JACK VARTOOGIAN, NY: 61bc, 156t.

JUDITH WELLER: *The Garment Worker* 128t; LUCIA WILSON CONSULTANCY: Ivar Mjell 2–3, 13br, 164; Collection of THE WHITNEY MUSEUM OF AMERICAN ART, NY: 198cla, 198c, 198clb, 199t, 199ca, 199cr, 199crb (purchase with funds from a public fundraising campaign in May 1982. One half of the funds were contributed by the Robert Wood Johnson Jr. Charitable Trust. Additional major donations were given by The Lauder Foundation; the Robert Lehman Foundation, Inc.; the Howard and Jean Lipman Foundation, Inc; an anonymous donor; The TM Evans Foundation, Inc.; MacAndrews & Forbes Group Incorporated; the DeWitt Wallace Fund, Inc; Martin & Agnes Gruss; Anne Phillips; Mr and Mrs Laurance S. Rockefeller; the Simon Foundation, Inc.; Marylou Whitney; Bankers Trust Company; Mr and Mrs Kenneth N Dayton; Joel and Anne Ehrenkranz; Irvin and Kenneth Feld; Flora Whitney Miller. More than 500 individuals from 26 states and abroad also contributed to the campaign), 199bl, 199br (purchased with funds from the Mr and Mrs Arthur G Altschul Purchase Fund, the Joan and Lester Avnet Purchase Fund, the Edgar William and Bernice Chrysler Garbisch Purchase Fund, the Mrs Robert C Graham Purchase Fund in honour of John I H Baur, the Mrs Percy Uris Purchase Fund and the Henry Schnakenberg Purchase Fund in honour of Juliana Force); WHEELER PICTURES: 78t.

YU YU YANG: *Untitled,* 1973, 57br.

Back endpaper: © METROPOLITAN TRANSIT AUTHORITY.

DORLING KINDERSLEY *TRAVEL GUIDES*

TITLES AVAILABLE

THE GUIDES THAT SHOW YOU WHAT OTHERS ONLY TELL YOU

COUNTRY GUIDES

AUSTRALIA • CANADA • FRANCE • GREAT BRITAIN
GREECE: ATHENS & THE MAINLAND • THE GREEK ISLANDS
IRELAND • ITALY • MEXICO • PORTUGAL • SCOTLAND
SOUTH AFRICA • SPAIN • THAILAND

REGIONAL GUIDES

BARCELONA & CATALONIA • CALIFORNIA
FLORENCE & TUSCANY • FLORIDA • HAWAII
JERUSALEM & THE HOLY LAND • LOIRE VALLEY
MILAN & THE LAKES • NAPLES WITH POMPEII & THE
AMALFI COAST • PROVENCE & THE COTE D'AZUR • SARDINIA
SEVILLE & ANDALUSIA • SICILY • VENICE & THE VENETO
GREAT PLACES TO STAY IN EUROPE

CITY GUIDES

AMSTERDAM • BERLIN • BUDAPEST • DUBLIN • ISTANBUL
LISBON • LONDON • MADRID • MOSCOW • NEW YORK
PARIS • PRAGUE • ROME • SAN FRANCISCO
ST PETERSBURG • SYDNEY • VIENNA • WARSAW

TRAVEL MAPS

AUSTRALIA • FRANCE • FLORIDA
GREAT BRITAIN & IRELAND • ITALY • SPAIN

DK TRAVEL GUIDES PHRASE BOOKS

CONTINUALLY UPDATED

The Manhattan Subway

How to Use this Map

Transit Authority subway service operates 24 hours a day, but not all trains operate at all times. Train identification letters or numbers below station names on this map show the basic, seven-day-a-week service from 6am to midnight. A **bold** letter or number at a station indicates that trains always operate and always stop at the station between 6am and midnight. A light letter or number indicates that the train either does not operate at all times or sometimes skips the station. This portion of the NYC Subway Map covers only central Manhattan. A free copy of the complete subway map is available from all subway stations. A large-scale map is also posted at each station. For specific inquiries, call the NYCTA Travel Information Center at (718) 330-1234 at any time, or see their website: www.mta.nyc.ny.us/nyct/subway/index

Throughout this guide, the subway station closest to each sight is listed. For more details on traveling on the New York subway, see pages 374–5.